Figure 1.3, The Technical and
Sociocultural Dimensions of the Project
Management Process

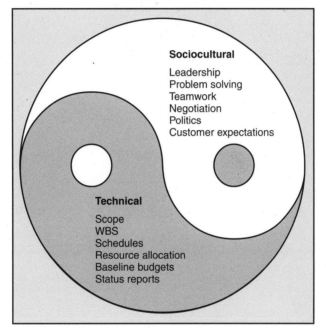

Project
Management

The Managerial Process

The McGraw-Hill/Irwin Series, Operations and Decision Sciences

OPERATIONS MANAGEMENT

Bowersox, Closs, and Cooper
Supply Chain Logistics Management
First Edition

Burt, Dobler, and Starling
World Class Supply Management
Seventh Edition

Chase, Jacobs, and Aquilano
Operations Management for Competitive Advantage
Tenth Edition

Davis and Heineke
Operations Management: Integrating Manufacturing and Services
Fifth Edition

Davis and Heineke
Managing Services
First Edition

Finch
Operations Now
Second Edition

Flaherty
Global Operations Management
First Edition

Fitzsimmons and Fitzsimmons
Service Management
Fourth Edition

Gehrlein
Operations Management Cases
First Edition

Gray and Larson
Project Management
Third Edition

Harrison and Samson
Technology Management
First Edition

Hill
Manufacturing Strategy: Text & Cases
Third Edition

Hopp and Spearman
Factory Physics
Second Edition

Jacobs and Whybark
Why ERP?
First Edition

Knod and Schonberger
Operations Management
Seventh Edition

Lambert and Stock
Strategic Logistics Management
Third Edition

Leenders and Fearon
Purchasing and Supply Chain Management
Twelfth Edition

Melnyk and Swink
Value-Driven Operations Management
First Edition

Moses, Seshadri, and Yakir
HOM Operations Management Software
First Edition

Nahmias
Production and Operations Analysis
Fifth Edition

Nicholas
Competitive Manufacturing Management
First Edition

Olson
Introduction to Information Systems Project Management
Second Edition

Pinto and Parente
SimProject: A Project Management Simulation for Classroom Instruction
First Edition

Schroeder
Operations Management: Contemporary Concepts and Cases
Second Edition

Seppanen, Kumar, and Chandra
Process Analysis and Improvement
First Edition

Simchi-Levi, Kaminsky, and Simchi-Levi
Designing and Managing the Supply Chain
Second Edition

Stevenson
Operations Management
Eighth Edition

Vollmann, Berry, Whybark and Jacobs
Manufacturing Planning & Control Systems
Fifth Edition

Zipkin
Foundations of Inventory Management
First Edition

QUANTITATIVE METHODS AND MANAGEMENT SCIENCE

Hillier and Hillier
Introduction to Management Science
Second Edition

Project
Management

The Managerial Process

Third Edition

Clifford F. Gray
Oregon State University

Erik W. Larson
Oregon State University

Boston   Burr Ridge, IL   Dubuque, IA   Madison, WI   New York   San Francisco   St. Louis
Bangkok   Bogotá   Caracas   Kuala Lumpur   Lisbon   London   Madrid   Mexico City
Milan   Montreal   New Delhi   Santiago   Seoul   Singapore   Sydney   Taipei   Toronto

**McGraw-Hill
Irwin**

PROJECT MANAGEMENT: THE MANAGERIAL PROCESS

Published by McGraw-Hill/Irwin, a business unit of The McGraw-Hill Companies, Inc., 1221
Avenue of the Americas, New York, NY, 10020. Copyright © 2006, 2003, 2000 by The
McGraw-Hill Companies, Inc. All rights reserved. No part of this publication may be reproduced
or distributed in any form or by any means, or stored in a database or retrieval system, without
the prior written consent of The McGraw-Hill Companies, Inc., including, but not limited to, in
any network or other electronic storage or transmission, or broadcast for distance learning.

Some ancillaries, including electronic and print components, may not be available to customers
outside the United States.

This book is printed on acid-free paper.

2 3 4 5 6 7 8 9 0 DOW/DOW 0 9 8 7 6 5

ISBN 0-07-297863-5

Editorial director: *Brent Gordon*
Executive editor: *Scott Isenberg*
Senior developmental editor: *Wanda J. Zeman*
Senior marketing manager: *Douglas Reiner*
Media producer: *Elizabeth Mavetz*
Project manager: *Jim Labeots*
Senior production supervisor: *Rose Hepburn*
Senior designer: *Adam Rooke*
Senior photo research coordinator: *Jeremy Cheshareck*
Photo researcher: *Julie Tesser*
Lead media project manager: *Cathy L. Tepper*
Supplement producer: *Gina F. DiMartino*
Developer, Media technology: *Brian Nacik*
Cover design: *Allison Traynham*
Typeface: *10.5/12 Times New Roman*
Compositor: *GTS—York, PA Campus*
Printer: *R. R. Donnelley*

Library of Congress Cataloging-in-Publication Data

Gray, Clifford F.
 Project management: the managerial process/Clifford F. Gray, Erik W. Larson.—3rd ed.
   p. cm.—(The McGraw-Hill/Irwin series Operations and decision sciences)
 Includes bibliographical references and index.
 ISBN 0-07-297863-5 (alk. paper)
 1. Project management. 2. Time management. 3. Risk management. I. Larson, Erik W.,
1952-II. Title. III. Series.
HD69.P75G72 2006
658.4'04—dc22
                                                    2004056943

www.mhhe.com

About the Authors

Clifford F. Gray

CLIFFORD F. GRAY is professor emeritus of management at the College of Business, Oregon State University. He continues to teach undergraduate and graduate project management courses overseas and in the United States; he has personally taught more than 100 executive development seminars and workshops. His research and consulting interests have been divided equally between operations management and project management; he has published numerous articles in these areas, plus a text on project management. He has also conducted research with colleagues in the International Project Management Association. Cliff has been a member of the Project Management Institute since 1976 and was one of the founders of the Portland, Oregon, chapter. He has been the president of Project Management International, Inc. (a training and consulting firm specializing in project management) since 1977. He received his BA in economics and management from Millikin University, M.B.A. from Indiana University, and doctorate in operations management from the College of Business, University of Oregon.

Erik W. Larson

ERIK W. LARSON is professor of project management in the department of management, marketing, and international business at the College of Business, Oregon State University. He teaches executive, graduate, and undergraduate courses on project management, organizational behavior, and leadership. His research and consulting activities focus on project management. He has published numerous articles on matrix management, product development, and project partnering. He has been a member of the Portland, Oregon, chapter of the Project Management Institute since 1984. In 1995 he worked as a Fulbright scholar with faculty at the Krakow Academy of Economics on modernizing Polish business education. He received a B.A. in psychology from Claremont McKenna College and a Ph.D. in management from State University of New York at Buffalo. He is a certified project management professional (PMP).

To Mary, Kevin, and Robert

                                           C.F.G.

To Ann, Mary, Rachel, and Victoria

                                           E.L.

Preface

Our motivation for writing this text was to provide students with a holistic, integrative view of project management. A holisitic view focuses on how projects contribute to the strategic goals of the organization. The linkages for integration include the process of selecting projects that best support the strategy of a particular organization and that in turn can be supported by the technical and managerial processes made available by the organization to bring projects to completion. The goals for prospective project managers are to understand the role of a project in their organizations and to master the project management tools, techniques, and interpersonal skills necessary to orchestrate projects from start to finish.

The role of projects in organizations is receiving increasing attention. Projects are becoming the major tool for implementing and achieving the strategic goals of the organization. In the face of intense, worldwide competition, many organizations have reorganized around a philosophy of innovation, renewal, and organizational learning to survive. This philosophy suggests an organization that is flexible and project driven. Project management has developed to the point where it is a professional discipline having its own body of knowledge and skills. Today it is nearly impossible to imagine anyone at any level in the organization who would not benefit from some degree of expertise in the process of managing projects.

Audience

This text is written for a wide audience. It covers concepts and skills that are used by managers to propose, plan, secure resources, budget, and lead project teams to successful completions of their projects. The text should prove useful to students and prospective project managers in helping them understand why organizations have developed a formal project management process to gain a competitive advantage. Readers will find the concepts and techniques discussed in enough detail to be immediately useful in new-project situations. Practicing project managers will find the text to be a valuable guide and reference when dealing with typical problems that arise in the course of a project. Managers will also find the text useful in understanding the role of projects in the missions of their organizations. Analysts will find the text useful in helping to explain the data needed for project implementation as well as the operations of inherited or purchased software. Members of the Project Management Institute will find the text is well structured to meet the needs of those wishing to prepare for PMP (Project Management Professional) certification. The text has in-depth coverage of the most critical topics found in PMI's *Project Management Body of Knowledge* (PIMBOK). People at all levels in the organization assigned to work on projects will find the text useful not only in providing them with a rationale for the use of project management tools and techniques but also because of the insights they will gain on how to enhance their contributions to project success.

Our emphasis is not only on how the management process works, but, more importantly, on *why* it works. The concepts, principles, and techniques are universally applicable. That is, the text does not specialize by industry type or project scope. Instead, the text is written for the individual who will be required to manage a variety of projects in a variety of different organizational settings. In the case of some small projects, a few of the steps of the techniques can be omitted, but the conceptual framework applies to all organizations in which projects are important to survival. The approach can be used in pure project organizations such as construction, research organizations, and engineering consultancy firms. At the same time, this approach will benefit organizations that carry out many small projects while the daily effort of delivering products or services continues.

Content

In this latest edition of the book, we have responded to feedback received from both students and teachers, which is deeply appreciated. As a result of the this feedback, the following changes have been made to the Third Edition:

- Expanded discussions of change management, managing conflict, communication plans, request for proposals (RFP), and project maturity models.
- Revised chapters on organizations (Chapter 3) and monitoring project performance (Chapter 13) to make their terminology consistent with the Project Management Body of Knowledge (PMBOK).
- The discussion of earned value has been completely revised to make it easier for students to understand.
- New student exercises have been added to several chapters. Several computer exercises have been revised.
- Examples and screenshots from MS Project are now embedded in the text.
- The "Snapshot from Practice" boxes feature a number of new examples of project management in action as well as new research highlights that continue to promote practical application of project management.

Overall the text addresses the major questions and issues the authors have encountered over their 50 combined years of teaching project management and consulting with practicing project managers in domestic and foreign environments. The following questions represent the issues and problems practicing project managers find consuming most of their effort: What is the strategic role of projects in contemporary organizations? How are projects prioritized? What organizational and managerial styles will improve chances of project success? How do project managers orchestrate the complex network of relationships involving vendors, subcontractors, project team members, senior management, functional managers, and customers that affect project success? What factors contribute to the development of a high-performance project team? What project management system can be set up to gain some measure of control? How do managers prepare for a new international project in a foreign culture? How does one pursue a career in project management?

Project managers must deal with all these concerns to be effective. All of these issues and problems represent linkages to an integrative project management view. The chapter content of the text has been placed within an overall framework that integrates these topics in a holistic manner. Cases and snapshots are included from the experiences of practicing managers. The future for project managers appears to be promising. Careers will be determined by success in managing projects.

Student Learning Aids

The Student CD-ROM accompanying the text includes study outlines, quizzes, selected exercises, videos, PowerPoint, Microsoft Project Video Tutorials and web links. The 120-day trial version of Microsoft Project software is included on its own CD-ROM free with the text.

SimProject, a project management simulation, developed by Jeffrey Pinto and Diane Parente of Pennsylvania State University—Erie, can be optionally bundled with this text for a modest additional cost. SimProject provides virtual experience in managing projects. Through the use of multiple scenarios and competitive and collaborative project teams, "firsthand" experience as a successful project manager is acquired. An appendix in the back of this text ties the simulation to the chapter sequence of the book.

Acknowledgments

We want first to acknowledge with special thanks and appreciation the contribution of Diane Parente, Pennsylvania State University—Erie, who prepared the SimProject extended case in the appendix. This case consists of a series of exercises tied to the chapters of this book that coordinate with and make use of SimProject, a project management simulation developed by Diane and her colleague at Penn State—Erie, Jeff Pinto. SimProject adds a hands-on, experiential dimension to this course.

In addition, we would like to thank Ed Blevins, DeVry University—Irving, for updating the Test Bank; Charlie Cook, University of West Alabama, for creating PowerPoint slides; and Julie Mehra for accuracy checking the text and Instructor's Resource Manual content.

Next, it is important to note that the text includes contributions from numerous students, colleagues, friends, and managers gleaned from professional conversations. We want them to know we sincerely appreciate their counsel and suggestions. Almost every exercise, case, and example in the text is drawn from a real-world project. Special thanks to managers who graciously shared their current project as ideas for exercises, subjects for cases, and examples for the text. Shlomo Cohen, Pat Taylor, and John Wold, whose work is printed, are gratefully acknowledged. Special gratitude is due Robert Breitbarth of Interact Management, who shared invaluable insights on prioritizing projects. University students and managers deserve special accolades for identifying problems with earlier drafts of the text and exercises.

We are indebted to the reviewers of the first and second edition who shared our commitment to elevating the instruction of project management. The reviewers include Paul S. Allen, Rice University; Denis F. Cioffi, George Washington University; Joseph D. DeVoss, DeVry Institute of Technology; Edward J. Glantz, Pennsylvania State University; Michael Godfrey, University of Wisconsin—Oshkosh; Robert Key, University of Phoenix; Dennis Krumwiede, Idaho State University; Nicholas C. Petruzzi, University of Illinois—Urbana/Champaign; William R. Sherrard, San Diego State University; S. Narayan Bodapati, Southern Illinois University at Edwardsville; Warren J. Boe, University of Iowa; Burton Dean, San Jose State University; Kwasi Amoako-Gyampah, University of North Carolina—Greensboro; Owen P. Hall, Pepperdine University; Bruce C. Hartman, University of Arizona; Richard Irving, York University; Robert T. Jones, DePaul University; Richard L. Luebbe, Miami University of Ohio; William Moylan, Lawrence Technological College of Business; Edward Pascal, University of Ottawa; James H. Patterson, Indiana University; Art Rogers, City University; Christy Strbiak, U.S. Air Force Academy; David A. Vaughan, City University; and Ronald W. Witzel, Keller Graduate School of Management.

In the third edition we continue to commit to improving the text content and improving instruction of project management. We are grateful to those reviewers who provided helpful critiques and insights. The reviewers for the third edition include Robert Bregman, University of Houston; Larry Cornwell, Bradley University; Edward L. Dollar, Southern Polytechnic State University; Michael Ensby, Clarkson University;

Abel Fernandez, University of the Pacific; Joan Hoopes, Marist College; Timothy Kloppenborg, Xavier University; Neal Lewis, University of Missouri—Rolla; Mary Meixell, George Mason University; Ali Mir, William Paterson University; Erin Sims, DeVry University—Pomona; Kenneth Solhem, DeVry University—Federal Way: Ali Zargar, San Jose State University; Dan Heiser, DePaul University; Randal Zentner, College of DuPage; Ross Hopkins, DeVry University—West Hills; Kenneth Pflieger, Potomac College; and James Holt, Washington State University. We thank you for your many thoughtful suggestions and for making our book better. Of course we accept responsibility for the final version of the text.

In addition, we would like to thank our colleagues in the College of Business at Oregon State University for their support and help in completing this project. In particular, we recognize Mark Pagell, Jimmy Yang, Prem Matheu, Jack Drexler, and Roger Graham for their helpful comments and suggestions. Special thanks go to Lori Emmons, Sharon Carlson, Ann Leen, and Cheryl Hoflich who helped prepare the manuscript. We also wish to thank the many students who helped us at different stages of this project, most notably Carrie Doran, Neil Young, Rebecca Keepers, Katie McAlexander, Katherine Knox, and Amanda Bosworth. Mary Gray deserves special credit for editing and working under tight deadlines.

Finally, we want to extend our thanks to all the people at McGraw-Hill/Irwin for their efforts and support. First, we'd like to thank Scott Isenberg for continuing to champion and provide editorial direction and guidance through all three editions of the book, and Wanda Zeman, whose superb management of the book's development has continued to add value to the book with each new edition of it. And we would also like to thank Jim Labeots, Rose Hepburn, Jeremy Cheshareck, Adam Rooke, Cathy Tepper, Elizabeth Mavetz, and Gina DeMartino for managing the final production, design, supplement, and media phases of the Third Edition.

Clifford F. Gray

Erik W. Larson

Note to Student

You will find the content of this text highly practical, relevant, and current. The concepts discussed are relatively simple and intuitive. As you study each chapter we suggest you try to grasp not only how things work, but why things work. You are encouraged to use the text as a handbook as you move through the three levels of competency:

I know.

I can do.

I can adapt to new situations.

Project management is both people and technical oriented. Project management involves understanding the cause-effect relationships and interactions among the socio-technical dimensions of projects. Improved competency in these dimensions will greatly enhance your competitive edge as a project manager.

The field of project management is growing in importance and at an exponential rate. It is nearly impossible to imagine a future management career that does not include management of projects. Résumés of managers will soon be primarily a description of the individual's participation in projects and their respective contributions.

Good luck on your journey through the text and on your future projects.

Brief Contents

Contents

Project Management

The Managerial Process

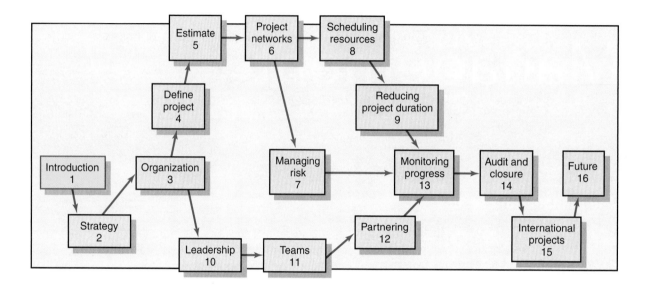

Modern Project Management

What Is a Project?

The Importance of Project Management

Project Management Today: An Integrative Approach

Summary

CHAPTER ONE

Modern Project Management

The whole discipline and art of project management is going to be the essence of management training, operational excellence, and value added.

Tom Peters, author, consultant

This is a good time to be reading a book about project management. Business leaders and experts have proclaimed that project management is the wave of the future. Project management provides people with a powerful set of tools that improves their ability to plan, implement, and manage activities to accomplish specific organizational objectives. But project management is more than just a set of tools; it is a results-oriented management style that places a premium on building collaborative relationships among a diverse cast of characters. Exciting opportunities await people skilled in project management.

The project approach has long been the style of doing business in the construction industry, U.S. Department of Defense contracts, and Hollywood as well as at big consulting firms. Now project management is spreading to all avenues of work. Today, project teams carry out everything from port expansions to hospital restructuring to upgrading information systems. The "Big Three" automakers credit their ability to recapture a significant share of the auto market to the use of project management teams, which quickly develop new cars that incorporate the latest automotive technology. The impact of project management is most profound in the area of information technology, where the new folk heroes are young professionals whose Herculean efforts lead to the constant flow of new hardware and software products.

Project management is not limited to the private sector. Project management is also a vehicle for doing good deeds and solving social problems. Endeavors such as providing emergency aid to a region devastated by a hurricane, devising a strategy for reducing crime and drug abuse within a city, or organizing a community effort to renovate a public playground would and do benefit from the application of modern project management skills and techniques.

Perhaps the best indicator of the growth and interest in project management can be seen in the rapid expansion of the Project Management Institute (PMI), a professional organization for project management specialists. Between 1993 and 1997, membership quadrupled to more than 24,000. Current membership is now over 139,000 with members in 125 countries. Since projects cover such a wide variety of industries, PMI has created Specific Interest Groups (SIGs) so people in different industries can share ideas about managing projects in their areas of interest, such as aerospace, automotive, construction, engineering, financial services, information technology, pharmaceuticals, and telecommunications.

Project management is not restricted to specialists. Managing projects are often a vital part of everyone's job. For example, Brian Vannoni, formerly of General Electric Plastics states:

> We have very few dedicated project managers. Our project managers might be process engineers, they might be scientists, they might be process control technicians, maintenance mechanics, degreed and nondegreed people. A short answer for GE Plastics is that anyone, any level, any function could be a project manager.*

Companies recognize that their entire organizational staff can benefit from being trained in project management, not just project management wannabes.

The growth of project management can also be seen in the classroom. Ten years ago major universities offered one or two classes in project management, primarily for engineers. Today, many universities offer multiple sections of project management classes, with the core group of engineers being supplemented by business students majoring in marketing, management information systems (MIS), and finance, as well as students from other disciplines such as oceanography, health sciences, computer sciences, and liberal arts. These students are finding that their exposure to project management is providing them with distinct advantages when it comes time to look for jobs. More and more employers are looking for graduates with project management skills. The logical starting point for developing these skills is understanding the uniqueness of a project and of project managers.

What Is a Project?

What do the following headlines have in common?

Next generation of high definition TVs enter the market.
Star Trek movie nears completion.
FARM AID concert raises millions for family farmers.
New football stadium breaks ground.
Portable fuel cells to replace conventional batteries.

All these events resulted from the management of projects. A project can be defined as follows:

> A project is a complex, nonroutine, one-time effort limited by time, budget, resources, and performance specifications designed to meet customer needs.

Like most organizational effort, the major goal of a project is to satisfy a customer's need. Beyond this fundamental similarity, the characteristics of a project help differentiate it from other endeavors of the organization. The major characteristics of a project are as follows:

1. An established objective.
2. A defined life span with a beginning and an end.
3. Usually, the involvement of several departments and professionals.
4. Typically, doing something that has never been done before.
5. Specific time, cost, and performance requirements.

First, projects have a defined objective—whether it is constructing a 12-story apartment complex by January 1 or releasing version 2.0 of a specific software package as

---

* Harold Kerzner, *Applied Project Management* (New York: John Wiley & Sons, 2000), p. 221.

quickly as possible. This singular purpose is often lacking in daily organizational life in which workers perform repetitive operations each day.

Second, because there is a specified objective, projects have a defined endpoint, which is contrary to the ongoing duties and responsibilities of traditional jobs. In many cases, individuals move from one project to the next as opposed to staying in one job. After helping to construct a desalination installation along the Gulf of Mexico, an engineer may next be assigned to construct an oil refinery plant in Malaysia.

Third, unlike much organizational work that is segmented according to functional specialty, projects typically require the combined efforts of a variety of specialists. Instead of working in separate offices under separate managers, project participants, whether they be engineers, financial analysts, marketing professionals, or quality control specialists, work closely together under the guidance of a project manager to complete a project.

The fourth characteristic of a project is that it is nonroutine and has some unique elements. This is not an either/or issue but a matter of degree. Obviously, accomplishing something that has never been done before, such as building a hybrid (electric/gas) automobile or landing two mechanical rovers on Mars, requires solving previously unsolved problems and breakthrough technology. On the other hand, even basic construction projects that involve established sets of routines and procedures require some degree of customization that makes them unique.

Finally, specific time, cost, and performance requirements bind projects. Projects are evaluated according to accomplishment, cost, and time spent. These triple constraints impose a higher degree of accountability than you typically find in most jobs. These three also highlight one of the primary functions of project management, which is balancing the trade-offs between time, cost, and performance while ultimately satisfying the customer.

What a Project Is Not   Projects should not be confused with everyday work. A project is not routine, repetitive work! Ordinary daily work typically requires doing the same or similar work over and over, while a project is done only once; a new product or service exists when the project is completed. Examine the list in Table 1.1 that compares routine, repetitive work and projects. Recognizing the difference is important because too often resources can be used up on daily operations which may not contribute to longer range organization strategies that require innovative new products.

The terms *program* and *project* are often used interchangeably in practice, which sometimes causes confusion. Programs and projects are similar in the sense that they both are directed toward goals and require plans and resources to reach their goals. Both use similar tools, methods, and policies. The differences lie primarily in scope and time horizon. *A program is a series of coordinated, related, multiple projects that continue over extended time intended to achieve a goal.* A program is a higher level *group* of projects targeted at a common goal. The classic example is the U.S. space program to place a space station on the moon to serve as a springboard to other space explorations.

TABLE 1.1 **Comparison of Routine Work with Projects**	Routine, Repetitive Work	Projects
	Taking class notes	Writing a term paper
	Daily entering sales receipts into the accounting ledger	Setting up a sales kiosk for a professional accounting meeting
	Responding to a supply-chain request	Developing a supply-chain information system
	Practicing scales on the piano	Writing a new piano piece
	Routine manufacture of an Apple iPod	Designing an iPod that is approximately 2×4 inches, interfaces with PC, and stores 10,000 songs
	Attaching tags on a manufactured product	Wire-tag projects for GE and Wal Mart

The Project Life Cycle

Another way of illustrating the unique nature of project work is in terms of the project life cycle. Some project managers find it useful to use the project life cycle as the cornerstone for managing projects. The life cycle recognizes that projects have a limited life span and that there are predictable changes in level of effort and focus over the life of the project. There are a number of different life-cycle models in project management literature. Many are unique to a specific industry or type of project. For example, a new software development project may consist of five phases: definition, design, code, integration/test, and maintenance. A generic cycle is depicted in Figure 1.1.

The project life cycle typically passes sequentially through four stages: defining, planning, executing, and delivering. The starting point begins the moment the project is given the go-ahead. Project effort starts slowly, builds to a peak, and then declines to delivery of the project to the customer.

1. **Defining stage:** Specifications of the project are defined; project objectives are established; teams are formed; major responsibilities are assigned.
2. **Planning stage:** The level of effort increases, and plans are developed to determine what the project will entail, when it will be scheduled, whom it will benefit, what quality level should be maintained, and what the budget will be.
3. **Executing stage:** A major portion of the project work takes place—both physical and mental. The physical product is produced (a bridge, a report, a software program). Time, cost, and specification measures are used for control. Is the project on schedule, on budget, and meeting specifications? What are the forecasts of each of these measures? What revisions/changes are necessary?
4. **Delivering stage:** Includes the two activities: delivering the project product to the customer and redeploying project resources. Delivery of the project might include customer training and transferring documents. Redeployment usually involves releasing project equipment/materials to other projects and finding new assignments for team members.

FIGURE 1.1
Project Life Cycle

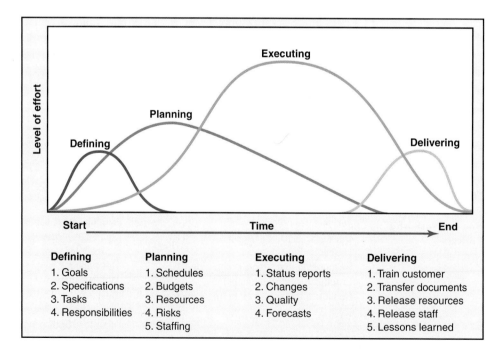

In practice, the project life cycle is used by some project groups to depict the timing of major tasks over the life of the project. For example, the design team might plan a major commitment of resources in the defining stage, while the quality team would expect their major effort to increase in the latter stages of the project life cycle. Because most organizations have a portfolio of projects going on concurrently, each at a different stage of each project's life cycle, careful planning and management at the organization and project levels are imperative.

The Project Manager

Management decides and implements the ways and means to effectively and efficiently utilize human and nonhuman resources to reach predetermined objectives. In a small sense project managers perform the same functions as other managers. That is, they plan, schedule, motivate, and control. Various types of managers exist because they fill special needs. For example, the marketing manager specializes in distributing a product or service; the production manager specializes in conversion of resource inputs to outputs; the financial manager ensures adequate funds are available to keep the organization viable. The project manager is unique because she/he manages temporary, nonrepetitive activities and frequently acts independently of the formal organization.

Project managers are expected to marshal resources to complete a fixed-life project on time, on budget, and within specifications. Project managers are the direct link to the customer and must manage the interface between customer expectations and what is feasible and reasonable. They provide direction, coordination, and integration to the project team, which is often made up of part-time participants loyal to their functional departments. Project managers are responsible for performance (frequently with too little authority). They must ensure that appropriate trade-offs are made between the time, cost, and performance requirements of the project. At the same time, unlike their functional counterparts, project managers generally possess only rudimentary technical knowledge to make such decisions. Instead, they must orchestrate the completion of the project by inducing the right people, at the right time, to address the right issues and make the right decisions. Clearly, project management is a unique and challenging profession. This text is intended to provide the necessary knowledge, perspective, and tools to enable students to accept the challenge.

The Importance of Project Management

Project management is no longer a special-need management. It is rapidly becoming a standard way of doing business. See Snapshot from Practice: Project Management at Work. An increasing percentage of the typical firm's effort is being devoted to projects. The future promises an increase in the importance and the role of projects in contributing to the strategic direction of organizations. Several reasons why this is the case are briefly discussed below.

Compression of the Product Life Cycle

One of the most significant driving forces behind the demand for project management is the shortening of the product life cycle. For example, today in high-tech industries the product life cycle is averaging 1 to 3 years. Only 30 years ago, life cycles of 10 to 15 years were not uncommon. *Time to market* for new products with short life cycles has become increasingly important. A common rule of thumb in the world of high-tech product development is that a six-month project delay can result in a 33 percent loss in product revenue share. Speed, therefore, becomes a competitive advantage; more and

Ryan McVay/Getty Images.

Investments in info-tech projects are indicative of rapid innovation within organizations. A few selected high profile organizations and their projects are described below. Although info-tech projects are hot, projects cut across small and large firms in diverse industries such as construction, biotechnology, nanotechnology, aerospace, and public transportation.

1. **Company: Krispy Kreme**
   Project: Network 320 stores to manage their inventory and take orders
   Payoff: New system provides many benefits: coordination alerts store managers of too much inventory; quick notification of the arrival of damaged goods at store; reduction of

more organizations are relying on cross-functional project teams to get new products and services to the market as quickly as possible.

Global Competition

Today's open market demands not only *cheaper* products and services but also *better* products and services. This has led to the emergence of the quality movement across the world with ISO 9000 certification a requirement for doing business. ISO 9000 is a family of international standards for quality management and assurance. These standards cover design, procurement, quality assurance, and delivery processes for everything from banking to manufacturing. Quality management and improvement invariably involve project management. For many, their first exposure to project management techniques has been in quality workshops.

Increased pressures to reduce costs have not only led to the migration of U.S. manufacturing operations to Mexico and Asia, which by itself is a significant project, but also a transformation in how organizations try to achieve results. See e.Schwab Snapshot from Practice. More and more work is being classified as projects. Individuals are being assigned responsibility to achieve a specific objective within a given budget and by problem orders down from 26,000 to less than 3,000; district managers can now handle 320 stores, up from 144 three years ago.

2. **Company: Mattel (Toy manufacturer)**
   Cut Design Time Project: Move product design and licensing on line
   Payoff: Instead of molding prototypes (e.g., Hot Wheels or Barbie doll), virtual models are electronically sent directly to manufacturing sites. Approvals for new products have been reduced from 14 to 5 weeks. Revenue is expected to increase by 200 million.

3. **Company: Nike**
   Project: Online supply-chain link to manufacturing partners
   Payoff: Lead time for new shoe development has been reduced from nine months to six. Better forecasting has reduced speculation on what to produce from 30 percent to 3 percent. These efficiencies have upped Nike's gross margin 2.1 percent.

4. **Company: FBI**
   Project: Digitizing millions of fingerprint cards and connecting law enforcement agencies to the data base
   Payoff: Local law enforcement departments can have the FBI check against 46 million sets of fingerprints and respond within two hours. In addition, the FBI conducts background checks for private enterprises (e.g., schools, insurance and securities industry, private security agencies). This latter service resulted in revenue of 152 million for one year.

5. **Company: Kinko's**
   Project: Replace 51 training sites with e-learning network
   Payoff: E-courses online are available to 20,000 employees. Courses range from products, to policies, to new product rollouts. Kinko's expects to save around $10 million a year on employee training. Kinko's is now moving into training for customers—such as making banners, holiday cards, and jazzy transparencies. Stores offering online customer training saw revenues rise 27 percent versus 11 percent in non-online stores.

6. **Company: BMW**
   Project: Build cars to specific customer orders
   Payoff: Updating supply chain from suppliers to customer allows customer (or salesperson) to use the Internet to order cars without altering production-line efficiency; delivery date is delivered in five seconds. Suppliers are notified when order is confirmed so parts arrive just-in-time for production. Cars are off the production line in 11 to 12 days and can be in the United States in 12 additional days. Eighty percent of European buyers design their own custom Beemer. Thirty percent of U.S. buyers access the custom service with the number increasing each year.

7. **Company: Sony**
   Project: Produce and use a secure website to rescue *Lord of the Rings* schedule
   Payoff: Important special effects for the film *Two Towers* fell behind schedule. Coordination between New Zealand, London, and the U.S. became a nightmare. A secure website using special custom software allowed all sites to download and edit over 100 scenes. Simultaneously, each site could use a digital pointer to discuss specific details or pull up specific footage. The one million dollar cost was small relative to the potential wasted cost of missing the promotions and ads deadlines.

*Adapted from Heather Green, "The Web," *Business Week,* November 24, 2003, pp. 82–104.

a specified deadline. Project management, with its triple focus on time, cost, and performance, is proving to be an efficient, flexible way to get things done.

Knowledge Explosion

The growth in new knowledge has increased the complexity of projects because projects encompass the latest advances. For example, building a road 30 years ago was a somewhat simple process. Today, each area has increased in complexity, including materials, specifications, codes, aesthetics, equipment, and required specialists. Similarly, in today's digital, electronic age it is becoming hard to find a new product that does not contain at least one microchip. Product complexity has increased the need to integrate divergent technologies. Project management has emerged as an important discipline for achieving this task.

Corporate Downsizing

The last decade has seen a dramatic restructuring of organizational life. Downsizing (or rightsizing if you are still employed) and sticking to core competencies have become necessary for survival for many firms. Middle management is a mere skeleton of the past. In

Main Street in the 1950s, malls in the 1970s, superstores in the 1990s—since World War II we have seen a fundamental shift in the retailing paradigm with each new generation, and now we are on the verge of another revolution: e-commerce. Experts agree that Internet retail operations will fundamentally change customers' expectations about convenience, speed, comparability, price, and service. Furthermore, project management will be a driving force behind this revolution. A case in point is the development of e.Schwab and the transformation of a discount brokerage firm into an online brokerage firm.

Charles R. Schwab founded The Charles Schwab Corporation in 1971 as a traditional brokerage company and in 1974 became a pioneer in the discount brokerage business. Schwab's journey into e-commerce began in late 1995 with a series of messages to chief information officer Dawn Lepore from one of her research teams. The group wanted to show her some experimental software that would allow Schwab's different computer systems to talk to one another. It was the sort of project that software designers love: challenging, technically complicated, and intended to solve an obscure problem that was difficult to explain to anyone but other techies. Lepore scheduled a demonstration and invited one of the company's biggest technology nuts, Charles Schwab himself, to attend.

The application the engineers chose was a very simple Web-based stock trade. Their program allowed a Schwab server to take an order from a Web browser on a PC, route it through all of Schwab's sophisticated backend systems and mainframes, execute it, and send a confirmation back to the PC. At the time, most existing Web trading systems required that orders be printed out and entered by hand into another system, defeating the point of automated trading. As it turns out, Lepore's computer researchers were less interested in online brokerage than in winning Lepore's approval to continue research on their obscure middleware project. But Lepore and Schwab instantly recognized the implications of the patched-together demo. Says Schwab, "I fell off my chair."

Within weeks an independent project team was assigned to get Web trading up and running at Schwab. The team consisted of Schwab executives and an Israeli engineer named Gideon Sassoon, whom Lepore had hired away from IBM to head technology development for the team. Working in secrecy at first, the team grew to 30 people and evolved into a separate electronic brokerage unit, called e.Schwab, which bypassed Schwab's normal hierarchy and reported directly to co-CEO David Pottruck.

A handful of deep-discount brokerages, such as E*Trade and Ameritrade, were racing to perfect Web trading at the same time. "We had to figure out how to compete with these small brokerages," says Pottruck. "So we needed a group that felt like they did: nimble, unshackled from the larger bureaucracy." And indeed, the early days were packed with intense, freewheeling meetings in which everyone could fit into one room and shout ideas back and forth.

By the middle of 1996, e.Schwab was ready. Investors had to send in a physical check (or wire transfer) to open an e.Schwab account, but after that they could trade any security available through a regular account—stocks, mutual funds, options—by logging onto e.Schwab's website. They would pay a flat $39 (quickly dropped to $29.95) for any stock trade up to 1,000 shares. The only publicity for the launch of e.Schwab was an announcement at the annual shareholders' meeting.

Despite the lack of fanfare, the new service was an immediate success. Says Sasson, "We were totally unprepared. Customers began voting with their keyboards, and in two weeks we reached 25,000 Web accounts—our goal for the entire year." By the end of 1997, all online accounts, both at e.Schwab and at regular Schwab, had grown to 1.2 million. By the end of the third quarter of 1998, 58 percent of total trades at Schwab were Web transactions. This percent has grown to over 80 percent in recent years.

*Erick Schonfeld, "Schwab Puts It All Online," Fortune (December 7, 1998), pp. 94–99.

today's flatter and leaner organizations, where change is a constant, project management is replacing middle management as a way of ensuring that things get done. Corporate downsizing has also led to a change in the way organizations approach projects. Companies outsource significant segments of project work, and project managers have to manage not only their own people but also their counterparts in different organizations.

Increased Customer Focus

Increased competition has placed a premium on customer satisfaction. Customers no longer simply settle for generic products and services. They want customized products and services that cater to their specific needs. This mandate requires a much closer working relationship between the provider and the receiver. Account executives and sales representatives are assuming more of a project manager's role as they work with their organization to satisfy the unique needs and requests of clients.

Increased customer attention has also prompted the development of customized products and services. For example, 10 years ago buying a set of golf clubs was a relatively simple process: You picked out a set based on price and feel. Today, there are golf clubs for tall players and short players, clubs for players who tend to slice the ball and clubs for those who hook the ball, high-tech clubs with the latest metallurgic discovery guaranteed to add distance, and so forth. Project management is critical both to development of customized products and services and to sustaining lucrative relationships with customers.

Rapid Development of Third World and Closed Economies

The collapse of the Soviet Empire and the gradual opening of Asian Communist countries have created an explosion of pent-up demand within these societies for all manner of consumer goods and infrastructure development. Western firms are scrambling to introduce their products and services to these new markets, and many firms are using project management techniques to establish distribution channels and foreign bases of operations. These historical changes have created a tremendous market for core project work in the areas of heavy construction and telecommunications as eastern European and Asian countries strive to revitalize their inefficient industries and decrepit infrastructures.

Small Projects Represent Big Problems

The velocity of change required to remain competitive or simply keep up has created an organizational climate in which hundreds of projects are implemented concurrently. This climate has created a multiproject environment and a plethora of new problems. Sharing and prioritizing resources across a portfolio of projects is a major challenge for senior management. Many firms have no idea of the problems involved with inefficient management of small projects. Small projects typically carry the same or more risk as do large projects. Small projects are perceived as having little impact on the bottom line because they do not demand large amounts of scarce resources and/or money. Because so many small projects are going on concurrently and because the perception of the inefficiency impact is small, measuring inefficiency is usually nonexistent. Unfortunately, many small projects soon add up to large sums of money. Many customers and millions of dollars are lost each year on small projects in product and service organizations.

Many small projects can eat up the people resources of a firm and represent hidden costs not measured in the accounting system. Organizations with many small projects going on concurrently face the most difficult project management problems. A key question becomes one of how to create an organizational environment that supports multiproject management. A process is needed to prioritize and develop a portfolio of small projects that supports the mission of the organization.

In summary, there are a variety of environmental forces interacting in today's business world that contribute to the increased demand for good project management across all industries and sectors. Project management appears to be ideally suited for a business environment requiring accountability, flexibility, innovation, speed, and continuous improvement.

Project Management Today—An Integrative Approach

Some project managers have used pieces of systems that are useful for managing projects. For example, networks, bar charts, job costing, task forces, partnering, and scheduling all have been used—sometimes very successfully and other times with poor results. As the world becomes more competitive, the importance of managing the process of project management and "getting it right the first time" takes on new meaning. Piecemeal systems fail to tie to the overall strategies of the firm. Piecemeal project priority systems fail to connect the selected projects to resources. Piecemeal tools and techniques fail to be integrated throughout the project life cycle. Piecemeal approaches fail to balance the application of project planning and control methods with appropriate adjustments in the organization's culture to support project endeavors.

Today, emphasis is on development of an integrated project management process that focuses all project effort toward the strategic plan of the organization and reinforces mastery of both the project management tools/techniques and the interpersonal skills necessary to orchestrate successful project completion. For some organizations, integrating projects with strategy will require reengineering the entire business management process. For others, integration will mean carefully establishing linkages among the piecemeal systems already in place and altering the focus to one of a total system. At the individual level, for some professionals to become effective project managers will require augmenting their leadership and team-building skills with modern project planning and control methods. For others it will require complementing their administrative skills with the capacity to inspire and lead a divergent cast of professionals to project completion.

Integration in project management directs attention to two key areas. The first area is integration of projects with the strategic plan of the organization. The second area is integration within the process of managing actual projects. Each of these areas is examined next.

Integration of Projects with the Strategic Plan

In some organizations, selection and management of projects often fail to support the strategic plan of the organization. Strategic plans are written by one group of managers, projects selected by another group, and projects implemented by another. These independent decisions by different groups of managers create a set of conditions leading to conflict, confusion, and—frequently—an unsatisfied customer. Under these conditions, resources of the organization are wasted in non-value-added activities/projects.

An integrated project management system is one in which all of the parts are interrelated. A change in any one of the parts will influence the whole. Every organization has a customer it is seeking to satisfy. The customer sets the raison d'être for the organization. Mission, objectives, and strategies are set to meet the needs of customer(s). Development of a mission, objectives, and organization strategies depend on the external and internal environmental factors. External environmental factors are usually classified as political, social, economic, and technological; they signal opportunities or threats in setting the direction for the organization. Internal environmental factors are frequently classified as strengths and weaknesses such as management, facilities, core competencies, and financial condition. The outcome of the analysis of all these environmental factors is a set of strategies designed to best meet the needs of customers. But this is only the first step (see Figure 1.2).

Implementing strategies is the most difficult step. Strategies are typically implemented through projects. Creative minds always propose more projects than there are resources. The key is selecting from the many proposals those projects that make the largest and most balanced contribution to the objectives and strategies (and thus, customers) of the organization. This means prioritizing projects so that scarce resources are allocated to the right projects. Once a project has been selected for implementation, the focus switches to the project management process that sets the stage for how the project will be implemented or delivered.

Integration within the Process of Managing Actual Projects

There are two dimensions within the project management process (see Figure 1.3). The first dimension is the technical side of the management process, which consists of the formal, disciplined, pure logic parts of the process. The technical side relies on the

FIGURE 1.2
Integrated
Management
of Projects

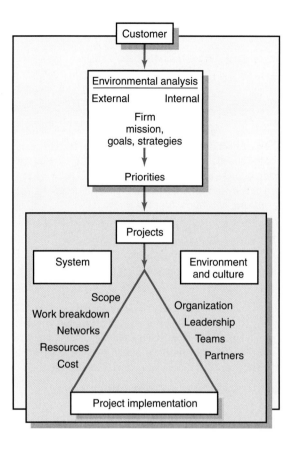

FIGURE 1.3
The Technical
and Sociocultural
Dimensions of the
Project Management
Process

The phrase "works well with others" has long been a staple on grade school report cards; now, in the IT world, it's the No. 1 criterion for management candidates. In a nationwide survey conducted in 1999, 27 percent of chief information officers (CIOs) cited strong interpersonal skills as the single most important quality for reaching management levels. Advanced technical skills came in second, receiving 23 percent of the response.

The project was sponsored by RHI Consulting, which provides information technology professionals on a project basis. An independent research firm was hired to administer the survey. Over 1,400 CIOs responded to the questionnaire.

Survey respondents were also asked:

In 2005, how frequently will employees in your IT department work on project-based teams with members of other departments throughout the company?

Their responses:		
Very frequently	57%	
Somewhat frequently	26%	
Somewhat infrequently	10%	
Very infrequently	6%	
Never	1%	

Greg Scileppi, RHI Consulting's executive director, recommends that IT professionals develop their interpersonal skills. "The predominance of project teams has created a corresponding need for strong communication and team-player abilities. Technical staff put these skills to test daily as they work with employees at all levels to create and implement IT solutions ranging from simple troubleshooting to corporate web initiatives and system wide upgrades."

*Joanita M. Nellenbach, "People Skills Top Technical Knowledge, CIOs Insist," PMNetwork (August 1999), pp. 7–8.

formal information system available. This dimension includes planning, scheduling, and controlling projects. Clear project scope statements are written to link the project and customer and to facilitate planning and control. Creation of the deliverables and work breakdown structures facilitate planning and monitoring the progress of the project. The work breakdown structure serves as a database that links all levels in the organization, major deliverables, and all work—right down to the tasks in a work package. Effects of project changes are documented and traceable. Thus, any change in one part of the project is traceable to the source by the integrated linkages of the system. This integrated information approach can provide all project managers and the customer with decision information appropriate to their level and needs. A successful project manager will be well trained in the technical side of managing projects.

The second dimension is the sociocultural side of the project management process. In contrast with the orderly world of project planning, this dimension involves the much messier, often contradictory and paradoxical world of implementation. It centers on creating a temporary social system within a larger organizational environment that combines the talents of a divergent set of professionals working to complete the project. See Research Highlight: Works Well with Others. Project managers must shape a project culture that stimulates teamwork and high levels of personal motivation as well as a capacity to quickly identify and resolve problems that threaten project work. This dimension also involves managing the interface between the project and external environment. Project managers have to assuage and shape expectations of customers, sustain the political support of top management, negotiate with their functional counterparts, monitor subcontractors, and so on. Overall, the manager must build a cooperative social network among a divergent set of allies with different standards, commitments, and perspectives.

Some suggest that the technical dimension represents the "science" of project management while the sociocultural dimension represents the "art" of managing a project. To be successful, a manager must be a master of both. Unfortunately, some project managers become preoccupied with the planning and technical dimension of project management. Often their first real exposure to project management is through project management software, and they become infatuated with network charts, Gantt diagrams, and performance variances and attempt to manage a project from a distance. Conversely, there are other managers who manage projects by the "seat of their pants," relying heavily on team dynamics and organizational politics to complete a project. Good project managers balance their attention to both the technical and sociocultural dimensions of project management.

Summary

There are powerful environmental forces contributing to the rapid expansion of project management approaches to business problems and opportunities. A project is defined as a nonroutine, one-time effort limited by time, resources, and performance specifications designed to meet customer needs. One of the distinguishing characteristics of project management is that it has both a beginning and an end and typically consists of four phases: defining, planning, executing, and delivering. Effective project management begins with selecting and prioritizing projects that support the firm's mission and strategy. Successful implementation requires both technical and social skills. Project managers have to plan and budget projects as well as orchestrate the contributions of others.

Text Overview

This text is written to provide the reader with a comprehensive, integrative understanding of the project management process. The text focuses both on the science of project management and the art of managing projects. Following this introductory chapter, Chapter 2 focuses on how organizations go about evaluating and selecting projects. Special attention is devoted to the importance of linking project selection to the mission and strategy of the firm. The organizational environment in which projects are implemented is the focus of Chapter 3. The traditional discussion of matrix management and other organizational forms is augmented by a discussion of the role the culture of an organization plays in the implementation of projects.

The next six chapters focus on developing a plan for the project; after all, project success begins with a good plan. Chapter 4 deals with defining the scope of the project and developing a work breakdown structure (WBS). The challenge of formulating cost and time estimates is the subject of Chapter 5. Chapter 6 focuses on utilizing the information from the WBS to create a project plan in the form of a timed and sequenced network of activities.

Risks are a potential threat to project management, and Chapter 7 examines how organizations and managers identify and manage risks associated with project work. Resource allocation is added to the plan in Chapter 8 with special attention devoted to how resource limitations impact the project schedule. Finally, Chapter 9 examines strategies for reducing ("crashing") project time either prior to the initiation of the project or in response to problems or new demands placed on the project.

Chapters 10 through 12 focus on project implementation and the sociocultural side of project management, beginning with Chapter 10, which focuses on the role of the project manager as a leader and stresses the importance of managing project stakeholders within the organization. Chapter 11 focuses on the core project team; it combines the latest information on team dynamics with leadership skills/techniques for developing a high-performance project team. Chapter 12 continues the theme of managing project stakeholders by discussing how to manage external relations such as those with contractors, customers, and suppliers.

Chapter 13 focuses on the kinds of information managers use to monitor project progress, with special attention devoted to the key concept of earned value. Issues surrounding the termination or completion of the project are dealt with in Chapter 14. Implementation of project management in multicultural, international environments is the subject of Chapter 15. Finally, Chapter 16 looks briefly toward the future of project management and includes a special segment on pursuing a career in project management.

Throughout this text you will be exposed to the major aspects of the project management system. However, a true understanding of project management comes not from knowing what a scope statement is, or the critical path, or partnering with contractors, but from comprehending how the different elements of the project management system interact to determine the fate of a project. The key to success, then, becomes managing conflicting demands and the interaction among different elements of a project, not the elements themselves. For example, project managers must manage the interactions among scope, cost, schedule, team, and customer expectations. They must manage the interactions between the project management information system and the people who provide the data and use it. They must manage the interactions between the core project team and the outsiders they depend on. If, by the end of this text, you come to appreciate these key points of balancing your skills in the technical and sociocultural dimensions and managing the interactions among them, you should have a distinct competitive advantage over others aspiring to work in the field of project management.

Key Terms	Program	Project	Sociotechnical
	ISO 9000	Project life cycle	perspective

Review Questions

1. Define a project. What are four characteristics that help differentiate projects from other functions carried out in the daily operations of the organization?
2. What are some of the key environmental forces that have changed the way projects are managed? What has been the effect of these forces on the management of projects?
3. Why is the implementation of projects important to strategic planning and the project manager?
4. The technical and sociocultural dimensions of project management are two sides to the same coin. Explain.
5. What is meant by an integrative approach to project management? Why is this approach important in today's environment?

Exercises

1. Review the front page of your local newspaper, and try to identify all the projects contained in the articles. How many were you able to find?
2. Individually identify what you consider to be the greatest achievements accomplished by mankind in the last five decades. Now share your list with three to five other students in the class, and come up with an expanded list. Review these accomplishments in terms of the definition of a project. What does your review suggest about the importance of project management?

3. Individually identify projects assigned in previous terms. Were both sociocultural and technical elements factors in the success or difficulties in the projects?

4. Check out the Project Management Institute's home page at *www.pmi.org*.

   a. Review general information about PMI as well as membership information.

   b. See if there is a PMI chapter in your state. It not, where is the closest one?

   c. From the news link, access information on PMI's Project Management Body of Knowledge (PMBOK), or go directly to it at *www.pmi.org/publictn/pmboktoc.htm*. What is PMBOK?

   d. Explore other links that PMI provides. What do these links tell you about the nature and future of project management?

Note: If you have any difficulty accessing any of the Web addresses listed here or elsewhere in the text, you can find up-to-date addresses on the home page of Dr. Erik Larson, coauthor of this text: *www.bus.oregonstate.edu/faculty/larson*.

References

Benko, C. and F. W. McFarlan, *Connecting the Dots* (Boston: HBS Press, 2003).

Cohen, D. J. and R. J. Graham, *The Project Manager's MBA* (San Francisco: Jossey-Bass, 2001).

Kerzner, H. *Project Management: A Systems Approach to Planning, Scheduling, and Controlling* (New York: Wiley, 2003).

Peters, T. *PM Network,* January 2004, Vol. 18, No. 1, p. 19.

Stewart, T. A. "The Corporate Jungle Spawns a New Species: The Project Manager," *Fortune* (September 1996), pp. 14–15.

Wysocki, B. "Flying Solo: High-Tech Nomads Write New Program for Future of Work," *The Wall Street Journal* (August 19, 1996), p. 1.

Case

A Day in the Life

Rachel, the project manager of a large information systems project, arrives at her office early to get caught up with work before her co-workers and project team arrive. However, as she enters the office she meets Neil, one of her fellow project managers, who also wants to get an early start on the day. Neil has just completed a project overseas. They spend 10 minutes socializing and catching up on personal news.

It takes Rachel 10 minutes to get to her office and settle in. She then checks her voice mail and turns on her computer. She was at her client's site the day before until 7:30 P.M. and has not checked her e-mail or voice mail since 3:30 P.M. the previous day. There are 7 phone messages, 16 e-mails, and 4 notes left on her desk. She spends 15 minutes reviewing her schedule and "to do" lists for the day before responding to messages that require immediate attention.

Rachel spends the next 25 minutes going over project reports and preparing for the weekly status meeting. Her boss, who just arrived at the office, interrupts her. They spend 20 minutes discussing the project. He shares a rumor that a team member is using stimulants on the job. She tells him that she has not seen anything suspicious but will keep an eye on the team member.

The 9:00 A.M. project status meeting starts 15 minutes late because two of the team members have to finish a job for a client. Several people go to the cafeteria to get coffee and doughnuts while others discuss last night's baseball game. The team members arrive, and the remaining 45 minutes of the progress review meeting surface project issues that have to be addressed and assigned for action.

After the meeting Rachel goes down the hallway to meet with Victoria, another IS project manager. They spend 30 minutes reviewing project assignments since the two of them share personnel. Victoria's project is behind schedule and in need of help. They broker a deal that should get Victoria's project back on track.

She returns to her office and makes several phone calls and returns several e-mails before walking downstairs to visit with members of her project team. Her intent is to follow up on an issue that had surfaced in the status report meeting. However, her simple, "Hi guys, how are things going?" elicits a stream of disgruntled responses from the "troops." After listening patiently for over 20 minutes, she realizes that among other things several of the client's managers are beginning to request features that were not in the original project scope statement. She tells her people that she will get on this right away.

Returning to her office she tries to call her counterpart John at the client firm but is told that he is not expected back from lunch for another hour. At this time, Eddie drops by and says, "How about lunch?" Eddie works in the finance office and they spend the next half hour in the company cafeteria gossiping about internal politics. She is surprised to hear that Jonah Johnson, the director of systems projects, may join another firm. Jonah has always been a powerful ally.

She returns to her office, answers a few more e-mails, and finally gets through to John. They spend 30 minutes going over the problem. The conversation ends with John promising to do some investigating and to get back to her as soon as possible.

Rachel puts a "Do not disturb" sign on her door, and lies down in her office. She listens to the third and fourth movement of Ravel's string quartet in F on headphones.

Rachel then takes the elevator down to the third floor and talks to the purchasing agent assigned to her project. They spend the next 30 minutes exploring ways of getting necessary equipment to the project site earlier than planned. She finally authorizes express delivery.

When she returns to her office, her calendar reminds her that she is scheduled to participate in a conference call at 2:30. It takes 15 minutes for everyone to get online. During this time, Rachel catches up on some e-mail. The next hour is spent exchanging information about the technical requirements associated with a new version of a software package they are using on systems projects like hers.

Rachel decides to stretch her legs and goes on a walk down the hallway where she engages in brief conversations with various co-workers. She goes out of her way to thank Chandra for his thoughtful analysis at the status report meeting. She returns to find that John has left a message for her to call him back ASAP. She contacts John, who informs her that, according to his people, her firm's marketing rep had made certain promises about specific features her system would provide. He doesn't know how this communication breakdown occurred, but his people are pretty upset over the situation. Rachel thanks John for the information and immediately takes the stairs to where the marketing group resides.

She asks to see Mary, a senior marketing manager. She waits 10 minutes before being invited into her office. After a heated discussion, she leaves 40 minutes later with Mary agreeing to talk to her people about what was promised and what was not promised.

She goes downstairs to her people to give them an update on what is happening. They spend 30 minutes reviewing the impact the client's requests could have on the project schedule. She also shares with them the schedule changes she and Victoria had agreed to. After she says good night to her team, she heads upstairs to her boss's office and spends 20 minutes updating him on key events of the day. She returns to her office and spends 30 minutes reviewing e-mails and project documents. She logs on to the MS project schedule of her project and spends the next 30 minutes working with "what-if" scenarios. She reviews tomorrow's schedule and writes some personal reminders before starting off on her 30-minute commute home.

1. How effectively do you think Rachel spent her day?
2. What does the case tell you about what it is like to be a project manager?

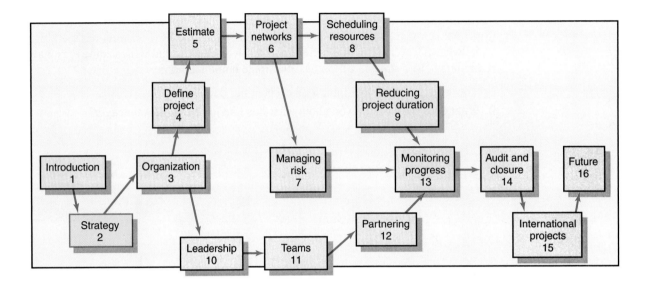

CHAPTER TWO

Organization Strategy and Project Selection

Strategy is implemented through projects. Every project should have a clear link to the organization's strategy.

Project managers commonly complain that projects appear out of nowhere. Comments such as the following are samples of those heard in practice:

- Where did this project come from?
- Should I stop working on this project and start on the new one?
- Why are we doing this project?
- How can all these projects be first priority?
- Where are we going to get the resources to do this project?

There are too many organizations in which many managers cannot identify a project's priority and link it with the strategic plan. This is not good management! Every project should contribute value to the organization's strategic plan, which is designed to meet the future needs of its customers. Ensuring a strong linkage between the strategic plan and projects is a difficult task that demands constant attention from top and middle management. The larger and more diverse an organization, the more difficult it is to create and maintain this strong link. Ample evidence still suggests that many organizations have not developed a process that clearly aligns project selection to the strategic plan. The result is poor utilization of the organization's resources—people, money, equipment, and core competencies. Conversely, organizations that have a coherent link of projects to strategy have more cooperation across the organization, perform better on projects, and have fewer projects.

How can an organization ensure this link and alignment? The answer requires integration of projects with the strategic plan. Integration assumes the existence of a strategic plan and a process for prioritizing projects by their contribution to the plan. A crucial factor to ensure the success of integrating the plan with projects lies in the creation of a process that is open and published for all participants to review. This chapter presents an overview of the importance of strategic planning and the process for developing a strategic plan. Typical problems encountered when strategy and projects are not linked are noted. A generic methodology that ensures integration by creating very strong linkages of project selection and priority to the strategic plan is then discussed. The intended outcomes are clear organization focus, best use of scarce organization resources (people, equipment, capital), and improved communication across projects and departments.

Why Project Managers Need to Understand Strategy

Project management historically has been preoccupied solely with the planning and execution of projects. Strategy was considered to be under the purview of senior management. This is old-school thinking. New-school thinking recognizes that project management is at the apex of strategy and operations. Aaron Shenhar speaks to this issue when he states, "…it is time to expand the traditional role of the project manager from an operational to a more strategic perspective. In the modern evolving organization, project managers will be focused on business aspects, and their role will expand from getting the job done to achieving the business results and winning in the market place."

There are two main reasons why project managers need to understand their organization's mission and strategy. The first reason is so they can make appropriate decisions and adjustments. For example, how a project manager would respond to a suggestion to modify the design of a product to enhance performance will vary depending upon whether his company strives to be a product leader through innovation or to achieve operational excellence through low cost solutions. Similarly, how a project manager would respond to delays may vary depending upon strategic concerns. A project manager will authorize overtime if her firm places a premium on getting to the market first. Another project manager will accept the delay if speed is not essential.

J. P. Descamps has observed that project managers who do not understand the role their project plays in accomplishing the strategy of their organization tend to make the following serious mistakes:

- Focusing on problems or solutions that have low priority strategically
- Focusing on the immediate customer rather than the whole market place and value chain
- Overemphasizing technology as an end in and of itself, resulting in projects that wander off pursuing exotic technology that does not fit the strategy or customer need
- Trying to solve every customer issue with a product or service rather than focusing on the 20 percent with 80 percent of the value (Pareto's Law)
- Engaging in a never-ending search for perfection that no one except the project team really cares about

The second reason project managers need to understand their organization's strategy is so that they can be effective project advocates. Project managers have to be able to demonstrate to senior management how their project contributes to their firm's mission. Protection and continued support come from being aligned with corporate objectives. Project managers also need to be able to explain to team members and other stakeholders why certain project objectives and priorities are critical. This is essential for getting buy-in on contentious trade-off decisions.

For these reasons project managers will find it valuable to have a keen understanding of strategic management and project selection processes, which are discussed next.

The Strategic Management Process: An Overview

Strategic management is the process of assessing "what we are" and deciding and implementing "what we intend to be and how we are going to get there." Strategy describes how an organization intends to compete with the resources available in the existing and perceived future environment.

Two major dimensions of strategic management are responding to changes in the external environment and allocating scarce resources of the firm to improve its competitive position. Constant scanning of the external environment for changes is a major

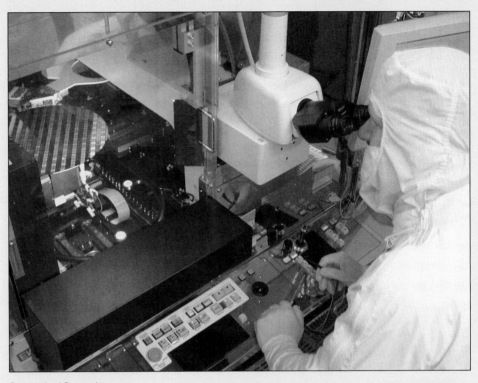

Courtesy Intel Corporation.

INTEL CEO, Craig R. Barrett, is planning his last hurrah only 15 months before his retirement to chairman of the board. His vision for INTEL is to move beyond computers: think INTEL everywhere. Barrett says, "Everything in the world is going digital." He wants INTEL chips to be the guts of every digital device on the planet—especially in the communications, consumer electronics, and entertainment industries. Think—cell phones, wireless home networks, video players, flat panel TVs—INTEL's expertise fits right in.

He is hitting the market today with a chip technology called WiMax "that can be used to deliver high speed Internet access throughout a small city (or 30 miles) for about $100,000, which is about one-tenth the cost of rolling out fiber optic lines today." (A competitor, WiFi, has a range of about 200 feet.) Cable and phone companies are very interested because of low entry costs.

Some critics believe Barrett's shotgun approach is too risky. He doesn't see it that way. Rather than following INTEL's past go-it-alone approach to new products, he wants INTEL to forge closer ties with customers by designing products they need rather than designing products no one asked for. He admits going into consumer markets will be a challenge and a half. He intends to provide financial support and cooperation for companies creating new products that will use INTEL chips. Barrett feels the risk of providing financial support for smaller companies creating new products is low, even if some go bust. If most of the new products take off, risk is minimized because their markets will lead to increasing demand for new, larger, and faster PCs where INTEL manufacturing dominates cost.

Implementing the new vision will not keep INTEL's manufacturing from remaining on the cutting edge. By 2005 five new factories will manufacture 12-inch wafers printed with 90-nanometer circuit lines, just 0.1 percent the width of a human hair. These plants are expected to slash chip costs in half.

The mission has been set: Create INTEL chips to meet the need of new digital products. Right or wrong, everyone in the organization knows the game plan and can focus their efforts in this new consumer-oriented direction. Projects related to digital products will be ranked high priority.

*Adapted from Cliff Edwards, "What is CEO Craig Barrett up to?" *Business Week*, March 8, 2004, pp. 56–64.

requirement for survival in a dynamic competitive environment. The second dimension is the internal responses to new action programs aimed at enhancing the competitive position of the firm. The nature of the responses depends on the type of business, environment volatility, competition, and the organizational culture.

Strategic management provides the theme and focus of the future direction of the organization. It supports consistency of action at every level of the organization. It encourages integration because effort and resources are committed to common goals and strategies. See Snapshot from Practice: Move Beyond Computers. It is a continuous, iterative process aimed at developing an integrated and coordinated long-term plan of action. Strategic management positions the organization to meet the needs and requirements of its customers for the long term. With the long-term position identified, objectives are set, and strategies are developed to achieve objectives and then translated into actions by implementing projects. Strategy can decide the survival of an organization. Most organizations are successful in *formulating* strategies for what course(s) they should pursue. However, the problem in many organizations is *implementing* strategies—that is, making them happen. Integration of strategy formulation and implementation often does not exist.

The components of strategic management are closely linked, and all are directed toward the future success of the organization. Strategic management requires strong links among mission, goals, objectives, strategy, and implementation. The mission gives the general purpose of the organization. Goals give global targets within the mission. Objectives give specific targets to goals. Objectives give rise to formulation of strategies to reach objectives. Finally, strategies require actions and tasks to be implemented. In most cases the actions to be taken represent projects. Figure 2.1 shows a schematic of the strategic management process and major activities required.

Four Activities of the Strategic Management Process

The typical sequence of activities of the strategic management process is outlined here; a description of each activity then follows:

1. Review and define the organizational mission.
2. Set long-range goals and objectives.
3. Analyze and formulate strategies to reach objectives.
4. Implement strategies through projects.

Review and Define the Organizational Mission

The mission identifies "what we want to become" or the raison d'être. Mission statements identify the scope of the organization in terms of its product or service. A written mission statement provides focus for decision making when shared by organizational managers and employees. Everyone in the organization should be keenly aware of the organization's mission. For example, at one large consulting firm, partners who fail to recite the mission statement on demand are required to buy lunch. The mission statement communicates and identifies the purpose of the organization to all stakeholders. Mission statements can be used for evaluating organization performance.

Traditional components found in mission statements are major products and services, target customers and markets, and geographical domain. In addition, statements frequently include organizational philosophy, key technologies, public image, and contribution to society. Including such factors in mission statements relates directly to business success.

Mission statements change infrequently. However, when the nature of the business changes or shifts, a revised mission statement may be required. For example, Steve Jobs of Apple computer envisioned the use of computer technology beyond the PC desktop. His mission was to look at computer technology as the vehicle for work and

FIGURE 2.1
Strategic Management Process

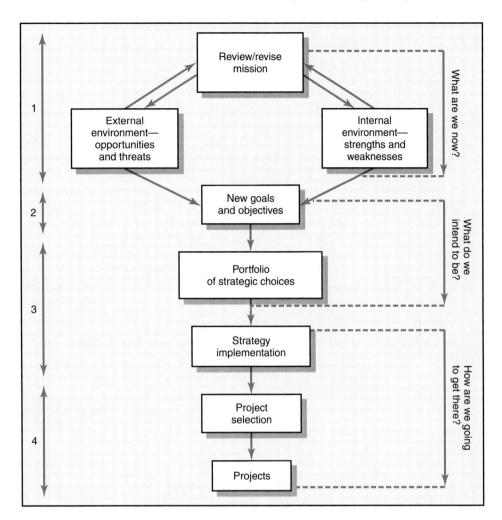

entertainment. As a result he developed the iPod for selling music and masterminded the development of animated movies such as *Finding Nemo* through the Pixar organization. The latter resulted in the breakaway of Pixar from Disney, which marketed the animated movies. As a result, Pixar will need to revise their mission statement to be more specific.

More specific mission statements tend to give better results because of a tighter focus. Mission statements decrease the chance of false directions by stakeholders. For example, compare the phrasing of the following mission statements:

Provide hospital design services.

Provide voice/data design services.

Provide information technology services.

Increase shareholder value.

Provide high-value products to our customer.

Clearly, the first two statements leave less chance for misinterpretation than the others. A rule-of-thumb test for a mission statement is, if the statement can be anybody's mission statement, it will not provide the guidance and focus intended. The mission sets the parameters for developing objectives.

Long-Range Goals and Objectives

Objectives translate the organization mission into specific, concrete, measurable terms. Organizational objectives set targets for all levels of the organization. Objectives pinpoint the direction managers believe the organization should move toward. Objectives answer in detail *where* a firm is headed and *when* it is going to get there. Typically, objectives for the organization cover markets, products, innovation, productivity, quality, finance, profitability, employees, and consumers. In every case, objectives should be as operational as possible. That is, objectives should include a time frame, be measurable, be an identifiable state, and be realistic. Doran created the memory device shown in Exhibit 2.1 which is useful when writing objectives.

Each level below the organizational objectives should support the higher-level objectives in more detail; this is frequently called cascading of objectives. For example, if a firm making leather luggage sets an objective of achieving a 40 percent increase in sales through a research and development strategy, this charge is passed to the marketing, production, and R&D departments. The R&D department accepts the firm's strategy as their objective, and their strategy becomes the design and development of a new "pull-type luggage with hidden retractable wheels." At this point the objective becomes a project to be implemented—to develop the retractable wheel luggage for market within six months within a budget of $200,000. In summary, organizational objectives drive your projects.

Analyze and Formulate Strategies to Reach Objectives

Formulating strategy answers the question of *what* needs to be done to reach objectives. Strategy formulation includes determining and evaluating alternatives that support the organization's objectives and selecting the best alternative. The first step is a realistic evaluation of the past and current position of the enterprise. This step typically includes an analysis of "who are the customers" and "what are their needs as they (the *customers*) see them."

The next step is an assessment of the internal and external environments. What are the internal strengths and weaknesses of the enterprise? Examples of internal strengths or weaknesses could be core competencies, such as technology, product quality, management talent, low debt, and dealer networks. Managers can alter internal strengths and weaknesses. Opportunities and threats usually represent external forces for change such as technology, industry structure, and competition. Competitive benchmarking tools are sometimes used here to assess current and future directions. Opportunities and threats are the flip sides of each other. That is, a threat can be perceived as an opportunity, or vice versa. Examples of perceived external threats could be a slowing of the economy, a maturing life cycle, exchange rates, or government regulation. Typical opportunities are increasing demand, emerging markets, and demographics. Managers or individual firms have limited opportunities to influence such external environmental factors; however, in recent years notable exceptions have been new technologies such as Apple using the iPod to create a market to sell music. The keys are to attempt to forecast fundamental industry changes and stay in a proactive mode rather than a reactive one. This assessment of the external and internal environments is known as the SWOT analysis (strengths, weaknesses, opportunities, and threats).

EXHIBIT 2.1
Characteristics of Objectives

S	Specific	Be specific in targeting an objective
M	Measurable	Establish a measurable indicator(s) of progress
A	Assignable	Make the objective assignable to one person for completion
R	Realistic	State what can realistically be done with available resources
T	Time related	State when the objective can be achieved, that is, duration

Photodisc Red/Getty Images.

During the early 1980s Jan Carlzon was appointed chief operating officer for Scandinavian Airlines (SAS). At this time, the entire airline industry was in the midst of a slump, and SAS was about to record a second straight year of losses. Carlzon halted the practice of instituting across-the-board cuts and instead focused on developing a strategic mission that would make SAS profitable during a time of zero market growth. The strategy was to make SAS known as the best airline in the world for the frequent business traveler. SAS realized that business travelers were the most stable part of the market and tended to purchase full-fare tickets as opposed to discounted tickets. Furthermore, business travelers tended to have unique needs that would allow SAS to develop services to attract their full-fare business.

Under Carlzon's leadership, SAS scrutinized every project and expense as to whether it contributed to improving the service to the frequent business traveler. If the answer was no, no matter what it was or how dear it was to those within SAS, it was cut. Projects such as developing vacation packages to the Mediterranean were eliminated, and overall SAS was able to cut $40 million in nonessential expenses. At the same time, Carlzon persuaded the SAS board to invest $45 million and increase operating expenses $12 million a year for 147 different projects designed to attract and serve the frequent business traveler. They launched a comprehensive punctuality campaign, improved the traffic hub in Copenhagen, and offered customer service courses for more than 12,000 staff members.

SAS dropped first-class seating and created "Euro-Class" at full-fare coach prices. They installed movable partitions in their aircraft to separate the Euro-Class section from the others. They were among the first airlines to create comfortable lounges at the terminals with telephone and telex services for Euro-Class passengers. They gave Euro-Class travelers separate, express check-in counters, more comfortable seats, and better food.

The results were startling. Within three years SAS increased the number of full-fare business passengers by 23 percent at a time when the overall market was stagnant. *Fortune* magazine conducted a survey that named SAS the best airline for business travelers in the world. The SAS story illustrates how a clear mission allows an organization to concentrate its limited resources on those projects that increase the profitability and success of the firm.

*Jan Carlzon, *Moments of Truth* (New York: Harper & Row, 1987).

From this analysis, critical issues and a portfolio of strategic alternatives are identified. These alternatives are compared with the current portfolio and available resources; strategies are then selected that should support the basic mission and objectives of the organization. Critical analysis of the strategies includes asking questions: Does the strategy take advantage of our core competencies? Does the strategy exploit our competitive advantage? Does the strategy maximize meeting customers' needs? Does the strategy fit within our acceptable risk range?

Strategy formulation ends with cascading objectives or tasks assigned to lower divisions, departments, or individuals. Formulating strategy might range around 20 percent of management's effort, while determining *how* strategy will be implemented might consume 80 percent.

Implement Strategies through Projects

Implementation answers the question of *how* strategies will be realized, given available resources. The conceptual framework for strategy implementation lacks the structure and discipline found in strategy formulation. Implementation requires action and completing tasks; the latter frequently means mission-critical projects. Therefore, implementation must include attention to several key areas.

First, completing tasks requires allocation of resources. Resources typically represent funds, people, management talents, technological skills, and equipment. Frequently, implementation of projects is treated as an "addendum" rather than an integral part of the strategic management process. However, multiple objectives place conflicting demands on organizational resources. Second, implementation requires a formal and informal organization that complements and supports strategy and projects. Authority, responsibility, and performance all depend on organization structure and culture. Third, planning and control systems must be in place to be certain project activities necessary to ensure strategies are effectively performed. Fourth, motivating project contributors will be a major factor for achieving project success. Finally, an area receiving more attention in recent years is prioritizing projects. Although the strategy implementation process is not as clear as strategy formulation, all managers realize that, without implementation, success is impossible.

The Need for an Effective Project Portfolio Management System

Implementation of projects without a strong priority system linked to strategy creates problems. Three of the most obvious problems are discussed below. A project portfolio system can go a long way to reduce, or even eliminate, the impact of these problems.

Problem 1: The Implementation Gap

In organizations with short product life cycles, it is interesting to note that frequently participation in strategic planning and implementation includes participants from all levels within the organization. However, in perhaps 80 percent of the remaining product and service organizations, top management pretty much formulates strategy and leaves strategy implementation to functional managers. Within these broad constraints, more detailed strategies and objectives are developed by the functional managers. The fact that these objectives and strategies are made *independently* at different levels by functional groups within the organization hierarchy causes manifold problems.

Some symptoms of organizations struggling with strategy disconnect and unclear priorities are presented here.

- Conflicts frequently occur among functional managers and cause lack of trust.
- Frequent meetings are called to establish or renegotiate priorities.
- People frequently shift from one project to another, depending on current priority. Employees are confused about which projects are important.

- People are working on multiple projects and feel inefficient.
- Resources are not adequate.

Because clear linkages do not exist, the organizational environment becomes dysfunctional, confused, and ripe for ineffective implementation of organization strategy and, thus, of projects. The implementation gap refers to the lack of understanding and consensus of organization strategy among top and middle-level managers.

A scenario the authors have seen repeated several times follows. Top management picks their top 20 projects for the next planning period, without priorities. Each functional department—marketing, finance, operations, engineering, information technology, and human resources—selects projects from the list. Unfortunately independent department priorities across projects are not homogenous. A project that rates first in the IT department can rate 10th in the finance department. Implementation of the projects represents conflicts of interest with animosities developing over organization resources.

If this condition exists, how is it possible to effectively implement strategy? The problem is serious. One study found that only about 25 percent of *Fortune* 500 executives believe there is a strong linkage, consistency, and/or agreement between the strategies they formulate and implementation. Middle managers considered organizational strategy to be under the purview of others or not in their realm of influence. It is the responsibility of senior management to set policies that show a distinct link between organizational strategy and objectives and projects that implement those strategies. The research of Fusco suggests the implementation gap and prioritizing projects are still overlooked by many organizations. He surveyed 280 project managers and found that 24 percent of their organizations did not even publish or circulate their objectives; in addition, 40 percent of the respondents reported that priorities among competing projects were not clear, while only 17 percent reported clear priorities.

Problem 2: Organization Politics

Politics exist in every organization and can have a significant influence on which projects receive funding and high priority. This is especially true when the criteria and process for selecting projects are ill-defined and not aligned with the mission of the firm. Project selection may be based not so much on facts and sound reasoning, but rather on the persuasiveness and power of people advocating projects.

The term "sacred cow" is often used to denote a project that a powerful, high-ranking official is advocating. Case in point, a marketing consultant confided that he was once hired by the marketing director of a large firm to conduct an independent, external market analysis for a new product the firm was interested in developing. His extensive research indicated that there was insufficient demand to warrant the financing of this new product. The marketing director chose to bury the report and made the consultant promise never to share this information with anyone. The director explained that this new product was the "pet idea" of the new CEO, who saw it as his legacy to the firm. He went on to describe the CEO's irrational obsession with the project and how he referred to it as his "new baby." Like a parent fiercely protecting his child, the marketing director believed that he would lose his job if such critical information ever became known.

Having a project sponsor can play a significant role in the selection and successful implementation of product innovation projects. Project sponsors are typically high-ranking managers who endorse and lend political support for the completion of a specific project. They are instrumental in winning approval of the project and in protecting the project during the critical development stage. Savvy project managers recognize the importance of having "friends in higher courts" who can advocate for their case and protect their interests.

The significance of corporate politics can be seen in the ill-fated ALTO computer project at Xerox during the mid-1970s. The project was a tremendous technological success; it developed the first workable mouse, the first laser printer, the first user-friendly software, and the first local area network. All of these developments were five years ahead of their nearest competitor. Over the next five years this opportunity to dominate the nascent personal computer market was squandered because of internal in-fighting at Xerox and the absence of a strong project sponsor.

Politics can play a role not only in project selection but also in the aspirations behind projects. Individuals can enhance their power within an organization by managing extraordinary and critical projects. Power and status naturally accrue to successful innovators and risk takers rather than to steady producers. Similarly, managers can become heroes within their organization by leading projects that contribute significantly to the organization's mission or solve a pressing crisis. Many ambitious managers pursue high-profile projects as a means for moving quickly up the corporate ladder. For example, Lee Iacocca's career was built on successfully leading the design and development of the highly successful Ford Mustang.

Many would argue that politics and project management should not mix. A more proactive response is that projects and politics invariably mix and that effective project managers recognize that any significant project has political ramifications. Likewise, top management needs to develop a system for identifying and selecting projects that reduces the impact of internal politics and fosters the selection of the best projects for achieving the mission and strategy of the firm.

Problem 3: Resource Conflicts and Multitasking

Most project organizations exist in a multiproject environment. This environment creates the problems of project interdependency and the need to share resources. For example, what would be the impact on the labor resource pool of a construction company if it should win a contract it would like to bid on? Will existing labor be adequate to deal with the new project—given the completion date? Will current projects be delayed? Will subcontracting help? Which projects will have priority? Competition among project managers can be contentious. All project managers seek to have the best people for their projects. The problems of sharing resources and scheduling resources across projects grow exponentially as the number of projects rises. In multiproject environments the stakes are higher and the benefits or penalties for good or bad resource scheduling become even more significant than in most single projects.

Resource sharing also leads to multitasking. Multitasking involves starting and stopping work on one task to go and work on another project, and then returning to the work on the original task. People working on several tasks concurrently are far less efficient, especially where conceptual or physical shutdown and startup are significant. Multitasking adds to delays and costs. Changing priorities exacerbate the multitasking problems even more. Likewise, multitasking is more evident in organizations that have too many projects for the resources they command.

The number of small and large projects in a portfolio almost always exceeds the available resources (typically by a factor of three to four times the available resources). This capacity overload inevitably leads to confusion and inefficient use of scarce organizational resources. The presence of an implementation gap, of power politics, and of multitasking adds to the problem of which projects are allocated resources first. Employee morale and confidence suffer because it is difficult to make sense of an ambiguous system. A multiproject organization environment faces major problems without a priority system that is clearly linked to the strategic plan.

EXHIBIT 2.2

Benefits of Project Portfolio Management

- Builds discipline into project selection process.
- Links project selection to strategic metrics.
- Prioritizes project proposals across a common set of criteria, rather than on politics or emotion.
- Allocates resources to projects that align with strategic direction.
- Balances risk across all projects.
- Justifies killing projects that do not support organization strategy.
- Improves communication and supports agreement on project goals.

In essence, to this point we have suggested that many organizations have no meaningful process for addressing the problems we have described. The first and most important change that will go a long way in addressing these and other problems is the development and use of a meaningful project priority process for project selection.

How can the implementation gap be narrowed so that understanding and consensus of organizational strategies run through all levels of management? How can power politics be minimized? Can a process be developed in which projects are consistently prioritized to support organizational strategies? Can the prioritized projects be used to allocate scarce organizational resources—for example, people, equipment? Can the process encourage bottom-up initiation of projects that support clear organizational targets?

What is needed is a set of integrative criteria and a process for evaluating and selecting projects that support higher-level strategies and objectives. A single-project priority system that ranks projects by their contribution to the strategic plan would make life easier. Easily said, but difficult to accomplish in practice. Organizations that managed independent projects and allocated resources ad hoc have shifted focus to selecting the right portfolio of projects to achieve their strategic objectives. This is a quickening trend. The advantages of successful project portfolio systems are becoming well recognized in project-driven organizations. See Exhibit 2.2, which lists a few key benefits; the list could easily be extended.

A project portfolio system is discussed next with emphasis on selection criteria, which is where the power of the portfolio system is established.

A Portfolio Management System

Succinctly put, portfolio management ensures projects are aligned with strategic goals and prioritized appropriately. Portfolio management provides information to make better business decisions. Since there are usually more projects clamoring for resources than are available, it is important to follow a logical and defined process for selecting the projects to implement.

Design of a project portfolio system should include classification of a project, selection criteria depending upon classification, sources of proposals, evaluating proposals, and managing the portfolio of projects.

Classification of the Project

Many organizations find they have three different kinds of projects in their portfolio: *compliance* and emergency (must do), *operational,* and *strategic* projects. Compliance projects are typically those needed to meet regulatory conditions required to operate in a region; hence, they are called "must do" projects. Emergency projects, such as rebuilding a soybean factory destroyed by fire, meet the must do criterion. Compliance and emergency projects usually have penalties if they are not implemented.

Operational projects are those that are needed to support current operations. These projects are designed to improve efficiency of delivery systems, reduce product costs, and improve performance. TQM projects are examples of operational projects. Finally, strategic projects are those that directly support the organization's long-run mission. They frequently are directed toward increasing revenue or market share. Examples of strategic projects are new products, research and development. (See Figure 2.2).

The strategic value of a proposed project must be determined before it can be placed in the project portfolio. Under rare circumstances, there are projects that "must" be selected. These compliance or emergency projects are those that must be implemented or the firm will fail or suffer dire penalties or consequences. For example, a manufacturing plant must install an electrostatic filter on top of a smokestack in six months or close down. EU courts are trying to force Microsoft to open their software architecture to allow competing software firms to be compatible and interact with Microsoft. This decision may become a compliance project for Microsoft. Any project placed in the "must" category ignores other selection criteria. A rule of thumb for placing a proposed project in this category is that 99 percent of the organization stakeholders would agree that the project must be implemented; there is no perceived choice but to implement the project. All other projects are selected using selection criteria linked to organization strategy.

Selection Criteria

Although there are many criteria for selecting projects, selection criteria are typically identified as *financial* and *nonfinancial*. A short description of each is given next, followed by a discussion of their use in practice.

Financial Models For most managers financial criteria are the preferred method to evaluate projects. These models are appropriate when there is a high level of confidence associated with estimates of future cash flows. Two models and examples are demonstrated here—payback and net present value (NPV).

> **Project A** has an initial investment of $700,000 and projected cash inflows of $225,000 for 5 years.
> **Project B** has an initial investment of $400,000 and projected cash inflows of $110,00 for 5 years.

1. The payback model measures the time it will take to recover the project investment. Shorter paybacks are more desirable. Payback is the simplest and most widely used model. Payback emphasizes cash flows, a key factor in business. Some managers use the payback model to eliminate unusually risky projects (those with lengthy payback periods). The major limitations of payback are that it ignores the time value of

FIGURE 2.2
Portfolio of Projects by Type

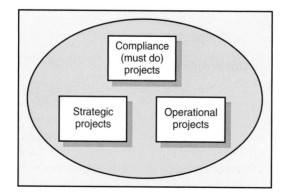

money, assumes cash inflows for the investment period (and not beyond), and does not consider profitability. Payback formula is

$$\text{Payback period (yrs)} = \text{Estimated Project Cost/Annual savings}$$

Exhibit 2.3 compares the payback for Project A and Project B. The payback for Project A is 3.1 years and for Project B is 3.6 years. Using the payback method both projects are acceptable since both return the initial investment in less than five years and have returns on the investment of 32.1 and 27.5 percent.

2. The net present value (NPV) model uses management's minimum desired rate-of-return (discount rate, for example, 20 percent) to compute the present value of all net cash inflows. If the result is positive, (the project meets the minimum desired rate of return) it is eligible for further consideration. If the result is negative, the project is rejected. Thus, higher positive NPV's are desirable. Excel uses this formula

$$\text{Project NPV} = I_0 + \sum_{t=1}^{n} \frac{F_t}{(1 + k)^t} \qquad \text{where}$$

I_0 = Initial investment (since it is an outflow, the number will be negative)

F_t = net cash inflow for period t

k = required rate of return

EXHIBIT 2.3   Example Comparing Two Projects: Net Present Value (NPV) and Payback Method

	A	B	C	D	E	F	G	H	I	J
1										
2				Exhibit 2.3						
3										
4				Example Comparing Two Projects Using NPV						
5	**Project A**		Year 0	Year 1	Year 2	Year 3	Year 4	Year 5	Total	Formulas
6	Required rate of return	15%								
7	Outflows		–$700,000						–$700,000	
8	Inflows			$225,000	$225,000	$225,000	$225,000	$225,000	$1,125,000	
9	Net Inflows			$225,000	$225,000	$225,000	$225,000	$425,000	$425,000	Project A: =C7+NPV(B6,D9:H9)
10	NPV	$54,235								
11										
12										
13	**Project B**									
14	Required rate of return	15%								
15	Outflows		–$400,000						–$400,000	
16	Inflows			$110,000	$110,000	$110,000	$110,000	$110,000	$550,000	
17	Net inflows			$110,000	$110,000	$110,000	$110,000	$110,000	$150,000	Project B: =C15+NPV(B14,D17:H17)
18	NPV	–$31,283								
19										
20										
21										
22	NPV comparison: Accept Project A---NPV is positive									
23	Reject Project B---NPV is negative									
24										
25										
26										
27				Example Comparing Two Projects Using the Payback Method						
28										
29				Project A		Project B				
30										
31										
32		Investment		$700,000		$400,000				Project A Payback =(D32/D33)
33		Annual savings		$225,000		$110,000				Project B Payback: =(F32/F33)
34										
35		Payback period*		3.1 years		3.6 years				
36										
37		Rate of return**		32.1%		27.5%				Project A: =(D33/D32)
38										Project B: =(F33/F32)
39	Project A: Accept. Less than 5 years and exceeds 15% desired rate									
40										
41	Project B: Accept. Less than 5 years.									
42										
43	* Note: Payback does not use the time value of money									
44	** Note: Rate of return is reciprocal of Payback									
45										

Exhibit 2.3 presents the NPV model using Microsoft Excel software. The NPV model Accepts project A, which has a *positive* NPV of $54,235. Project B is rejected since the NPV is *negative* $31,263. Compare the NPV results with the payback results. The NPV model is more realistic because it considers the time value of money, cash flows, and profitability.

When using the NPV model, the discount rate (return on investment hurdle rate) can differ for different projects. For example, the expected ROI on strategic projects is frequently set higher than operational projects. Similarly, ROI's can differ for riskier versus safer projects. The criteria for setting the ROI hurdle rate should be clear and applied consistently.

Nonfinancial Criteria

Financial return, while important, does not always reflect strategic importance. The sixties and seventies saw firms become overextended by diversifying too much. Now the prevailing thinking is that long term survival is dependent upon developing and maintaining core competencies. Companies have to be disciplined in saying no to potentially profitable projects that are outside the realm of their core mission. This requires other criteria be considered beyond direct financial return. For example, a firm may support projects that do not have high profit margins for other strategic reasons including:

To capture larger market share
To make it difficult for competitors to enter the market
To develop an enabler product, which by its introduction will increase sales in more profitable products
To develop core technology that will be used in next generation products
To reduce dependency on unreliable suppliers
To prevent government intervention and regulation

Less tangible criteria may also apply. Organizations may support projects to restore corporate image or enhance brand recognition. Many organizations are committed to corporate citizenship and support community development projects.

Since no single criterion can reflect strategic significance, portfolio management requires multi-criteria screening models. These models typically weight individual criteria so those projects that contribute to the most important strategic objectives are given higher consideration.

Multi-Weighted Scoring Models

A weighted scoring model typically uses several weighted selection criteria to evaluate project proposals. Weighted scoring models will generally include qualitative and/or quantitative criteria. Each selection criterion is asssigned a weight. Scores are assigned to each criterion for the project, based on its importance to the project being evaluated. The weights and scores are multiplied to get a total weighted score for the project. Using these multiple screening criteria, projects can then be compared using the weighted score. Projects with higher weighted scores are considered better.

Selection criteria need to mirror the critical success factors of an organization. For example, 3M set a target that 25 percent of the company's sales would come from products fewer than four years old versus the old target of 20 percent. Their priority system for project selection strongly reflects this new target. On the other hand, failure to pick the right factors will render the screening process "useless" in short order.

Figure 2.3 represents a project scoring matrix using some of the factors found in practice. The screening criteria selected are shown across the top of the matrix (e.g., stay within core competencies . . . ROI of 18 percent plus). Management weights each

FIGURE 2.3
Project Screening Matrix

Criteria / Weight	Stay within core competencies	Strategic fit	Urgency	25% of sales from new products	Reduce defects to less than 1%	Improve customer loyalty	ROI of 18% plus	Weighted total
	2.0	3.0	2.0	2.5	1.0	1.0	3.0	
Project 1	1	8	2	6	0	6	5	66
Project 2	3	3	2	0	0	5	1	27
Project 3	9	5	2	0	2	2	5	56
Project 4	3	0	10	0	0	6	0	32
Project 5	1	10	5	10	0	8	9	102
Project 6	6	5	0	2	0	2	7	55
⋮								
Project *n*	5	5	7	0	10	10	8	83

criterion (a value of 0 to a high of, say, 3) by its relative importance to the organization's objectives and strategic plan. Project proposals are then submitted to a project priority team or project office.

Each project proposal is then evaluated by its relative contribution/value added to the selected criteria. Values of 0 to a high of 10 are assigned to each criterion for each project. This value represents the project's fit to the specific criterion. For example, project 1 appears to fit well with the strategy of the organization since it is given a value of 8. Conversely, project 1 does nothing to support reducing defects (its value is 0). Finally, this model applies the management weights to each criterion by importance using a value of 1 to 3. For example, ROI and strategic fit have a weight of 3, while urgency and core competencies have weights of 2. Applying the weight to each criterion, the priority team derives the weighted total points for each project. For example, project 5 has the highest value of 102 $[(2 \times 1) + (3 \times 10) + (2 \times 5) + (2.5 \times 10) + (1 \times 0) + (1 \times 8) + (3 \times 9) = 102]$ and project 2 a low value of 27. If the resources available create a cutoff threshold of 50 points, the priority team would eliminate projects 2 and 4. (Note: Project 4 appears to have some urgency, but it is not classified as a "must" project. Therefore, it is screened with all other proposals.) Project 5 would receive first priority, project *n* second, and so on. See the adjacent Snapshot from Practice for a variation of this method. In rare cases where resources are severely limited and project proposals are similar in weighted rank, it is prudent to pick the project placing less demand on resources. Weighted multiple criteria models similar to this one are rapidly becoming the dominant choice for prioritizing projects.

At this point in the discussion it is wise to stop and put things into perspective. While selection models like the one above may yield numerical solutions to project selection decsions, models should not make the final decisions—the people using the models should. No model, no matter how sophisticated, can capture the total reality it is meant to represent. Models are tools for guiding the evaluation process so

AP/Wide World Photos.

The Transrapid Shanghai train is deemed a great engineering success. The magnetic levitation train travels at 267 miles per hour (430 kph) from the Pudong International Airport to close to Shanghai's business center in less than eight minutes.

Although the super fast train is deemed an engineering and technical success, it has not been a financial success. The train can carry 453 passengers on a trip, but the trains are riding virtually empty; a total of only 500 to 600 passengers ride the train in a day. The train now operates on a reduced schedule. Basically, the price per ride is well beyond what most Chinese families can afford. Second-class tickets are 75 yuan (US$9), and first-class tickets cost 150 yuan (US$18). The return on investment has been severely under expectations. The link between final customer needs and the financial case was not a top priority. Imposed project deadline (operate before 2003), scope reduction (shift to a station away from downtown), and apparent misconception of community needs all contribute to poor utilization of the train. The current model actually forces people to leave the train, wait, and then take public transportation to downtown Shanghai; time lost and cost have not convinced potential riders of the benefits of using the train.

The project demonstrates a classic error of not linking customer need with return on investment. The political strategy outweighed public needs.

*———, "Case Analysis: A Derailed Vision," *PM Network,* vol. 18, no. 4 (April 2004) p. 1.

that the decision-makers will consider relevant issues and reach a meeting of the minds as to what projects should be supported and not supported. This is a much more subjective process than calculations suggest. See Snapshot from Practice: A Derailed Vision.

Applying a Selection Model

Project Classification   It is not necessary to have exactly the same criteria for the different types of projects discussed above (strategic and operations). However, experience shows most organizations use similar criteria across all types of projects, with perhaps one or two criteria specific to the type of project—e.g., strategic breakthrough versus operational.

Regardless of criteria differences among different types of projects, the most important criterion for selection is the project's fit to the organization strategy. Therefore, this criterion should be consistent across all types of projects and carry a high priority relative to other criteria. This uniformity across all priority models used can keep departments from suboptimizing the use of organization resources. Anyone generating a project proposal should classify their proposal by type, so the appropriate criteria can be used to evaluate their proposal.

Selecting a Model   In the past, financial criteria were used almost to the exclusion of other criteria. However, in the last two decades we have witnessed a dramatic shift to include multiple criteria in project selection. Concisely put, profitability alone is simply not an adequate measure of contribution; however, it is still an important criterion, especially for projects that enhance revenue and market share such as breakthrough R & D projects.

Today, senior management is interested in identifying the potential mix of projects that will yield the best use of human and capital resources to maximize return on investment in the long run. Factors such as researching new technology, public image, ethical position, protection of the environment, core competencies, and strategic fit might be important criteria for selecting projects. Weighted scoring criteria seem the best alternative to meet this need.

Weighted scoring models result in bringing projects to closer alignment with strategic goals. If the scoring model is published and available to everyone in the organization, some discipline and credibility is attached to the selection of projects. The number of wasteful projects using resources is reduced. Politics and "sacred cow" projects are exposed. Project goals are more easily identified and communicated using the selection criteria as corroboration. Finally, using a weighted scoring approach helps project managers understand how their project was selected, how their project contributes to organization goals, and how it compares with other projects. Project selection is one of the most important decisions guiding the future success of an organization.

Criteria for project selection are the area where the power of portfolio starts to manifest itself. New projects are aligned with the strategic goals of the organization. With a clear method for selecting projects in place, project proposals can be solicited.

Sources and Solicitation of Project Proposals

As you would guess, projects should come from anyone who believes their project will add value to the organization. However, many organizations restrict proposals from specific levels or groups within the organization. This could be an opportunity lost. Good ideas are not limited to certain types or classes of organization stakeholders. Encourage and keep solicitations open to all sources—internal and external sponsors.

Figures 2.4 A and B provide an example of a proposal form for major projects. Note that this form includes a preliminary risk assessment as well as problem definition and project objectives. Risk analysis is the subject of Chapter 7.

In some cases organizations will solicit ideas for projects when the knowledge requirements for the project are not available in the organization. Typically, the organization will issue an RFP (Request for Proposal) to contractors/vendors with adequate experience to implement the project. In one example, a hospital published an RFP that asked for a bid to design and build a new operating room that uses the latest technology. Several architecture firms submitted bids to the hospital. The bids for the project were evaluated internally against other potential projects. When the project was accepted as a

FIGURE 2.4A
Major Project Proposal

Date _____				Number _____

Project Title _____

Responsible Manager _____ Project Manager _____

☐ _____	☐ General support	☐ Quality	☐ Legal	☐ New product
☐ _____	☐ _____	☐ Cost reduction	☐ Replacement	☐ Capacity
☐ _____	☐ _____	☐ _____	☐ _____	☐ _____

YES ☐ NO ☐ The project will take more than 500 labor hours?
YES ☐ NO ☐ The project is a one-time effort? (will not occur on a regular basis)
YES ☐ NO ☐ The project proposal was reviewed by the product manager?

Problem definition

Describe the problem/opportunity.

_____

Goal definition

Describe the project goal.

_____

Objective definition

Performance: Quantify the savings/benefits you expect from the project.

Cost: Labor hours, materials, methods, equipment?

Schedule: Overall duration in months.

go, other criteria were used to select the best qualified bidder. See Appendix 2.1 of this chapter for a complete description of requests for proposal (RFP).

Ranking Proposals and Selection of Projects

Culling through so many proposals to identify those that add the most value requires a structured process. Figure 2.5 shows a flow chart of a screening process beginning with the creation of an idea for a project.

Data and information are collected to assess the value of the proposed project to the organization and for future backup. If the sponsor decides to pursue the project on the basis of the collected data, it is forwarded to the project priority team (or the project office). Note that the sponsor knows which criteria will be used to accept or reject the project. Given the selection criteria and current portfolio of projects, the priority team rejects or accepts the project. If the project is accepted, the priority team sets implementation in motion.

FIGURE 2.4B
Risk Analysis

What are the three major risks for this project?

1.

2.

3.

		Risk 1 above	
What is the probability of the above risks occurring?	0 to 1.0 none high	Risk 2 above	
		Risk 3 above	
What is the impact on project success if these risks do occur?	0 to 10 none high	Risk 1 above	
		Risk 2 above	
		Risk 3 above	

Resources available? _____ Yes _____ No

Current project status

Start date _____ Estimated finish date _____

Status: ☐ Active ☐ On hold

Update:

Priority team action: ☐ Accepted ☐ Returned

☐ Discovery—project not defined   ☐ Duplicate to: _____

☐ Operational—proposal not a project   Project # [   ]

☐ Need more information—to prioritize project   ☐ Completed project

Figure 2.6 is a partial example of an evaluation form used by a large company to prioritize and select new projects. The form distinguishes between must and want objectives. If a project does not meet designated "must" objectives, it is not considered and removed from consideration. Organization (or division) objectives have been ranked and weighted by their relative importance—for example "Improve external customer service" carries a relative weight of 83 when compared to other want objectives. The want objectives are directly linked to objectives found in the strategic plan.

Impact definitions represent a further refinement to the screening system. They are developed to gauge the predicted impact a specific project would have on meeting a particular objective. A numeric scheme is created and anchored by defining criteria. To illustrate how this works, let's examine the $5 million in new sales objective. A "0" is assigned if the project will have no impact on sales or less than $100,000, a "1" is given if predicted sales are more than $100,000 but less than $500,000, a "2" if greater than $500,000. These impact assessments are combined with the relative importance of

FIGURE 2.5
Project Screening
Process

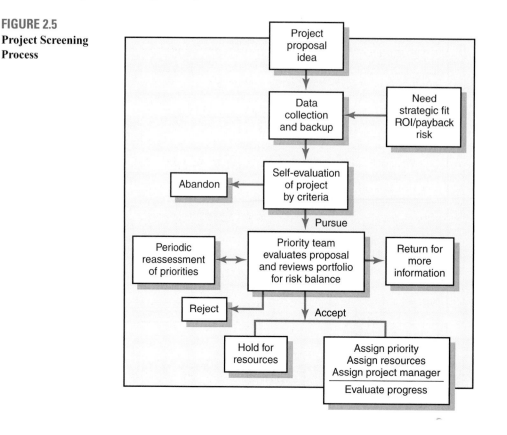

each objective to determine the predicted overall contribution of a project to strategic objectives. For example, project 26 creates an opportunity to fix field problems, has no effect on sales, and will have major impact on customer service. On these three objectives, project 26 would receive a score of 265 [99 + 0 + (2 × 83)]. Individual weighted scores are totaled for each project and are used to prioritize projects.

Responsibility for Prioritizing

Prioritizing can be an uncomfortable exercise for managers. Prioritizing means discipline, accountability, responsibility, constraints, reduced flexibility, and loss of power. Top management commitment means more than giving a blessing to the priority system; it means management will have to rank and weigh, in concrete terms, the objectives and strategies they believe to be most critical to the organization. This public declaration of commitment can be risky if the ranked objectives later prove to be poor choices, but setting the course for the organization is top management's job. The good news is, if management is truly trying to direct the organization to a strong future position, a good project priority system supports their efforts and develops a culture in which everyone is contributing to the goals of the organization.

Managing the Portfolio System

Managing the portfolio takes the selection system one step higher in that the merits of a particular project are assessed within the context of existing projects. At the same time it involves monitoring and adjusting selection criteria to reflect the strategic focus of the organization. This requires constant effort. The priority system can be managed

FIGURE 2.6
Priority Analysis

Must objectives		Must meet if impacts	...26	27	28	29
			Project number			
All activities meet current legal, safety, and environmental standards		Yes-Meets objective No-Does not meet obj N/A-No impact	**n/a**			
All new products will have a complete market analysis		Yes-Meets objective No-Does not meet obj N/A-No impact	**yes**			
Want objectives	Relative Importance 1-100	**Single project impact definitions**	Weighted score	Weighted score	Weighted score	Weighted score
Provides immediate response to field problems ㉚	**99**	0 ≤ Does not address ① = Opportunity to fix 2 ≥ Urgent problem	**99**			
Create $5 million in new sales by 20xx ⑮	**88**	⓪ < $100,000 1 = $100,000–500,000 2 > $500,000	**0**			
Improve external customer service ⑱	**83**	0 ≤ Minor impact 1 = Significant impact ② ≥ Major impact	**166**			
Total weighted score						
Priority						

by a small group of key employees in a small organization. Or, in larger organizations, the priority system can be managed by the project office or the enterprise management group.

Senior Management Input

Management of a portfolio system requires two major inputs from senior management. First, senior management must provide guidance in establishing selection criteria that strongly align with the current organization strategies. Second, senior management must annually decide how they wish to balance the available organizational resources (people and capital) among the different types of projects. A preliminary decision of balance must be made by top management (e.g., 20 percent compliance, 50 percent strategic, and 30 percent operational) before project selection takes place, although the balance may be changed when the projects submitted are reviewed. Given these inputs the priority team or project office can carry out its many responsibilities, which include supporting project sponsors and representing the interests of the total organization.

The Priority Team Responsibilities

The priority team, or project office, is responsible for publishing the priority of every project and ensuring the process is open and free of power politics. For example, most organizations using a priority team or project office use an electronic bulletin board to disperse the current portfolio of projects, the current status of each project, and current issues. This open communication discourages power plays. Over time the priority team evaluates the progress of the projects in the portfolio. If this whole process is managed well, it can have a profound impact on the success of an organization.

Constant scanning of the external environment to determine if organizational focus and/or selection criteria need to be changed is imperative! Periodic priority review and changes need to keep current with the changing environment and keep a unified vision of organization focus. Regardless of the criteria used for selection, each project should be evaluated by the same criteria. If projects are classified by must do, operation, and strategic, each project in its class should be evaluated by the same criteria. Enforcing the project priority system is crucial. Keeping the whole system open and aboveboard is important to maintaining the integrity of the system and keeping new, young executives from going around the system. For example, communicating which projects are approved, project ranks, current status of in-process projects, and any changes in priority criteria will discourage people from bypassing the system.

Balancing the Portfolio for Risks and Types of Projects

A major responsibility of the priority team is to balance projects by type, risk, and resource demand. This requires a total organization perspective. Hence, a proposed project that ranks high on most criteria may not be selected because the organization portfolio already includes too many projects with the same characteristics—e.g., project risk level, use of key resources, high cost, nonrevenue producing, long durations. Balancing the portfolio of projects is as important as project selection. Organizations need to evaluate each new project in terms of what it adds to the project mix. Short-term needs need to be balanced with long-term potential. Resource usage needs to be optimized across all projects not just the most important project.

David and Jim Matheson studied R&D organizations and developed a matrix that could be used for assessing a project portfolio (see Figure 2.7). The vertical axis

FIGURE 2.7
Project Portfolio Matrix

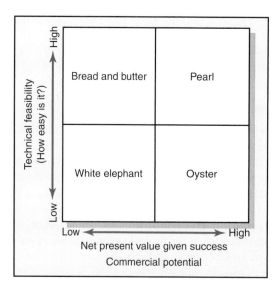

reflects a project's probability of success. The horizontal axis reflects potential commercial value. The grid has four quadrants, each with different project dimensions.

Bread-and-butter projects typically involve evolutionary improvements to current products and services. Examples include software upgrades and manufacturing cost reduction efforts.

Pearls represent revolutionary commercial advances using proven technical advances. Examples include next-generation integrated circuit chip and subsurface imaging to locate oil and gas.

Oysters involve technological breakthroughs with high commercial payoffs. Examples include embryonic DNA treatments and new kinds of metal alloys.

White elephants are projects that at one time showed promise but are no longer viable. Examples include products for a saturated market or a potent energy source with toxic side effects.

The Mathesons report that organizations often have too many white elephants and too few pearls and oysters. To maintain strategic advantage they recommend that organizations capitalize on pearls, eliminate or reposition white elephants and balance resources devoted to bread-and-butter and oyster projects to achieve alignment with overall strategy. Although their research centers on R&D organizations, their observations appear to hold true for all types of project organizations.

Summary

Multiple competing projects, limited skilled resources, dispersed virtual teams, time to market pressures, and limited capital serve as forces for the emergence of project portfolio management that provides the infrastructure for managing multiple projects and linking business strategy with project selection. The most important element of this system is the creation of a ranking system that utilizes multiple criteria that reflect the mission and strategy of the firm. It is critical to communicate priority criteria to all organizational stakeholders so that the criteria can be the source of inspiration for new project ideas.

Every significant project selected should be ranked and the results published. Senior management must take an active role in setting priorities and supporting the priority system. Going around the priority system will destroy its effectiveness. The project priority team needs to consist of seasoned managers who are capable of asking tough questions and distinguishing facts from fiction. Resources (people, equipment, and capital) for major projects must be clearly allocated and not conflict with daily operations or become an overload task.

The priority team needs to not only scrutinize significant projects in terms of their strategic value but also their fit with the portfolio of projects currently being implemented. Highly ranked projects may be deferred or even turned down if they upset the current balance among risks, resources, and strategic initiatives. Project selection must be based not only on the merits of the specific project but also on what it contributes to the current project portfolio mix. This requires a holistic approach to aligning projects with organizational strategy and resources.

Key Terms

Balanced scorecard	Priority system	Sacred cow
Implementation gap	Priority team	Strategic management
Net present value	Project portfolio	process
Organizational politics	Project screening	
Payback	matrix	

Review Questions

1. Describe the major components of the strategic management process.

2. Explain the role projects play in the strategic management process.

3. How are projects linked to the strategic plan?

4. The portfolio of projects is typically represented by compliance, strategic, and operations projects. What impact can this classification have on project selection?

5. Why does the priority system described in this chapter require that it be open and published? Does the process encourage bottom-up initiation of projects? Does it discourage some projects? Why?

6. Describe an operative system that will prioritize projects by their contribution to the strategic plan. How does this system assist in allocating organization resources and avoiding overcommitment of resources? How does your system differ from the case study model?

7. Why should an organization not rely only on ROI to select projects?

Exercises

1. You manage a hotel resort located on the South Beach on the Island of Kauai in Hawaii. You are shifting the focus of your resort from a traditional fun-in-the-sun destination to eco-tourism. How would you classify the following projects in terms of compliance, strategic, and operational?

   a. Convert the pool heating system from electrical to solar power.

   b. Build a 4-mile nature hiking trail.

   c. Renovate the horse barn.

   d. Replace the golf shop that accidentally burned down after being struck by lightning.

   e. Launch a new promotional campaign with Hawaii Airlines.

   f. Convert 12 adjacent acres into a wildlife preserve.

   g. Update all the bathrooms in condos that are 10 years old or older.

   h. Change hotel brochures to reflect eco-tourism image.

   i. Test and revise disaster response plan.

   j. Introduce wireless internet service in café and lounge areas.

   How easy was it to classify these projects? What made some projects more difficult than others?

2. Two new software projects are proposed to a young, start-up company. The Alpha project will cost $150,000 to develop and is expected to have annual net cash flow of $40,000. The Beta project will cost $200,000 to develop and is expected to have annual net cash flow of $50,000. The company is very concerned about their cash flow. Using the payback period, which project is better from a cash flow standpoint? Why?

3. A five-year project has a projected net cash flow of $15,000, $25,000, $30,000, $20,000, and $15,000 in the next five years. It will cost $50,000 to implement the project. If the required rate of return is 20 percent, conduct a discounted cash flow calculation to determine the NPV.

4. What would happen to the NPV of the above project if the inflation rate was expected to be 5 percent in each of the next five years?

5. You work for the 3T company which expects to earn at least 18 percent on its investments. You have to choose between two similar projects. On page 45 is the cash

information for each project. Your analysts predict that inflation rate will be a stable 3 percent over the next 7 years. Which of the two projects would you fund if the decision is based only on financial information? Why?

Omega Year	Inflow	Outflow	Netflow	Alpha Year	Inflow	Outflow	Netflow
Y0	0	$225,000	−225,000	Y0	0	$300,000	−300,000
Y1	0	190,000	−190,000	Y1	$ 50,000	100,000	−50,000
Y2	$ 150,000	0	150,000	Y2	150,000	0	150,000
Y3	220,000	30,000	190,000	Y3	250,000	50,000	200,000
Y4	215,000		215,000	Y4	250,000		250,000
Y5	205,000	30,000	175,000	Y5	200,000	50,000	150,000
Y6	197,000		197,000	Y6	180,000		180,000
Y7	100,000	30,000	70,000	Y7	120,000	30,000	90,000
Total	1,087,000	505,000	582,000	Total	1,200,000	530,000	670,000

6. The Custom Bike Company has set up a weighted scoring matrix for evaluation of potential projects. Below are three projects under consideration.

   a. Using the scoring matrix below, which project would you rate highest? Lowest?

   b. If the weight for "Strong Sponsor" is changed from 2.0 to 5.0, will the project selection change? What are the three highest weighted project scores with this new weight?

   c. Why is it important that the weights mirror critical strategic factors?

Project Screening Matrix

Criteria / Weight	Strong sponsor	Supports business strategy	Urgency	10% of sales from new products	Competition	Fill market gap	Weighted total
	2.0	5.0	4.0	3.0	1.0	3.0	
Project 1	9	5	2	0	2	5	
Project 2	3	7	2	0	5	1	
Project 3	6	8	2	3	6	8	
Project 4	1	0	5	10	6	9	
Project 5	3	10	10	1	8	0	

References

Benko, C., and F. W. McFarlan, *Connecting the Dots: Aligning Projects With Objectives in Unpredictable Times* (Boston: Harvard Business School Press, 2003).

Bigelow, D., "Want to Ensure Quality? Think Project Portfolio Management," *PM Network,* vol. 16 (1) April 2002, pp. 16–17.

Cohen, D., and R. Graham, *The Project Manager's MBA* (San Francisco: Jossey-Bass, 2001), pp. 58–59.

Descamps, J. P., "Mastering the Dance of Change: Innovation as a Way of Life," *Prism,* Second Quarter, 1999, pp. 61–67.

Doran, G. T., "There's a Smart Way to Write Management Goals and Objectives," *Management Review* (November 1981), pp. 35–36.

Floyd, S. W., and B. Woolridge, "Managing Strategic Consensus: The Foundation of Effectiveness Implementation," *Academy of Management Executives,* vol. 6 (4) 1992, pp. 27–39.

Foti, R., "Louder Than Words," *PM Network,* December 2002, pp. 22–27.

Frank, L., "On Demand," *PM Network,* vol. 18 (4) April 2004, pp. 58–62.

Fusco, J. C., "Better Policies Provide the Key to Implementing Project Management," *Project Management Journal,* vol. 28 (3) 1997, pp. 38–41.

Hutchens, G., "Doing the Numbers," *PM Network,* vol. 16 (4) March 2002, p. 20.

Johnson, R. E., "Scrap Capital Project Evaluations," *Chief Financial Officer* (May 1998), p. 14.

Kaplan, R. S., and D. P. Norton, "The Balanced Scorecard-Measures That Drive Performance," *Harvard Business Review,* January-February 1992, pp. 73–79.

Kenny, J., "Effective Project Management for Strategic Innovation and Change in an Organizational Context," *Project Management Journal,* vol. 34 (1) 2003, pp. 45–53.

Kharbanda, O. P., and J. K. Pinto, *What Made Gertie Gallop: Learning From Project Failures* (New York: Van Nostrand Reinhold, 1996), pp. 106–11, 263–83.

Leifer, R., C. M. McDermott, G. C. O'Connor, L. S. Peters, M. Price, and R. W. Veryzer, *Radical Innovation: How Mature Companies Can Outsmart Upstarts* (Boston: Harvard Business School Press, 2000).

Matheson, D., and J. Matheson, *The Smart Organization* (Boston: Harvard Business School Press, 1998), pp. 203–209.

Shenhar, A., "Strategic Project Leadership: Focusing Your Project on Business Success," *Proceedings of the Project Management Institute Annual Seminars & Symposium,* San Antonio, Texas, October 3–10, 2002, CD.

Woodward, H., "Winning in a World Limited Project Spending," *Proceedings of the Project Management Institute Global Congress North America,* Baltimore, Maryland, September 18–12, 2003, CD.

Case

Hector Gaming Company

Hector Gaming Company (HGC) is an educational gaming company specializing in young children's educational games. HGC has just completed their fourth year of operation. This year was a banner year for HGC. The company received a large influx of capital for growth by issuing stock privately through an investment banking firm. It appears the return on investment for this past year will be just over 25 percent with zero debt! The growth rate for the last two years has been approximately 80 percent each year. Parents and grandparents of young children have been buying HGC's products almost as fast as they are developed. Every member of the 56-person firm is enthusiastic and looking forward to helping the firm grow to be the largest and best educational gaming company in the world. The founder of the firm, Sally Peters, has been written up in *Young Entrepreneurs* as "the young entrepreneur to watch." She has been able to develop an organization culture in which all stakeholders are committed to innovation, continuous improvement, and organization learning.

Last year, 10 top managers of HGC worked with McKinley Consulting to develop the organization's strategic plan. This year the same 10 managers had a retreat in Aruba to formulate next year's strategic plan using the same process suggested by McKinley Consulting. Most executives seem to have a consensus of where the firm should go in the intermediate and long term. But there is little consensus on how this should be accomplished. Peters, now president of HGC, feels she may be losing control. The frequency of conflicts seems to be increasing. Some individuals are always requested for any new project created. When resource conflicts occur among projects, each project manager believes his or her project is most important. More projects are not meeting deadlines and are coming in over budget. Yesterday's management meeting revealed some top HGC talent have been working on an international business game for college students. This project does not fit the organization vision or market niche. At times it seems everyone is marching to his or her own drummer. Somehow more focus is needed to ensure everyone agrees on *how* strategy should be implemented, given the resources available to the organization.

Yesterday's meeting alarmed Peters. These emerging problems are coming at a bad time. Next week HGC is ramping up the size of the organization, number of new products per year, and marketing efforts. Fifteen new people will join HGC next month. Peters is concerned that policies be in place that will ensure the new people are used most productively. An additional potential problem looms on the horizon. Other gaming companies have noticed the success HGC is having in their niche market; one company tried to hire a key product development employee away from HGC. Peters wants HGC to be ready to meet any potential competition head on and to discourage any new entries into their market. Peters knows HGC is project driven; however, she is not as confident that she has a good handle on how such an organization should be managed—especially with such a fast growth rate and potential competition closer to becoming a reality. The magnitude of emerging problems demands quick attention and resolution.

Peters has hired you as a consultant. She has suggested the following format for your consulting contract. You are free to use another format if it will improve the effectiveness of the consulting engagement.

What is our major problem?

Identify some symptoms of the problem.

What is the major cause of the problem?

Provide a detailed action plan that attacks the problem. Be specific and provide examples that relate to HGC.

Film Prioritization

The purpose of this case is to give you experience in using a project priority system that ranks proposed projects by their contribution to the organization's objectives and strategic plan.

COMPANY PROFILE

The company is the film division for a large entertainment conglomerate. The main office is located in Anaheim, California. In addition to the feature film division, the conglomerate includes theme parks, home videos, a television channel, interactive games, and theatrical productions. The company has been enjoying steady growth over the past 10 years. Last year total revenues increased by 12 percent to $21.2 billion. The company is engaged in negotiations to expand its theme park empire to mainland China and Poland. The film division generated $274 million in revenues, which was an increase of 7 percent over the past year. Profit margin was down 3 percent to 16 percent because of the poor response to three of the five major film releases for the year.

COMPANY MISSION

The mission for the firm:

> Our overriding objective is to create shareholder value by continuing to be the world's premier entertainment company from a creative, strategic, and financial standpoint.

The film division supports this mission by producing four to six high-quality, family entertainment films for mass distribution each year. In recent years, the CEO of the company has advocated that the firm take a leadership position in championing environmental concerns.

COMPANY "MUST" OBJECTIVES

Every project must meet the must objectives as determined by executive management. It is important that selected film projects not violate such objectives of high strategic priority. There are three must objectives:

1. All projects meet current legal, safety, and environmental standards.
2. All film projects should receive a PG or lower advisory rating.
3. All projects should not have an adverse effect on current or planned operations within the larger company.

COMPANY "WANT" OBJECTIVES

Want objectives are assigned weights for their relative importance. Top management is responsible for formulating, ranking, and weighting objectives to ensure that projects support the company's strategy and mission. The following is a list of the company's want objectives:

1. Be nominated for and win an academy award for Best Picture of the Year.
2. Create at least one new animated character each year that can star in a cartoon or TV series.

3. Generate additional merchandise revenue (action figures, dolls, interactive games, music CDs).
4. Raise public consciousness about environmental issues and concerns.
5. Generate profit in excess of 18 percent.
6. Advance the state of the art in film animation, and preserve the firm's reputation.
7. Provide the basis for the development of a new ride at a company-owned theme park.

ASSIGNMENT

You are a member of the priority team in charge of evaluating and selecting film proposals. Use the provided evaluation form to formally evaluate and rank each proposal. Be prepared to report your rankings and justify your decisions.

Assume that all of the projects have passed the estimated hurdle rate of 14 percent ROI. In addition to the brief film synopsis, the proposals include the following financial projections of theater and video sales: 80 percent chance of ROI, 50 percent chance of ROI, and 20 percent chance of ROI.

For example, for proposal #1 (Dalai Lama) there is an 80 percent chance that it will earn at least 8 percent return on investment (ROI), a 50-50 chance the ROI will be 18 percent, and a 20 percent chance that the ROI will be 24 percent.

FILM PROPOSALS

PROJECT PROPOSAL 1: MY LIFE WITH DALAI LAMA

An animated, biographical account of the Dalai Lama's childhood in Tibet based on the popular children's book, *Tales from Nepal.* The Lama's life is told through the eyes of "Guoda," a field snake, and other local animals who befriend the Dalai and help him understand the principles of Buddhism.

Probability	80%	50%	20%
ROI	8%	18%	24%

PROJECT PROPOSAL 2: HEIDI

A remake of the classic children's story with music written by award-winning composers Syskle and Obert. The big-budget film will feature top-name stars and breathtaking scenery of the Swiss Alps.

Probability	80%	50%	20%
ROI	2%	20%	30%

PROJECT PROPOSAL 3: THE YEAR OF THE ECHO

A low-budget documentary that celebrates the career of one of the most influential bands in rock-and-roll history. The film will be directed by new-wave director Elliot Cznerzy and will combine concert footage and behind-the-scenes interviews spanning the 25-year history of the rock band, the Echos. In addition to great music, the film will focus on the death of one of the founding members from a heroin overdose and reveal the underworld of sex, lies, and drugs in the music industry.

Probability	80%	50%	20%
ROI	12%	14%	18%

PROJECT PROPOSAL 4: ESCAPE FROM RIO JAPUNI

An animated feature set in the Amazon rainforest. The story centers around Pablo, a young jaguar who attempts to convince warring jungle animals that they must unite and escape the devastation of local clear cutting.

Probability	80%	50%	20%
ROI	15%	20%	24%

PROJECT 5: NADIA!

The story of Nadia Comaneci, the famous Romanian gymnast who won three gold medals at the 1976 Summer Olympic Games. The low-budget film will document her life as a small child in Romania and how she was chosen by Romanian authorities to join their elite, state-run, athletic program. The film will highlight how Nadia maintained her independent spirit and love for gymnastics despite a harsh, regimented training program.

Probability	80%	50%	20%
ROI	8%	15%	20%

PROJECT 6: KEIKO—ONE WHALE OF A STORY

The story of Keiko, the famous killer whale, will be told by an imaginary offspring Seiko, who in the distant future is telling her children about their famous grandfather. The big-budget film will integrate actual footage of the whale within a realistic animated environment using state-of-the-art computer imagery. The story will reveal how Keiko responded to his treatment by humans.

Probability	80%	50%	20%
ROI	6%	18%	25%

PROJECT 7: GRAND ISLAND

The true story of a group of junior-high biology students who discover that a fertilizer plant is dumping toxic wastes into a nearby river. The moderate-budget film depicts how students organize a grassroots campaign to fight local bureaucracy and ultimately force the fertilizer plant to restore the local ecosystem.

Probability	80%	50%	20%
ROI	9%	15%	20%

**Project Priority
Evaluation Form**

Must objectives	Must meet if impacts	1	2	3	4	5	6	7
Meets all safety and environmental standards	Y = yes N = no N/A = not applicable							
PG or G rating	Y = yes N = no N/A = not applicable							
No adverse effect on other operations	Y = yes N = no N/A = not applicable							

Want objectives	Relative Importance 1–100	Single project impact definitions	Weighted Score	Weighted Score	Weighted Score	Weighted Score	Weighted Score	Weighted Score	Weighted Score
Be nominated for Best Picture of the Year	60	0 ≤ No potential 1 ≥ Low potential 2 > High potential							
Generate additional merchandise	10	0 ≤ No potential 1 ≥ Low potential 2 > High potential							
Create a new, major animated character	20	0 ≤ No potential 1 ≥ Low potential 2 > High potential							
Raise environmental concerns	55	0 ≤ No potential 1 ≥ Low potential 2 > High potential							
Generate profit greater than 18%	70	0 ≤ 18% 1 ≥ 18% 2 > 22%							
Advance state of film animation	40	0 ≤ No impact 1 ≥ Some impact 2 > Great impact							
Provide basis for new theme ride	10	0 ≤ No potential 1 ≥ Low potential 2 > High potential							
		Total weighted score							
		Priority							

Appendix 2.1

Request for Proposal (RFP)

Once an organization selects a project, the customer or project manager is frequently responsible for developing a request for proposal (RFP) for the project or sections of the project.

The responsible project manager will require input data from all stakeholders connected to the activities covered in the RFP. The RFP will be announced to external contractors/vendors with adequate experience to implement the project. For example, government projects frequently advertise with a "request for proposal" to outside contractors for roads, buildings, airports, military hardware, space vehicles. Similarly, businesses use RFPs to solicit bids for building a clean room, developing a new manufacturing process, delivering software for insurance billing, conducting a market survey. In all of these examples, requirements and features must be in enough detail that contractors have a clear description of the final deliverable that will meet the customer's needs. In most cases the RFP also specifies an expected format for the contractor's bid proposal so the responses of different contractors can be fairly evaluated. Although we typically think of RFPs for external contractors, in some organizations RFPs are used internally; that is, the organization sends out an RFP to different divisions or departments.

The content of the RFP is extremely important. In practice, the most common error is to offer an RFP that lacks sufficient detail. This lack of detail typically results in conflict issues, misunderstandings, often legal claims between the contractor and owner, and, in addition, an unsatisfied customer. All RFPs are different, but the outline in Figure A1.1 is a good starting point for the development of a detailed RFP. Each step is briefly described next.

1. Summary of needs and request for action. The background and a simple description of the final project deliverable are given first. For example, through simulated war games, the U.S. Navy has found their giant warships of the past are too vulnerable against today's technology (an example is the Silkworm antiship missiles). In addition, the Navy's mission has shifted to supporting ground forces and peacekeeping missions, which require getting closer to shore. As a result, the Navy is revamping ships for near-shore duty. The Navy will select three designs for further refinement from the responses to its RFP. In general, it is expected that the new ship will be capable of at least 55 knots, measure between 80 and 250 feet in length, and be fitted with radar absorbing panels to thwart guided missiles.

2. Statement of work detailing the scope and major deliverables. For example, if the project involves a market research survey, the major deliverables could be design, data collection, data analysis, and providing recommendations by February 21, 2006, for a cost not to exceed $300,000.

3. Deliverable specifications/requirements, features, and tasks. This step should be very comprehensive so bid proposals from contractors can be validated and later used for control. Typical specifications cover physical features such as size, quantity, materials, speed, and color. For example, an IT project might specify requirements for hardware, software, and training in great detail. Tasks required to complete deliverables can be included if they are known.

4. Responsibilities—vendor and customer. Failing to spell out the responsibilities for both parties is notorious for leading to serious problems when the contractor implements the project. For example, who pays for what? (If the contractor is to be on site, will the contractor be required to pay for office space?) What are the

FIGURE A1.1
Request for Proposal

1. Summary of needs and request for action
2. Statement of work (SOW) detailing the scope and major deliverables
3. Deliverable specifications/requirements, features, and tasks
4. Responsibilities—vendor and customer
5. Project schedule
6. Costs and payment schedule
7. Type of contract
8. Experience and staffing
9. Evaluation criteria

limits and exclusions for the contractor? (For example, who will supply test equipment?) What communication plan will be used by the contractor and owner? If escalation of an issue becomes necessary, what process will be used? How will progress be evaluated? Well-defined responsibilities will avoid many unforeseen problems later.

5. Project schedule. This step is concerned with getting a "hard" schedule which can be used for control and evaluating progress. Owners are usually very demanding in meeting the project schedule. In today's business environment, time-to-market is a major "hot button" that influences market share, costs, and profits. The schedule should spell out what, who, and when.

6. Costs and payment schedule. The RFP needs to set out very clearly how, when, and the process for determining costs and conditions for progress payments.

7. Type of contract. Essentially there are two types of contracts—fixed-price and cost-plus. Fixed price contracts agree on a price or lump sum in advance, and it remains as long as there are no changes to the scope provisions of the agreement. This type is preferred in projects that are well defined with predictable costs and minimal risks. The contractor must exercise care estimating cost because any underestimating of costs will cause the contractor's profit to be reduced. In cost-plus contracts the contractor is reimbursed for all or some of the expenses incurred during performance of the contract. This fee is negotiated in advance and usually involves a percent of total costs. "Time and materials" plus a profit factor are typical of cost-plus contracts. Both types of contracts can include incentive clauses for superior performance in time and cost, or in some cases, penalties—for example, missing the opening date of a new sports stadium.

8. Experience and staffing. The ability of the contractor to implement the project may depend on specific skills; this necessary experience should be specified, along with assurance such staff will be available for this project.

9. RFP evaluation criteria. The criteria for evaluating and awarding the project contract should be specified. For example, selection criteria frequently include methodology, price, schedule, and experience; in some cases these criteria are weighted. Use of the outline in Figure A1.1 will help to ensure key items in the proposal are not omitted. A well-prepared RFP will provide contractors with sufficient guidelines to prepare a proposal that clearly meets the project and customer's needs.

SELECTION OF CONTRACTOR FROM BID PROPOSALS

Interested contractors respond to project RFPs with a written bid proposal. It is likely that several contractors will submit bid proposals to the customer.

The final step in the RFP process is to select the contractor who best meets the requirements requested in the RFP. The selection criteria given in the RFP are used to evaluate which contractor is awarded the contract to implement the project. Losing contractors should be given an explanation of the key factors that lead to the selection of the winning contractor/vendor; appreciation for their participation and effort should be acknowledged.

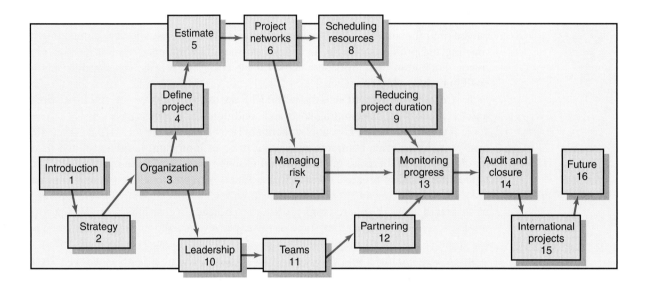

Organization: Structure and Culture	
Project Management Structures	
Choosing the Appropriate Project Management Structure	
Organizational Culture	
Implications of Organizational Culture for Organizing Projects	
Summary	
Appendix 3.1: How Culture Is Created and Communicated in Organizations	

CHAPTER THREE

Organization: Structure and Culture

Matrix management works, but it sure is difficult at times. All matrix managers must keep up their health and take Stress-Tabs.

—A Project Manager

Once management approves a project then the question becomes, how will the project be implemented? This chapter examines four different project management structures used by firms to implement projects: functional organization, dedicated project teams, matrix, and network organization. Although not exhaustive, these structures and their variant forms represent the major approaches for organizing projects. The advantages and disadvantages of each of these structures are discussed as well as some of the critical factors that might lead a firm to choose one form over others.

Whether a firm chooses to complete projects within the traditional functional organization or through some form of matrix arrangement is only part of the story. Anyone who has worked for more than one organization realizes that there are often considerable differences in how projects are managed within certain firms with similar structures. Working in a matrix system at AT&T is different from working in a matrix environment at Hewlett-Packard. Many researchers attribute these differences to the organizational culture at AT&T and Hewlett-Packard. A simple explanation of *organizational culture* is that it reflects the "personality" of an organization. Just as each individual has a unique personality, so each organization has a unique culture. Toward the end of this chapter, we examine in more detail what organizational culture is and the impact that the culture of the parent organization has on organizing and managing projects.

Both the project management structure and the culture of the organization constitute major elements of the environment in which projects are implemented. It is important for project managers and participants to know the "lay of the land" so that they can avoid obstacles and take advantage of pathways to complete their projects.

Project Management Structures

A project management system provides a framework for launching and implementing project activities within a parent organization. A good system appropriately balances the needs of both the parent organization and the project by defining the interface between the project and parent organization in terms of authority, allocation of resources, and eventual integration of project outcomes into mainstream operations.

Many business organizations have struggled with creating a system for organizing projects while managing ongoing operations. One of the major reasons for this struggle is that projects contradict fundamental design principles associated with traditional organizations. First, projects are unique, one-time efforts with a distinct beginning and end. Most organizations are designed to efficiently manage ongoing activities. Efficiency is achieved primarily by breaking down complex tasks into simplified, repetitive activities, as symbolized by assembly-line production methods. Projects by their very nature are not routine and are therefore an anomaly in these work environments.

A second reason businesses find it difficult to effectively organize projects is that most projects are multidisciplinary in nature because they require the coordinated efforts of a variety of specialists to be completed. For example, a new-product development project will likely involve the combined efforts of people from design, marketing, manufacturing, and finance. However, most organizations are departmentalized according to functional expertise with specialists from design, marketing, manufacturing, and finance residing in different units. Many researchers have noted that these groupings naturally develop unique customs, norms, values, and working styles that inhibit "integration" across functional boundaries. Not only are there "departmental silos", but managing projects poses the additional dilemma of who is in charge of the project. In most organizations authority is distributed hierarchically across functional lines. Because projects span across functional areas, identifying and legitimizing project management authority is often problematic.

Organizing Projects within the Functional Organization

One approach to organizing projects is to simply manage them within the existing functional hierarchy of the organization. Once management decides to implement a project, the different segments of the project are delegated to the respective functional units with each unit responsible for completing its segment of the project (see Figure 3.1). Coordination is maintained through normal management channels. For example, a tool manufacturing firm decides to differentiate its product line by offering a series of tools specially designed for left-handed individuals. Top management decides to implement the project, and different segments of the project are distributed to appropriate areas. The industrial design department is responsible for modifying specifications to conform to the needs of left-handed users. The production department is responsible for devising the means for producing new tools according to these new design specifications. The marketing department is responsible for gauging demand and price as well as identifying distribution outlets. The overall project will be managed within the normal hierarchy, with the project being part of the working agenda of top management.

The functional organization is also commonly used when, given the nature of the project, one functional area plays a dominant role in completing the project or has a dominant interest in the success of the project. Under these circumstances, a high-ranking manager in that area is given the responsibility of coordinating the project. For example, the transfer of equipment and personnel to a new office would be managed by a top-ranking manager in the firm's facilities department. Likewise, a project involving the upgrading of the management information system would be managed by the information systems department. In both cases, most of the project work would be done within the specified department and coordination with other departments would occur through normal channels.

FIGURE 3.1   Functional Organizations

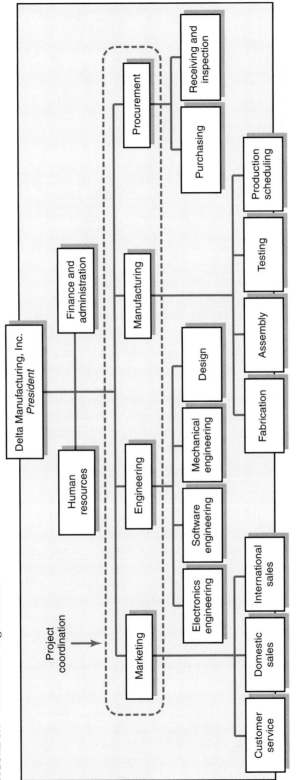

There are advantages and disadvantages for using the existing functional organization to administer and complete projects. The major advantages are the following:

1. **No Change.** Projects are completed within the basic functional structure of the parent organization. There is no radical alteration in the design and operation of the parent organization.

2. **Flexibility.** There is maximum flexibility in the use of staff. Appropriate specialists in different functional units can temporarily be assigned to work on the project and then return to their normal work. With a broad base of technical personnel available within each functional department, people can be switched among different projects with relative ease.

3. **In-Depth Expertise.** If the scope of the project is narrow and the proper functional unit is assigned primary responsibility, then in-depth expertise can be brought to bear on the most crucial aspects of the project.

4. **Easy Post-Project Transition.** Normal career paths within a functional division are maintained. While specialists can make significant contributions to projects, their functional field is their professional home and the focus of their professional growth and advancement.

Just as there are advantages for organizing projects within the existing functional organization, there are also disadvantages. These disadvantages are particularly pronounced when the scope of the project is broad and one functional department does not take the dominant technological and managerial lead on the project:

1. **Lack of Focus.** Each functional unit has its own core routine work to do; sometimes project responsibilities get pushed aside to meet primary obligations. This difficulty is compounded when the project has different priorities for different units. For example, the marketing department may consider the project urgent while the operations people considered it only of secondary importance. Imagine the tension if the marketing people have to wait for the operations people to complete their segment of the project before they proceed.

2. **Poor Integration.** There may be poor integration across functional units. Functional specialists tend to be concerned only with their segment of the project and not with what is best for the total project.

3. **Slow.** It generally takes longer to complete projects through this functional arrangement. This is in part attributable to slow response time—project information and decisions have to be circulated through normal management channels. Furthermore, the lack of horizontal, direct communication among functional groups contributes to rework as specialists realize the implications of others' actions after the fact.

4. **Lack of Ownership.** The motivation of people assigned to the project can be weak. The project may be seen as an additional burden that is not directly linked to their professional development or advancement. Furthermore, because they are working on only a segment of the project, professionals do not identify with the project. Lack of ownership discourages strong commitment to project-related activities.

Organizing Projects as Dedicated Teams

At the other end of the structural spectrum is the creation of independent project teams. These teams operate as separate units from the rest of the parent organization. Usually a full-time project manager is designated to pull together a core group of specialists who work full time on the project. The project manager recruits necessary personnel from both within and outside the parent company. The subsequent team is physically separated from the parent organization and given marching orders to complete the project (see Figure 3.2).

FIGURE 3.2 **Dedicated Project Team**

Courtesy Lockheed Martin.

In project management folklore, skunk works is code for a small, dedicated team assigned to a breakthrough project. The first skunk works was created more than a half a century ago by Clarence L. "Kelly" Johnson at Lockheed Aerospace Corporation. Kelly's project had two objectives: 1) to create a jet fighter, the Shooting Star, and 2) to do it as fast as possible. Kelly and a small band of engineering mavericks operated as a dedicated team unencumbered by red tape and the bureaucratic delays of the normal R&D process. The name was coined by team member Irvin Culver after the moonshine brewery (skonk works) deep in the forest in the popular cartoon strip Lil'Abner. The homemade whisky was euphemistically called kickapoo joy juice.

The project was a spectacular success. In just 43 days, Johnson's team of 23 engineers and teams of support personnel put together the first American fighter to fly at more than 500 miles per hour. Lockheed has continued to use Skunk Works to develop a string of high speed jets, including the F117 Stealth Fighter. Lockheed Martin has an official Skunk Works division. Their charter is:

The Skunk Works is a concentration of a few good people solving problems far in advance—and at a fraction of the cost—by applying the simplest, most straightforward methods possible to develop and produce new products.

*Miller, J., *Lockheed Martin's Skunk Works,* (New York: Speciality Publications, 1996).

The interface between the parent organization and the project teams will vary. In some cases the parent organization prescribes administrative and financial control procedures over the project. In other cases, firms allow the project manager maximum freedom to get the project done given the resources originally assigned to the project. Lockheed Martin has used this approach to develop next generation jet airplanes. See Snapshot from Practice: Skunk Works.

In the case of firms where projects are the dominant form of business, such as a construction firm or a consulting firm, the entire organization is designed to support project teams. Instead of one or two special projects, the organization consists of sets of quasi-independent teams working on specific projects. The main responsibility of traditional functional departments is to assist and support these project teams. For example, the marketing department is directed at generating new business that will lead to more projects, while the human resource department is responsible for managing a variety of personnel issues as well as recruiting and training new employees. This type of organization is referred to in the literature as a *Projectized* form of organization and is graphically portrayed in Figure 3.3.

As in the case of functional organization, the dedicated project team approach has strengths and weaknesses. The following are recognized as strengths:

1. **Simple.** Other than taking away resources in the form of specialists assigned to the project, the functional organization remains intact with the project team operating independently.
2. **Fast.** Projects tend to get done more quickly when participants devote their full attention to the project and are not distracted by other obligations and duties. Furthermore, response time tends to be quicker under this arrangement because most decisions are made within the team and are not deferred up the hierarchy.
3. **Cohesive.** A high level of motivation and cohesiveness often emerges within the project team. Participants share a common goal and personal responsibility toward the project and the team.

FIGURE 3.3 **Project Organization Structure**

One of the advantages of creating dedicated project teams is that project participants from different functional areas can develop into a highly cohesive work team that is strongly committed to completing the project. While such teams often produce Herculean efforts in pursuit of project completion, there is a negative dimension to this commitment that is often referred to in the literature as *projectitis*. A we–they attitude can emerge between project team members and the rest of the organization. The project team succumbs to *hubris* and develops a holier-than-thou attitude that antagonizes the parent organization. People not assigned to the project become jealous of the attention and prestige being showered on the project team, especially when they believe that it is their hard work that is financing the endeavor. The tendency to assign project teams exotic titles such as "Silver Bullets" and "Tiger Teams," as well as give them special perks, tends to intensify the gap between the project team and the parent organization.

Such appears to have been the case with Apple's highly successful Macintosh development team. Steve Jobs, who at the time was both the chairman of Apple and the project manager for the Mac team, pampered his team with perks including at-the-desk massages, coolers stocked with freshly squeezed orange juice, a Bosendorfer grand piano, and first-class plane tickets. No other employees at Apple got to travel first class. Jobs considered his team to be the elite of Apple and had a tendency to refer to everyone else as "Bozos" who "didn't get it." Engineers from the Apple II division, which was the bread and butter of Apple's sales, became incensed with the special treatment their colleagues were getting.

One evening at Ely McFly's, a local watering hole, the tensions between Apple II engineers seated at one table and those of a Mac team at another boiled over. Aaron Goldberg, a long-time industry consultant, watched from his barstool as the squabbling escalated. "The Mac guys were screaming, 'We're the future!' The Apple II guys were screaming, 'We're the money!' Then there was a geek brawl. Pocket protectors and pens were flying. I was waiting for a notebook to drop, so they would stop and pick up the papers."

Although comical from a distance, the discord between the Apple II and Mac groups severely hampered Apple's performance during the 1980s. John Sculley, who replaced Steve Jobs as chairman of Apple, observed that Apple had evolved into two "warring companies" and referred to the street between the Apple II and Macintosh buildings as "the DMZ" (demilitarized zone).

*Carlton, J., *Apple: The Inside Story of Intrigue, Egomania, and Business Blunders* (New York: Random House, 1997), pp. 13–14; Sculley, J., *Odyssey: Pepsi to Apple … A Journey of Adventure, Ideas, and the Future* (New York: Harper & Row, 1987), pp. 270–79.

4. **Cross-Functional Integration.** Specialists from different areas work closely together and, with proper guidance, become committed to optimizing the project not their respective areas of expertise.

In many cases, the project team approach is the optimum approach for completing a project when you view it solely from the standpoint of what is best for completing the project. Its weaknesses become more evident when the needs of the parent organization are taken into account:

1. **Expensive.** Not only have you created a new management position (project manager), but resources are also assigned on a full-time basis. This can result in duplication of efforts across projects and a loss of economies of scale.

2. **Internal Strife.** Sometimes dedicated project teams take on an entity of their own and a disease known as projectitis develops. See Snapshot from Practice: Projectitis—The Dark Side. A strong we–they divisiveness emerges between the project team and the parent organization. This divisiveness can undermine not only the integration of the eventual outcomes of the project into mainstream operations but also the assimilation of project team members back into their functional units once the project is completed.

3. **Limited Technological Expertise.** Creating self-contained teams inhibits maximum technological expertise being brought to bear on problems. Technical expertise is limited somewhat to the talents and experience of the specialists assigned to the project. While nothing prevents specialists from consulting with others in the functional division, the we–they syndrome and the fact that such help is not formally sanctioned by the organization discourage this from happening.

4. **Difficult Post-Project Transition.** Assigning full-time personnel to a project creates the dilemma of what to do with personnel after the project is completed. If other project work is not available, then the transition back to their original functional departments may be difficult because of their prolonged absence and the need to catch up with recent developments in their functional area.

Organizing Projects within a Matrix Arrangement

Matrix management is a hybrid organizational form in which a horizontal project management structure is "overlaid" on the normal functional hierarchy. In a matrix system, there are usually two chains of command, one along functional lines and the other along project lines. Instead of delegating segments of a project to different units or creating an autonomous team, project participants report simultaneously to both functional and project managers.

Companies apply this matrix arrangement in a variety of different ways. Some organizations set up temporary matrix systems to deal with specific projects, while "matrix" may be a permanent fixture in other organizations. Let us first look at its general application and then proceed to a more detailed discussion of finer points. Consider Figure 3.4. There are three projects currently under way: A, B, and C. All three project managers (PM A-C) report to a director of project management, who supervises all projects. Each project has an administrative assistant, although the one for project C is only part time.

Project A involves the design and expansion of an existing production line to accommodate new metal alloys. To accomplish this objective, project A has assigned to it 3.5 people from manufacturing and 6 people from engineering. These individuals are assigned to the project on a part-time or full-time basis, depending on the project's needs during various phases of the project. Project B involves the development of a new product that requires the heavy representation of engineering, manufacturing, and marketing. Project C involves forecasting changing needs of an existing customer base. While these three projects, as well as others are being completed, the functional divisions continue performing their basic, core activities.

The matrix structure is designed to optimally utilize resources by having individuals work on multiple projects as well as being capable of performing normal functional duties. At the same time, the matrix approach attempts to achieve greater integration by creating and legitimizing the authority of a project manager. In theory, the matrix approach provides a dual focus between functional/technical expertise and project requirements that is missing in either the project team or functional approach to project management. This focus can most easily be seen in the relative input of functional managers and project managers over key project decisions (see Table 3.1).

In principle every major project decision and action must be negotiated. The project manager is responsible for integrating functional input and overseeing the completion of the project. Functional managers are responsible for overseeing the functional contribution to the project.

Different Matrix Forms

In practice there are really different kinds of matrix systems, depending on the relative authority of the project and functional managers. Functional, lightweight, or *weak matrix* are titles given to matrices in which the balance of authority strongly favors the functional managers. *Balanced,* or middleweight *matrix* is used to describe the traditional matrix arrangement. Project, heavyweight, or *strong matrix* is used to describe a matrix in which the balance of authority is strongly on the side of the project manager.

FIGURE 3.4   Matrix Organization Structure

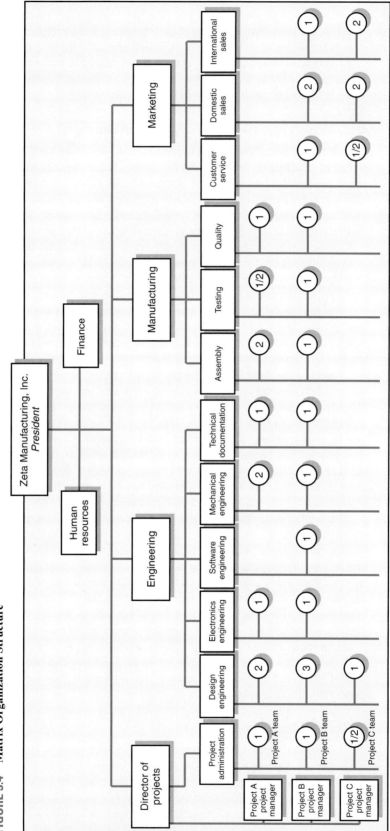

TABLE 3.1 **Division of Project Manager and Functional Manager Responsibilities in a Matrix Structure**

Project Manager	Negotiated Issues	Functional Manager
What has to be done?	Who will do the task?	How will it be done?
When should the task be done?	Where will the task be done?	
How much money is available to do the task?	Why will the task be done?	How will the project involvement impact normal functional activities?
How well has the total project been done?	Is the task satisfactorily completed?	How well has the functional input been integrated?

The relative difference in power between functional managers and project managers is reflected along a number of related dimensions. One such dimension is level of reporting relationship. A project manager who reports directly to the CEO has more clout than a marketing manager who reports to a director of marketing. Location of project activities is another subtle but important factor. A project manager wields considerably more influence over project participants if they work in his office than if they perform their project-related activities in their functional offices. Likewise, the percentage of full-time staff assigned to the project contributes to relative influence. Full-time status implies transfer of obligations from functional activities to the project.

One other factor is who is responsible for conducting performance appraisals and compensation decisions. In a weak matrix, the project manager is not likely to have any direct input into the evaluation of participants who worked on the project. This would be the sole responsibility of the functional manager. Conversely, in a strong matrix, the project manager's evaluation would carry more weight than the functional manager's. In a balanced matrix, either input from both managers is sought, or the project manager makes recommendations to the functional manager, who is responsible for the formal evaluation of individual employees. Often companies will brag that they use a strong, project-oriented matrix only to find upon closer examination that the project managers have very little say over the evaluation and compensation of personnel.

Ultimately, whether the matrix is weak or strong, a functional or project matrix is determined by the extent to which the project manager has direct authority over participants. Authority may be determined informally by the persuasive powers of managers involved and the perceived importance of the project or formally by the prescribed powers of the project manager. Here is a thumbnail sketch of the three kinds of matrices:

- **Weak matrix**—This form is very similar to a functional approach with the exception that there is a formally designated project manager responsible for coordinating project activities. Functional managers are responsible for managing their segment of the project. The project manager basically acts as a staff assistant who draws the schedules and checklists, collects information on status of work, and facilitates project completion. The project manager has indirect authority to expedite and monitor the project. Functional managers call most of the shots and decide who does what and when the work is completed.

- **Balanced matrix**—This is the classic matrix in which the project manager is responsible for defining what needs to be accomplished while the functional managers are concerned with how it will be accomplished. More specifically, the project manager establishes the overall plan for completing the project, integrates the contribution of the different disciplines, sets schedules, and monitors progress. The functional managers are responsible for assigning personnel and executing their segment of the project according to the standards and schedules set by the project manager. The merger of "what and how" requires both parties to work closely together and jointly approve technical and operational decisions.

- **Strong matrix**—This form attempts to create the "feel" of a project team within a matrix environment. The project manager controls most aspects of the project, including scope trade-offs and assignment of functional personnel. The project manager controls when and what specialists do and has final say on major project decisions. The functional manager has title over her people and is consulted on a need basis. In some situations a functional manager's department may serve as a "subcontractor" for the project, in which case they have more control over specialized work. For example, the development of a new series of laptop computers may require a team of experts from different disciplines working on the basic design and performance requirements within a project matrix arrangement. Once the specifications have been determined, final design and production of certain components (i.e., power source) may be assigned to respective functional groups to complete.

Matrix management both in general and in its specific forms has unique strengths and weaknesses. The advantages and disadvantages of matrix organizations in general are noted below, while only briefly highlighting specifics concerning different forms:

1. **Efficient.** Resources can be shared across multiple projects as well as within functional divisions. Individuals can divide their energy across multiple projects on an as-needed basis. This reduces duplication required in a projectized structure.

2. **Strong Project Focus.** A stronger project focus is provided by having a formally designated project manager who is responsible for coordinating and integrating contributions of different units. This helps sustain a holistic approach to problem solving that is often missing in the functional organization.

3. **Easier Post-Project Transition.** Because the project organization is overlaid on the functional divisions, specialists maintain ties with their functional group, so they have a homeport to return to once the project is completed.

4. **Flexible.** Matrix arrangements provide for flexible utilization of resources and expertise within the firm. In some cases functional units may provide individuals who are managed by the project manager. In other cases the contributions are monitored by the functional manager.

The strengths of the matrix structure are considerable. Unfortunately, so are the potential weaknesses. This is due in large part to the fact that a matrix structure is more complicated and the creation of multiple bosses represents a radical departure from the traditional hierarchical authority system.

Furthermore, one does not install a matrix structure overnight. Experts argue that it takes 3–5 years for a matrix system to fully mature. So many of the problems described below represent growing pains.

1. **Dysfunctional Conflict.** The matrix approach is predicated on tension between functional managers and project managers who bring critical expertise and perspectives to the project. Such tension is viewed as a necessary mechanism for achieving an appropriate balance between complex technical issues and unique project requirements. While the intent is noble, the effect is sometimes analogous to opening Pandora's box. Legitimate conflict can spill over to a more personal level, resulting from conflicting agendas and accountabilities. Worthy discussions can degenerate into heated arguments that engender animosity among the managers involved.

2. **Infighting.** Any situation in which equipment, resources, and people are being shared across projects and functional activities lends itself to conflict and competition for

scarce resources. Infighting can occur among project managers, who are primarily interested in what is best for their project.

3. **Stressful.** Matrix management violates the management principle of unity of command. Project participants have at least two bosses—their functional head and one or more project managers. Working in a matrix environment can be extremely stressful. Imagine what it would be like to work in an environment in which you are being told to do three conflicting things by three different managers.

4. **Slow.** In theory, the presence of a project manager to coordinate the project should accelerate the completion of the project. In practice, decision making can get bogged down as agreements have to be forged across multiple functional groups. This is especially true for the balanced matrix.

When the three variant forms of the matrix approach are considered, we can see that advantages and disadvantages are not necessarily true for all three forms of matrix. The strong matrix is likely to enhance project integration, diminish internal power struggles, and ultimately improve control of project activities and costs. On the downside, technical quality may suffer because functional areas have less control over their contributions. Finally, projectitis may emerge as the members develop a strong team identity.

The weak matrix is likely to improve technical quality as well as provide a better system for managing conflict across projects because the functional manager assigns personnel to different projects. The problem is that functional control is often maintained at the expense of poor project integration. The balanced matrix can achieve better balance between technical and project requirements, but it is a very delicate system to create and manage and is more likely to succumb to many of the problems associated with the matrix approach.

Organizing Projects within Network Organizations

The turn of the century has seen a radical shift in the organizational architecture of business firms. Corporate downsizing and cost control have combined to produce what we call "network organizations." In theory, network organization is an alliance of several organizations for the purpose of creating products or services for customers. This collaborative structure typically consists of several satellite organizations bee hived around a "hub" or "core firm." The core firm coordinates the network process and provides one or two core competencies, such as marketing or product development. For example, Cisco Systems mainly designs new products and utilizes a constellation of suppliers, contract manufacturers, assemblers, and other partners to deliver products to their customers. Nike, another prime example of a network organization, provides marketing expertise for its sports footwear and apparel. The key organizing principle is that, instead of doing everything in-house, a firm can outsource key activities to other businesses with the requisite competencies.

The shift toward network organizations is readily apparent in the film industry. During the golden era of Hollywood, huge, vertically integrated corporations made movies. Studios such as MGM, Warner Brothers, and 20th Century-Fox owned large movie lots and employed thousands of full-time specialists—set designers, camera people, film editors, directors, and even actors. Today, most movies are made by a collection of individuals and small companies who come together to make films project-by-project. This structure allows each project to be staffed with the talent most suited to its demands rather than choosing from only those people the studio employs.

Network projects have been the bread and butter of the construction industry. Whether it is building a dream house or a desalination plant, clients typically hire general contracting firms who subcontract trade people and professional organizations to perform specific segments of construction. This approach is now being applied to a wide range of projects. For example, see Figure 3.5.

Figure 3.5 depicts a situation in which a new mountain bike is being developed. The genesis for the bike comes from a mechanical engineer who developed the idea in her garage. The inventor negotiates a contract with a bicycle firm to develop and manufacture the bike. The bicycle company in turn creates a project team of manufacturers, suppliers, and marketing firms to create the new bike. Each participant adds requisite expertise to the project. The bicycle firm brings its brand name and distribution channels to the project. Tool and die firms provide customized parts which are delivered to a manufacturing firm that will produce the bikes. Marketing firms refine the design, develop packaging, and test-market potential names. A project manager is assigned by the bicycle firm to work with the inventor and the other parties to complete the project.

The advantages of network projects are many:

1. **Cost Reduction.** Companies can secure competitive prices for contracted services, especially if the work can be outsourced offshore. Furthermore, overhead costs are dramatically cut since the company no longer has to internally maintain the contracted services.

2. **High Level of Expertise.** A high level of expertise and technology can be brought to bear on the project. A company no longer has to keep up with technological advances. Instead, it can focus on developing its core compentencies and hire firms with the know-how to work on relevant segments of the project.

3. **Flexible.** Organizations are no longer constrained by their own resources but can pursue a wide range of projects by combining their resources with talents of other companies. Small companies can instantly go global by working with foreign partners.

FIGURE 3.5
Mountain Bicycle Network Project

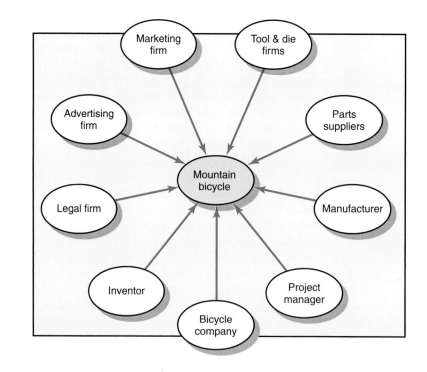

The disadvantages of network projects are less well documented:

1. **Coordination Breakdowns.** Coordination of professionals from different organizations can be challenging, especially if the project work requires close collaboration and mutual adjustment. This form of project management structure tends to work best when each party, as in the case of most construction projects, is responsible for a well-defined, independent deliverable.

2. **Loss of Control.** There is potential loss of control over the project. The core team depends on other organizations that they do not have direct authority over. While long-term survival of participating organizations depends on performance, a project may falter when one partner fails to deliver.

3. **Conflict.** Network projects are more prone to interpersonal conflict since the different participants do not share the same values, priorities, and culture. Trust, which is essential to project success, can be difficult to forge when interactions are limited and people come from different organizations.

Many network projects operate in a virtual environment in which people are linked by computers, faxes, computer-aided design systems, and video teleconferencing. They rarely, if ever, see one another face-to-face. On other projects participants from different organizations work closely together, for example at a construction site or in shared office space. In either case, people come and go as services are needed, much like a matrix structure, but they are not formal members of one organization, just technical experts who form a temporary alliance with an organization, fulfill their contractual obligations, and then move on to the next project.

Since projects involving collaboration of partners from different organizations is quickly becoming the norm, Chapter 12 is devoted to this subject.

Choosing the Appropriate Project Management Structure

There is growing empirical evidence that project success is directly linked to the amount of autonomy and authority project managers have over their projects. See Research Highlight: Relative Effectiveness of Different Project Management Structures. However, most of this research is based on what is best for managing specific projects. It is important to remember what was stated in the beginning of the chapter—that the best system balances the needs of the project with those of the parent organization. So what project structure should an organization use? This is a complicated question with no precise answers. A number of issues need to be considered at both the organization and project level.

Organization Considerations

At the organization level, the first question that needs to be asked is how important is project management to the success of the firm? What percentage of core work involves projects? If over 75 percent of work involves projects, then an organization should consider a fully projectized organization. If an organization has both standard products and projects, then a matrix arrangement would appear to be appropriate. If an organization has very few projects, then a less formal arrangement is probably all that is required. Temporary task forces could be created on an as-needed basis and the organization could outsource project work.

A second key question is resource availability. Remember, matrix evolved out of the necessity to share resources across multiple projects and functional domains while at the same time creating legitimate project leadership. For organizations that cannot afford to tie up critical personnel on individual projects, a matrix system would appear

Larson and Gobeli studied the relative efficacy of different project management structures. Their work is based on a sample of more than 1,600 project professionals and managers actively involved in project management within their organizations. Among the findings they report are the rated effectiveness of different structures for product development and construction projects. These results are summarized in Figure 3.6 and indicate a strong preference for either the project team or strong matrix. Both the functional approach and the weak matrix were rated ineffective, and the balanced matrix was considered only marginally effective.

Because these ratings may have been tempered by self-interest, with project managers advocating forms that give them more formal authority, the ratings of project managers were compared with those of top management and functional managers. No significant differences were found; the weak matrix and functional organization were considered the least effective even by functional managers.

This research was published at a time when matrix management was receiving a lot of negative press and when popular management media were advocating the dedicated project team approach. A key finding was that matrix management can be as effective as a project team—if the project manager is given significant control over project activities. The support is not without reservations; as one project manager reported, "Matrix management works, but it sure is difficult at times. All matrix managers must keep up their health and take Stress Tabs."

FIGURE 3.6   **Rated Effectiveness of Different Project Structures by Type of Project**

*Larson, E. W. and D. H. Gobeli, "Matrix Management: Contradictions and Insights," *California Management Review,* vol. 29, no. 4 (Summer 1987), p. 137.

to be appropriate. An alternative would be to create a dedicated team but outsource project work when resources are not available internally.

Within the context of the first two questions, an organization needs to assess current practices and what changes are needed to more effectively manage projects. A strong, project matrix is not installed overnight. The shift toward a greater emphasis on projects has a host of political implications that need to be worked through, requiring time and strong leadership. For example, we have observed many companies that make the transition from a functional organization to a matrix organization begin with a weak, functional matrix. This is due in part to resistance by functional and department managers toward transferring authority to project managers. With time, these matrix structures eventually evolve into a project matrix. Many organizations have created Project Management Offices to support project management efforts. See Snapshot from Practice: The PM Program Office.

As more and more companies embrace project management as a critical vehicle for realizing corporate objectives, they are creating centralized project management offices (PMOs) to oversee and improve the management of projects. PMO functions vary widely by organization and need. In some cases, they serve as a simple clearinghouse for project management information. In other cases, they recruit, train, and assign managers to specific projects. As PMOs mature and evolve over time, they become full-service providers of project management expertise within a firm. The different services PMOs may provide include the following:

- Creating and maintaining the internal project management information system.
- Recruiting and selecting project managers both within and outside the organization.
- Establishing standardized project planning and reporting methodologies.
- Training personnel in project management techniques and tools.
- Auditing ongoing and recently completed projects.
- Developing comprehensive risk management programs.
- Providing in-house project management consulting and mentoring services.

- Maintaining an internal project management library containing critical documents, including project plans, funding papers, test plans, audit reports, and so forth.
- Establishing and benchmarking best practices in project management.
- Maintaining and tracking the portfolio of projects within an organization.

A good example of how project management offices evolve is the global project office (GPO) at Citibank's Global Corporate Bank. GPO originated at the grassroots level within the small world of Operations and Technology for Global Cash Management. Committed to bringing order to the chaos of managing projects, GPO instituted training programs and professional project management practices on a very small scale. Soon the success of GPO-supported projects caught the eye of upper management. Within three years the department was expanded to offer a full range of PMO services across Citibank's entire banking operation. GPO's mission is to establish project management as a core competency throughout the entire Citibank organization.

*Block, T. R. and J. D. Frame, "Today's Project Office: Gauging Attitudes," *PM Network,* August, 2001; Gradante, W. and D. Gardner, "Managing Projects from the Future, Not from the Past," *Proceedings of the 29th Annual Project Management Institute 1998 Seminars and Symposium* (Newtown Square, PA: Project Management Institute, 1998), pp. 289–94.

Project Considerations

At the project level, the question is how much autonomy the project needs in order to be successfully completed. Hobbs and Ménard identify seven factors that should influence the choice of project management structure:

- Size of project.
- Strategic importance.
- Novelty and need for innovation.
- Need for integration (number of departments involved).
- Environmental complexity (number of external interfaces).
- Budget and time constraints.
- Stability of resource requirements.

The higher the levels of these seven factors, the more autonomy and authority the project manager and project team need to be successful. This translates into using either a dedicated project team or a project matrix structure. For example, these structures should be used for large projects that are strategically critical and are new to the company, thus requiring much innovation. These structures would also be appropriate for complex, multidisciplinary projects that require input from many departments, as well as for projects that require constant contact with customers to assess their expectations. Dedicated project teams should also be used for urgent projects in which the nature of the work requires people working steadily from beginning to end.

Many firms that are heavily involved in project management have created a flexible management system that organizes projects according to project requirements. For example, Chaparral Steel, a mini-mill that produces steel bars and beams from scrap metal, classifies projects into three categories: advanced development, platform, and incremental. Advanced development projects are high-risk endeavors involving the creation of a breakthrough product or process. Platform projects are medium-risk projects involving system upgrades that yield new products and processes. Incremental projects are low-risk, short-term projects that involve minor adjustments in existing products and processes. At any point in time, Chaparral might have 40–50 projects underway, of which only one or two are advanced, three to five are platform projects, and the remainder are small, incremental projects. The incremental projects are almost all done within a weak matrix with the project manager coordinating the work of functional subgroups. A strong matrix is used to complete the platform projects, while dedicated project teams are typically created to complete the advanced development projects. More and more companies are using this "mix and match" approach to managing projects.

Organizational Culture

The decision for combining a discussion of project management structures and organizational cultures in this chapter can be traced to a conversation we, the authors, had with two project managers who work for a medium-sized information technology firm.

The managers were developing a new operating platform that would be critical to the future success of their company. When they tried to describe how this project was organized, one manager began to sketch out on a napkin a complicated structure involving 52 different teams, each with a project leader and a technical leader! In response to our further probing to understand how this system worked, the manager stopped short and proclaimed, "The key to making this structure work is the culture in our company. This approach would never work at company Y, where I worked before. But because of our culture here we are able to pull it off."

This comment, our observations of other firms, and research suggest there is a strong connection between project management structure, organizational culture, and project success. We have observed organizations successfully manage projects within the traditional functional organization because the culture encouraged cross-functional integration. Conversely we have seen matrix structures break down because the culture of the organization did not support the division of authority between project managers and functional managers. We have also observed companies relying on independent project teams because the dominant culture would not support the innovation and speed necessary for success.

What Is Organizational Culture?

Anyone who has traveled abroad has experienced the phenomenon of culture. The architecture is different from that at home. The food is not what the traveler commonly eats, nor do the natives necessarily adhere to a particular routine of breakfast, lunch, and dinner. People dress differently. They often speak a different language.

Beneath these obvious differences, the traveler probably discerns sometimes subtle but significant differences in how people interact and spend their time. For example, one of the authors encountered such differences while working in Poland with several Polish colleagues to complete a significant segment of a project that was due by the end of the day. They were on the verge of completing the work when, at 4:00 P.M., everyone stopped what they were doing and went home. Unlike a work culture in the

United States, where it was expected that everyone would stay to finish the work, there is a clear division between work time and personal time in Poland, and it was taboo to expect or require people to work beyond business hours.

Although perhaps less pronounced, organizational cultures are similar to cultures of different countries. Think about the differences in physical layout, dress, pace, and tone of communication encountered in your local bank, department store, or medical clinic. Likewise, anyone who has worked in several organizations encounters significant differences in the norms, values, and customs of individual organizations.

Organizational culture refers to a system of shared norms, beliefs, values, and assumptions which binds people together, thereby creating shared meanings. This system is manifested by customs, norms, and habits that exemplify the values and beliefs of the organization. Culture reflects the personality of the organization and, similar to an individual's personality, can enable us to predict attitudes and behaviors of organizational members. Culture is also one of the defining aspects of an organization that sets it apart from other organizations even in the same industry.

Research suggests that there are 10 primary characteristics which, in aggregate, capture the essence of an organization's culture:

1. **Member identity**—the degree to which employees identify with the organization as a whole rather than with their type of job or field of professional expertise.
2. **Team emphasis**—the degree to which work activities are organized around groups rather than individuals.
3. **Management focus**—the degree to which management decisions take into account the effect of outcomes on people within the organization.
4. **Unit integration**—the degree to which units within the organization are encouraged to operate in a coordinated or interdependent manner.
5. **Control**—the degree to which rules, policies, and direct supervision are used to oversee and control employee behavior.
6. **Risk tolerance**—the degree to which employees are encouraged to be aggressive, innovative, and risk seeking.
7. **Reward criteria**—the degree to which rewards such as promotion and salary increases are allocated according to employee performance rather than seniority, favoritism, or other nonperformance factors.
8. **Conflict tolerance**—the degree to which employees are encouraged to air conflicts and criticisms openly.
9. **Means versus end orientation**—the degree to which management focuses on outcomes rather than on techniques and processes used to achieve those results.
10. **Open-systems focus**—the degree to which the organization monitors and responds to changes in the external environment.

As shown in Figure 3.7, each of these dimensions exists on a continuum. Assessing an organization according to these 10 dimensions provides a composite picture of the organization's culture. This picture becomes the basis for feelings of shared understanding that the members have about the organization, how things are done, and the way members are supposed to behave.

Culture performs several important functions in organizations. An organization's culture *provides a sense of identity* for its members. The more clearly an organization's shared perceptions and values are stated, the more strongly people can identify with their organization and feel a vital part of it. Identity generates commitment to the organization and reasons for members to devote energy and loyalty to the organization.

FIGURE 3.7
Key Dimensions Defining an Organization's Culture

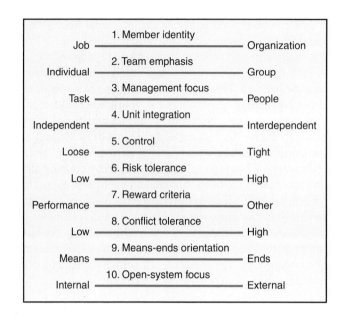

A second important function is that culture *helps legitimize the management system* of the organization. Culture helps clarify authority relationships and provides reasons why people are in a position of authority and why their authority should be respected. Furthermore, culture through myths, stories, and symbols helps people reconcile incongruities between ideal and actual behavior.

Most importantly, organizational culture *clarifies and reinforces standards of behavior.* Culture helps define what is permissible and inappropriate behavior. These standards span a wide range of behavior from dress code and working hours to challenging the judgment of superiors and collaborating with other departments. Ultimately, culture *helps create social order* within an organization. Imagine what it would be like if members didn't share similar beliefs, values, and assumptions—chaos! The customs, norms, and ideals conveyed by the culture of an organization provide the stability and predictability in behavior that is essential for an effective organization. See Snapshot from Practice: Software Development Teams at Microsoft for an example of this.

Although our discussion of organizational culture may appear to suggest one culture dominates the entire organization, in reality this is rarely the case. "Strong" or "thick" are adjectives used to denote a culture in which the organization's core values and customs are widely held and widely shared within the entire organization. Conversely, a "thin" or "weak" culture is one that is not widely shared or practiced within a firm.

Even within a strong organizational culture, there are likely to be subcultures often aligned within specific departments or specialty areas. As noted earlier in our discussion of project management structures, it is not uncommon for norms, values, and customs to develop within a specific field or profession such as marketing, finance, or operations. Similarly, countercultures can emerge within organizations that reflect a different set of values, beliefs, and customs—often in direct contradiction with the culture espoused by top management. How pervasive these subcultures and countercultures are affects the strength of the culture of the organization and the extent to which culture influences members' actions and responses.

Microsoft Corporation is the leading computer software company in the world. Microsoft's success stems in part from a corporate culture that supports teams of software developers to create and refine new products. No matter how big the project—even a complex one such as the development of the successful Windows 2000 operating system—the project is broken down into small parts that can be handled by teams of about 12 developers. The segment of the project each team is assigned is further subdivided so that each developer is assigned a specific part of the project to work on. Developers with greater experience are given more responsibilities than new members of the team, but the entire team knows that project success depends on the sum of their individual inputs.

Team members provide considerable support for each other. It is not uncommon to see two team members hunched over a computer screen trying to solve a problem. Team members can also be stern critics if a team member fails to perform at an acceptable level.

Developers are granted considerable autonomy in performing their work. At the same time behavior at Microsoft is governed by shared work culture that almost everyone follows. One set of informal rules governs the basic issue of working hours. Developers are free to adopt whatever work schedule suits them. If a developer has a sudden insight at midnight, it is not unusual for people to work until dawn. Likewise, if a developer's child is sick, the developer can stay home to take care of the child, and do makeup work at some other time. Along with these "rules" on flexible working hours, almost all developers abide by another norm: They put in the hours necessary to get the job done, even if it requires staying up all night to work on a particularly difficult part of a program.

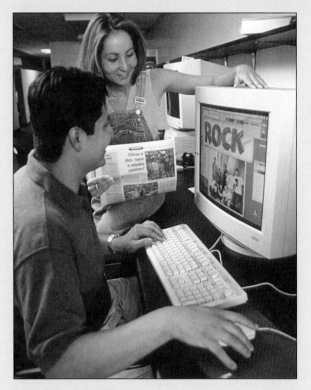

Michael Newman/PhotoEdit.

*Rebello, K., "Inside Microsoft," *Business Weekly*, July 15, 1996, pp. 56–67; Filipczak B., "Beyond the Gates of Microsoft," *Training*, September 1992, pp. 37–44.

Identifying Cultural Characteristics

Deciphering an organization's culture is a highly interpretative, subjective process that requires assessment of both current activities and past history. The student of culture cannot simply rely on what people report about their culture. The physical environment in which people work, as well as how people act and respond to different events that occur, must be examined. Figure 3.8 contains a worksheet for diagnosing the culture of an organization. Although by no means exhaustive, the checklist often yields clues about the norms, customs, and values of an organization:

1. **Study the physical characteristics of an organization.** What does the external architecture look like? What image does it convey? Is it unique? Are the buildings and offices the same quality for all employees? Or are modern buildings and fancier offices reserved for senior executives or managers from a specific department? What are the customs concerning dress? What symbols does the organization use to signal authority and status within the organization? These physical characteristics can shed light on who has real power within the organization, the extent to which the organization is internally differentiated, and how formal the organization is in its business dealings.

FIGURE 3.8
Organizational Culture Diagnosis Worksheet

I. Physical Characteristics
Architecture, office layout, decor, attire

_____
_____
_____

II. Public Documents
Annual reports, internal newsletters, vision statements

_____
_____
_____

III. Behavior
Pace, language, meetings, issues discussed,
decision-making style, communication patterns, rituals

_____
_____
_____

IV. Folklore
Stories, anecdotes, heroines, heroes, villains

_____
_____
_____

2. **Read about the organization.** Examine annual reports, mission statements, press releases, and internal newsletters. What do they describe? What principles are espoused in these documents? Do the reports emphasize the people who work for the organization and what they do or the financial performance of the firm? Each emphasis reflects a different culture. The first demonstrates concern for the people who make up the company. The second may suggest a concern for results and the bottom line.

3. **Observe how people interact within the organization.** What is their pace—is it slow and methodical or urgent and spontaneous? What rituals exist within the organization? What values do they express? Meetings can often yield insightful information. Who are the people at the meetings? Who does the talking? To whom do they talk? How candid is the conversation? Do people speak for the organization or for the individual department? What is the focus of the meetings? How much time is spent on various issues? Issues that are discussed repeatedly and at length are clues about the values of the organization's culture.

4. **Interpret stories and folklore surrounding the organization.** Finally, either through talking directly to people from other organizations or in daily conversations with co-workers, an observer can begin to gain a deeper sense of an organization's culture. Pay particular attention to the stories and anecdotes that are passed on within the organization; they often yield useful evidence about the important qualities of the culture. Look for similarities among stories told by different people. The subjects highlighted in recurring stories often reflect what is important to an organization's culture. For example, many of the stories that are repeated at Versatec, a Xerox subsidiary that makes graphic plotters for computers, involve their flamboyant cofounder, Renn Zaphiropoulos. According to company folklore, one of the very first things Renn did when the company was formed was to assemble the top management team at his home. They then devoted the weekend to handmaking a beautiful teak conference table around which all future decisions would be made. This table came to symbolize the importance of teamwork and maintaining high standards of performance, two essential qualities of the culture at Versatec.

Try to identify who the heroes and villains are in the folklore company. What do they suggest about the culture's ideals? Returning to the Versatec story, when the company was eventually purchased by Xerox many employees expressed concern that Versatec's informal, play hard/work hard culture would be overwhelmed by the bureaucracy at Xerox. Renn rallied the employees to superior levels of performance by arguing that if they exceeded Xerox's expectations they would be left alone. Autonomy has remained a fixture of Versatec's culture long after Renn's retirement.

It is also important to pay close attention to the basis for promotions and rewards. Are promotions based on accomplishments and performance or tenure and loyalty to the organization? What do people see as the keys to getting ahead within the organization? What contributes to downfalls? These last two questions can yield important insights into the qualities and behaviors which the organization honors as well as the cultural taboos and behavioral land mines that can derail a career. For example, one project manager confided that a former colleague was sent to project management purgatory soon after publicly questioning the validity of a marketing report. From that point on, the project manager was extra careful to privately consult the marketing department whenever she had questions about their data.

With practice an observer can assess how strong the dominant culture of an organization is and the significance of subcultures and countercultures. Furthermore, learners can discern and identify where the culture of an organization stands on the 10 cultural dimensions presented earlier and, in essence, begin to build a cultural profile for a firm. Based on this profile, conclusions can be drawn about specific customs and norms that need to be adhered to as well as those behaviors and actions that violate the norms of a firm.

Implications of Organizational Culture for Organizing Projects

Project managers have to be able to operate in several, potentially diverse, organizational cultures. First, they have to interact with the culture of their parent organization as well as the subcultures of various departments (e.g., marketing, accounting). Second, they have to interact with the project's client or customer organizations. Finally, they have to interact in varying degrees with a host of other organizations connected to the project. These organizations include suppliers and vendors, subcontractors, consulting firms, government and regulatory agencies, and, in many cases, community groups. Many of these organizations are likely to have very different cultures. Project managers have to be able to read and speak the culture they are working in to develop strategies, plans, and responses that are likely to be understood and accepted. Still, the emphasis of this chapter is on the relationship between organizational culture and project management structure, and it is necessary to defer further discussion of these implications until Chapters 10–12 which focus on leadership, team building, and partnering.

Earlier we stated that we believe there are strong relationships among project management structure, organizational culture, and successful project management. To explore these relationships further, let us return to the dimensions that can be used to characterize the culture of an organization. When examining these dimensions we could hypothesize that certain aspects of the culture of an organization would support successful project management while other aspects would deter or interfere with effective management. Figure 3.9 attempts to identify which cultural characteristics create an environment conducive to completing most complex projects involving people from different disciplines.

FIGURE 3.9

Cultural Dimensions of an Organization Supportive of Project Management

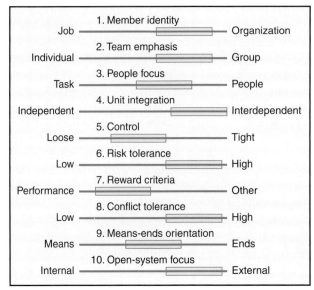

Note that, in many cases, the ideal culture is not at either extreme. For example, a fertile project culture would likely be one in which management balances its focus on the needs of both the task and the people. An optimal culture would balance concern with output (ends) and processes to achieve those outcomes (means). In other cases, the ideal culture would be on one end of a dimension or the other. For example, because most projects require collaboration across disciplines, it would be desirable that the culture of the organization emphasize working in teams and identifying with the organization, not just the professional domain. Likewise it would be desirable that the culture support a certain degree of risk taking and a reasonably high conflict tolerance.

One organization that appears to approach this ideal profile is 3M. 3M has received acclaim for creating an entrepreneurial culture within a large corporate framework. The essence of its culture is captured in phrases that have been chanted often by 3Mers throughout its history: "Encourage experimental doodling." "Hire good people and leave them alone." "If you put fences around people, you get sheep. Give people the room they need." Freedom and autonomy to experiment are reflected in the "15 percent rule," which encourages technical people to spend up to 15 percent of their time on projects of their own choosing and initiative. This fertile culture has contributed to 3M's branching out into more than 60,000 products and 40 separate product divisions.

The metaphor we choose to describe the relationship between organizational culture and project management is that of a riverboat trip. Culture is the river and the project is the boat. Organizing and completing projects within an organization in which the culture is conducive to project management is like paddling downstream: much less effort is required, and the natural force of the river generates progress toward the destination. In many cases, the current can be so strong that steering is all that is required. Such is the case for projects that operate in a project-friendly environment where teamwork and cross-functional cooperation are the norms, where there is a deep commitment to excellence, and where healthy conflict is voiced and dealt with quickly and effectively.

Conversely, trying to complete a project in an organization in which several important features of the dominant culture inhibit effective project management is like paddling upstream: much more time, effort, and attention are needed to reach the destination. This would be the situation in cultures that discourage teamwork and

After a decade of declining sales and profits, Digital Equipment Corporation (DEC) was acquired in 1998 by Compaq Computer. Many analysts attributed the decline at DEC to management of the company's structure prior to the ousting of its founder and CEO, Kenneth H. Olsen, in 1992.

Olsen created a matrix structure to manage DEC's new-product development. In the early days of the computer industry, companies had the time and opportunity to perfect a product's technical capabilities because the product cycles were slow. In the matrix, rival product teams worked side by side on different designs. When one superior design emerged, it was chosen for further development. The winning teams became organizational heroes and rose quickly in the corporation, earning the right to lead future product teams and claim a larger share of the company resources. The other teams were disbanded so that their members could work on other products.

At first this system worked well and led to early successes. But soon DEC began to lose ground as a result of increased competition in the computer industry, which placed a premium on speed to market. As DEC faltered, resources tightened, and the product teams began to compete with each other for scarce company resources such as marketing and engineering support. Intense rivalries broke out among product teams. Many key members left because they felt that their careers were in jeopardy because DEC rewarded only winners.

As a result of the increased competition among teams, the product teams did not pool knowledge and expertise, and integration between functions declined. Instead of providing flexibility and efficient use of resources, the matrix structure at DEC resulted in inertia, infighting, and slow development time.

*"Through the Mill," *The Economist,* vol. 33, no. 7880 (September 10, 1994), p. 76; McWilliams, G., "Crunch time at DEC," *Business Week* (May 4, 1992), pp. 30–33.

cooperation, that have a low tolerance for conflict, where risks are to be avoided, and where getting ahead is based less on performance and more on cultivating favorable relationships with superiors. In such cases, the project manager and her people not only have to overcome the natural obstacles of the project but also have to overcome the prevailing negative forces inherent in the culture of the organization. See Snapshot from Practice: Matrix Problems at DEC.

The implications of this analogy are obvious but important. Greater project authority and resources are necessary to complete projects that encounter a strong, negative cultural current. Conversely, less formal authority and fewer dedicated resources are needed to complete projects in which the cultural currents generate behavior and cooperation essential to project success. The key issue is the degree of interdependency between the parent organization and the project team and the corresponding need to create a unique project culture conducive to successful project completion.

In cases where the prevalent organizational culture supports the behaviors essential to project completion, a weaker project management structure can be effective. For example, one of the major reasons Chaparral Steel is able to use a functional matrix to successfully complete incremental projects is that its culture contains strong norms for cooperation. Conversely, one of the reasons behind the failure of Kodak's "Factory of the Future" project in the mid-1980s was that the culture at that time did not support project management.

When the parent organization possesses a dominant culture that inhibits collaboration and innovation among disciplines and groups of people, it is advisable to insulate the project team from the dominant culture by creating a self-sufficient, dedicated project team. If a dedicated project team is impossible because of resource constraints, then at least a project matrix should be used where the project manager has centralized control over the project. In both cases, the managerial strategy is to create a distinct subculture within the project team in which a new set of norms, customs, and values evolve that will be conducive to project completion.

Under extreme circumstances this project culture could even represent a counterculture in that many of the norms and values are the antithesis of the dominant, parent culture. Such was the case when IBM decided to develop their personal computer quickly in 1980. They knew that the project could get bogged down by the overabundance of computer knowledge and bureaucracy in the company. They also realized that they would have to work closely with suppliers and make use of many non-IBM parts if they were to get to the market quickly. This was not the IBM way at the time, so IBM established the PC project team in a warehouse in Boca Raton, Florida, far from corporate headquarters and other corporate development facilities that existed within the organization.

Summary

This chapter examined two major characteristics of the parent organization that affect the implementation and completion of projects. The first is the formal structure of the organization and how it chooses to organize and manage projects. Although the individual project manager may have very little say as to how the firm chooses to manage projects, he or she must be able to recognize the options available as well as the inherent strengths and weaknesses of different approaches.

Three basic project management structures were described and assessed as to their weaknesses and strengths. Only under unique circumstances can a case be made for managing a project within the normal functional hierarchy. When thinking only in terms of what is best for the project, the creation of an independent project team is clearly favored. However, the most effective project management system appropriately balances the needs of the project with those of the parent organization. Matrix structures emerged out of the parent organization's need to share personnel and resources across multiple projects and operations while creating legitimate project focus. The matrix approach is a hybrid organizational form that combines elements of both the functional and project team forms in an attempt to realize the advantages of both.

Matrix management, while good in theory, has often proven difficult to implement. Many firms have abandoned a matrix after several years of experimentation, citing it as a totally unworkable structure prone to anarchy. Others have found it to be quite effective. These mixed results may, in part, be attributable to the fact that there are different kinds of matrices depending on the relative influence of the functional managers and the project managers.

The second major characteristic of the parent organization that was discussed in this chapter is the concept of organizational culture. Organizational culture is the pattern of beliefs and expectations shared by an organization's members. Culture includes the behavioral norms, customs, shared values, and the "rules of the game" for getting along and getting ahead within the organization. It is important for project managers to be "culture sensitive" so that they can develop strategies and responses that are likely to be understood and accepted as well as avoid violating key norms that would jeopardize their effectiveness within the organization.

The interaction between project management structure and organizational culture is a complicated one. We have suggested that in certain organizations, culture encourages the implementation of projects. In this environment the project management structure used plays a less decisive role in the success of the project. Conversely, for other organizations in which the culture stresses internal competition and differentiation, just the opposite may be true. The prevailing norms, customs, and attitudes inhibit effective project management, and the project management structure plays a more decisive role in the successful implementation of projects. At a minimum, under adverse cultural conditions, the project manager needs to have significant authority over the project team; under more extreme conditions firms should use dedicated project teams to complete critical projects. In both cases, the managerial strategy should be to insulate project work from the dominant culture so that a more positive "subculture" can emerge among project participants.

The project management structure of the organization and the culture of the organization are major elements of the environment in which a project is initiated. Subsequent chapters will examine how project managers and professionals work within this environment to successfully complete projects.

The emergence of network organizations consisting of different companies working together to produce new products and services is reshaping the project management landscape. It is rare to find significant projects being done 100 percent internally. The key is being able to coordinate the efforts of participants from other organizations.

Key Terms			
Balanced matrix	Network organization	Strong matrix
Dedicated project	Organizational culture	Weak matrix
team	Projectitis	
Matrix	Projectized organization	

Review Questions

1. What are the relative advantages and disadvantages of the functional, matrix, virtual, and dedicated team approaches to managing projects?
2. What distinguishes a weak matrix from a strong matrix?
3. Under what conditions would it be advisable to use a project matrix instead of a dedicated project team?
4. Why is it important to assess the culture of an organization before deciding what project management structure should be used to complete a project?
5. What do you believe is more important for successfully completing a project—the formal project management structure or the culture of the parent organization?

Exercises

1. Going to college is analogous to working in a matrix environment in that most students take more than one class and must distribute their time across multiple classes. What problems does this situation create for you? How does it affect your performance? How could the system be better managed to make your life less difficult and more productive?
2. You work for LL Company, which manufacturers high-end optical scopes for hunting rifles. LL Company has been the market leader for the past 20 years and has decided to diversify by applying its technology to develop a top-quality binocular. What kind of project management structure would you recommend they use for this project? What information would you like to have to make this recommendation, and why?
3. You work for Barbata Electronics. Your R&D people believe they have come up with an affordable technology that will double the capacity of exisiting MP3 players and uses audio format that is superior to MP3. The project is code named KYSO (Knock Your Socks Off). What kind of project management structure would you recommend they use for the KYSO project? What information would you like to have to make this recommendation and why?
4. This chapter discussed the role of values and beliefs in forming an organization's culture. The topic of organization culture is big business on the Internet. Many companies use their Web pages to describe their mission, vision, and corporate values and beliefs. There also are many consulting firms that advertise how they help organizations to change their culture. The purpose of this exercise is for you to obtain information pertaining to the organizational culture for two different companies. You can go about this task by very simply searching on the key words "organizational

culture" or "corporate vision and values." This search will identify numerous companies for you to use to answer the following questions. You may want to select companies that you would like to work for in the future.

    a. What are the espoused values and beliefs of the companies?

    b. Use the checklist on p. 76 to assess the Web page. What does the Web page reveal about the culture of this organization? Would this culture be conducive to effective project management?

5. Use the cultural dimensions listed in Figure 3.7 to assess the culture of your school. Instead of employees, consider students, and instead of management, use faculty. For example, member identity refers to the degree to which students identify with the school as a whole rather than their major or option. Either as individuals or in small groups rate the culture of your school on the 10 dimensions.

    a. What dimensions were easy to evaluate and which ones were not?

    b. How strong is the culture of your school?

    c. What functions does the culture serve for your school?

    d. Do you think the culture of your school is best suited to maximizing your learning? Why or why not?

    e. What kind of projects would be easy to implement in your school and what kind of projects would be difficult given the structure and culture of your school? Explain your answer.

6. You work as an analyst in the marketing department for Springfield International (SI). SI uses a weak matrix to develop new services. Management has created an extremely competitive organizational culture that places an emphasis upon achieving results above everything else. One of the project managers that you have been assigned to help has been pressuring you to make his project your number one priority. He also wants you to expand the scope of your work on his project beyond what your marketing manager believes is necessary or appropriate. The project manager is widely perceived as a rising star within SI. Up to now you have been resisting the project manager's pressure and complying with your marketing manager's directives. However, your most recent interchange with the project manager ended by his saying, "I'm not happy with the level of help I am getting from you and I will remember this when I become VP of Marketing." How would you respond and why?

References

Block, T. R. and Frame, J. D., *The Project Office—A Key to Managing Projects Effectively* (Menlo Park, CA: Crisp Publications, 1998).

Block, T. R. and J. D. Frame, "Today's Project Office: Gauging Attitudes," *PM Network,* August, 2001.

Bowen, H. K., Clark, K. B., Holloway, C. A., and Wheelwright, S. C., *The Perpetual Enterprise Machine* (New York: Oxford University Press, 1994).

Brown, S. and Eisenhardt, K. R., "Product development: Past research, present findings, and future directions," *Academy of Management Review,* 20 (2) 1995, pp. 343–78.

Cameron, K. S. and Quinn, R. E., *Diagnosing and Changing Organizational Culture: Based on the Competing Values Framework,* (Upper Saddle River, NJ: Prentice Hall, 1999).

Carlton, J., Apple: *The Inside Story of Intrigue, Egomania, and Business Blunders* (New York: Random House, 1997), pp. 13–14.

Collins, J. C. and Porras, J. I., *Built to Last: The Successful Habits of Visionary Companies* (New York: HarperCollins, 1994), pp. 150–58.

Deal, T. E. and Kennedy, A. A., *Corporate Cultures: The Rites and Rituals of Corporate Life* (Reading, MA: Addison-Wesley, 1982).

De Laat, P. B., "Matrix Management of Projects and Power Struggles: A Case Study of an R&D Laboratory," *IEEE Engineering Management Review,* (Winter, 1995).

Gallagher, R. S., *The Soul of an Organization: Understanding the Values That Drive Successful Corporate Cultures* (Chicago: Dearborn Trade Publishing, 2002).

Gradante, W. and Gardner, D., "Managing Projects from the Future, Not from the Past," Proceedings of the 29th Annual Project Management Institute 1998 Seminars and Symposium (Newtown Square, PA: Project Management Institute, 1998), pp. 289–94.

Graham, R. J. and Englund, R. L., *Creating an Environment for Successful Projects: The Quest to Manage Project Management* (San Francisco: Jossey-Bass, 1997).

Gray, C., Dworatschek, S., Gobeli, D. H., Knoepfel, H., and Larson, E. W., "International Comparison of Project Organization Structures: Use and Effectiveness," *International Journal of Project Management,* vol. 8, no. 1 (February 1990), pp. 26–32.

Hacki, R. and J. Lighton, "The Future of the Networked Company," *McKinsey Quarterly,* no. 3, 2000, pp. 26–39.

Harrison, M. T. and Beyer, J. M., *The Culture of Organizations* (Englewood Cliffs, NJ: Prentice Hall, 1993).

Hobbs, B. and Ménard, P., "Organizational Choices for Project Management," in Paul Dinsmore (ed.), *The AMA Handbook of Project Management* (New York: AMACOM, 1993).

Hobday, M., "The Project-Based Organization: An Ideal Form for Managing Complex Products and Systems?" *Research Policy,* vol. 29, 7, 2000.

Hofstede, G., Neuijen, B., Ohayv, D. D., and Sanders, D., "Measuring Organizational Culture: A Qualitative and Quantitative Study Across Twenty Cases," *Administrative Science Quarterly* (June 1990), pp. 286–316.

Jassawalla, A. R. and Sashittal, H. C., "Cultures that Support Product-Innovation Processes," *Academy of Management Executive,* 15 (3) 2002, pp. 42–54.

Johnson, C. L., Smith, M., and Geary, L. Kelly, *More Than My Share in All,* (Washington, D.C.: Smithsonian Institute Publications, 1990).

Kerzner, H., *In Search of Excellence in Project Management* (New York: Von Nostrand Reinhold, 1997).

Larson, E. W. "Project Management Structures" in *The Handbook for Managing Projects,* Peter Morris & Jeffrey Pinto (Eds.), (Irwin, 2004).

Larson, E. W. and Gobeli, D. H., "Organizing for Product Development Projects," *Journal of Product Innovation Management,* vol. 5 (1988), pp. 180–90.

Larson, E. W. and Gobeli, D. H., "Project Management Structures: Is There a Common Language?" *Project Management Journal,* vol. 16, no. 2 (June 1985), pp. 40–44.

Larson, E. W., and Gobeli, D. H., "Matrix Management: Contradictions and Insights," *California Management Review,* vol. 29, no. 4 (Summer 1987), p. 137.

Laslo, Z. and Goldberg, A. I., "Matrix Structures and Performance: The Search for Optimal Adjustments to Organizational Objectives?", *IEEE Transactions in Engineering Management,* vol. 48, 2, 2001.

Lawrence, P. R. and Lorsch, J. W., *Organization and Environment* (Homewood, IL: Irwin, 1969).

Majchrzak, A. and Wang, Q., "Breaking the Functional Mind-Set in Process Organizations," *Harvard Business Review,* (Sept.–Oct. 1996), pp. 93–99.

Miles, R. E. and Snow, C. C., "The New Network Firm: A Spherical Structure Built on a Human Investment Philosophy," *Organizational Dynamics,* (Spring 1995), pp. 5–18.

Miles, R. E., Snow, C. C., Mathews, J. A., Miles, G. and Coleman, H. J., "Organizing in The Knowledge Age: Anticipating the Cellular Form," *Academy of Management Executive,* 11 (4), 1997: 7–24.

Miller, J., *Lockheed Martin's Skunk Works* (New York: Speciality Publications, 1996).

Olson, E. M., Walker, O. C. Jr., and Ruekert, R. W., "Organizing for Effective New Product Development: The Moderating Role of Product Innovativeness," *Journal of Marketing,* vol. 59 (January), 1995, pp. 48–62.

O'Reilly, C. A., Chatman, J., and Caldwell, D. F., "People and Organizational Culture: A Profile Comparison Approach to Assessing Person-Organization Fit," *Academy of Management Journal,* vol. 34, no. 3 (September 1991), pp. 487–516.

Pettegrew, A. M., "On Studying Organizational Culture," *Administrative Science Quarterly,* vol. 24, no. 4 (1979), pp. 570–81.

Rebello, K., "Inside Microsoft," *Business Weekly,* July 15, 1996, pp. 56–67; B. Filipczak, "Beyond the Gates of Microsoft," *Training,* September 1992, pp. 37–44.

Schein, E., *Organizational Culture and Leadership: A Dynamic View* (San Francisco, CA: Jossey-Bass, 1985).

Sculley, J., *Odyssey: Pepsi to Apple . . . A Journey of Adventure, Ideas, and the Future* (New York: Harper & Row, 1987), pp. 270–79.

Shenhar, A. J., "From Theory to Practice: Toward a Typology of Project Management Styles," *IEEE Transactions in Engineering Management,* 41 (1) 1998, pp. 33–48.

Shenhar, A. J., Dvir D., Lechler T., and Poli, M., "One Size Does Not Fit All–True for Projects, True for Frameworks," Frontiers of Project Management Research and Application, Proceedings of PMI Research Conference, Seattle, 2002, pp. 99–106.

Smith, P. G. and Reinertsen, D. G., *Developing Products in Half the Time* (New York: Van Nostrand Reinhold, 1995).

Stuckenbruck, L. C., *Implementation of Project Management* (Upper Darby, PA: Project Management Institute, 1981).

Youker, R., "Organizational Alternatives for Project Management," *Project Management Quarterly,* vol. 8 (March 1977), pp. 24–33.

Case

Moss and McAdams Accounting Firm

Bruce Palmer had worked for Moss and McAdams (M&M) for six years and was just promoted to account manager. His first assignment was to lead an audit of Johnsonville Trucks. He was quite pleased with the five accountants who had been assigned to his team, especially Zeke Olds. Olds was an Army vet who returned to school to get a double major in accounting and computer sciences. He was on top of the latest developments in financial information systems and had a reputation for coming up with innovative solutions to problems.

M&M was a well-established regional accounting firm with 160 employees located across six offices in Minnesota and Wisconsin. The main office, where Palmer worked, was in Green Bay, Wisconsin. In fact, one of the founding members, Seth Moss, played briefly for the hometown NFL Packers during the late 1950s. M&M's primary services were corporate audits and tax preparation. Over the last two years the partners decided to move more aggressively into the consulting business. M&M projected that consulting would represent 40 percent of their growth over the next five years.

M&M operated within a matrix structure. As new clients were recruited, a manager was assigned to the account. A manager might be assigned to several accounts, depending on the size and scope of the work. This was especially true in the case of tax preparation projects, where it was not uncommon for a manager to be assigned to 8 to 12 clients. Likewise, senior and staff accountants were assigned to multiple account teams. Ruby Sands was the office manager responsible for assigning personnel to different accounts at the Green Bay office. She did her best to assign staff to multiple projects under the same manager. This wasn't always possible, and sometimes accountants had to work on projects led by different managers.

M&M, like most accounting firms, had a tiered promotion system. New CPAs entered as junior or staff accountants. Within two years, their performance was reviewed and they were either asked to leave or promoted to senior accountant. Sometime during their fifth or sixth year, a decision was made to promote them to account manager. Finally, after 10 to 12 years with the firm, the manager was considered for promotion to partner. This was a very competitive position. During the last five years, only 20 percent of account managers at M&M had been promoted to partner. However, once a partner, they were virtually guaranteed the position for life and enjoyed significant increases in salary, benefits, and prestige. M&M had a reputation for being a results-driven organization; partner promotions were based on meeting deadlines, retaining clients, and generating revenue. The promotion team based its decision on the relative performance of the account manager in comparison to his or her cohorts.

One week into the Johnsonville audit, Palmer received a call from Sands to visit her office. There he was introduced to Ken Crosby, who recently joined M&M after working nine years for a Big 5 accounting firm. Crosby was recruited to manage special consulting projects. Sands reported that Crosby had just secured a major consulting project with Springfield Metals. This was a major coup for the firm: M&M had competed against two Big 5 accounting firms for the project. Sands went on to explain that she was working with Crosby to put together his team. Crosby insisted that Zeke Olds be assigned to his team. Sands told him that this would be impossible because Olds was already assigned to work on the Johnsonville audit. Crosby persisted, arguing that Olds's expertise was essential to the Springfield project. Sands decided to work out a compromise and have Olds split time across both projects.

At this time Crosby turned to Palmer and said, "I believe in keeping things simple. Why don't we agree that Olds works for me in the mornings and you in the afternoons. I'm sure we can work out any problems that come up. After all, we both work for the same firm."

SIX WEEKS LATER

Palmer could scream whenever he remembered Crosby's words, "After all, we both work for the same firm." The first sign of trouble came during the first week of the new arrangement when Crosby called, begging to have Olds work all of Thursday on his project. They were conducting an extensive client visit, and Olds was critical to the assessment. After Palmer reluctantly agreed, Crosby said he owed him one. The next week when Palmer called Crosby to request that he return the favor, Crosby flatly refused and said any other time but not this week. Palmer tried again a week later and got the same response.

At first Olds showed up promptly at 1:00 P.M. at Palmer's office to work on the audit. Soon it became a habit to show up 30 to 60 minutes late. There was always a good reason. He was in a meeting in Springfield and couldn't just leave, or an urgent task took longer than planned. One time it was because Crosby took his entire team out to lunch at the new Thai restaurant—Olds was over an hour late because of slow service. In the beginning Olds would usually make up the time by working after hours, but Palmer could tell from conversations he overheard that this was creating tension at home.

What probably bothered Palmer the most were the e-mails and telephone calls Olds received from Crosby and his team members during the afternoons when he was supposed to be working for Palmer. A couple of times Palmer could have sworn that Olds was working on Crosby's project in his (Palmer's) office.

Palmer met with Crosby to talk about the problem and voice his complaints. Crosby acted surprised and even a little bit hurt. He promised things would change, but the pattern continued.

Palmer was becoming paranoid about Crosby. He knew that Crosby played golf with Olds on the weekends and could just imagine him badmouthing the Johnsonville project and pointing out how boring auditing work was. The sad fact was that there probably was some truth to what he was saying. The Johnsonville project was getting bogged down, and the team was slipping behind schedule. One of the contributing factors was Olds's performance. His work was not up to its usual standards. Palmer approached Olds about this, and Olds became defensive. Olds later apologized and confided that he found it difficult switching his thinking from consulting to auditing and then back to consulting. He promised to do better, and there was a slight improvement in his performance.

The last straw came when Olds asked to leave work early on Friday so that he could take his wife and kids to a Milwaukee Brewers baseball game. It turned out Springfield Metals had given Crosby their corporate tickets, and he decided to treat his team with box seats right behind the Brewers dugout. Palmer hated to do it, but he had to refuse the request. He felt guilty when he overheard Olds explaining to his son on the telephone why they couldn't go to the game.

Palmer finally decided to pick up the phone and request an urgent meeting with Sands to resolve the problem. He got up enough nerve and put in the call only to be told that Sands wouldn't be back in the office until next week. As he put the receiver down, he thought maybe things would get better.

TWO WEEKS LATER

Sands showed up unexpectedly at Palmer's office and said they needed to talk about Olds. Palmer was delighted, thinking that now he could tell her what had been going on. But before he had a chance to speak, Sands told him that Olds had come to see her yesterday. She told him that Olds confessed that he was having a hard time working on both Crosby's and Palmer's projects. He was having difficulty concentrating on the auditing work in the afternoon because he was thinking about some of the consulting issues that had emerged during the morning. He was putting in extra hours to try to meet both of the projects' deadlines, and this was creating problems at home. The bottom line was that he was stressed out and couldn't deal with the situation. He asked that he be assigned full-time to Crosby's project. Sands went on to say that Olds didn't blame

Palmer, in fact he had a lot of nice things to say about him. He just enjoyed the consulting work more and found it more challenging. Sands concluded by saying, "We talked some more and ultimately I agreed with him. I hate to do this to you, Bruce, but Olds is a valuable employee, and I think this is the best decision for the firm."

1. If you were Palmer at the end of the case, how would you respond?
2. What, if anything, could Palmer have done to avoid losing Olds?
3. What advantages and disadvantages of a matrix type organization are apparent from this case?
4. What could the management at M&M do to more effectively manage situations like this?

Case

ORION Systems (A)*

The office erupted into cheers when it was announced over the PA system that ORION had just been awarded the government contract to build the next generation of high-speed, light-rail trains. Everyone came over to shake Mike Rosas's hand and congratulate him. It was well known that Rosas would be the project manager for this important project, which would be code named Jaguar. Once the celebration subsided, Rosas gazed out the window and thought about what he had just gotten himself into.

The Jaguar project would be a high-profile project that would affect procurement of future contracts with the government. Increased competition had raised performance expectations regarding completion time, quality, reliability, and cost. He knew that major changes in how ORION organized and managed projects would be necessary to meet the expectations of the Jaguar project.

PROJECT MANAGEMENT AT ORION

ORION was a division of a large aerospace company with 7,000 employees. ORION evolved from a project organization into a matrix structure to conserve costs and better utilize limited resources. At any point in time, ORION could be working on three to five large projects such as the Jaguar project and 30 to 50 smaller projects. Project managers negotiated personnel assignments with the VP of operations, who ultimately decided project assignments. It was not uncommon for an engineer to be working on two to three projects during a week.

Figure C3.1 portrays how new-product development projects were organized at ORION. Project management was limited only to the design and development of the new product. Once the final design and prototype were completed, they were turned over to manufacturing for production and delivery to the customer. A four-person management team oversaw the completion of the project and their responsibilities are briefly described here:

- *Project manager*—responsible for all aspects of design and development of the product.
- *Planning and control manager*—responsible for building an overall project network, scheduling, managing the budget, controlling and evaluating the design and development program, and preparing status reports.

---

* Prepared by Shlomo Cohen.

FIGURE C3.1
**Organization of
Product Development
Projects at ORION**

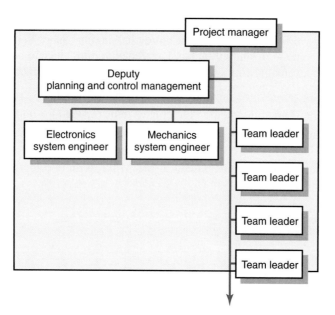

- *Electronics system engineer*—responsible for providing technical expertise on electronic systems issues.

- *Mechanics system engineer*—responsible for providing technical expertise on mechanical system issues.

The core work was completed by 12 to 20 design teams. Each team had a leader, who was responsible for designing, developing, building, and testing a specific subsystem of the product. The size of individual teams varied from 5 to 15 engineers, depending on the scope of their work. These engineers split time across multiple projects.

Design engineers ran the show at ORION, and manufacturing, marketing, and other groups were expected to follow their lead. The special status of the design engineers was reinforced by the fact that they were actually paid on higher pay curves than the manufacturing engineers.

The overall product development and manufacturing process is captured in the master plan chart (Figure C3.2). New-product design and development evolves

FIGURE C3.2   Traditional Master Plan at ORION

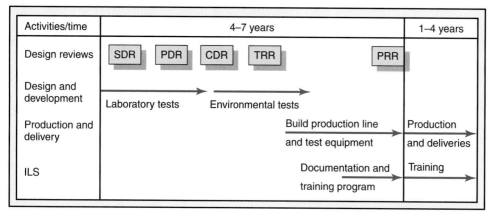

around five major reviews: system design review (SDR), preliminary design review (PDR), critical design review (CDR), test readiness review (TRR), and production readiness review (PRR).

Design and development work begins within the laboratory and progresses to field tests of specific subsystems and ultimately final product prototypes. Once completed, the design and prototype are turned over to manufacturing, which begins building the production line for the new product. Manufacturing also develops the necessary test equipment to confirm that manufactured components perform correctly. During this time, integrated logistical support (ILS) teams prepare product documentation, users' manuals, maintenance programs, and training programs for the customers who will be using the product. It typically takes ORION six to seven years to develop and manufacture a product such as the Jaguar.

ORION just completed a major assessment of how projects are managed. Below is a brief description of some of the major problems that were identified:

- *Higher than expected production costs.* Once products were developed, there was a tendency for them to be "thrown over the wall" to manufacturing to produce. Very little design for manufacturability was done, and the production ramp was complicated, inefficient, and stressful to the people in the plant.
- *Quality concerns.* Increased competition had raised customer expectations with regard to quality. Customers expected fewer defects and longer replacement schedules. ORION had a tendency to deal with quality issues after the fact, initiating quality improvements after the production process was set up. Not enough attention was devoted to incorporating quality considerations into the original design of products.
- *Problems with customer support.* User manuals and technical documentation sometimes failed to address all of a customer's concerns, and the follow-up training was not always adequately prepared. These problems contributed to increased costs in customer service and a decline in customer satisfaction.
- *Lack of strong project ownership.* While everyone accepted that a matrix arrangement was the only way to accommodate all the projects at ORION, the shifting back and forth of personnel across multiple projects took its toll on the progress of individual projects. Members often failed to identify with individual projects and develop the sense of excitement that contributed to superior performance. The shuffling of personnel slowed down progress because additional time had to be devoted to bringing returning members up to speed on current developments.
- *Scope creep.* ORION was renowned for its engineering prowess. However, there was a tendency for design engineers to get so absorbed with the science of the project that they lost focus on the practical considerations. This led to costly delays and sometimes design modifications that were inconsistent with customer requirements.

Rosas was aware of these and other concerns as he sat down with his staff to figure out the best way to organize the new Jaguar project.

1. What recommendations would you make to Rosas about organizing the Jaguar project, and why?
2. How would you change the organizational chart and master plan to reflect these changes?

ORION Systems (B)

ROSAS'S PLAN

Rosas and his staff worked hard over the past week to develop a plan to establish a new standard for completing projects at ORION. The Jaguar project management team will be expanded to seven managers, who will be responsible for overseeing the completion of the project from design to delivery to the customer. A brief description of the responsibilities for the three new positions follows (see Figure C3.3):

- *Production manager*—responsible for raising production issues during the design phase; responsible for building and managing the production line.
- *ILS (integrated logistical support) manager*—responsible for all activities that require project/customer support after delivery including customer training, documentation, and equipment testing.
- *QA (quality assurance) manager*—responsible for implementing a quality program that will enhance the reliability, availability and maintainability of the product.

These seven managers (the three just described plus the four discussed in Part A) will coordinate the completion of the project and see that their respective disciplines are factored into all major decisions. Rosas, as project manager, will work toward achieving consensus, but he will have the authority to intervene and make decisions if necessary.

The core work will be completed by 35 teams. Each team will have a "leader," who will be responsible for designing, developing, building, and testing a specific subsystem of the project. They will also be responsible for the quality and productivity of the subsystems and for doing the work on time and within budget.

FIGURE C3.3
Proposed Project Organization for the Jaguar Project

FIGURE C3.4   Jaguar Master Plan

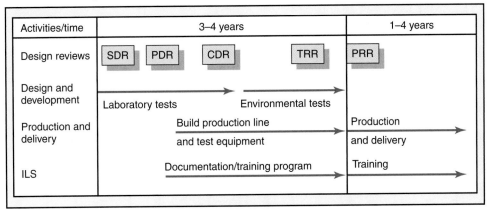

Individual teams will consist of 5 to 12 members, and Rosas insists that at least half of each team be assigned to work full time on the project. This will help ensure continuity and enhance commitment to the project.

The second key feature to the plan is the development of the overall master plan for the project. This involves abandoning the traditional sequential approach to product development and adopting a concurrent engineering approach to the project (see Figure C3.4).

Once the system design is reviewed and approved, different teams will begin working within the laboratory to design, develop, and test specific subsystems and components. Soon after this has begun the ILS team will start gathering information and preparing product documentation. Once the PDR is completed, the production teams will begin designing the necessary production lines. The CDR will include not only resolution of major technical questions but also a plan for manufacturing. Once the CDR is completed, project teams will begin field tests under a variety of different environmental conditions according to government specifications. Subsequent design refinements will be closely coordinated with manufacturing and ILS teams so that, ideally, ORION will be ready to begin producing the Jaguar upon completion of the PRR.

Rosas believes that the phasing of the production and documentation work alongside the core development work will accelerate project completion, reduce production costs, and contribute to customer satisfaction.

1. What are the major changes between this plan and the way ORION has managed projects in the past?
2. How well do you believe these changes deal with the problems identified in Part A?
3. Who is likely to support this plan? Who is not likely to support this plan?

Appendix 3.1

How Culture Is Created and Communicated in Organizations

To understand, interpret, and even change the culture of an organization, it is useful to understand how that culture evolved and how it is communicated to its members. Most experts trace the origins of an organization's culture to the personality, values, and habits of the individual(s) responsible for founding the organization. For example,

Bill Gates has been described as personally aggressive, competitive, highly disciplined, and willing to put in long hours on the job. These same characteristics have been used to describe the Microsoft organization, the software giant he founded and currently heads. While the roots of culture may be traced to the personality of the founding members, as organizations grow in size and encounter new challenges, their culture evolves and is sustained by a complex set of mechanisms summarized in Figure A3.1.

SELECTION OF NEW MEMBERS

The explicit goal of the recruitment process is to identify and hire individuals with the requisite skills, knowledge, and experience to perform jobs within an organization. Part of performing work within an organization is the ability to work with others and fit into the culture of the organization. Companies are paying increased attention to assessing the personal values and habits of applicants to determine whether they are compatible with the culture of the organization. For example, Compaq computers is known to hire candidates who are easy to get along with and who feel comfortable with the consensus decision-making style they use. They actively screen out loners or stellar performers with big egos. Conversely, Microsoft has a reputation for hiring aggressive, competitive employees.

The importance of selection as a means of sustaining or changing the culture of an organization cannot be underestimated. Experience has taught companies that it is much more difficult and costly to get rid of people who do not fit in than to invest extra time and effort to ensure that new hires are compatible with the culture of the organization. This is why it is not uncommon today for the selection and hiring process to be extended over a battery of interviews in which one of the primary objectives is to determine how well the applicant will "fit in."

METHODS FOR SUSTAINING CULTURE

No matter how careful an organization is in recruiting and hiring personnel, new employees need to be indoctrinated in the culture of the organization. Just like all Marines go through boot camp to prove their worthiness and learn the "Marine Way," new employees experience a less intense socialization process, where they are tested and learn the norms, customs, and ideals of the organization.

Formal Statement of Principles

It has become fashionable for companies to explicitly publish their values and operating principles in company documents. For example, the Kaufman and Broad Home Corporation, located in Los Angeles, states its mission as follows:

We build homes to meet people's dreams.

Objectives

- We are fiercely determined to continue to succeed. We intend to provide the best quality housing for our customers, a superior return to our shareholders, and a chance for every employee to make a difference and share in our success.

Vision

- We strive to be the leading home builder in each market in which we operate. We intend to lead the way in home building well into the twenty-first century.

Core Values

- It is our intention to deliver a quality product . . . 100 percent of the time.
- We believe that the true test of quality is customer satisfaction.
- There are no good excuses.
- We strive to be on the cutting edge of product development and innovative design.
- We don't just build homes, we build neighborhoods.
- This business is built around people. We want self-directed winners who have high personal integrity.
- All people at Kaufman and Broad have clout. We all work for the same ultimate boss, our customers.
- We respect the dignity of those with whom we deal. We always try to be fair.
- We are committed to steady growth and improved earnings; we will not overemphasize short-term results.

These corporate principles and philosophies are generally reviewed during new employee orientation sessions and are augmented by stories to underscore their significance. It should be noted that simply stating what the values and principles of a firm are will be meaningless unless they are visibly supported by the other methods.

Top Management Behavior

Just as the founder's personality is critical to the initial formation of a company's culture, many experts argue that top management plays a critical role in sustaining and shaping the culture of a firm. First, they serve as exemplars of the culture of the organization. As such, members look to them as role models to be emulated and to be analyzed to determine those qualities and habits the organization cherishes. Second, members interpret from top managers' actions what is truly important to the firm. For example, imagine the president of a firm announcing that improving customer satisfaction is the firm's number one priority. Now imagine the different impact this statement would have on the organization if, after this declaration, the president disappears behind a wall of business as usual as opposed to personally leading a series of focus groups to determine specific customer needs and complaints.

Reaction to Crisis

Organizations are sometimes confronted with defining moments in their history in which their values and priorities are tested and most clearly manifested. For example, during the mid-1980s the local Hewlett-Packard (HP) plant was operating at less than 40 percent capacity. Rumors abounded that there would be corresponding lay-offs and massive transfers. However, one of the dominating principles of the culture at HP has always been a commitment to human resources. Instead of draconian lay-offs, management of the plant responded by scheduling a nine-day work schedule over two weeks, representing a 10 percent cut in salary for everyone. They also encouraged employees to go on sabbaticals and pursue advanced degrees while maintaining benefits and job assurance. In doing so the firm sent a clear message to its employees about the importance of human resources. This response has become deeply ingrained in the corporation's folklore and, in turn, now serves to reinforce this aspect of its culture.

Allocation of Rewards and Status

Employees also learn about their organization's culture through its reward systems. The rewards and punishments attached to various behaviors convey to employees the priorities and values of both the individual manager and the organization. Imagine the different signals that are being sent if a worthy subordinate who was justifiably critical of a top management proposal is promoted versus transferred to a less prestigious area within the firm. Likewise, what values are being communicated when an employee is discovered engaging in unethical behavior and is verbally reprimanded as opposed to being fired?

It is important to note that organizations may be quite ineffective in rewarding behavior consistent with their espoused values and principles. Employees are adroit at pointing out inconsistencies between what management says and does. These inconsistencies undermine management credibility as well as help create a weak culture that contributes to ineffective organizational performance.

Rituals, Stories, and Symbols

A significant portion of an organization's culture is transmitted and reinforced symbolically. Symbolic communication is a sign or an act that means something more than itself—it is something invested with a particular, subjective meaning. Although symbolic communication is indirect, it can act as an "evocative" mechanism for rousing, channeling, and domesticating powerful emotions. To appreciate how much feeling symbols evoke, consider the response to the raising of a national flag at the Olympics or the meaning of Yassir Arafat standing or not standing when the Israeli national anthem is being played.

Organizational Rituals

Organizational rituals are defined as formal and customarily repeated acts that convey basic norms and values throughout the organization. The function of rituals is to give concrete expression to deeply held cultural values. The variety of ritualistic behaviors includes the annual company picnic and Christmas party, employee morale surveys, TGIF gatherings, weekly staff meetings, and going-away parties. Companies that are committed to building a strong culture that supports their basic values and principles invest considerable attention in organizational rituals. Take, for example, the Sequent Corporation, an information technology firm located in Portland, Oregon. As it turns out, 85 percent of their business is typically shipped out during the last week of the quarter. It has become the custom for everyone at Sequent from the president to the janitor to volunteer to work one shift in the loading area during this time. According to the president, this custom reinforces a variety of important corporate values, including "We're in the business of building products," and "None of us are too big to get our hands dirty."

Stories, Myths, and Legends

Many of the underlying beliefs and values of an organization's culture are expressed as legends and stories that become part of the organization's folklore. These stories and legends are a way of transmitting the existing culture from senior employees to new ones; they serve to emphasize important aspects of that culture. For example, employees at Prince Corp., now a division of Johnson Controls Inc., tell a story of founder Ed Prince, who was helping employees load finished materials onto a railroad car. When they discovered they needed a lubricant to perform the job, he tossed the keys to his new Cadillac to a young employee he had never met, handed him a $100 bill, and told him to go get some WD-40. The story ends with the employee returning with the product, the car, and Prince's change. By repeating this story, employees emphasize the importance of everyone pitching in to help get the job done and the high value placed on trust.

Material Symbols

Nike Corporate Headquarters in Portland, Oregon, doesn't look like normal head office operations. The first thing a visitor sees when driving into the grounds is a professionally groomed soccer field. Within the hall of the main building is a large mural of Michael Jordan. Intermixed within the network of modern offices are state-of-the-art athletic facilities for almost every sport imaginable. The employees are uniformly young and athletic. Fiercely contested basketball games are played during the workday. The entire operation communicates a play hard/work hard, competitive environment.

In sharp contrast to Nike is Amazon.com, where frugality is a key corporate value. Beyond the online bookseller's popular website is a drab 1960s, four-story headquarters in downtown Seattle. All desks are made from doors (total cost: $130). Monitors are propped up on telephone books to avoid the cost of monitor stands. "By watching your overhead you can spend more on business expansion," explains Amazon.com founder and CEO Jeff Bezos.

Size and layout of offices are other material symbols that reflect corporate values. For example, for many companies the size of an office and its floor number reflects how much status and real power the manager has. Conversely, many companies have tried to promote egalitarianism by opting for cubicle arrangements in which all departments are on the same floor and office space is standardized.

REMOVAL OF DEVIANTS

Just as members assess those people who are being rewarded to determine what the organization values, they assess people who are asked to leave to identify what kind of people and behavior management disapproves of. It is perfectly natural for individuals to gossip about reasons a former member left. These explanations help clarify what is acceptable and unacceptable behavior. Whenever possible, management needs to spell out the reasons individuals were discharged or left voluntarily so that the correct causes are understood.

APPENDIX SUMMARY

An organization's culture can have a profound impact on members' attitudes and behavior. Top management is devoting more time and attention to developing a unique culture that will provide them with a competitive advantage in today's business world. See the Snapshot from Practice: Culture Change at Hewlett-Packard for an example of trying to change the culture of an organization.

"The Rules of The Garage signify a new way of engaging with each other, a new way of cooperating. I believe these rules represent the essence of who we are and how we will work together in the future."

Carly Fiorina

Carly Fiorina is taking Hewlett Packard back to the future by reformulating the California-based technology company's legendary culture, known as the H-P Way. "The H-P Way is about innovation; trust and respect and integrity; contribution to community; and performance," says Fiorina, H-P's first CEO hired from outside the company. The problem, she argues, is that employees have distorted these values over the years. "The H-P Way has been misinterpreted and twisted as a gentle bureaucracy of entitlement instead of performance-based meritocracy."

To establish a more performance-based culture, Fiorina launched the "Rules of the Garage," a set of cultural values with symbolic reference to the Palo Alto garage where founders William Hewlett

and David Packard started the company in 1939. The rules include such principles as the customer defines whether a job is well done, radical ideas are not bad ideas, invent new ways of working, if your job does not make a contribution it does not leave the garage, and a belief that by working together we can change the world. To reinforce these values, Fiorina introduced a customer-focused bonus system, integrated the company's 83 decentralized business units, and laid off thousands of employees.

If the Rules of the Garage don't change H-P's culture, Fiorina is counting that a merger with Houston-based Compaq Computer will do the trick. Firoina calls the merger "a catalyst that would rejuvenate the H-P Way," forcing H-P employees to adopt Compaq's fast-moving, customer-driven culture.

*http://www.hp.com.sg/about-hp/rule_garage.html; D. Olive, "Fiorina: A Woman in a Hurry," *National Post,* September 5, 2001; M. Veverka, "Carly's Challenge," *Barron's,* August 13, 2001, pp. 21–27; "H-P's Employee-Friendly Culture in Flux," *Sacramento (CA) Business Journal,* August 3, 2001, p. 3; J. Foley, "Hewlett-Packard Reaches a Cultural Crossroads," *Information Week,* July 23, 2001, p. 40.

APPENDIX REVIEW QUESTIONS

1. What are the mechanisms that are used to sustain the culture of an organization?
2. Which mechanism do you believe has the biggest effect on the culture of an organization and why?

APPENDIX EXERCISE

1. Select an organization you have been or currently are a member of (e.g., work organization, athletic team, fraternity). Assess the organization's culture in terms of the roles that rituals and stories play in communicating the norms, expectations, and values of the organization. How are the cultural values communicated symbolically?
2. Review the Snapshot "Culture Change at H-P: From the H-P Way to Rules of the Garage."
   a. Search the internet using the key words "H-P Way" and "Rules of the Garage" to find information about cultural changes at Hewlett-Packard. What does this information suggest about how easy it is to change the culture of an organization?
   b. How does "Rules of the Garage" support effective project management?

APPENDIX REFERENCES

Abrahams, J., *The Mission Statement Book,* (New York: Ten-Speed Press, 1995): pp. 350–51.

Dandridge, T. C., "Symbols' Function and Use" In L. R. Pondy et al., eds., *Organizational Symbolism 1, Monographs in Organizational Behavior and Industrial Relations,* (Greenwich, CT: JAI Press, 1983), p. 166.

Deal, T. E. and A. A. Kennedy, *Corporate Cultures: The Rites and Rituals of Corporate Life,* (Reading, MA: Addison-Wesley, 1982).

Gallagher, R. S., *The Soul of an Organization: Understanding the Values That Drive Successful Corporate Cultures* (Chicago: Dearborn Trade Publishing, 2002).

Kerr, J. and J. W. Slocum, "Managing Corporate Culture Through Reward Systems," *Academy of Management Executive,* 1 (2) May 1987: pp. 99–108.

Larson, E. W. and J. King, "The Systemic Distortion of Information: An Ongoing Challenge to Management," *Organizational Dynamics,* 24 (3) 1996: pp. 49–62.

Schein, E., *Organizational Culture and Leadership: A Dynamic View,* (San Francisco: Jossey-Bass, 1985).

Trice, H. M. and J. M. Beyer, *The Culture of Organizations,* (Englewood Cliffs, NJ: Prentice Hall, 1993).

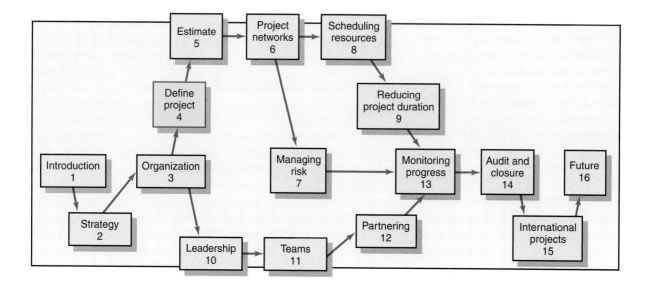

CHAPTER FOUR

Defining the Project

Select a dream
Use your dream to set a goal
Create a plan
Consider resources
Enhance skills and abilities
Spend time wisely
Start! Get organized and go
. . . it is one of those acro-whatevers,
said Pooh. *

One of the best ways to meet the needs of the customer and major project stakeholders is to use an integrated project planning and control system that requires selective information. Project managers who manage a single, small project can plan and schedule the project tasks without a formal planning and information system. However, when the project manager must manage several small projects or a large, complex project, a threshold is quickly reached in which the project manager can no longer cope with the detail.

This chapter describes a disciplined, structured method for selectively collecting information to use through all phases of the project life cycle, to meet the needs of all stakeholders (e.g., customer, project manager), and to measure performance against the strategic plan of the organization. The method suggested is a selective outline of the project called the *work breakdown structure*. The early stages of developing the outline serve to ensure that all tasks are identified and that participants of the project have an understanding of what is to be done. Once the outline and its detail are defined, an integrated information system can be developed to schedule work and allocate budgets. This baseline information is later used for control.

In addition, we will present a variant of the work breakdown structure called *process breakdown structure*. The five generic steps described herein provide a structured approach for collecting the project information necessary for planning, scheduling, and controlling the project. These steps and the development of project networks found in the next chapters all take place concurrently, and several iterations are typically required to develop dates and budgets that can be used to manage the project. The old saying, "We can control only what we have planned" is true; therefore, defining the project is the first step.

---

* Roger E. Allen and Stephen D. Allen, *Winnie-the-Pooh on Success* (New York: Penguin, 1997), p. 10.

Step 1: Defining the Project Scope

Defining the project scope sets the stage for developing a project plan. Project scope is a definition of the end result or mission of your project—a product or service for your client/customer. The primary purpose is to define as clearly as possible the deliverable(s) for the end user and to focus project plans. As fundamental and essential as scope definition appears, it is frequently overlooked by project leaders of well-managed, large corporations.

Research clearly shows that a poorly defined scope or mission is the most frequently mentioned barrier to project success. For example, a study by Smith and Tucker of a large petroleum refinery plant project found that poor scope definition for major segments of the project had the greatest negative impact on cost and schedule. In a larger study involving more than 1,400 project managers in the United States and Canada, Gobeli and Larson found that approximately 50 percent of the planning problems relate to unclear definition of scope and goals. These and other studies suggest a strong correlation between project success and clear scope definition. The scope document directs focus on the project purpose throughout the life of the project for the customer and project participants.

The scope should be developed under the direction of the project manager and customer. The project manager is responsible for seeing that there is agreement with the owner on project objectives, deliverables at each stage of the project, technical requirements, and so forth. For example, a deliverable in the early stage might be specifications; for the second stage, three prototypes for production; for the third, a sufficient quantity to introduce to market; and finally, marketing promotion and training.

Your project scope definition is a document that will be published and used by the project owner and project participants for planning and measuring project success. *Scope* describes what you expect to deliver to your customer when the project is complete. Your project scope should define the results to be achieved in specific, tangible, and measurable terms.

Employing a Project Scope Checklist

Clearly, project scope is the keystone interlocking all elements of a project plan. To ensure that scope definition is complete, you may wish to use the following checklist:

Project Scope Checklist

---
1. Project objective
2. Deliverables
3. Milestones
4. Technical requirements
5. Limits and exclusions
6. Reviews with customer

---

1. **Project objective.** The first step of project scope definition is to define the overall objective to meet your customer's need(s). For example, as a result of extensive market research a computer software company decides to develop a program that automatically translates verbal sentences in English to Russian. The project should be completed within three years at a cost not to exceed $1.5 million. Another example is to design and produce a completely portable, hazardous waste, thermal treatment system in 13 months at a cost not to exceed $13 million. The project objective answers the questions of what, when, and how much.

2. **Deliverables.** The next step is to define major deliverables—the expected outputs over the life of the project. For example, deliverables in the early design phase of a project might be a list of specifications. In the second phase deliverables could be software coding and a technical manual. The next phase could be to test prototypes. The final phase could be final tests and approved software.

3. **Milestones.** A milestone is a significant event in a project that occurs at a point in time. The milestone schedule shows only major segments of work; it represents first, rough-cut estimates of time, cost, and resources for the project. The milestone schedule is built using the deliverables as a platform to identify major segments of work and an end date—for example, testing complete and finished by July 1 of the same year. Milestones should be natural, important control points in the project. Milestones should be easy for all project participants to recognize.

4. **Technical requirements.** More frequently than not, a product or service will have technical requirements to ensure proper performance. For example, a technical requirement for a personal computer might be the ability to accept 120-volt alternating current or 240-volt direct current without any adapters or user switches. Another well-known example is the ability of 911 emergency systems to identify the caller's phone number and location of the phone. Examples from IS projects include speed and capacity of database systems and connectivity with alternative systems. For understanding the importance of key requirements, see Snapshot from Practice: Big Bertha.

5. **Limits and exclusions.** The limits of scope should be defined. Failure to do so can lead to false expectations and to expending resources and time on the wrong problem. Examples of limits are: local air transportation to and from base camps will be outsourced; system maintenance and repair will be done only up to one month after final inspection; client will be billed for additional training beyond that prescribed in the contract. Exclusions further define the boundary of the project by stating what is not included. Examples include: data will be collected by the client, not the contractor; a house will be built, but no landscaping or security devices added; software will be installed, but no training given.

6. **Reviews with customer.** Completion of the scope checklist ends with a review with your customer—internal or external. The main concern here is the understanding and agreement of expectations. Is the customer getting what he or she desires in deliverables? Does the project definition identify key accomplishments, budgets, timing, and performance requirements? Are questions of limits and exclusions covered? Clear communication in all these issues is imperative to avoid claims or misunderstanding.

In summary, close liaison with your customer is necessary to develop a project definition that meets all the requirements of the customer. Clear scope definition ensures you will know when a change in scope occurs. A clear project scope definition is the primary prerequisite for development of your work breakdown structure. Scope definition provides an administrative plan that is used to develop your operational plan. Scope definition should be as brief as possible but complete; one or two pages are typical for small projects. See Snapshot from Practice: Scope Statement on p. 104.

The above checklist is generic. Different industries and companies will develop unique checklists and templates to fit their needs and specific kinds of projects. Many companies engaged in contracted work refer to scope statements as *statements of work* (SOW). Other organizations use the term *project charter*. However, *project charter* has different meanings in the world of project management. One meaning is an expanded version of the scope statement, described above, that might include such items as risk limits, customer needs, spending limits, and even team composition. A second meaning,

Big Bertha II versus
the USGA's COR
Requirements*

In 1991 Callaway Golf Equipment introduced their Big Bertha driver and revolutionized the golf equipment business. Big Bertha—named after the World War I German long-distance cannon—was much larger than conventional woods and lacked a hosel (the socket in the head of the club into which the shaft is inserted) so that the weight could be better distributed throughout the head. This innovative design gave the clubhead a larger sweet spot, which allowed a player to strike the golf ball off-center and not suffer much loss in distance or accuracy. Callaway has maintained its preeminent position in the golf industry by utilizing space-age technology to extend the accuracy and distance of golf equipment.

In 2000 Callaway introduced the Big Bertha ERC II forged titanium driver. The driver was technologically superior to any driver on the market. However, there was one big problem. The new version of Bertha did not conform to the coefficient of restitution (COR) requirement established by the United States Golf Association (USGA). As a result it was barred from use by golfers in North America who intended to play by USGA's Rules of Golf.

The USGA believed that the rapid technological advances in golf equipment made by Callaway Golf and other golf manufacturers were threatening the integrity of the game. Players were hitting balls so much farther and straighter that golf courses around the world were being redesigned to make them longer and more difficult.

So in 1998 the USGA established performance thresholds for all new golf equipment. In order to prevent manufacturers from developing more powerful clubs, the USGA limited the COR of new golf equipment to 0.83. The COR was calculated by firing a golf ball at a driver out of a cannon-like machine at 109 miles per hour. The speed that the ball returned to the cannon could not exceed 83 percent of its initial speed (90.47 mph). The USGA called the ratio of incoming to outgoing velocity the coefficient of restitution (COR). The intent of the USGA COR threshold was to limit the distance that golf balls could be hit since studies indicated that 0.01 increase in COR resulted in two extra yards of carry. The Big Bertha ERC II's COR was 0.86.

After numerous efforts to get USGA to change its technical requirements, Callaway's engineers went back to the drawing board and in 2002 introduced Great Big Bertha II which conformed to USGA's 0.83 COR restriction.

*Gamble, John E. "Callaway Golf Company: Sustaining Advantage in a Changing Industry," in A. A. Thompson, J. E. Gamble, and A. J. Strickland, *Strategy: Winning in the Marketplace,* Boston, MA: McGraw-Hill/Irwin, 2004, pp. C204–C228.

which dates back to the original use of the word, charter, is a document that authorizes the project manager to initiate and lead the project. This document is issued by upper management and provides the project manager with written authority to use organizational resources for project activities.

Many projects suffer from scope creep, which is the tendency for the project scope to expand over time—usually by changing requirements, specifications, and priorities.

As we have already suggested, scope creep can be reduced by carefully writing your scope statement. A scope statement that is too broad is an invitation for scope creep. Scope creep can have a positive or negative effect on the project, but in most cases scope creep means added costs and possible project delays. Changes in requirements, specifications, and priorities frequently result in cost overruns and delays. Examples are abundant—Denver airport baggage handling system; Boston's new freeway system ("The Big Dig"), China's fast train in Shanghai; and the list goes on. On software development projects, scope creep is manifested in bloated products in which added functionality undermines ease of use.

If the project scope needs to change, it is critical to have a sound change control process in place that records the change and keeps a log of all project changes. The log identifies the change, impact, and those responsible for accepting or rejecting a proposed change.

Change control is the topic of Chapter 7. Project managers in the field constantly suggest that dealing with changing requirements is one of their most perplexing problems.

Step 2: Establishing Project Priorities

Quality and the ultimate success of a project are traditionally defined as meeting and/or exceeding the expectations of the customer and/or upper management in terms of cost (budget), time (schedule), and performance (scope) of the project (see Figure 4.1). The interrelationship among these criteria varies. For example, sometimes it is necessary to compromise the performance and scope of the project to get the project done quickly or less expensively. Often the longer a project takes, the more expensive it becomes. However, a positive correlation between cost and schedule may not always be true. Other times project costs can be reduced by using cheaper, less efficient labor or equipment that extends the duration of the project. Likewise, as will be seen in Chapter 9, project managers are often forced to expedite or "crash" certain key activities by adding additional labor, thereby raising the original cost of the project.

One of the primary jobs of a project manager is to manage the trade-offs among time, cost, and performance. To do so, project managers must define and understand the nature of the priorities of the project. They need to have a candid discussion with the project customer and upper management to establish the relative importance of each criterion. One technique that is useful for this purpose is completing a priority matrix for the project that identifies which criterion is constrained, which should be enhanced, and which can be accepted:

Constrain. The original parameter is fixed. The project must meet the completion date, specifications and scope of the project, or budget.

FIGURE 4.1
**Project Management
Trade-offs**

PROJECT OBJECTIVE

To construct a high-quality, custom home within five months at cost not to exceed $150,000.

DELIVERABLES

- A 2,200-square-foot, 2½-bath, 3-bedroom, finished home.
- A finished garage, insulated and sheetrocked.
- Kitchen appliances to include range, oven, microwave, and dishwasher.
- High-efficiency gas furnace with programmable thermostat.

MILESTONES

1. Permits approved—March 5
2. Foundation poured—March 14
3. Drywall in. Framing, sheathing, plumbing, electrical, and mechanical inspections passed—May 25
4. Final inspection—June 7

TECHNICAL REQUIREMENTS

1. Home must meet local building codes.
2. All windows and doors must pass NFRC class 40 energy ratings.
3. Exterior wall insulation must meet an "R" factor of 21.
4. Ceiling insulation must meet an "R" factor of 38.
5. Floor insulation must meet an "R" factor of 25.
6. Garage will accommodate two large-size cars and one 20-foot Winnebago.
7. Structure must pass seismic stability codes.

LIMITS AND EXCLUSIONS

1. The home will be built to the specifications and design of the original blueprints provided by the customer.
2. Owner responsible for landscaping.
3. Refrigerator is not included among kitchen appliances.
4. Air conditioning is not included but prewiring is included.
5. Contractor reserves the right to contract out services.
6. Contractor responsible for subcontracted work.
7. Site work limited to Monday through Friday, 8:00 A.M. to 6:00 P.M.

CUSTOMER REVIEW

John and Joan Smith

Enhance. Given the scope of the project, which criterion should be optimized? In the case of time and cost, this usually means taking advantage of opportunities to either reduce costs or shorten the schedule. Conversely, with regards to performance, enhancing means adding value to the project.

Accept. For which criterion is it tolerable not to meet the original parameters? When trade-offs have to be made, is it permissible for the schedule to slip, to reduce the scope and performance of the project, or to go over budget?

Figure 4.2 displays the priority matrix for the development of a new cable modem. Because *time* to market is important to sales, the project manager is instructed to take advantage of every opportunity to reduce completion time. In doing so, going over *budget* is acceptable though not desirable. At the same time, the original *performance* specifications for the modem as well as reliability standards cannot be compromised.

Priorities vary from project to project. For example, for many software projects time to market is critical, and companies like Microsoft may defer original scope requirements to later versions in order to get to the market first. Alternatively, for special event projects (conferences, parades, tournaments) time is constrained once the date has been announced, and if the budget is tight, the project manager will compromise the scope of the project in order to complete the project on time.

Some would argue that all three criteria are always constrained and that good project managers should seek to optimize each criterion. If everything goes well on a project and no major problems or setbacks are encountered, their argument may be valid. However, this situation is rare, and project managers are often forced to make tough decisions that benefit one criterion while compromising the other two. The purpose of this

FIGURE 4.2
Project Priority Matrix

	Time	Performance	Cost
Constrain		◯	
Enhance	◯		
Accept			◯

exercise is to define and agree on what the priorities and constraints of the project are so that when "push comes to shove," the right decisions can be made.

Although there is a very strong tendency in practice to "constrain" one criterion and then "enhance" the remaining two, this approach does not help to define priorities for decision making. We have found that companies that force the use of all three criteria have a much sounder basis for group consensus and decision making.

There are likely to be natural limits to the extent managers can constrain, optimize, or accept any one criterion. It may be acceptable for the project to slip one month behind schedule but no further or to exceed the planned budget by as much as $20,000. Likewise, it may be desirable to finish a project a month early, but after that cost conservation should be the primary goal. Some project managers document these limits as part of creating the priority matrix.

In summary, developing a decision priority matrix for a project is a useful exercise. It provides a forum for clearly establishing priorities with customers and top management so as to create shared expectations and avoid misunderstandings. The priority information is essential to the planning process, where adjustments can be made in the scope, schedule, and budget allocation. Finally, the matrix is useful midway in the project for approaching a problem that must be solved.

One caveat must be mentioned; during the course of a project, priorities may change. The customer may suddenly need the project completed one month sooner, or new directives from top management may emphasize cost saving initiatives. The project manager needs to be vigilant in order to anticipate and confirm changes in priorities and make appropriate adjustments.

Step 3: Creating the Work Breakdown Structure

Major Groupings Found in a WBS

Once the scope and deliverables have been identified, the work of the project can be successively subdivided into smaller and smaller work elements. The outcome of this hierarchical process is called the work breakdown structure (WBS). The WBS is a map of the project. Use of WBS helps to assure project managers that all products and work elements are identified, to integrate the project with the current organization, and to establish a basis for control. Basically, the WBS is an outline of the project with different levels of detail.

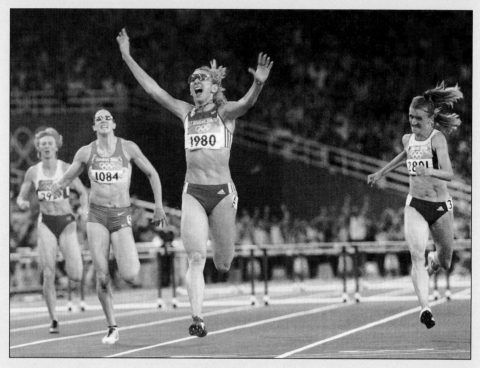

AP/Wide World Photos.

Figure 4.3 shows the major groupings commonly used in the field to develop a hierarchical WBS. The WBS begins with the project as the final deliverable. Major project work deliverables/systems are identified first; then the subdeliverables necessary to accomplish the larger deliverables are defined. The process is repeated until the subdeliverable detail is small enough to be manageable and where one person can be responsible. This subdeliverable is further divided into work packages. Because the lowest subdeliverable usually includes several work packages, the work packages are grouped by type of work—for example, hardware, programming, testing. These groupings within a subdeliverable are called cost accounts. This grouping facilitates a system for monitoring project progress by work, cost, and responsibility.

How WBS Helps the Project Manager

The WBS defines all the elements of the project in a hierarchical framework and establishes their relationships to the project end item(s). Think of the project as a large work package that is successively broken down into smaller work packages; the total project is the summation of all the smaller work packages. This hierarchical structure facilitates evaluation of cost, time, and technical performance at all levels in the

In the realm of event project management, the Olympic Games rank as one of the premier achievements.

PROJECT DEFINITION

Objective: To stage the Year 2004 Summer Olympic Games at specified locations in Greece beginning August 13 at a cost of $5.2 billion.

Client: Activities are underwritten by the Greek government. Many stakeholders and customers, e.g., citizens of Athens, local and national governments, the Greek people, the International Olympic Organization, the international community as a whole, the athletes, and Greek and international business communities.

Scope: Organizing all Games and ceremonies. Putting in place all technology and resources required to stage the Games. Handling public relations and fundraising.

Criteria for success: Trouble-free performance of Games. Level of public enthusiasm and enjoyment. Economic activity generated within Athens and Greece. Continued interest in future Olympic Games.

Project team: Athens Organizing Committee Olympic Games (AOCOG) was appointed as the project managers by legislation. Other organizations directly contributing to the success of the Games, such as the International Olympic Committee, Greek Olympic Committee, Athens City Council, and Olympic Coordination Authority (Greek government) have been made party to the Host City Contract. Olympic Coordination Authority is responsible for all the infrastructure projects, most of which are either already under way or are being reprogrammed to accommodate the Games.

Completion of these projects on time is vital to the success of the Olympic Games.

WBS: The work breakdown structure for the project includes the following major areas: events; venues and facilities including accommodation; transport; media facilities and coordination; telecommunications; security arrangements; medical care; human resources including volunteers; cultural olympiad; pre-games training; information technology projects; opening and closing ceremonies; public relations; financing; test games and trial events; and sponsorship management and control of ambush marketing. Each of these items could be treated as a project in its own right. Precision coordination will be necessary to ensure that these, and therefore the entire Games project, are delivered on time.

Time, obviously, is the most critical dimension of the Athens 2004 Olympic Games project. Early on initial delays and confusion caused the IOC to consider moving the Olympics to a different city. This threat galvanized the Greek efforts. At the end of a three year, around the clock construction blitz, Olympic organizers finally silenced critics with all the venues ready for the August 13 opening ceremony. As in the past, Olympics cost was the dimension sacrificed with the projected cost doubling to the $8 to 12 billion range. The Greeks were also forced to scale back the scope of construction and compromise on quality. While the glass roof centerpiece for the Olympic Stadium was preserved, delays caused cancellation of a similar roof for the aquatic center. Secondary projects designed to spruce up the city had to be scaled back or cut. Unfinished work was hidden behind huge banners. Ribbons and flags were used to divert attention from sidewalks that were never smoothed out or the dreary concrete buildings that didn't get fresh paint.

organization over the life of the project. The WBS also provides management with information appropriate to each level. For example, top management deals primarily with major deliverables, while first-line supervisors deal with smaller subdeliverables and work packages.

As WBS is developed, organizational units and individuals are assigned responsibility for accomplishment of work packages. This integrates the work and the organization. In practice, this process is sometimes called OBS, the organization breakdown structure, which will be further discussed later in the chapter.

The WBS also makes it possible to plan, schedule, and budget. It gives a framework for tracking cost and work performance. Use of the structure provides the opportunity to "roll up" (sum) the budget and actual costs of the smaller work packages into larger work elements so that performance can be measured by organizational units and work accomplishment.

The WBS defines communication channels and assists in understanding and coordinating many parts of the project. The structure shows the work and organizational units responsible and suggests where written communication should be directed. Problems can be quickly addressed and coordinated because the structure integrates work and responsibility.

FIGURE 4.3
Hierarchical
Breakdown
of the WBS

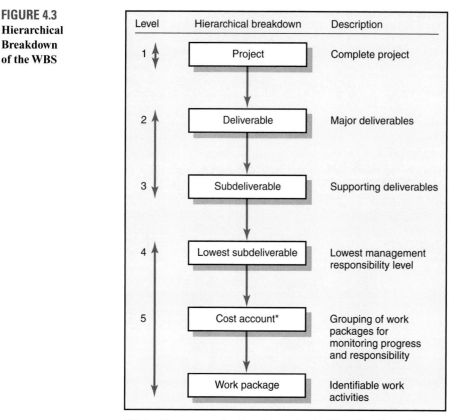

*This breakdown groups work packages by type of work within a deliverable and allows assignment of responsibility to an organizational unit. This extra step facilitates a system for monitoring project progress (discussed in Chapter 13).

WBS Development

Figure 4.4 shows a simplified WBS for development of a new personal computer project. At the top of the chart (level 1) is the project end item—a deliverable product or service. Note how the levels of the structure can represent information for different levels of management. For example, level 1 information represents the total project objective and is useful to top management; levels 2, 3, and 4 are suitable for middle management; and level 5 is for first-line managers.

Level 2 shows a partial list of deliverables necessary to develop the personal computer. One deliverable is the disk storage unit (shaded), which is made up of three subdeliverables—external USB, optical, and hard disks. Finally, the hard disk requires four subdeliverables—motor, circuit board, chassis frame, and read/write head. These subdeliverables represent the lowest manageable elements of the project. Each subdeliverable requires work packages that will be completed by an assigned organizational unit. Each deliverable will be successively divided in this manner. It is not necessary to divide all elements of the WBS to the same level.

The lowest level of the WBS is called a *work package*. Work packages are short-duration tasks that have a definite start and stop point, consume resources, and represent cost. Each work package is a control point. A work package manager is responsible for seeing that the package is completed on time, within budget, and according to technical specifications. Practice suggests a work package should not exceed 10 workdays or

FIGURE 4.4   Work Breakdown Structure

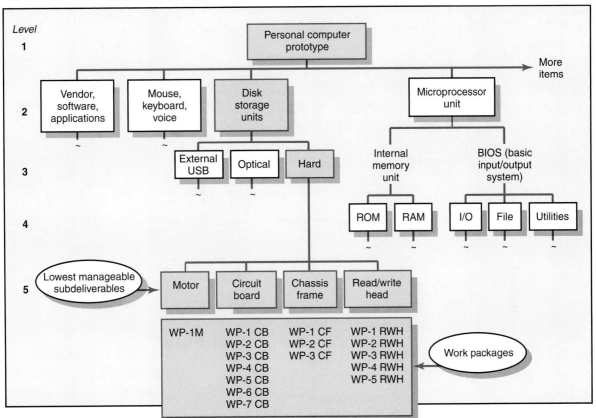

one reporting period. If a work package has a duration exceeding 10 days, check or monitoring points should be established within the duration, say, every three to five days, so progress and problems can be identified before too much time has passed. Each work package of the WBS should be as independent of other packages of the project as possible. No work package is described in more than one subdeliverable of the WBS.

There is an important difference between the last work breakdown subdeliverable and a work package. Typically, a work breakdown subdeliverable includes the outcomes of more than one work package from perhaps two or three departments. Therefore, the subdeliverable does not have a duration of its own and does not consume resources or cost money directly. (In a sense, of course, a duration for a particular work breakdown element can be derived from identifying which work package must start first [earliest] and which package will be the latest to finish; the difference becomes the duration for the subdeliverable.) The resources and costs for the subdeliverable are simply the summation of the resources and costs for all the work packages in the work subdeliverable. This is the basis for the term *project rollup*—starting with the work package, costs and resources can be "rolled up" into the higher elements. The higher elements are used to identify deliverables at different phases in the project and to develop status reports during the execution stage of the project life cycle. Thus, the work package is the basic unit used for planning, scheduling, and controlling the project.

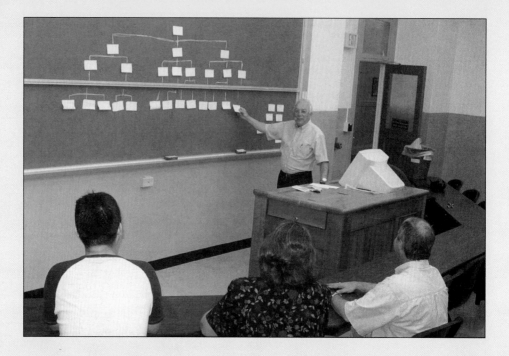

Figure 4.4 represents the classic WBS in which the project is broken down to the lowest manageable deliverable and subsequent work packages and cost accounts. Many situations do not require this level of detail. This begs the questions of how far you should break down the work.

There is no set answer to this question. However, here are some tips given by project managers:

Break down the work until you can do an estimate that is accurate enough for your purposes. If you are doing a ball-park estimate to see if the project is worthy of serious consideration, you probably do not need to break it down beyond major deliverables. On the other hand, if you are pricing a project to submit a competitive bid, then you are likely to go down to the work package level.

The WBS should conform to how you are going to schedule work. For example, if assignments are made in terms of days, then tasks should be limited as best as possible to one day or more to complete. Conversely, if hours are the smallest unit for scheduling, then work can be broken down to one-hour increments.

Final activities should have clearly defined start/end events. Avoid open-ended tasks like "research" or "market analysis." Take it down to the next level in which deliverables/outcomes are more clearly defined. Instead of ending with market analysis include items such as identify market share, list user requirements, or write a problem statement.

If accountability and control are important, then break the work down so that one individual is clearly responsible for the work. For example, instead of stopping at product design, take it to the next level and identify specific components of the design (i.e., electrical schematics, power source, etc.) that different individuals will be responsible for creating.

The bottom line is that the WBS should provide the level of detail needed to manage the specific project successfully.

To review, each work package in the WBS

1. Defines work (what).
2. Identifies time to complete a work package (how long).
3. Identifies a time-phased budget to complete a work package (cost).
4. Identifies resources needed to complete a work package (how much).
5. Identifies a single person responsible for units of work (who).
6. Identifies monitoring points for measuring progress.

Creating a WBS from scratch can be a daunting task. Project managers should take advantage of relevant examples from previous projects to begin the process.

WBSs are products of group efforts. If the project is small, the entire project team may be involved breaking down the project into its components. For large, complex projects, the people responsible for the major deliverables are likely to meet to establish the first two levels of deliverables. In turn, further detail would be delegated to the people responsible for the specific work. Collectively this information would be gathered and integrated into a formal WBS by a project support person. The final version would be reviewed by the inner echelon of the project team. Relevant stakeholders (most notably customers) would be consulted to confirm agreement and revise when appropriate.

Project teams developing their first WBS frequently forget that the structure should be end-item, output oriented. First attempts often result in a WBS that follows the organization structure—design, marketing, production, finance. If a WBS follows the organization structure, the focus will be on the organization function and processes rather than the project output or deliverables. In addition, a WBS with a process focus will become an accounting tool that records costs by function rather than a tool for "output" management. Every effort should be made to develop a WBS that is output oriented in order to concentrate on concrete deliverables. See Snapshot from Practice: Creating a WBS for more advice on creating a WBS. Organizational unit responsibility can be tied to the WBS by grouping the work packages of a deliverable into a cost account while still maintaining the focus on completing the deliverable. This process is discussed next.

Step 4: Integrating the WBS with the Organization

An integral part of the WBS is to define the organizational units responsible for performing the work. In practice, the outcome of this process is the organization breakdown structure (OBS). The OBS depicts how the firm has organized to discharge work responsibility. The purposes of the OBS are to provide a framework to summarize organization unit work performance, identify organization units responsible for work packages, and tie the organizational unit to cost control accounts. Recall, cost accounts group similar work packages (usually under the purview of a department). The OBS defines the organization subdeliverables in a hierarchical pattern in successively smaller and smaller units. Frequently, the traditional organization structure can be used. Even if the project is completely performed by a team, it is necessary to break down the team structure for assigning responsibility for budgets, time, and technical performance.

As in the WBS, the OBS assigns the lowest organizational unit the responsibility for work packages within a cost account. Herein lies one major strength of using WBS and OBS; they can be *integrated* as shown in Figure 4.5. The intersection of work packages and the organizational unit creates a project control point (cost account) that integrates work and responsibility. The intersection of the WBS and OBS represents the set of work packages necessary to complete the subdeliverable located immediately above and the organizational unit on the left responsible for accomplishing the packages at the intersection. Later we will use the intersection as a cost account for management control of projects. For example, the circuit board element requires completion of work packages whose primary responsibility will include the design, production, test, and software departments. Control can be checked from two directions—outcomes and responsibility. In the execution phase of the project, progress can be tracked vertically on deliverables (client's interest)

FIGURE 4.5 Integration of WBS and OBS

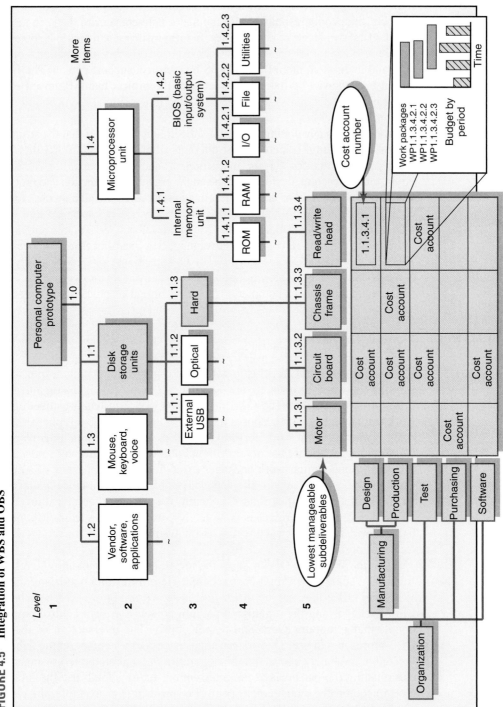

TABLE 4.1A
Sorted by WBS

		Direct Labor Budget	
1.1.3	Hard drive	1,660	
1.1.3.1	Motor	10	
	Purchasing		10
1.1.3.2	Circuit board	1,000	
	Design		300
	Production		400
	Testing		120
	Software		180
1.1.3.3	Chassis frame	50	
	Production		50
1.1.3.4	Read/write head	600	
	Design		300
	Production		200
	Testing		100

TABLE 4.1B
Sorted by OBS

		Direct Labor Budget	
Design		600	
1.1.3.2	Circuit board		300
1.1.3.4	Read/write head		300
Production		650	
1.1.3.2	Circuit board		400
1.1.3.3	Chassis frame		50
1.1.3.4	Read/write head		200
Testing		220	
1.1.3.2	Circuit board		120
1.1.3.4	Read/write head		100
Purchasing		10	
1.1.3.1	Motor		10
Software		180	
1.1.3.2	Circuit board		180
Total		1,660	

and tracked horizontally by organization responsibility (management's interest). Although it is possible to graphically show an integrated WBS/OBS (e.g., Figure 4.5) for demonstration purposes, software programs do not draw diagrams as we have shown. The graphic output requirements for large projects make such graphic descriptions impractical by sheer size alone. Typical software packages allow project managers to sort by WBS and/or OBS, which simply presents the information in another form. See Tables 4.1 A and 4.1 B.

Step 5: Coding the WBS for the Information System

Gaining the maximum usefulness of a breakdown structure depends on a coding system. The codes are used to define levels and elements in the WBS, organization elements, work packages, and budget and cost information. The codes allow reports to be consolidated at any level in the structure. The most commonly used scheme in practice is numeric indention. An example for the new computer project and the "Disk storage units" in Figure 4.5 is presented here:

1.0   Computer project
    1.1   Disk storage units
        1.1.1   External USB
        1.1.2   Optical
        1.1.3   Hard
            1.1.3.1   Motor
                1.1.3.1.1   Sourcing work package
                    ·
                    ·
            1.1.3.4   Read/write head
                1.1.3.4.1   Cost account
                1.1.3.4.2   Cost account
                    1.1.3.4.2.1   WP
                    1.1.3.4.2.2   WP
                    1.1.3.4.2.3   WP
                1.1.3.4.3   Cost account
                    ·
                    ·
                    ·
                        etc.

Note the project identification is 1.0. Each successive indention represents a lower element or work package. Ultimately the numeric scheme reaches down to the work package level, and all tasks and elements in the structure have an identification code. The "cost account" is the focal point because all budgets, work assignments, time, cost, and technical performance come together at this point.

This coding system can be extended to cover large projects. Additional schemes can be added for special reports. For example, adding a "–3" after the code could indicate a site location, an elevation, or a special account such as labor. Some letters can be used as special identifiers such as "M" for materials or "E" for engineers. You are not limited to only 10 subdivisions (0–9); you can extend each subdivision to large numbers—for example, .1–.99 or .1–.9999. If the project is small, you can use whole numbers. The following example is from a large, complex project:

$$3R–237A–P2–33.6$$

where 3R identifies the facility, 237A represents elevation and the area, P2 represents pipe two inches wide, and 33.6 represents the work package number. In practice most organizations are creative in combining letters and numbers to minimize the length of WBS codes.

Project Rollup

Recall that the intersection of the WBS and OBS represents a control point, called a cost account by project managers. The work packages and cost accounts serve as a database from which all other planning, scheduling, and controlling processes are coordinated. Cost accounts include one or more work packages. Each work package

FIGURE 4.6   **Work Package Estimates**

WP Description	*Final version*			Page _1_ of _1_			

WP ID _1.1.3.2_   Project _PC proto_

Deliverable _Circuit board_   Date _9/29/XX_

Original Unit _Software_   Estimator _RMG_

WP Duration _3_ work weeks   Total Budget $ _265_

Time-Phased Budget ($)

Work periods

Labor costs	Rate	1	2	3	4	5	Total
Code	$ XX/hr	50	30	20			$100
Document	$ XX/hr		10	15			25
Publish	$ XX/hr			5			5
Total labor		50	40	40			($130)
Materials			20				20
Equipment	$ XX/hr	50	15	50			115
Other ___							
Total direct		100	75	90			$265

has time, budget, resource, responsibility, and control points that can be used to track project progress. Figure 4.6 shows an example of an oversimplified version of a work package with a time-phased budget (without dates). This work package represents one work package in the circuit board deliverable assigned to the software department. Using only the direct labor cost factor, you can get an overview of how it is possible to roll up the project costs for the circuit board and across organizational units.

Figure 4.7 shows hypothetical labor costs and work packages for the hard disk storage element of the personal computer prototype project. The intersection of circuit board and production shows two work packages in the cost account with budgets of $140 and $260, which total $400. Rollup to the circuit board element (summation of all cost accounts below the element) is $1,000. The hard disk element, which includes all first-level elements, has a budget of $1,660. The rollup for the organizational units operates in a similar fashion. For example, the design department has responsibility for the work packages found in the circuit board and read/write head cost accounts. These accounts each have a labor budget of $300, or a total of $600. The manufacturing section has a total budget of $1,250. Of course, the total for the organization delivering the hard disk element is the same as the total budget of all elements rolled up to the hard disk element. This ability to consolidate and integrate using the rollup process demonstrates the potential value of the WBS for managing the project. Remember, the units do not have to be money; the units can be resources,

FIGURE 4.7   **Direct Labor Budget Rollup (000)**

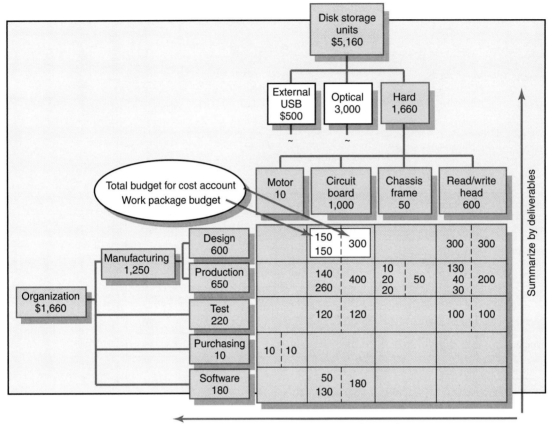

labor hours, materials, time, or any units that contribute to the completion of deliverables. However, at the cost account level, the units have to be the same throughout the structure.

Process Breakdown Structure

The WBS is best suited for design and build projects that have tangible outcomes such as an off-shore mining facility or a new car prototype. The project can be decomposed or broken down into major deliverables, subdeliverables, further subdeliverables, and ultimately to work packages. It is more difficult to apply WBS to less tangible, *process-oriented* projects in which the final outcome is a product of a series of steps or phases. Here, the big difference is that the project evolves over time with each phase affecting the next phase. IT projects typically fall in this category—for example, creating an extranet website or an internal software database system. Process projects are driven by performance requirements, not by plans/blueprints. Some practitioners choose to utilize what we refer to as a process breakdown structure (PBS) instead of the classic WBS.

Figure 4.8 provides an example of a PBS for a software development project. Instead of being organized around deliverables, the project is organized around phases. Each of the five major phases can be broken down into more specific activities until a

FIGURE 4.8   **PBS for Software Development Project**

sufficient level of detail is achieved to communicate what needs to be done to complete that phase. People can be assigned to specific activities, and a complementary OBS can be created just as is done for the WBS. Deliverables are not ignored but are defined as outputs required to move to the next phase.

Checklists that contain the phase exit requirements are developed to manage project progress. These checklists provide the means to support phase walk-throughs and reviews. Checklists vary depending upon the project and activities involved but typically include the following details:

- Deliverables needed to exit a phase and begin a new one.
- Quality checkpoints to ensure that deliverables are complete and accurate.
- Sign-offs by all responsible stakeholders to indicate that the phase has been successfully completed and that the project should move on to the next phase.

As long as exit requirements are firmly established and deliverables for each phase are well defined, the PBS provides a suitable alternative to the WBS for projects that involve extensive development work.

Responsibility Matrices

In many cases, the size and scope of the project do not warrant an elaborate WBS or OBS. One tool that is widely used by project managers and task force leaders of small projects is the *responsibility matrix* (RM). The RM (sometimes called a linear responsibility chart) summarizes the tasks to be accomplished and who is responsible for what on a project. In its simplest form an RM consists of a chart listing all the project

FIGURE 4.9 **Responsibility Matrix for a Market Research Project**

Task	Richard	Dan	Dave	Linda	Elizabeth
Identify target customers	R	S		S	
Develop draft questionnaire	R	S	S		
Pilot-test questionnaire		R		S	
Finalize questionnaire	R	S	S	S	
Print questionnaire					R
Prepare mailing labels					R
Mail questionnaires					R
Receive and monitor returned questionnaires				R	S
Input response data			R		
Analyze results		R	S	S	
Prepare draft of report	S	R	S	S	
Prepare final report	R		S		

Project Team (column group header above Richard, Dan, Dave, Linda, Elizabeth)

R = Responsible
S = Supports/assists

activities and the participants responsible for each activity. For example, Figure 4.9 illustrates an RM for a market research study. In this matrix the R is used to identify the committee member who is responsible for coordinating the efforts of other team members assigned to the task and making sure that the task is completed. The S is used to identify members of the five-person team who will support and/or assist the individual responsible. Simple RMs like this one are useful not only for organizing and assigning responsibilities for small projects but also for subprojects of large, more complex projects.

More complex RMs not only identify individual responsibilities but also clarify critical interfaces between units and individuals that require coordination. For example, Figure 4.10 is an RM for a larger, more complex project to develop a new piece of test equipment. Notice that within each cell a numeric coding scheme is used to define the nature of involvement on that specific task. Such an RM extends the WBS/OBS and provides a clear and concise method for depicting responsibility, authority, and communication channels.

Responsibility matrices provide a means for all participants in a project to view their responsibilities and agree on their assignments. They also help clarify the extent or type of authority exercised by each participant in performing an activity in which two or more parties have overlapping involvement. By using an RM and by defining authority, responsibility, and communications within its framework, the relationship between different organizational units and the work content of the project are made clear.

Clearly defining your project is the first and most important step in planning. The absence of a clearly defined project plan consistently shows up as the major reason for project failures. Whether you use a WBS, OBS, PBS, or responsibility matrix will depend primarily on the size of your project. Whatever method you use, the defining of your project should be adequate enough to allow for good control as the project is being implemented.

FIGURE 4.10 Responsibility Matrix for the Conveyor Belt Project

Deliverables	Organization							
	Design	Development	Documentation	Assembly	Testing	Purchasing	Quality Assur.	Manufacturing
Architechural design	1	2			2		3	3
Hardware specifications	2	1				2	3	
Kernel specifications	1	3						3
Utilities specification	2	1			3			
Hardware design	1			3		3		3
Disk drivers	3	1	2					
Memory management	1	3			3			
Operating system documentation	2	2	1					3
Prototypes	5		4	1	3	3	3	4
Integrated acceptance test	5	2	2		1		5	5

1 Responsible
2 Support
3 Consult
4 Notification
5 Approval

119

Summary

The project scope definition, priorities, and breakdown structure are the keys to nearly every aspect of managing the project. The scope definition provides focus and emphasis on the end item(s) of the project. Establishing project priorities allows managers to make appropriate trade-off decisions. The structure helps ensure all tasks of the project are identified and provides two views of the project—one on deliverables and one on organization responsibility. The WBS avoids having the project driven by organization function or by a finance system. The structure forces attention to realistic requirements of personnel, hardware, and budgets. Use of the structure provides a powerful framework for project control that identifies deviations from plan, identifies responsibility, and spots areas for improved performance. No well-developed project plan or control system is possible without a disciplined, structured approach. The WBS, OBS, and cost account codes provide this discipline. The WBS will serve as the database for developing the project network which establishes the timing of work, people, equipment, and costs.

PBS is often used for process-based projects with ill-defined deliverables. In small projects responsibility matrices may be used to clarify individual responsibility.

Key Terms

Cost account	Process breakdown	Work breakdown structure
Milestone	structure (PBS)	(WBS)
Organization breakdown	Responsibility matrix	Work package
structure (OBS)	Scope creep	
Priority matrix	Scope statement	

Review Questions

1. What questions does a project objective answer? What would be an example of a good project objective?
2. What is the difference between a project limit and a project exclusion?
3. What does it mean if the priorities of a project include: Time-Constrain, Scope-Accept, and Cost-Enhance?
4. What kinds of information are included in a cost account?
5. What kinds of information are included in a work package?
6. What is a time-phased budget in a work package?
7. What is a "project rollup," and how does the project manager use this information?
8. When would it be appropriate to create a responsibility matrix rather than a full-blown WBS?

Exercises

1. You are in charge of organizing a dinner-dance concert for a local charity. You have reserved a hall that will seat 30 couples and have hired a jazz combo.
   a. Develop a scope statement for this project that contains examples of all the elements. Assume that the event will occur in 4 weeks and provide your best guess estimate of the dates for milestones.
   b. What would the priorities likely be for this project?
2. In small groups, identify real life examples of a project that would fit each of the following priority scenarios:
   a. Time-constrained, Scope-enhanced, Cost-accept
   b. Time-accept, Scope-constrained, Cost-accept
   c. Time-constrained, Scope-accept, Cost-enhanced

3. Develop a WBS for a project in which you are going to build a bicycle. Try to identify all of the major components and provide three levels of detail.

4. You are the father or mother of a family of four (kids ages 13 and 15) planning a weekend camping trip. Develop a responsibility matrix for the work that needs to be done prior to starting your trip.

5. Develop a WBS for a local stage play. Be sure to identify the deliverables and organizational units (people) responsible. How would you code your system? Give an example of the work packages in one of your cost accounts. Develop a corresponding OBS which identifies who is responsible for what.

6. Use an example of a project you are familiar with or are interested in. Identify the deliverables and organizational units (people) responsible. How would you code your system? Give an example of the work packages in one of your cost accounts.

References

Ashley, D. B., et al., "Determinants of Construction Project Success," *Project Management Journal,* 18 (2) June 1987, p. 72.

Chilmeran, A. H., "Keeping Costs on Track," *PM Network,* 19 (2) 2004, pp. 45–51.

Gobeli, D. and E. Larson, "Business Affecting Project Success," *R. Bruines and P. Menard, eds., Measuring Success* (Newton Square, PA: Project Management Institute, 1986), pp. 22–29.

Ingebretsen, M., "Taming the Beast," *PM Network,* July 2003, pp. 30–35.

Katz, D. M., "Case Study: Beware 'Scope Creep' on ERP Projects," *CFO.com,* March 27, 2001.

Kerzner, H., *Project Management: A Systems Approach to Planning, 8th edition* (New York: Van Nostrand Reinhold, 2003).

Lewis, J. P., *Project Planning, Scheduling and Controlling, 3rd edition* (Burr Ridge, IL: McGraw-Hill, 2000).

Luby, R. E., D. Peel, and W. Swahl, "Component-Based Work Breakdown Structure" *Project Management Journal,* 26 (2) December 1995, pp. 38–44.

Murch, R., *Project Management: Best Practices for IT Professionals* (Upper Darby, NJ: Prentice Hall, 2001).

Pinto, J. K. and D. P. Slevin, "Critical Success Factors Across the Project Life Cycle," *Project Management Journal,* 19 (3) June 1988, p. 72.

Pitagorsky, G., "Realistic Project Planning Promotes Success," *Engineer's Digest,* 29 (1) 2001.

PMI Standards Committee, *Guide to the Project Management Body of Knowledge* (Newton Square, PA: Project Management Institute 2000).

Posner, B. Z., "What it Takes to be a Good Project Manager," *Project Management Journal,* 18 (1) March 1987, p. 52.

Raz, T. and S. Globerson, "Effective Sizing and Content Definition of Work Packages," *Project Management Journal,* 29 (4) 1998, pp. 17–23.

Smith, M. A. and R. L. Tucker, "Early Projection Problem-Assessment of Impact and Cause," *1984 Proceedings* (Newton Square, PA: Project Management Institute, 1984), p. 226.

Tate, K. and K. Hendrix, "Chartering IT Projects," *Proceedings, 30th Annual, Project Management Institute* (Philadelphia, PA. 1999), CD.

Zimmerman, E., "Preventing Scope Creep," *Manage,* February 2000.

Case

Manchester United Soccer Club

Nicolette Larson was loading the dishwasher with her husband, Kevin, and telling him about the first meeting of the Manchester United Tournament Organizing Committee. Larson, a self-confessed "soccer mom," had been elected tournament director and was responsible for organizing the club's first summer tournament.

Manchester United Soccer Club (MUSC) located in Manchester, New Hampshire, was formed in 1992 as a way of bringing recreational players to a higher level of competition and preparing them for the State Olympic Development Program and/or high school teams. The club currently has 24 boys and girls (ranging in age from under 9 to 16) on teams affiliated with the Hampshire Soccer Association and the Granite State Girls Soccer League. The club's board of directors decided in the fall to sponsor a summer invitational soccer tournament to generate revenue. Given the boom in youth soccer, hosting summer tournaments has become a popular method for raising funds. MUSC teams regularly compete in three to four tournaments each summer at different locales in New England. These tournaments have been reported to generate between $50,000 and $70,000 for the host club.

MUSC needs additional revenue to refurbish and expand the number of soccer fields at the Rock Rimmon soccer complex. Funds would also be used to augment the club's scholarship program, which provides financial aid to players who cannot afford the $450 annual club dues.

Nicolette gave her husband a blow-by-blow account of what transpired during the first tournament committee meeting that night. She started the meeting by having everyone introduce themselves and by proclaiming how excited she was that the club was going to sponsor its own tournament. She then suggested that the committee brainstorm what needed to be done to pull off the event; she would record their ideas on a flipchart.

What emerged was a free-for-all of ideas and suggestions. One member immediately stressed the importance of having qualified referees and spent several minutes describing in detail how his son's team was robbed in a poorly officiated championship game. This was followed by other stories of injustice on the soccer field. Another member suggested that they needed to quickly contact the local colleges to see if they could use their fields. The committee spent more than 30 minutes talking about how they should screen teams and how much they should charge as an entry fee. An argument broke out over whether they should reward the winning teams in each age bracket with medals or trophies. Many members felt that medals were too cheap, while others thought the trophies would be too expensive. Someone suggested that they seek local corporate sponsors to help fund the tournament. The proposed sale of tournament T-shirts and sweatshirts was followed by a general critique of the different shirts parents had acquired at different tournaments. One member advocated that they recruit an artist he knew to develop a unique silk-screen design for the tournament. The meeting adjourned 30 minutes late with only half of the members remaining until the end. Nicolette drove home with seven sheets of ideas and a headache.

As Kevin poured a glass of water for the two aspirin Nicolette was about to take, he tried to comfort her by saying that organizing this tournament would be a big project not unlike the projects he works on at his engineering and design firm. He offered to sit down with her the next night and help her plan the project. He suggested that the first thing they needed to do was to develop a WBS for the project.

1. Develop a draft of the work breakdown structure for the tournament that contains at least three levels of detail. What are the major deliverables associated with hosting an event such as a soccer tournament?
2. How would developing a WBS alleviate some of the problems that occurred during the first meeting and help Nicolette organize and plan the project?
3. Where can Nicolette find additional information to help her develop a WBS for the tournament?
4. How could Nicolette and her task force use the WBS to generate cost estimates for the tournament? Why would this be useful information?

Estimate 5	→ **Project networks** 6 → **Scheduling resources** 8

Define project 4

Reducing project duration 9

Introduction 1

Organization 3

Managing risk 7

Monitoring progress 13

Audit and closure 14

Future 16

Strategy 2

Leadership 10 → **Teams** 11

Partnering 12

International projects 15

Estimating Project Times and Costs

Factors Influencing the Quality of Estimates

Estimating Guidelines for Times, Costs, and Resources

Macro versus Micro Estimating

Methods for Estimating Project Times and Costs

Level of Detail

Developing Budgets

Types of Costs

Refining Estimates and Contingency Funds

Creating a Database for Estimating

Summary

Appendix 5.1: Learning Curves for Estimating

CHAPTER FIVE

Estimating Project Times and Costs

Project estimation is indeed a yardstick for project cost control. And if the yardstick is faulty, you start on the "wrong foot." . . . we exhort you not to underestimate the estimate.*

Given the urgency to start work on the project, managers sometimes minimize or avoid the effort to follow through on estimating project time and cost. This attitude is a huge mistake and costly. There are important reasons to make the effort and incur the cost of estimating for your project. Exhibit 5.1 summarizes some key reasons.

Estimating is the process of forecasting or approximating the time and cost of completing project deliverables. The processes used are unique to the organization; you can't buy the processes off the shelf. However, in practice, estimating processes are frequently classified as top-down (macro)/bottom-up (micro). Top-down estimates are usually derived from analogy, group consensus, or mathematical relationships. Bottom-up estimates are typically based on estimates of elements found in the work breakdown structure. In a few situations both methods are used and reasons for any differences are reconciled.

All project stakeholders prefer accurate cost and time estimates, but they also understand the inherent uncertainty in all projects. Inaccurate estimates lead to false expectations and consumer dissatisfaction. Accuracy is improved with greater effort, but is it worth the time and cost—estimating costs money! Many factors can mitigate estimating accuracy and effort. Project estimating becomes a task of balancing the expectations of major stakeholders and the need for control while the project is implemented.

Cost, time, and budget estimates are the lifeline for control; they serve as the standard for comparison of actual and plan throughout the life of the project. Project rollup and project status reports depend on reliable estimates as the major input for measuring variances and taking corrective action. Ideally, the project manager, and in most cases the customer, would prefer to have a database of detailed schedule and cost estimates for every work package in the project. Regrettably, such detailed data gathering is not always possible or practical and other methods are used to develop project estimates.

Factors Influencing the Quality of Estimates

A typical statement in the field is the desire to "have a 95 percent probability of meeting time and cost estimates." *Past experience* is a good starting point for developing time and cost estimates. But past experience estimates must almost always be refined

---

* O. P. Kharbanda and Jeffrey K. Pinto, *What Made Gertie Gallop: Learning from Project Failures* (New York: Von Nostrand Reinhold, 1996), p. 73.

EXHIBIT 5.1
Why Estimating Time and Cost Are Important

- Estimates are needed to support good decisions.
- Estimates are needed to schedule work.
- Estimates are needed to determine how long the project should take and its cost.
- Estimates are needed to determine whether the project is worth doing.
- Estimates are needed to develop cash flow needs.
- Estimates are needed to determine how well the project is progressing.
- Estimates are needed to develop time-phased budgets and establish the project baseline.

by other considerations to reach the 95 percent probability level. Factors related to the uniqueness of the project will have a strong influence on the accuracy of estimates. Project, people, and external factors all need to be considered to improve quality of estimates for project times and costs.

Planning Horizon

The quality of the estimate depends on the *planning horizon;* estimates of current events are close to 100 percent accurate but are reduced for more distant events. The accuracy of time and cost estimates should improve as you move from the conceptual phase to the point where individual work packages are defined.

Project Duration

Time to implement new *technology* has a habit of expanding in an increasing, nonlinear fashion. Sometimes poorly written scope specifications for new technology result in errors in estimating times and costs. Long-duration projects increase the uncertainty in estimates.

People

The *people* factor can also introduce errors in estimating times and cost. For example, accuracy of estimates depends on the skills of the people making the estimates. A close match of people skills to the task will influence productivity and learning time. Similarly, whether members of the project team have worked together before on similar projects will influence the time it takes to coalesce into an effective team. Sometimes factors such as staff turnover can influence estimates. It should be noted that adding new people to a project increases time spent communicating. Typically, people have only five to six productive hours available for each working day; the other hours are taken up with indirect work, such as meetings, paperwork, answering e-mail.

Project Structure and Organization

Which *project structure* is chosen to manage the project will influence time and cost estimates. One of the major advantages of a dedicated project team discussed earlier is the speed gained from concentrated focus and localized project decisions. This speed comes at an additional cost of tying up personnel full time. Conversely, projects operating in a matrix environment may reduce costs by more efficiently sharing personnel across projects but may take longer to complete since attention is divided and coordination demands are higher.

Padding Estimates

In some cases people are inclined to pad estimates. For example, if you are asked how long it takes you to drive to the airport, you might give an average time of 30 minutes, assuming a 50/50 chance of getting there in 30 minutes. If you are asked the fastest you could possibly get there, you might reduce the driving time to 20 minutes. Finally, if you are asked how long the drive would take if you absolutely had to be there to meet with the president, it is likely you would increase the estimate to say 50 minutes to ensure not being late. In work situations where you are asked for time and cost estimates, most of us are inclined to add a little padding to increase the probability and reduce the risk of being late. If everyone at all levels of the project adds a little padding to reduce risk, the project duration and cost are seriously overstated. This phenomenon causes some managers or owners to call for a 10–15 percent cut in time and/or cost for the project. Of course the next time the game is played, the person estimating cost and/or time will pad the estimate to 20 percent or more. Clearly such games defeat chances for realistic estimates, which is what is needed to be competitive.

Organization Culture

Organization culture can significantly influence project estimates. In some organizations padding estimates is tolerated and even privately encouraged. Other organizations place a premium on accuracy and strongly discourage estimating gamesmanship. Organizations vary in the importance they attach to estimates. The prevailing belief in some organizations is that detailed estimating takes too much time and is not worth the effort or that it's impossible to predict the future. Other organizations subscribe to the belief that accurate estimates are the bedrock of effective project management. Organization culture shapes every dimension of project management; estimating is not immune to this influence.

Other Factors

Finally, *nonproject factors* can impact time and cost estimates. For example, equipment downtime can alter time estimates. National holidays, vacations, and legal limits, can influence project estimates. Project priority can influence resource assignment and impact time and cost.

Project estimating is a complex process. The quality of time and cost estimates can be improved when these variables are considered in making the estimates. Estimates of time and cost together allow the manager to develop a time-phased budget, which is imperative for project control. Before discussing macro and micro estimating methods for times and costs, a review of estimating guidelines will remind us of some of the important "rules of the game" that can improve estimating.

Estimating Guidelines for Times, Costs, and Resources

Managers recognize time, cost, and resource estimates must be accurate if project planning, scheduling, and controlling are to be effective. However, there is substantial evidence suggesting poor estimates are a major contributor to projects that have failed. Therefore, every effort should be made to see that initial estimates are as accurate as possible since the choice of no estimates leaves a great deal to luck and is not palatable to serious project managers. Even though a project has never been done before, a manager can follow seven guidelines to develop useful work package estimates.

1. **Responsibility.** At the work package level, estimates should be made by the person(s) most familiar with the task. Draw on their expertise! Except for supertechnical tasks, those responsible for getting the job done on schedule and within budget are usually first-line supervisors or technicians who are experienced and familiar with the type of work involved. These people will not have some preconceived, imposed duration for a deliverable in mind. They will give an estimate based on experience and best judgment. A secondary benefit of using those responsible is the hope they will "buy in" to seeing that the estimate materializes when they implement the work package.

If those involved are not consulted, it will be difficult to hold them responsible for failure to achieve the estimated time. Finally, drawing on the expertise of team members who will be responsible helps to build communication channels early.

2. **Use several people to estimate.** It is well known that a cost or time estimate usually has a better chance of being reasonable and realistic when several people with relevant experience and/or knowledge of the task are used. True, people bring different biases based on their experience. But discussion of the individual differences in their estimate leads to consensus and tends to eliminate extreme estimate errors. This approach is similar to the Delphi estimating method, which can also be used.

3. **Normal conditions.** When task time, cost, and resource estimates are determined, they are based on certain assumptions. *Estimates should be based on normal conditions, efficient methods, and a normal level of resources.* Normal conditions are sometimes difficult to discern, but it is necessary to have a consensus in the organization as to what normal conditions mean in this project. If the normal workday is eight hours, the time estimate should be based on an eight-hour day. Similarly, if the normal workday is two shifts, the time estimate should be based on a two-shift workday. Any time estimate should reflect efficient methods for the resources normally available. The time estimate should represent the normal level of resources—people or equipment. For example, if three programmers are available for coding or two road graders are available for road construction, time and cost estimates should be based on these normal levels of resources unless it is anticipated the project will change what is currently viewed as "normal." In addition, possible conflicts in demand for resources on parallel or concurrent activities should not be considered at this stage. The need for adding resources will be examined when resource scheduling is discussed in a later chapter.

4. **Time units.** Specific time units to use should be selected early in the development phase of the project network. *All task time estimates need consistent time units.* Estimates of time must consider whether normal time is represented by calendar days, workdays, workweeks, person days, single shift, hours, minutes, etc. In practice the use of workdays is the dominant choice for expressing task duration. However, in projects such as a heart transplant operation, minutes probably would be more appropriate as a time unit. One such project that used minutes as the time unit was the movement of patients from an old hospital to an elegant new one across town. Since there were several life-endangering moves, minutes were used to ensure patient safety so proper emergency life-support systems would be available if needed. The point is, network analysis requires a standard unit of time. When computer programs allow more than one option, some notation should be made of any variance from the standard unit of time. If the standard unit of time is a five-day workweek and the estimated activity duration is in calendar days, it must be converted to the normal workweek.

5. **Independence.** Estimators should treat each task as independent of other tasks that might be integrated by the WBS. Use of first-line managers usually results in considering tasks independently; this is good. Top managers are prone to aggregate many tasks into one time estimate and then deductively make the individual task time estimates add to the total. If tasks are in a chain and performed by the same group or department, it is best not to ask for all the time estimates in the sequence at once to avoid the tendency for a planner or a supervisor to look at the whole path and try to adjust individual task times in the sequence to meet an arbitrary imposed schedule or some rough "guesstimate" of the total time for the whole path or segment of the project. This tendency does not reflect the uncertainties of individual activities and generally results in optimistic task time estimates. In summary, each task time estimate should be considered independently of other activities.

6. **Contingencies.** *Work package estimates should not include allowances for contingencies.* The estimate should assume normal or average conditions even though every work package will not materialize as planned. For this reason top management needs to create an extra fund for contingencies that can be used to cover unforeseen events.

7. **Adding risk assessment to the estimate helps to avoid surprises to stakeholders.** It is obvious some tasks carry more time and cost risks than others. For example, a new technology usually carries more time and cost risks than a proven process. Simply identifying the degree of risk lets stakeholders consider alterative methods and alter process decisions. A simple breakdown by optimistic, most likely, and pessimistic for task time could provide valuable information regarding time and cost. See Chapter 7 for further discussion of project risk.

Where applicable, these guidelines will greatly help to avoid many of the pitfalls found so often in practice.

Macro versus Micro Estimating

Since estimating efforts cost money, the time and detail devoted to estimating is an important decision. Statements similar to those below strongly influence the decision to use macro (top-down) or micro estimates (bottom-up).

Rough order of magnitude is good enough. Spending time on detailed estimating wastes money.

Time is everything; our survival depends on getting there first! Time and cost accuracy is not an issue.

The project is internal. We don't need to worry about cost.

The uncertainty is so great, spending time and money on estimates is a waste.

The project is so small, we don't need to bother with estimates. Just do it.

They used an initial estimate "for strategic decisions" and then we had to live with it.

We were burned once. I want a detailed estimate of every task by the people responsible.

These statements indicate there are sound reasons for using macro or micro estimates. Table 5.1 depicts conditions that suggest when one approach is preferred over another.

Top-down estimates usually are derived from someone who uses experience and/or information to determine the project duration and total cost. These estimates are sometimes made by top managers who have very little knowledge of the processes used to complete the project. For example, a mayor of a major city making a speech noted that a new law building would be constructed at a cost of $23 million and would be ready for occupancy in two and one-half years. Although the mayor probably asked for an

TABLE 5.1 Conditions for Preferring Top-Down or Bottom-Up Time and Cost Estimates	Condition	Macro Estimates	Micro Estimates
	Strategic decision making	X	
	Cost and time important		X
	High uncertainty	X	
	Internal, small project	X	
	Fixed-price contract		X
	Customer wants details		X
	Unstable scope	X	

estimate from someone, the estimate could have come from a luncheon meeting with a local contractor who wrote an estimate (guesstimate) on a napkin. This is an extreme example, but in a relative sense this scenario is frequently played out in practice. But the question is, *do these estimates represent low-cost, efficient methods? Do the top-down estimates of project time and cost become a self-fulfilling prophecy in terms of setting time and cost parameters?*

If possible and practical, you want to push the estimating process down to the work package level for bottom-up estimates that establish low-cost, efficient methods. This process can take place after the project has been defined in detail. Good sense suggests project estimates should come from the people most knowledgeable about the estimate needed. The use of several people with relevant experience with the task can improve the time and cost estimate. The bottom-up approach at the work package level can serve as a check on cost elements in the WBS by rolling up the work packages and associated cost accounts to major deliverables. Similarly, resource requirements can be checked. Later, the time, resource, and cost estimates from the work packages can be consolidated into time-phased networks, resource schedules, and budgets that are used for control.

In conclusion, the ideal approach is for the project manager to allow enough time for both the top-down and bottom-up estimates to be worked out so a complete plan based on reliable estimates can be offered to the customer. In this way false expectations are minimized for all stakeholders and negotiation is reduced. The bottom-up approach also provides the customer with an opportunity to compare the low-cost, efficient method approach with any imposed restrictions. For example, if the project completion duration is imposed at two years and your bottom-up analysis tells you the project will take two and one-half years, the client can now consider the trade-off of the low-cost method versus compressing the project to two years—or in rare cases canceling the project. Similar trade-offs can be compared for different levels of resources or increases in technical performance. The assumption is any movement away from the low-cost, efficient method will increase costs—e.g., overtime. The preferred approach in defining the project is to make rough top-down estimates, develop the WBS/OBS, make bottom-up estimates, develop schedules and budgets, and reconcile differences between top-down and bottom-up estimates. Hopefully, these steps will be done *before* final negotiation with either an internal or external customer. With both top-down and bottom-up approaches, managers must be sensitive to factors that can influence project estimates.

Methods for Estimating Project Times and Costs

Macro Approaches for Estimating Project Times and Costs

At the strategic level macro estimating methods are used to evaluate the project proposal. Sometimes much of the information needed to derive accurate time and cost estimates is not available in the initial phase of the project—for example, design is not finalized. In these situations macro estimates are used until the tasks in the WBS are clearly defined.

Consensus Methods

This method simply uses the pooled experience of senior and/or middle managers to estimate the total project duration and cost. This typically involves a meeting where experts discuss, argue, and ultimately reach a decision as to their best guess estimate. Firms seeking greater rigor will use the Delphi method to make these macro estimates. See Snapshot from Practice: The Delphi Method.

Originally developed by the RAND Corporation in 1969 for technological forecasting, the *Delphi Method* is a group decision process about the likelihood that certain events will occur. The Delphi Method makes use of a panel of experts familiar with the kind of project in question. The notion is that well-informed individuals, calling on their insights and experience, are better equipped to estimate project costs/times than theoretical approaches or statistical methods. Their responses to estimate questionnaires are anonymous, and they are provided with a summary of opinions.

Experts are then encouraged to reconsider, and if appropriate to change their previous estimate in light of the replies of other experts. After two or three rounds it is believed that the group will converge toward the "best" response through this consensus process. The midpoint of responses is statistically categorized by the median score. In each succeeding round of questionnaires, the range of responses by the panelists will presumably decrease and the median will move toward what is deemed to be the "correct" estimate.

One distinct advantage of the Delphi Method is that the experts never need to be brought together physically. The process also does not require complete agreement by all panelists, since the majority opinion is represented by the median. Since the responses are anonymous, the pitfalls of ego, domineering personalities and the "bandwagon or halo effect" in responses are all avoided. On the other hand, future developments are not always predicted correctly by iterative consensus nor by experts, but at times by creative, "off the wall" thinking.

It is important to recognize that these first, macro estimates are only a rough cut and typically occur in the "conceptual" stage of the project. The top-down estimates are helpful in initial development of a complete plan. However, such estimates are sometimes significantly off the mark because little detailed information is gathered. At this level individual work items are not identified. Or, in a few cases, the top-down estimates are not realistic because top management "wants the project." Nevertheless, the initial top-down estimates are helpful in determining whether the project warrants more formal planning, which would include more detailed estimates. Be careful that macro estimates made by senior managers are not dictated to lower level managers who might feel compelled to accept the estimates even if they believe resources are inadequate.

Although your authors prefer to avoid the macro approach if possible, we have witnessed surprising accuracy in estimating project duration and cost in isolated cases. Some examples are building a manufacturing plant, building a distribution warehouse, developing air control for skyscraper buildings, and road construction. However, we have also witnessed some horrendous miscalculations, usually in areas where the technology is new and unproven. Macro methods can be useful if experience and judgment have been accurate in the past.

Ratio Methods

Macro methods (sometimes called parametric) are usually top down and use ratios, or surrogates, to estimate project times or costs. Macro approaches are often used in the concept or "need" phase of a project to get an initial duration and cost estimate for the project. For example, contractors frequently use number of square feet to estimate the cost and time to build a house; that is, a house of 2,700 square feet might cost $110 per square foot (2,700 feet × $110 per foot equals $297,000). Likewise, knowing the square feet and dollars per square foot, experience suggests it should take approximately 100 days to complete. Two other common examples of macro cost estimates are the cost for a new plant estimated by capacity size, or a software product estimated by features and complexity.

Apportion Method

This method is an extension to the ratio method. Apportionment is used when projects closely follow past projects in features and costs. Given good historical data, estimates can be made quickly with little effort and reasonable accuracy. This method is very common in projects that are relatively standard but have some small variation or customization.

131

Anyone who has borrowed money from a bank to build a house has been exposed to this process. Given an estimated total cost for the house, banks and the FHA (Federal Housing Authority) pay out money to the contractor by completion of specific segments of the house. For example, foundation might represent 3 percent of the total loan, framing 25 percent, electric plumbing and heating 15 percent, etc. Payments are made as these items are completed. An analogous process is used by some companies that apportion costs to deliverables in the WBS—given average cost percentages from past projects. Figure 5.1 presents an example similar to one found in practice. Assuming the total project cost is estimated, using a macro estimate, to be $500,000, the costs are apportioned as a percent of the total cost. For example, the costs apportioned to the "Document" deliverable are 5 percent of the total, or $25,000. The subdeliverables "Doc-1 and Doc-2" are allocated 2 and 3 percent of the total—$10,000 and $15,000, respectively.

Function Point Methods for Software and System Projects

In the software industry, software development projects are frequently estimated using weighted macro variables called "function points" or major parameters such as number of inputs, number of outputs, number of inquiries, number of data files, and number of interfaces. These weighted variables are adjusted for a complexity factor and added. The total adjusted count provides the basis for estimating the labor effort and cost for a project (usually using a regression formula derived from data of past projects). This latter method assumes adequate historical data by type of software project for the industry—for example, MIS systems. In the U.S. software industry, one person month represents on average five function points. A person working one month can generate on average (across all types of software projects) about five function points. Of course each organization needs to develop its own average for its specific type of work. Such historical data provide a basis for estimating the project duration. Variations of this top-down approach are used by companies such as IBM, Bank of America, Sears Roebuck, H-P, AT & T, Ford Motors, GE, Du Pont and many others. See Table 5.2 and Table 5.3 for a simplified example of function point count methodology.

FIGURE 5.1 **Apportion Method of Allocating Project Costs Using the Work Breakdown Structure**

TABLE 5.2
Simplified Basic Function Point Count Process for a Prospective Project or Deliverable

	Complexity Weighting			
Element	**Low**	**Average**	**High**	**Total**
Number of *inputs*	_____ × 2 +	_____ × 3 +	_____ × 4	= _____
Number of *outputs*	_____ × 3 +	_____ × 6 +	_____ × 9	= _____
Number of *inquiries*	_____ × 2 +	_____ × 4 +	_____ × 6	= _____
Number of *files*	_____ × 5 +	_____ × 8 +	_____ × 12	= _____
Number of *interfaces*	_____ × 5 +	_____ × 10 +	_____ × 15	= _____

TABLE 5.3
Example: Function Point Count Method

Software Project 13: Patient Admitting and Billing			
15	Inputs	Rated complexity as low	(2)
5	Outputs	Rated complexity as average	(6)
10	Inquiries	Rated complexity as average	(4)
30	Files	Rated complexity as high	(12)
20	Interfaces	Rated complexity as average	(10)

Application of Complexity Factor					
Element	**Count**	**Low**	**Average**	**High**	**Total**
Inputs	15	× 2			= 30
Outputs	5		× 6		= 30
Inquiries	10		× 4		= 40
Files	30			× 12	= 360
Interfaces	20		× 10		= 200
				Total	660

From historical data the organization developed the weighting scheme for complexity found in Table 5.2. Function points are derived from multiplying the number of kinds of elements by weighted complexity.

Table 5.3 shows the data collected for a specific task or deliverable: Patient Admitting and Billing—the number of inputs, outputs, inquiries, files and interfaces along with the expected complexity rating. Finally, the application of the element count is applied and the function point count total is 660. Given this count and the fact that one person month has historically been equal to 5 function points, the job will require 132 person months (660/5 = 132). Assuming you have ten programmers who can work on this task, the duration would be approximately 13 months. The cost is easily derived by multiplying the labor rate per month times 132 person months. For example, if the monthly programmer rate is $4000, then the estimated cost would be $528,000 (132 × 4000). Although function point metrics are useful, their accuracy depends on adequate historical data, currency of data, and relevancy of the project/deliverable to past averages.

Learning Curves

Some projects require that the same task, group of tasks, or product be repeated several times. Managers know intuitively that the time to perform a task improves with repetition. This phenomenon is especially true of tasks that are labor intensive. In these circumstances the pattern of improvement phenomenon can be used to predict the reduction in time to perform the task. From empirical evidence across *all* industries, the pattern of this improvement has been quantified in the *learning curve* (also known as improvement curve, experience curve, and industrial progress curve), which is described by the following relationship:

Each time the output quantity doubles, the unit labor hours are reduced at a constant rate.

In practice the improvement ratio may vary from 60 percent, representing very large improvement, to 100 percent representing no improvement at all. Generally, as the difficulty of the work decreases the expected improvement also decreases and the improvement ratio that is used becomes greater. One significant factor to consider is the proportion of labor in the task in relation to machine-paced work. Obviously, a lower percentage of improvement can occur only in operations with high labor content. Appendix 5.1 at the end of the chapter provides a detailed example of how the improvement phenomenon can be used to estimate time and cost for repetitive tasks.

The main disadvantage of macro approaches to estimating is simply that the time and cost for a specific task are not considered. Grouping many tasks into a common basket encourages errors of omission and the use of imposed times and costs.

Micro estimating methods are usually more accurate than macro methods. The bottom-up approach at the work package level can serve as a check on cost elements in the WBS by rolling up the work packages and associated cost accounts to major deliverables. Similarly, resource requirements can be checked. Later, the time, resource, and cost estimates from the work packages can be consolidated into time-phased networks, resource schedules, and budgets that are used for control.

Micro Approaches for Estimating Project Times and Costs

Template Method

If the project is similar to past projects, the costs from past projects can be used as a starting point for the new project. Differences in the new project can be noted and past times and costs adjusted to reflect these differences. For example, a ship repair dry-dock firm has a set of standard repair projects (i.e., templates for overhaul, electrical, mechanical) that are used as starting points for estimating the cost and duration of any new project. Differences from the appropriate standardized project are noted (for times, costs, and resources) and changes are made. This approach enables the firm to develop a potential schedule, estimate costs, and develop a budget in a very short time span. Development of such templates in a database can quickly reduce estimate errors.

Parametric Procedures Applied to Specific Tasks

Just as parametric techniques such as cost per square foot can be the source of macro estimates, the same technique can be applied to specific tasks. For example, as part of an MS Office 2000 conversion project, 36 different computer workstations needed to be converted. Based on past conversion projects, the project manager determined that on average one person could convert three workstations per day. Therefore the task of converting the 36 workstations would take three technicians four days [(36/3)/3]. Similarly, to estimate the wallpapering allowance on a house remodel, the contractor figured a cost of $5 per square yard of wallpaper and $2 per yard to install it, for a total cost of $7. By measuring the length and height of all the walls she was able to calculate the total area in square yards and multiply it by $7.

Detailed Estimates for the WBS Work Packages

Probably the most reliable method for estimating time and cost is to use the WBS and to ask the people responsible for the work package to make the estimates. They know from experience or know where to find the information to estimate work package durations—especially those that depend on labor hours and costs. When work packages have significant uncertainty associated with the time to complete, it is a prudent policy to require three time estimates—low, average, and high. Figure 5.2 presents a template training form using three time estimates for work packages by three different estimators. The form illustrates how this information can identify large differences among estimators and how the use of averages can give a more balanced time estimate. This time estimating approach gives the project manager and owner an opportunity to assess the risks associated with project times (and thus, costs). The approach helps to reduce surprises as the project progresses. The three-time estimate approach also provides a basis for assessing risk and determining the contingency fund. (See Chapter 7 for a discussion of contingency funds.)

A Hybrid: Phase Estimating

This approach begins with a macro estimate for the project and then refines estimates for phases of the project as it is implemented. Some projects by their nature cannot be rigorously defined because of the uncertainty of design or the final product. Although rare, such projects do exist. These projects are often found in aerospace projects, IT projects, new technology projects, and construction projects where design is incomplete. In these projects, phase or life-cycle estimating is frequently used.

Phase estimating is used when an unusual amount of uncertainty surrounds a project and it is impractical to estimate times and costs for the entire project. Phase estimating uses a two-estimate system over the life of the project. A detailed estimate is developed for the immediate phase and a macro estimate is made for the remaining phases of the project. Figure 5.3 depicts the phases of a project and the progression of estimates over its life.

FIGURE 5.2 **SB45 Support Cost Estimate Worksheet**

Project Number: *17*

Project Manager: *Kathleen Walling*

Project Description: *Road Diversion Project*

Date: 5 - 07

		Estimator 1			Estimator 2			Estimator 3			Estimator Averages			Ratio*
		Low	Aver.	High	Low	Aver.	High	Low	Aver.	High	Aver.	Aver.	Aver.	Range/
WBS	**Description**	Est.	Est.	Est.	Est.	Est.	Est.	Est.	Est.	Est.	Low		High	Aver.
ID		Days	Days	Days	Days	Days	Days	Days	Days	Days	Days	Days	Days	
102	Engineering	95	100	105	97	100	103	93	96	100	95.0	98.7	102.7	0.08
103	Project Management	14	15	17	14	16	18	13	14	15	13.7	15.0	16.7	0.20
104	R/W Property Acceptances	44	48	52	45	50	52	43	46	49	44.0	48.0	51.0	0.15
105	Base Maps	36	38	40	36	37	39	35	36	37	35.7	37.0	38.7	0.08
106	Coordinate Utilities	7	8	9	7	8	9	8	9	10	7.3	8.3	9.3	0.24
107	EPA Acceptance	13	14	15	14	15	16	13	15	17	13.3	14.7	16.0	0.18
108	Alignment Surveys	32	35	38	32	35	37	32	34	35	32.0	34.7	36.7	0.13
•														
•														
•					* Note: = ABS (Average Low - Average High)/Average									
•					This ratio indicates the degree of variability in the estimates									

Estimate accuracy improves with more detailed planning. The extent of this improvement varies by type of project. The table below is developed to reflect this observation. For example, information technology projects that determine their time and cost estimates in the conceptual stage can expect their "actuals" to err up to 200 percent over cost and duration and, perhaps, as much as 30 percent under estimates. Conversely, estimates for buildings, roads, etc., made after the work packages are clearly defined have a smaller error in actual costs and times of 15 percent over estimate and 5 percent less than estimate. Although these estimates vary by project, they can serve as ballpark numbers for project stakeholders selecting how project time and cost estimates will be derived.

Time and Cost Estimate Accuracy by Type of Project

	Bricks and Mortar	Information Technology
Conceptual stage	+60% to −30%	+200% to −30%
Deliverables defined	+30% to −15%	+100% to −15%
Work packages defined	+15% to −5%	+50% to −5%

For example, when the project need is determined, a macro estimate of the project cost and duration is made so analysis and decisions can be made. Simultaneously a detailed estimate is made for deriving project specifications and a macro estimate for the remainder of the project. As the project progresses and specifications are solidified, a detailed estimate for design is made and a macro estimate for the remainder of the project is computed. Clearly, as the project progresses through its life cycle and more information is available, the reliability of the estimates should be improving.

Phase estimating is preferred by those working on projects where the final product is not known and the uncertainty is very large—for example, the integration of wireless phones and computers. The commitment to cost and schedule is only necessary over the next phase of the project and commitment to unrealistic future schedules and costs based on poor information is avoided. This progressive macro/micro method provides a stronger basis for using schedule and cost estimates to manage progress during the next phase.

Unfortunately your customer—internal or external—will want an accurate estimate of schedule and cost the moment the decision is made to implement the project. Additionally, the customer who is paying for the project often perceives phase estimating as a blank check because costs and schedules are not firm over most of the project life cycle. Even though the reasons for phase estimating are sound and legitimate, most customers have to be sold on its legitimacy. A major advantage for the customer is the

FIGURE 5.3
Phase Estimating over Project Life Cycle

Phase	Need 1	Specifications 2	Design 3	Produce 4	Deliver 5
1		Macro estimate			
2		Detailed estimate	Macro estimate		
3			Detailed estimate	Macro estimate	
4				Detailed estimate	Macro estimate
5					Detailed estimate

Practicing project managers advocate keeping the level of detail to a minimum. But there are limits to this suggestion. One of the most frequent errors of new project managers is to forget that the task time estimate will be used to control schedule and cost performance. A frequent rule of thumb used by practicing project managers says that a task duration should not exceed 5 workdays or at the most 10 workdays, if workdays are the time units used for the project. Such a rule probably will result in a more detailed network, but the additional detail pays off in controlling schedule and cost as the project progresses.

Suppose the task is "build prototype computer-controlled conveyor belt," the time estimate is 40 workdays, and the budget $300,000. It may be better to divide the task into seven or eight smaller tasks for control purposes. If one of the smaller tasks gets behind because of problems or a poor time estimate, it will be possible to take corrective action quickly and avoid delaying successive tasks and the project. If the single task of 40 workdays is used, it is possible that no corrective action would be taken until day 40, since many people have a tendency to "wait and see" or avoid admitting they are behind or passing on bad news; the result may mean far more than 5 days behind schedule.

The 5- to 10-day rule of thumb applies to cost and performance goals. If using the rule of thumb suggested above results in too many network tasks, an alternative is available, but it has conditions. The activity time can be extended beyond the 5- to 10-day rule only *IF* control monitoring checkpoints for segments of the task can be established so clear measures of progress can be identified by a specific percent complete.

This information is invaluable to the control process of measuring schedule and cost performance—for example, payments for contract work are paid on "percent complete" basis. Defining a task with clear definable start and end points and intermediate points enhances the chances of early detection of problems, corrective action, and on-time project completion.

opportunity to change features, re-evaluate, or even cancel the project in each new phase. In conclusion, phase estimating is very useful in projects that possess huge uncertainties concerning the final nature (shape, size, features) of the project.

Level of Detail

Level of detail is different for different levels of management. At any level the detail should be no more than is necessary and sufficient. Top management interests usually center on the total project and major milestone events that mark major accomplishments—e.g., "Build Oil Platform in the North Sea" or "Complete Prototype." Middle management might center on one segment of the project or one milestone. First-line managers' interests may be limited to one task or work package. One of the beauties of WBS is the ability to aggregate network information so each level of management can have the kind of information necessary to make decisions.

Getting the level of detail in the WBS to match management needs for effective implementation is crucial, but the delicate balance is difficult to find. See Snapshot from Practice: Level of Detail. The level of detail in the WBS varies with the complexity of the project; the need for control; the project size, cost, duration; and other factors. If the structure reflects excessive detail, there is a tendency to break the work effort into department assignments. This tendency can become a barrier to success, since the emphasis will be on departmental outcomes rather than on deliverable outcomes. Excessive detail also means more unproductive paperwork. Note that if the level of the WBS is increased by one, the number of cost accounts may increase geometrically. On the other hand, if the level of detail is not adequate, an organization unit may find the structure falls short of meeting its needs. Fortunately, the WBS has built-in flexibility. Participating organization units may expand their portion of the structure to meet their special needs. For example, the engineering department may wish to further break their work on a deliverable into smaller packages by electrical, civil, and mechanical. Similarly, the marketing department may wish to break their new product promotion into TV, radio, periodicals, and newspapers.

Developing Budgets

Time-Phased Budgets

Cost estimates are not a budget. A cost estimate becomes a budget when it is time-phased. Time-phasing project work is the anchor point for project cost control. Without time phasing it is near impossible to have any timely and reliable cost control! Time phasing starts with the time estimate for the work package. In Figure 5.4 the work package has a duration of three weeks; at this point there is *no way of knowing when* the work package time-phased expenses will be incurred. This work package duration and others are used to develop the project network that schedules when work packages will start and finish. The time-phased budgets for work packages are then assigned to scheduled time periods to determine the financial requirements for each period over the life of the project. These time-phased budgets should mirror how the actual cash needs will occur because these budgets will be used for project cost control.

Perceptions of costs and budgets vary depending on their users. The project manager must be very aware of these differences when setting up the project budget and when communicating these differences to others. Figure 5.5 depicts these different perceptions. The project manager can commit costs months before the resource is used. This information is useful to the financial officer of the organization in forecasting future cash outflows. The project manager is interested in when the budgeted cost is expected to occur, when the budgeted cost actually is charged (earned), and when the actual cost emerges; the respective timings of these three cost figures are used to measure project schedule and cost variances.

FIGURE 5.4
Work Package Estimates

WP Description	*Final version*				Page *1* of *1*	

WP ID	*1.1.3.2*				Project	*PC Proto*

Deliverable	*Circuit board*				Date	*9/29/XX*

Original Unit	*Software*				Estimator	*RMG*

WP Duration *3* Work Weeks					Total Budget $ *265*	

Time-Phased Budget ($)

Work periods

Direct costs	Rate	1	2	3	4	5	Total
Code	$ XX/hr	50	30	20			$100
Document	$ XX/hr		10	15			25
Publish	$ XX/hr			5			5
Total labor		50	40	40			**$130**
Materials			20				20
Equipment	$ XX/hr	50	15	50			115
Other _____							
Total direct		100	75	90			**$265**

FIGURE 5.5
Three Views of Cost

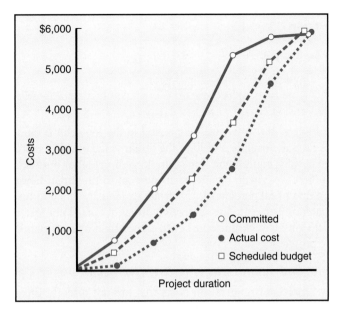

Types of Costs

The accuracy of the cost estimate improves as you move from the conceptual phase of the project to the point where individual items (work packages) are defined. Assuming work packages are defined, detailed cost estimates can be made. Here are typical kinds of costs found in a project:

1. Direct costs
   a. Labor
   b. Materials
   c. Equipment
   d. Other
2. Project overhead costs
3. General and administrative (G&A) overhead costs

The total project cost estimate is broken down in this fashion to sharpen the control process and improve decision making.

Direct Costs

These costs are clearly chargeable to a specific work package. Direct costs can be influenced by the project manager, project team, and individuals implementing the work package. These costs represent real cash outflows and must be paid as the project progresses; therefore, direct costs are usually separated from overhead costs. Lower-level project rollups frequently include only direct costs.

Direct Overhead Costs

Direct overhead rates more closely pinpoint which resources of the organization are being used in the project. Direct overhead costs can be tied to project deliverables or work packages. Examples include the salary of the project manager and temporary rental space for the project team. Although overhead is not an immediate out-of-pocket

FIGURE 5.6
Contract Bid
Summary Costs

Direct costs	$80,000
Direct overhead	$20,000
G&A overhead (20%)	$20,000
Profit (20%)	$24,000
Total bid	$144,000

expense, it is *real* and must be covered in the long run if the firm is to remain viable. These rates are usually a ratio of the dollar value of the resources used—e.g., direct labor, materials, equipment. For example, a direct labor burden rate of 20 percent would add a direct overhead charge of 20 percent to the direct labor cost estimate. A direct charge rate of 50 percent for materials would carry an additional 50 percent charge to the material cost estimate. Selective direct overhead charges provide a more accurate project (job or work package) cost, rather than using a blanket overhead rate for the whole project.

General and Administrative (G&A) Overhead Costs

These represent organization costs that are not directly linked to a specific project. These costs are carried for the duration of the project. Examples include organization costs across all products and projects such as advertising, accounting, and senior management above the project level. Allocation of G&A costs varies from organization to organization. However, G&A costs are usually allocated as a percent of total direct cost, or a percent of the total of a specific direct cost such as labor, materials, or equipment.

Given the totals of direct and overhead costs for individual work packages, it is possible to cumulate the costs for any deliverable or for the entire project. A percentage can be added for profit if you are a contractor. A breakdown of costs for a proposed contract bid is presented in Figure 5.6.

Refining Estimates and Contingency Funds

As described earlier in Chapter 4, detailed work package estimates are aggregated and "rolled up" by deliverable to estimate the total direct cost of the project. Similarly, estimated durations are entered into the project network to establish the project schedule and determine the overall duration of the project. Experience tells us that for many projects the total estimates do not materialize and the actual costs and schedule of some projects significantly exceed original work package–based estimates. See Snapshot from Practice: How Do You Estimate the Cost of a Nuclear Power Plant? for a dramatic example of this. In order to compensate for the problem of actual cost and schedule exceeding estimates, some project managers adjust total costs by some multiplier (i.e., total estimated costs × 1.20).

The practice of adjusting original estimates by 20 or even 100 percent begs the question of why, after investing so much time and energy on detailed estimates, could the numbers be so far off? There are a number of reasons for this, most of which can be traced to the estimating process and the inherent uncertainty of predicting the future. Some of these reasons are discussed below.

* **Interaction costs are hidden in estimates.** According to the guidelines, each task estimate is supposed to be done independently. However, tasks are rarely completed in a vacuum. Work on one task is dependent upon prior tasks, and the hand-offs between tasks require time and attention. For example, people working on prototype

O. P. Kharbanda in his book (co-authored with Jeffrey Pinto), *What Made Gertie Gallop: Learning from Project Failures* makes the important point that estimating is as much an art as a skill. For example, early in his career (1960s), he was involved with the fabrication of a nuclear reactor in India at a time when the local facilities were not geared for such sophisticated jobs. Having had no experience in building complex equipment with (almost) unheard of tolerances and precision, it was virtually impossible to create a reasonable advance estimate of the cost. The estimators did the best they could, then added a little more than normal margin before quoting a price to the client.

Soon after, O. P. happened to attend a week-long international nuclear power conference that included stalwarts in this field from all over the world. About midweek, he was fortunate to come face-to-face with the chief engineer of the company that had supplied the first reactor to India, identical in design to the one his company had recently bid on. This was the chance of a lifetime to finally get the inside information on accurate cost estimating. In fact, the expert confessed that his company lost "their shirt" on the Indian reactor. Then in reply to the innocent question, "How do you estimate a nuclear reactor?" the expert answered with cool confidence, "Do your normal cautious estimating, add more than normal margin and then after a short pause, double it!" O. P. confessed that in their ignorance, they had skipped the last vital step, but this short, casual conversation proved most valuable. "We were forewarned, we took it seriously, and got forearmed. It saved us several millions of dollars."

development need to interact with design engineers after the design is completed, whether to simply ask clarifying questions or to make adjustments in the original design. Similarly, the time necessary to coordinate activities is typically not reflected in independent estimates. Coordination is reflected in meetings and briefings as well as time necessary to resolve disconnects between tasks. Time, and therefore cost, devoted to managing interactions rises exponentially as the number of people and different disciplines involved increases on a project.

- **Normal conditions do not apply.** Estimates are supposed to be based on normal conditions. While this is a good starting point, it rarely holds true in real life. This is especially true when it comes to the availability of resources. Resource shortages, whether in the form of people, equipment, or materials, can extend original estimates. For example, under normal conditions four bulldozers are typically used to clear a certain site size in five days, but the availability of only three bulldozers would extend the task duration to eight days. Similarly, the decision to outsource certain tasks can increase costs as well as extend task durations since time is added to acclimating outsiders to the particulars of the project and the culture of the organization.

- **Things go wrong on projects.** Design flaws are revealed after the fact, extreme weather conditions occur, accidents happen, and so forth. Although you shouldn't plan for these risks to happen when estimating a particular task, the likelihood and impact of such events need to be considered.

- **Changes in project scope and plans.** As one gets further and further into the project, a manager obtains a better understanding of what needs to be done to accomplish the project. This may lead to major changes in project plans and costs. Likewise, if the project is a commercial project, changes often have to be made midstream to respond to new demands by the customer and/or competition. Unstable project scopes are a major source of cost overruns. While every effort should be made up front to nail down the project scope, it is becoming increasingly difficult to do so in our rapidly changing world.

The reality is that for many projects not all of the information needed to make accurate estimates is available, and it is impossible to predict the future. The dilemma is that without solid estimates, the credibility of the project plan is eroded. Deadlines become meaningless, budgets become rubbery, and accountability becomes problematic.

So how do organizations deal with these challenges? First, they do the best job they can revising estimates based on relevant information prior to establishing the baseline schedule and budget. Second, they create contingency funds and time buffers to deal with uncertainty. Finally, they have a change management system in place so that the baseline budget and schedule can be revised when events warrant it. Each of these actions will be briefly discussed below.

Adjusting Estimates   Effective organizations adjust estimates of specific tasks once risks, resources, and particulars of the situation have been more clearly defined. They recognize that the rolled up estimates generated from a detailed estimate based on the WBS are just the starting point. As they delve further into the project-planning process, they make appropriate revisions both in the time and cost of specific activities. They factor the final assignment of resources into the project budget and schedule. For example, when they realize that only three instead of four bulldozers are available to clear a site, they adjust both the time and cost of that activity. They adjust estimates to account for specific actions to mitigate potential risks on the project. For example, to reduce the chances of design code errors, they would add the cost of independent testers to the schedule and budget. Finally, organizations adjust estimates to take into account abnormal conditions. For example, if soil samples reveal excessive ground water, then they adjust foundation costs and times.

Contingency Funds and Time Buffers   Contingency funds and time buffers are created to offset uncertainty. Adding contingency reduces the likelihood that actual costs will overrun estimates and the project will take longer than planned. In general, the less well defined the project, the greater the contingency.

It is important that contingency allowances be independent of the original time and cost estimates! These allowances need to be clearly distinguished to avoid time and budget game playing.

Contingency can be added to specific activities or work packages or to the project as a whole. Activity contingency is an amount added by the estimator to the initial estimate of an activity or work package to account for known uncertainties. Contingencies include such things as design changes, unreliable estimates, and risks associated with specific activities. For example, the backup plan against the risk that the project is behind schedule is to use the more expensive overnight delivery service. Note that once the risk has passed, the specific contingency fund should be cut from the project budget and not used elsewhere. This practice discourages the tendency to expend whatever is available in the budget when costs rise.

In addition to assigning contingencies for specific tasks or activities, project managers create an overall project contingency. The amount, both in terms of time and cost, is proportional to the uncertainty inherent in the project. Hence, projects with greater uncertainty are allotted a higher contingency amount. When possible the percentage contingency is derived from historical records of similar projects. For example, if previous software development projects on the average take 25 percent longer than planned, then this percentage would be added as a contingency. This contingency is used to account for hidden interaction costs as well as risks and uncertainties that cannot be pinpointed to specific tasks, such as fluctuation in exchange rates, resource shortages, untested assumptions, and changes in the market.

Changing Baseline Schedule and Budget   Sometimes events dictate reformulating the budget and schedule. Examples of such events include changes in the product concept, insurmountable technical barriers, labor strikes, legal entanglements, political upheaval, and skyrocketing wage and material costs. In these cases the original estimates no longer apply, and a new baseline budget and schedule need to be created. This should only be done after careful consultation with all of the major stakeholders and should be implemented through a formal change management system. Change management and contingency funds will be discussed further in Chapter 7.

Obtaining accurate estimates is a challenge. Committed organizations accept the challenge of coming up with meaningful estimates and invest heavily in developing their capacity to do so. They understand that without an honest attempt to come up with the best estimates possible, all else is a crapshoot. Accurate estimates reduce uncertainty and provide a discipline for effectively managing projects.

Creating a Database for Estimating

The best way to improve estimates is to collect and archive data on past project estimates and actuals. Saving historical data—estimates and actuals—provides a knowledge base for improving project time and cost estimating. Creating an estimating database is a "best practice" among leading project management organizations.

Some organizations have large estimating departments of professional estimators—e.g., Boeing, Kodak, IBM—that have developed large time and cost databases. Others collect these data through the project office. This database approach allows the project estimator to select a specific work package item from the database for inclusion. The estimator then makes any necessary adjustments concerning the materials, labor, and equipment. Of course any items not found in the database can be added to the project—and ultimately to the database if desired. Again, the quality of the database estimates depends on the experience of the estimators, but over time the data quality should improve. Such structured databases serve as feedback for estimators and as benchmarks for cost and time for each project. In addition, comparison of estimate and actual for different projects can suggest the degree of risk inherent in estimates. See Figure 5.7 for the structure of a database similar to those found in practice.

FIGURE 5.7
Estimating Database Templates

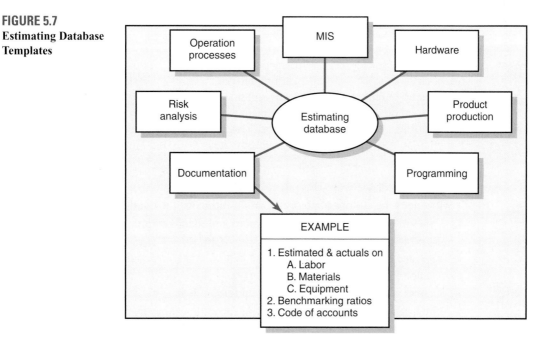

Summary

Quality time and cost estimates are the bedrock of project control. Past experience is the best starting point for these estimates. The quality of estimates is influenced by other factors such as people, technology, and downtimes. The key for getting estimates that represent realistic average times and costs is to have an organization culture that allows errors in estimates without incriminations. If times represent average time, we should expect that 50 percent will be less than the estimate and 50 percent will exceed the estimate. It should also be recognized that once work gets behind, it tends to stay behind. The use of teams that are highly motivated can help in keeping task times and costs near the average. For this reason, it is crucial to get the team to buy into time and cost estimates.

Using top-down (macro) estimates is good for initial and strategic decision making or in situations where the costs associated with developing better estimates have little benefit. However, in most cases the bottom-up approach (micro) to estimating is preferred and more reliable because it assesses each work package, rather than the whole project, section, or deliverable of a project. Estimating time and costs for each work package facilitates development of the project network and a time-phased budget, which are needed to control schedule and cost as the project is implemented. Using the estimating guidelines will help eliminate many common mistakes made by those unacquainted with estimating times and costs for project control. Establishing a time and cost estimating database fits well with the learning organization philosophy.

The level of time and cost detail should follow the old saying of "no more than is necessary and sufficient." Managers must remember to differentiate between committed outlays, actual costs, and scheduled costs. It is well known that up-front efforts in clearly defining project objectives, scope, and specifications vastly improve time and cost estimate accuracy.

Finally, how estimates are gathered and how they are used can affect their usefulness for planning and control. The team climate, organization culture, and organization structure can strongly influence the importance attached to time and cost estimates and how they are used in managing projects.

Key Terms

Apportionment methods	Interaction costs	Phase estimating
Contingency funds	Learning curves	Ratio methods
Delphi method	Macro and micro estimating	Template method
Direct costs	Overhead costs	Time and cost databases
Function points	Padding estimates	Time-phased budgets

Review Questions

1. Why are accurate estimates critical to effective project management?
2. How does the culture of an organization influence the quality of estimates?
3. What are the differences between micro and macro estimating approaches? Under what conditions would you prefer one over the other?
4. What are the major types of costs? Which costs are controllable by the project manager?
5. When is phase-time estimating appropriate?
6. Why is it important to separate contingency allowances from original estimates?

Exercises

1. Mrs. Tolstoy and her husband, Serge, are planning their dream house. The lot for the house sits high on a hill with a beautiful view of the Appalachian Mountains. The plans for the house show the size of the house to be 2,900 square feet. The average price for a lot and house similar to this one has been $120 per square foot. Fortunately, Serge is a retired plumber and feels he can save money by installing the plumbing himself. Mrs. Tolstoy feels she can take care of the interior decorating.

   The following average cost information is available from a local bank that makes loans to local contractors and disperses progress payments to contractors when specific tasks are verified as complete.

24%	Excavation and framing complete
8%	Roof and fireplace complete
3%	Wiring roughed in
6%	Plumbing roughed in
5%	Siding on
17%	Windows, insulation, walks, plaster, and garage complete
9%	Furnace installed
4%	Plumbing fixtures installed
10%	Exterior paint, light fixtures installed, finish hardware installed
6%	Carpet and trim installed
4%	Interior decorating
4%	Floors laid and finished

   a. What is the estimated cost for the Tolstoy's house if they use contractors to complete all of the house?

   b. Estimate what the cost of the house would be if the Tolstoys use their talents to do some of the work themselves.

2. Below is a project WBS with cost apportioned by percents. If the total project cost is estimated to be $600,000, what are the estimated costs for the following deliverables?

   a. Design?

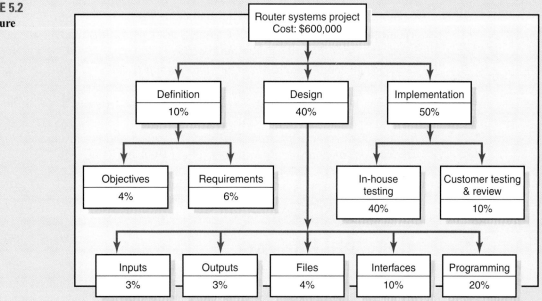

EXERCISE 5.2
WBS Figure

b. Programming?

c. In-house testing?

What weaknesses are inherent in this estimating approach?

3. Firewall Project XT. Using the "complexity weighting" scheme shown in Table 5.2 and the function point complexity weighted table shown below, estimate the total function point count. Assume historical data suggest five function points equal one person a month and six people can work on the project.

Complexity Weight Table		
Number of inputs	10	Rated complexity low
Number of outputs	20	Rated complexity average
Number of inquires	10	Rated complexity average
Number of files	30	Rated complexity high
Number of interfaces	50	Rated complexity high

a. What is the estimated project duration?

b. If 20 people are available for the project, what is the estimated project duration?

c. If the project must be complete in six months, how many people will be needed for the project?

References

Dalkey, N. C., D. L. Rourke, R. Lewis, and D. Snyder, *Studies in the Quality of Life: Delphi and Decision Making,* (Lexington, MA: Lexington Books, 1972).

Gray, N. S., "Secrets to Creating the Elusive 'Accurate Estimate'," *PM Network,* 15 (8) August 2001, p. 56.

Jeffery, R., G. C. Low, and M. Barnes, "A Comparison of Function Point Counting Techniques," *IEEE Transactions on Software Engineering,* 19 (5) 1993, pp. 529–32.

Jones, C., *Applied Software Measurement,* (New York: McGraw-Hill, 1991).

Jones, C., *Estimating Software Costs,* (New York: McGraw-Hill, 1998).

Kharbanda, O. P., and J. K. Pinto, *What Made Gertie Gallop: Learning from Project Failures,* (New York: Von Nostrand Reinhold, 1996).

Magne, E., K. Emhjellenm, and P. Osmundsen, "Cost Estimation Overruns in the North Sea," *Project Management Journal* 34 (1) 2003, pp. 23–29.

McLeod, G., and D. Smith, *Managing Information Technology Projects,* (Cambridge, MA: Course Technology, 1996).

Pressman, R. S., *Software Engineering: A Practitioner's Approach, 4th edition,* (New York: McGraw-Hill, 1997).

Symons, C. R., "Function Point Analysis: Difficulties and Improvements," *IEEE Transactions on Software Engineering,* 14 (1) 1988, pp. 2–11.

Case

Sharp Printing, AG

Three years ago the Sharp Printing (SP) strategic management group set a goal of having a color laser printer available for the consumer and small business market for less than $300. A few months later the senior management met off-site to discuss the new product. The results of this meeting were a set of general technical specifications along with major deliverables, a product launch date, and a cost estimate based on prior experience.

Shortly afterward, a meeting was arranged for middle management explaining the project goals, major responsibilities, the project start date, and importance of meeting the product launch date within the cost estimate. Members of all departments involved attended the meeting. Excitement was high. Although everyone saw the risks as high, the promised rewards for the company and the personnel were emblazoned in their minds. A few participants questioned the legitimacy of the project duration and cost estimates. A couple of R&D people were worried about the technology required to produce the high-quality product for less than $300. But given the excitement of the moment, everyone agreed the project was worth doing and doable. The color laser printer project was to have the highest project priority in the company.

Lauren was selected to be the project manager. She had 15 years of experience in printer design and manufacture, which included successful management of several projects related to printers for commercial markets. Since she was one of those uncomfortable with the project cost and time estimates, she felt getting good bottom-up time and cost estimates for the deliverables was her first concern. She quickly had a meeting with the significant stakeholders to create a WBS identifying the work packages and organizational unit responsible for implementing the work packages. Lauren stressed she wanted time and cost estimates from those who would do the work or were the most knowledgeable, if possible. Getting estimates from more than one source was encouraged. Estimates were due in two weeks.

The compiled estimates were placed in the WBS/OBS. The corresponding cost estimate seemed to be in error. The cost estimate was $1,250,000 over the senior management estimate; this represents about a 20 percent overrun! The time estimate from the developed project network was only four months over the top management time estimate. Another meeting was scheduled with the significant stakeholders to check the estimates and to brainstorm for alternative solutions; the cost and time estimates appeared to be reasonable. Some of the suggestions for the brainstorming session are listed below.

- Change scope.
- Outsource technology design.
- Use the priority matrix (found in Chapter 4) to get top management to clarify their priorities.
- Partner with another organization or build a research consortium to share costs and to share the newly developed technology and production methods.
- Cancel the project.
- Commission a break-even study for the laser printer.

Very little in the way of concrete savings was identified, although there was consensus that time could be compressed to the market launch date, but at additional costs.

Lauren met with the marketing (Connor), production (Kim), and design (Gage) managers who yielded some ideas for cutting costs, but nothing significant enough to have a large impact. Gage remarked, "I wouldn't want to be the one to deliver the message to top management that their cost estimate is $1,250,000 off! Good luck, Lauren."

At this point, what would you do if you were the project manager?

Appendix 5.1

Learning Curves for Estimating

A forecast estimate of the time required to perform a work package or task is a basic necessity for scheduling the project. In some cases, the manager simply uses judgment and past experience to estimate work package time, or may use historical records of similar tasks.

Most managers and workers intuitively know that improvement in the amount of time required to perform a task or group of tasks occurs with repetition. A worker can perform a task better/quicker the second time and each succeeding time she/he performs it (without any technological change). It is this pattern of improvement that is important to the project manager and project scheduler.

This improvement from repetition generally results in a reduction of labor hours for the accomplishment of tasks and results in lowers project costs. From empirical evidence across *all* industries, the pattern of this improvement has been quantified in the *learning curve* (also known as improvement curve, experience curve, and industrial progress curve), which is described by the following relationship:

Each time the output quantity doubles, the unit labor hours are reduced at a constant rate.

For example, assume that a manufacturer has a new contract for 16 prototype units and a total of 800 labor hours were required for the first unit. Past experience has indicated that on similar types of units the improvement rate was 80 percent. This relationship of improvement in labor hours is shown below:

Unit		Labor Hours
1		800
2	$800 \times .80 =$	640
4	$640 \times .80 =$	512
8	$512 \times .80 =$	410
16	$410 \times .80 =$	328

By using Table A5.1 unit values, similar labor hours per unit can be determined. Looking across the 16 unit level and down the 80 percent column, we find a ratio of .4096. By multiplying this ratio times the labor hours for the first unit, we obtained the per unit value.

$$.4096 \times 800 = 327.68$$

That is, the 16th unit should require close to 328 labor hours, assuming an 80 percent improvement ratio.

Obviously, a project manager may need more than a single unit value for estimating the time for some work packages. The cumulative values in Table A5.2 provide factors for computing the cumulative total labor hours of all units. In the previous example, for the first 16 units, the total labor hours required would be

$$800 \times 8.920 = 7,136 \text{ hours}$$

By dividing the total cumulative hours (7,136) by the units, the average unit labor hours can be obtained

$$7,136 \text{ labor hours}/16 \text{ units} = 446 \text{ average labor hours per unit}$$

Note how the labor hours for the 16th unit (328) differs from average for all 16 units (446). The project manager, knowing the average labor costs and processing costs, could estimate the total prototype costs. (The mathematical derivation of factors found in Tables A5.1 and A5.2 can be found in F. C. Jelen, and J. H. Black, *Cost and Optimization Engineering,* 2d ed. (New York: McGraw-Hill, 1983.)

FOLLOW-ON CONTRACT EXAMPLE

Assume the project manager gets a follow-on order of 74 units, how should she estimate labor hours and cost? Going to the cumulative Table A5.2 we find at the 80 percent ratio and 90 total units intersection—a 30.35 ratio.

800 × 30.35 =	24,280 labor hours for 90 units
Less previous 16 units =	7,136
Total follow-on order =	17,144 labor hours
17,144/74 equals 232 average labor hours per unit	

Labor hours for the 90th unit can be obtained from the Table A5.1 .2349 × 800 = 187.9 labor hours. (For ratios between given values, simply estimate.)

Exercise A5.1

Norwegian Satellite Development Company
Cost estimates
for
World Satellite Telephone Exchange Project

NSDC has a contract to produce eight satellites to support a worldwide telephone system (for Alaska Telecom, Inc.) that allows individuals to use a single, portable telephone in any location on earth to call in and out. NSDC will develop and produce the eight units. NSDC has estimated that the R&D costs will be NKr 12,000,000. Material costs are expected to be NKr 6,000,000. They have estimated the design and production of the first satellite will require 100,000 labor hours and an 80 percent improvement curve is expected. Skilled labor cost is NKr 300 per hour. Desired profit for all projects is 25 percent of total costs.

A. How many labor hours should the eighth satellite require?

B. How many labor hours for the whole project of eight satellites?

C. What price would you ask for the project? Why?

D. Midway through the project your design and production people realize that a 75 percent improvement curve is more appropriate. What impact does this have on the project?

E. Near the end of the project Deutsch Telefon AG has requested a cost estimate for four satellites identical to those you have already produced. What price will you quote them? Justify your price.

TABLE A5.1
Learning Curves Unit Values

Unit	60%	65%	70%	75%	80%	85%	90%	95%
1	1.0000	1.0000	1.0000	1.0000	1.0000	1.0000	1.0000	1.0000
2	.6000	.6500	.7000	.7500	.8000	.8500	.9000	.9500
3	.4450	.5052	.5682	.6338	.7021	.7729	.8462	.9219
4	.3600	.4225	.4900	.5625	.6400	.7225	.8100	.9025
5	.3054	.3678	.4368	.5127	.5956	.6857	.7830	.8877
6	.2670	.3284	.3977	.4754	.5617	.6570	.7616	.8758
7	.2383	.2984	.3674	.4459	.5345	.6337	.7439	.8659
8	.2160	.2746	.3430	.4219	.5120	.6141	.7290	.8574
9	.1980	.2552	.3228	.4017	.4930	.5974	.7161	.8499
10	.1832	.2391	.3058	.3846	.4765	.5828	.7047	.8433
12	.1602	.2135	.2784	.3565	.4493	.5584	.6854	.8320
14	.1430	.1940	.2572	.3344	.4276	.5386	.6696	.8226
16	.1296	.1785	.2401	.3164	.4096	.5220	.6561	.8145
18	.1188	.1659	.2260	.3013	.3944	.5078	.6445	.8074
20	.1099	.1554	.2141	.2884	.3812	.4954	.6342	.8012
22	.1025	.1465	.2038	.2772	.3697	.4844	.6251	.7955
24	.0961	.1387	.1949	.2674	.3595	.4747	.6169	.7904
25	.0933	.1353	.1908	.2629	.3548	.4701	.6131	.7880
30	.0815	.1208	.1737	.2437	.3346	.4505	.5963	.7775
35	.0728	.1097	.1605	.2286	.3184	.4345	.5825	.7687
40	.0660	.1010	.1498	.2163	.3050	.4211	.5708	.7611
45	.0605	.0939	.1410	.2060	.2936	.4096	.5607	.7545
50	.0560	.0879	.1336	.1972	.2838	.3996	.5518	.7486
60	.0489	.0785	.1216	.1828	.2676	.3829	.5367	.7386
70	.0437	.0713	.1123	.1715	.2547	.3693	.5243	.7302
80	.0396	.0657	.1049	.1622	.2440	.3579	.5137	.7231
90	.0363	.0610	.0987	.1545	.2349	.3482	.5046	.7168
100	.0336	.0572	.0935	.1479	.2271	.3397	.4966	.7112
120	.0294	.0510	.0851	.1371	.2141	.3255	.4830	.7017
140	.0262	.0464	.0786	.1287	.2038	.3139	.4718	.6937
160	.0237	.0427	.0734	.1217	.1952	.3042	.4623	.6869
180	.0218	.0397	.0691	.1159	.1879	.2959	.4541	.6809
200	.0201	.0371	.0655	.1109	.1816	.2887	.4469	.6757
250	.0171	.0323	.0584	.1011	.1691	.2740	.4320	.6646
300	.0149	.0289	.0531	.0937	.1594	.2625	.4202	.5557
350	.0133	.0262	.0491	.0879	.1517	.2532	.4105	.6482
400	.0121	.0241	.0458	.0832	.1453	.2454	.4022	.6419
450	.0111	.0224	.0431	.0792	.1399	.2387	.3951	.6363
500	.0103	.0210	.0408	.0758	.1352	.2329	.3888	.6314
600	.0090	.0188	.0372	.0703	.1275	.2232	.3782	.6229
700	.0080	.0171	.0344	.0659	.1214	.2152	.3694	.6158
800	.0073	.0157	.0321	.0624	.1163	.2086	.3620	.6098
900	.0067	.0146	.0302	.0594	.1119	.2029	.3556	.6045
1,000	.0062	.0137	.0286	.0569	.1082	.1980	.3499	.5998
1,200	.0054	.0122	.0260	.0527	.1020	.1897	.3404	.5918
1,400	.0048	.0111	.0240	.0495	.0971	.1830	.3325	.5850
1,600	.0044	.0102	.0225	.0468	.0930	.1773	.3258	.5793
1,800	.0040	.0095	.0211	.0446	.0895	.1725	.3200	.5743
2,000	.0037	.0089	.0200	.0427	.0866	.1683	.3149	.5698
2,500	.0031	.0077	.0178	.0389	.0606	.1597	.3044	.5605
3,000	.0027	.0069	.0162	.0360	.0760	.1530	.2961	.5530

TABLE A5.2
Learning Curves
Cumulative Values

Units	60%	65%	70%	75%	80%	85%	90%	95%
1	1.000	1.000	1.000	1.000	1.000	1.000	1.000	1.000
2	1.600	1.650	1.700	1.750	1.800	1.850	1.900	1.950
3	2.045	2.155	2.268	2.384	2.502	2.623	2.746	2.872
4	2.405	2.578	2.758	2.946	3.142	3.345	3.556	3.774
5	2.710	2.946	3.195	3.459	3.738	4.031	4.339	4.662
6	2.977	3.274	3.593	3.934	4.299	4.688	5.101	5.538
7	3.216	3.572	3.960	4.380	4.834	5.322	5.845	6.404
8	3.432	3.847	4.303	4.802	5.346	5.936	6.574	7.261
9	3.630	4.102	4.626	5.204	5.839	6.533	7.290	8.111
10	3.813	4.341	4.931	5.589	6.315	7.116	7.994	8.955
12	4.144	4.780	5.501	6.315	7.227	8.244	9.374	10.62
14	4.438	5.177	6.026	6.994	8.092	9.331	10.72	12.27
16	4.704	5.541	6.514	7.635	8.920	10.38	12.04	13.91
18	4.946	5.879	6.972	8.245	9.716	11.41	13.33	15.52
20	5.171	6.195	7.407	8.828	10.48	12.40	14.64	17.13
22	5.379	6.492	7.819	9.388	11.23	13.38	15.86	18.72
24	5.574	6.773	8.213	9.928	11.95	14.33	17.10	20.31
25	5.668	6.909	8.404	10.19	12.31	14.80	17.71	21.10
30	6.097	7.540	9.305	11.45	14.02	17.09	20.73	25.00
35	6.478	8.109	10.13	12.72	15.64	19.29	23.67	28.86
40	6.821	8.631	10.90	13.72	17.19	21.43	26.54	32.68
45	7.134	9.114	11.62	14.77	18.68	23.50	29.37	36.47
50	7.422	9.565	12.31	15.78	20.12	25.51	32.14	40.22
60	7.941	10.39	13.57	17.67	22.87	29.41	37.57	47.65
70	8.401	11.13	14.74	19.43	25.47	33.17	42.87	54.99
80	8.814	11.82	15.82	21.09	27.96	36.80	48.05	62.25
90	9.191	12.45	16.83	22.67	30.35	40.32	53.14	69.45
100	9.539	13.03	17.79	24.18	32.65	43.75	58.14	76.59
120	10.16	14.16	19.57	27.02	37.05	50.39	67.93	90.71
140	10.72	15.08	21.20	29.67	41.22	56.78	77.46	104.7
160	11.21	15.97	22.72	32.17	45.20	62.95	86.80	118.5
180	11.67	16.79	24.14	34.54	49.03	68.95	95.96	132.1
200	12.09	17.55	25.48	36.80	52.72	74.79	105.0	145.7
250	13.01	19.28	28.56	42.08	61.47	88.83	126.9	179.2
300	13.81	20.81	31.34	46.94	69.66	102.2	148.2	212.2
350	14.51	22.18	33.89	51.48	77.43	115.1	169.0	244.8
400	15.14	23.44	36.26	55.75	84.85	127.6	189.3	277.0
450	15.72	24.60	38.48	59.80	91.97	139.7	209.2	309.0
500	16.26	25.68	40.58	63.68	98.85	151.5	228.8	340.6
600	17.21	27.67	44.47	70.97	112.0	174.2	267.1	403.3
700	18.06	29.45	48.04	77.77	124.4	196.1	304.5	465.3
800	18.82	31.09	51.36	84.18	136.3	217.3	341.0	526.5
900	19.51	32.60	54.46	90.26	147.7	237.9	376.9	587.2
1,000	20.15	34.01	57.40	96.07	158.7	257.9	412.2	647.4
1,200	21.30	36.59	62.85	107.0	179.7	296.6	481.2	766.6
1,400	22.32	38.92	67.85	117.2	199.6	333.9	548.4	884.2
1,600	23.23	41.04	72.49	126.8	218.6	369.9	614.2	1001.
1,800	24.06	43.00	76.85	135.9	236.8	404.9	678.8	1116.
2,000	24.83	44.84	80.96	144.7	254.4	438.9	742.3	1230.
2,500	26.53	48.97	90.39	165.0	296.1	520.8	897.0	1513.
3,000	27.99	52.62	98.90	183.7	335.2	598.9	1047.	1791.

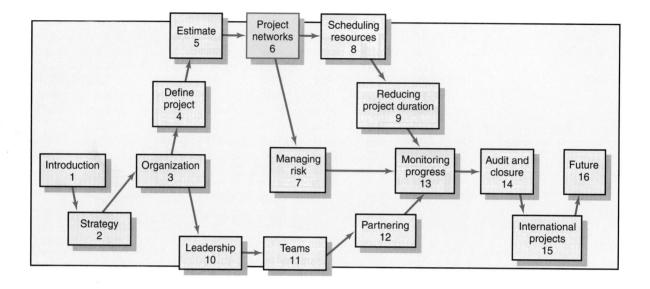

Developing a Project Plan

Developing the Project Network

From Work Package to Network

Constructing a Project Network

Activity-on-Node (AON) Fundamentals

Network Computation Process

Using the Forward and Backward Pass Information

Level of Detail for Activities

Practical Considerations

Extended Network Techniques to Come Closer to Reality

Summary

Appendix 6.1: Activity-on-Arrow Method

CHAPTER SIX

Developing a Project Plan

I had six honest serving men who taught me all I know: their names were what and how and why, and when and where and who.

Rudyard Kipling

Developing the Project Network

The project network is the tool used for planning, scheduling, and monitoring project progress. The network is developed from the information collected for the WBS and is a graphic flow chart of the project job plan. The network depicts the project activities that must be completed, the logical sequences, the interdependencies of the activities to be completed, and in most cases the times for the activities to start and finish along with the longest path(s) through the network—the *critical path*. The network is the framework for the project information system that will be used by the project managers to make decisions concerning project time, cost, and performance.

Developing the project networks takes time for someone or some group to develop; therefore, they cost money! Are networks really worth the struggle? The answer is definitely yes, except in cases where the project is considered trivial or very short in duration. The network is easily understood by others because the network presents a graphic display of the flow and sequence of work through the project. Once the network is developed, it is very easy to modify or change when unexpected events occur as the project progresses. For example, if materials for an activity are delayed, the impact can be quickly assessed and the whole project revised in only a few minutes with the computer. These revisions can be communicated to all project participants quickly (for example, via e-mail or project website).

The project network provides other invaluable information and insights. It provides the basis for scheduling labor and equipment. It enhances communication that melds all managers and groups together in meeting the time, cost, and performance objectives of the project. It provides an estimate of project duration rather than picking a project completion date from a hat or someone's preferred date. The network gives the times when activities can start and finish and when they can be delayed. It provides the basis for budgeting the cash flow of the project. It identifies which activities are "critical" and, therefore, should not be delayed if the project is to be completed as planned. It highlights which activities to consider if the project needs to be compressed to meet a deadline.

There are other reasons project networks are worth their weight in gold. Basically, project networks minimize surprises by getting the plan out early and allowing corrective feedback. A commonly heard statement from practitioners is that the project network represents three-quarters of the planning process. Perhaps this is an exaggeration, but it signals the perceived importance of the network to project managers in the field.

From Work Package to Network

Project networks are developed from the WBS. The project network is a visual flow diagram of the sequence, interrelationships, and dependencies of all the activities that must be accomplished to complete the project. *An activity is an element in the project that consumes time—for example, work or waiting.* Work packages from the WBS are used to build the activities found in the project network. An activity can include one or more work packages. The activities are placed in a sequence that provides for orderly completion of the project. Networks are built using nodes (boxes) and arrows (lines). The node depicts an activity, and the arrow shows dependency and project flow.

Integrating the work packages and the network represents a point where the management process often fails in practice. The primary explanations for this failure are that (1) different groups (people) are used to define work packages and activities and (2) the WBS is poorly constructed and not deliverable/output oriented. Integration of the WBS and project network is crucial to effective project management. The project manager must be careful to guarantee continuity by having some of the same people who defined the WBS and work packages develop the network activities.

Networks provide the project schedule by identifying dependencies, sequencing, and timing of activities, which the WBS is not designed to do. The primary inputs for developing a project network plan are work packages. Remember, a work package is defined independently of other work packages, has definite start and finish points, requires specific resources, includes technical specifications, and has cost estimates for the package. However, dependency, sequencing, and timing of each of these factors are not included in the work package. A network activity can include one or more work packages.

Figure 6.1 shows a segment of the WBS example from Chapter 4 and how the information is used to develop a project network. The lowest level deliverable in Figure 6.1 is "circuit board." The cost accounts (design, production, test, software) denote project work, organization unit responsible, and time-phased budgets for the work packages. Each cost account represents one or more work packages. For example, the design cost account has two work packages (D-1-1 and D-1-2)—specifications and documentation. The software and production accounts also have two work packages. Developing a network requires sequencing tasks from all work packages that have measurable work.

Figure 6.1 traces how work packages are used to develop a project network. You can trace the use of work packages by the coding scheme. For example, activity A uses work packages D-1-1 and D-1-2 (specifications and documentation), while activity C uses work package S-22-1. This methodology of selecting work packages to describe activities is used to develop the project network, which sequences and times project activities. Care must be taken to include all work packages. *The manager derives activity time estimates from the task times in the work package.* For example, activity B (proto 1) requires five weeks to complete; activity K (test) requires three weeks to complete. After computing the activity early and late times, the manager can schedule resources and time-phase budgets (with dates).

FIGURE 6.1
WBS/Work Packages to Network

Activity network for circuit board work packages

Constructing a Project Network

Terminology

Every field has its jargon that allows colleagues to communicate comfortably with each other about the techniques they use. Project managers are no exception. Here are some terms used in building project networks.

Activity. For project managers, an *activity* is an element of the project that requires time. It may or may not require resources. Typically an activity consumes time—either while people work or while people wait. Examples of the latter are time waiting for contracts to be signed, materials to arrive, drug approval by the government, budget clearance, etc. Activities usually represent one or more tasks from a work package. Descriptions of activities should use a verb/noun format: for example, develop product specifications.

Merge activity. This is an activity that has more than one activity immediately preceding it (more than one dependency arrow flowing to it).

Parallel activities. These are activities that can take place at the same time, if the manager wishes. However, the manager may choose to have parallel activities *not* occur simultaneously.

Path. A sequence of connected, dependent activities.

Critical path. When this term is used, it means the longest path(s) through the network; if an activity on the path is delayed, the project is delayed the same amount of time.

Event. This term is used to represent a point in time when an activity is started or completed. It does not consume time.

Burst activity. This activity has more than one activity immediately following it (more than one dependency arrow flowing from it).

Two Approaches

The two approaches used to develop project networks are known as *activity-on-node (AON)* and *activity-on-arrow (AOA). Both methods use two building blocks—the arrow and the node.* Their names derive from the fact that the former uses a node to depict an activity, while the second uses an arrow to depict an activity. From the first use of these two approaches in the late 1950s, practitioners have offered many enhancements; however, the basic models have withstood the test of time and still prevail with only minor variations in form.

In practice, the activity-on-node (AON) method has come to dominate most projects. Hence, this text will deal primarily with AON. However, for those who find their organization using the activity-on-arrow (AOA) approach, the chapter includes an appendix demonstrating AOA methods (Appendix 6.1). There are good reasons for students of project management to be proficient in both methods. Different departments and organizations have their "favorite" approaches and are frequently loyal to software that is already purchased and being used. New employees or outsiders are seldom in a position to govern choice of method. If subcontractors are used, it is unreasonable to ask them to change their whole project management system to conform to the approach you are using. The point is, a project manager should feel comfortable moving among projects that use either AON or AOA.

Basic Rules to Follow in Developing Project Networks

The following eight rules apply in general when developing a project network:

1. Networks flow typically from left to right.
2. An activity cannot begin until all preceding connected activities have been completed.
3. Arrows on networks indicate precedence and flow. Arrows can cross over each other.
4. Each activity should have a unique identification number.
5. An activity identification number must be larger than that of any activities that precede it.
6. Looping is not allowed (in other words, recycling through a set of activities cannot take place).

7. Conditional statements are not allowed (that is, this type of statement should not appear: If successful, do something; if not, do nothing).

8. Experience suggests that when there are multiple starts, a common start node can be used to indicate a clear project beginning on the network. Similarly, a single project end node can be used to indicate a clear ending.

Activity-on-Node (AON) Fundamentals

The wide availability of personal computers and graphics programs has served as an impetus for use of the activity-on-node (AON) method (sometimes called the *precedence diagram method*). Figure 6.2 shows a few typical uses of building blocks for the AON network construction. An **activity** is represented by a *node* (box). The node can take many forms, but in recent years the node represented as a rectangle (box) has dominated. The dependencies among activities are depicted by *arrows* between the rectangles (boxes) on the AON network. The arrows indicate how the activities are related and the sequence in which things must be accomplished. The length and slope of the arrow are arbitrary and set for convenience of drawing the network. The letters in the

FIGURE 6.2
Activity-on-Node Network Fundamentals

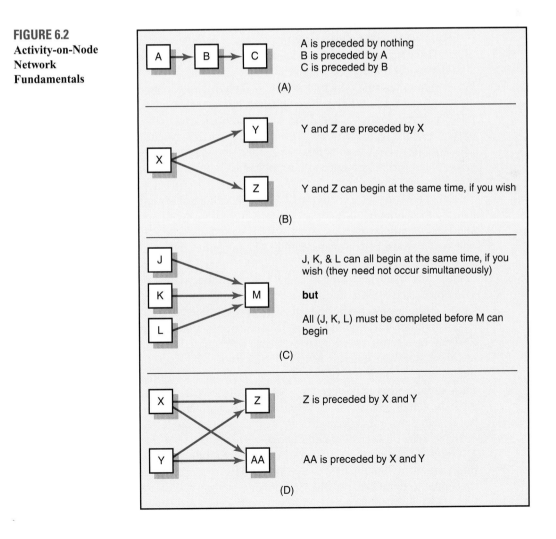

boxes serve here to identify the activities while you learn the fundamentals of network construction and analysis. In practice, activities have identification numbers and descriptions.

There are three basic relationships that must be established for activities included in a project network. The relationships can be found by answering the following three questions for each activity:

1. Which activities must be completed immediately *before* this activity? These activities are called *predecessor* activities.
2. Which activities must immediately *follow* this activity? These activities are called *successor* activities.
3. Which activities can occur *while* this activity is taking place? This is known as a *concurrent* or *parallel* relationship.

Sometimes a manager can use only questions 1 and 3 to establish relationships. This information allows the network analyst to construct a graphic flow chart of the sequence and logical interdependencies of project activities.

Figure 6.2A is analogous to a list of things to do where you complete the task at the top of the list first and then move to the second task, etc. This figure tells the project manager that activity A must be completed before activity B can begin, and activity B must be completed before activity C can begin.

Figure 6.2B tells us that activities Y and Z cannot begin until activity X is completed. This figure also indicates that activities Y and Z can occur concurrently or simultaneously if the project manager wishes; however, it is not a necessary condition. For example, pouring concrete driveway (activity Y) can take place while landscape planting (activity Z) is being accomplished, but land clearing (activity X) must be completed before activities Y and Z can start. Activities Y and Z are considered *parallel* activities. Parallel paths allow concurrent effort, which may shorten time to do a series of activities. Activity X is sometimes referred to as a *burst* activity because more than one arrow bursts from the node. The number of arrows indicates how many activities immediately follow activity X.

Figure 6.2C shows us activities J, K, and L can occur simultaneously if desired, and activity M cannot begin until activities J, K, and L are all completed. Activities J, K, and L are parallel activities. Activity M is called a *merge* activity because more than one activity must be completed before M can begin. Activity M could also be called a milestone.

In Figure 6.2D, activities X and Y are parallel activities that can take place at the same time; activities Z and AA are also parallel activities. But activities Z and AA cannot begin until activities X and Y are both completed.

Given these fundamentals of AON, we can practice developing a simple network. Remember, the arrows can cross over each other (e.g., Figure 6.2D), be bent, or be any length or slope. Neatness is not a criterion for a valid, useful network—only accurate inclusion of all project activities, their dependencies, and time estimates. Information for a simplified project network is given in Table 6.1. This project represents a new business center that is to be developed and the work and services the county engineering design department must provide as it coordinates with other groups—such as the business center owners and contractors.

Figure 6.3 shows the first steps in constructing the AON project network from the information in Table 6.1. We see that activity A (application approval) has nothing preceding it; therefore, it is the first node to be drawn. Next, we note that activities B, C, and D (construction plans, traffic study, and service availability check) are all preceded

TABLE 6.1
Network Information

	KOLL BUSINESS CENTER County Engineers Design Department	
Activity	**Description**	**Preceding Activity**
A	Application approval	None
B	Construction plans	A
C	Traffic study	A
D	Service availability check	A
E	Staff report	B, C
F	Commission approval	B, C, D
G	Wait for construction	F
H	Occupancy	E, G

by activity A. We draw three arrows and connect them to activities B, C, and D. This segment shows the project manager that activity A must be completed before activities B, C, and D can begin. After A is completed, B, C, and D can go on concurrently, if desired. Figure 6.4 shows the completed network with all of the activities and precedences depicted.

At this point our project network presents us with a graphic map of the project activities with sequences and dependencies. This information is tremendously valuable to those managing the project. However, estimating the duration for each activity will further increase the value of the network. A realistic project plan and schedule require reliable time estimates for project activities. The addition of time to the network allows us to estimate how long the project will take. When activities can or must start, when resources must be available, which activities can be delayed, and when the project is estimated to be complete are all determined from the times assigned. Deriving an

FIGURE 6.3
Koll Business Center—Partial Network

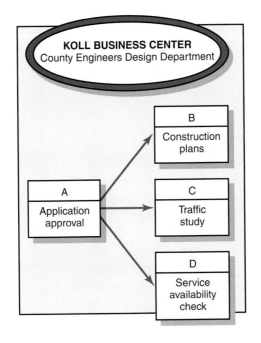

FIGURE 6.4 **Koll Business Center—Complete Network**

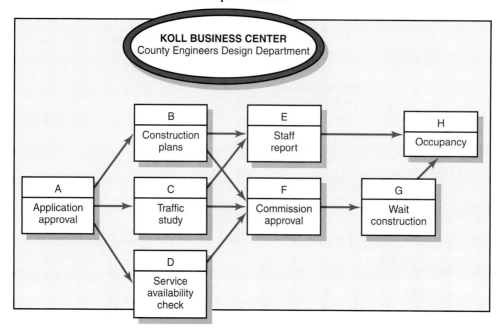

activity time estimate necessitates early assessment of resource needs in terms of material, equipment, and people. In essence the project network with activity time estimates links planning, scheduling, and controlling of projects.

Network Computation Process

Drawing the project network places the activities in the right sequence for computing start and finish times of activities. Activity time estimates are taken from the task times in the work package and added to the network (review Figure 6.2). Performing a few simple computations allows the project manager to complete a process known as the forward and backward pass. Completion of the *forward and backward pass* will answer the following questions:

Forward Pass—Earliest Times
1. How soon can the activity start? (early start—ES)
2. How soon can the activity finish? (early finish—EF)
3. How soon can the project be finished? (expected time—TE)

Backward Pass—Latest Times
1. How late can the activity start? (late start—LS)
2. How late can the activity finish? (late finish—LF)
3. Which activities represent the critical path (CP)? This is the longest path in the network which, when delayed, will delay the project.
4. How long can the activity be delayed? (slack or float—SL)

In practice small project networks (25 to 100 activities) are frequently developed using yellow Post-it® stickers. The meeting requirements and process for the project team are described herein.

The following are the requirements for such a project:

1. Project team members and a facilitator.
2. One yellow sticker (3 × 4 inches or larger) for each activity with the description of the activity printed on the sticker.
3. Erasable whiteboard with marker pen (a long, 4-foot-wide piece of butcher paper can be used in place of the whiteboard).

All of the yellow stickers are placed in easy view of all team members. The team begins by identifying those activity stickers that have no predecessors. Each of these activity stickers is then attached to the whiteboard. A start node is drawn, and a dependency arrow is connected to each activity.

Given the initial network start activities, each activity is examined for immediate successor activities. These activities are attached to the whiteboard and dependency arrows drawn. This process is continued until all of the yellow stickers are attached to the whiteboard with dependency arrows. (Note: The process can be reversed, beginning with those activities that have no successor activities and connecting them to a project end node. The predecessor activities are selected for each activity and attached to the whiteboard with dependency arrows marked.)

When the process is complete, the dependencies are recorded in the project software, which develops a computer-designed network along with the critical path(s) and early, late, and slack times. This methodology sensitizes team members early to the interdependencies among activities of the project. But more importantly, the methodology empowers team members by giving them input to the important decisions that they must implement later.

The terms in parentheses represent the acronyms used in most texts and computer programs and by project managers. The forward and backward pass process is presented next.

Forward Pass—Earliest Times

The forward pass starts with the first project activity(ies) and traces each path (chain of sequential activities) through the network to the last project activity(ies). As you trace along the path, you *add* the activity times. The longest path denotes the project

TABLE 6.2
Network Information

| | KOLL BUSINESS CENTER | | |
| | County Engineers Design Department | | |
Activity	Description	Preceding Activity	Activity Time
A	Application approval	None	5
B	Construction plans	A	15
C	Traffic study	A	10
D	Service availability check	A	5
E	Staff report	B, C	15
F	Commission approval	B, C, D	10
G	Wait for construction	F	170
H	Occupancy	E, G	35

completion time for the plan and is called the critical path (CP). Table 6.2 lists the activity times in workdays for the Koll Business Center example we used for drawing a network.

Figure 6.5 shows the network with the activity time estimate found in the node (see "Dur" for duration in the legend). For example, activity A has an activity duration of 5 workdays, and activity G has a duration of 170 workdays. The forward pass begins with the project start time, which is usually time zero. (Note: Calendar times can be

FIGURE 6.5   **Activity-on-Node Network**

computed for the project later in the planning phase.) In our Koll Center example, the early start time for the first activity (activity A) is zero. This time is found in the upper left corner of the activity A node in Figure 6.6. The early finish for activity A is 5 (ES + Dur = EF or 0 + 5 = 5). Next, we see that activity A is the predecessor for activities B, C, and D. Therefore, the earliest these activities can begin is the instant in time when activity A is completed; this time is 5 workdays. You can now see in Figure 6.6 that activities B, C, and D can all start the moment activity A is complete and, therefore, have an early start (ES) of 5. Using the formula ES + Dur = EF, the early finish (EF) times for activities B, C, and D are 20, 15, and 10. What is the ES for activity E, then, which is a merge activity? Is it 15 or 20? The answer is 20 because all activities immediately preceding activity E (B and C) must be completed before activity E can begin. Because activity B will take the longest to complete, it controls the ES of activity E. The same process is used for determining the ES for activity F. It is preceded by activities B, C, and D. The controlling early finish (EF) time is activity B, which has the longer early finish (20 versus 15 and 10) of the immediate predecessors (activities B, C, and D) of activity F. Stated differently, the forward pass assumes every activity will start the instant in time when the last of its predecessors is finished.

The forward pass requires that you remember just three things when computing early activity times:

1. You *add* activity times along each path in the network (ES + Dur = EF).
2. You carry the early finish (EF) to the next activity where it becomes its early start (ES), *unless*

FIGURE 6.6 **Activity-on-Node Network Forward Pass**

3. The next succeeding activity is a *merge* activity. In this case you select the *largest* early finish number (EF) of *all* its immediate predecessor activities.

In our example in Figure 6.6, the EF for activity F (30) is carried to activity G, where it becomes its ES (30). We see activity H is a merge activity and therefore find the largest EF of its immediate predecessors (activities E and G). In this case, the choice is between the EF times of 35 and 200; the choice for the ES of activity H is 200. The EF for activity H (235) becomes the earliest the project can be expected to be completed (TE) under normal conditions. The three questions derived from the forward pass have been answered; that is, early start (ES), early finish (EF), and the project duration (TE) times have been computed. The backward pass is the next process to learn.

Backward Pass—Latest Times

The backward pass starts with the last project activity(ies) on the network. You trace backward on each path *subtracting* activity times to find the late start (LS) and finish times (LF) for each activity. Before the backward pass can be computed, the late finish for the last project activity(ies) must be selected. In early planning stages, this time is usually set equal to the early finish (EF) of the last project activity (or in the case of multiple finish activities, the activity with the largest EF). In some cases an imposed project duration deadline exists, and this date will be used. Let us assume for planning purposes we can accept the EF project duration (TE) equal to 235 workdays. The LF for activity H becomes 235 workdays (EF = LF) (see Figure 6.7).

The backward pass is similar to the forward pass; you need to remember three things:

1. You *subtract* activity times along each path starting with the project end activity (LF − Dur = LS).

2. You carry the LS to the next preceding activity to establish its LF, *unless*

3. The next preceding activity is a *burst* activity; in this case you select the *smallest* LS of all its immediate successor activities to establish its LF.

Let's apply these rules to our Koll Center example. Beginning with activity H (occupancy) and an LF of 235 workdays, the LS for activity H is 200 workdays (LF − Dur = LS or 235 − 35 = 200). The LS for activity H becomes the LF for activities E and G. The LS for activities E and G becomes 185 (200 − 15 = 185) and 30 workdays (200 − 170 = 30), respectively. Next, the LS for activity G becomes the LF for activity F, and its LS becomes 20. At this point we see that activities B and C are *burst* activities that tie to activities E and F. The late finish for activity B is controlled by the LS of activities E and F. The LS for activity E is 185 days and for activity F, 20 days. Follow the arrows backward from activities E and F to activity B. Note that LS times for activities E and F have been placed to the right of the node so you can select the *smallest* time—20 days. The latest activity B can finish is 20 days, or activity F will be delayed and hence the project. The LF for activity C is identical to activity B because it is also controlled by the LS of activities E and F. Activity D simply picks up its LF from activity F. By computing the LS (LF − Dur = LS) for activities B, C, and D, we can determine the LF for activity A, which is a *burst* activity. You see that the finish of activity A is controlled by activity B, which has the smallest LS of activities B, C,

FIGURE 6.7   **Activity-on-Node Network Backward Pass**

Determining Slack (or Float)

When the forward and backward passes have been computed, it is possible to determine which activities can be delayed by computing "slack" or "float." Total slack or float for an activity is simply the difference between the LS and ES (LS − ES = SL) or between LF and EF (LF − EF = SL). For example, the slack for activity C is 5 days, for activity D is 10 days, and for activity G is zero (see Figure 6.8). *Total slack* tells us the amount of time an activity can be delayed and yet not delay the project. If slack of one activity in a path is used, the ES for all activities that follow in the chain will be delayed and their slack reduced. Use of total slack must be coordinated with all participants in the activities that follow in the chain.

After slack for each activity is computed, the critical path(s) is (are) easily identified. When the LF = EF for the end project activity, the critical path can be identified as those activities that also have LF = EF or a slack of zero (LF − EF = 0) (or LS − ES = 0). *The critical path is the network path(s) that has (have) the least slack in common.* This awkward arrangement of words is necessary because a problem arises when the project finish activity has an LF that differs from the EF found in the forward pass—for example, an imposed duration date. If this is the case, the slack on the critical path will *not* be zero; it will be the difference between the

FIGURE 6.8 **Activity-on-Node Network with Slack**

project EF and the imposed LF of the last project activity. For example, if the EF for the project is 235 days, but the imposed LF or target date is set at 220 days, all activities on the critical path would have a slack of minus 15 days. Of course, this would result in a late start of–15 days for the first project activity—a good trick if the project is to start now. Negative slack occurs in practice when the critical path is delayed.

In Figure 6.8 the critical path is marked with dashed arrows and nodes—activities A, B, F, G, and H. Delay of any of these activities will delay the total project by the same number of days. Critical activities typically represent about 10 percent of the activities of the project. Therefore, project managers pay close attention to the critical path activities to be sure they are not delayed. See Snapshot from Practice: The Critical Path.

Free Slack (Float)

An activity with free slack is unique because the activity can be delayed without delaying the ES of activities following it. Free slack is defined as the difference between the EF of an activity and the ES of the activity that follows it. Free slack can never be negative. Only activities that occur at the end of a chain of activities (usually where you have a merge activity) can have free slack. For example, if a single chain (path) of activities has 14 days slack, the last activity will have free slack, and the others will have none. Sometimes the chain is not very long; it can be only one activity. For example, in the Koll Business Center network (Figure 6.8), activity E is a chain of one and has free slack of 165 workdays (200 − 35 = 165). Activities C and D also have free slack of 5 and 10 days, respectively.

The critical path method (CPM) has long been considered the "Holy Grail" of project management. Here are comments made by veteran project managers when asked about the significance of the critical path in managing projects:

- I try to make it a point whenever possible to put my best people on critical activities or on those activities that stand the greatest chance of becoming critical.

- I pay extra attention when doing risk assessment to identifying those risks that can impact the critical path, either directly or indirectly, by making a noncritical activity so late that it becomes critical. When I've got money to spend to reduce risks, it usually gets spent on critical tasks.

- I don't have time to monitor all the activities on a big project, but I make it a point to keep in touch with the people who are working on critical activities. When I have the time, they are the ones I visit to find out firsthand how things are going. It's amazing how much more I can find out from talking to the rank and file who are doing the work and by reading the facial expressions of people—much more than I can gain from a number-driven status report.

- When I get calls from other managers asking to "borrow" people or equipment, I'm much more generous when it involves resources from working on noncritical activities. For example, if another project manager needs an electrical engineer who is assigned to a task with five days of slack, I'm willing to share that engineer with another project manager for two to three days.

- The most obvious reason the critical path is important is because these are the activities that impact completion time. If I suddenly get a call from above saying they need my project done two weeks earlier than planned, the critical path is where I schedule the overtime and add extra resources to get the project done more quickly. In the same way, if the project schedule begins to slip, it's the critical activities I focus on to get back on schedule.

The beauty of free slack is that changes in start and finish times for the free slack activity require less coordination with other participants in the project and give the project manager more flexibility than total slack. Because the activity is the last in the chain, delaying the activity up to the slack amount will not influence any following activities. For example, assume a chain of 10 activities. Delaying any of the other nine activities in the chain requires notifying the managers of the remaining activities in the chain that you will be late, so they can adjust their schedules because the slack is not available to them.

Using the Forward and Backward Pass Information

What does a slack of 10 workdays for activity D mean for the project manager? In this specific case it means activity D can be delayed 10 days. In a larger sense the project manager soon learns that slack is important because it allows flexibility in scheduling scarce project resources—personnel and equipment—that are used on more than one parallel activity or another project.

Knowing the four activity times of ES, LS, EF, and LF is invaluable for the planning, scheduling, and controlling phases of the project. The ES and LF tell the project manager the time interval in which the activity should be completed. For example, activity E must be completed within the time interval 20 and 200 workdays; the activity can start as early as day 20 or finish as late as day 200. Conversely, activity F (commission approval), must start on day 20, or the project will be delayed.

When the critical path is known, it is possible to tightly manage the resources of the activities on the critical path so no mistakes are made that will result in delays. In addition, if for some reason the project must be expedited to meet an earlier date, it is possible to select those activities, or combination of activities, that will cost the least to shorten the project. Similarly, if the critical path is delayed and the time must be made up by shortening some activity or activities on the critical path to make up any negative slack, it is possible to identify the activities on the critical path that cost the least to shorten. If there are other paths with very little slack, it may be necessary to shorten activities on those paths also.

Level of Detail for Activities

Time-phasing work and budgets of the project mandate careful definition of the activities that make up the project network. Typically an activity represents one or more tasks from a work package. How many tasks you include in each activity sets the level of detail. In some cases it is possible to end up with too much information to manage, and this can result in increased overhead costs. Managers of small projects have been able to minimize the level of detail by eliminating some of the preliminary steps to drawing networks. Larger firms also recognize the cost of information overload and are working to cut down the level of detail in networks and in most other dimensions of the project.

Practical Considerations

Network Logic Errors

Project network techniques have certain logic rules that must be followed. One rule is that conditional statements such as "if test successful build proto, if failure redesign" are not permitted. The network is not a decision tree; it is a project plan that we assume will materialize. If conditional statements were allowed, the forward and backward pass would make little sense. Although in reality a plan seldom materializes as we expect in every detail, it is a reasonable initial assumption. You shall see that once a network plan is developed, it is an easy step to make revisions to accommodate changes.

Another rule that defeats the project network and computation process is *looping*. Looping is an attempt by the planner to return to an earlier activity. Recall that the activity identification numbers should always be higher for the activities following an activity in question; this rule helps to avoid the illogical precedence relationships among the activities. An activity should only occur once; if it is to occur again, the activity should have a new name and identification number and should be placed in the right sequence on the network. Figure 6.9 shows an illogical loop. If this loop were allowed to exist, this path would perpetually repeat itself. Many computer programs catch this type of logic error.

FIGURE 6.9
Illogical Loop

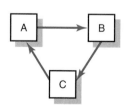

Activity Numbering

Each activity needs a unique identification code—usually a number. In practice very elegant schemes exist. Most schemes number activities in ascending order, that is, each succeeding activity has a larger number so that the flow of the project activities is toward project completion. It is customary to leave gaps between numbers (1, 5, 10, 15 . . .). Gaps are desirable so you can add missing or new activities later. Because it is nearly impossible to draw a project network perfectly, numbering networks is frequently not done until after the network is complete.

In practice you will find computer programs that accept numeric, alphabetic, or a combination of activity designations. Combination designations are often used to identify cost, work skill, departments, and locations. As a general rule, activity numbering systems should be ascending and as simple as possible. The intent is to make it as easy as you can for project participants to follow work through the network and locate specific activities.

Use of Computers to Develop Networks

All of the tools and techniques discussed in this chapter can be used with computer software currently available. Two examples are shown in Figures 6.10 and 6.11. Figure 6.10 presents a generic AON computer output for the Air Control project. The critical path is identified by the unshaded nodes (activities 1, 4, 6, 7, and 8). The activity description is shown on the top line of the activity node. The activity identification and duration are found on the right side of the node. The early start and early finish are on the left side of the node. The project starts on January 1 and is planned to finish February 14.

Figure 6.11 presents an early start Gantt bar chart. Bar charts are popular because they present an easy-to-understand, clear picture on a time-scaled horizon. They are used during planning, resource scheduling, and status reporting. The format is a two-dimensional representation of the project schedule, with activities down the rows and time across the horizontal axis. In this computer output the gray bars represent the activity durations. The extended lines from the bars represent slack. For example, "software development" has a duration of 18 time units (shaded area of the bar) and 20 days slack (represented by the extended line). The bar also indicates the activity has an early start of January 3, would end January 20, but can finish as late as February 9 because it has 20 days of slack. When calendar dates are used on the time axis, Gantt charts provide a clear overview of the project schedule and can be often found posted on the walls of project offices. Unfortunately, when projects have many dependency relationships, the dependency lines soon become overwhelming and defeat the simplicity of the Gantt chart.

Project management software can be a tremendous help in the hands of those who understand and are familiar with the tools and techniques discussed in this text. However, there is nothing more dangerous than someone using the software with little or no knowledge of how the software derives its output. Mistakes in input are very common and require someone skilled in the concepts, tools, and information system to recognize that errors exist so false actions are avoided.

Calendar Dates

Ultimately you will want to assign calendar dates to your project activities. If a computer program is not used, dates are assigned manually. Lay out a calendar of workdays (exclude nonworkdays), and number them. Then relate the calendar workdays to

FIGURE 6.10 Air Control Project

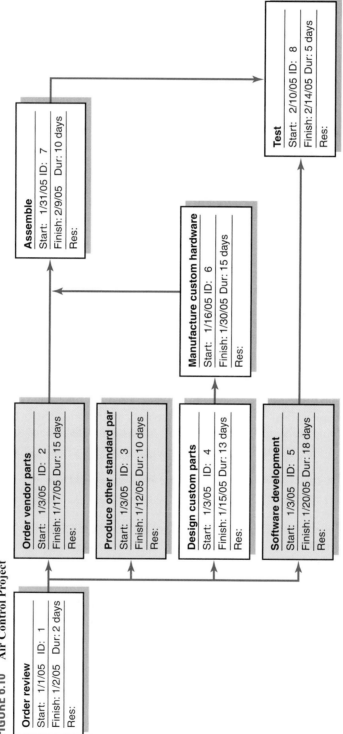

Order review
Start: 1/1/05 ID: 1
Finish: 1/2/05 Dur: 2 days
Res:

Order vendor parts
Start: 1/3/05 ID: 2
Finish: 1/17/05 Dur: 15 days
Res:

Produce other standard par
Start: 1/3/05 ID: 3
Finish: 1/12/05 Dur: 10 days
Res:

Design custom parts
Start: 1/3/05 ID: 4
Finish: 1/15/05 Dur: 13 days
Res:

Software development
Start: 1/3/05 ID: 5
Finish: 1/20/05 Dur: 18 days
Res:

Manufacture custom hardware
Start: 1/16/05 ID: 6
Finish: 1/30/05 Dur: 15 days
Res:

Assemble
Start: 1/31/05 ID: 7
Finish: 2/9/05 Dur: 10 days
Res:

Test
Start: 2/10/05 ID: 8
Finish: 2/14/05 Dur: 5 days
Res:

FIGURE 6.11   **Air Control Project**

ID	Duration	Task Name	Start	Finish	Late Start	Late Finish	Free Slack	Total Slack
1	2 days	Order review	Tue 1/1/05	Wed 1/2/05	Tue 1/1/05	Wed 1/2/05	0 days	0 days
2	15 days	Order vendor parts	Thu 1/3/05	Thu 1/17/05	Wed 1/16/05	Wed 1/30/05	13 days	13 days
3	10 days	Produce other standard parts	Thu 1/3/05	Sat 1/12/05	Mon 1/21/05	Wed 1/30/05	18 days	18 days
4	13 days	Design custom parts	Thu 1/3/05	Tue 1/15/05	Thu 1/3/05	Tue 1/15/05	0 days	0 days
5	18 days	Software development	Thu 1/3/05	Sun 1/20/05	Wed 1/23/05	Sat 2/9/05	20 days	20 days
6	15 days	Manufacture custom hardware	Wed 1/16/05	Wed 1/30/05	Wed 1/16/05	Wed 1/30/05	0 days	0 days
7	10 days	Assemble	Thu 1/31/05	Sat 2/9/05	Thu 1/31/05	Sat 2/9/05	0 days	0 days
8	5 days	Test	Sun 2/10/05	Thu 2/14/05	Sun 2/10/05	Thu 2/14/05	0 days	0 days

the workdays on your project network. Most computer programs will assign calendar dates automatically after you identify start dates, time units, nonworkdays, and other information.

Multiple Starts and Multiple Projects

Some computer programs require a common start and finish event in the form of a node—usually a circle or rectangle—for a project network. Even if this is not a requirement, it is a good idea because it avoids "dangler" paths. Dangler paths give the impression that the project does not have a clear beginning or ending. If a project has more than one activity that can begin when the project is to start, each path is a dangler path. The same is true if a project network ends with more than one activity; these unconnected paths are also called danglers. Danglers can be avoided by tying dangler activities to a common project start or finish node.

When several projects are tied together in an organization, using a common start and end node helps to identify the total planning period of all projects. Use of pseudo or dummy wait activities from the common start node allows different start dates for each project.

Extended Network Techniques to Come Closer to Reality

The method for showing relationships among activities in the last section is called the finish-to-start relationship because it assumes all immediate preceding connected activities must be completed before the next activity can begin. In an effort to come closer to the realities of projects, some useful extensions have been added. The use of *laddering* was the first obvious extension practitioners found very useful.

Laddering

The assumption that all immediate preceding activities must be 100 percent complete is too restrictive for some situations found in practice. This restriction occurs most frequently when one activity overlaps the start of another and has a long duration. Under the standard finish-to-start relationship, when an activity has a long duration and will delay the start of an activity immediately following it, the activity can be broken into segments and the network drawn using a *laddering* approach so the following activity can begin sooner and not delay the work. This segmenting of the larger activity gives the appearance of steps on a ladder on the network, thus the name. The classic example used in many texts and articles is laying pipe, because it is easy to visualize. The trench must be dug, pipe laid, and the trench refilled. If the pipeline is one mile long, it is not necessary to dig one mile of trench before the laying of pipe can begin or to lay one mile of pipe before refill can begin. Figure 6.12 shows how these overlapping activities might appear in an AON network using the standard finish-to-start approach.

Use of Lags

The use of *lags* has been developed to offer greater flexibility in network construction. *A lag is the minimum amount of time a dependent activity must be delayed to begin or end.* The use of lags in project networks occurs for two primary reasons:

1. When activities of long duration delay the start or finish of successor activities, the network designer normally breaks the activity into smaller activities to avoid the

FIGURE 6.12   **Example of Laddering Using Finish-to-Start Relationship**

long delay of the successor activity. Use of lags can avoid such delays and reduce network detail.

2. Lags can be used to constrain the start and finish of an activity.

The most commonly used relationship extensions are start-to-start, finish-to-finish, and combinations of these two. These relationship patterns are discussed in this section.

Finish-to-Start Relationship

The finish-to-start relationship represents the typical, generic network style used in the early part of the chapter. However, there are situations in which the next activity in a sequence must be delayed even when the preceding activity is complete. For example, removing concrete forms cannot begin until the poured cement has cured for two time units. Figure 6.13 shows this lag relationship for AON networks. Finish-to-start lags are frequently used when ordering materials. For example, it may take 1 day to place orders but take 19 days to receive the goods. The use of finish-to-start allows the activity duration to be only 1 day and the lag 19 days. This approach ensures the activity cost is tied to placing the order only rather than charging the activity for 20 days of work. This same finish-to-start lag relationship is useful to depict transportation, legal, and mail lags.

   The use of finish-to-start lags should be carefully checked to ensure their validity. Conservative project managers or those responsible for completion of activities have been known to use lags as a means of building in a "slush" factor to reduce the risk of being late. A simple rule to follow is that the use of finish-to-start lags must be justified and approved by someone responsible for a large section of the project. The legitimacy of lags is not usually difficult to discern. The legitimate use of the additional relationship shown can greatly enhance the network by more closely representing the realities of the project.

Start-to-Start Relationship

An alternative to segmenting the activities as we did earlier is to use a start-to-start relationship. Typical start-to-start relationships are shown in Figure 6.14. Figure 6.14A shows the start-to-start relationship with zero lag, while Figure 6.14B shows the same

FIGURE 6.13
Finish-to-Start
Relationship

X	Lag 2 →	Y

FIGURE 6.14
Start-to-Start
Relationship

relationship with a lag of five time units. It is important to note that the relationship may be used with or without a lag. If time is assigned, it is usually shown on the dependency arrow of an AON network.

In Figure 6.14B, activity Q cannot begin until five time units after activity P begins. This type of relationship typically depicts a situation in which you can perform a portion of one activity and begin a following activity before completing the first. This relationship can be used on the pipe-laying project. Figure 6.15 shows the project using an AON network. The start-to-start relationship reduces network detail and project delays by using lag relationships.

It is possible to find compression opportunities by changing finish-to-start relations to start-to-start relationships. A review of finish-to-start critical activities may point out opportunities that can be revised to be parallel by using start-to-start relationships. For example, in place of a finish-to-start activity "design house, then build foundation," a start-to-start relationship could be used in which the foundation can be started, say, five days (lag) after design has started—assuming the design of the foundation is the first part of the total design activity. This start-to-start relationship with a small lag allows a sequential activity to be worked on in parallel and to compress the duration of the critical path. This same concept is frequently found in projects in which concurrent engineering is used to speed completion of a project. Concurrent engineering, which is highlighted in the Snapshot from Practice: Concurrent Engineering, basically breaks activities into smaller segments so that work

FIGURE 6.15
Use of Lags to
Reduce Detail

In the old days, when a new product development project was initiated by a firm, it would start its sequential journey in the research and development department. Concepts and ideas would be worked out and the results passed to the engineering department, which sometimes reworked the whole product. This result would be passed to manufacturing, where it might be reworked once more in order to ensure the product could be manufactured using existing machinery and operations. Quality improvements were initiated after the fact once defects and improvement opportunities were discovered during production. This sequential approach to product development required a great deal of time, and it was not uncommon for the final product to be totally unrecognizable when compared to original specifications.

Given the emphasis on speed to the market, companies have abandoned the sequential approach to product development and have adopted a more holistic approach titled concurrent engineering. In a nutshell, *concurrent engineering* entails the active involvement of all the relevant specialty areas throughout the design and development process. The traditional chainlike sequence of finish-to-start relationships is replaced by a series of start-to-start lag relationships as soon as meaningful work can be initiated for the next phase. Figure 6.16 summarizes the dramatic gains in time to market achieved by this approach.

FIGURE 6.16 **New Product Development Process**

For example, this approach was used by Chrysler Corporation to design its new line of SC cars including the popular *Neon* sedan. From the very beginning specialists from marketing, engineering, design, manufacturing, quality assurance, and other relevant departments were involved in every stage of the project. Not only did the project meet all of its objectives, it was completed six months ahead of schedule.

*O. Suris, "Competitors Blinded by Chrysler's Neon," *The Wall Street Journal* (January 10, 1994).

can be done in parallel and the project expedited. Start-to-start relationships can depict the concurrent engineering conditions and reduce network detail. Of course, the same result can be accomplished by breaking an activity into small packages that can be implemented in parallel, but this latter approach increases the network and tracking detail significantly.

Finish-to-Finish Relationship

This relationship is found in Figure 6.17. The finish of one activity depends on the finish of another activity. For example, testing cannot be completed any earlier than four days after the prototype is complete. Note that this is not a finish-to-start relationship because the testing of subcomponents can begin before the prototype is completed, but four days of "system" testing is required after the prototype is finished.

Start-to-Finish Relationship

This relationship represents situations in which the finish of an activity depends on the start of another activity. For example, system documentation cannot end until three days after testing has started (see Figure 6.18). Here all the relevant information to complete the system documentation is produced after the first three days of testing.

Combinations of Lag Relationships

More than one lag relationship can be attached to an activity. These relationships are usually start-to-start and finish-to-finish combinations tied to two activities. For example, debug cannot begin until two time units after coding has started. Coding must be finished four days before debug can be finished (see Figure 6.19).

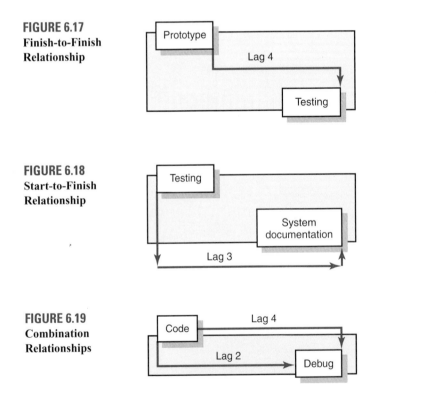

FIGURE 6.17
Finish-to-Finish Relationship

FIGURE 6.18
Start-to-Finish Relationship

FIGURE 6.19
Combination Relationships

An Example Using Lag Relationships—The Forward and Backward Pass

The forward and backward pass procedures are the same as explained earlier in the chapter for finish-to-start relationships (without lags). The modifying technique lies in the need to check each new relationship to see if it alters the start or finish time of another activity.

An example of the outcome of the forward and backward pass is shown in Figure 6.20. Order hardware depends upon the design of the system (start-to-start). Three days into the design of the system (activity A), it is possible to order the required hardware (activity B). It takes four days after the order is placed (activity B) for the hardware to arrive so it can begin to be installed (activity C). After two days of installing the software system (activity D), the testing of the system can begin (activity E). System testing (activity E) can be completed two days after the software is installed (activity D). Preparing system documentation (activity F) can begin once the design is completed (activity A), but it cannot be completed until two days after testing the system (activity E). This final relationship is an example of a finish-to-finish lag.

Note how an activity can have a critical finish and/or start. Activities E and F have critical finishes (zero slack), but their activity starts have 4 and 12 days of slack. It is only the finish of activities E and F that are critical. Conversely, activity A has zero slack to start but has five days of slack to finish. The critical path follows activity start

FIGURE 6.20   Network Using Lags

Hammock activities are frequently used to identify the use of fixed resources or costs over a segment of the project. Typical examples of hammock activities are inspection services, consultants, or construction management services. A hammock activity derives its duration from the time span between other activities. For example, a special color copy machine is needed for a segment of a tradeshow publication project. A hammock activity can be used to indicate the need for this resource and to apply costs over this segment of the project. This hammock is linked from the start of the first activity in the segment that uses the color copy machine to the end of the last activity that uses it. The hammock duration is simply the difference between the EF for the last activity and the ES of the first activity. The duration is computed after the forward pass and hence has no influence on other activity times. Figure 6.21 provides an example of a hammock activity used in a network. The duration for the hammock activity is derived from the early start of activity B and the early finish of activity F; that is, the difference between 13 and 5, or 8 time units. The hammock duration will change if any ES or EF in the chain-sequence changes. Hammock activities are very useful in assigning and controlling indirect project costs.

FIGURE 6.21 **Hammock Activity Example**

Another major use of hammock activities is to aggregate sections of a project. This is similar to developing a subnetwork, but the precedence is still preserved. This approach is sometimes used to present a "macro network" for upper management levels. Using a hammock activity to group activities can facilitate getting the right level of detail for specific sections of a project.

and finish constraints that occur due to the use of the additional relationships available and the imposed lags. You can identify the critical path in Figure 6.20 by following the dotted line on the network.

If a lag relationship exists, each activity must be checked to see if the start or finish is constrained. For example, in the forward pass the EF of activity E (test system) (18) is controlled by the finish of activity D (install software) and the lag of two time units (16 + 2 lag = 18). Finally, in the backward pass, the LS of activity A (design system) is controlled by activity B (order hardware) and the lag relationship to activity A (3 − 3 = 0).

Hammock Activities

Another of the extended techniques uses a *hammock activity*. This type of activity derives its name because it spans over a segment of a project. The hammock activity duration is determined *after* the network plan is drawn. The Snapshot from Practice: Hammock Activities describes how the hammock activity is used.

Summary

Many project managers feel the project network is their most valuable exercise and planning document. Project networks sequence and time-phase the project work, resources, and budgets. Work package tasks are used to develop activities for networks. Every project manager should feel comfortable working in an AON environment. The AON method uses nodes (boxes) for activities and arrows for dependencies. The forward and backward passes establish early and late times for activities. Although most project managers use computers to generate networks and activity times, they find a keen understanding of network development and the ability to compute activity times is invaluable in the field. Computers break down; input errors give false information; some decisions must be made without computer "what if" analysis. Project managers who are well acquainted with network development and AON methods and who are able to compute activity times will encounter fewer problems than project managers less well acquainted. Project networks help to ensure there are no surprises.

Several extensions and modifications have been appended to the original AON method. Lags allow the project planner to more closely replicate the actual conditions found in practice. The use of lags can result in the start or finish of an activity becoming critical. Some computer software simply calls the whole activity critical rather than identifying the start or finish as being critical. Caution should be taken to ensure that lags are not used as a buffer for possible errors in estimating time. Finally, hammock activities are useful in tracking costs of resources used for a particular segment of a project. Hammock activities can also be used to reduce the size of a project network by grouping activities for simplification and clarity. All of the discussed refinements to the original AON methodology contribute toward better planning and control of projects.

Key Terms

Activity	Concurrent engineering	Merge activity
Activity-on-arrow (AOA)	Critical path	Network sensitivity
	Early and late times	Parallel activity
Activity-on-node (AON)	Gantt chart	Slack/float—total and free
Burst activity	Hammock activity	
	Lag relationship	

Review Questions

1. How does the WBS differ from the project network?
2. How are WBS and project networks linked?
3. Why bother creating a WBS? Why not go straight to a project network and forget the WBS?
4. Why is slack important to the project manager?
5. What is the difference between free slack and total slack?
6. Why are lags used in developing project networks?
7. What is a hammock activity, and when is it used?

Exercises

Creating a Project Network

1. Here is a work breakdown structure for a wedding. Use the yellow sticky approach described in the Snapshot from Practice (see p. 161) to create a network for this project.

Note: Do not include summary tasks in the network (i.e., 1.4, Ceremony, is a summary task; 1.2, Marriage license, is not a summary task). Do not consider who would be doing the task in building the network. For example, do not arrange "hiring a band" to occur after "florist" because the same person is responsible for doing both tasks. Focus only on technical dependencies between tasks.

Hint: Start with the last activity (wedding reception), and work your way back to the start of the project. Build the logical sequence of tasks by asking the following question: In order to have or do this, what must be accomplished immediately before this? Once completed, check forward in time by asking this question: Is this task(s) the only thing that is needed immediately before the start of the next task?

Work Breakdown Structure

1. Wedding project
   - 1.1 Decide on date ·
   - 1.2 Marriage license
   - 1.3 Bridal arrangements
     - *1.3.1 Select attendants*
     - *1.3.2 Order dresses*
     - *1.3.3 Fit dresses*
   - 1.4 Ceremony
     - *1.4.1 Rent church*
     - *1.4.2 Florist*
     - *1.4.3 Create/print programs*
     - *1.4.4 Hire photographer*
     - *1.4.5 Wedding ceremony*
   - 1.5 Guests
     - *1.5.1 Develop guest list*
     - *1.5.2 Order invitations*
     - *1.5.3 Address and mail invitations*
     - *1.5.4 Track RSVPs*

1.6 Reception

   1.6.1 Reserve reception hall

   1.6.2 Food and beverage

      1.6.2.1 Choose caterer

      1.6.2.2 Decide on menu

      1.6.2.3 Make final order

   1.6.3 Hire band

   1.6.4 Decorate reception hall

   1.6.5 Wedding reception

Drawing AON Networks

2. Draw a project network from the following information.

Activity	Predecessor
A	None
B	A
C	A
D	A, B, C
E	D
F	D, E

3. Given the following information, draw a project network.

Activity	Predecessor
A	None
B	A
C	A
D	A
E	B
F	C, D
G	E
H	G, F

4. Use the following information to draw a project network.

Activity	Predecessor
A	None
B	A
C	A
D	B
E	B
F	C
G	D, E
H	F
I	F
J	G, H
K	J, I

5. Draw an AON project network from the following information.

Activity	Predecessor
A	None
B	None
C	None
D	A, B
E	C
F	D, E
G	E
H	F, G
I	H

6. Use the following information to draw a project network.

Activity	Predecessor
A	None
B	None
C	A
D	B
E	C, D
F	E
G	E
H	E
I	F
J	G, H
K	H, I, J

AON Network Times

7. From the following information, develop an AON project network. Complete the forward and backward pass, compute the activity slack, and identify the critical path.

Activity	Predecessor	Time (weeks)
A	None	4
B	A	5
C	A	4
D	B	3
E	C, D	6
F	D	2
G	E, F	5

What is the critical path?

How many weeks to complete?

What is the slack for activity F? For activity C?

8. The marketing department of a bank is developing a new mortgage plan for housing contractors. Draw a project network given the information below. Complete the forward and backward pass, compute the activity slack, and identify the critical path.

Activity	Predecessor	Time (weeks)
A	None	3
B	None	4
C	A	2
D	C	5
E	B	7
F	D, E	1
G	D	4
H	F, G	5

What is the critical path?

How many weeks to complete?

What is the slack for activity F? For activity G?

9. The project information for the custom order project of the Air Control Company is presented here. Draw a project network for this project. Compute the early and late activity times and the slack times. Identify the critical path.

ID	Activity	Predecessor	Time
A	Order review	None	2
B	Order standard parts	A	15
C	Produce standard parts	A	10
D	Design custom parts	A	13
E	Software development	A	18
F	Manufacture custom hardware	C, D	15
G	Assemble	B, F	10
H	Test	E, G	5

10. J. Wold, project manager of Print Software, Inc., wants you to prepare a project network; compute the early, late, and slack activity times; determine the planned project duration; and identify the critical path. His assistant has collected the following information for the Color Printer Drivers Software Project:

ID	Description	Predecessor	Time
A	External specifications	None	8
B	Review design features	A	2
C	Document new features	A	3
D	Write software	A	60
E	Program and test	B	60
F	Edit and publish notes	C	2
G	Review manual	D	2
H	Alpha site	E, F	20
I	Print manual	G	10
J	Beta site	H, I	10
K	Manufacture	J	12
L	Release and ship	K	3

11. A large eastern city is requesting federal funding for a park-and-ride project. One of the requirements in the request application is a network plan for the design phase of the project. Catherine Walker, the chief engineer, wants you to develop a project network plan to meet this requirement. She has gathered the activity time estimates and their dependencies shown here. Show your project network with the activity early, late, and slack times. Mark the critical path.

ID	Description	Predecessor	Time
A	Survey	None	5
B	Soils report	A	20
C	Traffic design	A	30
D	Lot layout	A	5
E	Approve design	B, C, D	80
F	Illumination	E	15
G	Drainage	E	30
H	Landscape	E	25
I	Signing	E	20
J	Bid proposal	F, G, H, I	10

12. Given the project network that follows, complete a bar chart for the project. Use the timeline to align your bars. Be sure to show slack for noncritical activities.

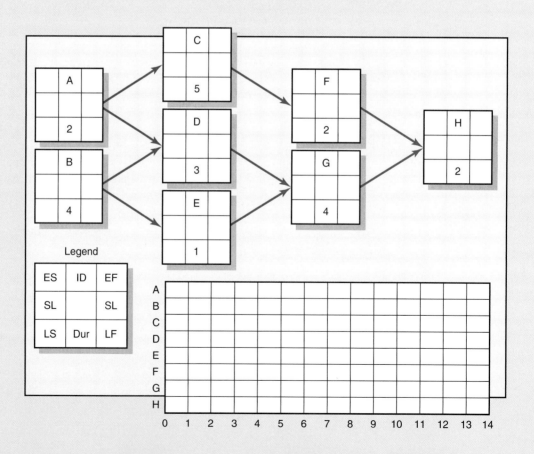

13. Given the project network that follows, complete a bar chart for the project. Use the timeline to align your bars. Be sure to show slack for noncritical activities.

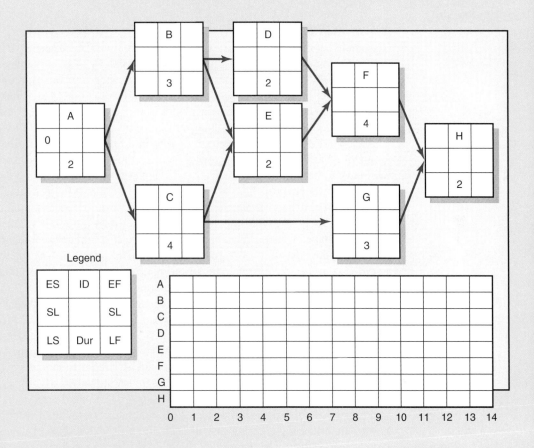

Computer Exercise

14. The planning department of an electronics firm has set up the activities for developing and production of a new CD Player. Given the information below, develop a project network using Microsoft Project. Assume a five-day workweek and the project starts on January 3, 2005.

Activity ID	Description	Activity Predecessor	Activity Time (weeks)
1	Staff	None	2
2	Develop market program	1	3
3	Select channels of distribution	1	8
4	Patent	1	12
5	Pilot production	1	4
6	Test market	5	4
7	Ad promotion	2	4
8	Set up for production	4, 6	16

The project team has requested that you create a network for the project, and determine if the project can be completed in 45 weeks.

15. Using Microsoft Project, set up the network and determine the critical path for Phase 1 of the project. The project workweek will be 6 days.

Whistler Ski Resort Project

Given the coming 2010 Winter Olympics in Vancouver and Whistler, BC, Canada, and the fact that the number of skiing visitors to Whistler has been increasing at an exciting rate, the Whistler Ski Association has been considering construction of another ski lodge and ski complex. The results of an economic feasibility study just completed by members of the staff show that a winter resort complex near the base of Whistler Mountain could be a very profitable venture. The area is accessible by car, bus, train, and air. The board of directors has voted to build the ten-million dollar complex recommended in the study. Unfortunately, due to the short summer season, the complex will have to be built in stages. The first stage (year 1) will contain a day lodge, chair lift, rope tow, generator house (for electricity), and a parking lot designed to accommodate 400 cars and 30 buses. The second and third stages will include a hotel, ice rink, pool, shops, two additional chair lifts, and other attractions. The board has decided that stage one should begin no later than April 1 and be completed by October 1, in time for the next skiing season. You have been assigned the task of project manager, and it is your job to coordinate the ordering of materials and construction activities to ensure the project's completion by the required date.

After looking into the possible sources of materials, you are confronted with the following time estimates. Materials for the chair lift and rope tow will take 30 days and 12 days, respectively, to arrive once the order is submitted. Lumber for the day lodge, generator hut, and foundations will take 9 days to arrive. The electrical and plumbing materials for the day lodge will take 12 days to arrive. The generator will take 12 days to arrive. Before actual construction can begin on the various facilities, a road to the site must be built; this will take 6 days. As soon as the road is in, clearing can begin concurrently on the sites of the day lodge, generator house, chair lift, and rope tow. It is estimated that the clearing task at each site will take 6 days, 3 days, 36 days, and 6 days, respectively. The clearing of the main ski slopes can begin after the area for the chair lift has been cleared; this will take 84 days.

The foundation for the day lodge will take 12 days to complete. Construction of the main framework will take an additional 18 days. After the framework is completed, electrical wiring and plumbing can be installed concurrently. These should take 24 and 30 days, respectively. Finally, the finishing construction on the day lodge can begin; this will take 36 days.

Installation of the chair lift towers can begin once the site is cleared, lumber delivered, and the foundation completed; all this takes 6 days, and the towers take 67 days. Also, when the chair lift site has been cleared, construction of a permanent road to the upper towers can be started; this will take 24 days. While the towers are being installed, the electric motor to drive the chair lift can be installed; the motor can be installed in 24 days. Once the towers are completed and the motor installed, it will take 3 days to install the cable and an additional 12 days to install the chairs.

Installation of the towers for the rope tow can begin once the site is cleared and the foundation is built and poured; it takes 4 days to build the foundation, pour the concrete and let it cure, and 20 days to install the towers for the rope tow. While the towers are being erected, installation of the electric motor to drive the rope tow can begin; this activity will take 24 days. After the towers and motor are installed, the rope tow can be strung in 1 day. The parking lot can be cleared once the rope tow is finished; this task will take 18 days.

The foundation for the generator house can begin at the same time as the foundation for the lodge; this will take 6 days. The main framework for the generator house can begin once the foundation is completed; framing will take 12 days. After the house is framed, the diesel generator can be installed in 18 days. Finishing construction on the generator house can now begin and will take 12 more days.

Assignment:

1. Identify the critical path on your network.
2. Can the project be completed by October 1?

Lag Exercises

16. From the following information, draw the project network. Compute the early, late, and slack times for each activity. Identify the critical path. (Hint: Draw the finish-to-start relationships first.)

ID	Duration	Finish-to-Start Predecessor	Finish-to-Start Lag	Additional Lag Relationships	Lag
A	5	None	0	None	0
B	10	A	0	None	0
C	15	A	0	Start-finish C to D	20
D	5	B	5	Start-start D to E	5
				Finish-finish D to E	25
E	20	B	0	Finish-finish E to F	0
F	15	D	0	None	0
G	10	C	10	Finish-finish G to F	10
H	20	F	0	None	

17. Given the following information, draw the project network. Compute the early, late, and slack times for the project network. Which activities on the critical path have only the start or finish of the activity on the critical path?

ID	Duration	Finish-to-Start Predecessor	Finish-to-Start Lag	Additional Lag Relationships	Lag
A	2	None	0	None	0
B	4	A	0	None	0
C	6	A	0	Finish-finish C to F	7
D	8	A	0	None	0
E	18	B	0	Finish-finish E to G	9
		C	10		
F	2	D	0	None	
G	5	F	0	Start-start G to H	10
H	5	None	0	None	0
I	14	E	0	Finish-finish I to J	5
J	15	G, H	0	None	

18. Given the information in the following lag exercises, compute the early, late, and slack times for the project network. Which activities on the critical path have only the start or finish of the activity on the critical path?

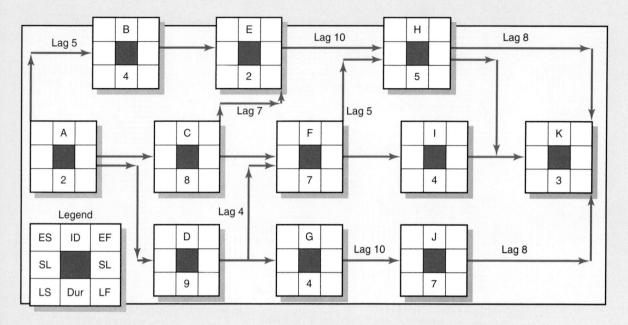

19. Given the network below, compute the early, late, and slack time for each activity.

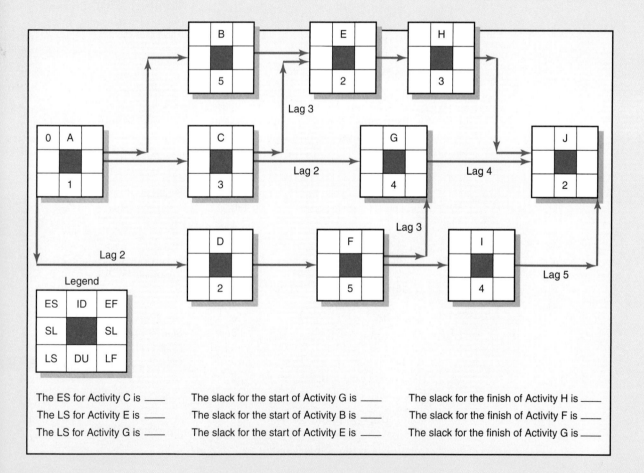

The ES for Activity C is ____   The slack for the start of Activity G is ____   The slack for the finish of Activity H is ____

The LS for Activity E is ____   The slack for the start of Activity B is ____   The slack for the finish of Activity F is ____

The LS for Activity G is ____   The slack for the start of Activity E is ____   The slack for the finish of Activity G is ____

Optical Disk Preinstallation Project

20. The optical disk project team has started gathering the information necessary to develop the project network—predecessor activities and activity times in weeks. The results of their meeting are found in the following table.

Activity	Description	Duration	Predecessor
1	Define scope	6	None
2	Define customer problems	3	1
3	Define data records and relationships	5	1
4	Mass storage requirements	5	2, 3
5	Consultant needs analysis	10	2, 3
6	Prepare installation network	3	4, 5
7	Estimate costs and budget	2	4, 5
8	Design section "point" system	1	4, 5
9	Write request proposal	5	4, 5
10	Compile vendor list	3	4, 5
11	Prepare mgmt. control system	5	6, 7
12	Prepare comparison report	5	9, 10
13	Compare system "philosophies"	3	8, 12
14	Compare total installation	2	8, 12
15	Compare cost of support	3	8, 12
16	Compare customer satisfaction level	10	8, 12
17	Assign philosophies points	1	13
18	Assign installation cost	1	14
19	Assign support cost	1	15
20	Assign customer satisfaction points	1	16
21	Select best system	1	11, 17, 18, 19, 20
22	Order system	1	21

The project team has requested that you create a network for the project, and determine if the project can be completed in 45 weeks.

Case

Nightingale Project—A

You are the assistant project manager to Rassy Brown, who is in charge of the Nightingale project. Nightingale was the code name given to the development of a handheld electronic medical reference guide. Nightingale would be designed for emergency medical technicians and paramedics who need a quick reference guide to use in emergency situations.

Rassy and her project team were developing a project plan aimed at producing 30 working models in time for MedCON, the biggest medical equipment trade show each year. Meeting the MedCON October 25 deadline was critical to success. All the major medical equipment manufacturers demonstrated and took orders for new products at

MedCON. Rassy had also heard rumors that competitors were considering developing a similar product, and she knew that being first to market would have a significant sales advantage. Besides, top management made funding contingent upon developing a workable plan for meeting the MedCON deadline.

The project team spent the morning working on the schedule for Nightingale. They started with the WBS and developed the information for a network, adding activities when needed. Then the team added the time estimates they had collected for each activity. Following is the preliminary information for activities with duration time and predecessors:

Activity	Description	Duration	Predecessor
1	Architectural decisions	10	None
2	Internal specifications	20	1
3	External specifications	18	1
4	Feature specifications	15	1
5	Voice recognition	15	2,3
6	Case	4	2,3
7	Screen	2	2,3
8	Speaker output jacks	2	2,3
9	Tape mechanism	2	2,3
10	Database	40	4
11	Microphone/soundcard	5	4
12	Pager	4	4
13	Barcode reader	3	4
14	Alarm clock	4	4
15	Computer I/O	5	4
16	Review design	10	5,6,7,8,9,10,11,12,13,14,15
17	Price components	5	5,6,7,8,9,10,11,12,13,14,15
18	Integration	15	16,17
19	Document design	35	16
20	Procure prototype components	20	18
21	Assemble prototypes	10	20
22	Lab test prototypes	20	21
23	Field test prototypes	20	19,22
24	Adjust design	20	23
25	Order stock parts	2	24
26	Order custom parts	2	24
27	Assemble first production unit	10	25, FS—8 time units 26, FS—13 time units
28	Test unit	10	27
29	Produce 30 units	15	28
30	Train sales representatives	10	29

Use any project network computer program available to you to develop the schedule for activities (see Case Appendix for further instructions)—noting late and early times, the critical path, and estimated completion for the project.

Prepare a short memo that addresses the following questions:

1. Will the project as planned meet the October 25th deadline?
2. What activities lie on the critical path?
3. How sensitive is this network?

Case

Nightingale Project—B

Rassy and the team were concerned with the results of your analysis. They spent the afternoon brainstorming alternative ways for shortening the project duration. They rejected outsourcing activities because most of the work was developmental in nature and could only be done in-house. They considered altering the scope of the project by eliminating some of the proposed product features. After much debate, they felt they could not compromise any of the core features and be successful in the marketplace. They then turned their attention to accelerating the completion of activities through overtime and adding additional technical manpower. Rassy had built into her proposal a discretionary fund of $200,000. She was willing to invest up to half of this fund to accelerate the project, but wanted to hold onto at least $100,000 to deal with unexpected problems. After a lengthy discussion, her team concluded that the following activities could be reduced at the specified cost:

- Development of voice recognition system could be reduced from 15 days to 10 days at a cost of $15,000.
- Creation of database could be reduced from 40 days to 35 days at a cost of $35,000.
- Document design could be reduced from 35 days to 30 days at a cost of $25,000.
- External specifications could be reduced from 18 days to 12 days at a cost of $20,000.
- Procure prototype components could be reduced from 20 days to 15 days at a cost of $30,000.
- Order stock parts could be reduced from 15 days to 10 days at a cost of $20,000.

Ken Clark, a development engineer, pointed out that the network contained only finish-to-start relationships and that it might be possible to reduce project duration by creating start-to-start lags. For example, he said that his people would not have to wait for all of the field tests to be completed to begin making final adjustments in the design. They could start making adjustments after the first 15 days of testing. The project team spent the remainder of the day analyzing how they could introduce lags into the network to hopefully shorten the project. They concluded that the following finish-to-start relationships could be converted into lags:

- Document design could begin 5 days after the start of the review design.
- Adjust design could begin 15 days after the start of field tests.
- Ordering stock parts could begin 5 days after the start of adjust design.
- Ordering custom parts could begin 5 days after the start of adjust design.
- Training sales personnel could begin 5 days after the start of unit test and completed 5 days after the production of 30 units.

As the meeting adjourns, Rassy turns to you and tells you to assess the options presented and try to develop a schedule that will meet the October 25th deadline. You are to prepare a report to be presented to the project team that answers the following questions:

1. Is it possible to meet the deadline?
2. If so, how would you recommend changing the original schedule (Part A) and why? Assess the relative impact of crashing activities versus introducing lags to shorten project duration.

3. What would the new schedule look like?

4. What other factors should be considered before finalizing the schedule?

CASE APPENDIX: TECHNICAL DETAILS

Create your project schedule and assess your options based on the following information:

1. The project will begin the first working day in January.

2. The following holidays are observed: January 1, Memorial Day (last Monday in May), July 4th, Labor Day (first Monday in September), Thanksgiving Day (fourth Thursday in November), December 25 and 26.

3. If a holiday falls on a Saturday, then Friday will be given as an extra day off; if it falls on a Sunday, then Monday will be given as a day off.

4. The project team works Monday through Friday.

5. If you choose to reduce the duration of any one of the activities mentioned, then it must be for the specified time and cost (i.e., you cannot choose to reduce database to 37 days at a reduced cost; you can only reduce it to 35 days at a cost of $35,000).

6. You can only spend up to $100,000 to reduce project activities; lags do not contain any additional costs.

Case

Pilot's Stadium Case

The G&E Company is preparing a bid to build the new 47,000 seat Pilot's baseball stadium. The construction must start on June 1, 2006, and be completed in time for the start of the 2009 season. A penalty clause of $50,000 per day of delay beyond April 1, 2009, is written into the contract.

Ben Keith, the president of the company expressed optimism at obtaining the contract and revealed that the company could net as much as $2 million on the project. He also said the prospects for future projects are quite good since there is projected renaissance in building ball parks with modern luxury boxes.

EXERCISE

Given the information provided in Table 6.3, construct a network schedule for the stadium project and answer the following questions:

1. Will the project be able to be completed by the April 1st deadline? How long will it take?

2. What is the critical path for the project?

3. Based on the schedule would you recommend that G&E pursue this contact? Why? Include a one-page Gantt chart for the stadium schedule.

CASE APPENDIX: TECHNICAL DETAILS OF THE BASEBALL STADIUM

The baseball stadium is an outdoor structure with a retractable roof. The project begins with clearing the site, an activity that lasts 60 days. Once the site is clear, work can start simultaneously on the structure itself and demolishing an adjacent building site. This demolition is necessary to create a construction stage for storing materials and equipment. It will take 30 days to demolish the buildings and another 30 days to set up the construction site.

The work on the stadium begins by driving 160 support pilings, which will take 120 days. Next comes the pouring of the lower concrete bowl (120 days). Once this is done and the construction site has been set up, then the pouring of the main concourse (120 days), the installation of the playing field (90 days), and the construction of the upper steel bowl can occur (120 days).

Once the concourse and upper bowl are completed, work can start simultaneously on building the luxury boxes (90 days), installing the seats (120 days), installing the scoreboard (30 days), and installing stadium infrastructure (120 days) which includes: bathrooms, lockers, restaurants, etc. Once the seats are installed then the steel canopy can be constructed (60 days) followed by the installation of the lights (30 days).

The retractable roof represents the most significant technical challenge to the project. Building the roof track supports (90 days) can begin after the lower concrete bowl is constructed. At this time the dimensions of the roof can be finalized and the construction of the roof at a separate site can begin (180 days). After the roof supports are completed then the roof tracks can be installed (90 days). Once the tracks and the roof are completed then the roof can be installed and made operational (90 days). Once all activities are completed it will take 15 days to inspect the stadium.

For purposes of this case assume the following:

1. The following holidays are observed: January 1, Memorial Day (last Monday in May), July 4th, Labor Day (first Monday in September), Thanksgiving Day (4th Thursday in November), December 25 and 26.

2. If a holiday falls on a Saturday then Friday will be given as an extra day off, and if it falls on a Sunday then Monday will be given as a day off.

3. The construction crew work Monday through Friday.

TABLE 6.3
Pilot's Stadium Case

ID	Activity	Duration	Predecessors
1	***Baseball Stadium***		
2	Clear stadium site	60 days	—
3	Demolish building	30 days	2
4	Set up construction site	70 days	3
5	Drive support piles	120 days	2
6	Power lower concrete bowl	120 days	5
7	Pour main concourse	120 days	3,6
8	Install playing field	90 days	3,6
9	Construct upper steel bowl	120 days	3,6
10	Install seats	120 days	7,9
11	Build luxury boxes	90 days	7,9
12	Install Jumbotron	30 days	7,9
13	Stadium infrastructure	120 days	7,9
14	Construct steel canopy	60 days	10
15	Light installation	30 days	14
16	Build roof supports	90 days	6
17	Construct roof	180 days	16
18	Install roof tracks	90 days	16
19	Install roof	90 days	17,18
20	Inspection	15 days	8,11,13,15,19

Appendix 6.1

Activity-on-Arrow Method

DESCRIPTION

The activity-on-arrow (AOA) approach also uses the arrow and node as network building blocks. However, in this approach *the arrow represents an individual project activity that requires time.* The length and slope of the arrow have no significance. *The node represents an event; it is usually presented as a small circle.* Events represent points in time but do not consume time. Each activity on the network has a start and end event node. For example, if the activity were "install software," the start event could be "start installing software" and the end event could be "finish software installation." Event nodes are numbered with the start node having a smaller number than the end event node (see Figure A6.1). These two numbers are used to identify the activity start node to finish node (79–80). As we shall see shortly, an event node can serve as a start or end node for one or more activities, and an end event node can serve as a start node for one or more activities that immediately follow.

Figure A6.2 illustrates several methods for showing AOA activity relationships in a project network. Figure A6.2A simply tells the project manager that activity X must be completed before activity Y can begin. Activity X can also be identified as activity 10–11. Note that event 11 is the finish event for activity X and the start event for activity Y. All AOA networks use this method to link activities and establish dependencies among activities.

Figure A6.2B tells us that activities R, S, and T are parallel, that is, independent, and can occur concurrently if the project manager wishes; however, activities R, S, and T must all be completed before activity U can begin. Observe how event 20 is a common ending event for activities R, S, and T and the start event for activity U. Figure 6.2C shows that activity M must be completed before activities N and O can begin. When activity M is complete, activities N and O are considered independent and can occur simultaneously if you wish. Event 54 is called a burst event because more than one activity arrow leaves (bursts from) it. Figure A6.2D tells us activity E and F can go on together, but both must be completed before activities G and H can begin. Event 23 is both a merge event and a burst event. Theoretically, an event is unlimited in the number of activities (arrows) that can lead into (merge) or out of (burst from) it. Figure A6.2E illustrates parallel paths A–C and B–D. Activity A must precede activity C and B precede D. Paths A–C and B–D are independent of each other. Let us apply these fundamentals to the simple Koll Business Center project.

FIGURE A6.1
AOA Network Building Blocks

FIGURE A6.2
Activity-on-Arrow
Network
Fundamentals

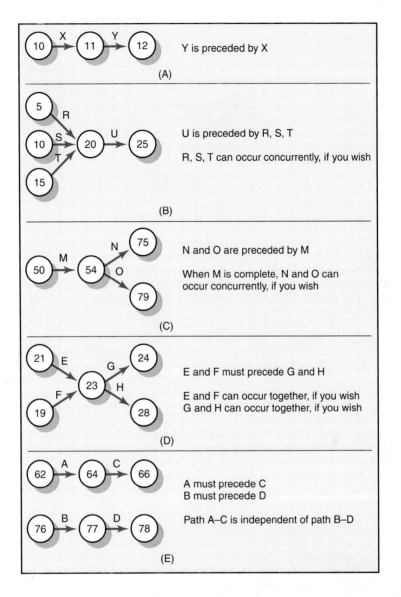

DESIGN OF AN AOA PROJECT NETWORK

You are now ready to use the information in Table A6.1 to draw an AOA network of the Koll Business Center. From the information given, the first four activities can be drawn as shown in Figure A6.3. Activity A (1–2) (Application approval) must be completed before activities B (2–4), C (2–3), and D (2–5) can begin.

At this point we run into a problem common in AOA networks. Activity E is preceded by activities B and C. The natural inclination is to draw your activity arrows for B and C from event 2 straight to event 4, which is the beginning event for activity E. However, the result would be that activities B and C would both have the same identification numbers (2–4). In cases like this where two or more activities are parallel and have the same start and finish nodes, a dummy activity is inserted to ensure each activity has its unique identification number. A dummy activity is depicted by a dashed arrow and its duration is zero. The dummy activity could be inserted before or after

TABLE A6.1
Network Information

	KOLL BUSINESS CENTER			
	County Engineers Design Department			
Activity	Description		Preceding Activity	Activity Time
A	Application approval		None	5
B	Construction plans		A	15
C	Traffic study		A	10
D	Service availability check		A	5
E	Staff report		B, C	15
F	Commission approval		B, C, D	10
G	Wait for construction		F	170
H	Occupancy		E, G	35

FIGURE A6.3
Partial Koll Business Center AOA Network

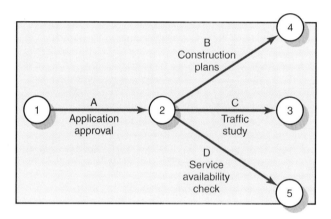

either activity B or C as shown in Figure A6.4 (see parts A through D). In Figure A6.4E we placed it after activity C with its own identification of X or 3–4.

Activity F in Figure A6.4E denotes another network problem in which activity dependencies exist but it is not convenient to connect the activities. In this case, the dummy activity can be used to maintain the logic of the network dependencies. Activity F is preceded by activities B, C, and D. Dummy activity Y (4–5) is necessary because activity B precedes both E and F. The dummy activity maintains the intended logic and sequence. Dummy activity 3–5 can be removed because it is redundant; that is, its removal does not change the intended relationships—the end event 4 precedes activity F. Typically, the first pass in drawing your network will include many dummy activities. After several passes forward and backward through the network, you will find ways to remove some of the dummy activities that are there solely to maintain logic. However, when two or more parallel activities have the same beginning and ending event nodes, dummy activities cannot be avoided. Figure A6.5 has a completed network for the Koll design project.

In this simple project network no activity networks cross over each other, a situation which is very rare. Remember the length and slope of the arrows is arbitrary. The activity durations are included and found below the arrows, near the middle. You should work through the AOA network exercises before moving to the next section. Your familiarity with the activity/event approach will help your initial understanding of the forward and backward pass on an AOA network.

FIGURE A6.4
Partial AOA Koll
Network

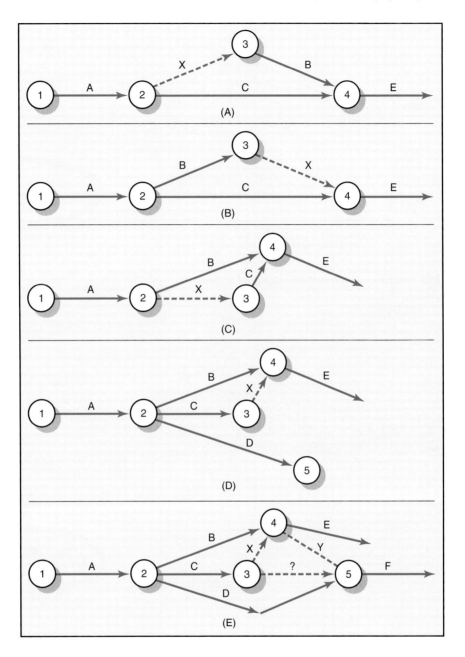

Forward Pass—Earliest Times

The forward pass in AOA uses the same concepts found in the AON procedure. The major difference lies in recognition and use of events to set early and late start and finish times for activities. Figure A6.6 shows the Koll design project with all the activity durations and early start and finish times. Also near each event is a box that will allow us to record event times and slack. In the field this box is sometimes called a "T-box" because the shape within the box forms the letter T. There are many variations of the T-box found in the field, but they all use the basic T format.

The forward pass starts with the first activity(ies) and traces each path through the network. As in AON, you *add* (cumulate) the activity times along the path. When you

FIGURE A6.5 **Activity-on-Arrow Network**

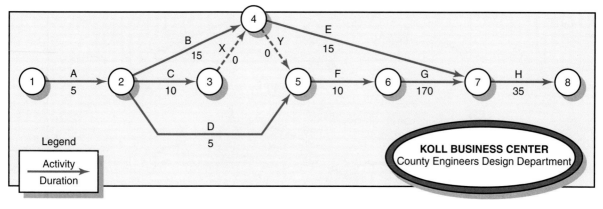

FIGURE A6.6 **Activity-on-Arrow Network Forward Pass**

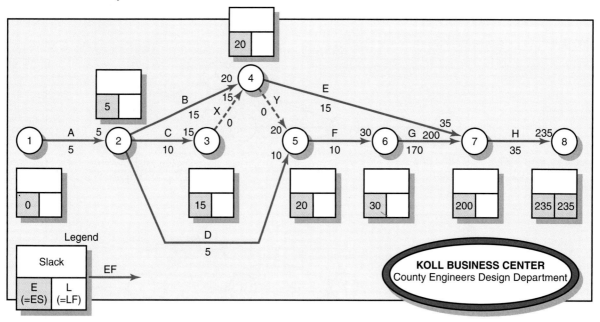

come to a merge event, you select the largest early finish (EF) of all the activities merging to that event. Let's work through Figure A6.6. Event 1 is the project start event; therefore, the earliest that event can occur is time zero. This early event time for event 1 is placed in the lower left side of the event box. The early event time is also the ES for any activity bursting from an event. Therefore, the zero in the box for event 1 is also the early start for activity A. The early finish for activity A is 5 workdays (ES + Dur = EF or 0 + 5 = 5). The EF for the activity is placed at the head of the arrow. The earliest event 2 can occur is the instant activity A is complete, which is 5 workdays; therefore, this time is placed in the lower left T-box of event 2. Again, note that the early event time is also the ES for any activity using the event as a start event. Hence, the ES for activities B, C, and D is 5 workdays. The EF for activity B is 20 (ES + Dur = EF), for activity C is 15, and for activity D is 10. (See the head of the arrow for each activity.) The ES for the dummy activity (3–4) is 15, and its EF is 15 (15 + 0 = 15). Although the dummy activity has zero duration, it must be included in the forward and backward pass computations.

At this point you must determine the early event times for events 4 and 5. Both are merge events that require selection among activities merging into these events. Event 4 has B and X, the dummy activity (3–4). The largest EF for these two activities (20 and 15) is 20, which controls the early event time for event 4. Similarly, event 5 is controlled by activities D and Y. Because activity Y has the largest early finish (20 versus 10 workdays for activity D), it establishes the early event time for event 5 and activity F. Times are cumulated until merge event 7. The EFs for activities E and G are 35 and 200 workdays, respectively. Thus, event 7 and activity H have early times of 200 workdays. The early finish for the project is 235 workdays. Assuming we accept this planned duration of 235 days for the project, the LF for event 8 becomes 235 days, and you are ready to compute the backward pass.

Backward Pass—Latest Times

The backward pass procedure is similar to that used in the AON procedure. You start with the last project event node(s) and *subtract* activity times along each path (LF − Dur = LS) until you reach a burst event. When this happens, you pick the *smallest* LS of all the activities bursting from the event; this number denotes the latest that event can occur and not delay the project. Let's trace the backward pass for part of the Koll design project.

Figure A6.7 displays the late times for the events and activities. The late start for activity H is 200 days (LF − Dur = LS or 235 − 35 = 200). This time is found at the tail of the arrow. Because event 7 is not a burst event, the late start for activity H becomes the late time for event 7. This procedure continues until you reach event 4, which is a burst event. The LS for activity E is 185 and for activity Y is 20. The smallest

FIGURE A6.7   Activity-on-Arrow Network Backward Pass

FIGURE A6.8   **Activity-on-Arrow Network Backward Pass, Forward Pass, and Slack**

time is 20 days and is the late time for event 4. The next burst event is event 2. Here the LS for activities B, C, and D are 5, 10, and 15 days, respectively. Activity B controls the late event time for event 2, which is 5 workdays. The late event time is also the LF for any activity using the event as an end event. For example, the late time for event 7 is 200 workdays; thus, activities E and G can finish no later than day 200, or the project will be delayed.

With the backward pass complete, the slack and critical path can be identified. Figure A6.8 presents the completed network. The event slack is entered above the T in the event box. Activity slack is the difference between LS and ES or LF and EF. For example, the slack for activity E is 165 days—LS − ES (185 − 20 = 165) or LF − EF (200 − 35 = 165). What are the slack values for activities B, C, and D? The answers are zero workdays (5 − 5 = 0 or 20 − 20 = 0), 5 workdays (10 − 5 = 5 or 20 − 15 = 5), and 10 workdays (15 − 5 = 10 or 20 − 10 = 10), respectively. The critical path is A, B, Y, F, G, H.

Compare the networks found in Figure A6.8 and in chapter text Figure 6.8 to see the similarities between the AOA and AON methods. As in the AON method, if the early and late time for the end project event are the same (L = E or LF = EF), the slack on the critical path will be zero. If the times are not the same, the slack on the critical path will equal the difference (L − E or LF − EF).

Computer-Generated Networks

Figure A6.9 presents a generic AOA computer output for the custom order project. AOA networks identify activities by the beginning and ending nodes—for example, the software development activity is identified as activity 2–6. Its duration is 18 time units; ES = 2; EF = 20; LS = 22; and LF = 40 time units. The critical path is 1, 2, 3, 4, 5, 6, 7. Compare the AOA computer output in Figure A6.9 with the AON computer output

FIGURE A6.9   **Air Control Inc. Custom Order Project—AOA Network Diagram**

TABLE A6.2
Comparison of AON and AOA Methods

AON Method

Advantages
1. No dummy activities are used.
2. Events are not used.
3. AON is easy to draw if dependencies are not intense.
4. Activity emphasis is easily understood by first-level managers.
5. The CPM approach uses deterministic times to construct networks.

Disadvantages
1. Path tracing by activity number is difficult. If the network is not available, computer outputs must list the predecessor and successor activities for each activity.
2. Network drawing and understanding are more difficult when dependencies are numerous.

AOA Method

Advantages
1. Path tracing is simplified by activity/event numbering scheme.
2. AOA is easier to draw if dependencies are intense.
3. Key events or milestones can easily be flagged.

Disadvantages
1. Use of dummy activities increases data requirements.
2. Emphasis on events can detract from activities. Activity delays cause events and projects to be late.

in chapter Figure 6.10. Bar charts are identical to those developed for AON networks; see Chapter Figure 6.11.

CHOICE OF METHOD—AON OR AOA

Your choice of method depends on the importance of various advantages and disadvantages of each method. Table A6.2 will assist you in making your choice.

SUMMARY

In AOA networks, dummy activities meet two needs. First, when two parallel activities have the same start and end nodes, a dummy must be inserted to give each activity a unique identification number (see activity X in Figure A6.8). Next, dummy activities can be used to clarify dependency relationships (see activity Y in Figure A6.8). Dummy activities are very useful when activity dependencies are far apart on the network. In AOA networks the early event time is the ES for any activity emanating from the event. Conversely, the late event time is the LF for any activity merging to the event. The major advantage of the AOA method is the avoidance of having to list all the predecessor and successor activities for each activity in the network so activity sequence and dependency can be traced when a network is not available or shows incomplete information. Computer output is reduced manyfold.

REVIEW QUESTIONS

1. How do the building blocks of AON and AOA differ?
2. What are the purposes of dummy or pseudo activities?
3. How do activities differ from events?

APPENDIX EXERCISES

1. Use the information found in the text exercises 3 and 4 to draw AOA networks. Include the activity and event times on the network as shown in Figure A6.8.
2. Use the information found in the text exercise 11 to draw an AOA network. Include the activity and event times on the network as shown in Figure A6.8.
3. Given the project network that follows, compute the early, late, and slack times for the project. Be sure to show the early finish and late start times on your network.

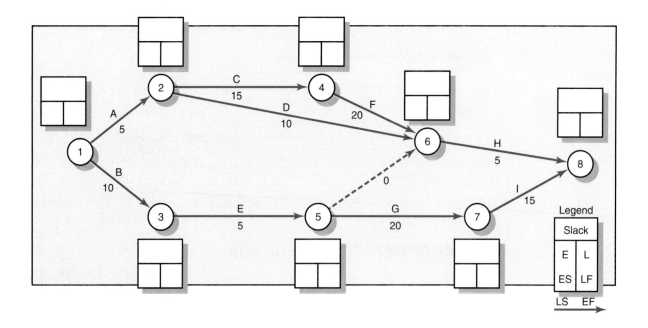

4. Given the project network that follows, compute the early, late, and slack times for the project. Be sure to show the early finish and late start times on your network.

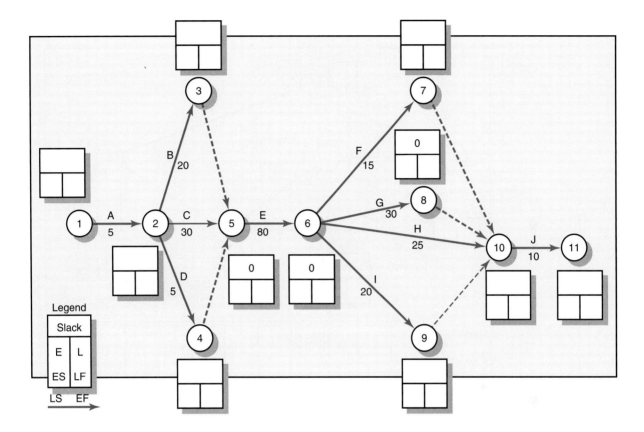

5. Given the project network that follows, complete the bar chart for this project. Use the timeline to align your bars. Be sure to use the legend to show slack for noncritical activities.

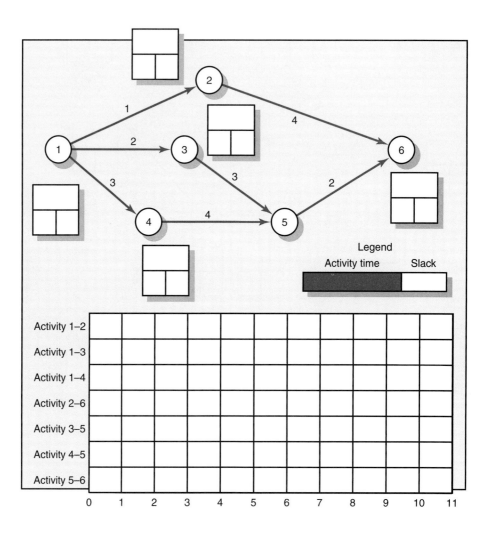

6. Given the project network that follows, draw a bar chart for this project. Use the timeline to align your bars. Be sure to show slack for noncritical activities.

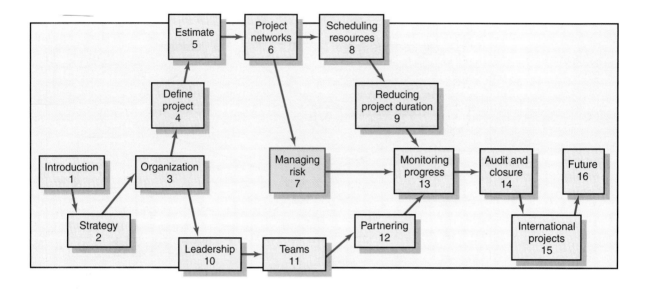

Managing Risk

Risk Management Process

Step 1: Risk Identification

Step 2: Risk Assessment

Step 3: Risk Response Development

Contingency Planning

Contingency Funding and Time Buffers

Step 4: Risk Response Control

Change Control Management

Summary

Appendix 7.1: PERT and PERT Simulation

CHAPTER SEVEN

Managing Risk

Great deeds are usually wrought at great risk.
—Herodotus, Greek historian

Every project manager understands risks are inherent in projects. No amount of planning can overcome *risk,* or the inability to control chance events. In the context of projects, risk is an uncertain event or condition that, if it occurs, has a positive or negative effect on project objectives. A risk has a cause and, if it occurs a consequence. For example, a cause may be a flu virus or change in scope requirements. The event is that team members get striken with the flu or the product has to be redesigned. If either of these uncertain events occurs, it will impact the cost, schedule, and quality of the project.

Some potential risk events can be identified before the project starts—such as equipment malfunction or change in technical requirements. Risks can be anticipated consequences, like schedule slippages or cost overruns. Risks can be beyond imagination like the September 11, 2001, attack on the Twin Towers in New York City. While risks can have positive consequences such as unexpected price reduction in materials, the focus of this chapter is on what can go wrong and the risk management process.

Risk management attempts to recognize and manage potential and unforeseen trouble spots that may occur when the project is implemented. Risk management identifies as many risk events as possible (what can go wrong), minimizes their impact (what can be done about the event before the project begins), manages responses to those events that do materialize (contingency plans), and provides contingency funds to cover risk events that actually materialize.

Risk Management Process

Figure 7.1 presents a graphic model of the risk management dilemma. The chances of a risk event occurring (e.g., an error in time estimates, cost estimates, or design technology) are greatest in the concept, planning, and start-up phases of the project. The cost impact of a risk event in the project is less if the event occurs earlier rather than later. The early stages of the project represent the period when the opportunity for minimizing the impact or working around a potential risk exists. Conversely, as the project passes the halfway mark, the cost of a risk event occurring increases rapidly. For example, the risk event of a design flaw occurring after a prototype has been made has a greater cost or time impact than if the event occurred in the startup phase of the project. Clearly, identifying project risk events and deciding a response before the project begins is a more prudent approach than not attempting to manage risk.

FIGURE 7.1
Risk Event Graph

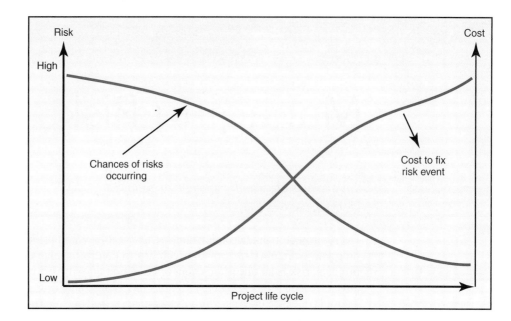

The cost of mismanaged risk control early on in the project is magnified by the ill-fated 1999 NASA Mars Climate Orbiter. Investigations revealed that Lockheed Martin botched the design of critical navigation software. While flight computers on the ground did calculations based on pounds of thrust per second, the spacecraft's computer software used metric systems called newtons. A check to see if the values were compatible was never done.

"Our check and balances processes did not catch an error like this that should have been caught," said Ed Weiler, NASA's associate administrator for space science. "That is the bottom line. Processes that were in place were not followed." (*Orlando Sentinel,* 1999.) After the nine-month journey to the Red Planet the $125 million probe approached Mars at too low an altitude and burned up in the planet's atmosphere.

Risk management is a proactive approach rather than reactive. It is a preventive process designed to ensure that surprises are reduced and that negative consequences associated with undesirable events are minimized. It also prepares the project manager to take risk when a time, cost, and/or technical advantage is possible. Successful management of project risk gives the project manager better control over the future and can significantly improve chances of reaching project objectives on time, within budget, and meeting required technical (functional) performance.

The sources of project risks are unlimited. There are sources external to the organization, such as inflation, market acceptance, exchange rates, and government regulations. In practice, these risk events are often referred to as "threats" to differentiate them from those that are not within the project manager's or team's responsibility area. (Later we will see budgets for such risk events are placed in a "management reserve" contingency budget.) Since such external risks are usually considered before the decision to go ahead with the project, they will be excluded from the discussion of project risks. However, external risks are extremely important and must be addressed.

The major components of the risk management process are depicted in Figure 7.2. Each step will be examined in more detail in the remainder of the chapter.

FIGURE 7.2
**The Risk
Management Process**

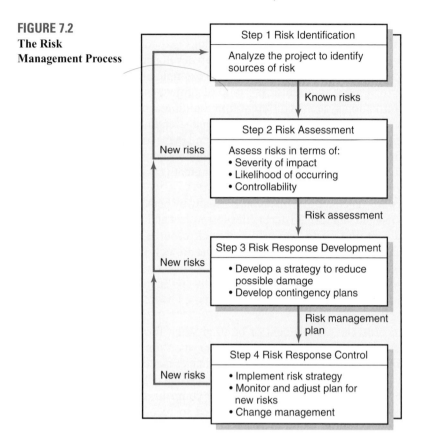

Step 1 Risk Identification

Analyze the project to identify sources of risk

→ Known risks

New risks

Step 2 Risk Assessment

Assess risks in terms of:
• Severity of impact
• Likelihood of occurring
• Controllability

→ Risk assessment

New risks

Step 3 Risk Response Development

• Develop a strategy to reduce possible damage
• Develop contingency plans

→ Risk management plan

New risks

Step 4 Risk Response Control

• Implement risk strategy
• Monitor and adjust plan for new risks
• Change management

Step 1: Risk Identification

The risk management process begins by trying to generate a list of all the possible risks that could affect the project. Typically the project manager pulls together, during the planning phase, a risk management team consisting of core team members and other relevant stakeholders. The team uses brainstorming and other problem identifying techniques to identify potential problems. Participants are encouraged to keep an open mind and generate as many probable risks as possible. More than one project has been bushwhacked by an event that members thought was preposterous in the beginning. Later during the assessment phase, participants will have a chance to analyze and filter out unreasonable risks.

One common mistake that is made early in the risk identification process is to focus on consequences and not on the events that could produce consequences. For example, team members may identify failing to meet schedule as a major risk. What they need to focus on are the events that could cause this to happen (i.e., poor estimates, adverse weather, shipping delays, etc.). Only by focusing on actual events can potential solutions be found.

The focus in the beginning should be on risks that can affect the whole project as opposed to a specific section of the project or network. After the macro risks have been identified, specific areas can be checked. An effective tool for identifying specific risks is the work breakdown structure (WBS). Use of the WBS reduces the chance a risk event will be missed. On large projects multiple risk teams are organized around specific deliverables and submit their risk management reports to the project manager.

A risk profile is another tool that can help management teams identify and eventually analyze risks. A risk profile is a list of questions that address traditional areas of uncertainty on a project. These questions have been developed and refined from previous, similar projects. Figure 7.3 provides a partial example of a risk profile.

Good risk profiles are tailored to the type of project in question. For example, building an information system is different from building a new car. They are organization specific. Risk profiles recognize the unique strengths and weaknesses of the firm. Finally, risk profiles address both technical and management risks. For example, the profile shown in Figure 7.3 asks questions about design (*Does the design depend upon unrealistic assumptions?*) and work environment (*Do people cooperate across functional boundaries?*).

Risk profiles are generated and maintained usually by personnel from the project office. They are updated and refined during the postproject audit (see Chapter 14). These profiles, when kept up to date, can be a powerful resource in the risk management process. The collective experience of the firm's past projects resides in their questions.

It is even possible to acquire good risk profiles. Many consulting firms sell them as part of their project management services. The Software Engineering Institute offers in its *Continuous Risk Management Guidebook* a detailed list of questions for evaluating risks on software projects.

Historical records can complement or be used when formal risk profiles are not available. Project teams can investigate what happened on similar projects in the past to identify potential risks. For example, a project manager can check the on-time performance of selected vendors to gauge the threat of shipping delays. IT project managers can access "best practices" papers detailing other companies' experiences converting software systems. Inquiries should not be limited to recorded data. Savvy project managers tap the wisdom of others by seeking the advice of veteran project managers.

The risk identification process should not be limited to just the core team. Input from customers, sponsors, subcontractors, vendors, and other stakeholders should be solicited. Relevant stakeholders can be formally interviewed or included on the risk

FIGURE 7.3
Partial Risk Profile for Product Development Project

Technical Requirements

Are the requirements stable?

Design

Does the design depend on unrealistic or optimistic assumptions?

Testing

Will testing equipment be available when needed?

Development

Is the development process supported by a compatible set of procedures, methods, and tools?

Schedule

Is the schedule dependent upon the completion of other projects?

Budget

How reliable are the cost estimates?

Quality

Are quality considerations built into the design?

Management

Do people know who has authority for what?

Work Environment

Do people work cooperatively across functional boundaries?

Staffing

Is staff inexperienced or understaffed?

Customer

Does the customer understand what it will take to complete the project?

Contractors

Are there any ambiguities in contractor task definitions?

management team. Not only do these players have a valuable perspective, but by involving them in the risk management process they also become more committed to project success.

One of the keys to success in risk identification is attitude. While a "can do" attitude is essential during implementation, project managers have to encourage critical thinking when it comes to risk identification. The goal is to find problems before they happen, and participants need to believe in Murphy's law—"anything that can go wrong, will go wrong."

The WBS and risk profiles are useful tools for making sure no stones are left unturned. At the same time, when done well the number of risks identified can be overwhelming and a bit discouraging. Initial optimism can be replaced with griping and cries of "what have we gotten ourselves into?" It is important that project managers set the right tone and complete the risk management process so members regain confidence in themselves and the project.

Step 2: Risk Assessment

Step 1 produces a list of potential risks. Not all of these risks deserve attention. Some are trivial and can be ignored, while others poise serious threats to the welfare of the project. Managers have to develop methods for sifting through the list of risks eliminating inconsequential or redundant ones and stratifying worthy ones in terms of importance and need for attention.

Scenario analysis is the easiest and most commonly used technique for analyzing risks. Team members assess each risk in terms of:

1. The undesirable event.
2. All the outcomes of the event's occurrence.
3. The magnitude or severity of the event's impact.
4. Chances/probability of the event happening.
5. When the event might occur in the project.
6. Interaction with other parts of this or other projects.

For example, assume the chances of a resource shortage of a particular skill are about 80 percent. The outcomes could be a delayed project, tighter scheduling and less flexibility, increased cost, etc. The impact could be a 10 percent increase in cost and a 5 percent delay in project duration. The shortage will show up in the design stage of the project. A delay in this project may delay other projects or require a change in priorities. Having this information available facilitates the assessment of each risk event worthy of attention.

Documentation of scenario analyses can be seen in various risk assessment forms used by companies. Figure 7.4 is a partial example of a risk assessment form used on an IS project involving the upgrade from Windows Office 97 to Windows Office 2000XP. The project team identified risks, including interface problems with current software systems, the system freezing after installation, end-users resisting and complaining about the changes, and hardware equipment malfunctioning. In addition to assessing the chances, severity, and when the event is likely to occur, the project team also assessed whether they would be able to detect that the event was going to occur in time to take mitigating action. Notice that the team rated the detection difficulty "high" (#5) for the system freezing since systems crash without warning, while "user backlash" was rated medium (#3) because a ground swell of resistance could be detected before there is open rebellion.

FIGURE 7.4
Risk Assessment Form

Risk Event	Likelihood	Impact	Detection Difficulty	When
Interface problems	4	4	4	Conversion
System freezing	2	5	5	Start-up
User backlash	4	3	3	Postinstallation
Hardware malfunctioning	1	5	5	Installation

Often organizations find it useful to categorize the severity of different risks into some form of risk assessment matrix. The matrix is typically structured around the impact and likelihood of the risk event. For example, the risk matrix presented in Figure 7.5 consists of a 5 × 5 array of elements with each element representing a different set of impact and likelihood values.

The matrix is divided into red, yellow, and green zones representing major, moderate, and minor risks, respectively. The red zone is centered on the top right corner of the matrix (high impact/high likelihood), while the green zone is centered on the bottom left corner (low impact/low likelihood). The moderate risk, yellow zone extends down the middle of the matrix. Since impact is generally considered more important than likelihood (a 10-percent chance of losing $1,000,000 is usually considered a more severe risk than a 90 percent chance of losing $1,000), the red zone (major risk) extends farther down the high impact column.

Using the Windows Office 2000 project again as an example, interface problems and system freezing would be placed in the red zone (major risk), while user backlash and hardware malfunctioning would be placed in the yellow zone (moderate risk).

FIGURE 7.5
Risk Severity Matrix

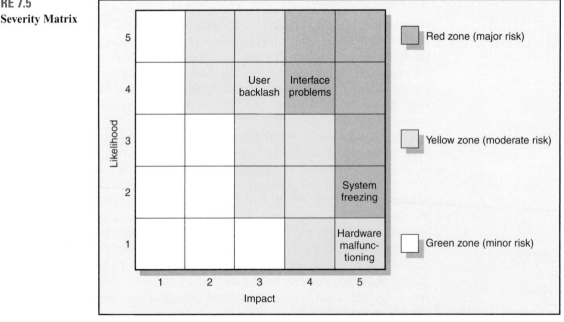

The risk severity matrix provides a basis for prioritizing which risks to address. Red zone risks receive first priority followed by yellow zone risks. Green zone risks are typically considered inconsequential and ignored unless their status changes.

Failure Mode and Effects Analysis (FMEA) extends the risk severity matrix by including ease of detection in the equation:

$$\text{Impact} \times \text{Probability} \times \text{Detection} = \text{Risk Value}$$

Each of the three dimensions is rated according to a five-point scale. For example, detection is defined as the ability of the project team to discern that the risk event is imminent. A score of 1 would be given if even a chimpanzee could spot the risk coming. The highest detection score of 5 would be given to events that could only be discovered after it is too late (i.e., system freezing). Similar anchored scales would be applied for severity of impact and the probability of the event occurring. The weighting of the risks is then based on their overall score. For example, a risk with an impact in the "1" zone with a very low probability and an easy detection score might score a 1 ($1 \times 1 \times 1 = 1$). Conversely, a high-impact risk with a high probability and impossible to detect would score 125 ($5 \times 5 \times 5 = 125$). This broad range of numerical scores allows for easy stratification of risk according to overall significance.

Probability Analysis

There are many statistical techniques available to the project manager that can assist in assessing project risk. Decision trees have been used to assess alternative courses of action using expected values. Statistical variations of net present value (NPV) have been used to assess cash flow risks in projects. Correlations between past projects' cash flow and S-curves (cumulative project cost curve—baseline—over the life of the project) have been used to assess cash flow risks.

PERT (program evaluation and review technique) and PERT simulation can be used to review activity and project risk. PERT and related techniques take a more macro perspective by looking at overall cost and schedule risks. Here the focus is not on individual events but on the likelihood the project will be completed on time and within budget. These methods are useful in assessing the overall risk of the project and the need for such things as contingency funds, resources, and time. The use of PERT simulation is increasing because it uses the same data required for PERT, and software to perform the simulation is readily available.

Basically PERT simulation assumes a statistical distribution (range between optimistic and pessimistic) for each activity duration; it then simulates the network (perhaps over 1,000 simulations) using a random number generator. The outcome is the relative probability, called a criticality index, of an activity becoming critical under the many different, possible activity durations for each activity. PERT simulation also provides a list of potential critical paths and their respective probabilities of occurring. Having this information available can greatly facilitate identifying and assessing schedule risk. (See Appendix 7.1 at the end of this chapter for a more detailed description and discussion.)

Scenario Analysis: Semiquantitative

Project managers are often reluctant to use or provide probabilities for risk analysis. The challenge is to get the project team to articulate risk in words. This information can be very practical and, at the same time, provide some of the benefits of probability and utility theory.

The scenario analysis begins with the *baseline schedule,* which typically represents average time and implies there is a 50/50 chance of completing the project schedule early or late. Risk team members are checked to be sure they are 90 (or 95) percent confident that the schedule's duration is about average.

Second, the risk team assesses the baseline schedule assuming "everything goes right." A new *best-case schedule* is developed. The team is asked to confirm they are 90 percent confident that there is at least a 10 percent chance that the best-case schedule can be reached if everything goes right. Note that this schedule actually represents an opportunity for project compression by taking steps to avoid or reduce risks.

Third, the risk team assumes the worst case, which implies that the identified risk events will occur. Murphy's law will dominate the project. A *worst-case schedule* is developed. The team is asked to confirm they are 90 percent confident that there is a 90 percent chance they can meet the worst-case schedule if the risk events occur.

Finally, as a reality check on the three schedules—best, baseline, and worst—team members are asked to suggest how much of their own money they would be willing to wager on each schedule. This open process usually results in some small revisions of schedules, but it also brings the team close to agreeing that the schedules are reasonable. Figure 7.6 depicts three hypothetical schedules for a project, known as 10, 50, and 90 percent schedules. That is, the team is 90 percent confident there is a 10 percent chance of reaching the best-case schedule of 470 days, a 50 percent chance of meeting the baseline schedule of 500 days, and a 90 percent chance of meeting the worst-case schedule of 590 days. Graphing these three schedules and documenting time estimates, costs, and assumptions is a powerful mechanism that is very useful in explaining to the customer and senior management the uncertainties and effects of risk on a project.

FIGURE 7.6 Risk Schedules

While the project is implemented, the actual schedule can be plotted against the 10, 50, and 90 percent schedules. The bottom section of Figure 7.6 shows an "actual" tracked schedule for the hypothetical project. On day 300 it is estimated that the project will take 250 more days; this is 50 days more than the baseline and 40 days less than the worst-case schedule.

One approach used by practicing project managers, semiquantitative scenario analysis, is described in the Snapshot from Practice: Semiquantitative Risk Approach. This approach uses time because most risk events are time dependent, impact project delays, and are easily understood by risk team members. (Note that a similar approach can be used for budget.)

The quasiquantitative scenario approach described in the Snapshot from Practice takes basic scenario analysis one step further. By using numbers to verify impacts, it serves as a reality check on identified risks and analysis. A major outcome of the process is a "bracketing" of the project risk and possible durations. By running the three schedules before the project begins, it is possible to examine what decisions may have to be made; "what if" questions can be addressed. For example, if a risk event occurs, what impact will it have on other projects? This approach is also very useful in explaining to project members the risks inherent in a project.

Step 3: Risk Response Development

When a risk event is identified and assessed, a decision must be made concerning which response is appropriate for the specific event. Responses to risk can be classified as mitigating, avoiding, transferring, sharing, or retaining.

Mitigating Risk

Reducing risk is usually the first alternative considered. There are basically two strategies for mitigating risk: (1) reduce the likelihood that the event will occur and/or (2) reduce the impact that the adverse event would have on the project. An example of the former can be found in an information systems project. The project team was responsible for installing a new operating system in their parent company. Before implementing the project, the team tested the new system on a smaller isolated network. By doing so they discovered a variety of problems and were able to come up with solutions prior to implementation. The team still encountered problems with the installation but the number and severity were greatly reduced. Other examples of reducing the probability of risks occurring are scheduling outdoor work during the summer months, investing in up-front safety training, and choosing high-quality materials and equipment.

When the concerns are that duration and costs have been underestimated, managers will augment estimates to compensate for the uncertainties. It is common to use a ratio between old and new project to adjust time or cost. The ratio typically serves as a constant. For example if past projects have taken 10 minutes per line of computer code, a constant of 1.10 (which represents a 10 percent increase) would be used for the proposed project time estimates because the new project is more difficult than prior projects.

An alternative mitigation strategy is to reduce the impact of the risk if it occurs. For example, a bridge-building project illustrates risk reduction. A new bridge project for a coastal port was to use an innovative, continuous cement-pouring process developed by an Australian firm to save large sums of money and time. The major risk was that the continuous pouring process for each major section of the bridge could not be interrupted. Any interruption would require that the whole cement section (hundreds of cubic yards) be torn down and started over. An assessment of possible risks centered on delivery of the cement from the cement factory. Trucks could be delayed, or the factory could break down. Such risks would result in tremendous rework costs and delays. Risk was reduced by having two additional portable cement plants built nearby on different highways within 20 miles of the bridge project in case the main factory supply was interrupted. These two portable plants carried raw materials for a whole bridge section, and extra trucks were on immediate standby each time continuous pouring was required. Similar risk reduction scenarios are apparent in system and software development projects where parallel innovation processes are used in case one fails. Finally, the Dome to Dust Snapshot from Practice details the steps Controlled Demolition took to minimize damage when they imploded the Seattle Kingdome.

On March 26, 2000, the largest concrete domed structure in the world was reduced to a pile of rubble in a dramatic implosion lasting less than 20 seconds. According to Mark Loizeaux, whose Maryland-based Controlled Demolition Inc. was hired to bring the 24-year-old Seattle Kingdome down, "We don't blow things up. We use explosives as an engine, but gravity is the catalyst that will bring it down."

Destroying the Kingdome was the most complicated of the 7,000 demolitions Loizeaux's company has undertaken. Nearly three months of preparations were needed to implode the dome at a total cost of $9 million. The Kingdome was considered to be one of the strongest structures in the world containing over 25,000 tons of concrete with each of its 40 vaulted ribs incorporating seven lengths of two-and-one-quarter-inch reinforcing steel bar.

Strands of orange detonating cord—basically dynamite in a string that explodes at the lightning pace of 24,000 feet per second—connected six pielike divisions of the Kingdome to a nearby control center.

Throughout each section, Controlled Demolition workers drilled nearly 1,000 holes and packed them with high-velocity gelatin explosives the size of hot dogs. Large charges were placed about one-third of the way up each dome rib, smaller charges were put farther up the ribs. When the detonation button was pushed, blasting caps set off a chain reaction of explosions in each section reducing the stadium to rubble.

While the actual implosion was a technical tour-de-force, risk management was a critical part of the project's success.

To minimize damage to surrounding buildings, the explosive charges were wrapped in a layer of chain-link fencing covered with thick sheets of geotextile polypropylene fabric to contain flying concrete. Nearby buildings were protected in various manners depending on the structure and proximity to the Dome. Measures included sealing air-handling units, taping seams on doors and windows, covering floors and windows with plywood and draping reinforced polyethylene sheeting around the outside.

To help absorb the impact, air-conditioning units removed from the interior were stacked with other material to create a barrier around the perimeter of the work area.

Hundreds of police officers and security personnel were used to cordon off an area extending roughly 1,000 feet from the Dome from overzealous spectators. Traffic was closed for a larger area. Accommodations were provided for people and pets who lived within the restricted zone.

Eight water trucks, eight sweeper units, and more than 100 workers were deployed immediately after the blast to control dust and begin the cleanup.

As a side note, one-third of the concrete will be crushed and used in the foundation of a new $430 million outdoor football stadium which is being built in its place. The rest of the concrete will be carted away and used in roadbeds and foundations throughout the Seattle area.

*New York Times—Sunday Magazine (March 19, 2000); Seattle Times (March 27, 2000) website.

Avoiding Risk

Risk avoidance is changing the project plan to eliminate the risk or condition. Although it is impossible to eliminate all risk events, some specific risks may be avoided before you launch the project. For example, adopting proven technology instead of experimental technology can eliminate technical failure. Choosing an Australian supplier as opposed to an Indonesian supplier would virtually eliminate the chance that political unrest would disrupt the supply of critical materials. See the WAP versus JAVA Snapshot from Practice to see how Ellipsus Systems avoided a potentially critical technical risk.

Transferring Risk

Passing risk to another party is common; this transfer does not change risk. Passing risk to another party almost always results in paying a premium for this exemption. Fixed-price contracts are the classic example of transferring risk from an owner to a contractor. The contractor understands his or her firm will pay for any risk event that materializes; therefore, a monetary risk factor is added to the contract bid price. Before deciding to transfer risk, the owner should decide which party can best control activities that would lead to the risk occurring. Also, is the contractor capable of absorbing the risk? Clearly identifying and documenting responsibility for absorbing risk is imperative. Another more obvious way to transfer risk is insurance. However, in most

Ellipsus Systems, AB, located in Vaxjo, Sweden, is a software design company whose products link corporate computer systems to mobile phones. Critical to the company's success is making the right technology decisions, especially around the standards and protocols its software uses. As wireless and mobile devices continue to take hold, there are two major emerging technical standards. One standard is WAP (Wireless Application Protocol). The second standard, Java, is based on Internet programming standards created by Sun Microsystems.

Rikard Kjellberg, one of Ellipsus's founders, was facing a conundrum: which standard to use? In one, Java was dominant; in the other, WAP was dominant. WAP was first to market. It generated huge excitement, and as Nokia prepared to launch the first wireless phone in late 1999, engineers across Europe left secure jobs to form WAP start-ups. At the same time some negative perceptions were developing about systems based on the WAP standard. Due to the slow response time, a Swedish newspaper ran a story titled, "WAP is Crap." Java, on the other hand, had yet to establish itself with no commercial handsets available at the time.

Kjellberg's solution was to have projects in his company's portfolio based on both standards. Ellipsus built early prototypes of both systems and took them to a trade show, with both systems sitting side by side. "We knew within an hour which way to go," says Douglas Davies, the COO. Ellipsus began securing million dollar contracts to supply its Java-based system to leading U.S. operators.

*David Pringle, "How the U.S. took the wireless lead away from Europe," *The Wall Street Journal Europe,* 20 February 2002 http://www.network365.com/news.jsp?id=145 (accessed 10, November 2003).

cases this is impractical because defining the project risk event and conditions to an insurance broker who is unfamiliar with the project is difficult and usually expensive. Of course, low-probability and high-consequence risk events such as acts of God are more easily defined and insured. Performance bonds, warranties, and guarantees are other financial instruments used to transfer risk.

Sharing Risk

Risk sharing allocates proportions of risk to different parties. An example of risk sharing was the Airbus A340. Research and development risks were allocated among European countries including Britain and France. Alternatively, the entertainment industry formed a consortium to define a common operating format for Digital Video Disc (DVD) to ensure compatibility across products. Other forms of risk sharing are emerging.

Sharing risk has drawn more attention in recent years as a motivation for reducing risk and, in some cases, cutting project cost. Partnering (see Chapter 12) between an owner and contractors has prompted the development of continuous improvement procedures to encourage contractors to suggest innovative ways for project implementation. The new method will probably include additional start-up costs and the risk that the new process may not work. Usually the risk costs and benefits of the improved process are shared on a 50/50 basis between the owner and contracting firms.

Retaining Risk

In some cases a conscious decision is made to accept the risk of an event occurring. Some risks are so large it is not feasible to consider transferring or reducing the event (e.g., an earthquake or flood). The project owner assumes the risk because the chance of such an event occurring is slim. In other cases risks identified in the budget reserve can simply be absorbed if they materialize. The risk is retained by developing a contingency plan to implement if the risk materializes. In a few cases a risk event can be ignored and a cost overrun accepted should the risk event occur.

The more effort given to risk response before the project begins, the better the chances are for minimizing project surprises. Knowing that the response to a risk event will be retained, transferred, or shared greatly reduces stress and uncertainty when the risk event occurs. Again, control is possible with this structured approach.

Contingency Planning

A contingency plan is an alternative plan that will be used if a possible foreseen risk event becomes a reality. The contingency plan represents actions that will reduce or mitigate the negative impact of the risk event. Like all plans, the contingency plan answers the questions of what, where, when, and how much action will take place. The absence of a contingency plan, when a risk event occurs, can cause a manager to delay or postpone the decision to implement a remedy. This postponement can lead to panic, and acceptance of the first remedy suggested. Such after-the-event decision making under pressure can be potentially dangerous and costly. Contingency planning evaluates alternative remedies for possible foreseen events before the risk event occurs and selects the best plan among alternatives. This early contingency planning facilitates a smooth transition to the remedy or work-around plan. The availability of a contingency plan can significantly increase the chances for project success.

Conditions for activating the implementation of the contingency plan should be decided and clearly documented. The plan should include a cost estimate and identify the source of funding. All parties affected should agree to the contingency plan and have authority to make commitments. Because implementation of a contingency plan embodies disruption in the sequence of work, all contingency plans should be communicated to team members so that surprise and resistance are minimized.

Here is an example: A high-tech niche computer company intends to introduce a new "platform" product at a very specific target date. The project's 47 teams all agree delays will not be acceptable. Their contingency plans for two large component suppliers demonstrate how seriously risk management is viewed. One supplier's plant sits on the San Andreas Fault. The contingency plan has an alternative supplier, who is constantly updated, producing a replica of the component in another plant. Another supplier in Toronto, Canada, presents a delivery risk on their due date because of potential bad weather. This contingency plan calls for a chartered plane (already contracted to be on standby) if overland transportation presents a delay problem. To outsiders these plans must seem a bit extreme, but in high-tech industries where time to market is king, risks of identified events are taken seriously.

Risk response matrices such as the one shown in Figure 7.7 are useful for summarizing how the project team plans to manage risks that have been identified. Again, the Windows Office 2000 XP project (see Figure 7.7) is used to illustrate this kind of matrix. The first step is to identify whether to reduce, share, transfer, or accept the risk. The team decided to reduce the chances of the system freezing by experimenting with a prototype of the system. Prototype experimentation not only allows them to identify

FIGURE 7.7
Risk Response Matrix

Risk Event	Response	Contingency Plan	Trigger	Who Is Responsible
Interface problems	Reduce	Work around until help comes	Not solved within 24 hours	Nils
System freezing	Reduce	Reinstall OS	Still frozen after one hour	Emmylou
User backlash	Reduce	Increase staff support	Call from top management	Eddie
Equipment malfunctions	Transfer	Order different brand	Replacement doesn't work	Jim

and fix conversion "bugs" before the actual installation, but it also yields information that could be useful in enhancing acceptance by end-users. The project team is then able to identify and document changes between the old and new system that will be incorporated in the training the users receive. The risk of equipment malfunctioning is transferred by choosing a reliable supplier with a strong warranty program.

The next step is to identify contingency plans in case the risk still occurs. For example, if interface problems prove insurmountable, then the team would attempt a work-around until vendor experts arrived to help solve the problem. If the system freezes after installation, the team will first try to reinstall the software. If user dissatisfaction is high, then the IS department will provide more staff support. If the team is unable to get reliable equipment from the original supplier, then it will order a different brand from a second dealer. The team also needs to discuss and agree what would "trigger" implementation of the contingency plan. In the case of the system freezing, the trigger is not being able to unfreeze the system within one hour or, in the case of user backlash, an angry call from top management. Finally, the individual responsible for monitoring the potential risk and initiating the contingency plan needs to be assigned. Smart project managers establish protocols for contingency responses before they are needed. For an example of the importance of establishing protocols see the Risk Management at the Top of the World Snapshot from Practice on page 220.

Some of the most common methods for handling risk are discussed here.

Technical Risks

Technical risks are problematic; they can often be the kind that cause the project to be shut down. What if the system or process does not work? Contingency or backup plans are made for those possibilities that are foreseen. For example, Carrier Transcicold was involved in developing a new Phoenix refrigeration unit for truck-trailer applications. This new unit was to use rounded panels made of bonded metals, which at the time was new technology for Transicold. Furthermore, one of its competitors had tried unsuccessfully to incorporate similar bonded metals in their products. The project team was eager to make the new technology work, but it wasn't until the very end of the project that they were able to get the new adhesives to bond adequately to complete the project. Throughout the project, the team maintained a welded-panel fabrication approach just in case they were unsuccessful. If this contingency approach had been needed, it would have increased production costs, but the project still would have been completed on time.

In addition to backup strategies, project managers need to develop methods to quickly assess whether technical uncertainties can be resolved. The use of sophisticated CAD programs has greatly helped resolve design problems. At the same time, Smith and Reinertsen, in their book *Developing Products in Half the Time,* argue that there is no substitute for making something and seeing how it works, feels, or looks. They suggest that one should first identify the high-risk technical areas, then build models or design experiments to resolve the risk as quickly as possible. By isolating and testing the key technical questions early on in a project, project feasibility can be quickly determined and necessary adjustments made such as reworking the process or in some cases closing down the project. Usually the owner and project manager make decisions concerning technical risks.

Schedule Risks

Managing scheduling risk usually requires trade-off decisions. It is ironic that practicing managers actually increase schedule risk by some of their decisions. Three of those situations are examined on page 221.

Snapshot from Practice

Risk Management at the Top of the World*

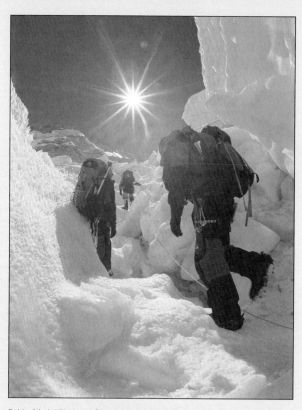

Bobby Model/National Geographic Image Collection.

Into Thin Air, Jon Krakauer's gripping account of an ill-fated attempt to climb Mount Everest in which six climbers died, provides testimony to the risks of extreme mountain climbing. Thirteen days after the tragedy, David Breashears successfully led a film crew to the summit. Their footage can be seen in the spectacular IMAX film, *Everest.*

Accounts of Mount Everest expeditions provide insights into project risk management. First, most climbers spend more than three weeks acclimating their bodies to high-altitude conditions. Native Sherpas are used extensively to carry supplies and set up each of the four base camps that will be used during the final stages of the climb. To reduce the impact of hypoxia, lightheadness, and disorientation caused by shortage of oxygen, most climbers use oxygen masks and bottles during the final ascent. If lucky enough not to be one of the first expeditions of the season, the path to the summit should be staked out and roped by previous climbers. Climbing guides receive last-minute weather reports by radio to confirm whether the weather conditions warrant the risk. Finally, for added insurance, most climbers join their Sherpas in an elaborate *puja* ritual intended to summon the divine support of the gods before beginning their ascent.

All of these efforts pale next to the sheer physical and mental rigors of making the final climb from base camp IV to the summit.

This is what climbers refer to as the "death zone" because beyond 26,000 feet the mind and body begin to quickly deteriorate despite supplemental oxygen. Under fair conditions it takes around 18 hours to make the round-trip to the top and back to the base camp. Climbers leave as early as 1:00 A.M. in order to make it back before night falls and total exhaustion sets in.

The greatest danger in climbing Mount Everest is not reaching the summit but making it back to the base camp. One out of every five climbers who make it to the summit dies during their descent. The key is establishing a contingency plan in case the climbers encounter hard going or the weather changes. Guides establish a predetermined turnaround time (i.e., 2:00 P.M.) to ensure a safe return no matter how close the climbers are to the summit. Accepting the time takes tremendous discipline. One who was caught up by time was solo climber Goran Krupp. He turned back 1,000 feet from the top after bicycling 8,000 miles from Stockholm to Katmandu!

Many lives have been lost by failing to adhere to the turnback time and pushing forward to the summit. As one climber put it, "With enough determination, any bloody idiot can get up the hill. The trick is to get back down alive."

*Jon Krakauer, *Into Thin Air* (New York: Doubleday, 1997), p. 190; Broughton Coburn, *Everest: Mountain without Mercy* (New York: National Geographic Society, 1997).

220

Use of Slack

When some managers see network slack, they cease to worry about completing their activity on time—why worry if there are 10 days of slack! Unfortunately, that slack may be needed by another activity on the path that now must start later and leave little or no slack available because the path slack has already been used up. Managing slack can be an excellent method for reducing schedule risk. Remember, use of slack moves more activities nearer their late start, and thus the risk of project delay is increased.

Imposed Duration Dates

Our experience suggests that about 80 percent of all projects have imposed duration dates. Usually this means someone (with authority) has determined that the project or milestone(s) can or must be completed by a specific date. Examples might be completing a road by January 1 or developing a video game for the Christmas market. The specified project duration is frequently a top-down decision that does not include bottom-up planning and often understates the normal time required to complete the project. If this is the case, meeting the required, specified project duration will result in activities being performed more rapidly than the normal, low-cost method. This hurried approach increases cost and the chance of activities being late and reduces flexibility in the total scheduling system. There are times when completing a project by an imposed duration is necessary (e.g., time to market to beat competition), but in almost all cases of imposed project durations, both risks of being late and greater costs are increased. The question is, "Is this simply poor planning, or is there a real necessity to manage projects by imposed durations?"

Compression of Project Schedules

Sometimes before or midway through the project, the need to shorten the project duration arises. Shortening project duration is accomplished by shortening (compressing) one or more activities on the critical path. Shortening an activity/work package duration increases direct cost. In addition, compressing the critical path decreases total slack on other paths, and more paths become critical or near critical. The more critical activities or near-critical activities there are, the higher the risk of delaying project completion. Some contingency plans can avoid costly procedures. For example, schedules can be altered by working activities in parallel or using start-to-start lag relationships. Also, using the best people for high-risk tasks can relieve or lessen the chance of some risk events occurring. Techniques for managing this situation are discussed in Chapter 9.

Cost Risks

Given some of the reported cost overruns, cost risks are significant and carry heavy consequences. Most cost risks are created in schedule and technical estimate errors and omissions. In addition, some management decisions actually increase cost risks. A few selected cost risks found in practice are discussed here.

Time/Cost Dependency Link

There is a dependency link between time and cost and technical problems and cost. For example, if the activity "develop process prototype" requires 50 percent more time than the original estimate, it can be expected that costs will also increase. Thus, time and cost do not occur independently. Neglecting to consider this interactive dependency can result in significant cost risk errors.

Cash Flow Decisions

Some cash flow decisions can heighten schedule risks. For example, financial analysts will make comparisons of an early-start schedule versus a late-start schedule. Theoretically, they conclude that by delaying activities, the future value of the money is greater than its value today (the money can earn interest). Alternatively, the money can be used elsewhere. The increased risk of reducing slack is sometimes ignored or significantly underestimated. Using the schedule to solve cash flow problems should be avoided if possible. If the schedule is used, it should be done with a clear recognition that the project will likely be completed both later and at a higher cost.

Price Protection Risks

Projects of long duration need some contingency for price changes—which are usually upward. The important point to remember when reviewing price is to avoid the trap of using one lump sum to cover price risks. For example, if inflation has been running about 3 percent, some managers add 3 percent for all resources used in the project. This lump-sum approach does not address exactly where price protection is needed and fails to provide for tracking and control. Price risks should be evaluated item by item. Some purchases and contracts will not change over the life of the project. Those that may change should be identified and estimates made of the magnitude of change. This approach ensures control of the contingency funds as the project is implemented.

Funding Risks

What if the funding for the project is cut by 25 percent or completion projections indicate that costs will greatly exceed available funds? What are the chances of the project being canceled before completion? Seasoned project managers recognize that a complete risk assessment must include an evaluation of funding supply. This is especially true for publicly funded projects. Case in point was the ill-fated RAH-66 Comanche helicopter which was being developed for the U.S. Army by Sikorsky Aircraft Corp. and Boeing Co. Eight billion dollars had been invested to develop a new age combat and reconnaissance helicopter, when in February 2004, the Defense Department recommended that the project be canceled. The cancellation reflected a need to cut costs and a switch toward using unmanned aircraft for surveillance as well as attack missions.

Just as government projects are subject to changes in strategy and political agenda, business firms frequently undergo changes in priorities and top management. The pet projects of the new CEO replace the pet projects of the former CEO. Resources become tight and one way to fund new projects is to cancel other projects.

Severe budget cuts or lack of adequate funding can have a devastating effect on a project. Typically, when such a fate occurs, there is a need to scale back the scope of the project to what is possible. "All-or-nothing projects" are ripe targets to budget cutters. This was the case of the Comanche helicopter once the decision was made to move away from manned reconnaissance aircraft. Here the "chunkability" of the project can be an advantage. For example, freeway projects can fall short of the original intentions but still add value for each mile completed.

On a much smaller scale, similar funding risks may exist for more mundane projects. For example, a building contractor may find that due to a sudden downturn in the stock market the owners can no longer afford to build their dream house. Or an IS consulting firm may be left empty handed when a client files for bankruptcy. In the former case the contractor may have as a contingency selling the house on the open market, while unfortunately the consulting firm will have to join the long line of creditors.

Contingency Funding and Time Buffers

Contingency funds are established to cover project risks—identified and unknown. When, where, and how much money will be spent is not known until the risk event occurs. Project "owners" are often reluctant to set up project contingency funds that seem to imply the project plan might be a poor one. Some perceive the contingency fund as an add-on slush fund. Others say they will face the risk when it materializes. Usually such reluctance to establish contingency reserves can be overcome with documented risk identification, assessment, contingency plans, and plans for when and how funds will be disbursed.

The size and amount of contingency reserves depend on uncertainty inherent in the project. Uncertainty is reflected in the "newness" of the project, inaccurate time and cost estimates, technical unknowns, unstable scope, and problems not anticipated. In practice, contingencies run from 1 to 10 percent in projects similar to past projects. However, in unique and high-technology projects it is not uncommon to find contingencies running in the 20 to 60 percent range. Use and rate of consumption of reserves must be closely monitored and controlled. Simply picking a percentage of the baseline, say, 5 percent, and calling it the contingency reserve is not a sound approach. Also, adding up all the identified contingency allotments and throwing them into one pot is not conducive to sound control of the reserve fund.

In practice, the contingency reserve fund is typically divided into budget and management reserve funds for control purposes. Budget reserves are set up to cover identified risks; these reserves are those allocated to specific segments or deliverables of the project. Management reserves are set up to cover unidentified risks and are allocated to risks associated with the total project. The risks are separated because their use requires approval from different levels of project authority. Because all risks are probabilistic, the reserves are not included in the baseline for each work package or activity; they are only activated when a risk occurs. If an identified risk does not occur and its chance of occurring is past, the fund allocated to the risk should be deducted from the budget reserve. (This removes the temptation to use budget reserves for other issues or problems.) Of course if the risk does occur, funds are removed from the reserve and added to the cost baseline.

Budget Reserves

These reserves are identified for specific work packages or segments of a project found in the baseline budget or work breakdown structure. Budget reserves are for *identified* risks that have a low chance of occurring. Examples of variations covered by budget reserves are small design changes and time and cost estimate errors. For example, a reserve amount might be added to "computer coding" to cover the risk of "testing" showing a coding problem. The reserve amount is determined by costing out the accepted contingency or recovery plan. The budget reserve should be communicated to the project team. This openness suggests trust and encourages good cost performance. However, distributing budget reserves should be the responsibility of both the project manager and the team members responsible for implementing the specific segment of the project. If the risk does not materialize, the funds are returned to the management reserve. Thus, budget reserves decrease as the project progresses.

Management Reserves

These reserve funds are needed to cover major unforeseen risks and, hence, are applied to the total project. For example, a major scope change may appear necessary midway in the project. Because this change was not anticipated or identified, it is covered from the management reserve. Management reserves are established *after* budget reserves are identified and funds established. These reserves are independent of budget reserves and are controlled by the project manager and the "owner" of the project. The "owner" can be internal (top management) or external to the project organization. Most management reserves are set using historical data and judgments concerning the uniqueness and complexity of the project.

Placing technical contingencies in the management reserve is a special case. Identifying possible technical (functional) risks is often associated with a new, untried, innovative process or product. Because there is a chance the innovation may not work out, a fallback plan is necessary. This type of risk is beyond the control of the project manager. Hence, technical reserves are held in the management reserve and controlled by the owner or top management. The owner and project manager decide when the contingency plan will be implemented and the reserve funds used. It is assumed there is a high probability these funds will never be used.

Table 7.1 shows the development of a contingency fund estimate for a hypothetical project. Note how budget and management reserves are kept separate; control is easily tracked using this format.

Time Buffers

Just as contingency funds are established to absorb unplanned costs, managers use time buffers to cushion against potential delays in the project. And like contingency funds, the amount of time is dependent upon the inherent uncertainty of project. The more uncertain the project the more time should be reserved for the schedule. The strategy is to assign extra time at critical moments in the project. For example, buffers are added to

A. activities with severe risks.

B. merge activities that are prone to delays due to one or more preceding activities being late.

C. noncritical activities to reduce the likelihood that they will create another critical path.

D. activities that require scarce resources to ensure that the resources are available when needed.

In the face of overall schedule uncertainty, buffers are sometimes added to the end of the project. For example, a 300-working-day project may have a 30-day project buffer. While the extra 30 days would not appear on the schedule, it is available if

TABLE 7.1
Contingency Fund Estimate (Thousands of Dollars)

Activity	Budget Baseline	Budget Reserve	Project Budget
Design	$500	$15	$515
Code	900	80	980
Test	20	2	22
Subtotal	$1,420	$97	$1,517
Management reserve	—	—	50
Total	$1,420	$97	$1,567

needed. Like management reserves, this buffer typically requires the authorization of top management. A more systematic approach to buffer management is discussed in the Chapter 8 Appendix on critical chain project management.

Step 4: Risk Response Control

The last step in the risk management process is risk control—executing the risk response strategy, monitoring triggering events, initiating contingency plans, and watching for new risks. Establishing a change management system to deal with events that require formal changes in the scope, budget, and/or schedule of the project is an essential element of risk control.

Project managers need to monitor risks just like they track project progress. Risk assessment and updating needs to be part of every status meeting and progress report system. The project team needs to be on constant alert for new, unforeseen risks. Management needs to be sensitive that others may not be forthright in acknowledging new risks and problems. Admitting that there might be a bug in the design code or that different components are not compatible reflects poorly on individual performance. If the prevailing organizational culture is one where mistakes are punished severely, then it is only human nature to protect oneself. Similarly, if bad news is greeted harshly and there is a propensity to "kill the messenger," participants will be reluctant to speak freely. The tendency to suppress bad news is compounded when individual responsibility is vague and the project team is under extreme pressure from top management to get the project done quickly.

Project managers need to establish an environment in which participants feel comfortable raising concerns and admitting mistakes. The norm should be that mistakes are acceptable, hiding mistakes is intolerable. Problems should be embraced not denied. Participants should be encouraged to identify problems and new risks. Here a positive attitude by the project manager toward risks is a key.

On large, complex projects it may be prudent to repeat the risk identification/ assessment exercise with fresh information. Risk profiles should be reviewed to test to see if the original responses held true. Relevant stakeholders should be brought into the discussion. While this may not be practical on an ongoing basis, project managers should touch base with them on a regular basis or hold special stakeholder meetings to review the status of risks on the project.

A second key for controlling the cost of risks is documenting responsibility. This can be problematic in projects involving multiple organizations and contractors. Responsibility for risk is frequently passed on to others with the statement, "That is not my worry." This mentality is dangerous. Each identified risk should be assigned (or shared) by mutual agreement of the owner, project manager, and the contractor or person having line responsibility for the work package or segment of the project. It is best to have the line person responsible approve the use of budget reserve funds and monitor their rate of usage. If management reserve funds are required, the line person should play an active role in estimating additional costs and funds needed to complete the project. Having line personnel participate in the process focuses attention on the management reserve, control of its rate of usage, and early warning of potential risk events. If risk management is not formalized, responsibility and responses to risk will be ignored—*it is not my area.*

The bottom line is that project managers and team members need to be vigilant in monitoring potential risks and identify new land mines that could derail a project. Risk assessment has to be part of the working agenda of status meetings and when new risks emerge they need to be analyzed and incorporated into the risk management process.

Change Control Management

A major element of the risk control process is change management. Every detail of a project plan will not materialize as expected. Coping with and controlling project changes present a formidable challenge for most project managers. Changes come from many sources such as the project customer, owner, project manager, team members, and occurrence of risk events. Most changes easily fall into three categories:

1. Scope changes in the form of design or additions represent big changes; for example, customer requests for a new feature or a redesign that will improve the product.
2. Implementation of contingency plans, when risk events occur, represent changes in baseline costs and schedules.
3. Improvement changes suggested by project team members represent another category.

Because change is inevitable, a well-defined change review and control process should be set up early in the project planning cycle.

Change control systems involve reporting, controlling, and recording changes to the project baseline. (Note: Some organizations consider change control systems part of configuration management.) In practice most change control systems are designed to accomplish the following:

FIGURE 7.8

Change Control Process

1. Identify proposed changes.
2. List expected effects of proposed change(s) on schedule and budget.
3. Review, evaluate, and approve or disapprove changes formally.
4. Negotiate and resolve conflicts of change, conditions, and cost.
5. Communicate changes to parties affected.
6. Assign responsibility for implementing change.
7. Adjust master schedule and budget.
8. Track all changes that are to be implemented.

As part of the project communication plan, stakeholders define up front the communication and decision-making process that will be used to evaluate and accept changes. The process can be captured in a flow diagram like the one presented in Figure 7.8. On small projects this process may simply entail approval of a small group of stakeholders. On larger projects more elaborate decision-making processes are established, with different processes being used for different kinds of change. For example, changes in performance requirements may require multiple sign-offs, including the project sponsor and client, while switching suppliers may be authorized by the project manager. Regardless of the nature of the project, the goal is to establish the process for introducing necessary changes in the project in a timely and effective manner.

Of particular importance is assessing the impact of the change on the project. Often solutions to immediate problems have adverse consequence on other aspects of a project. For example, in overcoming a problem with the exhaust system for a hybrid automobile, the design engineers contributed to the prototype exceeding weight parameters. It is important that the implications of changes are assessed by people with appropriate expertise and perspective. On construction projects this is often the responsibility of the architecture firm, while "software architects" perform a similar function on software development efforts.

Organizations use change request forms and logs to track proposed changes. An example of a simplified change request form is depicted in Figure 7.9. Typically change request forms include a description of the change, the impact of not approving

FIGURE 7.9
Sample Change Request

Project name *Irish/Chinese culture exchange*	Project sponsor *Irish embassy*
Request number _12_	Date *June 6, 2xxx*
Originator *Jennifer McDonald*	Change requested by *Chinese culture office*

Description of requested change

1. *Request river dancers to replace small Irish dance group.*
2. *Request one combination dance with river dancers and China ballet group.*

Reason for change

River dancers will enhance stature of event. The group is well known and loved by Chinese people.

Areas of impact of proposed change–describe each on separate sheet

- [X] Scope
- [X] Cost
- [ ] Other _____
- [ ] Schedule
- [ ] Risk

Disposition	Priority	Funding Source
[ ] Approve	[ ] Emergency	[ ] Mgmt. reserve
[X] Approve as amended	[X] Urgent	[ ] Budget reserve
[ ] Disapprove	[ ] Low	[X] Customer
[ ] Deferred		[ ] Other

Sign-off Approvals

Project manager *William O'Mally*	Date *June 12, 2xxx*
Project sponsor *Kenneth Thompson*	Date *June 13, 2xxx*
Project customer *Hong Lee*	Date *June 18, 2xxx*
Other _____	Date _____

the change, the impact of the change on project scope/schedule/cost, and defined signature paths for review as well as a tracking log number.

An abridged version of a change request log for a construction project is presented in Figure 7.10. These logs are used to monitor change requests. They typically summarize the status of all outstanding change requests and include such useful information as source and date of the change, document codes for related information, cost estimates, and the current status of the request.

Every approved change must be identified and integrated into the plan of record through changes in the project WBS and baseline schedule. The plan of record is the current official plan for the project in terms of scope, budget, and schedule. The plan of record serves as a change management benchmark for future change requests as well as the baseline for evaluating project progress.

FIGURE 7.10   **Change Request Log**

OWNER REQUESTED CHANGE STATUS REPORT—OPEN ITEMS							OSU—WEATHERFORD
RC#	DESCRIPTION	REFERENCE DOCUMENT	**DATES**		AMOUNT	STATUS	COMMENTS
			DATE REC'D	DATE SUBMIT			
51	Sewer work offset				−188129	OPEN	FUNDING FROM OTHER SOURCE
52	Stainless Plates at restroom Shower Valves	ASI 56	1/5/2004	3/30/2004	9308	APPROVED	
53	Waterproofing Options	ASI 77	1/13/2004		169386	OPEN	
54	Change Electrical floor box spec change	RFI 113	12/5/2003	3/29/2004	2544	SUBMIT	
55	VE Option for Style and rail doors	Door samples	1/14/2004		−20000	ROM	
56	Pressure Wash C tower	Owner request	3/15/2004	3/30/2004	14861	SUBMIT	
57	Fire Lite glass in stairs	Owner request			8000	QUOTE	ROM BASED ON FIRELITE NT
58	Cyber Café added tele/OFOI equipment	ASI 65	1/30/2004	3/29/2004	4628	APPROVED	
59	Additional Dampers in C wing	ASI 68	2/4/2004	3/29/2004	1085	SUBMIT	
60	Revise Corridor ceilings	ASI 72	2/13/2004	3/31/2004	−3755	SUBMIT	

OPEN—Requires Estimate   SUBMIT—RC letter submitted   ASI—Architect's Supplemental Instructions
ROM—Rough Order magnitde   APPROVED—RC letter approved   RFI—Request for Information
QUOTE—Subcontractor quotes   REVISE—RC letter to be reviewed

If the change control system is not integrated with the WBS and baseline, project plans and control will soon self-destruct. Thus, one of the keys to a successful change control process is document, document, document! The benefits derived from change control systems are the following:

1. Inconsequential changes are discouraged by the formal process.
2. Costs of changes are maintained in a log.
3. Integrity of the WBS and performance measures is maintained.
4. Allocation and use of budget and management reserve funds are tracked.
5. Responsibility for implementation is clarified.
6. Effect of changes is visible to all parties involved.
7. Implementation of change is monitored.
8. Scope changes will be quickly reflected in baseline and performance measures.

Clearly, change control is important and requires that someone or some group be responsible for approving changes, keeping the process updated, and communicating changes to the project team and relevant stakeholders. Project control depends heavily on keeping the change control process current. This historical record can be used for satisfying customer inquiries, identifying problems in postproject audits, and estimating future project costs.

Summary

To put the processes discussed in this chapter in proper perspective one should recognize that the essence of project management is risk management. Every technique in this book is really a risk management technique. Each in its own way tries to prevent something bad from happening. Project selection systems try to reduce the likelihood that projects will not contribute to the mission of the firm. Project scope statements, among other things, are designed to avoid costly misunderstandings and reduce scope creep. Work breakdown structures reduce the likelihood that some vital part of the project will be omitted or that the budget estimates are unrealistic. Teambuilding reduces the likelihood of dysfunctional conflict and breakdowns in coordination. All of the techniques try to increase stakeholder satisfaction and increase the chances of project success.

From this perspective managers engage in risk management activities to compensate for the uncertainty inherent in project management and that things never go according to plan. Risk management is proactive not reactive. It reduces the number of surprises and leads to a better understanding of the most likely outcomes of negative events.

Although many managers believe that in the final analysis, risk assessment and contingency depend on subjective judgment, some standard method for identifying, assessing, and responding to risks should be included in all projects. The very process of identifying project risks forces some discipline at all levels of project management and improves project performance.

Contingency plans increase the chance that the project can be completed on time and within budget. Contingency plans can be simple "work-arounds" or elaborate detailed plans. Responsibility for risks should be clearly identified and documented. It is desirable and prudent to keep a reserve as a hedge against project risks. Budget reserves are linked to the WBS and should be communicated to the project team. Control of management reserves should remain with the owner, project manager, and line person responsible. Use of contingency reserves should be closely monitored, controlled, and reviewed throughout the project life cycle.

Experience clearly indicates that using a formal, structured process to handle possible foreseen and unforeseen project risk events minimizes surprises, costs, delays, stress, and misunderstandings. Risk management is an iterative process that occurs throughout the lifespan of the project. When risk events occur or changes are necessary, using an effective change control process to quickly approve and record changes will facilitate measuring performance against schedule and cost. Ultimately successful risk management requires a culture in which threats are embraced not denied and problems are identified not hidden.

Key Terms

Avoiding risk
Budget reserve
Change management system
Contingency plan
Management reserve
Mitigating risk
Risk
Risk profile
Risk severity matrix
Scenario analysis
Sharing risk
Time buffer
Transferring risk

Review Questions

1. Project risks can/cannot be eliminated if the project is carefully planned. Explain.
2. The chances of risk events occurring and their respective costs increasing change over the project life cycle. What is the significance of this phenomenon to a project manager?
3. What is the difference between avoiding a risk and accepting a risk?

4. What is the difference between mitigating a risk and contingency planning?

5. Explain the difference between budget reserves and management reserves.

6. How are the work breakdown structure and change control connected?

7. What are the likely outcomes if a change control process is not used? Why?

Exercises

1. Gather a small team of students. Think of a project most students would understand; the kinds of tasks involved should also be familiar. Identify and assess major and minor risks inherent to the project. Decide on a response type. Develop a contingency plan for two to four identified risks. Estimate costs. Assign contingency reserves. How much reserve would your team estimate for the whole project? Justify your choices and estimates.

2. You have been assigned to a project risk team of five members. Because this is the first time your organization has formally set up a risk team for a project, it is hoped that your team will develop a process that can be used on all future projects. Your first team meeting is next Monday morning. Each team member has been asked to prepare for the meeting by developing, in as much detail as possible, an outline that describes how you believe the team should proceed in handling project risks. Each team member will hand out their proposed outline at the beginning of the meeting. Your outline should include but not be limited to the following information:
    a. Team objectives.
    b. Process for handling risk events.
    c. Team activities.
    d. Team outputs.

3. The Manchester United Soccer Tournament project team has identified the following potential risks to their project:
    a. Referees failing to show up at designated games.
    b. Fighting between teams.
    c. Pivotal error committed by a referee that determines the outcome of a game.
    d. Abusive behavior along the sidelines by parents.
    e. Inadequate parking.
    f. Not enough teams sign up for different age brackets.
    g. Serious injury.

    How would you recommend that they respond (i.e., avoid, accept, . . .) to these risks and why?

4. Search the World Wide Web (WWW) using the key words: "best practices, project management." What did you find? How might this information be useful to a project manager?

References

Baker, B., and R. Menon, "Politics and Project Performance: The Fourth Dimension of Project Management," *PM Network,* 9 (11) November 1995, pp. 16–21.

Carr, M. J., S. L. Konda, I. Monarch, F. C. Ulrich, and C. F. Walker, "Taxonomy-Based Risk Identification," *Technical Report CMU/SEI-93-TR 6, Software Engineering Institute,* Carnegie Mellon University, Pittsburgh, 1993.

Graves, R., "Qualitative Risk Assessment," *PM Network,* 14 (10) October 2000, pp. 61–66.

Gray, C. F., and R. Reinman, "PERT Simulation: A Dynamic Approach to the PERT Technique," *Journal of Systems Management,* March 1969, pp. 18–23.

Hamburger, D. H., "The Project Manager: Risk Taker and Contingency Planner," *Project Management Journal,* 21 (4) 1990, pp. 11–16.

Hulett, D. T., "Project Schedule Risk Assessment," *Project Management Journal,* 26 (1) 1995, pp. 21–31.

Ingebretson, Mark, "In No Uncertain Terms," *PM Network,* 2002, pp. 28–32.

Levine, H. A., "Risk Management for Dummies: Managing Schedule, Cost and Technical Risk, and Contingency," *PM Network,* 9 (10) October 1995, pp. 31–33.

"Math Mistake Proved Fatal to Mars Orbiter," *The Orlando Sentinel,* November 23, 1999.

Pritchard, C. L., "Advanced Risk–How Big Is Your Crystal Ball?" Proceedings of the 31st Annual Project Management Institute 2000 Seminars and Symposium, (Houston, TX, 2000) CD, pp. 933–36.

Project Management Body of Knowledge, (Newton Square, PA: Project Management Institute, 2000), pp. 127–46.

Schuler, J. R., "Decision Analysis in Projects: Monte Carlo Simulation," *PM Network,* 7 (1) January 1994, pp. 30–36.

Silverstein, Ken, "Closing the Circuit," *PM Network,* August, 2003, pp. 40–45.

Smith, P. G., and D. G. Reinersten, *Developing Products in Half the Time* (New York: Van Nostrand, 1995).

Smith, P. G., and G. M. Merritt. *Proactive Risk Management: Controlling Uncertainty in Product Development* (New York: Productivity Press, 2002).

Case

Alaska Fly-Fishing Expedition*

You are sitting around the fire at a lodge in Dillingham, Alaska, discussing a fishing expedition you are planning with your colleagues at Great Alaska Adventures (GAA). Earlier in the day you received a fax from the president of BlueNote, Inc. The president wants to reward her top management team by taking them on an all-expense-paid fly-fishing adventure in Alaska. She would like GAA to organize and lead the expedition.

You have just finished a preliminary scope statement for the project (see below). You are now brainstorming potential risks associated with the project.

1. Brainstorm potential risks associated with this project. Try to come up with at least five different risks.
2. Use a risk assessment matrix similar to Figure 7.4 to analyze identified risks.
3. Develop a risk response matrix similar to Figure 7.7 to outline how you would deal with each of the risks.

PROJECT SCOPE STATEMENT

PROJECT OBJECTIVE

To organize and lead a five-day fly-fishing expedition down the Tikchik River system in Alaska from June 21 to 25 at a cost not to exceed $18,000.

---

* This case was prepared with the assistance of Stuart Morigeau.

DELIVERABLES

- Provide air transportation from Dillingham, Alaska, to Camp I and from Camp II back to Dillingham.
- Provide river transportation consisting of two eight-man drift boats with outboard motors.
- Provide three meals a day for the five days spent on the river.
- Provide four hours fly-fishing instruction.
- Provide overnight accommodations at the Dillingham lodge plus three four-man tents with cots, bedding, and lanterns.
- Provide four experienced river guides who are also fly fishermen.
- Provide fishing licenses for all guests.

MILESTONES

1. Contract signed January 22.
2. Guests arrive in Dillingham June 20.
3. Depart by plane to Base Camp I June 21.
4. Depart by plane from Base Camp II to Dillingham June 25.

TECHNICAL REQUIREMENTS

1. Fly in air transportation to and from base camps.
2. Boat transportation within the Tikchik River system.
3. Digital cellular communication devices.
4. Camps and fishing conform to state of Alaska requirements.

LIMITS AND EXCLUSIONS

1. Guests are responsible for travel arrangements to and from Dillingham, Alaska.
2. Guests are responsible for their own fly-fishing equipment and clothing.
3. Local air transportation to and from base camps will be outsourced.
4. Tour guides are not responsible for the number of King Salmon caught by guests.

CUSTOMER REVIEW

The president of BlueNote, Inc.

Case

Silver Fiddle Construction

You are the president of Silver Fiddle Construction (SFC), which specializes in building high-quality, customized homes in the Grand Junction, Colorado, area. You have just been hired by the Czopeks to build their dream home. You operate as a general contractor and employ only a part-time bookkeeper. You subcontract work to local trade professionals. Housing construction in Grand Junction is booming. You are tentatively scheduled to complete 11 houses this year. You have promised the Czopeks that the final costs will range from $290,000 to $320,000 and that it will take five months to complete the house once groundbreaking has begun. The Czopeks are willing to have the project delayed in order to save costs.

You have just finished a preliminary scope statement for the project (see below). You are now brainstorming potential risks associated with the project.

1. Identify potential risks associated with this project. Try to come up with at least five different risks.
2. Use a risk assessment matrix similar to Figure 7.4 to analyze identified risks.
3. Develop a risk response matrix similar to Figure 7.7 to outline how you would deal with each of the risks.

PROJECT SCOPE STATEMENT

PROJECT OBJECTIVE

To construct a high-quality, custom home within five months at a cost not to exceed $320,000.

DELIVERABLES

- A 2,500-square-foot, 2½-bath, 3-bedroom, finished home.
- A finished garage, insulated and sheetrocked.
- Kitchen appliances to include range, oven, microwave, and dishwasher.
- High-efficiency gas furnace with programmable thermostat.

MILESTONES

1. Permits approved July 5.
2. Foundation poured July 12.
3. "Dry in"—framing, sheathing, plumbing, electrical, and mechanical inspections—passed September 25.
4. Final inspection November 7.

TECHNICAL REQUIREMENTS

1. Home must meet local building codes.
2. All windows and doors must pass NFRC class 40 energy ratings.
3. Exterior wall insulation must meet an "R" factor of 21.
4. Ceiling insulation must meet an "R" factor of 38.
5. Floor insulation must meet an "R" factor of 25.
6. Garage will accommodate two cars and one 28-foot-long Winnebago.
7. Structure must pass seismic stability codes.

LIMITS AND EXCLUSIONS

1. The home will be built to the specifications and design of the original blueprints provided by the customer.
2. Owner is responsible for landscaping.
3. Refrigerator is not included among kitchen appliances.
4. Air conditioning is not included, but house is prewired for it.
5. SFC reserves the right to contract out services.

CUSTOMER REVIEW

"Bolo" and Izabella Czopek.

Case

Javacom LAN Project*

Javacom is a small, information systems consulting firm located in Meridian, Louisiana. Javacom has just been hired to design and install a local area network (LAN) for the city of Meridian's social welfare agency. You are the manager for the project, which includes two Javacom professionals and one intern from a local university. You have just finished a preliminary scope statement for the project (see below). You are now brainstorming potential risks associated with the project.

1. Identify potential risks associated with this project. Try to come up with at least five different risks.
2. Use a risk assessment matrix similar to Figure 7.4 to analyze identified risks.
3. Develop a risk response matrix similar to Figure 7.7 to outline how you would deal with each of the risks.

PROJECT SCOPE STATEMENT

PROJECT OBJECTIVE

To design and install a local area network (LAN) within one month with a budget not to exceed $82,000 for the Meridian Social Service Agency.

DELIVERABLES

- Twenty workstations.
- Server with dual Pentium processor.
- Two Hewlett-Packard laser jet Si/Si MX printers.
- Windows NT server and workstation operating system.
- Four hours of introduction training for client's personnel.
- Sixteen hours of training for client network administrator.
- Fully operational LAN system.

MILESTONES

1. Hardware January 22.
2. Setting users' priority and authorization January 26.
3. In-house whole network test completed February 1.
4. Client site test completed February 2.
5. Training completed February 16.

TECHNICAL REQUIREMENTS

1. Workstations with 17-inch monitors, Pentium II processor, 128 MB RAM, 4 MB SVGA, 32X CD-ROM, zip drive, Ethernet card, 4.0 GB hard drive.
2. PCI 64 Ethernet LAN interface cards and Ethernet connections (must transmit at least 100 mbps).
3. System must support Windows NT platform and be Y2K compliant.

LIMITS AND EXCLUSIONS

1. System maintenance and repair only up to one month after final inspection.
2. Warranties transferred to client.

* This case was prepared with the assistance of Budiyoso Kurniawai.

3. Only responsible for installing software designated by the client two weeks before the start of the project.

4. Client will be billed for additional training beyond that prescribed in the contract.

CUSTOMER REVIEW

Director of the city of Meridian's Social Service Agency.

Appendix 7.1

PERT and PERT Simulation

PERT—PROGRAM EVALUATION REVIEW TECHNIQUE

In 1958 the Special Office of the Navy and the Booze, Allen, and Hamilton consulting firm developed PERT (program evaluation and review technique) to schedule the more than 3,300 contractors of the Polaris submarine project and to cover uncertainty of activity time estimates.

PERT is almost identical to the critical path method (CPM) technique except it assumes each activity duration has a range that follows a statistical distribution. PERT uses three time estimates for each activity. Basically, this means each activity duration can range from an optimistic time to a pessimistic time, and a weighted average can be computed for each activity. Because project activities usually represent work, and because work tends to stay behind once it gets behind, the PERT developers chose an approximation of the *beta distribution* to represent activity durations. This distribution is known to be flexible and can accommodate empirical data that do not follow a normal distribution. The activity durations can be skewed more toward the high or low end of the data range. Figure A7.1A depicts a *beta* distribution for activity durations that is skewed toward the right and is representative of work that tends to stay late once it is behind. The distribution for the project duration is represented by a normal (symmetrical) distribution shown in Figure A7.1B. The project distribution represents the sum of the weighted averages of the activities on the critical path(s).

Knowing the weighted average and variances for each activity allows the project planner to compute the probability of meeting different project durations. Follow the steps described in the hypothetical example given next. (The jargon is difficult for those not familiar with statistics, but the process is relatively simple after working through a couple of examples.)

FIGURE A7.1 Activity and Project Frequency Distributions

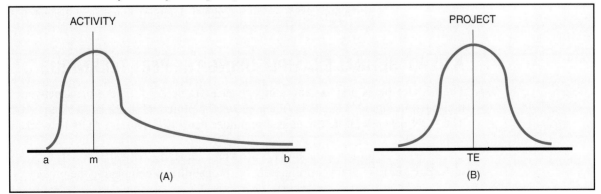

The weighted average activity time is computed by the following formula:

$$t_e = \frac{a + 4m + b}{6}$$ (7.1)

where t_e = weighted average activity time

   a = optimistic activity time (1 chance in 100 of completing the activity earlier under *normal* conditions)

   b = pessimistic activity time (1 chance in 100 of completing the activity later under *normal* conditions)

   m = most likely activity time

When the three time estimates have been specified, this equation is used to compute the weighted average duration for each activity. The average (deterministic) value is placed on the project network as in the CPM method and the early, late, slack, and project completion times are computed as they are in the CPM method.

The variability in the activity time estimates is approximated by the following equations: Equation 7.2 represents the standard deviation for the *activity*. Equation 7.3 represents the standard deviation for the *project*. Note the standard deviation of the activity is squared in this equation; this is also called variance. This sum includes only activities on the critical path(s) or path being reviewed.

$$\sigma_{t_e} = \left(\frac{b - a}{6}\right)$$ (7.2)

$$\sigma_{T_E} = \sqrt{\Sigma \sigma t_e^2}$$ (7.3)

Finally, the average project duration (T_E) is the sum of all the average activity times along the critical path (sum of t_e), and it follows a normal distribution.

Knowing the average project duration and the variances of activities allows the probability of completing the project (or segment of the project) by a specific time to be computed using standard statistical tables. The equation below (Equation 7.4) is used to compute the "Z" value found in statistical tables (Z = number of standard deviations from the mean), which, in turn, tells the probability of completing the project in the time specified.

$$Z = \frac{T_S - T_E}{\sqrt{\Sigma \sigma_{te^2}}}$$ (7.4)

where T_E = critical path duration

   T_S = scheduled project duration

   Z = probability (of meeting scheduled duration) found in statistical Table A7.2

A HYPOTHETICAL EXAMPLE USING THE PERT TECHNIQUE

The activity times and variances are given in Table A7.1. The project network is presented in Figure A7.2. This figure shows the project network as AOA and AON. The AON network is presented as a reminder that PERT can use AON networks as well as AOA.

The expected project duration (T_E) is 64 time units; the critical path is 1, 2, 3, 5, 6, or A, B, C, E, F. With this information, the probability of completing the project by a

TABLE A7.1
Activity Times and Variances

Activity	a	m	b	t_e	$[(b - a)/6]^2$
1–2	17	29	47	30	25
2–3	6	12	24	13	9
2–4	16	19	28	20	4
3–5	13	16	19	16	1
4–5	2	5	14	6	4
5–6	2	5	8	5	1

FIGURE A7.2
Hypothetical Network

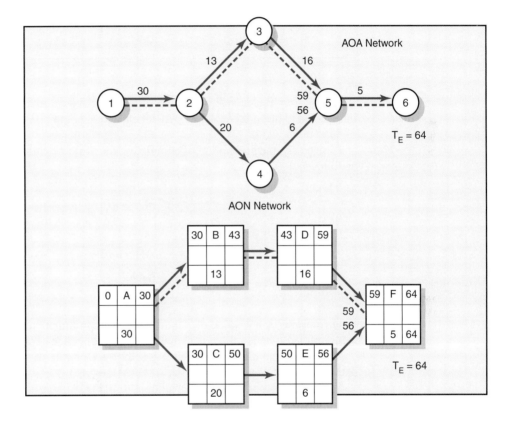

specific date can easily be computed using standard statistical methods. For example, what is the probability the project will be completed before a scheduled time (T_S) of 67? The normal curve for the project would appear as shown in Figure A7.3.

Using the formula for the Z value, the probability can be computed as follows:

$$Z = \frac{T_S - T_E}{\sqrt{\Sigma \sigma_{t_e}^2}}$$

$$= \frac{67 - 64}{\sqrt{25 + 9 + 1 + 1}}$$

$$= \frac{+3}{\sqrt{36}}$$

$$= +0.50$$

$$P = 0.69$$

FIGURE A7.3
Possible Project
Durations

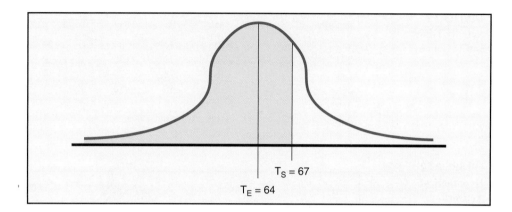

$T_S = 67$

$T_E = 64$

Reading from Table A7.2, a *Z* value of $+0.5$ gives a probability of 0.69, which is interpreted to mean there is a 69 percent chance of completing the project on or before 67 time units.

Conversely, the probability of completing the project by time period 60 is computed as follows:

$$Z = \frac{60 - 64}{\sqrt{25 + 9 + 1 + 1}}$$

$$= \frac{-4}{\sqrt{36}}$$

$$= -0.67$$

$$P \approx 0.26$$

From Table A7.2, a Z value of -0.67 gives an approximate probability of 0.26, which is interpreted to mean there is about a 26 percent chance of completing the project on or before 60 time units. Note that this same type of calculation can be made for any path or segment of a path in the network.

When such probabilities are available to management, trade-off decisions can be made to accept or reduce the risk associated with a particular project duration. For example, if the project manager wishes to improve the chances of completing the project by 64 time units, at least two choices are available. First, management can spend money up front to change conditions that will reduce the duration of one or more activities on the critical path. A more prudent, second alternative would be to allocate money to a contingency fund and wait to see how the project is progressing as it is implemented.

TABLE A7.2

Z Value	Probability	Z Value	Probability
−2.0	0.02	+2.0	0.98
−1.5	0.07	+1.5	0.93
−1.0	0.16	+1.0	0.84
−0.7	0.24	+0.7	0.76
−0.5	0.31	+0.5	0.69
−0.3	0.38	+0.3	0.62
−0.1	0.36	+0.1	0.54

Case

International Capital, Inc.—Part A

International Capital, Inc. (IC), is a small investment banking firm that specializes in securing funds for small- to medium-sized firms. IC is able to use a standardized project format for each engagement. Only activity times and unusual circumstances change the standard network. Beth Brown has been assigned to this client as project manager partner and has compiled the network information and activity times for the latest client below:

Activity	Description	Immediate Predecessor
A	Start story draft using template	—
B	Research client firm	—
C	Create "due diligence" rough draft	A, B
D	Coordinate needs proposal with client	C
E	Estimate future demand and cash flows	C
F	Draft future plans for client company	E
G	Create and approve legal documents	C
H	Integrate all drafts into first-draft proposal	D, F, G
I	Line up potential sources of capital	G, F
J	Check, approve, and print final legal proposal	H
K	Sign contracts and transfer funds	I, J

	Time in Workdays		
Activity	Optimistic	Most Likely	Pessimistic
A	4	7	10
B	2	4	8
C	2	5	8
D	16	19	28
E	6	9	24
F	1	7	13
G	4	10	28
H	2	5	14
I	5	8	17
J	2	5	8
K	17	29	45

MANAGERIAL REPORT

Brown and other broker partners have a policy of passing their plan through a project review committee of colleagues. This committee traditionally checks that all details are covered, times are realistic, and resources are available. Brown wishes you to develop a report that presents a planned schedule and expected project completion time in workdays. Include a project network in your report. The average duration for a sourcing capital project is 70 workdays. IC partners have agreed it is good business to set up projects with a 95 percent chance of attaining the plan. How does this project stack up with the average project? What would the average have to be to ensure a 95 percent chance of completing the project in 70 workdays?

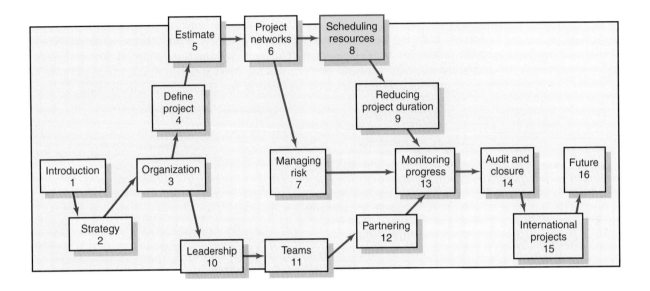

Scheduling Resources
The Problem
Types of Project Constraints
Classification of a Scheduling Problem
Resource Allocation Methods
Computer Demonstration of Resource-Constrained Scheduling
Splitting/Multitasking
Benefits of Scheduling Resources
Assigning Project Work
Multiproject Resource Schedules
Summary
Appendix 8.1: Critical-Chain Approach

CHAPTER EIGHT

Scheduling Resources

Project network times are not a schedule until resources have been assigned.

There are always more project proposals than there are available resources. The priority system needs to select projects that best contribute to the organization's objectives, within the constraints of the resources available. If all projects and their respective resources are computer scheduled, the feasibility and impact of adding a new project to those in process can be quickly assessed. With this information the project priority team will add a new project only if resources are available to be formally committed to that specific project. This chapter examines methods of scheduling resources so the team can make realistic judgments of resource availability and project durations. The project manager uses the same schedule for implementing the project. If changes occur during project implementation, the computer schedule is easily updated and the effects easily assessed.

The Problem

After staff and other resources were assigned to her project, a project manager listed the following questions that still needed to be addressed:

- Will the assigned labor and/or equipment be adequate and available to deal with my project?
- Will outside contractors have to be used?
- Do unforeseen resource dependencies exist? Is there a new critical path?
- How much flexibility do we have in using resources?
- Is the original deadline realistic?

Clearly, this project director has a good understanding of the problems she is facing. Any project scheduling system should facilitate finding quick, easy answers to these questions.

The planned network and activity project duration times found in previous chapters fail to deal with resource usage and availability. The time estimates for the work packages and network times were made independently with the implicit assumption that resources would be available. This may or may not be the case. If resources are adequate but the demand varies widely over the life of the project, it may be desirable to even out resource demand by delaying noncritical activities (using slack) to lower peak demand and, thus, increase resource utilization. This process is called *resource leveling* or *smoothing.* On the other hand, if resources are not adequate to meet peak demands, the late start of some activities must be delayed, and the duration of the project may be increased. This process is called *resource-constrained scheduling.* One research study by your author of more than 50 projects found that planned project network durations were increased 38 percent when resources were scheduled.

Because the costs of failing to consider resource usage and availability are hidden or not obvious, resource scheduling in practice is often not done or does not get the attention it deserves. The consequences of failing to schedule limited resources are a costly activity and project delays usually manifest themselves midway in the project when quick corrective action is difficult. An additional consequence of failing to schedule resources is ignoring the peaks and valleys of resource usage over the duration of the project. Because project resources are usually overcommitted and because resources seldom line up by availability and need, procedures are needed to deal with these problems. This chapter addresses methods available to project managers for dealing with resource utilization and availability through resource leveling and resource-constrained scheduling.

Types of Project Constraints

Project constraints impede or delay the start of activities. The result is a reduction in slack shown on the planned network, a decrease in scheduling flexibility, a possible decrease in the number of parallel activities, and an increase in the likelihood of delaying the project. Three project constraints need to be considered in scheduling.

Technical or Logic Constraints

These constraints usually address the *sequence* in which project activities must occur. The project network depicts technical constraints. A project network for framing a house might show three activities of (1) pour foundation, (2) build frame, and (3) cover roof in a sequence. A network for a new software project could place the activities of (1) design, (2) code, and (3) test in the network as a sequence. In other words, you cannot logically perform activity 2 until 1 is completed, etc. (see Figure 8.1A).

FIGURE 8.1
Constraint Examples

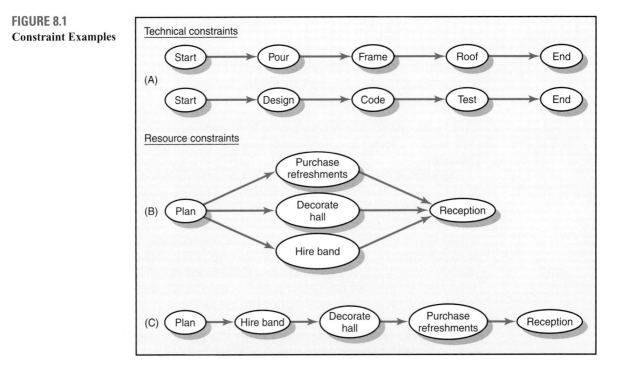

Physical Constraints

In rare situations there are physical constraints that cause activities that would normally occur in parallel to be constrained by contractual or environmental conditions. For example, renovation of a ship compartment might allow only one person to perform an activity because of space limitations. Another example would be erection of a tower and nearby ground work. The procedures for handling physical constraints are similar to those used for resource constraints.

Resource Constraints

The absence or shortage of resources can drastically alter technical constraints. A project network planner may assume adequate resources and show activities occurring in parallel. However, parallel activities hold potential for resource conflicts. For example, assume you are planning a wedding reception that includes four activities—(1) plan, (2) hire band, (3) decorate hall, and (4) purchase refreshments. Each activity takes one day. Activities 2, 3, and 4 could be done in parallel by different people. There is no technical reason or dependency of one on another (see Figure 8.1B). However, if one person must perform all activities, the resource constraint requires the activities be performed in sequence or series. Clearly the consequence is a delay of these activities and a very different set of network relationships (see Figure 8.1C). Note that the resource dependency takes priority over the technological dependency but *does not violate the technological dependency;* that is, hire, decorate, and purchase may now have to take place in sequence rather than concurrently, but they must all be completed before the reception can take place.

The interrelationships and interactions among time and resource constraints are complex for even small project networks. Some effort to examine these interactions before the project begins frequently uncovers surprising problems. Project managers who do not consider resource availability in moderately complex projects usually learn of the problem when it is too late to correct. A deficit of resources can significantly alter project dependency relationships, completion dates, and project costs. Project managers must be careful to schedule resources to ensure availability in the right quantities and at the right time. Fortunately, there are computer software programs that can identify resource problems during the early project planning phase when corrective changes can be considered. These programs only require activity resource needs and availability information to schedule resources.

Kinds of Resource Constraints

Resources are people, equipment, and material that can be drawn on to accomplish something. In projects the availability or unavailability of resources will often influence the way projects are managed. The major resources projects managers must marshal, schedule, and manage on a daily basis are people, materials, equipment, and working capital.

1. People   This is the most obvious and important project resource. Human resources are usually classified by the skills they bring to the project—for example, programmer, mechanical engineer, welder, inspector, marketing director, supervisor. In rare cases some skills are interchangeable, but usually with a loss of productivity. The many differing skills of human resources add to the complexity of scheduling projects.

2. Materials   Project materials cover a large spectrum: for example, chemicals for a scientific project, concrete for a road project, survey data for a marketing project.

Material availability and shortages have been blamed for the delay of many projects. When it is known that a lack of availability of materials is important and probable, materials should be included in the project network plan and schedule. For example, delivery and placement of an oil rig tower in a Siberian oil field has a very small time window during one summer month. Any delivery delay means a one-year, costly delay. Another example in which material was the major resource scheduled was the resurfacing and replacement of some structures on the Golden Gate Bridge in San Francisco. Work on the project was limited to the hours between midnight and 5:00 A.M. with a penalty of $1,000 per minute for any work taking place after 5:00 A.M. Scheduling the arrival of replacement structures was an extremely important part of managing the five-hour work-time window of the project. Scheduling materials has also become important in developing products where time-to-market can result in loss of market share.

3. Equipment   Equipment is usually presented by type, size, and quantity. In some cases equipment can be interchanged to improve schedules, but this is not typical. Equipment is often overlooked as a constraint. The most common oversight is to assume the resource pool is more than adequate for the project. For example, if a project needs one earth-moving tractor six months from now and the organization owns four, it is common to assume the resource will not delay the pending project. However, when the earth-moving tractor is due on-site in six months, all four machines in the pool might be occupied on other projects. In multiproject environments it is prudent to use a common resource pool for all projects. This approach forces a check of resource availability across all projects and reserves the equipment for specific project needs in the future. Recognition of equipment constraints before the project begins can avoid high crashing or delay costs.

4. Working Capital   In a few project situations such as construction, working capital is treated as a resource because it is limited in supply. If working capital is readily available, a project manager may work on many activities concurrently. If working capital is in short supply because progress payments are made monthly, materials and labor usage may have to be restricted to conserve cash. This situation represents a cash flow problem.

Classification of a Scheduling Problem

Most of the scheduling methods available today require the project manager to classify the project as either *time constrained* or *resource constrained.* Project managers need to consult their priority matrix (see Figure 4.2) to determine which case fits their project. One simple test to determine if the project is time or resource constrained is to ask, "If the critical path is delayed, will resources be added to get back on schedule?" If the answer is yes, assume the project is time constrained; if no, assume the project is resource constrained.

> A time-constrained project is one that must be completed by an imposed date. If required, resources can be added to ensure the project is completed by a specific date. Although time is the critical factor, resource usage should be no more than is necessary and sufficient.
>
> A resource-constrained project is one that assumes the level of resource available cannot be exceeded. If the resources are inadequate, it will be acceptable to delay the project, but as little as possible.

In scheduling terms, time constrained means time (project duration) is fixed and resources are flexible, while resource constrained means resources are fixed and time is flexible. Methods for scheduling these projects are presented in the next section.

Resource Allocation Methods

Assumptions

Ease of demonstrating the allocation methods available requires some limiting assumptions to keep attention on the heart of the problem. The rest of the chapter depends entirely on the assumptions noted here. First, splitting activities will not be allowed. This means once an activity is placed in the schedule, assume it will be worked on continuously until it is finished; hence, an activity cannot be started, stopped for a period of time, and then finished. Second, the level of resource used for an activity cannot be changed. These limiting assumptions do not exist in practice, but simplify learning. It is easy for new project managers to deal with the reality of splitting activities and changing the level of resources when they meet them on the job.

Time-Constrained Projects: Smoothing Resource Demand

Scheduling time-constrained projects focuses on resource *utilization*. When demand for a specific resource type is erratic, it is difficult to manage, and utilization may be very poor. Practitioners have attacked the utilization problem using resource leveling techniques that balance or smooth demand for a resource. Basically, all leveling techniques delay noncritical activities by using positive slack to reduce peak demand and fill in the valleys for the resources. An example will demonstrate the basic procedure for a time-constrained project. See Figure 8.2.

For the purpose of demonstration, the Botanical Garden project uses only one resource (backhoes); all backhoes are interchangeable. The top bar chart shows the activities on a time scale. The dependencies are shown with the vertical connecting arrows. The horizontal arrows following activities represent activity slack (for example, irrigation requires six days to complete and has six days slack). The number of backhoes needed for each task is shown in the shaded activity duration block (rectangle). After the land has been scarified and the plan laid out, work can begin on the walkways, irrigation, and fencing and retaining walls simultaneously. The middle chart shows the resource profile for the backhoes. For periods 4 through 10, four backhoes are needed.

Because this project is declared time constrained, the goal will be to reduce the peak requirement for the resource and thereby increase the utilization of the resource. A quick examination of the ES (early start) resource load chart suggests only two activities have slack that can be used to reduce the peak—fence and walls provide the best choice for smoothing the resource needs. Another choice could be irrigation, but it would result in an up and down resource profile. The choice will probably center on the activity that is perceived as having the least risk of being late. The smoothed resource loading chart shows the results of delaying the fence and walls activity. Note the differences in the resource profiles. The important point is the resources needed over the life of the project have been reduced from four to three (25 percent). In addition the profile has been smoothed, which should be easier to manage.

The Botanical Garden project schedule reached the three goals of smoothing:

- The peak of demand for the resource was reduced.
- Resources over the life of the project have been reduced.
- The fluctuations in resource demand were minimized.

The latter improves the utilization of resources. Backhoes are not easily moved from location to location. There are costs associated with changing the level of resources needed. The same analogy applies to the movement of people back and forth among

FIGURE 8.2 **Botanical Garden**

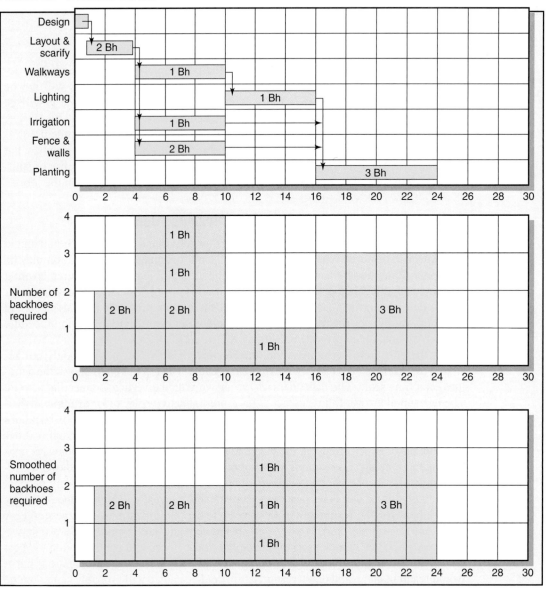

projects. It is well known that people are more efficient if they can focus their effort on one project rather than multitasking their time among, say, three projects.

The downside of leveling is a loss of flexibility that occurs from reducing slack. The risk of activities delaying the project also increases because slack reduction can create more critical activities and/or near-critical activities. Pushing leveling too far for a perfectly level resource profile is risky. Every activity then becomes critical.

The Botanical Garden example gives a sense of the time-constrained problem and the smoothing approach. However, in practice the magnitude of the problem is very complex for even small projects. Manual solutions are not practical. Fortunately, the software packages available today have very good routines for leveling project resources. Typically, they use activities that have the most slack to level project resources. The rationale is those activities with the most slack pose the least risk. Although this is generally true, other risk factors such as reduction of flexibility to use reassigned resources on other activities or the nature of the activity (easy, complex) are not addressed using such a simple rationale. It is easy to experiment with many alternatives to find the one that best fits your project and minimizes risk of delaying the project.

Resource-Constrained Projects

When the number of people and/or equipment is not adequate to meet peak demand requirements and it is impossible to obtain more, the project manager faces a resource-constrained problem. Something has to give. The trick is to prioritize and allocate resources to minimize project delay without exceeding the resource limit or altering the technical network relationships.

The resource scheduling problem is a large combinatorial one. This means even a modest-size project network with only a few resource types might have several thousand feasible solutions. A few researchers have demonstrated *optimum* mathematical solutions to the resource allocation problem but only for small networks and very few resource types. The massive data requirements for larger problems make pure mathematical solutions (e.g., linear programming) impractical. An alternative approach to the problem has been the use of heuristics (rules of thumb) to solve large combinatorial problems. These practical decision or priority rules have been in place for many years.

Heuristics do not always yield an optimal schedule, but they are very capable of yielding a "good" schedule for very complex networks with many types of resources. The efficiency of different rules and combinations of rules has been well documented. However, because each project is unique, it is wise to test several sets of heuristics on a network to determine the priority allocation rules that minimize project delay. The computer software available today makes it very easy for the project manager to create a good resource schedule for the project. A simple example of the heuristic approach is illustrated here.

Heuristics allocate resources to activities to minimize project delay; that is, heuristics prioritize which activities are allocated resources and which activities are delayed when resources are not adequate. The following scheduling heuristics have been found to consistently minimize project delay over a large variety of projects. Schedule activities using the following heuristic priority rules in the order presented:

1. Minimum slack.
2. Smallest duration.
3. Lowest activity identification number.

The parallel method is the most widely used approach to apply heuristics. The parallel method is an iterative process that starts at the first time period of the project and schedules period-by-period any activities eligible to start. In any period when two or more activities require the same resource, the priority rules are applied. For example, if in period 5 three activities are eligible to start (i.e., have the same ES) and require the same resource, the first activity placed in the schedule would be the activity with the least slack (rule 1). However, if all activities have the same slack, the next rule would be invoked (rule 2), and the activity with the smallest duration would be placed in the schedule first. In very rare cases, when all eligible activities have the same slack and the same duration, the tie is broken by the lowest activity identification number (rule 3), since each activity has a unique ID number.

When a resource limit has been reached, the early start (ES) for succeeding activities not yet in the schedule will be delayed (and all successor activities not having free slack) and their slack reduced. In subsequent periods the procedure is repeated until the project is scheduled. The procedure is demonstrated below; see Figure 8.3. The shaded areas in the resource loading chart represent the "scheduling interval" of the *time constrained* schedule (ES through LF). You can schedule the resource any place *within* the interval and not delay the project. Scheduling the activity beyond the LF will delay the project.

The programmers are limited to three. Follow the actions described in Figures 8.3 and 8.4. Note how the limit of three programmers starts to delay the project.

The Parallel Method:

Period	Action
0–1	Only activity 1 is eligible. It requires 2 programmers.
	Load activity 1 into schedule.
1–2	No activities are eligible to be scheduled.
2–3	Activities 2, 3, and 4 are eligible to be scheduled. Activity 3 has the least slack (0)—apply rule 1.
	Load Activity 3 into schedule.
	Activity 2 is next with slack of 2; however, activity 2 requires 2 programmers and only 1 is available.
	Delay activity 2. Update ES = 3, slack = 1.
	The next eligible activity is activity 4, since it only requires 1 programmer.
	Load activity 4 into schedule.

——————————————————————— See Figure 8.4 ———————————————————————

Period	Action
3–4	Activity 2 is eligible but exceeds limit of 3 programmers in pool.
	Delay activity 2. Update ES = 4, slack = 0.
4–5	Activity 2 is eligible but exceeds limit of 3 programmers in pool.
	Delay activity 2. Update ES = 5, slack = −1.
	Delay activity 7. Update ES = 11, slack = −1.
5–6	Activity 2 is eligible but exceeds limit of 3 programmers in pool.
	Delay activity 2. Update ES = 6, slack = −2.
	Delay activity 7. Update ES = 12, slack = −2.
6–7	Activities 2, 5, and 6 are eligible with slack of −2, 2, and 0, respectively.
	Load activity 2 into schedule (rule 1).
	Because activity 6 has 0 slack, it is the next eligible activity.
	Load activity 6 into schedule (rule 1).
	The programmer limit of 3 is reached.
	Delay activity 5. Update ES = 7, slack = 1.
7–8	Limit is reached. No programmers available.
	Delay activity 5. Update ES = 8, slack = 0.
8–9	Limit is reached. No programmers available.
	Delay activity 5. Update ES = 9, slack = −1.
9–10	Limit is reached. No programmers available.
	Delay activity 5. Update ES = 10 slack = −2.
10–11	Activity 5 is eligible.
	Load activity 5 into schedule.
	(Note: Activity 6 does not have slack because there are no programmers available—3 maximum.)
11–12	No eligible activities.
12–13	Activity 7 is eligible.
	Load activity 7 into schedule.

FIGURE 8.3   **Resource-Constrained Schedule through Period 2–3**

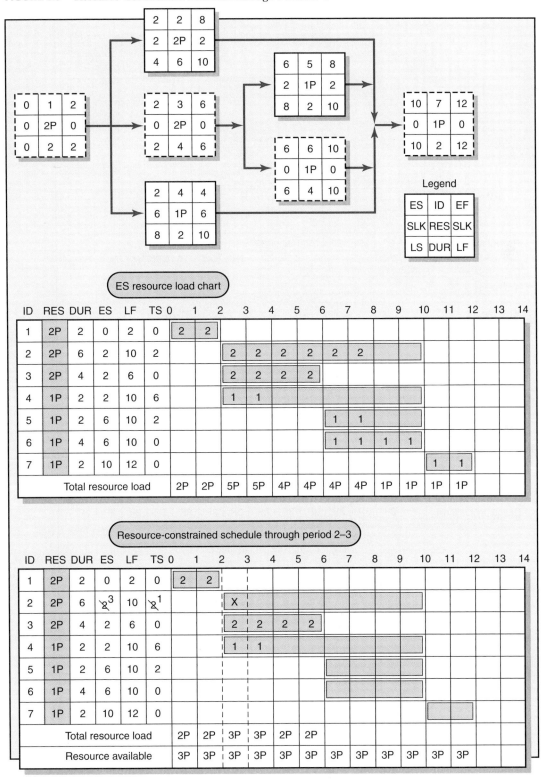

FIGURE 8.4 **Resource-Constrained Schedule through Period 5–6**

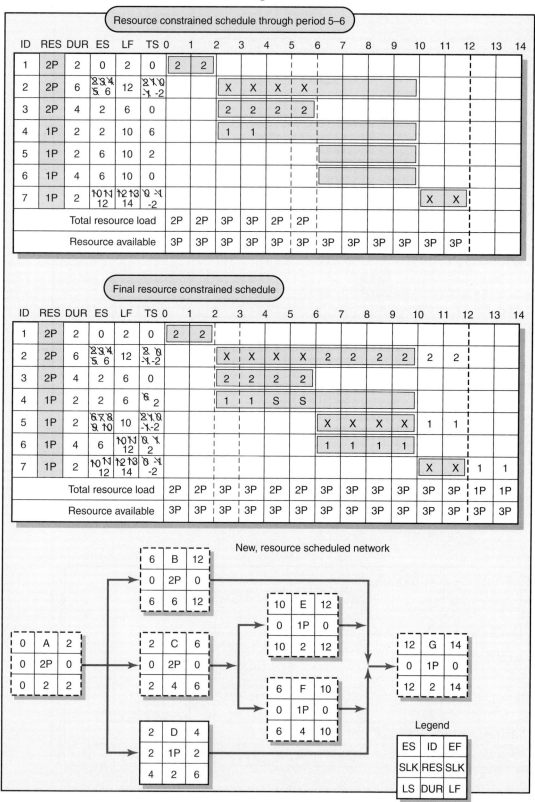

Observe how it is necessary to update each period to reflect changes in activity early start and slack times so the heuristics can reflect changing priorities. The network in Figure 8.4 on the preceding page reflects the new schedule date of 14 time units, rather than the time-constrained project duration of 12 time units. The network has also been revised to reflect new start, finish, and slack times for each activity. Note that activity 6 is still critical and has a slack of 0 time units because no resources are available (they are being used on activities 2 and 5). Compare the slack for each activity found in Figures 8.3 and 8.4; slack has been reduced significantly. Note that activity 4 has only 2 units of slack rather than what appears to be 6 slack units. This occurs because only three programmers are available, and they are needed to satisfy the resource requirements of activities 2 and 5. Note that even though the project duration has increased from 12 to 14 time units, the number of critical activities (1, 2, 3, 5, 6, 7) has increased from four to six.

Computer Demonstration of Resource-Constrained Scheduling

Fortunately, project management software is capable of assessing and resolving complicated resource-constrained schedules using heuristics similar to what was described above. We will use the EMR project to demonstrate how this is done using MS Project 2002. It is important to note that the software is not "managing" the project. The software is simply a tool the project manager uses to view the project from different perspectives and conditions. See the Snapshot from Practice on page 257 for more tips on assessing resource problems.

EMR is the name given to the development of a handheld electronic medical reference guide to be used by emergency medical technicians and paramedics. Figure 8.5 contains a time-limited network for the design phase of the project. For the purpose of this example, we assume that only design engineers are required for the tasks and that the design engineers are interchangeable. The number of engineers required to perform each task is noted in the network, where 500 percent means five design engineers are needed for the activity. For example, activity 5, feature specs, requires four design engineers (400 percent). The project begins January 1, 2005, and ends February 14, 2005, a duration of 45 workdays. The time-limited (constrained) bar chart for the project is shown in Figure 8.6. This bar chart incorporates the same information used to develop the project network, but presents the project in the form of a bar chart along a time line.

Finally, a resource usage chart is presented for a segment of the project—January 15 to January 23; see Figure 8.7A. Observe that the time-limited project requires 21 design engineers on January 18 and 19 (168 hrs/8 hrs per engineer = 21 engineers). This segment represents the peak requirement for design engineers for the project. However, due to the shortage of design engineers and commitments to other projects, only eight engineers can be assigned to the project. This creates overallocation problems more clearly detailed in Figure 8.7B, which is a resource loading chart for design engineers. Notice that the peak is 21 engineers and the limit of 8 engineers is shown by the gray shaded area.

To resolve this problem we use the "leveling" tool within the software and first try to solve the problem by leveling only within slack. This solution would preserve the original finish date. However, as expected, this does not solve all of the allocation problems. The next option is to allow the software to apply scheduling heuristics and level outside of slack. The new schedule is contained in the revised, resource-limited

FIGURE 8.5 EMR Project Network View Schedule before Resources Leveled

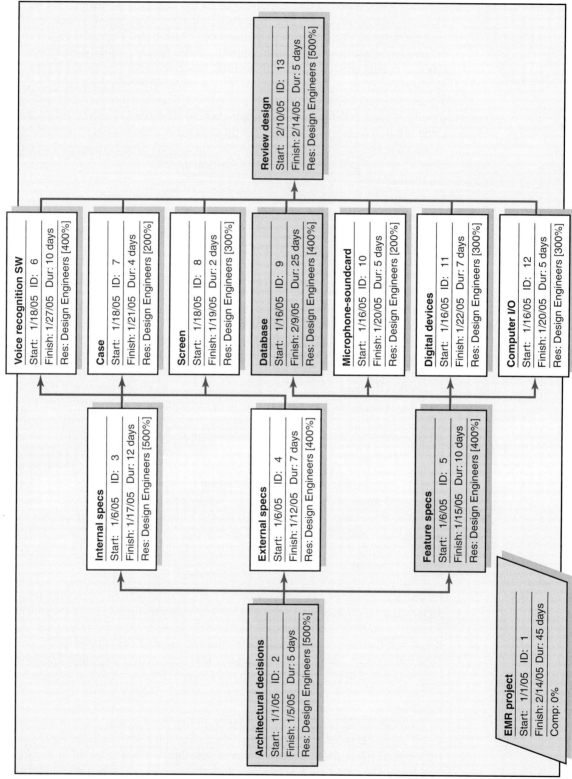

Voice recognition SW
Start: 1/18/05   ID: 6
Finish: 1/27/05   Dur: 10 days
Res: Design Engineers [400%]

Case
Start: 1/18/05   ID: 7
Finish: 1/21/05   Dur: 4 days
Res: Design Engineers [200%]

Screen
Start: 1/18/05   ID: 8
Finish: 1/19/05   Dur: 2 days
Res: Design Engineers [300%]

Database
Start: 1/16/05   ID: 9
Finish: 2/9/05   Dur: 25 days
Res: Design Engineers [400%]

Microphone-soundcard
Start: 1/16/05   ID: 10
Finish: 1/20/05   Dur: 5 days
Res: Design Engineers [200%]

Digital devices
Start: 1/16/05   ID: 11
Finish: 1/22/05   Dur: 7 days
Res: Design Engineers [300%]

Computer I/O
Start: 1/16/05   ID: 12
Finish: 1/20/05   Dur: 5 days
Res: Design Engineers [300%]

Review design
Start: 2/10/05   ID: 13
Finish: 2/14/05   Dur: 5 days
Res: Design Engineers [500%]

Internal specs
Start: 1/6/05   ID: 3
Finish: 1/17/05   Dur: 12 days
Res: Design Engineers [500%]

External specs
Start: 1/6/05   ID: 4
Finish: 1/12/05   Dur: 7 days
Res: Design Engineers [400%]

Feature specs
Start: 1/6/05   ID: 5
Finish: 1/15/05   Dur: 10 days
Res: Design Engineers [400%]

Architectural decisions
Start: 1/1/05   ID: 2
Finish: 1/5/05   Dur: 5 days
Res: Design Engineers [500%]

EMR project
Start: 1/1/05   ID: 1
Finish: 2/14/05   Dur: 45 days
Comp: 0%

FIGURE 8.6 EMR Project before Resources Added

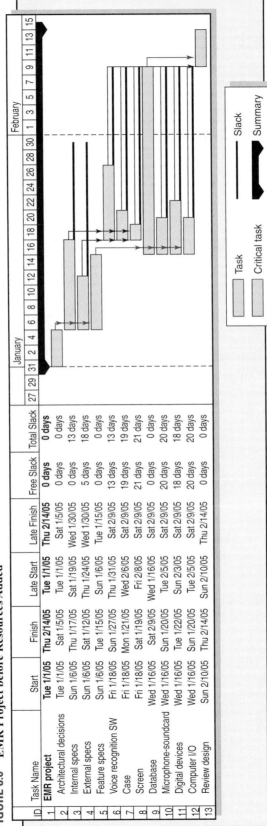

ID	Task Name	Start	Finish	Late Start	Late Finish	Free Slack	Total Slack
1	**EMR project**	**Tue 1/1/05**	**Thu 2/14/05**	**Tue 1/1/05**	**Thu 2/14/05**	**0 days**	**0 days**
2	Architectural decisions	Tue 1/1/05	Sat 1/5/05	Tue 1/1/05	Sat 1/5/05	0 days	0 days
3	Internal specs	Sun 1/6/05	Thu 1/17/05	Sat 1/19/05	Wed 1/30/05	0 days	13 days
4	External specs	Sun 1/6/05	Sat 1/12/05	Thu 1/24/05	Wed 1/30/05	5 days	18 days
5	Feature specs	Sun 1/6/05	Tue 1/15/05	Sun 1/6/05	Tue 1/15/05	0 days	0 days
6	Voice recognition SW	Fri 1/18/05	Sun 1/27/05	Thu 1/31/05	Sat 2/9/05	13 days	13 days
7	Case	Fri 1/18/05	Mon 1/21/05	Wed 2/6/05	Sat 2/9/05	19 days	19 days
8	Screen	Fri 1/18/05	Sat 1/19/05	Fri 2/8/05	Sat 2/9/05	21 days	21 days
9	Database	Wed 1/16/05	Sat 2/9/05	Wed 1/16/05	Sat 2/9/05	0 days	0 days
10	Microphone-soundcard	Wed 1/16/05	Sun 1/20/05	Tue 2/5/05	Sat 2/9/05	20 days	20 days
11	Digital devices	Wed 1/16/05	Tue 1/22/05	Sun 2/3/05	Sat 2/9/05	18 days	18 days
12	Computer I/O	Wed 1/16/05	Sun 1/20/05	Tue 2/5/05	Sat 2/9/05	20 days	20 days
13	Review design	Sun 2/10/05	Thu 2/14/05	Sun 2/10/05	Thu 2/14/05	0 days	0 days

253

FIGURE 8.7A   EMR Project—Time-Constrained Resource Usage View, January 15–23, 2005

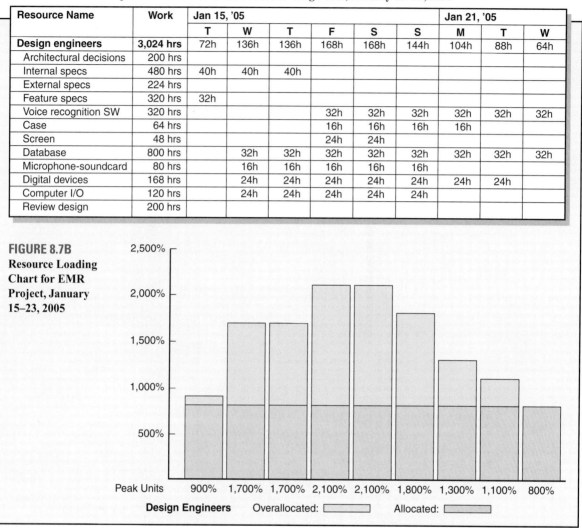

Resource Name	Work	Jan 15, '05						Jan 21, '05		
		T	W	T	F	S	S	M	T	W
Design engineers	**3,024 hrs**	72h	136h	136h	168h	168h	144h	104h	88h	64h
Architectural decisions	200 hrs									
Internal specs	480 hrs	40h	40h	40h						
External specs	224 hrs									
Feature specs	320 hrs	32h								
Voice recognition SW	320 hrs				32h	32h	32h	32h	32h	32h
Case	64 hrs				16h	16h	16h	16h		
Screen	48 hrs				24h	24h				
Database	800 hrs		32h	32h	32h	32h	32h	32h	32h	32h
Microphone-soundcard	80 hrs		16h	16h	16h	16h	16h			
Digital devices	168 hrs		24h	24h	24h	24h	24h	24h	24h	
Computer I/O	120 hrs		24h	24h	24h	24h	24h			
Review design	200 hrs									

FIGURE 8.7B

Resource Loading Chart for EMR Project, January 15–23, 2005

Peak Units   900%   1,700%   1,700%   2,100%   2,100%   1,800%   1,300%   1,100%   800%

Design Engineers   Overallocated: ▢   Allocated: ▢

network chart presented in Figure 8.8. The resource-limited project network indicates the project duration has now been extended to 2/26/05, or 57 workdays (versus 45 days time limited). The critical path is now 2, 3, 9, 13.

Figure 8.9 presents the project bar chart and the results of leveling the project schedule to reflect the availability of only eight design engineers. The application of the heuristics can be seen in the scheduling of the internal, external, and feature specification activities. All three activities were originally scheduled to start immediately after activity 1, architectural decisions.

This is impossible, since the three activities collectively require 14 engineers. The software chooses to schedule activity 5 first because this activity is on the original critical path and has zero slack (heuristic # 1). Next, and concurrently, activity 4, is chosen over activity 3 because activity 4 has a shorter duration (heuristic # 2); internal specs, activity 3, is delayed due to the limitation of 8 design engineers. Notice that the original critical path no longer applies because of the resource dependencies created by having only eight design engineers.

FIGURE 8.8 EMR Project Network View Schedule after Resources Leveled

EMR project
Start: 1/1/05   ID: 1
Finish: 2/26/05 Dur: 57 days
Comp: 0%

Architectural decisions
Start: 1/1/05   Dur: 5 days
Finish: 1/5/05   Dur: 5 days
Res: Design Engineers [500%]

Internal specs
Start: 1/16/05 ID: 3
Finish: 1/27/05 Dur: 12 days
Res: Design Engineers [500%]

External specs
Start: 1/6/05   ID: 4
Finish: 1/12/05 Dur: 7 days
Res: Design Engineers [400%]

Feature specs
Start: 1/6/05   ID: 5
Finish: 1/15/05 Dur: 10 days
Res: Design Engineers [400%]

Voice recognition SW
Start: 2/2/05   ID: 6
Finish: 2/11/05 Dur: 10 days
Res: Design Engineers [400%]

Case
Start: 2/12/05 ID: 7
Finish: 2/15/05 Dur: 4 days
Res: Design Engineers [200%]

Screen
Start: 2/16/05 ID: 8
Finish: 2/17/05 Dur: 2 days
Res: Design Engineers [300%]

Database
Start: 1/28/05 ID: 9
Finish: 2/21/05 Dur: 25 days
Res: Design Engineers [400%]

Microphone-soundcard
Start: 1/16/05 ID: 10
Finish: 1/20/05 Dur: 5 days
Res: Design Engineers [200%]

Digital devices
Start: 1/26/05 ID: 11
Finish: 2/1/05   Dur: 7 days
Res: Design Engineers [300%]

Computer I/O
Start: 1/21/05 ID: 12
Finish: 1/25/05 Dur: 5 days
Res: Design Engineers [300%]

Review design
Start: 2/22/05 ID: 13
Finish: 2/26/05 Dur: 5 days
Res: Design Engineers [500%]

FIGURE 8.9 EMR Project Resources Leveled

ID	Task Name	Start	Finish	Late Start	Late Finish	Free Slack	Total Slack
1	**EMR project**	**Tue 1/1/05**	**Thu 2/26/05**	**Tue 1/1/05**	**Tue 2/26/05**	**0 days**	**0 days**
2	Architectural decisions	Tue 1/1/05	Sat 1/5/05	Tue 1/1/05	Sat 1/5/05	0 days	0 days
3	Internal specs	Wed 1/16/05	Sun 1/27/05	Sun 1/20/05	Thu 1/31/05	0 days	4 days
4	External specs	Sun 1/6/05	Sat 1/12/05	Fri 1/25/05	Thu 1/31/05	15 days	19 days
5	Feature specs	Sun 1/6/05	Tue 1/15/05	Sun 1/6/05	Tue 1/15/05	0 days	0 days
6	Voice recognition SW	Sat 2/2/05	Mon 2/11/05	Tue 2/12/05	Thu 2/21/05	10 days	10 days
7	Case	Tue 2/12/05	Fri 2/15/05	Mon 2/18/05	Thu 2/21/05	6 days	6 days
8	Screen	Sat 2/16/05	Sun 2/17/05	Wed 2/20/05	Thu 2/21/05	4 days	4 days
9	Database	Mon 1/28/05	Thu 2/21/05	Mon 1/28/05	Thu 2/21/05	0 days	0 days
10	Microphone-soundcard	Wed 1/16/05	Sun 1/20/05	Sun 2/17/05	Thu 2/21/05	32 days	32 days
11	Digital devices	Sat 1/26/05	Fri 2/1/05	Fri 2/15/05	Thu 2/21/05	20 days	20 days
12	Computer I/O	Mon 1/21/05	Fri 1/25/05	Sun 2/17/05	Thu 2/21/05	27 days	27 days
13	Review design	Fri 2/22/05	Tue 2/26/05	Fri 2/22/05	Tue 2/26/05	0 days	0 days

One of the strengths of today's project management software is the ability to identify and provide options for resolving resource allocation problems. A project manager who uses MS Project to plan projects shared with us the following checklist for dealing with resource conflicts after preliminary assignment of resources has been made.

1. Assess whether you have overallocation problems (see *Red* in the resource sheet view.)

2. Identify where and when conflicts occur by examining the resource usage view.

3. Resolve the problem by
   a. Replacing overallocated resources with appropriate resources that are available. Then ask if this solves the problem.

   If not:

   b. Use the leveling tool and choose the level within slack option.

   i. Does this solve the problem? (Are resources still over-allocated?)

   ii. Check the sensitivity of the network and ask if this is acceptable.

   If not:

   c. Consider splitting tasks.

   i. Make sure to readjust task durations to take into account additional start-up and shutdown time.

4. If 3 does not work then either:
   a. Use level tool default option and ask if you can live with the new completion date.

   If not:

   b. Negotiate for additional resources to complete the project.

   If not possible

   c. Consider reducing project scope to meet deadline.

While this checklist makes specific references to MS Project, the same steps can be used with most project management software.

Compare the bar chart in Figure 8.9 with the time-limited bar chart in Figure 8.6. For example, note the different start dates for activity 8 (screen). In the time-limited plan (Figure 8.6), the start date for activity 8 is 1/18, while the start date in the resource limited schedule (Figure 8.9) is 2/26, over a month later!

While resource bar graphs are commonly used to illustrate overallocation problems, we prefer to view resource usage tables like the one presented in Figure 8.7A. This table tells you when you have an overallocation problem and identifies activities that are causing the overallocation.

The Impacts of Resource-Constrained Scheduling

Like leveling schedules, the limited resource schedule usually reduces slack, reduces flexibility by using slack to ensure delay is minimized, and increases the number of critical and near-critical activities. Scheduling complexity is increased because resource constraints are added to technical constraints; start times may now have two constraints. The traditional critical path concept of sequential activities from the start to the end of the project is no longer meaningful. The resource constraints can break the sequence and leave the network with a set of disjointed critical activities. Conversely, parallel activities can become sequential. Activities with slack on a time-constrained network can change from critical to noncritical.

Splitting/Multitasking

Splitting or multitasking is a scheduling technique used to get a better project schedule and/or to increase resource utilization. A planner splits the continuous work included in an activity by interrupting the work and sending the resource to another activity for a period of time and then having the resource resume work on the original

FIGURE 8.10
Splitting/
Multitasking

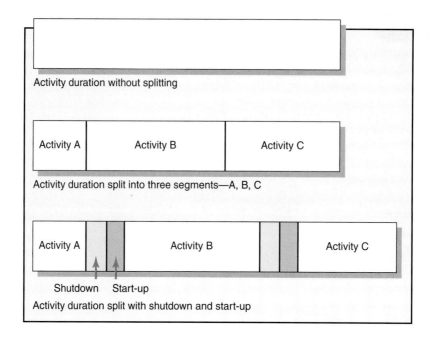

Activity duration without splitting

| Activity A | Activity B | Activity C |

Activity duration split into three segments—A, B, C

| Activity A | | Activity B | | | Activity C |

Shutdown   Start-up

Activity duration split with shutdown and start-up

activity. Splitting can be a useful tool if the work involved does not include large start-up or shutdown costs—for example, moving equipment from one activity location to another. The most common error is to interrupt "people work," where there are high conceptual start-up and shutdown costs. For example, having a bridge designer take time off to work on the design problem of another project may cause this individual to lose four days shifting conceptual gears in and out of two activities. The cost may be hidden, but it is real. Figure 8.10 depicts the nature of the splitting problem. The original activity has been split into three separate activities: A, B, and C. The shutdown and start-up times lengthen the time for the original activity.

Some have argued that the propensity to deal with resource shortages by multitasking is a major reason why projects fail to meet schedule. We agree. Planners should avoid the use of splitting as much as possible, except in situations where splitting costs are known to be small or when there is no alternative for resolving the resource problem. Computer software offers the splitting option for each activity; use it sparingly. See Snapshot from Practice: Assessing Resource Allocation.

Benefits of Scheduling Resources

It is important to remember that, if resources are truly limited and activity time estimates are accurate, the resource-constrained schedule *will* materialize as the project is implemented—*not* the time-constrained schedule! Therefore, failure to schedule limited resources can lead to serious problems for a project manager. The benefit of creating this schedule *before* the project begins leaves time for considering reasonable alternatives. If the scheduled delay is unacceptable or the risk of being delayed too high, the assumption of being resource constrained can be reassessed. Cost-time trade-offs can be considered. In some cases priorities may be changed. See Snapshot from Practice: U.S. Forest Service Resource Shortage.

A major segment of work in managing U.S. Forest Service (USFS) forests is selling mature timber to logging companies that harvest the timber under contract conditions monitored by the Service. The proceeds are returned to the federal government. The budget allocated to each forest depends on the two-year plan submitted to the U.S. Department of Agriculture.

Olympic Forest headquarters in Olympia, Washington, was developing a two-year plan as a basis for funding. All of the districts in the forest submitted their timber sale projects (numbering more than 50) to headquarters, where they were compiled and aggregated into a project plan for the whole forest. The first computer run was reviewed by a small group of senior managers to determine if the plan was reasonable and "doable." Management was pleased and relieved to note all projects appeared to be doable in the two-year time frame until a question was raised concerning the computer printout. "Why are all the columns in these projects labeled 'RESOURCE' blank?" The response from an engineer was, "We don't use that part of the program."

The discussion that ensued recognized the importance of resources in completing the two-year plan and ended with a request to "try the program with resources included." The new output was startling. The two-year program turned into a three-and-a-half-year plan because of the shortage of specific labor skills such as road engineer and environmental impact specialist. Analysis showed that adding only three skilled people would allow the two-year plan to be completed on time. In addition, further analysis showed hiring only a few more skilled people, beyond the three, would allow an extra year of projects to also be compressed into the two-year plan. This would result in additional revenue of more than $3 million. The Department of Agriculture quickly approved the requested extra dollars for additional staff to generate the extra revenue.

Resource schedules provide the information needed to prepare time-phased work package budgets with dates. Once established, they provide a quick means for a project manager to gauge the impact of unforeseen events such as turnover, equipment breakdowns, or transfer of project personnel. Resource schedules also allow project managers to assess how much flexibility they have over certain resources. This is useful when they receive requests from other managers to borrow or share resources. Honoring such requests creates goodwill and an "IOU" that can be cashed in during a time of need.

Assigning Project Work

When making individual assignments, project managers should match, as best they can, the demands and requirements of specific work with the qualifications and experience of available participants. In doing so, there is a natural tendency to assign the best people the most difficult tasks. Project managers need to be careful not to overdo this. Over time these people may grow to resent the fact that they are always given the toughest assignments. At the same time, less experienced participants may resent the fact that they are never given the opportunity to expand their skill/knowledge base. Project managers need to balance task performance with the need to develop the talents of people assigned to the project.

Project managers not only need to decide who does what but who works with whom. A number of factors need to be considered in deciding who should work together. First, to minimize unnecessary tension, managers should pick people with compatible work habits and personalities but who complement each other (i.e., one person's weakness is the other person's strength). For example, one person may be brilliant at solving complex problems but sloppy at documenting his or her progress. It would be wise to pair this person with an individual who is good at paying attention to details. Experience is another factor. Veterans should be teamed up with new hires—not only so they can share their experience but also to help socialize the newcomers to the customs and norms of the organization. Finally, future needs should be considered. If managers have some people who have never worked together before but who have to later on in the project, they may be wise to take advantage of opportunities to have these people work together early on so that they can become familiar with each other. Finally, see the Snapshot in Practice: Managing Geeks for some interesting thoughts about how Novell, Inc., puts together teams.

Multiproject Resource Schedules

For clarity we have discussed key resource allocation issues within the context of a single project. In reality resource allocation generally occurs in a multiproject environment where the demands of one project have to be reconciled with the needs of other projects. Organizations must develop and manage systems for efficiently allocating and scheduling resources across several projects with different priorities, resource requirements, sets of activities, and risks. The system must be dynamic and capable of accommodating new projects as well as reallocating resources once project work is completed. While the same resource issues and principles that apply to a single project also apply to this multiproject environment, application and solutions are more complex, given the interdependency among projects.

The following lists three of the more common problems encountered in managing multiproject resource schedules. Note that these are macro manifestations of single-project problems that are now magnified in a multiproject environment:

1. **Overall schedule slippage.** Because projects often share resources, delays in one project can have a ripple effect and delay other projects. For example, work on one software development project can grind to a halt because the coders scheduled for the next critical task are late in completing their work on another development project.

2. **Inefficient resource utilization.** Because projects have different schedules and requirements, there are peaks and valleys in overall resource demands. For example, a firm may have a staff of 10 electricians to meet peak demands when, under normal conditions, only 5 electricians are required.

3. **Resource bottlenecks.** Delays and schedules are extended as a result of shortages of critical resources that are required by multiple projects. For example, at one Lattice Semiconductor facility, project schedules were delayed because of competition over access to test equipment necessary to debug programs. Likewise, several projects at a U.S. forest area were extended because there was only one silviculturist on the staff.

To deal with these problems, more and more companies create project offices or departments to oversee the scheduling of resources across multiple projects. One approach to multiple project resource scheduling is to use a first come–first served rule. A project queue system is created in which projects currently underway take precedence over new projects. New project schedules are based on the projected availability of resources. This queuing tends to lead to more reliable completion estimates and is preferred on contracted projects that have stiff penalties for being late. The disadvantages of this deceptively simple approach are that it does not optimally utilize resources or take into account the priority of the project. See the Snapshot from Practice: Multiple Project Resource Scheduling.

Many companies utilize more elaborate processes for scheduling resources to increase the capacity of the organization to initiate projects. Most of these methods approach the problem by treating individual projects as part of one big project and adapting the scheduling heuristics previously introduced to this "megaproject." Project schedulers monitor resource usage and provide updated schedules based on progress and resource availability across all projects. One major improvement in project management software in recent years is the ability to prioritize resource allocation to specific projects. Projects can be prioritized in ascending order (e.g., 1, 2, 3, 4, . . .), and these priorities will override scheduling heuristics so that resources go to the project highest on the priority list. (Note: This improvement fits perfectly with organizations that use project priority models similar to those described in Chapter 2.) Centralized project scheduling also makes it easier to identify resource bottlenecks that stifle progress on projects. Once identified, the impact of the bottlenecks can be documented and used to justify acquiring additional equipment, recruiting critical personnel, or delaying the project.

Finally, many companies are using outsourcing as a means for dealing with their resource allocation problems. In some cases, a company will reduce the number of projects they have to manage internally to only core projects and outsource noncritical projects to contractors and consulting firms. In other cases, specific segments of projects are outsourced to overcome resource deficiencies and scheduling problems. Companies may hire temporary workers to expedite certain activities that are falling behind schedule or contract project work during peak periods when there are insufficient internal resources to meet the demands of all projects. The ability to more efficiently manage the ebbs and flows of project work is one of the major driving forces behind outsourcing today.

Summary

Usage and availability of resources are major problem areas for project managers. Attention to these areas in developing a project schedule can point out resource bottlenecks before the project begins. Project managers should understand the ramifications of failing to schedule resources. The results of resource scheduling are frequently significantly different from the results of the standard CPM method.

With the rapid changes in technology and emphasis on time-to-market, catching resource usage and availability problems before the project starts can save the costs of crashing project activities later. Any resource deviations from plan and schedule that occur when the project is being implemented can be quickly recorded and the effect noted. Without this immediate update capability, the real negative effect of a change may not be known until it happens. Tying resource availability to a multiproject, multiresource system supports a project priority process that selects projects by their contribution to the organization's objectives and strategic plan.

Assignment of individuals to projects may not fit well with those assigned by computer software routines. In these cases overriding the computer solution to accommodate individual differences and skills is almost always the best choice.

Key Terms

Heuristic	Resource-constrained	Splitting
Leveling/smoothing	projects	Time-constrained
Multitasking	Resource profile	projects

Review Questions

1. How does resource scheduling tie to project priority?
2. How does resource scheduling reduce flexibility in managing projects?
3. Present six reasons scheduling resources is an important task.
4. How can outsourcing project work alleviate the three most common problems associated with multiproject resource scheduling?
5. Explain the risks associated with leveling resources, compressing or crashing projects, and imposed durations or "catch-up" as the project is being implemented.

Exercises

1. Given the network plan that follows, compute the early, late, and slack times. What is the project duration? Using any approach you wish (e.g., trial and error), develop a loading chart for resources, Electrical Engineers (EE), and resource, Mechanical Engineers (ME). Assume only one of each resource exists. Given your resource schedule, compute the early, late, and slack times for your project. Which activities are now critical? What is the project duration now? Could something like this happen in real projects?

2. Given the network plan that follows, compute the early, late, and slack times. What is the project duration? Using any approach you wish (e.g., trial and error), develop a loading chart for resources Carpenters (C) and Electricians (E). Assume only one Carpenter is available and two Electricians are available. Given your resource schedule, compute the early, late, and slack times for your project. Which activities are now critical? What is the project duration now?

3. Compute the early, late, and slack times for the activities in the network that follows, assuming a time-constrained network. Which activities are critical? What is the time constrained project duration?

Note: Recall, in the schedule resource load chart the *time constrained* "scheduling interval (ES through LF) has been shaded. Any resource scheduled beyond the shaded area will delay the project.

Assume you are a computer using a software that schedules projects by the parallel method and following heuristics. Schedule only one period at a time!

Minimum slack

Smallest duration

Lowest identification number

Keep a log of each activity change and update you make each period—e.g., period 0–1, 1–2, 2–3, etc. (Use a format similar to the one on page 248.) The log should include any changes or updates in ES and slack times each period, activities scheduled, and activities delayed. (Hint: Remember to maintain the technical dependencies of the network.) Use the resource load chart to assist you in scheduling (see pages 249–250).

List the order in which you scheduled the activities of the project. Which activities of your schedule are now critical?

Recompute your slack for each activity given your new schedule. What is the slack for activity 1? 4? 5?

4. Develop a resource schedule in the loading chart that follows. Use the parallel method and heuristics given. Be sure to update each period as the computer would do. Note: Activities 2, 3, 5, and 6 use two of the resource skills. Three of the resource skills are available.

Complete a time-constrained plan in the project network.

Use the following heuristics:
  Minimum slack
  Smallest duration
  Lowest identification number

List the order in which your activities are scheduled
/_____ /_____ /_____ /
/_____ /_____ /_____ /

Develop a resource-constrained schedule in the loading chart below.

ID	RES	DUR	ES	LF	SLK	0	1	2	3	4	5	6	7	8	9	10	11	12	13	14	15
1	1	4	0	5	1																
2	2	5	0	5																	
3	2	4	4	10																	
4	1	5	5	10																	
5	2	3																			
6	2	2																			

Resources scheduled

| Resources available | 3 | 3 | 3 | 3 | 3 | 3 | 3 | 3 | 3 | 3 | 3 | 3 | 3 | 3 | 3 |

What is the schedule slack for 1_____, 2_____, and 4_____?
Which activities are critical now? _____

5. Develop a resource schedule in the loading chart that follows. Use the parallel method and heuristics given. Be sure to update each period as the computer would do. Note: Activities 1, 2, 3, 5, and 6 use two of the resource skills. Three of the resource skills are available.

Complete a time-constrained plan in the project network.

Use the following heuristics:
Minimum slack
Smallest duration
Lowest identification number

List the order in which your activities are scheduled
/_____ /_____ /_____ /
/_____ /_____ /_____ /

Legend

ES	ID	EF
SLK		SLK
LS	DUR	LF

Resource

ID	RES	DUR	ES	LF	SLK	0	1	2	3	4	5	6	7	8	9	10	11	12	13	14	15	16
1	2	2	0	2	0	2	2																
2	2	3	2	6	1																	
3	2	4	2	6	0																	
4	1	2																				
5	2	2																				
6	2	3																				
Resources scheduled																						
Resources available					3	3	3	3	3	3	3	3	3	3	3	3	3	3	3	3	3

What is the schedule slack for 1_____, 2_____3, and 4_____?
Which activities are critical now? _____

6. You have prepared the following schedule for a project in which the key resource is a backhoe. This schedule is contingent on having 3 backhoes. You receive a call from your partner, Brooker, who desperately needs 1 of your backhoes. You tell Brooker you would be willing to let him have the backhoe if you are still able to complete your project in 11 months.

Develop a resource schedule in the loading chart that follows to see if it is possible to complete the project in 11 months with only 2 backhoes. Be sure to record the order in which you schedule the activities using scheduling heuristics. Activities 5 and 6 require 2 backhoes, while activities 1, 2, 3, and 4 require 1 backhoe. No splitting of activities is possible. Can you say yes to Brooker's request?

7. Develop a resource schedule in the loading chart that follows. Use the parallel method and heuristics given. Be sure to update each period as the computer would do. Note: Activities 1, 3, 5, and 6 use two of the resource skills. Three of the resource skills are available.

Use the following heuristics:
Minimum slack
Smallest duration
Lowest identification number

List the order in which your activities are scheduled
/_____ /_____ /_____ /
/_____ /_____ /_____ /

ID	RES	DUR	ES	LF	SLK	0	1	2	3	4	5	6	7	8	9	10	11	12	13
1	2	2	0	3	1														
2	2	3	0	3	0														
3	2	3	2	7	2														
4	1	4	3	7	0														
5	2	2	3	7	2														
6	2	1	7	8	0														
Resources scheduled																			
Resources available					3	3	3	3	3	3	3	3	3	3	3	3	3

What is the schedule slack for 1_____, 2_____, and 4_____ after loading?
Which activities are critical now? _____

References   Arrow, K. J., and L. Hurowicz, *Studies in Resource Allocation Process* (New York: Cambridge University Press, 1997).

Brucker, P., A. Drexl, R. Mohring, L. Newmann, and E. Pesch, "Resource-constrained Project Scheduling: Notation, Classification, Models and Methods," *European Journal of Operational Research,* 112 (1), 1999, pp. 3–42.

Burgess, A. R., and J. B. Kellebrew, "Variations in Activity Level on Cyclical Arrow Diagrams," *Journal of Industrial Engineering,* Vol. 13 March–April 1962, pp. 76–83.

Charnes, A., and W. W. Cooper, "A Network Interpretation and Direct Sub Dual Algorithm for Critical Path Scheduling," *Journal of Industrial Engineering,* July–August 1962.

Demeulemeester, E. L., and W. S. Herroelen, *Project Scheduling: A Research Handbook* (Norwell, Mass: Kluwer Academic Publishers, 2002).

Fendly, L. G., "Towards the Development of a Complete Multi Project Scheduling System," *Journal of Industrial Engineering,* Vol. 19, 1968, pp. 505–155.

Reinersten, D., "Is it Always a Bad Idea to Add Resources to a Late Project?" *Electric Design,* October 30, 2000, pp. 17–18.

Talbot, B. F., and J. H. Patterson, "Optimal Methods for Scheduling Under Resource Constraints," *Project Management Journal,* December 1979.

Wiest, J. D., "A Heuristic Model for Scheduling Large Projects with Unlimited Resources," *Management Science,* Vol. 18, February 1967, pp. 359–77.

Woodworth, B. M., and C. J. Willie, "A Heuristic Algorithm for Resource Leveling in Multiproject, Multiresource Scheduling," *Decision Sciences,* Vol. 6, July 1975, pp. 525–40.

Woodworth, B. M., and S. Shanahan, "Identifying the Critical Sequence in a Resource Constrained Project," *International Journal of Project Management,* 6 (2) 1988, pp. 89–96.

Case

Power Train, Ltd.

We have smashing systems for reporting, tracking, and controlling costs on design projects. Our planning of projects is better than any I have seen at other companies. Our scheduling seemed to serve us well when we were small and we had only a few projects. Now that we have many more projects and schedule using multiproject software, there are too many occasions when the right people are not assigned to the projects deemed important to our success. This situation is costing us big money, headaches, and stress!

Claude Jones, VP, Design and Operations

HISTORY

Power Train, Ltd. (PT), was founded in 1960 by Daniel Gage, a skilled mechanical engineer and machinist. Prior to founding PT he worked for three years as design engineer for a company that designed and built transmissions for military tanks and trucks. It was a natural transition for Dan to start a company designing and building power trains for farm tractor companies. Today, Dan is no longer active in the management of PT but is still revered as its founder. He and his family still own 25 percent of the company, which went public in 1988. PT has been growing at a 6 percent clip for the last five years but expects industry growth to level off as supply exceeds demand.

Today, PT continues its proud tradition of designing and building the best-quality power trains for manufacturers of farm tractors and equipment. The company employs 178 design engineers and has about 1,800 production and support staff. Contract design projects for tractor manufacturers represent a major portion of PT's revenue. At any given time, about 45 to 60 design projects are going on concurrently. A small portion of their design work is for military vehicles. PT only accepts military contracts that involve very advanced, new technology and are cost plus.

A new phenomenon has attracted management of PT to look into a larger market. Last year a large Swedish truck manufacturer approached PT to consider designing power trains for its trucks. As the industry consolidates, the opportunities for PT should increase because these large firms are moving to more outsourcing to cut infrastructure costs and stay very flexible. Only last week a PT design engineer spoke to a German truck manufacturing manager at a conference. The German manager was already exploring outsourcing of drive trains to Porsche and was very pleased to be reminded of PT's expertise in the area. A meeting is set up for next month.

CLAUDE JONES

Claude Jones joined PT in 1989 as a new MBA from the University of Edinburgh. He worked as a mechanical engineer for U.K. Hydraulics for five years prior to returning to school for the MBA. "I just wanted to be part of the management team and where the action is." Jones moved quickly through the ranks. Today he is the vice president of design and operations. Sitting at his desk, Jones is pondering the conflicts and confusion that seem to be increasing in scheduling people to projects. He gets a real rush at the thought of designing power trains for large trucks; however, given their current project scheduling problems, a large increase in business would only compound their problems. Somehow these conflicts in scheduling have to be resolved before any serious thought can be given to expanding into design of power transmissions for truck manufacturers.

Jones is thinking of the problems PT had in the last year. The MF project is the first to come to mind. The project was not terribly complex and did not require their best design engineers. Unfortunately, the scheduling software assigned one of the most creative and expensive engineers to the MF project. A similar situation, but reversed, happened on the Deer project. This project involved a big customer and new hydrostatic technology for small tractors. In this project the scheduling software assigned engineers who were not familiar with small tractor transmissions. Somehow, thinks Jones, the right people need to be scheduled to the right projects. Upon reflection, this problem with scheduling has been increasing since PT went to multiproject scheduling. Maybe a project office is needed to keep on top of these problems.

A meeting with the information technology team and software vendors was positive but not very helpful because these people are not really into detailed scheduling problems. The vendors provided all sorts of evidence suggesting the heuristics used—least slack, shortest duration, and identification number—are absolutely efficient in scheduling people and minimizing project delays. One project software vendor, Lauren, kept saying their software would allow PT to customize the scheduling of projects and people to almost any variation selected. Lauren repeated over and over, "If the standard heuristics do not meet your requirements, create your own heuristics that do." Lauren even volunteered to assist in setting up the system. But she is not willing to spend time on the problem until PT can describe to her exactly what criteria will be used (and their sequence) to select and schedule people to projects.

WHAT NEXT?

Potential expansion into the truck power train business is not feasible until the confusion in project scheduling is solved or reduced significantly. Jones is ready to tackle this problem, but he is not sure where to start.

Appendix 8.1

The Critical-Chain Approach

In practice, project managers carefully manage slack on sensitive resource-limited projects. For example, some managers use an early start schedule and prohibit use of slack on any activity or work package to be used unless authorized by the project manager. Progress by percent complete and by remaining time are carefully monitored and reported to catch any activities that beat estimated completion times so that succeeding activities can start ahead of schedule—on critical and noncritical activities. Monitoring and encouraging of early completion of estimated times ensure that the time gained is used to start a succeeding activity earlier and time is not wasted. The intent is to save the slack as a time buffer to complete the project early or to cover delay problems that may creep up on critical activities or paths.

Eliyahu Goldratt, who championed the "theory of constraints" in his popular book *The Goal,* advocates an alternative approach to managing slack. He has coined the term "critical-chain" to recognize that the project network may be constrained by both resource and technical dependencies. Each type of constraint can create task dependencies, and in the case of resource constraints, new task dependencies can be created! Remember, the critical resource shifted the critical path. Visit Figure 8.4 again. The critical-chain (C-C) refers to the longest string of dependencies that exist on the project. Chain is used instead of path, since the latter tends to be associated with just technical dependencies not resource dependencies. Goldratt uses the C-C concept to develop strategies for accelerating the completion of projects. These strategies are based on his observations about time estimates of individual activities.

TIME ESTIMATES

Goldratt argues that there is a natural tendency for people to add safety (just-in-case) time to their estimations. It is believed that those who estimate activity times provide an estimate that has about an 80 to 90 percent chance of being completed on or before the estimated time. Hence, the median time (50/50 chance) is overestimated by approximately 30 to 40 percent. For example, a programmer may estimate that there is a 50/50 chance that he can complete an activity in five days. However, to ensure success and to protect against potential problems, he adds three days of safety time and reports that it will take eight days to complete the task. In this case the median (50/50) time is overestimated by approximately 60 percent. If this hidden contingency is pervasive across a project, then most activities in theory should be completed ahead of schedule. Remember, the programmer still has a 50/50 chance of completing the assignment within five days or less.

This situation raises an interesting paradox. Why, if there is a tendency to overestimate activity durations, do so many projects come in behind schedule? Goldratt offers several explanations:

- *Parkinson's law:* Work fills the time available. Why hustle to complete a task today when it isn't due until tomorrow?
- *Self-protection:* Participants fail to report early finishes out of fear that management will adjust their future standards and demand more next time.
- *Dropped baton:* Early finishes may not lead to the start of the next activity because people assigned to perform the next activity are not ready to start work early. The time gained is therefore lost.
- *Excessive multitasking:* This phenomenon adds time to the completion of tasks.

- *Resource bottlenecks:* Delays are caused by limited availability of critical resources.
- *Student syndrome:* There is a tendency to delay the start of tasks until you absolutely have to.

The dropped baton and student syndrome explanations deserve further discussion. Goldratt uses the metaphor of a relay race to describe the impact of poor coordination between resources. Just like a runner's time is lost if the next runner is not ready to receive the baton, so is the time gained from completing a task early if the next group of people are not ready to receive the project work.

Goldratt also asserts that just as students delay writing a term paper until the last minute, workers delay starting tasks when they perceive that they have more than enough time to complete the task. The problem with delaying the start of a task is that obstacles are often not detected until the task is underway. By postponing the start of the task, the opportunity to cope with these obstacles and complete the task on time is compromised.

CRITICAL-CHAIN IN ACTION

Goldratt's solution to reducing project time overruns is to insist on people using the "true 50/50" activity time estimates (rather than estimates which have an 80 to 90 percent chance of being completed before the estimated time); the 50/50 estimates result in a project duration about one-half the low risk of 80 to 90 percent estimates. Using 50/50 estimates will discourage Parkinson's law, the student syndrome, and self protection from coming into play and in turn should increase productivity on individual tasks. Similarly, the compressed time schedule reduces the likelihood of the dropped baton effect.

Goldratt recommends inserting time buffers into the schedule to act as "shock absorbers" to protect the project completion date against task durations taking longer than the 50/50 estimate. The rationale is that by using 50/50 estimates you are in essence taking out all of the "safety" in individual tasks. He also recommends using portions of this collective safety strategically by inserting time buffers where potential problems are likely to occur. First, since all activities along the critical chain have inherent *uncertainty* that is difficult to predict, project duration is uncertain. Therefore, a project time buffer is added to the expected *project duration*—say 50 percent of the aggregate of the hidden contingencies of activity durations. Second, *feeder* buffers are added to the network where noncritical paths merge with the critical chain. These buffers serve to protect the critical path from being delayed. Third, *resource* time buffers are inserted where scarce resources are needed for an activity. Resource time buffers come in at least two forms. One form is a time buffer attached to a critical resource to ensure that the resource is on call and available when needed. This preserves the relay race. The second form of time buffer is added to activities preceding the work of a scarce resource. This kind of buffer protects against resource bottlenecks by increasing the likelihood that the preceding activity will be completed when the resource is available. All buffers reduce the risk of the project duration being late and increase the chance of early project completion.

CRITICAL-CHAIN VERSUS TRADITIONAL SCHEDULING APPROACH

To illustrate how C-C affects scheduling lets compare it with the traditional approach to project scheduling. We will first resolve resource problems the way described in Chapter 8 and then the C-C method. Figure A8.1A shows the *planned* Air Control project network without any concern for resources. That is, activities are assumed to be independent and resources will be made available and/or are interchangeable. Figure A8.1B depicts the bar chart for the project. The green bars represent the durations of critical activities; the clear bars represent the durations of noncritical activities; the light gray

FIGURE A8.1A   Air Control Project: Time Plan without Resources

Order review
Early start: 0   ID: 1
Early finish: 2   Dur: 2 days

Order vendor parts
Early start: 2   ID: 2
Early finish: 17   Dur: 15 days

Produce std. parts
Early start: 2   ID: 3
Early finish: 20   Dur: 18 days

Design custom parts
Early start: 2   ID: 4
Early finish: 15   Dur: 13 days

Software development
Early start: 2   ID: 5
Early finish: 20   Dur: 18 days

Manufacture custom parts
Early start: 15   ID: 6
Early finish: 30   Dur: 15 days

Assemble
Early start: 30   ID: 7
Early finish: 40   Dur: 10 days

Test
Early start: 40   ID: 8
Early finish: 45   Dur: 5 days

Project duration 45 days

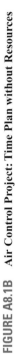

FIGURE A8.1B   Air Control Project: Time Plan without Resources

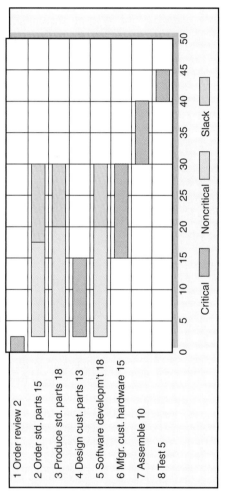

1 Order review 2
2 Order std. parts 15
3 Produce std. parts 18
4 Design cust. parts 13
5 Software developm't 18
6 Mfgr. cust. hardware 15
7 Assemble 10
8 Test 5

Critical   Noncritical   Slack

0   5   10   15   20   25   30   35   40   45   50

bars represent slack. Note that the duration is 45 days and the critical path is represented by activities 1, 4, 6, 7, and 8.

Parallel activities hold potential for resource conflicts. This is the case in this project. Ryan is the resource for activities 3 and 6. If you insert Ryan in the bar chart in Figure A8.1B for activities 3 and 6, you can see activity 3 overlaps activity 6 by five days—an impossible situation. Because Ryan cannot work two activities simultaneously and no other person can take his place, a resource dependency exists. The result is that two activities (3 and 6) that were assumed to be independent now become dependent. Something has to give! Figure A8.2A shows the Air Control project network with the resources included. A pseudo-dashed arrow has been added to the network to indicate the resource dependency. The bar chart in Figure A8.2B reflects the revised schedule resolving the overallocation of Ryan. Given the new schedule, slack for some activities has changed. More importantly, the critical path has changed. It is now 1, 3, 6, 7, 8. The resource schedule shows the new project duration to be 50 days rather than 45 days.

Now let's apply the C-C approach to the Air Control project. Figure A8.3 details many of the changes. First, notice that task estimates now represent approximations of the 50/50 rule. Second, observe that not all of the activities on the critical-chain are technically linked. Manufacturing custom parts is included because of previously defined resource dependency. Third, a project time buffer is added at the end of schedule. Finally, feeder buffers are inserted at each point where a noncritical activity merges with the critical chain.

The impact the C-C approach has on the project schedule can best be seen in the Gantt chart presented in Figure A8.4. Notice first the late start times for each of the three noncritical activities. For example, under the critical path method, order vendor parts and software development would be scheduled to begin immediately after the order review. Instead they are scheduled later in the project. Three-day feeder buffers have been added to each of these activities to absorb any delays that might occur in these activities. Finally, instead of taking 50 days the project is now estimated to take only 27 days with a 10-day project buffer!

This example provides an opportunity for explaining the differences between buffers and slack. Slack is spare time inherent in the schedule of noncritical activities and can be determined by differences between the early start and late start of a specific activity. Buffers, on the other hand, are dedicated time blocks reserved to cover most likely contingencies and are monitored closely so, if they are not needed, subsequent activities can proceed on schedule. Buffers are needed in part because the estimates are based on 50/50 approximations, and therefore roughly half of the activities will take longer than planned. To protect against these extended activity durations, buffers are inserted to minimize the impact on the schedule. Buffers are not part of the project schedule and are used only when sound management dictates it.

While not depicted in the figures, an example of a resource buffer would be to add six days to Ryan's schedule (remember he is the critical resource that caused the schedule to be extended). This would ensure that he could continue to work on the project beyond the 18th day in case either produce standard parts and/or manufacture custom hardware takes longer than planned. Progress on these two tasks would be monitored closely, and his schedule would be adjusted accordingly.

C-C AND MULTITASKING

Buffers do not address the insidious effects of pervasive multitasking, especially in a multiproject environment where workers are juggling different project assignments. Goldratt has three recommendations that will help to reduce the impact of multitasking:

1. Reduce the number of projects so people are not assigned to as many projects concurrently.

FIGURE A8.2A Air Control Project: Schedule with Resources Limited

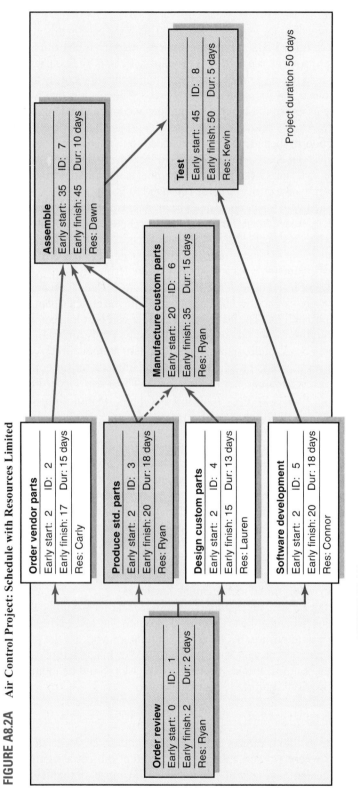

Project duration 50 days

Order review
Early start: 0	ID: 1
Early finish: 2	Dur: 2 days
Res: Ryan	

Order vendor parts
Early start: 2	ID: 2
Early finish: 17	Dur: 15 days
Res: Carly	

Produce std. parts
Early start: 2	ID: 3
Early finish: 20	Dur: 18 days
Res: Ryan	

Design custom parts
Early start: 2	ID: 4
Early finish: 15	Dur: 13 days
Res: Lauren	

Software development
Early start: 2	ID: 5
Early finish: 20	Dur: 18 days
Res: Connor	

Manufacture custom parts
Early start: 20	ID: 6
Early finish: 35	Dur: 15 days
Res: Ryan	

Assemble
Early start: 35	ID: 7
Early finish: 45	Dur: 10 days
Res: Dawn	

Test
Early start: 45	ID: 8
Early finish: 50	Dur: 5 days
Res: Kevin	

FIGURE A8.2B Air Control Project: Schedule with Resources Limited

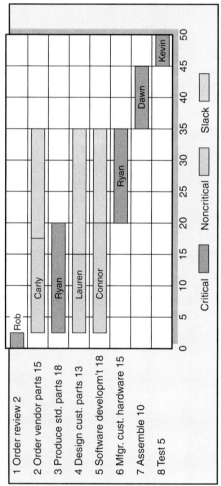

1 Order review 2
2 Order vendor parts 15
3 Produce std. parts 18
4 Design cust. parts 13
5 Software developm't 18
6 Mfgr. cust. hardware 15
7 Assemble 10
8 Test 5

Critical   Noncritical   Slack

FIGURE A8.3 Air Control Project: Critical-Chain Network

FIGURE A8.4
Air Control Project Gantt Chart: Critical-Chain Network

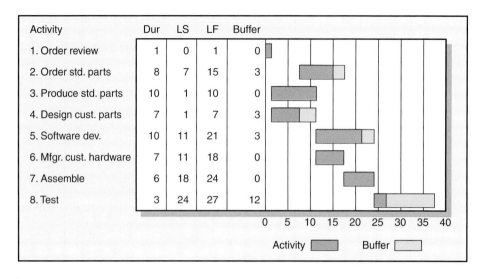

Activity	Dur	LS	LF	Buffer
1. Order review	1	0	1	0
2. Order std. parts	8	7	15	3
3. Produce std. parts	10	1	10	0
4. Design cust. parts	7	1	7	3
5. Software dev.	10	11	21	3
6. Mfgr. cust. hardware	7	11	18	0
7. Assemble	6	18	24	0
8. Test	3	24	27	12

2. Control start dates of projects to accommodate resource shortages. Don't start projects until sufficient resources are available to work full time on the project.
3. Contract (lock in) for resources *before* the project begins.

MONITORING PROJECT PERFORMANCE

The C-C method uses buffers to monitor project time performance. Remember that as shown in Figure A8.3 a project buffer is used to insulate the project against delays along the critical-chain. For monitoring purposes, this buffer is typically divided into three zones—OK, Watch, and Act, respectively. As the buffer begins to decrease and moves into the second zone, alarms are set off to seek corrective action. (For additional sources see endnote 2.) To be truly effective, buffer management requires comparing buffer usage with actual progress on the project. For example, if the project is 75 percent complete and you have only used 50 percent of the project buffer, then the project is in pretty good shape. Conversely, if the project is only 25 percent complete and 50 percent of the buffer has already been used, you are in trouble and corrective action is needed. A method for estimating percentage complete is described in Chapter 13.

THE C-C METHOD TODAY

C-C has generated considerable debate within the project management community. While sound in theory, support at this time is limited but growing. For example, Harris Semiconductor was able to build a new automated wafer fabrication facility within 13 months using C-C methods when the industry standard for such a facility is 26–36 months. The Israeli aircraft industry has used C-C techniques to reduce average maintenance work on aircraft from two months to two weeks. The U.S. Air Force and Navy as well as Boeing, Lucent Technologies, Intel, GM, and 3M are applying critical-chain principles to their multi-project environments.

C-C is not without critics. First, C-C does not address the biggest cause of project delays, which is an ill-defined and unstable project scope. Second, some critics challenge Goldratt's assumptions about human behavior. They question the tendency of experts to pad estimates and that employees act deliberately against the organization for their own interest and benefit. They also object to the insinuation that trained professionals would exhibit the student syndrome habits. Right or wrong, for some there is an implied element of distrust and lack of faith in the employee's expertise in the C-C approach. The harshest critics see C-C as a highly manipulative system in which people are set up for failure with the hope that this added pressure will increase productivity.

The key to implementing theory into practice is the culture of the organization. If the organization honors noble efforts that fail to meet estimates as it does efforts that do meet estimates, then greater acceptance will occur. Conversely, if management treats honest failure differently from success, then resistance will be high. Organizations adopting the C-C approach have to invest significant energy to obtaining "buy-in" on the part of all participants to its core principles and allaying the fears that this system may generate.

SUMMARY

Regardless of where one stands in the debate, the C-C approach deserves credit for bringing resource dependency to the forefront, highlighting the modern ills of multi-tasking, and forcing us to rethink conventional methods of project scheduling.

EXERCISE

1. Check out the Goldratt Institute's homepage at *http://www.goldratt.com* for current information on the application of critical-chain techniques to project management.
2. Apply critical-chain scheduling principles to the Print Software, Inc., project presented in Chapter 6 on page 183. Revise the estimated time durations by 50 percent except round up the odd time durations (i.e., 3 becomes 4). Draw a C-C network diagram similar to the one contained in Figure A8.3 for the Print Software project as well as a Gantt chart similar to Figure A8.4. How would these diagrams differ from the ones generated using the traditional scheduling technique?

APPENDIX REFERENCES

Goldratt, *Critical Chain* (Great Barrington, MA: North River Press, 1997).

Herroelen, W., R. Leus, and E. Demeulemeester, "Critical Chain Project Scheduling: Do Not Oversimplify," *Project Management Journal,* Vol. 33 (4), 2002, pp. 48–60.

Leach, L. P., "Critical Chain Project Management," *Proceedings of 29th Annual Project Management Institute, 1998, Seminars and Symposium,* (Newtown, PA: Project Management Institute, 1998), pp. 1239–44.

Levine, H. A., "Shared Contingency: Exploring the Critical Chain," *PM Network,* October, 1999, pp. 35–38.

Newbold, R. C., *Project Management in the Fast Lane: Applying the Theory of Constraints,* (Baton Roca, FL: St. Lucie Press, 1998).

Noreen, E., D. Smith, and J. Mackey, *The Theory of Constraints and it's Implication for Management Accounting* (Barrington, MA: North River Press, 1995).

Raz, T., R. Barnes, and D. Dvir, "A Critical Look at Critical Chain Project Management," *Project Management Journal,* December 2003, pp. 24–32.

Sood, S., "Taming Uncertainty: Critical-Chain Buffer Management Helps Minimize Risk in the Project Equation," *PM Network,* March 2003, pp. 57–59.

Zalmanson, E., "Readers Feedback," *PM Network,* Vol. 15 (1), 2001, p. 4.

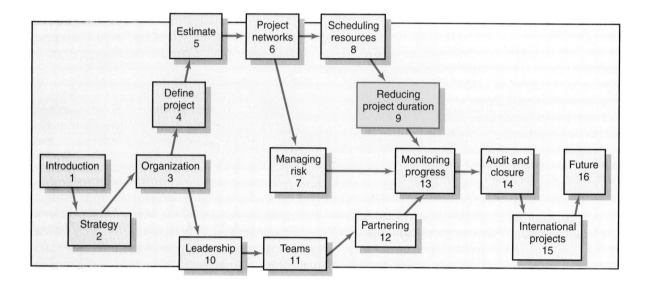

Reducing Project Duration

Rationale for Reducing Project Duration

Options for Accelerating Project Completion

Project Cost–Duration Graph

Constructing a Project Cost–Duration Graph

Practical Considerations

What if Cost, Not Time, Is the Issue?

Summary

CHAPTER NINE

Reducing Project Duration

When do you need it?
Yesterday.

Imagine the following scenarios:

> After finalizing your project schedule, you realize the estimated completion date is two months beyond what your boss publicly promised an important customer.

> Two months into the project, you realize that you are already three weeks behind the drop dead date for the project.

> Four months into a project top management changes its priorities and now tells you that money is not an issue. Complete the project ASAP!

What do you do?

This chapter addresses strategies for reducing project duration either prior to setting the baseline for the project or in the midst of project execution. Choice of options is based on the constraints surrounding the project. Here the project priority matrix introduced in Chapter 4 comes into play. For example, there are many more options available for reducing project time if you are not resource constrained than if you cannot spend more than your original budget. We will begin first by examining the reasons for reducing project duration followed by a discussion of different options for accelerating project completion. The chapter will conclude with the classic time-cost framework for selecting which activities to "crash." Crash is a term that has emerged in the Project Management lexicon for shortening the duration of an activity or project beyond when it can be normally done.

Rationale for Reducing Project Duration

There are few circumstances in which a project manager or owner would not wish to reduce the time to complete a project. Reducing the time of a critical activity in a project can be done but almost always results in a higher direct cost; thus, the manager faces a cost-time trade-off problem—is the reduction in time worth the additional cost? Cost-time situations focus on reducing the critical path that determines the project completion date. See Snapshot from Practice: Northridge Earthquake.

There are many good reasons for attempting to reduce the duration of a project. One of the more common reasons is known in the field as an "imposed" project duration date. For example, a politician makes a public statement that a new law building will be available in two years. Or the president of a software company remarks in a speech that new technologically advanced software will be available in one year. Such statements too often become imposed project duration dates—without any consideration of the

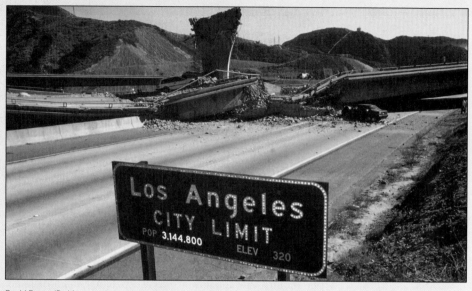

David Butow/Corbis.

On January 17, 1994, a 6.8-magnitude earthquake struck the Los Angeles basin, near suburban Northridge, causing 60 deaths, thousands of injuries, and billions of dollars in property damage. Nowhere was the destructive power of nature more evident than in the collapsed sections of the freeway system that disrupted the daily commute of an estimated 1 million Los Angelians. The Northridge earthquake posed one of the greatest challenges to the California Department of Transportation (CalTrans) in its nearly 100-year history. To expedite the recovery process, Governor Pete Wilson signed an emergency declaration allowing CalTrans to streamline contracting procedures and offer attractive incentives for completing work ahead of schedule. For each day that the schedule was beaten, a sizable bonus was to be awarded. Conversely, for each day over the deadline, the contractor would be penalized the same amount. The amount ($50,000 to $200,000) varied depending on the importance of the work.

The incentive scheme proved to be a powerful motivator for the freeway reconstruction contractors. C. C. Myers, Inc., of Rancho Cordova, California, won the contract for the reconstruction of the Interstate 10 bridges. Myers pulled out all stops to finish the project in a blistering 66 days—a whopping 74 days ahead of schedule—and earning a $14.8 million bonus! Myers took every opportunity to save time and streamline operations. They greatly expanded the workforce. For example, 134 ironworkers were employed instead of the normal 15. Special lighting equipment was set up so that work could be performed around the clock.

Likewise, the sites were prepared and special materials were used so that work could continue despite inclement weather that would normally shut down construction. The work was scheduled much like an assembly line so that critical activities were followed by the next critical activity. A generous incentive scheme was devised to reward teamwork and reach milestones early. Carpenters and ironworkers competed as teams against each other to see who could finish first.

Although C. C. Myers received a substantial bonus for finishing early, they spent a lot of money on overtime, bonuses, special equipment, and other premiums to keep the job rolling along. CalTrans supported Myers's efforts. With reconstruction work going on 24 hours a day, including jackhammering and pile-driving, CalTrans temporarily housed many families in local motels. CalTrans even erected a temporary plastic soundwall to help reduce the construction noise traveling to a nearby apartment complex. The double-layer curtain, 450 feet long and 20 feet high, was designed to reduce construction noise by 10 decibels.

Despite the difficulties and expense incurred by around-the-clock freeway building, most of Los Angeles cheered CalTrans's quake recovery efforts. The Governor's Office of Planning and Research issued a report concluding that for every day the Santa Monica Freeway was closed, it cost the local economy more than $1 million.

*Jerry B. Baxter, "Responding to the Northridge Earthquake," *PM Network* (November 1994), pp. 13–22.

problems or cost of meeting such a date. The project duration time is set while the project is in its "concept" phase before or without any detailed scheduling of all the activities in the project. This phenomenon is very common in practice! Unfortunately, this practice almost always leads to a higher-cost project than one that is planned using low-cost, efficient methods and detailed planning. In addition, quality is sometimes compromised to meet deadlines. More importantly, these increased costs of imposed duration dates are seldom recognized or noted by project participants. Imposed project durations are a fact of life for project managers.

In recent years emphasis on time-to-market has taken on new importance because of intense global competition and rapid technological advances. The *market* imposes a project duration date. For example, a rule of thumb for moderate- to high-technology firms is that a six-month delay in bringing a product to market can result in a gross profit loss or market share of about 30 percent. In these cases, high-technology firms typically assume that the time savings and avoidance of lost profits are worth any additional costs to reduce time without any formal analysis. It is interesting to observe how more serious analysis occurs in recession periods when cash flows are tight.

Incentive contracts in partnering arrangements can make reduction of project time rewarding—usually for both the project contractor and owner. For example, a contractor finished a bridge across a lake 18 months early and received more than $6 million for the early completion. The availability of the bridge to the surrounding community 18 months early to reduce traffic gridlock made the incentive cost to the community seem small to users. In another example, in a partnering continuous improvement arrangement, the joint effort of the owner and contractor resulted in early completion of a river lock and a 50/50 split of the savings to the owner and contractor.

Another reason for reducing project time occurs when unforeseen delays—for example, adverse weather, design flaws, and equipment breakdown—cause substantial delays midway in the project. Getting back on schedule usually requires compressing the time on some of the remaining critical activities. The additional costs of getting back on schedule need to be compared with the costs of being late.

Sometimes very high overhead or goodwill costs are recognized before the project begins. In these cases it is prudent to examine the direct costs of shortening the critical path versus the overhead and/or goodwill cost savings. Usually there are opportunities to shorten a few critical activities at less than the daily overhead rate or perceived goodwill cost. Under specific conditions (which are not rare), huge savings are possible with little risk.

Finally there are times when it is important to reassign key equipment and/or people to new projects. Under these circumstances, the cost of compressing the project can be compared with the costs of not releasing key equipment or people.

Options for Accelerating Project Completion

Managers have several effective methods for crashing specific project activities when resources are not constrained. Several of these are summarized below:

Adding Resources

The most common method for shortening project time is to assign additional staff and equipment to activities. There are limits, however, as to how much speed can be gained by adding staff. Doubling the size of the workforce will not necessarily reduce completion time by half. The relationship would be correct only when tasks can be partitioned so minimal communication is needed between workers, as in harvesting a

In the face of increasing time-to-market pressures, many bio-tech firms are turning to outsourcing to expedite the drug development process. Panos Kalaritis, vice president of operations for Irix Pharmaceuticals, says that outsourcing process development can accelerate a drug's evolution by allowing a pharmaceutical company to continue research while a contractor works on process optimization. Susan Dexter of Lonza Biologics identified different types of outsourcing contracts including agreements for product development, clinical trial supplies, in-market or commercial supplies, and technology transfer. Often, she said, a given project can encompass more than one of the above stages over a period of several years.

Using a contractor, said Paul Henricks business manager for Patheon Inc., gives the client company access to specialized knowledge and infrastructure as well as flexible resources and capacity. The sponsoring company can also manage risks by sharing responsibilities through outsourcing.

"Communication is key to a successful outsourcing relationship," said Dan Gold, vice president of process development for Covance, which was formerly Corning Bio. "Contractors and sponsors should both assign project managers, and the two must work together to maintain, track, and document project completion. There must be a concerted effort on the part of both parties to work as partners to complete the project."

*Mathew Lerner, "Outsourcing in Bio-Technology Picks Up Speed," *Chemical Market Reporter,* Vol. 251, No. 14, p. 17.

crop by hand or repaving a highway. Most projects are not set up that way; additional workers increase the communication requirements to coordinate their efforts. For example, doubling a team by adding two workers requires six times as much pair-wise intercommunication than is required in the original two-person team. Not only is more time needed to coordinate and manage a larger team, there is the additional delay of training the new people and getting them up to speed on the project. The end result is captured in Brooks' law: Adding manpower to a late software project makes it later.

Frederick Brooks formulated this principle based on his experience as a project manager for IBM's System/360 software project during the early 1960s. Subsequent research concluded that adding more people to a late project does not necessarily cause the project to be later. The key is whether the new staff is added early so there is sufficient time to make up for lost ground once the new members have been fully assimilated.

Outsourcing Project Work

A common method for shortening the project time is to subcontract an activity. The subcontractor may have access to superior technology or expertise that will accelerate the completion of the activity. For example, contracting for a backhoe can accomplish in two hours what it can take a team of laborers two days to do. Likewise, by hiring a consulting firm that specializes in ADSI programming, a firm may be able to cut in half the time it would take for less experienced, internal programmers to do the work. Subcontracting also frees up resources that can be assigned to a critical activity and will ideally result in a shorter project duration. See Snapshot from Practice: Outsourcing Bio-Tech.

Scheduling Overtime

The easiest way to add more labor to a project is not to add more people, but to schedule overtime. If a team works 50 hours a week instead of 40, it might accomplish 25 percent more. By scheduling overtime you avoid the additional costs of coordination and communication encountered when new people are added. If people involved are salaried workers, there may be no real additional cost for the extra work. Another advantage is that there are fewer distractions when people work outside normal hours.

Overtime has disadvantages. First, hourly workers are typically paid time and a half for overtime and double time for weekends and holidays. Sustained overtime work by salaried employees may incur intangible costs such as divorce, burnout, and turnover. The latter is a key organizational concern when there is a shortage of workers.

Furthermore, it is an oversimplification to assume that, over an extended period of time, a person is as productive during his or her eleventh hour at work as during his or her third hour of work. There are natural limits to what is humanly possible, and extended overtime may actually lead to an overall decline in productivity when fatigue sets in.

Despite the potential disadvantages, overtime and working longer hours is the preferred choice for accelerating project completion, especially when the project team is salaried.

Establish a Core Project Team

As discussed in Chapter 3, one of the advantages of creating a dedicated core team to complete a project is speed. Assigning professionals full time to a project avoids the hidden cost of multitasking in which people are forced to juggle the demands of multiple projects. Professionals are allowed to devote their undivided attention to a specific project. This singular focus creates a shared goal that can bind a diverse set of professionals into a highly cohesive team capable of accelerating project completion. Factors that contribute to the emergence of high-performing project teams will be discussed in detail in Chapter 11.

Do It Twice—Fast and Correctly

If you are in a hurry, try building a "quick and dirty" short-term solution, then go back and do it the right way. For example, the Rose Garden stadium in Portland, Oregon, was supposed to be completely finished in time for the start of the 1995–1996 National Basketball Association (NBA) season. Delays made this impossible, so the construction crew set up temporary bleachers to accommodate the opening-night crowd. The additional costs of doing it twice are often more than compensated for by the benefits of satisfying the deadline.

A project manager has fewer options for accelerating project completion when additional resources are either not available or the budget is severely constrained. This is especially true once the schedule has been established. Below are some of these options.

Fast-Tracking

Sometimes it is possible to rearrange the logic of the project network so that critical activities are done in parallel (concurrently) rather than sequentially. This alternative is a good one if the project situation is right. When this alternative is given serious attention, it is amazing to observe how creative project team members can be in finding ways to restructure sequential activities in parallel. As noted in Chapter 6, one of the most common methods for restructuring activities is to change a finish-to-start relationship to a start-to-start relationship. For example, instead of waiting for the final design to be approved, manufacturing engineers can begin building the production line as soon as key specifications have been established. Changing activities from sequential to parallel usually requires closer coordination among those responsible for the activities affected but can produce tremendous time savings.

Critical-Chain

Critical-chain (C-C) project management is designed to accelerate project completion. As discussed in Chapter 8, the jury is still out in terms of its applicability. Still C-C principles appear sound and worthy of experimentation if speed is essential. At the same time, it would be difficult to apply C-C project management midstream in a project. C-C requires considerable training and a shift in habits and perspectives that take time to adopt. Although there have been reports of immediate gains, especially in terms of completion times, a long-term management commitment is probably necessary to reap full benefits. See the Snapshot from Practice: The Fastest House in the World for an extreme example of C-C application.

AP/Wide World Photos.

On March 13, 1999, Habitat for Humanity New Zealand built a fully operational, four-bedroom house in Auckland in 3 hours, 44 minutes, and 59 seconds from floor to roof complete with curtains, running showers, lawn, and fence. In doing so they became the fastest house builders in the world.

"We made a significant decimation of the record," said Habitat New Zealand's Chief Executive Graeme Lee. "The previous record of 4 hours, 39 minutes, 8 seconds, held by a Habitat chapter in Nashville, USA, was made with a three-bedroom home, and we built one with four bedrooms and used only 140 volunteers on the site." The rules provide for construction to commence from an established floor platform. The house is complete when it meets the local building code, and the family can move in.

The project took 14 months to plan. Critical-chain principles were applied using ProChain Software to finalize project schedule. The critical-chain was recalculated 150–200 times and then analyzed to optimize the resulting new sequence of operations. This reiterative process was used to progressively develop the fastest plan.

One of the keys to efficiency was the use of "Laserbilt" prefabricated walls made from 36mm particleboard using technology that had been invented by a company in New Zealand. Another time saver was the use of a crane which lowered the wooden roof frame (built on adjacent land) onto the four walls.

Once the roof was on the walls, roofing iron was put on. Meanwhile, the wall sheathing was attached to outside walls and windows fitted, with painters almost painting the face of the hammers as sheath nailing was completed. Inside, vinyl was laid first in the utility areas while painters started in the bedrooms. After the vinyl, the bathrooms were fitted and curtains hung. On the outside, while the roofing was being installed, decks and steps were constructed, a front path laid, mail box and clothesline installed, wooden fence constructed around the perimeter, three trees planted, and lawns leveled and seeded.

Postproject assessment revealed that even further time could have been gained. The management rule was to be "One tradesperson in one room at one time," but enthusiasm took over and people were doing whatever they could wherever they could, especially toward the end. The project manager estimated that if greater discipline had been exercised and if people moved out of the house as soon as they had completed their task, another 15 minutes would have been shaved from the record.

Habitat for Humanity is an international charitable organization that builds simple, affordable houses and sells them on a no-interest, no-profit basis to needy families.

*"A 4 Bedroom House in 3 Hours, 44 Minutes & 59 Seconds," Avraham Y. Goldratt Institute, www.goldratt.com. "Fastest House in the World," Habitat for Humanity International, www.habitat.org.

Reducing Project Scope

Probably the most common response for meeting unattainable deadlines is to reduce or scale back the scope of the project. This invariably leads to a reduction in the functionality of the project. For example, the new car will average only 25 mpg instead of 30, or the software product will have fewer features than originally planned. While scaling back the scope of the project can lead to big savings in both time and money, it may come at a cost of reducing the value of the project. If the car gets lower gas mileage, will it stand up to competitive models? Will customers still want the software minus the features?

The key to reducing a project scope without reducing value is to reassess the true specifications of the project. Often requirements are added under best-case, blue-sky scenarios and represent desirables, but not essentials. Here it is important to talk to the customer and/or project sponsors and explain the situation—you can get it your way but not until February. This may force them to accept an extension or to add money to expedite the project. If not, then a healthy discussion of what the essential requirements are and what items can be compromised in order to meet the deadline needs to take place. More intense re-examination of requirements may actually improve the value of the project by getting it done more quickly and for a lower cost.

Calculating the savings of reduced project scope begins with the work breakdown structure. Reducing functionality means certain tasks, deliverables, or requirements can be reduced or even eliminated. These tasks need to be found and the schedule adjusted. Focus should be on changes in activities on the critical path.

Compromise Quality

Reducing quality is always an option, but it is rarely acceptable or used. If quality is sacrificed, it may be possible to reduce the time of an activity on the critical path.

In practice the methods most commonly used to crash projects are scheduling overtime, outsourcing, and adding resources. Each of these maintains the essence of the original plan. Options that depart from the original project plan include do it twice, fast-tracking, and phase project delivery. Rethinking of project scope, customer needs, and timing become major considerations for these techniques.

Project Cost–Duration Graph

Nothing on the horizon suggests that the need to shorten project time will change. The challenge for the project manager is to use a quick, logical method to compare the benefits of reducing project time with the cost. When sound, logical methods are absent, it is difficult to isolate those activities that will have the greatest impact on reducing project time at least cost. This section describes a procedure for identifying the costs of reducing project time so that comparisons can be made with the benefits of getting the project completed sooner. The method requires gathering direct and indirect costs for specific project durations. Critical activities are searched to find the lowest direct-cost activities that will shorten the project duration. Total cost for specific project durations are computed and then compared with the benefits of reducing project time—before the project begins or while it is in progress.

Explanation of Project Costs

The general nature of project costs is illustrated in Figure 9.1. The total cost for each duration is the sum of the indirect and direct costs. Indirect costs continue for the life of the project. Hence, any reduction in project duration means a reduction in indirect

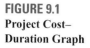

FIGURE 9.1
Project Cost–
Duration Graph

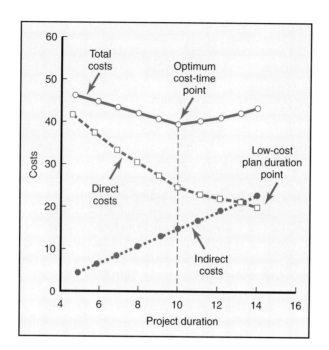

costs. Direct costs on the graph grow at an increasing rate as the project duration is reduced from its original planned duration. With the information from a graph such as this for a project, managers can quickly judge any alternative such as meeting a time-to-market deadline. Further discussion of indirect and direct costs is necessary before demonstrating a procedure for developing the information for a graph similar to the one depicted in Figure 9.1.

Project Indirect Costs

Indirect costs generally represent overhead costs such as supervision, administration, consultants, and interest. Indirect costs cannot be associated with any particular work package or activity, hence the term. Indirect costs vary directly with time. That is, any reduction in time should result in a reduction of indirect costs. For example, if the daily costs of supervision, administration, and consultants are $2,000, any reduction in project duration would represent a savings of $2,000 per day. If indirect costs are a significant percentage of total project costs, reductions in project time can represent very real savings (assuming the indirect resources can be utilized elsewhere).

Project Direct Costs

Direct costs commonly represent labor, materials, equipment, and sometimes subcontractors. Direct costs are assigned directly to a work package and activity, hence the term. The ideal assumption is that direct costs for an activity time represent normal costs, which typically mean low-cost, efficient methods for a normal time. When project durations are imposed, direct costs may no longer represent low-cost, efficient methods. Costs for the imposed duration date will be higher than for a project duration developed from ideal normal times for activities. Because direct costs are assumed to be developed from normal methods and time, any reduction in activity time should add to the costs of the activity. The sum of the costs of all the work packages or activities represents the total direct costs for the project.

The major plight faced in creating the information for a graph similar to Figure 9.1 is computing the direct cost of shortening individual critical activities and then finding the total direct cost for each project duration as project time is compressed; the process requires selecting those critical activities that cost the least to shorten. (Note: The graph implies that there is always an optimum cost-time point. This is only true if shortening a schedule has incremental indirect cost savings exceeding the incremental direct cost incurred. However, in practice there are almost always several activities in which the direct costs of shortening are less than the indirect costs.)

Constructing a Project Cost–Duration Graph

There are three major steps required to construct a project cost–duration graph:

1. Find total direct costs for selected project durations.
2. Find total indirect costs for selected project durations.
3. Sum direct and indirect costs for these selected durations.

The graph is then used to compare additional cost alternatives for benefits. Details of these steps are presented here.

Determining the Activities to Shorten

The most difficult task in constructing a cost–duration graph is finding the total direct costs for specific project durations over a relevant range. The central concern is to decide which activities to shorten and how far to carry the shortening process. Basically, managers need to look for critical activities that can be shortened with the *smallest increase in cost per unit of time.* The rationale for selecting critical activities depends on identifying the activity's normal and crash times and corresponding costs. *Normal time* for an activity represents low-cost, realistic, efficient methods for completing the activity under normal conditions. Shortening an activity is called *crashing.* The shortest possible time an activity can realistically be completed in is called its *crash time.* The direct cost for completing an activity in its crash time is called *crash cost.* Both normal and crash times and costs are collected from personnel most familiar with completing the activity. Figure 9.2 depicts a hypothetical cost–duration graph for an activity.

The normal time for the activity is 10 time units, and the corresponding cost is $400. The crash time for the activity is five time units and $800. The intersection of the normal time and cost represents the original low-cost, early-start schedule. The crash point represents the maximum time an activity can be compressed. The heavy line connecting the normal and crash points represents the slope, which assumes the cost of reducing the time of the activity is constant *per unit of time.* The assumptions underlying the use of this graph are as follows:

1. The cost-time relationship is linear.
2. Normal time assumes low-cost, efficient methods to complete the activity.
3. Crash time represents a limit—the greatest time reduction possible under realistic conditions.
4. Slope represents cost *per unit of time.*
5. All accelerations must occur within the normal and crash times.

FIGURE 9.2

Activity Graph

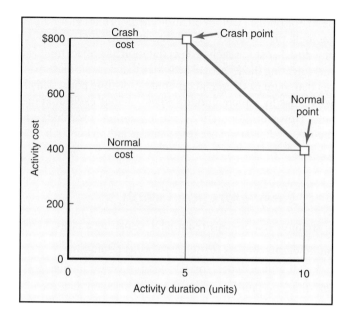

Knowing the slope of activities allows managers to compare which critical activities to shorten. The less steep the cost slope of an activity, the less it costs to shorten one time period; a steeper slope means it will cost more to shorten one time unit. The cost per unit of time or slope for any activity is computed by the following equation:

$$\text{Cost slope} = \frac{\text{Rise}}{\text{Run}} = \frac{\text{Crash cost} - \text{Normal cost}}{\text{Normal time} - \text{Crash time}}$$

$$= \frac{CC - NC}{NT - CT} = \frac{\$800 - \$400}{10 - 5}$$

$$= \frac{\$400}{5} = \$80 \text{ per unit of time}$$

In Figure 9.2 the rise is the *y* axis (cost) and the run is the *x* axis (duration). The slope of the cost line is $80 for each time unit the activity is reduced; the limit reduction of the activity time is five time units. Comparison of the slopes of all critical activities allows us to determine which activity(ies) to shorten to minimize total direct cost. Given the preliminary project schedule (or one in progress) with all activities set to their early-start times, the process of searching critical activities as candidates for reduction can begin. The total direct cost for each specific compressed project duration must be found.

A Simplified Example

Figure 9.3a presents normal and crash times and costs for each activity, the computed slope and time reduction limit, the total direct cost, and the project network with a duration of 25 time units. Note the total direct cost for the 25-period duration is $450. This is an anchor point to begin the procedure of shortening the critical path(s) and finding the total direct costs for each specific duration less than 25 time units. The maximum time reduction of an activity is simply the difference between the normal and crash times for an activity. For example, activity D can be reduced from a normal

FIGURE 9.3
Cost–Duration
Trade-off Example

time of 11 time units to a crash time of 7 time units, or a maximum of 4 time units. The positive slope for activity D is computed as follows:

$$\text{Slope} = \frac{\text{Crash cost} - \text{Normal cost}}{\text{Normal time} - \text{Crash time}} = \frac{\$150 - \$50}{11 - 7}$$

$$= \frac{\$100}{4} = \$25 \text{ per period reduced}$$

The network shows the critical path to be activities A, D, F, G. Because it is impossible to shorten activity G, activity A is circled because it is the least-cost candidate; that is, its slope ($20) is less than the slopes for activities D and F ($25 and $30). Reducing activity A one time unit cuts the project duration to 24 time units but increases the total direct costs to $470 ($450 + $20 = $470). Figure 9.3b reflects these changes. The duration of activity A has been reduced to two time units; the "x" indicates the activity cannot be reduced any further. Activity D is circled because it costs the least

FIGURE 9.4
Cost–Duration
Trade-off Example
(continued)

($25) to shorten the project to 23 time units. Compare the cost of activity F. The total direct cost for a project duration of 23 time units is $495 (see Figure 9.4a).

Observe that the project network in Figure 9.4a now has two critical paths—A, C, F, G and A, D, F, G. Reducing the project to 22 time units will require that activity F be reduced; thus, it is circled. This change is reflected in Figure 9.4b. The total direct cost for 22 time units is $525. This reduction has created a third critical path—A, B, E, G; all activities are critical. The least-cost method for reducing the project duration to 21 time units is the combination of the circled activities C, D, E which cost $30, $25, $30, respectively, and increase total direct costs to $610. The results of these changes are depicted in Figure 9.4c. Although some activities can still be reduced (those without the "x" next to the activity time), no activity or combination of activities will result in a reduction in the project duration.

With the total direct costs for the array of specific project durations found, the next step is to collect the indirect costs for these same durations. These costs are typically a rate per day and are easily obtained from the accounting department. Figure 9.5 presents the total direct costs, total indirect costs, and total project costs. These same

FIGURE 9.5
Summary Costs by Duration

Project duration	Direct costs	+	Indirect costs	=	Total costs
25	450		400		$850
24	470		350		820
23	495		300		795
22	525		250		775
21	610		200		810

FIGURE 9.6
Project Cost–Duration Graph

costs are plotted in Figure 9.6. This graph shows that the optimum cost-time duration is 22 time units and $775. Assuming the project will actually materialize as planned, any movement away from this time duration will increase project costs. The movement from 25 to 22 time units occurs because, in this range, the absolute slopes of the indirect costs are greater than the direct cost slopes.

Practical Considerations

Using the Project Cost–Duration Graph

This graph, as presented in Figures 9.1 and 9.6, is valuable to compare any proposed alternative or change with the optimum cost and time. More importantly, the creation of such a graph keeps the importance of indirect costs in the forefront of decision making. Indirect costs are frequently forgotten in the field when the pressure for action is intense. Finally, such a graph can be used before the project begins or while the project is in progress. Creating the graph in the preproject planning phase without an imposed duration is the first choice because normal time is more meaningful. Creating the graph in the project planning phase with an imposed duration is less desirable because normal time is made to fit the imposed date and is probably not low cost. Creating the graph after the project has started is the least desirable because some alternatives may be ruled out of the decision process. Managers may choose not to use the formal procedure demonstrated. However, regardless of the method used, the principles and concepts inherent in the formal procedure are highly applicable in practice and should be considered in any cost–duration trade-off decision.

Crash Times

Collecting crash times for even a moderate-size project can be difficult. The meaning of crash time is difficult to communicate. What is meant when you define crash time as "the shortest time you can realistically complete an activity"? Crash time is open to different interpretations and judgments. Some estimators feel very uncomfortable providing crash times. Regardless of the comfort level, the accuracy of crash times and costs is frequently rough at best, when compared with normal time and cost.

Linearity Assumption

Because the accuracy of compressed activity times and costs is questionable, the concern of some theorists—that the relationship between cost and time is not linear but curvilinear—is seldom a concern for practicing managers. Reasonable, quick comparisons can be made using the linear asumption. The simple approach is adequate for most projects. There are rare situations in which activities cannot be crashed by single time units. Instead, crashing is "all or nothing." For example, activity A will take 10 days (for say $1,000) or it will take 7 days (for say $1,500), but no options exist in which activity A will take 8 or 9 days to complete. In a few rare cases of very large, complex, long-duration projects, the use of present value techniques may be useful; such techniques are beyond the scope of this text.

Choice of Activities to Crash Revisited

The cost–time crashing method relies on choosing the cheapest method for reducing the duration of the project. There are other factors that should be assessed beyond simply cost. First, the timing of activities needs to be considered. Crashing a critical activity early in the project may result in wasted money if some other critical activity is finished early or some noncritical path becomes the new critical path. In such cases, the money spent early is gone and no benefit comes from early completion by crashing the activity. Conversely, it may be wise to crash an early critical activity when later activities are likely to be delayed and absorb the time gained. Then the manager would still have the option of crashing final activities to get back on schedule.

A second consideration is the impact crashing would have on the morale and motivation of the project team. If the least-cost method repeatedly signals a subgroup to accelerate progress, fatigue and resentment may set in. Conversely, if overtime pay is involved, other team members may resent not having access to this benefit. This situation can lead to tension within the entire project team. Good project managers gauge the response that crashing activities will have on the entire project team.

Finally, the inherent risks involved in crashing particular activities need to be considered. Some activities are riskier to crash than others. For example, accelerating the completion of a software design code may not be wise if it increases the likelihood of errors surfacing downstream. Conversely, it may be wise to crash a more expensive activity if there are fewer inherent risks involved.

Michael Newman/Photo Edit.

The focus of this chapter has been on how project managers crash activities by typically assigning additional manpower and equipment to cut significant time off of scheduled tasks. Project managers often encounter situations in which they need to motivate individuals to accelerate the completion of a specific, critical task. Imagine the following scenario.

Brue Young just received a priority assignment from corporate headquarters. The preliminary engineering sketches that were due tomorrow need to be e-mailed to the West Coast by 4:00 P.M. today so that the model shop can begin construction of a prototype to present to top management. He approaches Danny Whitten, the draftsman responsible for the task, whose initial response is, "That's impossible!" While he agrees that it would be very difficult he does not believe that it is as impossible as Danny suggests or that Danny truly believes that. What should he do?

He tells Danny that he knows this is going to be a rush job, but he is confident that he can do it. When Danny balks, he responds, "I tell you what, I'll make a bet with you. If you are able to finish the design by 4:00, I'll make sure you get two of the company's tickets to tomorrow night's Celtics–Knicks basketball game." Danny accepts the challenge, works feverishly to complete the assignment, and is able to take his daughter to her first professional basketball game.

Conversations with project managers reveal that many use bets like this one to motivate extraordinary performance. These bets range from tickets to sporting and entertainment events to gift certificates at high-class restaurants to a well-deserved afternoon off. For bets to work they need to adhere to the principles of expectancy theory of motivation. Boiled down to simple terms, expectancy theory rests on three key questions:

1. Can I do it (Is it possible to meet the challenge)?

2. Will I get it (Can I demonstrate that I met the challenge and can I trust the project manager will deliver his/her end of the bargain)?

3. Is it worth it (Is the payoff of sufficient personal value to warrant the risk and extra effort)?

If in the mind of the participant the answer to any of these three questions is no, then the person is unlikely to accept the challenge. However, when the answers are affirmative, then the individual is likely to accept the bet and be motivated to meet the challenge.

Bets can be effective motivational tools and add an element of excitement and fun to project work. But, the following practical advice should be heeded:

1. The bet has greater significance if it also benefits family members or significant others. Being able to take a son or daughter to a professional basketball game allows that individual to "score points" at home through work. These bets also recognize and reward the support project members receive from their families and reinforces the importance of their work to loved ones.

2. Bets should be used sparingly; otherwise everything can become negotiable. They should be used only under special circumstances that require extraordinary effort.

3. Individual bets should involve clearly recognizable individual effort, otherwise others may become jealous and discord may occur within a group. As long as others see it as requiring truly remarkable, "beyond the call of duty" effort, they will consider it fair and warranted.

Time Reduction Decisions and Sensitivity

Should the project owner or project manager go for the optimum cost-time? The answer is, "It depends." Risk must be considered. Recall from our example that the optimum project time point represented a reduced project cost and was less than the original normal project time (review Figure 9.6). The project direct-cost line near the normal point is usually relatively flat. Because indirect costs for the project are usually greater in the same range, the optimum cost-time point is less than the normal time point. Logic of the cost-time procedure suggests managers should reduce the project duration to the lowest total cost point and duration.

How far to reduce the project time from the normal time toward the optimum depends on the *sensitivity* of the project network. A network is sensitive if it has several critical or near-critical paths. In our example project movement toward the optimum time requires spending money to reduce critical activities, resulting in slack reduction and/or more critical paths and activities. Slack reduction in a project with several near-critical paths increases the risk of being late. The practical outcome can be a higher total project cost if some near-critical activities are delayed and become critical; the money spent reducing activities on the original critical path would be wasted. Sensitive networks require careful analysis. The bottom line is that compression of projects with several near-critical paths reduces scheduling flexibility and increases the risk of delaying the project. The outcome of such analysis will probably suggest only a partial movement from the normal time toward the optimum time.

There is a positive situation where moving toward the optimum time can result in very real, large savings—this occurs when the network is *insensitive*. A project network is insensitive if it has a dominant critical path, that is, no near-critical paths. In this project circumstance, movement from the normal time point toward the optimum time will *not* create new or near-critical activities. The bottom line here is that the reduction of the slack of noncritical activities increases the risk of their becoming critical only slightly when compared with the effect in a sensitive network. Insensitive networks hold the greatest potential for real, sometimes large, savings in total project costs with a minimum risk of noncritical activities becoming critical.

Insensitive networks are not a rarity in practice; they occur in perhaps 25 percent of all projects. For example, a light rail project team observed from their network a dominant critical path and relatively high indirect costs. It soon became clear that by spending some dollars on a few critical activities, very large savings of indirect costs could be realized. Savings of several million dollars were spent extending the rail line and adding another station. The logic found in this example is just as applicable to small projects as large ones. Insensitive networks with high indirect costs can produce large savings.

Ultimately, deciding if and which activities to crash is a judgment call requiring careful consideration of the options available, the costs and risks involved, and the importance of meeting a deadline.

What if Cost, Not Time, Is the Issue?

In today's fast-paced world, there appears to be a greater emphasis on getting things done quickly. Still, organizations are always looking for ways to get things done cheaply. This is especially true for fixed-bid projects, where profit margin is derived from the difference between the bid and actual cost of the project. Every dollar saved is a dollar in your pocket. Sometimes, in order to secure a contract, bids are tight, which puts added pressure on cost containment. In other cases, there are financial incentives tied to cost containment.

Even in situations where cost is transferred to customer, there is pressure to reduce cost. Cost overruns make for unhappy customers and can damage future business opportunities. Budgets can be fixed or cut, and when contingency funds are exhausted, then cost overruns have to be made up with remaining activities.

As discussed earlier, shortening project duration may come at the expense of over-time, adding additional personnel, and using more expensive equipment and/or mate-rials. Conversely, sometimes cost savings can be generated by extending the duration of a project. This may allow for a smaller workforce, less-skilled (expensive) labor, and even cheaper equipment and materials to be used. Below are some of the more com-monly used options for cutting costs.

Reduce Project Scope

Just as scaling back or reducing the scope of the project can gain time, delivering less than what was originally planned also produces significant savings. Again, calculating the savings of a reduced project scope begins with the work breakdown structure. How-ever, since time is not the issue, you do not need to focus on critical activities.

Have Owner Take on More Responsibility

One way of reducing project costs is identifying tasks that customers can do them-selves. Homeowners frequently use this method to reduce costs on home improvement projects. For example, to reduce the cost of a bathroom remodel, a homeowner may agree to paint the room instead of paying the contractor to do it. On IS projects, a cus-tomer may agree to take on some of the responsibility for testing equipment or provid-ing in-house training. Naturally, this arrangement is best negotiated before the project begins. Customers are less receptive to this idea if you suddenly spring it on them. An advantage of this method is that, while costs are lowered, the original scope is retained. Clearly this option is limited to areas in which the customer has expertise and the capability to pick up the tasks.

Outsourcing Project Activities or Even the Entire Project

When estimates exceed budget, it not only makes sense to re-examine the scope but also search for cheaper ways to complete the project. Perhaps instead of relying on internal resources, it would be more cost effective to outsource segments or even the entire project, opening up work to external price competition. Specialized subcontrac-tors often enjoy unique advantages, such as material discounts for large quantities, as well as equipment that not only gets the work done more quickly but also less expen-sively. They may have lower overhead and labor costs. For example, to reduce costs of software projects, many American firms outsource work to firms operating in India where the salary of a software engineer is one-eighth that of an American software en-gineer. However, outsourcing means you have less control over the project and will need to have clearly definable deliverables.

Brainstorming Cost Savings Options

Just as project team members can be a rich source of ideas for accelerating project activities, they can offer tangible ways for reducing project costs. For example, one project manager reported that his team was able to come up with over $75,000 worth of cost saving suggestions without jeopardizing the scope of the project. Project managers should not underestimate the value of simply asking if there is a cheaper, better way.

Summary

The need for reducing the project duration occurs for many reasons such as imposed duration dates, time-to-market considerations, incentive contracts, key resource needs, high overhead costs, or simply unforeseen delays. These situations are very common in practice and are known as cost-time trade-off decisions. This chapter presented a logical, formal process for assessing the implications of situations that involve shortening the project duration. Crashing the project duration increases the *risk* of being late. How far to reduce the project duration from the normal time toward the optimum depends on the *sensitivity* of the project network. A sensitive network is one that has several critical or near-critical paths. Great care should be taken when shortening sensitive networks to avoid increasing project risks. Conversely, insensitive networks represent opportunities for potentially large project cost savings by eliminating some overhead costs with little downside risk.

Alternative strategies for reducing project time were discussed within the context of whether or not the project is resource limited. Project acceleration typically comes at a cost of either spending money for more resources or compromising the scope of the project. If the latter is the case, then it is essential that all relevant stakeholders be consulted so that everyone accepts the changes that have to be made. One other key point is the difference in implementing time-reducing activities in the midst of project execution versus incorporating them into the project plan. You typically have far fewer options once the project is underway than before it begins. This is especially true if you want to take advantage of the new scheduling methodologies such as fast-tracking and critical-chain. Time spent up front considering alternatives and developing contingency plans will lead to time savings in the end.

Key Terms

Crash point	Fast-tracking	Phase project delivery
Crash time	Indirect costs	Project cost–duration
Direct costs	Outsourcing	graph

Review Questions

1. What are the advantages and disadvantages of reducing project scope to accelerate a project? What can be done to reduce the disadvantages?
2. Why is scheduling overtime a popular choice for getting projects back on schedule? What are the potential problems for relying on this option?
3. Identify five indirect costs you might find on a moderately complex project. Why are these costs classified as indirect?
4. How can a cost–duration graph be used by the project manager? Explain.
5. Reducing the project duration increases the risk of being late. Explain.
6. It is possible to shorten the critical path and save money. Explain how.

Exercises

1. Draw a project network from the following information.

Activity	Predecessor	Duration
A	None	2
B	A	4
C	A	3
D	A	2
E	B	3
F	C	6
G	C, D	5
H	E, F	6
I	G	5
J	H, I	5

Activities B and H can be shortened to a minimum of 2 weeks. Which activity would you shorten to reduce the project duration by 2 weeks? Why?

2. Assume the network and data that follow. Compute the total direct cost for each project duration. If the indirect costs for each project duration are $400 (19 time units), $350 (18), $300 (17), and $250 (16), compute the total project cost for each duration. Plot the total direct, indirect, and project costs for each of these durations on a cost-time graph. What is the optimum cost-time schedule for the project? What is this cost?

Act.	Crash Cost (Slope)	Maximum Crash Time	Normal Time	Normal Cost
A	20	1	3	50
B	60	2	5	60
C	40	1	3	70
D	0	0	10	50
E	50	3	6	100
F	100	3	7	90
G	70	1	5	50
				$470

3. Given the data and information that follow, compute the total direct cost for each project duration. If the indirect costs for each project duration are $90 (15 time units), $70 (14), $50 (13), $40 (12), and $30 (11), compute the total project cost for each duration. What is the optimum cost-time schedule for the project? What is this cost?

Act.	Crash Cost (Slope)	Maximum Crash Time	Normal Time	Normal Cost
A	20	1	5	50
B	60	2	3	60
C	0	0	4	70
D	10	1	2	50
E	60	3	5	100
F	100	1	2	90
G	30	1	5	50
H	40	0	2	60
I	200	1	3	200
				$730

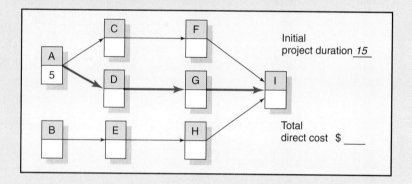

Initial
project duration _15_

Total
direct cost $____

4. If the indirect costs for each duration are $1,200 for 16 weeks, $1,130 for 15 weeks, $1,000 for 14 weeks, $900 for 13 weeks, $860 for 12 weeks, $820 for 11 weeks and $790 for 10 weeks, compute the total costs for each duration. Plot these costs on a graph. What is the optimum cost-time schedule?

Act.	Crash Cost (Slope)	Maximum Crash Time	Normal Time	Normal Cost
A	10	1	4	30
B	70	2	7	60
C	0	0	1	80
D	20	2	4	40
E	50	3	5	110
F	200	3	5	90
G	30	1	2	60
H	40	1	2	70
I	0	0	2	140
				$680

Time unit = 1 week

Project duration _16_

Total
direct cost $ ____

5. If the indirect costs for each duration are $300 for 27 weeks, $240 for 26 weeks, $180 for 25 weeks, $120 for 24 weeks, $60 for 23 weeks, and $50 for 22 weeks, compute the direct, indirect and total costs for each duration. What is the optimum cost-time schedule? The customer offers you $10 dollars for every week you shorten the project from your original network. Would you take it? If so for how many weeks?

Act.	Crash Cost (Slope)	Maximum Crash Time	Normal Time	Normal Cost
A	80	2	10	40
B	30	3	8	10
C	40	1	5	80
D	50	2	11	50
E	100	4	15	100
F	30	1	6	20
				$300

Time unit = 1 week

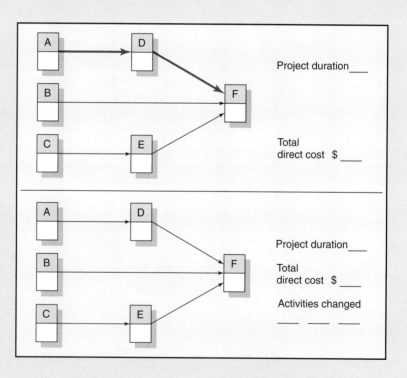

6. Use the information contained below to compress one time unit per move using the least cost method. Reduce the schedule until you reach the crash point of the network. For each move identify what activity(s) was crashed, the adjusted total cost, and explain your choice if you have to choose between activities that cost the same.

   Note: Crash point of the network is the point in which the duration cannot be reduced any further.

| Activity ID | Slope | Maximum Crash Time | Direct Costs | | | |
| | | | Normal | | Crash | |
			Time	Cost	Time	Cost
A	—	0	4	$50	0	—
B	$40	3	5	70	2	$190
C	40	1	5	80	4	40
D	40	2	4	40	2	120
E	40	2	5	60	3	140
F	40	1	5	50	4	90
G	30	1	4	70	3	160
H	30	1	4	80	3	110
I	—	0	3	50	0	—

Total direct costs—$550

Completion time: _21_   Total cost $ _550_

References

Abdel-Hamid, T., and S. Madnick, *Software Project Dynamics: An Integrated Approach* (Englewood Cliffs, NJ: Prentice Hall, 1991).

Baker, B. M., "Cost/Time Trade-off Analysis for the Critical Path Method," *Journal of the Operational Research Society,* 48 (12), 1997, pp. 1241–44.

Brooks, F. P., Jr., *The Mythical Man-Month: Essays on Software Engineering Anniversary Edition* (Reading, MA: Addison-Wesley Longman, Inc., 1994), pp. 15–26.

DeMarco, T., *Slack: Getting Past Burnout, Busywork, and the Myth of Total Efficiency* (New York: Broadway, 2002).

Ibbs, C. W., S. A. Lee, and M. I. Li, "Fast-Tracking's Impact on Project Change," *Project Management Journal,* 29 (4), 1998, pp. 35–42.

Khang, D. B., and M. Yin, "Time, Cost, and Quality Tradeoff in Project Management," *International Journal of Project Management,* 17 (4), 1999, pp. 249–56.

Perrow, L. A., *Finding Time: How Corporations, Individuals, and Families Can Benefit From New Work Practices* (Ithaca, NY: Cornell University Press, 1997).

Roemer, T. R., Ahmadi, and R. Wang, "Time-cost Trade-offs in Overlapped Product Development," *Operations Research,* 48 (6) 2000, pp. 858–65.

Smith, P. G., and D.G. Reinersten, *Developing Products in Half the Time* (New York: Van Nostrand Reinhold, 1995).

Verzuh, E., *The Fast Forward MBA in Project Management* (New York: John Wiley, 1999).

Vroom, V. H., *Work and Motivation* (New York: John Wiley & Sons, 1964).

Case

International Capital, Inc.—Part B

Given the project network derived in Part A of the case from Chapter 7, Brown also wants to be prepared to answer any questions concerning compressing the project duration. This question will almost always be entertained by the accounting department, review committee, and the client. To be ready for the compression question, Brown has prepared the following data in case it is necessary to crash the project. (Use your weighted average times (t_e) computed in Part A of the International Capital case found in Chapter 7.)

Activity	Normal Cost	Maximum Crash Time	Crash Cost/Day
A	$ 3,000	3	$ 500
B	5,000	2	1,000
C	6,000	0	—
D	20,000	3	3,000
E	10,000	2	1,000
F	7,000	1	1,000
G	20,000	2	3,000
H	8,000	1	2,000
I	5,000	1	2,000
J	7,000	1	1,000
K	12,000	6	1,000

Total normal costs = $103,000

Using the data provided, determine the activity crashing decisions and best-time cost project duration. Given the information you have developed, what suggestions would you give Brown to ensure she is well prepared for the project review committee? Assume the overhead costs for this project are $700 per workday. Will this alter your suggestions?

Case

Whitbread World Sailboat Race

Each year countries enter their sailing vessels in the nine-month Round the World Whitbread Sailboat Race. In recent years, about 14 countries entered sailboats in the race. Each year's sailboat entries represent the latest technologies and human skills each country can muster.

Bjorn Ericksen has been selected as a project manager because of his past experience as a master helmsman and because of his recent fame as the "best designer of racing sailboats in the world." Bjorn is pleased and proud to have the opportunity to design, build, test, and train the crew for next year's Whitbread entry for his country. Bjorn has picked Karin Knutsen (as chief design engineer) and Trygve Wallvik (as master helmsman) to be team leaders responsible for getting next year's entry ready for the traditional parade of all entries on the Thames River in the United Kingdom, which signals the start of the race.

As Bjorn begins to think of a project plan, he sees two parallel paths running through the project—design and construction and crew training. Last year's boat will be used for training until the new entry can have the crew on board to learn maintenance tasks. Bjorn calls Karin and Trygve together to develop a project plan. All three agree the major goal is to have a winning boat and crew ready to compete in next year's competition at a cost of $3.2 million. A check of Bjorn's calendar indicates he has 45 weeks before next year's vessel must leave port for the United Kingdom to start the race.

THE KICKOFF MEETING

Bjorn asks Karin to begin by describing the major activities and the sequence required to design, construct, and test the boat. Karin starts by noting that design of the hull, deck, mast, and accessories should only take six weeks—given the design prints from past race entries and a few prints from other countries' entries. After the design is complete, the hull can be constructed, the mast ordered, sails ordered, and accessories ordered. The hull will require 12 weeks to complete. The mast can be ordered and will require a lead time of eight weeks; the seven sails can be ordered and will take six weeks to get; accessories can be ordered and will take 15 weeks to receive. As soon as the hull is finished, the ballast tanks can be installed, requiring two weeks. Then the deck can be built, which will require five weeks. Concurrently, the hull can be treated with special sealant and friction-resistance coating, taking three weeks. When the deck is completed and mast and accessories received, the mast and sails can be installed, requiring two weeks; the accessories can be installed, which will take six weeks. When all of these activities have been completed, the ship can be sea-tested, which should take five weeks. Karin believes she can have firm cost estimates for the boat in about two weeks.

Trygve believes he can start selecting the 12-man or woman crew and securing their housing immediately. He believes it will take six weeks to get a committed crew on-site and three weeks to secure housing for the crew members. Trygve reminds Bjorn that last year's vessel must be ready to use for training the moment the crew is on-site until the new vessel is ready for testing. Keeping the old vessel operating will cost $4,000 per week as long as it is used. Once the crew is on-site and housed, they can develop and implement a routine sailing and maintenance training program, which will take 15 weeks (using the old vessel). Also, once the crew is selected and on-site, crew equipment can be selected, taking only two weeks. Then crew equipment can be ordered; it will take five weeks to arrive. When the crew equipment and maintenance training program are complete, crew maintenance on the new vessel can begin; this should take 10 weeks. But crew maintenance on the new vessel cannot begin until the deck is complete and the mast, sails, and accessories have arrived. Once crew maintenance on the new vessel begins, the new vessel will cost $6,000 per week until sea training is complete. After the new ship maintenance is complete and while the boat is being tested, initial sailing training can be implemented; training should take seven weeks. Finally, after the boat is tested and initial training is complete, regular sea training can be implemented—weather permitting; regular sea training requires eight weeks. Trygve believes he can put the cost estimates together in a week, given last year's expenses.

Bjorn is pleased with the expertise displayed by his team leaders. But he believes they need to have someone develop one of those critical path networks to see if they can safely meet the start deadline for the race. Karin and Trygve agree. Karin suggests the cost estimates should also include crash costs for any activities that can be compressed and the resultant costs for crashing. Karin also suggests the team complete the following priority matrix for project decision making:

FIGURE C9.1
Project Priority Matrix: Whitbread Project

	Time	Performance	Cost
Constrain			
Enhance			
Accept			

TWO WEEKS LATER

Karin and Trygve submit the following cost estimates for each activity and corresponding crash costs to Bjorn (costs are in thousands of dollars):

Activity		Normal Time	Normal Cost	Crash Time	Crash Cost
A	Design	6	$ 40	4	$ 160
B	Build hull	12	1,000	10	1,400
C	Install ballast tanks	2	100	2	100
D	Order mast	8	100	7	140
E	Order sails	6	40	6	40
F	Order accessories	15	600	13	800
G	Build deck	5	200	5	200
H	Coat hull	3	40	3	40
I	Install accessories	6	300	5	400
J	Install mast and sails	2	40	1	80
K	Test	5	60	4	100
L	Sea trials	8	200	7	450
M	Select crew	6	10	5	20
N	Secure housing	3	30	3	30
O	Select crew equipment	2	10	2	10
P	Order crew equipment	5	30	5	30
Q	Routine sail and maintenance	15	40	12	130
R	Crew maintenance training	10	100	9	340
S	Initial sail training	7	50	5	350

Bjorn reviews the materials and wonders if the project will come in within the budget of $3.2 million and in 45 weeks. Advise the Whitbread team of their situation.

Case

The "Now" Wedding*

On December 31 of last year, Lauren burst into the family living room and announced that she and Connor (her college boyfriend) were going to be married. After recovering from the shock, her mother hugged her and asked, "When?" The following conversation resulted:

Lauren: January 21.

Mom: What?

Dad: The Now wedding will be the social hit of the year. Wait a minute. Why so soon?

Lauren: Because on January 30 Connor, who is in the National Guard, will be shipping out overseas. We want a week for a honeymoon.

Mom: But Honey, we can't possibly finish all the things that need to be done by then. Remember all the details that were involved in your sister's wedding? Even if we start tomorrow, it takes a day to reserve the church and reception hall, and they need at least 14 days' notice. That has to be done before we can start decorating, which takes 3 days. An extra $200 on Sunday would probably cut that 14 day notice to 7 days, though.

Dad: Oh, boy!

Lauren: I want Jane Summers to be my maid of honor.

Dad: But she's in the Peace Corps in Guatemala isn't she? It would take her 10 days to get ready and drive up here.

Lauren: But we could fly her up in two days and it would only cost $1,000.

Dad: Oh boy!

Mom: And catering! It takes 2 days to choose the cake and decorations, and Jack's Catering wants at least 5 days' notice. Besides, we'd have to have those things before we could start decorating.

Lauren: Can I wear your wedding dress, Mom?

Mother: Well, we'd have to replace some lace, but you could wear it, yes. We could order the lace from New York when we order the material for the bridesmaids' dresses. It takes 8 days to order and receive the material. The pattern needs to be chosen first, and that would take 3 days.

Dad: We could get the material here in 5 days if we paid an extra $20 to airfreight it. Oh, boy!

Lauren: I want Mrs. Jacks to work on the dresses.

Mom: But she charges $48 a day.

Dad: Oh, boy!

Mom: If we did all the sewing we could finish the dresses in 11 days. If Mrs. Jacks helped we could cut that down to 6 days at a cost of $48 for each day less than 11 days. She is very good too.

* This case was adapted from a case originally written by Professor D. Clay Whybark, University of North Carolina, Chapel Hill, N.C.

Lauren: I don't want anyone but her.

Mom: It would take another 2 days to do the final fitting and 2 more days to clean and press the dresses. They would have to be ready by rehearsal night. We must have rehearsal the night before the wedding.

Dad: Everything should be ready rehearsal night.

Mom: We've forgotten something. The invitations!

Dad: We should order the invitations from Bob's Printing shop, and that usually takes 7 days. I'll bet he would do it in 5 or 6 days if we slipped him an extra $20 for each day less than 7. Oh, boy!

Mom: It would take us 2 days to choose the invitation style before we could order them and we want the envelopes printed with our return address.

Lauren: Oh! That will be elegant.

Mom: The invitations should go out at least 10 days before the wedding. If we let them go any later, some of the relatives would get theirs too late to come and that would make them mad. I'll bet that if we didn't get them out until 8 days before the wedding, Aunt Ethel couldn't make it and she would reduce her wedding gift by $200.

Dad: Oh, boy!!

Mom: We'll have to take them to the Post office to mail them and that takes a day. Addressing would take three days unless we hired some part-time girls and we can't start until the printer is finished. If we hired the girls we could probably save two days by spending $40 for each day saved.

Lauren: We need to get gifts for the bridesmaids. I could spend a day and do that.

Mom: Before we can even start to write out those invitations we need a guest list. Heavens, that will take 4 days to get in order and only I can understand our address file.

Lauren: Oh, Mom:, I'm so excited. We can start each of the relatives on a different job.

Mom: Honey, I don't see how we can do it. Why, I've got to choose the invitations and patterns and reserve the church and . . .

Dad: Why don't you just take $3,000 and elope. Your sister's wedding cost me $2,400 and she didn't have to fly people up from Guatemala, hire extra girls and Mrs. Jacks, use airfreight, or anything like that.

1. Using a yellow sticky approach (see p. 110), develop a project network for the NOW Wedding.
2. Create a schedule for the Wedding using MS Project. Can you reach the deadline of January 21 for the Now Wedding? If you cannot, what would it cost to make the January 21 deadline and which activities would you change?

Case

The Now Wedding, Part B

Several complications arose during the course of trying to meet the deadline of January 20 for the Now wedding rehearsal. Since Lauren was adamant on having the wedding on January 21 (as was Connor for obvious reasons); the implications of each of these complications had to be assessed.

1. On January 1 the chairman of the Vestry Committee of the church was left unimpressed by the added donation and said he wouldn't reduce the notice period from 14 to 7 days.
2. Mother comes down with the three-day flu as she starts work on the guest list January 2.
3. Bob's Printing Service's press was down for one day on January 5th in order to replace faulty brushes in the electric motor.
4. The lace and dress material are lost in transit. Notice of the loss is received on January 10.

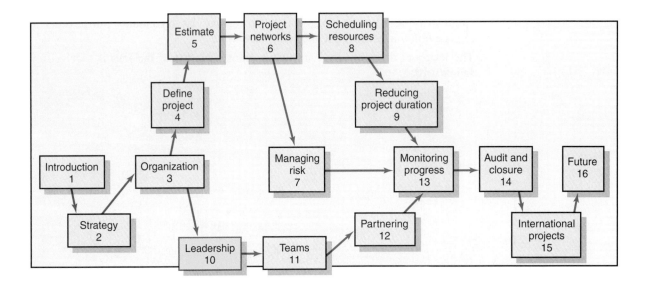

Estimate 5	Project networks 6	Scheduling resources 8
Define project 4		Reducing project duration 9
Introduction 1	Organization 3	Managing risk 7	Monitoring progress 13	Audit and closure 14	Future 16
Strategy 2	Leadership 10	Teams 11	Partnering 12	International projects 15

Leadership: Being an Effective Project Manager

Managing versus Leading a Project

Managing Project Stakeholders

Influence as Exchange

Social Network Building

Ethics and Project Management

Building Trust: The Key to Exercising Influence

Qualities of an Effective Project Manager

Summary

CHAPTER TEN

Leadership: Being an Effective Project Manager

I couldn't wait to be the manager of my own project and run the project the way I thought it should be done. Boy, did I have a lot to learn!

—first-time project manager

This chapter is based on the premise that one of the keys to being an effective project manager is building cooperative relationships among different groups of people to complete projects. Project success does not just depend on the performance of the project team. Success or failure often depends on the contributions of top management, functional managers, customers, suppliers, contractors, and others.

The chapter begins with a brief discussion of the differences between leading and managing a project. The importance of managing project stakeholders is then introduced. Managers require a broad influence base to be effective in this area. Different sources of influence are discussed and are used to describe how project managers build social capital. This management style necessitates constant interacting with different groups of people whom project managers depend on. Special attention is devoted to managing the critical relationship with top management and the importance of leading by example. The importance of gaining cooperation in ways that build and sustain the trust of others is emphasized. The chapter concludes by identifying personal attributes associated with being an effective project manager. Subsequent chapters will expand on these ideas in a discussion of managing the project team and working with people outside the organization.

Managing versus Leading a Project

In a perfect world, the project manager would simply implement the project plan and the project would be completed. The project manager would work with others to formulate a schedule, organize a project team, keep track of progress, and announce what needs to be done next, and then everyone would charge along. Of course no one lives in a perfect world, and rarely does everything go according to plan. Project participants get testy; they fail to complement each other; other departments are unable to fulfill their commitments; technical glitches arise; work takes longer than expected. The project manager's job is to get the project back on track. A manager expedites certain activities; figures out ways to solve technical problems; serves as peacemaker when tensions rise; and makes appropriate trade-offs among time, cost, and scope of the project.

However, project managers do more than put out fires and keep the project on track. They also innovate and adapt to ever-changing circumstances. They often have to deviate from what was planned and introduce significant changes in the project scope and schedule to respond to unforeseen threats or opportunities. For example, customers' needs may change, requiring significant design changes midway through the project. Competitors may release new products that dictate switching the time, cost, and scope priorities of the project. Working relationships among project participants may break down, requiring a reformulation of the project team. Ultimately, what was planned or expected in the beginning may be very different from what was accomplished by the end of the project.

Project managers are responsible for integrating assigned resources to complete the project according to plan. At the same time they need to initiate changes in plans and schedules as persistent problems make plans unworkable. In other words, managers want to keep the project going while making necessary adjustments along the way. According to Kotter these two different activities represent the distinction between management and leadership. Management is about coping with complexity, while leadership is about coping with change.

Good management brings about order and stability by formulating plans and objectives, designing structures and procedures, monitoring results against plans, and taking corrective action when necessary. Leadership involves recognizing and articulating the need to significantly alter the direction and operation of the project, aligning people to the new direction, and motivating them to work together to overcome hurdles produced by the change and to realize new objectives.

Strong leadership, while usually desirable, is not always necessary to successfully complete a project. Well-defined projects that encounter no significant surprises require little leadership, as might be the case in constructing a conventional apartment building in which the project manager simply administrates the project plan. Conversely, the higher the degree of uncertainty encountered on a project—whether in terms of changes in project scope, technological stalemates, breakdowns in coordination between people, and so forth—the more leadership is required. For example, strong leadership would be needed for a software development project in which the parameters are always changing to meet developments in the industry.

It takes a special person to perform both roles well. Some individuals are great visionaries who are good at exciting people about change. Too often though, these same people lack the discipline or patience to deal with the day-to-day drudgeries of managing. Likewise, there are other individuals who are very well organized and methodical but lack the ability to inspire others.

Strong leaders can compensate for their managerial weaknesses by having trusted assistants who oversee and manage the details of the project. Conversely, a weak leader can complement his or her strengths by having assistants who are good at sensing the need to change and rallying project participants. Still, one of the things that makes good project managers so valuable to an organization is that they have the ability to both manage and lead a project. In doing so they recognize the need to manage project interfaces and build a social network that allows them to find out what needs to be done and obtain the cooperation necessary to achieve it.

Managing Project Stakeholders

First-time project managers are eager to implement their own ideas and manage their people to successfully complete their project. What they soon find out is that project success depends on the cooperation of a wide range of individuals, many of whom do not directly report to them. For example, during the course of a system integration project, a project manager was surprised by how much time she was spending negotiating and working with vendors, consultants, technical specialists, and other functional managers:

> Instead of working with my people to complete the project, I found myself being constantly pulled and tugged by demands of different groups of people who were not directly involved in the project but had a vested interest in the outcome.

Too often when new project managers do find time to work directly on the project, they adopt a hands-on approach to managing the project. They choose this style not because they are power-hungry egomaniacs but because they are eager to achieve results. They become quickly frustrated by how slowly things operate, the number of people that have to be brought on board, and the difficulty of gaining cooperation. Unfortunately, as this frustration builds, the natural temptation is to exert more pressure and get more heavily involved in the project. These project managers quickly earn the reputation of "micro managing" and begin to lose sight of the real role they play on guiding a project.

Some new managers never break out of this vicious cycle. Others soon realize that authority does not equal influence and that being an effective project manager involves managing a much more complex and expansive set of interfaces than they had previously anticipated. They encounter a web of relationships that requires a much broader spectrum of influence than they felt was necessary or even possible.

For example, a significant project, whether it involves renovating a bridge, creating a new product, or installing a new information system, will likely involve in one way or another working with a number of different groups of stakeholders. First, there is the core group of specialists assigned to complete the project. This group is likely to be supplemented at different times by professionals who work on specific segments of the project. Second, there are the groups of people within the performing organization who are either directly or indirectly involved with the project. The most notable is top management, to whom the project manager is accountable. There are also other managers who provide resources and/or may be responsible for specific segments of the project, and administrative support services such as human resources, finance, etc. Depending on the nature of the project, there are a number of different groups outside the organization that influence the success of the project; the most important is the customer for which the project is designed (see Figure 10.1).

Each of these groups of individuals brings different expertise, standards, priorities, and agendas to the project. The sheer breadth and complexity of the relationships that need to be managed distinguishes project management from regular management. To be effective, a project manager must understand how these groups can affect the project and develop methods for managing the dependency. The nature of these dependencies is identified here:

- The **project team** manages and completes project work. Most participants want to do a good job, but they are also concerned with their other obligations and how their involvement on the project will contribute to their personal goals and aspirations.
- **Project managers** naturally compete with each other for resources and the support of top management. At the same time they often have to share resources and exchange information.
- **Administrative support** groups, such as human resources, information systems, purchasing agents, and maintenance, provide valuable support services. At the same time they impose constraints and requirements on the project such as the documentation of expenditures and the timely and accurate delivery of information.

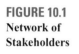

FIGURE 10.1
Network of
Stakeholders

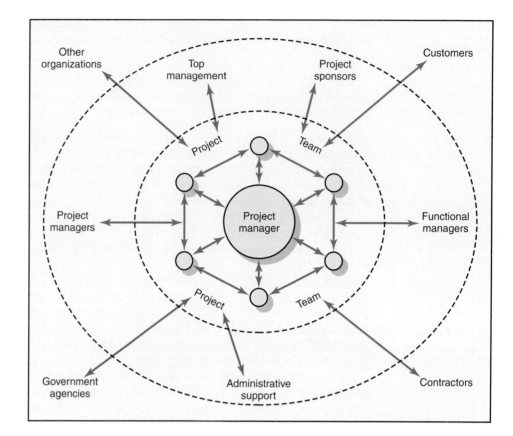

- **Functional managers,** depending on how the project is organized, can play a minor or major role toward project success. In matrix arrangements, they may be responsible for assigning project personnel, resolving technical dilemmas, and overseeing the completion of significant segments of the project work. Even in dedicated project teams, the technical input from functional managers may be useful, and acceptance of completed project work may be critical to in-house projects. Functional managers want to cooperate up to a point, but only up to a certain point. They are also concerned with preserving their status within the organization and minimizing the disruptions the project may have on their own operations.

- **Top management** approves funding of the project and establishes priorities within the organization. They define success and adjudicate rewards for accomplishments. Significant adjustments in budget, scope, and schedule typically need their approval. They have a natural vested interest in the success of the project, but at the same time have to be responsive to what is best for the entire organization.

- **Project sponsors** champion the project and use their influence to gain approval of the project. Their reputation is tied to the success of the project, and they need to be kept informed of any major developments. They defend the project when it comes under attack and are a key project ally.

- **Subcontractors** may do all the actual work, in some cases, with the project team merely coordinating their contributions. In other cases, they are responsible for

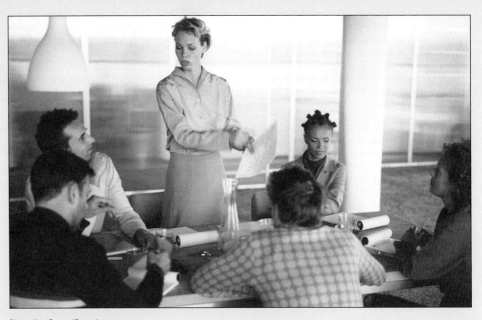

Photodisc Green/Getty Images.

Metaphors convey meaning beyond words. For example, a meeting can be described as being difficult or "like wading through molasses." A popular metaphor for the role of a project manager is that of *conductor*. The conductor of an orchestra integrates the divergent sounds of different instruments to perform a given composition and make beautiful music. Similarly, the project manager integrates the talents and contributions of different specialists to complete the project. Both have to be good at understanding how the different players contribute to the performance of the whole. Both are almost entirely dependent upon the expertise and know-how of the players. The conductor does not have command of all the musical instruments. Likewise, the project manager usually possesses only a small proportion of the technical knowledge to make decisions. As such, the conductor

and project manager both facilitate the performance of others rather than actually perform.

Conductors use their arms, baton, and other nonverbal gestures to influence the pace, intensity, and involvement of different musicians. Likewise, project managers orchestrate the completion of the project by managing the involvement and attention of project members. Project managers balance time and process and induce participants to make the right decisions at the right time just as the conductor induces the wind instruments to perform at the right moment in a movement. Each controls the rhythm and intensity of work by managing the tempo and involvement of the players. Finally, each has a vision that transcends the music score or project plan. To be successful they must both earn the confidence, respect, and trust of their players.

ancillary segments of the project scope. Poor work and schedule slips can affect work of the core project team. While contractors' reputations rest with doing good work, they must balance their contributions with their own profit margins and their commitments to other clients.

- **Government agencies** place constraints on project work. Permits need to be secured. Construction work has to be built to code. New drugs have to pass a rigorous battery of U.S. Food and Drug Administration tests. Other products have to meet safety standards, for example, Occupational Safety and Health Administration standards.

- **Other organizations,** depending on the nature of the project, may directly or indirectly affect the project. For example, suppliers provide necessary resources for completion of the project work. Delays, shortages, and poor quality can bring a project to a standstill. Public interest groups may apply pressure on government agencies. Customers often hire consultants and auditors to protect their interests on a project.

- **Customers** define the scope of the project, and ultimate project success rests in their satisfaction. Project managers need to be responsive to changing customer needs and requirements and to meeting their expectations. Customers are primarily concerned with getting a *good deal* and, as will be elaborated in Chapter 11, this naturally breeds tension with the project team.

These relationships are interdependent in that a project manager's ability to work effectively with one group will affect her ability to manage other groups. For example, functional managers are likely to be less cooperative if they perceive that top management's commitment to the project is waning. Conversely, the ability of the project manager to buffer the team from excessive interference from a client is likely to increase her standing with the project team.

The project management structure being used will influence the number and degree of external dependencies that will need to be managed. One advantage of creating a dedicated project team is that it reduces dependencies, especially within the organization, because most of the resources are assigned to the project. Conversely, a functional matrix structure increases dependencies, with the result that the project manager is much more reliant upon functional colleagues for work and staff.

The old-fashioned view of managing projects emphasized directing and controlling subordinates; the new perspective emphasizes managing project stakeholders and anticipating change as the most important jobs. Project managers need to be able to assuage concerns of customers, sustain support for the project at higher levels of the organization, quickly identify problems that threaten project work, while at the same time defend the integrity of the project and the interests of the project participants.

Within this web of relationships, the project manager must find out what needs to be done to achieve the goals of the project and build a cooperative network to accomplish it. Project managers must do so without the requisite authority to expect or demand cooperation. Doing so requires sound communication skills, political savvy, and a broad influence base.

Influence as Exchange

To successfully manage a project, a manager must adroitly build a cooperative network among divergent allies. Networks are mutually beneficial alliances that are generally governed by the law of reciprocity. The basic principle is that "one good deed deserves another, and likewise, one bad deed deserves another." The primary way to gain cooperation is to provide resources and services for others in exchange for future resources and services. This is the age-old maxim: "Quid pro quo (something for something)." Or in today's vernacular: "You scratch my back, I'll scratch yours."

Cohen and Bradford described the exchange view of influence as "currencies." If you want to do business in a given country, you have to be prepared to use the appropriate currency, and the exchange rates can change over time as conditions change. In

TABLE 10.1
Commonly Traded Organizational Currencies

Source: Adapted from A. R. Cohen and David L. Bradford, *Influence without Authority* (New York: John Wiley & Sons, 2005). Reprinted by permission of John Wiley & Sons, Inc.

Task-related currencies	
Resources	Lending or giving money, budget increases, personnel, etc.
Assistance	Helping with existing projects or undertaking unwanted tasks.
Cooperation	Giving task support, providing quicker response time, or aiding implementation.
Information	Providing organizational as well as technical knowledge.
Position-related currencies	
Advancement	Giving a task or assignment that can result in promotion.
Recognition	Acknowledging effort, accomplishments, or abilities.
Visibility	Providing a chance to be known by higher-ups or significant others in the organization.
Network/contacts	Providing opportunities for linking with others.
Inspiration-related currencies	
Vision	Being involved in a task that has larger significance for the unit, organization, customer, or society.
Excellence	Having a chance to do important things really well.
Ethical correctness	Doing what is "right" by a higher standard than efficiency.
Relationship-related currencies	
Acceptance	Providing closeness and friendship.
Personal support	Giving personal and emotional backing.
Understanding	Listening to others' concerns and issues.
Personal-related currencies	
Challenge/learning	Sharing tasks that increase skills and abilities.
Ownership/involvement	Letting others have ownership and influence.
Gratitude	Expressing appreciation.

the same way, what is valued by a marketing manager may be different from what is valued by a veteran project engineer, and you are likely to need to use different influence currency to obtain the cooperation of each individual. Although this analogy is a bit of an oversimplification, the key premise holds true that in the long run, "debit" and "credit" accounts must be balanced for cooperative relationships to work. Table 10.1 presents the commonly traded organizational currencies identified by Cohen and Bradford; they are then discussed in more detail in the following sections.

Task-Related Currencies

This form of influence comes directly from the project manager's ability to contribute to others' accomplishing their work. Probably the most significant form of this currency is the ability to respond to subordinates' requests for additional manpower, money, or time to complete a segment of a project. This kind of currency is also evident in sharing resources with another project manager who is in need. At a more personal level, it may simply mean providing direct assistance to a colleague in solving a technical problem.

Providing a good word for a colleague's proposal or recommendation is another form of this currency. Because most work of significance is likely to generate some form of opposition, the person who is trying to gain approval for a plan or proposal can be greatly aided by having a "friend in court."

Another form of this currency includes extraordinary effort. For example, fulfilling an emergency request to complete a design document in two days instead of the normal four days is likely to engender gratitude. Finally, sharing valuable information that would be useful to other managers is another form of this currency.

Position-Related Currencies

This form of influence stems from the manager's ability to enhance others' positions within their organization. A project manager can do this by giving someone a challenging assignment that can aid their advancement by developing their skills and abilities. Being given a chance to prove yourself naturally generates a strong sense of gratitude. Sharing the glory and bringing to the attention of higher-ups the efforts and accomplishments of others generate goodwill.

Project managers confide that a key strategy useful for gaining the cooperation of professionals in other departments and organizations is figuring out how to make these people look good to their bosses. For example, a project manager worked with a subcontractor whose organization was heavily committed to total quality management (TQM). The project manager made it a point in top-level briefing meetings to point out how quality improvement processes initiated by the contractor contributed to cost control and problem prevention.

Another variation of recognition is enhancing the reputation of others within the firm. "Good press" can pave the way for lots of opportunities, while "bad press" can quickly shut a person off and make it difficult to perform. This currency is also evident in helping to preserve someone's reputation by coming to the defense of someone unjustly blamed and making sure the right attributions are made.

Finally, one of the strongest forms of this currency is sharing contacts with other people. Helping individuals expand their own networks by introducing them to key people naturally engenders gratitude. For example, suggesting to a functional manager that he should contact Sally X if he wants to find out what is really going on in that department or to get a request expedited is likely to engender a sense of indebtedness.

Inspiration-Related Currencies

Perhaps the most powerful form of influence is based on inspiration. Most sources of inspiration derive from people's burning desire to make a difference and add meaning to their lives. Creating an exciting, bold vision for a project can elicit extraordinary commitment. For example, many of the technological breakthroughs associated with the introduction of the original Macintosh computer were attributed to the feeling that the project members had a chance to change the way people approached computers. A variant form of vision is providing an opportunity to do something really well. Being able to take pride in your work often drives many people.

Often the very nature of the project provides a source of inspiration. Discovering a cure for a devastating disease, introducing a new social program that will help those in need, or simply building a bridge that will reduce a major traffic bottleneck can provide opportunities for people to feel good about what they are doing and that they are making a difference. Inspiration operates as a magnet—pulling people as opposed to pushing people toward doing something.

Relationship-Related Currencies

These currencies have more to do with strengthening the relationship with someone than directly accomplishing the project tasks. The essence of this form of influence is forming a relationship that transcends normal professional boundaries and extends into the realm of friendship. Such relationships develop by giving personal and emotional backing. Picking people up when they are feeling down, boosting their confidence, and providing encouragement naturally breed goodwill. Sharing a sense of humor and making difficult times fun is another form of this currency. Similarly, engaging in non-work-related activities such as sports and family outings is another way relationships are naturally enhanced.

Perhaps the most basic form of this currency is simply listening to other people. Psychologists suggest that most people have a strong desire to be understood and that relationships break down because the parties stop listening to each other. Sharing personal secrets/ambitions and being a wise confidant also creates a special bond between individuals.

Personal-Related Currencies

This last form of currency deals with individual needs and an overriding sense of self-esteem. Some argue that self-esteem is a primary psychological need; the extent to which we can help others feel a sense of importance and personal worth will naturally generate goodwill. A project manager can enhance a colleague's sense of worth by sharing tasks that increase skills and abilities, delegating authority over work so that others experience ownership, and allowing individuals to feel comfortable stretching their abilities. This form of currency can also be seen in sincere expressions of gratitude for the contributions of others. Care, though, must be exercised in expressing gratitude since it is easily devalued when overused. That is, the first *thank you* is likely to be more valued than the twentieth.

The bottom line is that a project manager will be influential only insofar as she can offer something that others value. Furthermore, given the diverse cast of people a project manager depends on, it is important that she be able to acquire and exercise different influence currencies. The ability to do so will be constrained in part by the nature of the project and how it is organized. For example, a project manager who is in charge of a dedicated team has considerably more to offer team members than a manager who is given the responsibility of coordinating the activities of different professionals across different departments and organizations. In such cases, that manager will probably have to rely more heavily on personal and relational bases of influence to gain the cooperation of others.

Social Network Building

Mapping Dependencies

The first step to building a social network is identifying those on whom the project depends for success. The project manager and his or her key assistants need to ask the following questions:

- Whose cooperation will we need?
- Whose agreement or approval will we need?
- Whose opposition would keep us from accomplishing the project?

Many project managers find it helpful to draw a map of these dependencies. For example, Figure 10.2 contains the dependencies identified by a project manager responsible for installing a new financial software system in her company.

FIGURE 10.2
Dependencies for
Financial Software
Installation Project

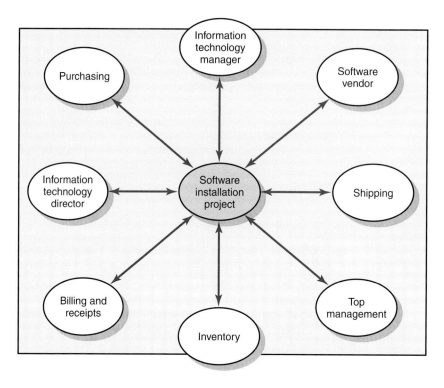

It is always better to overestimate rather than underestimate dependencies. All too often, otherwise talented and successful project managers have been derailed because they were blindsided by someone whose position or power they had not anticipated. After identifying whom you will depend on, you are ready to "step into their shoes" and see the project from their perspective:

- What differences exist between myself and the people on whom I depend (goals, values, pressures, working styles, risks)?
- How do these different people view the project (supporters, indifferents, antagonists)?
- What is the current status of the relationship I have with the people I depend on?
- What sources of influence do I have relative to those on whom I depend?

Once you start this analysis you can begin to appreciate what others value and what currencies you might have to offer as a basis on which to build a working relationship. You begin to realize where potential problems lie—relationships in which you have a current debit or no convertible currency. Furthermore, diagnosing another's point of view as well as the basis for their positions will help you anticipate their reactions and feelings about your decisions and actions. This information is vital for selecting the appropriate influence strategy and tactics and conducting win/win negotiations.

For example, after mapping her dependency network, the project manager who was in charge of installing the software system realized that she was likely to have serious problems with the manager of the receipts department, who would be one of the primary users of the software. She had no previous history of working with this individual but had heard through the grapevine that the manager was upset with the choice of software and that he considered this project to be another unnecessary disruption of his department's operation. Prior to project initiation the project manager arranged to have lunch with the manager, where she sat patiently and listened to his concerns. She invested additional time and attention to educate him and his staff about the benefits of the new software. She tried to minimize the disruptions the transition would cause in his department. She altered the implementation schedule to accommodate his preferences as to when the actual software would be installed and the subsequent training would occur. In turn, the receipts manager and his people were much more accepting of the change, and the transition to the new software went more smoothly than anticipated.

Management by Wandering Around (MBWA)

The preceding example illustrates the next step in building a supportive social network. Once you have established who the key players are that will determine success, then you initiate contact and begin to build a relationship with those players. Building this relationship requires a management style employees at Hewlett-Packard refer to as "management by wandering around" (MBWA) to reflect that managers spend the majority of their time outside their offices. MBWA is somewhat of a misnomer in that there is a purpose/pattern behind the "wandering." Through face-to-face interactions, project managers are able to stay in touch with what is really going on in the project and build cooperative relationships essential to project success.

Effective project managers initiate contact with key players to keep abreast of developments, anticipate potential problems, provide encouragement, and reinforce the objectives and vision of the project. They are able to intervene to resolve conflicts and prevent stalemates from occurring. In essence, they "manage" the project. By staying in touch with various aspects of the project they become the focal point for information on the project. Participants turn to them to obtain the most current and comprehensive information about the project which reinforces their central role as project manager.

We have also observed less-effective project managers who eschew MBWA and attempt to manage projects from their offices and computer terminals. Such managers proudly announce an open-door policy and encourage others to see them when a problem or an issue comes up. To them no news is good news. This allows their contacts to be determined by the relative aggressiveness of others. Those who take the initiative and seek out the project manager get too high a proportion of the project manager's attention. Those people less readily available (physically removed) or more passive get ignored. This behavior contributes to the adage, "Only the squeaky wheel gets greased," which produces resentment in those who believe they are more deserving.

While a significant amount of their time is devoted to the project team, effective project managers find the time to regularly interact with more distal stakeholders. They keep in touch with suppliers, vendors, top management, and other functional managers. In doing so they maintain familiarity with different parties, sustain friendships, discover opportunities to do favors, and understand the motives and needs of others. They remind people of commitments and champion the cause of their project. They also shape people's expectations (see Snapshot from Practice). Through frequent communication they alleviate people's concerns about the project, dispel rumors, warn people of potential problems, and lay the groundwork for dealing with setbacks in a more effective manner.

Unless project managers take the initiative to build a network of supportive relationships, they are likely to see a manager (or other stakeholder) only when there is bad news or when they need a favor (e.g., they don't have the data they promised or the

Dorothy Kirk, a project management consultant and program manager with Financial Solutions Group of Mynd, offers several keen insights about the art of managing stakeholder expectations:

... expectations are hardy. All they need to take root is the absence of evidence to the contrary. Once rooted, the unspoken word encourages growth. They can develop and thrive without being grounded in reality. For this reason, project managers do daily battle with unrealistic expectations.

She goes on to offer several tips for managing expectations:

- The way you present information can either clarify or muddy expectations. For example, if you estimate that a task will take 317 hours, you are setting high expectations by your precision. The stakeholder is likely to be unhappy if it takes 323 hours. The stakeholder will not be unhappy with 323 hours if you quoted an estimate of 300–325 hours.

- Recognize that it is only human nature to interpret a situation in one's best interest. For example, if you tell someone it will be done by January, you are inclined to interpret it to your advantage and assume you have to the end of January, while the other person believes it will be done January 1st.

- Seize every opportunity to realign expectations with reality. Too often we avoid opportunities to adjust expectations because we hold onto a false hope that things will somehow work out.

- Do not ask for stakeholder suggestions for improvement if you do not intend to do something with their input. Asking for their input raises expectations.

- State the obvious. What is obvious to you may be obscure to others.

- Don't avoid delivering bad news. Communicate openly and in person. Expect some anger and frustration. Do not get defensive in return. Be prepared to explain the impact of the problems. For example, never say the project is going to be late without being able to give a new date. Explain what you are doing to see that this does not continue to happen.

All stakeholders have expectations about the schedule, cost, and project benefits. Project managers need to listen for, understand, and manage these expectations.

*D. Kirk, "Managing Expectations," *PM Network,* August 2000, pp. 59–62.

project has slipped behind schedule). Without prior, frequent, easy give-and-take interactions around nondecisive issues, the encounter prompted by the problem is likely to provoke excess tension. The parties are more likely to act defensively, interrupt each other, and lose sight of the common problem.

Experienced project managers recognize the need to build relationships before they need them. They initiate contact with the key stakeholders at times when there are no outstanding issues or problems and therefore no anxieties and suspicions. On these social occasions, they engage in small talk and responsive banter. Astute project managers also seek to make deposits in their relationships with potentially important stakeholders. They respond to others' requests for aid, provide supportive counsel, and exchange information. In doing so they establish credit in that relationship, which will allow them to deal with more serious problems down the road. When one person views another as pleasant, credible, and helpful based on past contact, he or she is more likely to be responsive to requests for help and less confrontational when problems arise.

Managing Upward Relations

Research consistently points out that project success is strongly affected by the degree to which a project has the support of top management. Such support is reflected in an appropriate budget, responsiveness to unexpected needs, and a clear signal to others in the organization of the importance of cooperation.

Visible top management support is not only critical for securing the support of other managers within an organization, but it also is a key factor in the project manager's ability to motivate the project team. Nothing establishes a manager's right to lead more than her ability to defend. To win the loyalty of team members, project managers have

Ancona and Caldwell studied the performance of 45 new-product teams in five high-technology companies and produced some startling results. The most significant was that internal team dynamics were not related to performance. That is, high-performance teams were not distinguished by clearer goals, smoother workflow among members, or greater ability to satisfy the individual goals of team members. What related to team performance were level and intensity of external interactions between the project team and the rest of the organization. Ancona and Caldwell identified four key patterns of activity which contribute to creating a high-performance team:

1. *Ambassador* activities are aimed at representing the team to others and protecting the team from interference. The project manager typically takes on this responsibility, which involves buffering the team from political pressures and building support for the project within the hierarchy of the company.

2. *Task coordinator* activities are aimed at coordinating the team's efforts with other units and organizations. Unlike the ambassador role, which is focused upward, these are more lateral activities and involve negotiating and interacting with interested parties within the organization.

3. *Scouts* act as a scout on an expedition; that is, they go out from the team to bring back information about what is going on elsewhere in the organization. This is a much less focused task than task coordinator.

4. *Guard* activities differ from the other activities in that they are intended to keep information and resources inside the team, preventing drainage out of the group. A key guard activity is keeping necessary information secret until it is appropriate to share it.

Ancona and Caldwell found that the importance of these activities varies during the product development life cycle if the project team is to be successful. For example, scouting activities are more critical during the creation phase, when the product idea is being formulated and the team is being developed. Ambassador activities are especially critical during the development phase, when product specifications have been agreed upon and the major task is developing a prototype.

Ancona and Caldwell caution that their findings do not mean that teamwork and the internal operations of a project team are not important to project success. Effective team dynamics are necessary to successfully integrate information from outside sources and coordinate activities across groups. Their research supports the adage that problems and opportunities often lie at the borders of projects, and that one of the primary jobs of a project manager is to manage the interface between his or her team and the rest of the organization.

*D. G. Ancona, and D. Caldwell. "Improving the Performance of New-Product Teams," *Research Technology Management,* Vol. 33, No. 2 (March–April 1990), pp. 25–29.

to be effective advocates for their projects. They have to be able to get top management to rescind unreasonable demands, provide additional resources, and recognize the accomplishments of team members.

Perhaps because of the importance of this connection, working relationships with upper management is a common source of consternation. Comments we have heard from project managers about upper management include the following:

They don't know how much it sets us back losing Neil to another project.

I would like to see them get this project done with the budget they gave us.

I just wish they would make up their minds as to what is really important.

While it may seem counterintuitive for a subordinate to "manage" a superior, smart project managers devote considerable time and attention to influencing and garnering the support of top management. Project managers have to accept profound differences in perspective and become skilled at the art of persuading superiors.

Many of the tensions that arise between upper management and project managers are a result of differences in perspective. Project managers become naturally absorbed with what is best for their project. To them the most important thing in the world is their project. Top management should have a different set of priorities. They are concerned with what is best for the entire organization. It is only natural for these two interests to conflict at times. For example, a project manager may lobby intensively for additional personnel only to be turned down because top management believes that the other departments cannot afford a reduction in staff. Although frequent communication can minimize differences, the project manager has to accept the fact that top management is inevitably going to see the world differently.

Once project managers accept that disagreements with superiors are more a question of perspective than substance, they can focus more of their energy on the art of persuading upper management. But before they can persuade superiors, they must first prove loyalty. Loyalty in this context simply means that most of the time project managers have to show that they consistently follow through on requests and adhere to the parameters established by top management without a great deal of grumbling or fuss. Closely linked to loyalty is having credibility, which comes from an established track record of success. Once managers have proven loyalty to upper management, senior management is much more receptive to their challenges and requests.

FIGURE 10.3

The Significance of a Project Sponsor

Project managers have to cultivate strong ties with upper managers who are sponsoring the project. As noted earlier, these are high-ranking officials who championed approval and funding of the project; as such, their reputations are aligned with the project. Sponsors are also the ones who defend the project when it is under attack in upper circles of management. They shelter the project from excessive interference (see Figure 10.3). Project managers should *always* keep such people informed of any problems that may cause embarrassment or disappointment. For example, if costs are beginning to outrun the budget or a technical glitch is threatening to delay the completion of the project, managers make sure that the sponsors are the first to know.

When negotiating from a subordinate position for additional funds, resources, or extensions, project managers recognize that the timing of a request is critical. Asking for additional budget the day after disappointing third-quarter earnings are reported is going to be much more difficult than making a similar request four weeks later. Good project managers pick the optimum time to appeal to top management. They enlist their project sponsors to lobby their cause. They also realize there are limits to top management's accommodations. Here, the Lone Ranger analogy is appropriate—you have only so many silver bullets, so use them wisely.

When giving a status report to superiors, project managers must present the most positive image possible without stretching the truth. They should adapt their communication pattern to that of the senior group, making it a point to use buzzwords and jargon valued by superiors in their presentations. For example, one project manager recognized that top management had a tendency to use sports metaphors to describe business situations, so she framed a recent slip in schedule by admitting that "we lost five yards, but we still have two plays to make a first down." Smart project managers learn the language of top management and use it to their advantage.

Finally, a few project managers admit ignoring chains of command. If they are confident that top management will reject an important request and that what they want to do will benefit the project, they do it without asking permission. While acknowledging that this is very risky, they claim that bosses typically won't argue with success. (See Snapshot from Practice, Leading at the Edge, for a dramatic example of this.)

In 1914, the intrepid explorer Ernest Shackleton embarked on the *Endurance* with his team of seamen and scientists, intent upon crossing the unexplored Antarctic continent. What happened in the two years between their departure and their ultimate incredible rescue has rarely been matched in the annals of survival: a ship crushed by expanding ice pack ... a crew stranded on the floes of the frozen Weddell Sea ... two perilous treks in open boats across a raging Southern Ocean ... a team marooned on the wild, forlorn Elephant Island, stretched to the limits of human endurance.

This adventure provided the basis for the book, *Leading at the Edge: Leadership Lessons from the Extraordinary Saga of Shackleton's Antarctic Expedition* written by Dennis Perkins. Perkins provides numerous incidents of how Shackleton's personal example influenced the behavior of his beleaguered crew. For example, from the beginning of the Trans-Atlantic expedition to its end Shackleton consistently encouraged behavior that emphasized caring and respect:

> After the destruction of the *Endurance* Shackleton heated hot milk for the crew and went from tent to tent with the "life giving" drink. After the sail to the island of South Georgia, when the exhausted crew had landed, Shackleton took the first watch, which he kept for three hours instead of the usual one.

Crewmembers emulated the caring behaviors that Shackleton modeled. A good example of this occurred during one of the most dramatic moments in the *Endurance* saga. The food supply had dwindled to perilously low levels. Less than a week's supply remained, and the tiny ration of seal steak usually served at breakfast was eliminated. The waste meat generally used to feed the dogs was inspected for edible scraps.

Under these wretched conditions, and after a wet sleepless night, an argument broke out among some of the team members. Caught in the middle, one crew member (Greenstreet) spilled his tiny ration of powdered milk and shouted at the biologist (Clark). Alfred Lansing, described what happened next:

> Greenstreet paused to get his breath, and in that instant his anger was spent and he suddenly fell silent. Everyone else in the tent became quiet, too, and looked at Greenstreet, shaggy-haired, bearded, and filthy with blubber soot, holding his empty mug in

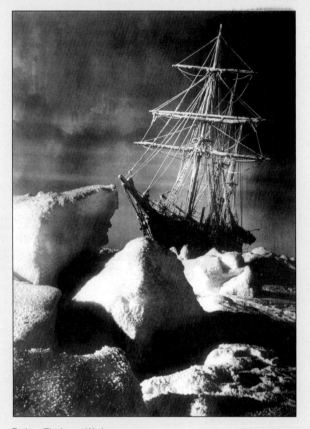

Topham/The Image Works.

his hand and looking helplessly down into the snow that had thirstily soaked up his precious milk. The loss was so tragic he seemed almost on the point of weeping. Without speaking, Clark reached out and poured some milk into Greenstreet's mug. Then Worsely, the Macklin, and Rickerson and Kerr, Orde-Lees, and finally Blackborrow. They finished in silence.

*Adapted from Dennis N. T. Perkins, *Leading at the Edge: Leadership Lessons from the Extraordinary Saga of Shackleton's Antarctica Expedition* (New York: AMACOM Press, 2000), pp. 94–95; and Alfred Lansing, *Endurance: Shackleton's Incredible Voyage* (New York: Carroll & Graf, 1998), p. 127.

Leading by Example

A highly visible, interactive management style is not only essential to building and sustaining cooperative relationships, it also allows project managers to utilize their most powerful leadership tool—their own behavior. Often, when faced with uncertainty, people look to others for cues as to how to respond and demonstrate a propensity to mimic the behavior of superiors. A project manager's behavior symbolizes how other people should work on the project. Through her behavior a project manager can influence how others act and respond to a variety of issues related to the project. To be

FIGURE 10.4

Leading by Example

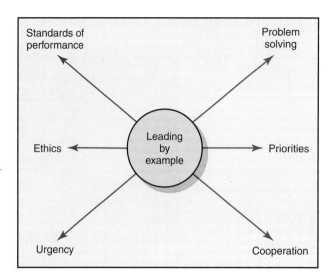

effective, project managers must "walk the talk" (see Figure 10.4). Six aspects of leading by example are discussed next.

Priorities

Actions speak louder than words. Subordinates and others discern project managers' priorities by how they spend their time. If a project manager claims that this project is critical and then is perceived as devoting more time to other projects, then all his verbal reassurances are likely to fall on deaf ears. Conversely, a project manager who takes the time to observe a critical test instead of simply waiting for a report affirms the importance of the testers and their work. Likewise, the types of questions project managers pose communicate priorities. By repeatedly asking how specific issues relate to satisfying the customer, a project manager can reinforce the importance of customer satisfaction.

Urgency

Through their actions project managers can convey a sense of urgency, which can permeate project activities. This urgency in part can be conveyed through stringent deadlines, frequent status report meetings, and aggressive solutions for expediting the project. The project manager uses these tools like a metronome to pick up the beat of the project. At the same time, such devices will be ineffective if there is not also a corresponding change in the project manager's behavior. If they want others to work faster and solve problems quicker, then they need to work faster. They need to hasten the pace of their own behavior. They should accelerate the frequency of their interactions, talk and walk more quickly, get to work sooner, and leave work later. By simply increasing the pace of their daily interaction patterns, project managers can reinforce a sense of urgency in others.

Problem Solving

How project managers respond to problems sets the tone for how others tackle problems. If bad news is greeted by verbal attacks, then others will be reluctant to be forthcoming. If the project manager is more concerned with finding out who is to blame instead of how to prevent problems from happening again, then others will tend to cover their tracks and cast the blame elsewhere. If, on the other hand, project managers focus more on how they can turn a problem into an opportunity or what can be learned from a mistake, then others are more likely to adopt a more proactive approach to problem solving.

Cooperation

How project managers act toward outsiders influences how team members interact with outsiders. If a project manager makes disparaging remarks about the "idiots" in the marketing department, then this oftentimes becomes the shared view of the entire team. If project managers set the norm of treating outsiders with respect and being responsive to their needs, then others will more likely follow suit.

Standards of Performance

Veteran project managers recognize that if they want participants to exceed project expectations then they have to exceed others' expectations of a good project manager. They establish a high standard for project performance through the quality of their daily interactions. They respond quickly to the needs of others, carefully prepare and run crisp meetings, stay on top of all the critical issues, facilitate effective problem solving, and stand firm on important matters.

Ethics

How others respond to ethical dilemmas that arise in the course of a project will be influenced by how the project manager has responded to similar dilemmas. In many cases, team members base their actions on how they think the project manager would respond. If project managers deliberately distort or withhold vital information from customers or top management, then they are signaling to others that this kind of behavior is acceptable. Project management invariably creates a variety of ethical dilemmas; this would be an appropriate time to delve into this topic in more detail.

Ethics and Project Management

Questions of ethics have already arisen in previous chapters that discussed padding of cost and time estimations, exaggerating pay-offs of project proposals, and so forth. Ethical dilemmas involve situations where it is difficult to determine whether conduct is right or wrong. Is it acceptable to falsely assure customers that everything is on track when, in reality, you are only doing so to prevent them from panicking and making matters worse?

In a survey of project managers, 81 percent reported that they encounter ethical issues in their work. These dilemmas range from being pressured to alter status reports, backdate signatures, or shade documentation to mask the reality of project progress to falsifying cost accounts, compromising safety standards to accelerate progress, and approving shoddy work.

Project management is complicated work, and, as such, ethics invariably involve gray areas of judgment and interpretation. For example, it is difficult to distinguish deliberate falsification of estimates from genuine mistakes or the willful exaggeration of project pay-offs from genuine optimism. It becomes problematic to determine whether unfulfilled promises were deliberate deception or an appropriate response to changing circumstances.

To provide greater clarity to business ethics, many companies and professional groups publish a code of conduct. Cynics see these documents as simply window dressing, while advocates argue that they are important, albeit limited, first steps. In practice, personal ethics do not lie in formal statutes but at the intersection of one's work, family, education, profession, religious beliefs, and daily interactions. Most project managers report that they rely on their own private sense of right and wrong—what one project manager called his "internal compass." One common rule of thumb for testing whether a response is ethical is to ask, "Imagine that whatever you did was going to be reported on the front page of your local newspaper. How would you like that? Would you be comfortable?"

"Think straight and talk straight" was the principle on which Arthur E. Andersen built his accounting firm in the early 1900s. It was a phrase his mother taught him and became the firm's motto. The commitment to integrity and a systematic, planned approach to work were instrumental in Arthur Andersen becoming one of the largest and best-known accounting firms in the world.

Working for Arthur Andersen was not for everyone. It could be a tough culture. It was much too hierarchical and top down for the more free spirited. Many people left after less than two years, believing the rewards did not warrant the demands that were made on them. Others learned to play by the rules and some even thrived. To remain in the firm, staff members were expected to work hard, respect authority of rank, and maintain a high level of conformity. In return they were rewarded with support, promotion, and the possibility of making partner. Those individuals who made a career with the firm grew old together, professionally and personally, and most had never worked anywhere else. To these survivors, Andersen was their second family, and they developed strong loyalties to the firm and its culture. (p. 133)

On October 23, 2001, David Duncan told his Enron project team that they needed to start complying with Andersen's new policy on handling audit documents. The policy had been instituted to make sure that the firm's extraneous paperwork could not be used in court cases. Although the document retention policy required that papers supporting the firm's opinions and audit be retained, it allowed a broad category of secondary documents to be destroyed. The team reacted with stunned silence to Duncan's directive. Then everyone got up and began racing to do what they had been told to do. No one asked Duncan to explain further. None asked whether what they were doing was wrong. No one questioned whether what he or she were doing might be illegal. Andersen's Houston staff just reacted, following orders without question.

On November 9, the day after the Securities Exchange Commission (SEC) issued a subpoena to Andersen, the shredding stopped. More than one ton of documents had been destroyed and 30,000 e-mails and Enron-related computer files erased. According to Andersen's legal defense team, the shredding was business as usual. The lawyers claimed that the shredding was standard practice for eliminating unnecessary files. To the SEC, it appeared to be the start of a deep cover-up operation. Subsequently one of the most respected accounting firms in the world closed its doors.

*Susan E. Squires, Cynthia J. Smith, Lorna McDougall, and William R. Yeak, *Inside Arthur Andersen: Shifting Values, Unexpected Consequences* (Upper Saddle, NJ: Prentice Hall, 2004).

Unfortunately, scandals at Enron, Worldcom, and Arthur Andersen have demonstrated the willingness of highly trained professionals to abdicate personal responsibility for illegal actions and to obey the directives of superiors (see Snapshot from Practice: The Collapse of Arthur Andersen). Top management and the culture of an organization play a decisive role in shaping members' beliefs of what is right and wrong. Many organizations encourage ethical transgressions by creating a "win at all cost" mentality. The pressures to succeed obscure consideration of whether the ends justify the means. Other organizations place a premium on "fair play" and command a market position by virtue of being trustworthy and reliable.

Many project managers claim that ethical behavior is its own reward. By following your own internal compass your behavior expresses your personal values. Others suggest that ethical behavior is doubly rewarding. You not only are able to fall asleep at night but you also develop a sound and admirable reputation. As will be explored in the next section, such a reputation is essential to establishing the trust necessary to exercise influence effectively.

Building Trust: The Key to Exercising Influence

We all know people who have influence but whom we do not trust; these individuals are often referred to as "political animals" or "jungle fighters." While these individuals are often very successful in the short run, the prevalent sense of mistrust prohibits long-term efficacy. Successful project managers not only need to be influential, they also need to exercise influence in a manner that builds and sustains the trust of others.

The significance of trust can be discerned by its absence. Imagine how different a working relationship is when you distrust the other party as opposed to trusting them. When people distrust each other, they often spend inordinate amounts of time and energy attempting to discern hidden agendas and the true meaning of communications and then securing guarantees to promises. They are much more cautious with each other and hesitant to cooperate. Here is what one line manager had to say about how he reacted to a project manager he did not trust:

> Whenever Jim approached me about something, I found myself trying to read between the lines to figure what was really going on. When he made a request, my initial reaction was "no" until he proved it.

Conversely, trust is the "lubricant" that maintains smooth and efficient interactions. When you are trusted, people are more likely to take your actions and intentions at face value when circumstances are ambiguous. Cohen and Bradford note that with trust, people will be less stringent about whether you are paying back in kind; they will extend you a larger line of credit and be more liberal in your repayment terms. Such flexibility is critical to project managers, especially during times of organizational change and uncertainty, when it is by definition more difficult to establish "fair exchange rates." For example, here is what a functional manager had to say about how he dealt with a project manager he trusted:

> If Sally said she needed something, no questions were asked. I knew it was important or she wouldn't have asked.

Trust is an elusive concept. It is hard to nail down in precise terms why some project managers are trusted and others are not. One popular way to understand trust is to see it as a function of character and competence. Character focuses on personal motives (i.e., does he or she want to do the right thing?), while competence focuses on skills necessary to realize motives (i.e., does he or she know the right things to do?).

Stephen Covey resurrected the significance of character in leadership literature in his best selling *Seven Habits of Highly Effective People*. Covey criticized popular management literature as focusing too much on shallow human relations skills and manipulative techniques, which he labeled the personality ethic. He argues that at the core of highly effective people is a character ethic that is deeply rooted in personal values and principles such as dignity, service, fairness, the pursuit of truth, and respect.

One of the distinguishing traits of character is consistency. When people are guided by a core set of principles, they are naturally more predictable because their actions are consistent with these principles. Another feature of character is openness. When people have a clear sense of who they are and what they value, they are more receptive to others. This trait provides them with the capacity to empathize and the talent to build consensus among divergent people. Finally, another quality of character is a sense of purpose. Managers with character are driven not only by personal ambitions but also for the common good. Their primary concern is what is best for their organization and the project, not what is best for themselves. This willingness to subordinate personal interests to a higher purpose garners the respect, loyalty, and trust of others.

The significance of character is summarized by the comments made by two team members about two very different project managers.

> At first everyone liked Joe and was excited about the project. But after a while, people became suspicious of his motives. He had a tendency to say different things to different people. People began to feel manipulated. He spent too much time with top management.

People began to believe that he was only looking out for himself. It was HIS project. When the project began to slip he jumped ship and left someone else holding the bag. I'll never work for that guy again.

My first impression of Jack was nothing special. He had a quiet, unassuming management style. Over time I learned to respect his judgment and his ability to get people to work together. When you went to him with a problem or a request, he always listened carefully. If he couldn't do what you wanted him to do, he would take the time to explain why. When disagreements arose he always thought of what was best for the project. He treated everyone by the same rules; no one got special treatment. I'd jump at the opportunity to work on a project with him again.

Character alone will not engender trust. We must also have confidence in the competency of individuals before we really trust them. We all know well-intended managers whom we like but do not trust. Although we may befriend these managers, we don't like to work with or for them. Competence is reflected at a number of different levels. First, there is task-related knowledge and skills reflected in the ability to answer questions, solve technical problems, and excel in certain kinds of work. Second, there is competence at an interpersonal level demonstrated in being able to listen effectively, communicate clearly, resolve arguments, provide encouragement, and so forth. Finally, there is organizational competence. This includes being able to run effective meetings, set meaningful objectives, reduce inefficiencies, and build a social network. Too often there is a tendency for young engineers and other professionals to place too much value on task or technical competence. They underestimate the significance of organizational skills. Veteran professionals, on the other hand, recognize the importance of management and place a greater value on organizational and interpersonal skills.

One problem new project managers experience is that it takes time to establish a sense of character and competency. Character and competency are often demonstrated when they are tested, such as when a tough call has to be made or when difficult problems have to be solved. Veteran project managers have the advantage of reputation and an established track record of success. Although endorsements from credible sponsors can help a young project manager create a favorable first impression, ultimately he or she will have to demonstrate character and competence during the course of dealings with others in order to gain their trust.

So far this chapter has addressed the importance of building a network of relationships to complete the project based on trust and reciprocity. The next section examines the nature of project management work and the personal qualities needed to excel at it.

Qualities of an Effective Project Manager

Project management is, at first glance, a misleading discipline in that there is an inherent logic in the progression from formulating a project scope statement, creating a WBS, developing a network, adding resources, finalizing a plan, and reaching milestones. However, when it comes to actually implementing and completing projects, this logic quickly disappears, and project managers encounter a much messier world, filled with inconsistencies and paradoxes (see Research Highlight). Effective project managers have to be able to deal with the contradictory nature of their work. Some of those contradictions are listed here:

* **Innovate and maintain stability.** Project managers have to put out fires, restore order, and get the project back on track. At the same time they need to be innovative and develop new, better ways of doing things. Innovations unravel stable routines and spark new disturbances that have to be dealt with.

Marianne Lewis and her colleagues studied how project managers cope with the multiple—and often conflicting and fluctuating—contingencies endemic to product development efforts. In their review of the literature, they found two seemingly contradictory prescriptions. One advocates an emergent style that involves facilitating team members' creativity, flexibility, and improvisation. The second approach recommends a more disciplined approach in which structure and procedures direct team efforts.

Advocates of emergent style view product development as inherently ambiguous. In this light, project managers focus on facilitating team members' improvisation and creativity, helping innovation emerge from the bottom up. Progress is monitored in terms of team members' experiential learning—that is, how their project focus, knowledge, and skills are developing as they interact with each other and the product itself.

In contrast, proponents of the planned style presume product development is more predictable and rational, best managed from top down. Management provides focus and structure, striving to direct team efforts and link project and organizational goals. Control is maintained in a tightly coupled system of milestones punctuated with formal reviews that enable critical assessments of design specifications and resource assignments.

Lewis collected data on 80 product development projects in a large chemical firm, whose products ranged from a new elevator system to a stick deodorant to new formulations of over-the-counter vitamins to agricultural chemicals. They looked at the relationship between emergent and planned styles and project performance. One of the strengths of their study is that they studied these styles over the length of the project.

The results suggest that meeting tenuous demands of innovation and efficiency requires paradoxical patterns of behavior. They found that successful product development may require managers (1) to use emergent and planned activities concurrently, (2) to go back and forth between styles as changes in project uncertainty occur, and (3) to make trade-offs between contending demands. For example, project managers have to exert strong leadership to keep teams focused on project objectives and schedule while providing them with freedom necessary to spark creativity and sustain motivation.

*Marianne W. Lewis, M. Ann Welsh, Gordon E. Dehler, and Stephen G. Green, "Product development tensions: Exploring contrasting styles of project management," *Academy of Management Journal*, 45 (3), 2002, pp. 546–564.

- **See the big picture while getting your hands dirty.** Project managers have to see the big picture and how their project fits within the larger strategy of their firm. There are also times when they must get deeply involved in project work and technology. If they don't worry about the details, who will?

- **Encourage individuals but stress the team.** Project managers have to motivate, cajole, and entice individual performers while at the same time maintaining teamwork. They have to be careful that they are considered fair and consistent in their treatment of team members while at the same time treating each member as a special individual.

- **Hands-off/Hands-on.** Project managers have to intervene, resolve stalemates, solve technical problems, and insist on different approaches. At the same time they have to recognize when it is appropriate to sit on the sidelines and let other people figure out what to do.

- **Flexible but firm.** Project managers have to be adaptable and responsive to events and outcomes that occur on the project. At the same time they have to hold the line at times and tough it out when everyone else wants to give up.

- **Team versus organizational loyalties.** Project managers need to forge a unified project team whose members stimulate one another to extraordinary performance. But at the same time they have to counter the excesses of cohesion and the team's resistance to outside ideas. They have to cultivate loyalties to both the team and the parent organization.

Managing these and other contradictions requires finesse and balance. Finesse involves the skillful movement back and forth between opposing behavioral patterns. For example, most of the time project managers actively involve others, move by increment, and seek consensus. There are other times when project managers must act as autocrats and take decisive, unilateral action. Balance involves recognizing the danger of extremes and that too much of a good thing invariably becomes harmful. For example, many managers have a tendency to always delegate the most stressful, difficult assignments to their best team members. This habit often breeds resentment among those chosen ("why am I always the one who gets the tough work?") and never allows the weaker members to develop their talents further.

There is no one management style or formula for being an effective project manager. The world of project management is too complicated for formulas. Successful project managers have a knack for adapting styles to specific circumstances of the situation.

So, what should one look for in an effective project manager? Many authors have addressed this question and have generated list after list of skills and attributes associated with being an effective manager. When reviewing these lists, one sometimes gets the impression that to be a successful project manager requires someone with superhuman powers. While we agree that not everyone has the right stuff to be an effective project manager, there are some core traits and skills that can be developed to successfully perform the job. Nine of these traits are noted below.

1. **Systems thinker.** Project managers must be able to take a holistic rather than a reductionist approach to projects. Instead of breaking up a project into individual pieces (planning, budget) and managing it by understanding each part, a systems perspective focuses on trying to understand how relevant project factors collectively interact to produce project outcomes. The key to success then becomes managing the interaction between different parts and not the parts themselves.

2. **Personal integrity.** Before you can lead and manage others, you have to be able to lead and manage yourself. Begin by establishing a firm sense of who you are, what you stand for, and how you should behave. This inner strength provides the buoyancy to endure the ups and downs of the project life cycle and the credibility essential to sustaining the trust of others.

3. **Proactive.** Good project managers take action before it is needed to prevent small concerns from escalating into major problems. They spend the majority of their time working within their sphere of influence to solve problems and not dwelling on things they have little control over. Project managers can't be whiners.

4. **High tolerance of stress.** Project management is not for the meek. Deadline pressures, technical uncertainties, and dealing with a variety of difficult, even stubborn professionals can generate a great deal of stress. People vary in their tolerance of stress. Physical exercise, a healthy diet, and a supportive homefront are necessary to endure the rigors of project management.

5. **General business perspective.** Because the primary role of a project manager is to integrate the contributions of different business and technical disciplines, it is important that a manager have a general grasp of business fundamentals and how the different functional disciplines interact to contribute to a successful business.

6. **Good communicator.** This one appears on every list and with good reason. Project managers have to be able to communicate with a wide variety of individuals. They not only have to be able to convey their ideas in an easily understandable manner, but they must also be empathic listeners, capable of drawing out the true meaning in what others are trying to say to them.

7. **Effective time management.** Time is a manager's scarcest resource. Project managers have to be able to budget their time wisely and quickly adjust their priorities. They need to balance their interactions so no one feels ignored.

8. **Skillful politician.** Project managers have to be able to deal effectively with a wide range of people and win their support and endorsement of their project. They need to be able to sell the virtues of their project without compromising the truth.

9. **Optimist.** Project managers have to display a can-do attitude. They have to be able to find rays of sunlight in a dismal day and keep people's attention positive. A good sense of humor and a playful attitude are often a project manager's greatest strength.

So how does one develop these traits? Workshops, self-study, and courses can upgrade one's general business perspective and capacity for systems thinking. Training programs can improve one's communication and political skills. People can also be taught stress and time management techniques. However, we know of no workshop or magic potion that can transform a pessimist into an optimist or provide a sense of purpose when there is not one. These qualities get at the very soul or being of a person. Optimism, integrity, and even being proactive are not easily developed if there is not already a predisposition to display them.

Summary

To be successful, project managers must build a cooperative network among a diverse set of allies. They begin by identifying who the key stakeholders on a project are, followed by a diagnosis of the nature of the relationships, and the basis for exercising influence. Effective project managers are skilled at acquiring and exercising a wide range of influence. They use this influence and a highly interactive management style to monitor project performance and initiate appropriate changes in project plans and direction. They do so in a manner that generates trust, which is ultimately based on others' perceptions of their character and competence.

Project managers are encouraged to keep in mind the following suggestions:

- *Build relationships before you need them.* Identify key players and what you can do to help them before you need their assistance. It is always easier to receive a favor after you have granted one. This requires the project manager to see the project in systems terms and to appreciate how it affects other activities and agendas inside and outside the organization. From this perspective they can identify opportunities to do good deeds and garner the support of others.

- *Be leery of the Golden Rule.* Many managers boil down managing to this basic premise: "Do unto others as you would wish them to do unto you." While there is a lot of wisdom embedded in this saying, there is one potential dangerous flaw. Others may not want what you want or need what you need. What is fair to you may not be perceived as fair by others. Empathy is needed to put yourself in their shoes to understand their specific desires and needs.

- *Trust is sustained through frequent face-to-face contact.* Trust withers through neglect. This is particularly true under conditions of rapid change and uncertainty that naturally engender doubt, suspicion, and even momentary bouts of paranoia. Project managers must maintain frequent contact with key stakeholders to keep abreast of developments, assuage concerns, engage in reality testing, and focus attention on the project. Frequent face-to-face interactions affirm mutual respect and trust in each other.

Ultimately, exercising influence in an effective and ethical manner begins and ends with how you view the other parties. Do you view them as potential partners or obstacles to your goals? If obstacles, then you wield your influence to manipulate and gain compliance and cooperation. If partners, you exercise influence to gain their commitment and support. People who view social network building as building partnerships see every interaction with two goals: resolving the immediate problem/concern and improving the working relationship so that next time it will be even more effective. Experienced project managers realize that "what goes around comes around" and try at all cost to avoid antagonizing players for quick success.

Key Terms

Law of reciprocity	Organizational	Social network
Leading by example	currencies	building
Management by wander-	Proactive	Stakeholder
ing around (MBWA)	Project sponsor	Systems thinking

Review Questions

1. Why is a conductor of an orchestra an appropriate metaphor for being a project manager? What aspects of project managing are not reflected by this metaphor? Can you think of other metaphors that would be appropriate?

2. What does the exchange model of influence suggest you do to build cooperative relationships to complete a project?

3. What differences would you expect to see between the kinds of influence currencies that a project manager in a functional matrix would use and the influence a project manager of a dedicated project team would use?

4. Why is it important to build a relationship before you need it?

5. Why is it critical to keep the project sponsor informed?

6. Why is trust a function of both character and competence?

7. Which of the nine traits/skills associated with being an effective project manager is the most important? The least important? Why?

Exercises

1. Access the Keirsey Temperament Sorter Questionnaire at *http://sunsite.unc.edu/ personality/keirsey.html*. Respond to the interactive questionnaire to identify your temperament type. Read supportive documents associated with your type. What does this material suggest are the kinds of projects that would best suit you? What does it suggest your strengths and weaknesses are as a project manager? How can you compensate for your weaknesses?

2. Access the Project Management Institute website at *www.pmi.org* and review the standards contained in PMI Member Ethical Standards section. How useful is the information for helping someone decide what behavior is appropriate and inappropriate?

   If you have difficulty accessing any of the Web addresses listed here or elsewhere in the book, you can find up-to-date addresses on the home page of Dr. Erik Larson, coauthor of this book, at *www.bus.orst.edu/faculty/larson*.

3. You are organizing an AIDS benefit concert in your hometown that will feature local heavy metal rock groups and guest speakers. Draw a dependency map identifying the major groups of people that are likely to affect the success of this project. Who do you think will be most cooperative? Who do you think will be the least cooperative? Why?

4. You are the project manager responsible for the overall construction of a new international airport. Draw a dependency map identifying the major groups of people that are likely to affect the success of this project. Who do you think will be most cooperative? Who do you think will be the least cooperative? Why?

5. Identify an important relationship (co-worker, boss, friend) in which you are having trouble gaining cooperation. Assess this relationship in terms of the influence currency model. What kinds of influence currency have you been exchanging in this relationship? Is the "bank account" for this relationship in the "red" or the "black"? What kinds of influence would be appropriate for building a stronger relationship with that person?

6. Each of the following six mini-case scenarios involve ethical dilemmas associated with project management. How would you respond to each situation, and why?

Jack Nietzche

You returned from a project staffing meeting in which future project assignments were finalized. Despite your best efforts, you were unable to persuade the director of project management to promote one of your best assistants, Jack Nietzche, to a project manager position. You feel a bit guilty because you dangled the prospect of this promotion to motivate Jack. Jack responded by putting in extra hours to ensure that his segments of the project were completed on time. You wonder how Jack will react to this disappointment. More importantly, you wonder how his reaction might affect your project. You have five days remaining to meet a critical deadline for a very important customer. While it won't be easy, you believed you would be able to complete the project on time. Now you're not so sure. Jack is halfway through completing the documentation phase, which is the last critical activity. Jack can be pretty emotional at times, and you are worried that he will blow up once he finds he didn't get the promotion. As you return to your office, you wonder what you should do. Should you tell Jack that he isn't going to be promoted? What should you say if he asks about whether the new assignments were made?

Seaburst Construction Project

You are the project manager for the Seaburst construction project. So far the project is progressing ahead of schedule and below budget. You attribute this in part to the good working relationship you have with the carpenters, plumbers, electricians, and machine operators who work for your organization. More than once you have asked them to give 110 percent, and they have responded.

One Sunday afternoon you decide to drive by the site and show it to your son. As you point out various parts of the project to your son, you discover that several pieces of valuable equipment are missing from the storage shed. When you start work again on Monday you are about to discuss this matter with a supervisor when you realize that all the missing equipment is back in the shed. What should you do? Why?

The Project Status Report Meeting

You are driving to a project status report meeting with your client. You encountered a significant technical problem on the project that has put your project behind schedule. This is not good news because completion time is the number one priority for the project. You are confident that your team can solve the problem if they are free to give their undivided attention to it and that with hard work you can get back on schedule. You also believe if you tell the client about the problem, she will demand a meeting with your team to discuss the implications of the problem. You can also expect her to send some of her personnel to oversee the solution to the problem. These interruptions will likely further delay the project. What should you tell your client about the current status of the project?

Gold Star LAN project

You work for a large consulting firm and were assigned to the Gold Star LAN project. Work on the project is nearly completed and your clients at Gold Star appear to be pleased with your performance. During the course of the project, changes in the original scope had to be made to accommodate specific needs of managers at Gold Star. The costs of these changes were documented as well as overhead and submitted to the centralized accounting department. They processed the information and submitted a change order bill for your signature. You are surprised to see the bill is 10 percent higher than what you submitted. You contact Jim Messina in the accounting office and ask if a mistake has been made. He curtly replies that no mistake was made and that management adjusted the bill. He recommends that you sign the document.

Greendale Bio-Tech

You are responsible for installing the new Double E production line. Your team has collected estimates and used the WBS to generate a project schedule. You have confidence in the schedule and the work your team has done. You report to top management that you believe that the project will take 110 days and be completed by March 5. The news is greeted positively. In fact , the project sponsor confides that orders do not have to be shipped until April 1st. You leave the meeting wondering whether you should share this information with the project team or not.

References

Anacona, D. G., and D. Caldwell, "Improving the Performance of New-Product Teams," *Research Technology Management,* 33 (2) March-April 1990, pp. 25–29.

Badaracco, J. L. Jr., and A. P. Webb, "Business Ethics: A View from the Trenches," *California Management Review,* 37 (2) Winter 1995, pp. 8–28.

Baker, B., "Leadership and the Project Manager," *PM Network,* December 2002, p. 20.

Baker, W. E., *Network Smart: How to Build Relationships for Personal and Organizational Success* (New York: McGraw-Hill, 1994).

Bennis, W., *On Becoming a Leader* (Reading, MA: Addison-Wesley, 1989).

Cabanis, J., "A Question of Ethics: The Issues Project Managers Face and How They Resolve Them," *PM Network,* December 1996, pp. 19–24.

Cohen, A. R., and D. L. Bradford, *Influence Without Authority* (New York: John Wiley & Sons, 1990).

Covey, S. R., *The Seven Habits of Highly Effective People* (New York: Simon & Schuster, 1989).

Gabarro, S. J. J., *The Dynamics of Taking Charge* (Boston: Harvard Business School Press, 1987).

Hill, L. A., *Becoming A Manager: Mastery of a New Identity* (Boston: Harvard Business School Press, 1992).

Kaplan, R. E., "Trade Routes: The Manager's Network of Relationships," *Organizational Dynamics,* 12 (4) Spring 1984, pp. 37–52.

Kirk, D., "Managing Expectations," *PM Network,* August 2000, pp. 59–62.

Kotter, J. P., "Power, Dependence, and Effective Management," *Harvard Business Review,* 55 (4) July–August 1977, pp. 125–36.

Kotter, J. P., "What Leaders Really Do," *Harvard Business Review,* 68 (3) May–June 1990, pp. 103–11.

Kouzes, J. M., and B. Z. Posner, *The Leadership Challenge* (San Francisco: Jossey-Bass, 1987).

Kouzes, J. M., and B. Z. Posner, *Celebrity: How Leaders Gain and Lose It. Why People Demand It* (San Francisco: Jossey-Bass, 1993).

Larson, E., and J. B. King, "The Systemic Distortion of Information: An Ongoing Management Challenge," *Organizational Dynamics,* 24 (3) Winter 1996, pp. 49–62.

Lewis, M. W., M. A. Welsh, G. E. Dehler, and S.G. Green, "Product Development Tensions: Exploring Contrasting Styles of Project Management," *Academy of Management Journal,* 45 (3) 2002, pp. 546–64.

Peters, L. H., "A Good Man in a Storm: An Interview with Tom West," *Academy of Management Executive,* 16 (4) 2002, pp. 53–63.

Peters, L. H., "Soulful Ramblings: An Interview with Tracy Kidder," *Academy of Management Executive,* 16 (4) 2002, pp. 45–52.

Peters, T., *Thriving on Chaos: Handbook For a Management Revolution* (New York: Alfred A. Knopf, 1988).

Pinto, J. L., and D. P. Sleven, "Critical Success Factors in Successful Project Implementation," *IEEE Transactions in Engineering Management,* 34 (1) 1987, pp. 22–27.

Pinto, J. L., and S. K. Mantel, "The Causes of Project Failure," *IEEE Transactions in Engineering Management,* 37 (4) 1990, pp. 269–76.

Posner, B. Z., "What it Takes to be an Effective Project Manager," *Project Management Journal,* March 1987, pp. 51–55.

Robb, D. J., "Ethics in Project Management: Issues, Practice, and Motive," *PM Network,* December 1996, pp. 13–18.

Sayles, L. R., *Leadership: Managing in Real Organizations* (New York: McGraw-Hill, 1989), pp. 70–78.

Sayles, L. R., *The Working Leader* (New York: Free Press, 1993).

Senge, P. M., *The Fifth Discipline* (New York: Doubleday, 1990).

Shenhar, A. J., and B. Nofziner, "A New Model for Training Project Managers," *Proceedings of the 28th Annual Project Management Institute Symposium,* 1997, pp. 301–6.

Shtub, A., J. F. Bard, and S. Globerson, *Project Management: Engineering, Technology, and Implementation* (Englewood Cliffs, NJ: Prentice Hall, 1994).

Verma, V. K., "Organizing Projects for Success: The Human Aspects of Project Management," Vol. 1 (Newton Square, PA: Project Management Institute, 1995), pp. 45–73.

Wysock, R. K., R. Beck, and D. B., Crane, *Effective Project Management* (New York: John Wiley & Sons, 1995).

Case

Western Oceanography Institute

It was already 72 degrees when Astrid Young pulled into the parking lot at the Western Oceanography Institute (WOI). The radio announcer was reminding listeners to leave out extra water for their pets because the temperature was going to be in the high 90s for the third straight day. Young made a mental note to call her husband, Jon, when she got to her office and make sure that he left plenty of water outside for their cat, Figaro. Young was three-quarters of the way through the Microsoft NT conversion project. Yesterday had been a disaster, and she was determined to get back on top of things.

ASTRID YOUNG

Astrid Young was a 27-year-old graduate of Western State University (WSU) with a B.S. degree in management information systems. After graduation she worked for five years at Evergreen Systems in Seattle, Washington. While at WSU she worked part time for an oceanography professor, Ahmet Green, creating a customized database for a research project he was conducting. Green was recently appointed director of WOI, and Young was confident that this prior experience was instrumental in her getting the job as information services (IS) director at the Institute. Although she took a significant pay cut, she jumped at the opportunity to return to her alma mater. Her job at Evergreen Systems had been very demanding. The long hours and extensive traveling had created tension in her marriage. She was looking forward to a normal job with reasonable hours. Besides, Jon would be busy pursuing his MBA at Western State. While at Evergreen, Young worked on Y2000 projects and installed NT servers. She was confident that she had the requisite technical expertise to excel at her new job.

Western Oceanography Institute was an independently funded research facility aligned with Western State University. Approximately 60 full- and part-time staff worked at the Institute. They worked on research grants funded by the National Science Foundation (NSF) and the United Nations (UN), as well as research financed by private industry. There were typically 7 to 8 major research projects under way at any one time as well as 20 to 25 smaller projects. One-third of the Institute's scientists had part-time teaching assignments at WSU and used the Institute to conduct their own basic research.

FIRST FOUR MONTHS AT WOI

Young worked at the Institute for four months prior to initiating the NT conversion project. She made a point of introducing herself to the various groups of people upon her arrival at the Institute. Still, her contact with the staff had been limited. She spent most of her time becoming familiar with WOI's information system, training her staff, responding to unexpected problems, and planning the conversion project. Young suffered from food allergies and refrained from informal staff lunches at nearby restaurants. She stopped regularly attending the biweekly staff meetings in order to devote more time to her work. She now only attended the meetings when there was a specific agenda item regarding her operation.

Last month the system was corrupted by a virus introduced over the Internet. She devoted an entire weekend to restoring the system to operation. A recurring headache was one of the servers code named "Poncho" that would occasionally shut down for no apparent reason. Instead of replacing it, she decided to nurse Poncho along until it was replaced by the new NT system. Her work was frequently interrupted by frantic calls from staff researchers who needed immediate help on a variety of computer-related problems. She was shocked at how computer illiterate some of the researchers were and how she had to guide them through some of the basics of e-mail management and database configuration. She did find time to help Assistant Professor Amanda Johnson on a project. Johnson was the only researcher to respond to Young's e-mail announcing that the IS staff was available to help on projects. Young created a virtual project office on the Internet so that Johnson could collaborate with colleagues from institutes in Italy and Thailand on a UN research grant. She looked forward to the day when she could spend more time on fun projects like that.

Young had a part-time team of five student assistants from the computer science department. At first she was not sure how freely she could delegate work to the students, and she closely supervised their work. She quickly realized that they were all very bright, competent workers who were anxious to leverage this work experience into a lucrative career upon graduation. She admitted that she sometimes had a hard time relating to students who were preoccupied with fraternity bashes and X-games. She lost her temper only once, and that was at Samantha Eggerts for failing to set up an adequate virus screening system that would have prevented the Internet corruption that occurred. She kept a close eye on Eggerts's work after that, but in time, Eggert proved her worth. Young saw a lot of herself in Eggerts's work habits.

THE MICROSOFT NT CONVERSION PROJECT

Young laid the groundwork for the NT conversion project in her recruitment interview with the director by arguing that conversion was a critical skill she would bring to the position. Once hired she was able to sell the director and his immediate staff on the project, but not without some resistance. Some associate directors questioned whether it was necessary to go through another conversion so soon after the Windows 95 conversion 16 months ago. Some of the researchers lobbied that the money would be better spent on installing a centralized air-conditioning system at WOI. Ultimately, the director signed off on the project after Young assured him that the conversion would be relatively painless and the Institute would then have a state-of-the-art information system.

The conversion was scheduled to take eight weeks to complete and consisted of four major phases: server setup, network installation, data migration, and workstation conversion. The project would be completed during the summer so that the student assistants could work full time on the project. Young and her student team would first need to purchase and set up seven new NT servers. They would then create a new local area network (LAN). Next they would migrate data to the new Oracle NT database. Finally, they would convert the existing 65 client computers into NT workstations capable of functioning on the new system. Young had been actively involved in four similar conversions when working at Evergreen Systems and was confident that she and her team could complete the project with a minimum of technical problems. She also believed that this conversion would not be traumatic to the staff at the Institute because the NT interface was very similar to the Windows 95 interface.

Young knew that in order for the project to be considered successful, there needed to be minimum disruption of daily staff functions. She held a staff briefing meeting to outline the scope of the project and the impact it would have on the Institute's operations. She was disappointed by the light attendance at the meeting. One problem was the irregular hours staff worked at WOI. Several of the researchers were night owls who preferred to work late into the night. Other staff traveled frequently. She ended up holding two other briefing meetings, including one in the evening. Still the attendance was less than desired.

The staff's major concerns were the amount of downtime that would occur and whether the software and databases they were currently using would work on the new system. Young assured them that most of the downtime would occur on the weekends and would be posted well in advance. The only disruption would be two hours necessary to convert their existing computer into a workstation. Young invested extra energy in researching the compatibility issue and sent an e-mail to everyone listing the software that was known to not work in the NT system. The only software problems involved specially written DOS v2.1 or older programs that would not function in the new NT operating environment. In one case, she assigned a student to rewrite and enhance the present program for a researcher. In the other case, she was able to persuade the staff member to use a newer, better program.

Young sent a second e-mail asking staff members to clean up their hard drives and get rid of old, obsolete files because the new NT software would take up considerably more space than the Windows 95 operating system. In some cases, she replaced existing hard drives with bigger drives so that this would not be a problem. She circulated a workstation conversion schedule by e-mail so that staff could pick a preferred time for when their computer would be down and when her assistants could upgrade the computer into a workstation. Seventy percent of the staff responded to the e-mail request, and she and her staff contacted the remaining staff by telephone to schedule the conversion.

The first six weeks of the project went relatively smoothly. The NT servers arrived on time and were installed and configured on schedule. The completion of the network was delayed three days when the fire marshal showed up earlier than planned to inspect the electrical wiring. Young had never met the marshal before and was surprised at how nit-picking he was. They failed the inspection, and it took three days to reschedule and pass inspection. Word about failing the fire inspection circulated the hallways at the Institute. One joker put a Smokey the Bear sign on the IS office door. Young later found out that as a result of a recent fire in town, the fire marshals had been instructed to be extra vigilant in their inspections.

Data migration to the new Oracle database took a little longer than planned because the new version was not as compatible with the old version as advertised. Still, this only added three days to the project. The project was entering the fourth and final phase—conversion of client computers into NT workstations. This phase involved her staff deleting the old operating system and installing new operating software in each computer at the Institute. Young had scheduled two hours per machine and had organized a daily workload of 10 computers so that adequate backup could be made just in case something went wrong.

Young chose to convert the director's office first and told Green that everything was going according to plan. Soon the project began to experience nagging problems. First, some of the staff forgot when they were scheduled to be converted. The team had to wait for them to abandon what they were doing so they could convert the computer. Second, the drivers on some of the computers were not compatible, and the team had to devote extra time downloading new drivers off the Internet. Third, a few of the staff failed to create adequate hard drive space to accommodate the new NT software. In most cases, the team worked with the staff member to delete or compress unnecessary files. One time the staff member could not be found, and Young had to decide which files to delete. This wasn't a problem since the hard drive contained computer games and ancient Word Perfect files. To compound matters, midway through the third day, one of the student assistants, Steve Stills, was diagnosed with a moderate case of carpal tunnel and was told to take two weeks off from computer work.

After three days only 22 computers had been converted to NT stations. Young ended the day by sending an e-mail to the remaining users apologizing for the delays and posting a revised schedule for their system configuration.

THE CALL

Young and her staff were working diligently on converting computers into NT workstations when she received an urgent call from the director's secretary requesting that she drop everything and come downstairs to the staff meeting. The secretary's voice appeared tense, and Young wondered what was up. As she gathered her things, the student assistant, Eggerts, cleared her throat and confided that there may be problems with some of the Institute's websites. She discovered yesterday that some of the links in the Web pages created using Netscape weren't working in the Microsoft environment. Young demanded to know why she wasn't told about this sooner. Eggerts confessed that she thought she had fixed the problem last night. Young told her that they would talk about this when she got back and left.

Young entered the meeting room and immediately recognized that there were more than the usual faces in attendance. The director welcomed her by saying, "We're glad you could find the time to visit with us. My staff meeting has just erupted into a series of complaints about your NT conversion project. As it turns out Dr. Phillips over here can't access his documents because his Word Perfect file mysteriously disappeared. Dr. Simon's geothermal assessment program, which he has used for the past seven years, doesn't seem to work anymore. Now it appears that the website we use to coordinate our research with the Oslo Institute is a mess. Everyone is complaining about how the revised installation schedule is going to disrupt work. I want to know why I wasn't informed about these problems. These guys want to lynch me for approving your project!"

1. How would you respond to the director?
2. What mistakes did Young make that contributed to the problems at the end of the case?
3. How could she have managed the conversion project better?

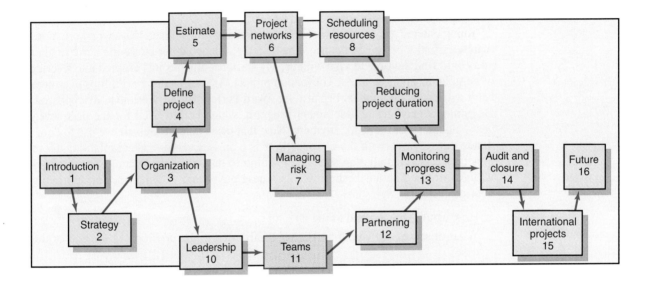

Managing Project Teams

The Five-Stage Team Development Model

Situational Factors Affecting Team Development

Building High-Performance Project Teams

Managing Virtual Project Teams

Project Team Pitfalls

Summary

CHAPTER ELEVEN

Managing Project Teams

The difference in productivity between an average team and a turned-on, high-performing team is not 10 percent, 20 percent, or 30 percent, but 100 percent, 200 percent, even 500 percent!

—Tom Peters, management consultant and writer

The magic and power of teams is captured in the term "synergy," which is derived from the Greek word *sunergos:* "working together." There is positive and negative synergy. The essence of positive synergy can be found in the phrase, "The whole is greater than the sum of the parts." Conversely, negative synergy occurs when the whole is less than the sum of the parts. Mathematically, these two states can be symbolized by the following equations:

$$\text{Positive Synergy } 1 + 1 + 1 + 1 + 1 = 10$$
$$\text{Negative Synergy } 1 + 1 + 1 + 1 + 1 = 2 \text{ (or even } -2)$$

Synergy perhaps can best be seen on a football field, a soccer pitch, or a basketball court. For example, the Chicago Bulls dominated professional basketball during the 1990s. Admittedly in Michael Jordan they had, if not the greatest, then one of the best players to ever play the game. Still, it wasn't until management found players to complement Jordan's abilities and Jordan himself accepted the fact that he had to play a team game that their reign of championships began. Positive synergy could be seen in how routinely the Bulls executed a fast break, where the combined actions of all five players produced an unchallenged slam dunk, or in their aggressive, denial defense, which stifled the performance of a much taller and more talented opponent. Negative synergy can be plainly seen in cellar-dwelling NBA teams where players ignore wide-open teammates to launch wild 3-point shots or when two or three members fail to hustle back on defense leaving a lone teammate to defend a 3-on-1 fast break. Teams that exhibit negative team synergy are often characterized as being underachievers, while champions become synonymous with teams that exhibit positive synergy.

Although less visible than in team sports, positive and negative synergy can also be observed and felt in the daily operations of project teams. Here is a description from one project manager we interviewed:

> Instead of operating as one big team we fractionalized into a series of subgroups. The marketing people stuck together as well as the systems guys. A lot of time was wasted gossiping and complaining about each other. When the project started slipping behind schedule, everyone started covering their tracks and trying to pass the blame on to others. After a while we avoided direct conversation and resorted to e-mail. Management finally pulled the plug and brought in another team to salvage the project. It was one of the worst project management experiences in my life.

This same manager fortunately was also able to recount a more positive experience:

> There was a contagious excitement within the team. Sure we had our share of problems and setbacks, but we dealt with them straight on and, at times, were able to do the impossible. We all cared about the project and looked out for each other. At the same time we challenged each other to do better. It was one of the most exciting times in my life.

The following is a set of characteristics commonly associated with high-performing teams that exhibit positive synergy:

1. The team shares a sense of common purpose, and each member is willing to work toward achieving project objectives.
2. The team identifies individual talents and expertise and uses them, depending on the project's needs at any given time. At these times, the team willingly accepts the influence and leadership of the members whose skills are relevant to the immediate task.
3. Roles are balanced and shared to facilitate both the accomplishment of tasks and feelings of group cohesion and morale.
4. The team exerts energy toward problem solving rather than allowing itself to be drained by interpersonal issues or competitive struggles.
5. Differences of opinion are encouraged and freely expressed.
6. To encourage risk taking and creativity, mistakes are treated as opportunities for learning rather than reasons for punishment.
7. Members set high personal standards of performance and encourage each other to realize the objectives of the project.
8. Members identify with the team and consider it an important source of both professional and personal growth.

High-performing teams become champions, create break-through products, exceed customer expectations, and get projects done ahead of schedule and under budget. They are bonded together by mutual interdependency and a common goal or vision. They trust each other and exhibit a high level of collaboration.

The Five-Stage Team Development Model

Just as infants develop in certain ways during their first months of life, many experts argue that groups develop in a predictable manner. One of the most popular models identifies five stages (see Figure 11.1) through which groups develop into effective teams:

1. **Forming.** During this initial stage the members get acquainted with each other and understand the scope of the project. They begin to establish ground rules by trying to find out what behaviors are acceptable with respect to both the project (what role they will play, what performance expectations are) and interpersonal relations (who's really in charge). This stage is completed once members begin to think of themselves as part of a group.
2. **Storming.** As the name suggests, this stage is marked by a high degree of internal conflict. Members accept that they are part of a project group but resist the constraints that the project and group put on their individuality. There is conflict over who will control the group and how decisions will be made. As these conflicts are

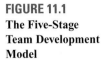

FIGURE 11.1

The Five-Stage Team Development Model

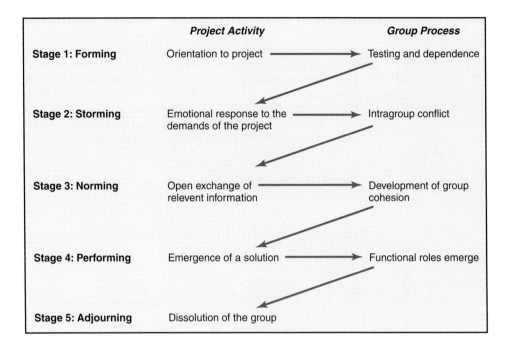

resolved, the project manager's leadership becomes accepted, and the group moves to the next stage.

3. **Norming.** The third stage is one in which close relationships develop and the group demonstrates cohesiveness. Feelings of camaraderie and shared responsibility for the project are heightened. The norming phase is complete when the group structure solidifies and the group establishes a common set of expectations about how members should work together.

4. **Performing.** The team operating structure at this point is fully functional and accepted. Group energy has moved from getting to know each other and how the group will work together to accomplishing the project goals.

5. **Adjourning.** For conventional work groups, performing is the last stage of their development. However, for project teams, there is a completion phase. During this stage, the team prepares for its own disbandment. High performance is no longer a top priority. Instead attention is devoted to wrapping up the project. Responses of members vary in this stage. Some members are upbeat, basking in the project team's accomplishments. Others may be depressed over loss of camaraderie and friendships gained during the project's life.

This model has several implications for those managing project teams. The first is that the project manager needs to devote initial attention to helping the group evolve quickly to the productive fourth (performing) phase. The second implication for project managers is that the model provides a framework for the group to understand its own development. Project managers have found it useful to share the model with their teams. It helps members accept the tensions of the storming phase, and it directs their focus to moving toward the more productive phases. The final implication is that it stresses the importance of the norming phase, which contributes significantly to the level of productivity experienced during the performing phase. Project managers, as we shall see, have to take an active role in shaping group norms that will contribute to ultimate project success.

Gersick's research suggests that groups don't develop in a universal sequence of stages as suggested by the five-phase model. Her research, which is based on the systems concept of *punctuated equilibrium,* found that the *timing* of when groups form and actually change the way they work is highly consistent. What makes this research appealing is that it is based on studies of more than a dozen field and laboratory task forces assigned to complete a specific project. This research reveals that each group begins with a unique approach to accomplishing its project that is set in its first meeting and includes the behavior and roles that dominate phase I. Phase I continues until one-half of the allotted time for project completion has expired (regardless of actual amount of time). At this midpoint, a major transition occurs that includes the dropping of the group's old norms and behavior patterns and the emergence of new behavior and working relationships that contribute to increased progress toward completing the project. The last meeting is marked by accelerated activity to complete the project. These findings are summarized in Figure 11.2.

FIGURE 11.2   The Punctuated Equilibrium Model of Group Development

The remarkable discovery in these studies was that each group experienced its transition at the same point in its calendar—precisely halfway between the first meeting and the completion deadline—despite the fact that some groups spent as little as an hour on their project while others spent six months. It was as if the groups universally experienced a midlife crisis at this point. The midpoint appeared to work like an alarm clock, heightening members' awareness that time was limited and they needed to get moving. Within the context of the five-stage model, it suggests that groups begin by combining the forming and norming stages, then go through a period of low performing, followed by storming, then a period of high performing, and finally adjourning.

Gersick's findings suggest that there are natural transition points during the life of teams in which the group is receptive to change and that such a moment naturally occurs at the scheduled midpoint of a project. However, a manager does not want to have to wait 6 months on a complicated 12-month project for a team to get its act together! Here it is important to note that Gersick's groups were working on relatively small-scale projects, i.e., a 4-person bank task force in charge of designing a new bank account in one month and a 12-person medical task force in charge of reorganizing two units of a treatment facility. In most cases no formal project plan was established. If anything, the results point to the importance of good project management and the need to establish deadlines and milestones. By imposing a series of deadlines associated with important milestones, it is possible to create multiple transition points for natural group development. For example, a 12-month construction project can be broken down into six to eight significant milestones with the challenge of meeting each deadline producing the prerequisite tension for elevating team performance.

*Connie J. Gersick, "Time and Transition in Work Teams: Toward a New Model of Group Development," *Academy of Management Journal,* Vol. 31, No. 1 (March 1988), pp. 9–41; and Connie J. Gersick, "Making Time Predictable Transitions in Task Groups," *Academy of Management Journal,* Vol. 32, No. 2 (June 1989), pp. 274–309.

Situational Factors Affecting Team Development

Experience and research indicate that high-performance project teams are much more likely to develop under the following conditions:

- There are 10 or fewer members per team.
- Members volunteer to serve on the project team.
- Members serve on the project from beginning to end.
- Members are assigned to the project full time.
- Members are part of an organization culture that fosters cooperation and trust.
- Members report solely to the project manager.
- All relevant functional areas are represented on the team.
- The project involves a compelling objective.
- Members are located within conversational distance of each other.

In reality, it is rare that a project manager is assigned a project that meets all of these conditions. For example, many projects' requirements dictate the active involvement of more than 10 members and may consist of a complex set of interlocking teams comprising more than 100 professionals. In many organizations, functional managers or central manpower offices assign project members with little input from the project manager. To optimize resource utilization, team member involvement may be part time, and/or participants may move in and out of the project team on an as-needed basis. In the case of ad hoc task forces, no member of the team works full time on the project. In many corporations an NIH (not invented here) culture exists that discourages collaboration across functional boundaries.

Team members often report to different managers, and, in some cases, the project manager will have no direct input over performance appraisals and advancement opportunities of team members. Key functional areas may not be represented during the entire duration of the project but may only be involved in a sequential manner. Not all projects have a compelling objective. It can be hard to get members excited about mundane projects such as a simple product extension or a conventional apartment complex. Finally, team members are often scattered across different corporate offices and buildings or, in the case of a virtual project, across the entire globe.

It is important for project managers and team members to recognize the situational constraints they are operating under and do the best they can. It would be naive to believe that every project team has the same potential to evolve into a high-performance team. Under less-than-ideal conditions, it may be a struggle just to meet project objectives. Ingenuity, discipline, and sensitivity to team dynamics are essential to maximizing the performance of a project team.

Building High-Performance Project Teams

Project managers play a key role in developing high-performance project teams. They recruit members, conduct meetings, establish a team identity, create a common sense of purpose or a shared vision, manage a reward system that encourages teamwork, orchestrate decision making, resolve conflicts that emerge within the team, and rejuvenate the team when energy wanes (see Figure 11.3). Project managers take advantage of situational factors that naturally contribute to team development while improvising around those factors that inhibit team development. In doing so they exhibit a highly

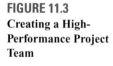

FIGURE 11.3
Creating a High-Performance Project Team

interactive management style that exemplifies teamwork and, as discussed in the previous chapter, manage the interface between the team and the rest of the organization.

Recruiting Project Members

The process of selecting and recruiting project members will vary across organizations. Two important factors affecting recruitment are the importance of the project and the management structure being used to complete the project. Often for high-priority projects that are critical to the future of the organization, the project manager will be given virtual carte blanche to select whomever he or she deems necessary. For less significant projects, the project manager will have to persuade personnel from other areas within the organization to join the team. In many matrix structures, the functional manager controls who is assigned to the project; the project manager will have to work with the functional manager to obtain necessary personnel. Even in a project team where members are selected and assigned full time to the project, the project manager has to be sensitive to the needs of others. There is no better way to create enemies within an organization than to be perceived as unnecessarily robbing other departments of essential personnel.

Experienced project managers stress the importance of asking for volunteers. However, this desirable step oftentimes is outside the manager's control. Still, the value of having team members volunteer for the project as opposed to being assigned cannot be overlooked. Agreeing to work on the project is the first step toward building personal commitment to the project. Such commitment will be essential to maintain motivation when the project hits hard times and extra effort is required.

When selecting and recruiting team members, project managers naturally look for individuals with the necessary experience and knowledge/technical skills critical for project completion. At the same time, there are less obvious considerations that need to be factored into the recruitment process:

- *Problem-solving ability.* If the project is complex and fuzzy, then a manager wants people who are good at working under uncertainty and have strong problem identification and solving skills. These same people are likely to be bored and less productive working on straightforward projects that go by the book.
- *Availability.* Sometimes the people who are most available are not the ones wanted for the team. Conversely, if members recruited are already overcommitted, they may not be able to offer much.

- *Technological expertise.* Managers should be wary of people who know too much about a specific technology. They may be technology buffs who like to study but have a hard time settling down and doing the work.
- *Credibility.* The credibility of the project is enhanced by the reputation of the people involved in the project. Recruiting a sufficient number of "winners" lends confidence to the project.
- *Political connections.* To begin to establish a cooperative relationship with a significant, but potentially uncooperative stakeholder group, managers would be wise to recruit individuals who already have a good working relationship with that group. This is particularly true for projects operating in a matrix environment in which a significant portion of the work will be under the domain of a specific functional department and not the core project team.
- *Ambition, initiative, and energy.* These qualities can make up for a lot of shortcomings in other areas and should not be underestimated.

After reviewing needed skills, the manager should try and find out through the corporate grapevine who is good, who is available, and who might want to work on the project. Some organizations may allow direct interviews. Often a manager will have to expend political capital to get highly prized people assigned to the project.

In matrix environments, the project manager will have to request appointments with functional managers to discuss project requirements for staffing. The following documents should be available at these discussions: an overall project scope statement, endorsements of top management, and a description of the tasks and general schedule that pertain to the people from their departments. Managers need to be precise as to what attributes they are seeking and why they are important. Good negotiation skills are necessary at this meeting. Functional managers should be encouraged to suggest names of people within their departments as candidates. If the project manager is asked to suggest names, it might be wise to say, "Well, I would really like Pegi Young, but I know how critical her work is. How about Billy Talbot?" If the conversation goes this way, the project manager may be able to cut a deal then and there and will want to be sure to put the agreement in writing immediately after the meeting as a memorandum of understanding.

If, on the other hand, the functional manager balks at the suggestions and the meeting is not progressing, the project manager should adroitly terminate the conversation with an understanding that the matter will be discussed again in a few days. This technique demonstrates persistence and a desire to do what it takes to resolve the issue. Ultimately, of course, the project manager will have to settle on the best offer. Managers should exercise care not to reveal how different members of the team were selected. The project might be crippled at the start if reluctantly assigned members are identified and the team perceives differences in attitude and commitment.

Conducting Project Meetings

The First Project Team Meeting

Research on team development confirms what we have heard from project managers: The first project kick-off meeting is critical to the early functioning of the project team. According to one veteran project manager:

> The first team meeting sets the tone for how the team will work together. If it is disorganized, or becomes bogged down with little sense of closure, then this can often become a self-fulfilling prophecy for subsequent group work. On the other hand, if it is crisply run, focusing on real issues and concerns in an honest and straightforward manner, members come away excited about being part of the project team.

There are typically three objectives project managers try to achieve during the first meeting of the project team. The first is to provide an overview of the project, including the scope and objectives, the general schedule, method, and procedures. The second is to begin to address some of the interpersonal concerns captured in the team development model: Who are the other team members? How will I fit in? Will I be able to work with these people? The third and most important objective is to begin to model how the team is going to work together to complete the project. The project manager must recognize that first impressions are important; her behavior will be carefully monitored and interpreted by team members. This meeting should serve as an exemplary role model for subsequent meetings and reflect the leader's style.

The meeting itself comes in a variety of shapes and forms. It is not uncommon in major projects for the kickoff meeting to involve one or two days, often at a remote site away from interruptions. This retreat provides sufficient time for preliminary introduction, to begin to establish ground rules, and to define the structure of the project. One advantage of off-site kickoff meetings is that they provide ample opportunity for informal interaction among members during breaks, meals, and evening activities; such informal interactions are critical to forming relationships.

However, many organizations do not have the luxury of holding elaborate retreats. In other cases the scope of project and level of involvement of different participants does not warrant such an investment of time. In these cases, the key operating principle should be KISS (keep it simple stupid!) Too often when constrained by time, project managers try to accomplish too much during the first meeting; in doing so, issues do not get fully resolved, and members come away with an information headache. Managers must remember that there are limits to how much information any one individual can absorb and that there will be opportunities in future meetings to establish ground rules and procedural matters. The primary goal is to run a productive meeting, and objectives should be realistic given the time available. If the meeting is only one hour, then the project manager should simply review the scope of the project, discuss how the team was formed, and provide an opportunity for members to introduce themselves to the team.

Establishing Ground Rules

Whether as part of an elaborate first meeting or during follow-up meetings, the project manager must quickly begin to establish operational ground rules for how the team will work together. These ground rules involve not only organizational and procedural issues but also normative issues on how the team will interact with each other. Although specific procedures will vary across organizations and projects, some of the major issues that need to be addressed include the following:

Planning Decisions
- How will the project plan be developed?
- What tools will be used to support the project?
- Will a specific project management software package be used? If so, which one?
- Who will enter the planning information?
- What are the specific roles and responsibilities of all the participants?
- Who needs to be informed of decisions? How will they be kept informed?
- What are the relative importance of cost, time, and performance?
- What are the deliverables of the project planning process?
- What format is appropriate for each deliverable?

Courtesy of NASA.

Donna Shirley's 35-year career as aerospace engineer reached a pinnacle in July 1997 when Sojourner—the solar-powered, self-guided, microwave-oven-sized rover—was seen exploring the Martian landscape in Pathfinder's spectacular images from the surface of the red planet. The event marked a milestone in space exploration: No vehicle had ever before roamed the surface of another planet. Shirley, a manager at the Jet Propulsion Laboratory's Mars Exploration Program, headed the mostly male team that designed and built Sojourner. In her insightful memoir, *Managing Martians*, written with Danelle Morton, she makes the following observation about managing creative teams:

> When you are managing really brilliant, creative people, at some point you find it's impossible to command or control them because

you can't understand what they are doing. Once they have gone beyond your ability to understand them, you have a choice to make as a manager. You can limit them and the project by your intelligence, which I think is the wrong way to do it. Or you can trust them and use your management skills to keep them focused on the goal.

A lot of bad managers get threatened when their "subordinates" know more than they do. They either hire people who are inferior to them so they can always feel in control or they bottleneck people who know something they don't so they can maintain control. The whole project suffers from the manager's insecurities.

*Donna Shirley and Danelle Morton, *Managing Martians* (New York: Broadway Books, 1998), pp. 88–89.

- Who will approve and sign off at the completion of each deliverable?
- Who receives each deliverable?

Tracking Decisions
- How will progress be assessed?
- At what level of detail will the project be tracked?
- How will team members get data from each other?
- How often will they get this data?
- Who will generate and distribute reports?
- Who needs to be kept informed about project progress, and how will they be informed?
- What content/format is appropriate for each audience?

- Meetings
  - Where will meetings be located?
  - What kind of meetings will be held?
  - Who will "run" these meetings?
  - How will agendas be produced?
  - How will information be recorded?

Managing Change Decisions

- How will changes be instituted?
- Who will have change approval authority?
- How will plan changes be documented and evaluated?

Relationship Decisions

- What department or organizations will the team need to interact with during the project?
- What are the roles and responsibilities of each organization (reviewer, approver, creator, user)?
- How will all involved parties be kept informed of deliverables, schedule dates, expectations, etc.?
- How will the team members communicate among themselves?
- What information will and won't be exchanged?

Checklists like these are only a guide; items should be added or deleted as needed. Many of these procedures will have already been established by precedent and will only have to be briefly reviewed. For example, *Microsoft Project* or *Primavera* may be the standard software tool for planning and tracking. Likewise, a specific firm is likely to have an established format for reporting status information. How to deal with other issues will have to be determined by the project team. When appropriate, the project manager should actively solicit input from the project team members and draw upon their experience and preferred work habits. This process also contributes to their buying into the operational decisions. Decisions should be recorded and circulated to all members.

During the course of establishing these operational procedures, the project manager, through word and deed, should begin working with members to establish the norms for team interaction. Below are examples of some of the norms researchers have found associated with high-performance teams.

- Confidentiality is maintained; no information is shared outside the team unless all agree to it.
- It is acceptable to be in trouble, but it is not acceptable to surprise others. Tell others immediately when deadlines or milestones will not be reached.
- There is zero tolerance for bulling a way through a problem or an issue.
- Agree to disagree, but when a decision has been made, regardless of personal feelings, move forward.
- Respect outsiders, and do not flaunt one's position on the project team.
- Hard work does not get in the way of having fun.

One way of making these norms more tangible is by creating a project team charter that goes beyond the scope statement of the project and states in explicit terms the norms and values of the team. This charter should be a collaborative effort on the part of the core team. Project managers can lead by proposing certain tenets, but they need to be open to suggestions from the team. Once there is general agreement to the rules

AP/Wide World Photos.

Mattel is the largest toy manufacturing company in the world with product lines that include Barbie dolls, Fisher-Price toys, and Hot Wheels. Mattel stumbled when it missed out on the girl empowerment trend in the late 1990s. Vowing never to have this happen again, Mattel re-engineered its product development processes by instituting Project Platypus.

Project Playtpus consists of people from a variety of functional areas who leave their regular jobs for three months and move out of Mattel headquarters to a separate location where they work collaboratively on new product ideas. Team members in Mattel's Project Platypus sometimes spend their days dropping eggs from a 14-foot ladder or throwing stuffed animals at each other. It is all part of team-building activities designed to get people to think differently and come up with creative ideas for new toys.

According to Ivy Ross, head of Mattel's girl design division, exercises such as devising a method to prevent an egg from breaking when dropped from 14 feet or throwing stuffed bunnies at a team-mate to release inhibitions are ways to get people to think outside the box and discover consumer trends and marketplace changes. "Other companies have skunk works," Ross says, "we have platypus. I looked up the definition and it said, 'an uncommon mix of different species.'"

The strength of the Platypus lies in its members' ability to build on one another's creative ideas. A key group norm is no one owns an idea. Everything belongs to the group, which helps eliminate competitiveness.

Project Platypus is also designed to encourage team bonding, so that people will continue to share ideas and collaborate once the creative ideas move further into product development and production. Previously, product development at Mattel involved a lot of "baton passing," as Ross puts it. Mattel now wants everyone to collaborate in a design and development process where there's a shared sense of ownership and achievement. Participants in the project work in a huge open space with no walls or cubicles. Desks are on wheels to encourage spontaneous sharing and collaboration. Project members can post their sketched ideas on the walls and invite others for suggestions.

The first Project Platypus effort is a new toy called Ello, a hybrid between a construction set and activity kit. Ello sets consist of interconnected pieces that allow children to explore their imagination to build anything from jewelry to buildings. Platypus project teams are continuing to work to develop two to three new product ideas a year.

*Chuck Salter, "Ivy Ross is Not Playing Around," *Fast Company,* Issue 64, November 2002, p. 104.

of conduct, each member signs the final document to symbolize commitment to the principles it contains. Unfortunately, in some cases this becomes a meaningless ritual because the charter is signed and filed away, never to be discussed again. To have a lasting effect, the charter has to be a legitimate part of the project monitoring system. Just as the team reviews progress toward project objectives, the team assesses the extent to which members are adhering to the principles in the charter.

Project managers play a major role in establishing team norms through personal example. If they freely admit mistakes and share what they have learned from them, other team members will begin to do the same. At the same time, project managers need to intervene when they believe such norms are being violated. They should talk to offenders privately and clearly state their expectations. The amazing thing about groups is that once a group is cohesive, with well-established norms, the members will police themselves so that the manager doesn't have to be the heavy. For example, one project manager confided that his team had a practice of having a small bean bag present at every meeting. If any one member felt that a colleague was shooting hot air or shading the truth, he or she was obligated to toss the bean bag at the speaker.

Managing Subsequent Project Meetings

The project kickoff meeting is one of several kinds of meetings required to complete a project. Other meetings include status report meetings, problem-solving meetings, and audit meetings. Issues unique to these meetings will be discussed in subsequent chapters. For now, here are some general guidelines for running effective meetings. They speak directly to the person chairing the meeting:

- Start meetings on time regardless of whether everyone is present.
- Prepare and distribute an agenda prior to the meeting.
- Identify an adjournment time.
- Periodically take time to review how effective previous meetings have been.
- Solicit recommendations and implement changes.
- Assign good recordkeeping.
- Review the agenda before beginning, and tentatively allocate time for each item.
- Prioritize issues so that adjustments can be made given time constraints.
- Encourage active participation of all members by asking questions instead of making statements.
- Summarize decisions, and review assignments for the next meeting.
- Prepare and distribute a summary of the meeting to appropriate people.
- Recognize accomplishments and positive behavior.

Meetings are often considered an anathema to productivity, but this does not have to be the case. The most common complaint is that meetings last too long. Establishing an agenda and adjournment time helps participants budget discussion time and provides a basis for expediting the proceedings. Recordkeeping can be an unwelcome, tedious task. Utilizing laptop computers to record decisions and information in real time can facilitate the communication process. Careful preparation and consistent application of these guidelines can make meetings a vital part of projects.

Establishing a Team Identity

One of the challenges project managers often face in building a team is the lack of full-time involvement of team members. Specialists work on different phases of the project and spend the majority of their time and energy elsewhere. They are often members of

Knight-Ridder's *Tallahassee Democrat,* like many American newspapers in the late 1980s, was struggling to survive in the face of declining revenues. Fred Mott, the general manager of the *Democrat,* was convinced that the key to the newspaper's future was becoming more customer-focused. Despite his best efforts, little progress was being made toward becoming a customer-driven newspaper. One area that was particularly problematic was advertising, where lost revenues due to errors could be as high as $10,000 a month.

Fred Mott decided to create a team of 12 of his best workers from all parts of the newspaper. They became known as the ELITE team because their mission was to "ELIminate The Errors." At first the team spent a lot of time pointing fingers at each other rather than coming to grips with the error problems at the newspaper. A key turning point came when one member produced what became known as "the rat tracks fax" and told the story behind it. It turns out a sloppily prepared ad arrived through a fax machine looking like "a rat had run across the page." Yet the ad passed through the hands of seven employees and probably would have been printed if it had not been totally unreadable. The introduction of this fax broke the ice, and the team started to admit that everyone—not

everyone else—was at fault. Then, recalls one member, "We had some pretty hard discussions. And there were tears at those meetings."

The emotional responses galvanized the group to the task at hand and bonded them to one another. The ELITE team looked carefully at the entire process by which an ad was sold, created, printed, and billed. When the process was examined, the team discovered patterns of errors, most of which could be attributed to bad communication, time pressures, and poor attitude. They made a series of recommendations that completely transformed the ad process at the *Democrat.* Under ELITE's leadership, advertising accuracy rose sharply and stayed above 99 percent. Lost revenues from errors dropped to near zero. Surveys showed a huge positive swing in advertiser satisfaction.

The impact of ELITE, however, went beyond numbers. The ELITE team's own brand of responsiveness to customer satisfaction spread to other parts of the newspaper. In effect this team of mostly frontline workers spearheaded a cultural transformation at the newspaper that emphasized a premium on customer service.

*Jon R. Katzenbach and Douglas K. Smith, *The Wisdom of Teams* (Boston: Harvard Business School Press, 1993), pp. 67–72. Copyright McKinsey & Co., Inc.

multiple teams, each competing for their time and allegiance. Project expert David Frame points out that for many of these specialists a specific project is an abstraction; as a consequence their level of motivation suffers. Project managers need to try to make the project team as tangible as possible to the participants by developing a unique team identity to which participants can become emotionally attached. Team meetings, co-location of team members, team names, and team rituals are common vehicles for doing so.

- *Effective use of meetings.* Periodic project team meetings provide an important forum for communicating project information. A less obvious function of project meetings is to help establish a concrete team identity. During project meetings, members see that they are not working alone. They are part of a larger project team, and project success depends on the collective efforts of all the team members. Timely gatherings of all the project participants help define team membership and reinforce a collective identity.

- *Co-location of team members.* The most obvious way to make the project team tangible is to have members work together in a common space. This is not always possible in matrix environments where involvement is part time and members are working on other projects and activities. A worthwhile substitute for co-location is the creation of a project office, sometimes referred to as the project war room or clubhouse. Such rooms are the common meeting place and contain the most significant project documentation. Frequently, their walls are covered with Gantt charts, cost graphs, and other output associated with project planning and control. These rooms serve as a tangible sign of project effort.

- *Creation of project team name.* The development of a team name such as the "A-Team" or "Casey's Crusaders" is a common device for making a team more tangible. Frequently an associated team logo is also created. Again the project manager should rely on the collective ingenuity of the team to come up with the appropriate name and logo. Such symbols then can be affixed to stationery, T-shirts, coffee mugs, etc., to help signify team membership.

- *Team rituals.* Just as corporate rituals help establish the unique identity of a firm, similar symbolic actions at the project level can contribute to a unique team subculture. For example, on one project members were given ties with stripes that corresponded to the number of milestones on the project. After reaching each milestone, members would gather and cut the next stripe off their ties to signify progress. Ralph Katz reports it was common practice for Digital Equipment's alpha chip design team to recognize people who found a bug in the design by giving them a phosphorescent toy roach. The bigger the bug that was discovered, the bigger the toy roach received. Such rituals help set project work apart from mainstream operations and reinforce a special status.

Creating a Shared Vision

Unlike project scope statements, which include specific cost, completion dates, and performance requirements, a *vision* involves the less tangible aspects of project performance. It refers to an image a project team holds in common about how the project will look upon completion, how they will work together, and/or how customers will accept the project. At its simplest level, a shared vision is the answer to the question, "What do we want to create?" Not everyone will have the same vision, but the images should be similar. Visions come in a variety of shapes and forms; they can be captured in a slogan or a symbol or can be written as a formal vision statement.

What a vision is, is not as important as what it does. A vision inspires members to give their best effort. (See A Good Man in a Storm Snapshot.) Moreover, a shared vision unites professionals with different backgrounds and agendas to a common aspiration. It helps motivate members to subordinate their individual agendas and do what is best for the project. As psychologist Robert Fritz puts it, "In the presence of greatness, pettiness disappears." Visions also provide focus and help communicate less tangible priorities, helping members make appropriate judgment calls. Finally, a shared vision for a project fosters commitment to the long term and discourages expedient responses that collectively dilute the quality of the project.

Visions can be surprisingly simple. For example, the vision for a new car could be expressed as a "pocket rocket." Compare this vision with the more traditional product description—"a sports car in the midprice range." The "pocket rocket" vision provides a much clearer picture of what the final product should be. Design engineers would immediately understand that the car will be both small and fast and that the car should be quick at the getaway, nimble in the turns, and very fast in the straightaways. Obviously, many details would have to be worked out, but the vision would help establish a common framework for making decisions.

There appear to be four essential qualities of an effective vision (see Figure 11.4): First, its essential qualities must be able to be communicated. A vision is worthless if it only resides in someone's head. Second, visions have to be challenging but also realistic. For example, a task force directed at overhauling the curriculum at the college of business at a state university is likely to roll its eyes if the dean announces that their vision is to compete against the Harvard Business School. Conversely, developing the best undergraduate business program in that state may be a realistic vision for that task force. Third, the project manager has to believe in the vision. Passion for the vision is an essential element of an effective vision. Finally, it should be a source of inspiration to others.

Once upon a time, back in 1976, Data General Corporation needed to come up quickly with a fast, reasonably priced 32-bit mini-computer to compete with Digital Equipment Corporation's VAX. Data General CEO Edson de Castro launched the Fountainhead Project and gave it the best people and ample resources to complete the 32-bit initiative. As a back-up to the Fountainhead project, Data General created the Eagle project within the Eclipse group under the leadership of Tom West. Work on both projects began in 1978.

In 1980 Data General announced its new computer. Featuring simplicity, power, and low cost. This computer was not the Fountainhead from the well funded "best" DG group but the Eagle from Tom West's under-funded Eclipse team. Tracy Kidder saw all this happen and told the story in *The Soul of a New Machine,* which won a Pulitzer Prize in 1982. This book, which Kidder thought might be of interest to a handful of computer scientists , has become a project management classic.

In the beginning of his book, Kidder introduces the readers to the book's protagonist Tom West by telling the story of him sailing a yacht across rough seas off the coast of New England. Kidder's title for the prologue was "A Good Man in a Storm."

Twenty years after the Kidder's book was published Tom West was interviewed by Lawrence Peters for the *Academy of Management Executive.* Below are some excerpts that capture Tom's views on managing innovative projects:

On selecting team members:

> You explain to a guy what the challenge was, and then see if his eyes light up.

On motivating team members:

> . . . Challenge was everything. People, especially creative technical people who really want to make a difference, will do whatever is possible or whatever is necessary. I've done this more than once, and I've repeated it over and over. It seems to work.

On the importance of having a vision:

> . . . you've got to find a rallying cry. You need to have something that can be described very simply and has that sort of ring of truth to an engineer that says "yes that's the thing to be doing right now." Otherwise you're going to be rolling rocks up hill all the time.

On the role of being a project manager:

> You have to act as a cheerleader. You have to act as the instructor. You have to constantly bring to mind what the purpose is and what's moving the ball towards the goal post, and what's running sideways, and you have to take up a lot of battles for them. I mean you really don't want your design engineer arguing with the guy in the drafting shop about why he ought to do it the designer's way. I can do that, and I can pull rank too, and sometimes I did just that.

*Tracy Kidder, *Soul of a New Machine.* (New York: Avon Books, 1981); Lawrence H. Peters, "'A Good Man in a Storm': An Interview with Tom West," *Academy of Management Executive*, Vol. 16, No. 4, 2002, pp. 53–60.

Once a project manager accepts the importance of building a shared vision, the next question is how to get a vision for a particular project. First, project managers don't get visions. They act as catalysts and midwives for the formation of a shared vision of a project team. In many cases visions are inherent in the scope and objectives of the project. People get naturally excited about being the first ones to bring a new technology to the

FIGURE 11.4
Requirements for an Effective Project Vision

market or solving a problem that is threatening their organization. Even with mundane projects, there are often ample opportunities for establishing a compelling vision. One way is to talk to various people involved in the project and find out early on what gets them excited about the project. For some it may be doing a better job than on the last project or the satisfaction in the eyes of the customers when the project is over. Many visions evolve reactively in response to competition. For example, the Kodak team responsible for developing the single-use FunSaver camera was driven by the vision of beating a similar effort by Fuji to the market.

Some experts advocate engaging in formal vision-building meetings. These meetings generally involve several steps, beginning with members identifying different aspects of the project and generating ideal scenarios for each aspect. For example, on a construction project the scenarios may include "no accidents," "no lawsuits," "winning a prize," or "how we are going to spend our bonus for completing the project ahead of schedule." The group reviews and chooses the scenarios that are most appealing and translates them into vision statements for the project. The next step is to identify strategies for achieving the vision statements. For example, if one of the vision statements is that there will be no lawsuits, members will identify how they will have to work with the owner and subcontractors to avoid litigation. Next, members volunteer to be the keeper of the flame for each statement. The vision, strategies, and the name of the responsible team member are published and distributed to relevant stakeholders.

In more cases than not, shared visions emerge informally. Project managers collect information about what excites participants about the project. They test bits of their working vision in their conversations with team members to gauge the level of excitement the early ideas elicit in others. To some extent they engage in basic market research. They seize opportunities to galvanize the team, such as a disparaging remark by an executive that the project will never get done on time or the threat of a competing firm launching a similar project. Consensus in the beginning is not essential. What is essential is a core group of at least one-third of the project team that is genuinely committed to the vision. They will provide the critical mass to draw others aboard. Once the language has been formulated to communicate the vision, then the statement needs to be a staple part of every working agenda, and the project manager should be prepared to deliver a "stump" speech at a moment's notice. When problems or disagreements emerge, all responses should be consistent with the vision.

Much has been written about visions and leadership. Critics argue that vision is a glorified substitute for shared goals. Others argue that it is one of the things that separates leaders from managers. The key is discovering what excites people about a project, being able to articulate this source of excitement in an appealing manner, and finally protecting and nurturing this source of excitement throughout the duration of the project.

Managing Project Reward Systems

Project managers are responsible for managing the reward system that encourages team performance and extra effort. One advantage they have is that often project work is inherently satisfying, whether it is manifested in an inspiring vision or simple sense of accomplishment. Projects provide participants with a change in scenery, a chance to learn new skills, and an opportunity to break out of their departmental cocoon. Another inherent reward is what was referred to in *The Soul of the New Machine* as "pinball"— project success typically gives team members an option to play another exciting game.

Still, many projects are underappreciated, boring, interfere with other more significant priorities, and are considered an extra burden. In some of these cases, the biggest reward is finishing the project so that team members can go back to what they really enjoy doing and what will yield the biggest personal payoffs. Unfortunately, when this attitude is the primary incentive, project quality is likely to suffer. In these circumstances, external rewards play a more important role in motivating team performance.

Most project managers we talk to advocate the use of group rewards. Because most project work is a collaborative effort, it only makes sense that the reward system would encourage teamwork. Recognizing individual members regardless of their accomplishments can distract from team unity. Project work is highly interdependent, so it can become problematic to distinguish who truly deserves additional credit. Cash bonuses and incentives need to be linked to project priorities. It makes no sense to reward a team for completing their work early if controlling cost was the number one priority.

One of the limitations of lump-sum cash bonuses is that all too often they are consumed by the household budget to pay the dentist or mechanic. To have more value, rewards need to have lasting significance. Many companies convert cash into vacation rewards, sometimes with corresponding time off. For example, there is one firm that rewarded a project team for getting the job done ahead of schedule with a four-day, all-expenses-paid trip to Walt Disney World for the members' entire families. That vacation not only will be remembered for years, but it also recognizes spouses and children who, in a sense, also contributed to the project's success. Similarly, other firms have been known to give members home computers and entertainment centers. Wise project managers negotiate a discretionary budget so that they can reward teams surpassing milestones with gift certificates to popular restaurants or tickets to sporting events. Impromptu pizza parties and barbecues are also used to celebrate key accomplishments.

Sometimes project managers have to use negative reinforcement to motivate project performance. For example, Ritti recounts the story of one project manager who was in charge of the construction of a new, state-of-the-art manufacturing plant. His project team was working with a number of different contracting firms. The project was slipping behind schedule, mostly because of a lack of cooperation among the different players. The project manager did not have direct authority over many key people, especially the contractors from the other companies. He did, however, have the freedom to convene meetings at his convenience. So the project manager instituted daily "coordination meetings," which were required of all the principals involved, at 6:00 A.M. The meetings continued for about two weeks until the project got back on schedule. At that time the project manager announced that the next meeting was canceled, and no further sunrise meetings were ever scheduled.

While project managers tend to focus on group rewards, there are times when they need to reward individual performance. This is done not only to compensate extraordinary effort but also to signal to the others what exemplary behavior is. More specifically, among the rewards they use to motivate and recognize individual contributions are the following:

- **Letters of commendation.** While project managers may not have responsibility for their team members' performance appraisals, they can write letters commending their project performance. These letters can be sent to the workers' supervisors to be placed in their personnel files.
- **Public recognition for outstanding work.** Superlative workers should be publicly recognized for their efforts. Some project managers begin each status review meeting with a brief mention of project workers who have exceeded their project goals.
- **Job assignments.** Good project managers recognize that, while they may not have much budgetary authority, they do have substantial control over who does what, with whom, when, and where. Good work should be rewarded with desirable job assignments. Managers should be aware of member preferences and, when appropriate, accommodate them.

- **Flexibility.** Being willing to make exceptions to rules, if done judiciously, can be a powerful reward. Allowing members to work at home when a child is sick or excusing a minor discretion can engender long-lasting loyalty.

We reiterate that individual rewards should be used judiciously, and the primary emphasis should be on group incentives. Nothing can undermine the cohesiveness of a team more than members beginning to feel that others are getting special treatment or that they are being treated unfairly. Camaraderie and collaboration can quickly vanish only to be replaced by bickering and obsessive preoccupation with group politics. Such distractions can absorb a tremendous amount of energy that otherwise would be directed toward completing the project. Individual rewards typically should be used only when everyone in the team recognizes that a member is deserving of special recognition.

Orchestrating the Decision-Making Process

Most decisions on a project do not require a formal meeting to discuss alternatives and determine solutions. Instead decisions are made in real time as part of the daily interaction patterns between project managers, stakeholders, and team members. For example, as a result of routine "how's it going?" question, a project manager discovers that a mechanical engineer is stuck trying to meet the performance criteria for a prototype he is responsible for building. The project manager and engineer go down the hallway to talk to the designers, explain the problem, and ask what, if anything, can be done. The designers distinguish which criteria are essential and which ones they think can be compromised. The project manager then checks with the marketing group to make sure the modifications are acceptable. They agree with all but two of the modifications. The project manager goes back to the mechanical engineer and asks whether the proposed changes would help solve the problem. The engineer agrees. Before authorizing the changes he calls the project sponsor, reviews the events, and gets the sponsor to sign off on the changes. This is an example of how, by practicing MBWA (management by wandering around), project managers consult team members, solicit ideas, determine optimum solutions, and create a sense of involvement that builds trust and commitment to decisions.

Still, projects encounter problems and decisions that require the collective wisdom of team members as well as relevant stakeholders. Group decision making should be used when it will improve the quality of important decisions. This is often the case with complex problems that require the input of a variety of different specialists. Group decision making should also be used when strong commitment to the decision is needed and there is a low probability of acceptance if only one person makes the decision. Participation is used to reduce resistance and secure support for the decision. Group decision making would be called for with controversial problems which have a major impact on project activities or when trust is low within the project team. Guidelines for managing group decision making are provided below.

Facilitating Group Decision Making

Project managers play a pivotal role in guiding the group decision-making process. They must remind themselves that their job is not to make a decision but to facilitate the discussion within the group so that the team reaches a consensus on the best possible solution. Consensus within this context does not mean that everyone supports the decision 100 percent, but that they all agree what the best solution is under the circumstances. Facilitating group decision making essentially involves four major steps. Each step is briefly described on page 361 with suggestions for how to manage the process.

1. **Problem identification.** The project manager needs to be careful not to state the problem in terms of choices (e.g., should we do X or Y?). Rather the project manager should identify the underlying problem to which these alternatives and probably others are potential solutions. This allows group members to generate alternatives, not just choose among them. One useful way of defining problems is to consider the gap between where a project is (i.e., the present state) and where it should be (desired state). For example, the project may be four days behind schedule or the prototype weighs two pounds more than the specifications. Whether the gap is small or large, the purpose is to eliminate it. The group must find one or more courses of action that will change the existing state into the desired one.

   If one detects defensive posturing during the problem identification discussion, then it may be wise to postpone the problem-solving step if possible. This allows for emotions to subside and members to gain a fresh perspective on the issues involved.

2. **Generating alternatives.** Once there is general agreement as to the nature of the problem(s), then the next step is to generate alternative solutions. If the problem requires creativity, then brainstorming is commonly recommended. Here the team generates a list of possible solutions on a flipchart or blackboard. During that time the project manager establishes a moratorium on criticizing or evaluating ideas. Members are encouraged to "piggyback" on other's ideas by extending them or combining ideas into a new idea. The object is to create as many alternatives as possible no matter how outlandish they may appear to be. Some project managers report that for really tough problems they have found it beneficial to conduct such sessions away from the normal work environment; the change in scenery stimulates creativity.

3. **Reaching a decision.** The next step is to evaluate and assess the merits of alternative solutions. During this phase it is useful to have a set of criteria for evaluating the merits of different solutions. In many cases the project manager can draw upon the priorities for the project and have the group assess each alternative in terms of its impact on cost, schedule, and performance as well as reducing the problem gap. For example, if time is critical, then the solution that solves the problem as quickly as possible would be chosen.

   During the course of the discussion the project manager attempts to build consensus among the group. This can be a complicated process. Project managers need to provide periodic summaries to help the group keep track of its progress. They must protect those members who represent the minority view and ensure that such views get a fair hearing. They need to guarantee that everyone has an opportunity to share opinions and no one individual or group dominates the conversation. It may be useful to bring a two-minute timer to regulate the use of air time. When conflicts occur, managers need to apply some of the ideas and techniques discussed in the next section.

   Project managers need to engage in consensus testing to determine what points the group agrees on and what are still sources of contention. They are careful not to interpret silence as agreement; they confirm agreement by asking questions. Ultimately, through thoughtful interaction, the team reaches a "meeting of the minds" as to what solution is best for the project.

4. **Follow-up.** Once the decision has been made and implemented, it is important for the team to find the time to evaluate the effectiveness of the decision. If the decision failed to provide the anticipated solution, then the reasons should be explored and the lessons learned added to the collective memory bank of the project team.

So far the discussion of team building has been directed primarily to significant projects that command the attention and involvement of assigned members. But what about projects that have low priority for team members: The perfunctory task forces that members begrudgingly join? The committee work people get assigned to do? The part-time projects that pull members away from the critical work they would rather be doing? Projects that cause members to privately question why they are doing this?

There is no magic wand available that transforms mildly interested, part-time project teams into high-performance teams. We interviewed several project managers about such project scenarios. They all agreed that these can be very difficult and frustrating assignments and that there are limits to what is possible. Still, they offered tips and advice for making the best of the situation. Most of these tips focus on building commitment to the project when it does not naturally exist.

One project manager advocated orchestrating a large "time" investment upfront on such projects—either in the form of a lengthy meeting or a significant early assignment. He viewed this as a form of down payment that members would forfeit if they didn't carry the project to completion.

Others emphasize interjecting as much fun into activities as possible. Here rituals discussed under building team identity come into play. People become committed because they enjoy working together on the project. One project manager even confided that the perfect attendance at her project meetings was due primarily to the quality of the doughnuts she provided.

Another strategy is to make the benefits of the project as real to the team members as possible. One project manager escalated commitment to a mandated accidents prevention task force by bringing accident victims to a project meeting. Another project manager brought the high-ranking project sponsor to recharge the team by reinforcing the importance of the project to the company.

Most project managers emphasized the importance of building a strong personal relationship with each of the team members. When this connection occurs, members work hard not so much because they really care about the project but because they don't want to let the project manager down. Although not couched in influence currency terms, these managers talked about getting to know each member, sharing contacts, offering encouragement, and extending a helping hand when needed.

Finally, all project managers cautioned that nothing should be taken for granted on low-priority projects. They recommend reminding people about meetings and bringing extra copies of materials to meetings for those who have forgotten them or can't find them. Project managers should remain in frequent contact with team members and remind them of their assignments. One manager summed it up best when he said, "Sometimes it all boils down to just being a good nag."

Managing Conflict within the Project

Disagreements and conflicts naturally emerge within a project team during the life of the project. Participants will disagree over priorities, allocation of resources, the quality of specific work, solutions to discovered problems, and so forth. Some conflicts support the goals of the group and improve project performance. For example, two members may be locked in a debate over a design trade-off decision involving different features of a product. They argue that their preferred feature is what the primary customer truly wants. This disagreement may force them to talk to or get more information from the customer, with the result that they realize neither feature is highly valued, but instead the customer wants something else. On the other hand, conflicts can also hinder group performance. Initial disagreements can escalate into heated arguments with both parties storming out of the room and refusing to work together.

Thamhain and Wilemon's research revealed that the sources of conflict change as projects progress along the project life cycle. Figure 11.5 summarizes the major sources of conflict in each phase.

During project definition, the most significant sources of conflict are priorities, administrative procedures, schedule, and resources. Disputes occur over the relative importance of the project compared with other activities, which project management structure to use (especially how much control the project manager should have), the personnel to be assigned, and the scheduling of the project into existing workloads.

During the planning phase, the chief source of conflict remains priorities, followed by schedules, procedures, and technical requirements. This is the phase where the

FIGURE 11.5
Conflict Intensity over the Project Life Cycle

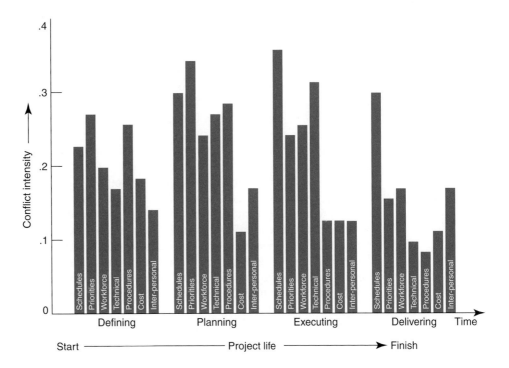

project moves from a general concept to a detailed set of plans. Disagreements often emerge over the final schedule, the availability of resources, communication and decision making procedures, and technical requirements for the project.

During the execution phase, friction arises over schedule slippage, technical problems, and staff issues. Milestones become more difficult to meet because of accumulating schedule slippages. This leads to tension within the team as delays prevent others from starting or completing their work. Managing the trade-offs between time, cost, and performance becomes paramount. Project managers must decide between letting the schedule slip, investing additional funds to get back on track, or scaling back the scope of the project in order to save time. Technical problems involve finding solutions to unexpected problems and integrating the contributions of different people. The strain of the project may be expressed in interpersonal conflicts as well as pressures to use resources more effectively.

During the delivery phase, schedules continue as the biggest source of conflict as schedule slippages make it more difficult to meet target completion dates. Pressures to meet objectives coupled with growing anxiety over future assignments increases interpersonal tensions. Technical problems are rare since most of them have been worked out during the earlier phases.

Encouraging Functional Conflict

The demarcation between functional and dysfunctional conflict is neither clear nor precise. In one team, members may exchange a diatribe of four-letter expletives and eventually resolve their differences. Yet in another project team, such behavior would create irreconcilable divisions and would prohibit the parties from ever working together productively again. The distinguishing criterion is how the conflict affects project performance, not how individuals feel. Members can be upset and dissatisfied with the interchange, but as long as the disagreement furthers the objectives of the project, then the conflict is functional. Project managers should recognize that conflict is an inevitable and even a desirable part of project work; the key is to encourage functional conflict and manage dysfunctional conflict.

A shared vision can transcend the incongruities of a project and establish a common purpose to channel debate in a constructive manner. Without shared goals there is no common ground for working out differences. In the previous example involving the design trade-off decision, when both parties agreed that the primary goal was to satisfy the customer, there was a basis for more objectively resolving the dispute. Therefore, agreeing in advance which priority is most important—cost, schedule, or scope—can help a project team decide what response is most appropriate.

Sometimes it's not the presence of conflict, but the absence of conflict that is the problem. Oftentimes as a result of compressed time pressures, self-doubt, and the desire to preserve team harmony, members are reluctant to voice objections. This hesitation robs the team of useful information that might lead to better solutions and the avoidance of critical mistakes. Project managers need to encourage healthy dissent in order to improve problem solving and innovation. They can demonstrate this process by asking tough questions and challenging the rationale behind recommendations. They can also orchestrate healthy conflict by bringing in people with different points of view to critical meetings.

Project managers can legitimize dissent within the team by designating someone to play the role of devil's advocate or by asking the group to take 15 minutes to come up with all the reasons the team should not pursue a course of action. Functional conflict plays a critical role in obtaining a deeper understanding of the issues and coming up with the best decisions possible.

One of the most important things project managers can do is model an appropriate response when someone disagrees or challenges their ideas. They need to avoid acting defensively and instead encourage critical debate. They should exhibit effective listening skills and summarize the key issues before responding. They should check to see if others agree with the opposing point of view. Finally, project managers should value and protect dissenters. Organizations have a tendency to create too many yes-men, and the emperor needs to be told when he doesn't have any clothes on.

Managing Dysfunctional Conflict

Managing dysfunctional conflict is a much more challenging task than encouraging functional conflict. First, dysfunctional conflict is hard to identify. A manager might have two highly talented professionals who hate each other's guts, but in the heat of competition they produce meritorious results. Is this a pleasant situation? No. Is it functional? Yes, as long as it contributes to project performance. Conversely, sometimes functional conflict degenerates into dysfunctional conflict. This change occurs when technical disagreements evolve into irrational, personality clashes or when failure to resolve an issue causes unnecessary delays in critical project work.

The second major difficulty managers face is that there is often no easy solution to dysfunctional conflict. Project managers have to decide among a number of different strategies to manage it; here are five possibilities:

1. **Mediate the conflict.** The manager intervenes and tries to negotiate a resolution by using reasoning and persuasion, suggesting alternatives and the like. One of the keys is trying to find common ground. In some cases the project manager can make the argument that the win/lose interchange has escalated to the point that it has become lose/lose for everyone and now is the time to make concessions.

2. **Arbitrate the conflict.** The manager imposes a solution to the conflict after listening to each party. The goal is not to decide who wins but to have the project win. In doing so, it is important to seek a solution that allows each party to save face; otherwise the decision may provide only momentary relief. One project manager admits that she has had great success using a King Solomon approach to resolving conflict. She confided she announces a solution that neither party will like and gives the opponents two hours to come up with a better solution they can both agree on.

3. **Control the conflict.** Reducing the intensity of the conflict by smoothing over differences or interjecting humor is an effective strategy. If feelings are escalating, the manager can adjourn the interaction and hope cooler heads prevail the next day. If the conflict continues to escalate, project assignments may need to be rearranged if possible so that two parties don't have to work together.

4. **Accept it.** In some cases the conflict will outlive the life of the project and, though a distraction, it is one the manager has to live with.

5. **Eliminate the conflict.** Sometimes the conflict has escalated to the point that it is no longer tolerable. In this case the manager removes the members involved from the project. If there is a clear villain then only he or she should be removed. If, as is often the case, both parties are at fault, then it would be wise if possible to eliminate both individuals. Their removal would give a clear signal to the others on the team that this kind of behavior is unacceptable.

In summary, project managers establish the foundation for functional conflict by establishing clear roles and responsibilities, developing common goals or a shared vision, and using group incentives that reward collaboration. Project managers have to be adroit at reading body language to identify unspoken disagreement. They also have to keep in touch with what is going on in a project to identify small problems that might escalate into big conflicts. Well-timed humor and redirecting the focus to what is best for the project can alleviate the interpersonal tensions that are likely to flare up on a project team.

Rejuvenating the Project Team

Over the course of a long project, a team sometimes drifts off course and loses momentum. The project manager needs to swing into action to realign the team with the project objectives and step on the pedal. There are both formal and informal ways of doing this. Informally, the project manager can institute new rituals like the "toy roaches" to reenergize a team. On one project that was experiencing rough going, the project manager stopped work and took the team bowling to relieve frustrations. On another project, a manager showed her team the movie, *The Shawshank Redemption* to rekindle hope and commitment to success.

Another option is to have the project sponsor give a pep talk to the "troops." In other cases, a friendly challenge can reinvigorate a team. For example, one project sponsor offered to cook a five-course meal if the project got back on track and hit the next milestone.

Sometimes more formal action needs to be taken. The project manager may recognize the need for a team-building session devoted to improving the work processes of the team. This meeting is particularly appropriate if she senses that the team is approaching a transition point in its development. The goal of such a session is to improve the project team's effectiveness through better management of project demands and group processes. It is an inward look by the team at its own performance, behavior, and culture for the purpose of eliminating dysfunctional behaviors and strengthening functional ones. The project team critiques its performance, analyzes its way of doing things, and attempts to develop strategies to improve its operation.

Oftentimes an external consultant is hired, or an internal staff specialist is assigned to facilitate the session. This process brings a more objective, outside perspective to the table, frees the project manager to be part of the process, and provides a specialist trained in group dynamics. Furthermore, if preliminary information is to be collected, team members may be more candid and open to an outsider. One caveat about using outside consultants is that too often managers resort to this as a method for dealing with a problem that they have been unable or unwilling to deal with. The marching order to the consultant is "fix my team for me." What the managers fail to recognize is that one of the keys to fixing the team is improving the working relationship between themselves and the remainder of the team. For such sessions to be effective, project managers have to be willing to have their own role scrutinized and be receptive to changing their own behavior and work habits based on the comments and suggestions of the project team.

Consultants use a wide variety of team-building techniques to elevate team performance. Here is a brief description of one of the more common approaches. The first step is to gather information and make a preliminary diagnosis of team performance. Whether through individual interviews or in a group forum, the consultant asks general questions about the project team performance, that is, what obstacles are getting in the way of the team being able to perform better? This information is summarized in terms of themes. When everyone has understood the themes, the group ranks them in terms of both their importance and the extent the team has ownership over them. This last dimension is critical. *Ownership* refers to whether the team has direct influence over the issue. For example, a team probably has little influence over delivery of contracted supplies, but team members do control how quickly they inform each other of sudden changes in plans. If the group becomes preoccupied with issues outside its control, the meeting can quickly evolve into a demoralizing gripe session. Therefore, the most important issues they have direct control over become the subjects of the agenda. During the course of the meeting, much interpersonal and group process information will be generated, and that is examined too. Thus, the group works on two sets of items: the agenda items and the items that emerge from the interaction of the participants. This is where the expertise of the external facilitator becomes critical for identifying interaction patterns and their implications for team performance.

As important problems are discussed, alternatives for action are developed. The team-building session concludes by deciding on specific action steps for remedying problems and setting target dates for who will do what, when. These assignments can be reviewed at project status meetings or at a special follow-up session.

It has become fashionable to link team-building activities with outdoor experiences. The outdoor experience—whether it is whitewater rafting down the Rogue River in Oregon or rock climbing in Colorado—places group members in a variety of physically challenging situations that must be mastered through teamwork, not individual effort. By having to work together to overcome difficult obstacles, team members are supposed to experience increased self-confidence, more respect for another's capabilities, and a greater commitment to teamwork. No empirical data are available to support such exotic endeavors other than the enthusiastic support of the participants. Such activities are likely to provide an intense common experience that may accelerate the social development of the team. Such an investment of time and money communicates the importance of teamwork and is considered by some a perk for being on the project. At the same time, unless the lessons from these experiences can be immediately transferred to actual project work, their significance is likely to vanish.

Managing Virtual Project Teams

Building a high-performance project team among a mixture of part-time and full-time members is a challenging task. Consider how much more challenging it is to build a team when members cannot engage in face-to-face interactions. Such would be the case for a virtual project team in which the team members are geographically situated so that they may seldom, if ever, meet face-to-face as a team. For example, Hewlett-Packard's integrated circuit business headquarters and a portion of the R&D facilities are located in Palo Alto, California; the two wafer fabrication operations are located in Corvallis, Oregon, and Fort Collins, Colorado; and the packaging assembly process is primarily in Singapore and Korea. It is not uncommon for professionals at each of these locations to be involved in the same project. When team members are spread across different time zones and continents, the opportunity for direct communication is severely limited. Electronic communication such as the Internet, e-mail, and teleconferencing takes on much more importance in virtual projects because this is the primary means of communication. See Managing Virtual Global Teams for an example of how this works.

Two of the biggest challenges involved in managing a virtual project team are developing trust and effective patterns of communication. Trust is crucial to virtual project management. Unlike working as a traditional team, where members can see whether someone has done what they say they have done, virtual team members depend on the word of distant members. At the same time, it can be difficult to trust someone whom you may have met only one or two times or not at all. Geographical separation also prohibits the informal social interactions that are often essential to building camaraderie among team members. As one virtual team member put it, "You can't have a beer together over the Internet."

So how can a project manager facilitate the development of trust within a virtual team? First, if it is impossible to hold a face-to-face meeting in the beginning, managers need to orchestrate the exchange of social information—who everyone is and some personal background information during the initial electronic interchange. Second, they need to set clear roles for each team member. Ideally, specific tasks should be assigned to each member so that they can make an immediate contribution to the project. Trust in virtual projects grows through team member reliability, consistency, and responsiveness. Finally, the project manager must consistently display enthusiasm and an action orientation in all messages; this spirit will hopefully spread to other team members.

The second major challenge for managing a virtual project team is to establish effective patterns of communication. E-mail and faxes are great for communicating facts—but not the feelings behind the facts; nor do they allow for real-time communication. Conference calls and project chat rooms can help, but they also have their limitations. Videoconferencing is a significant improvement over nonvisual electronic forms of communication. Still, it is a very expensive medium, and real-time interaction is available on only the most advanced and expensive systems. Even with the best system, managers have to overcome the problem of time zone differences, cultural nuances, and finding a convenient time for people to conference. Here are some tips for alleviating communication problems and enhancing the performance of virtual teams:

1. **Include face-to-face time if at all possible.** Hold an initial meeting for all team members so they can meet each other and socialize. Hold subsequent meetings at key junctures in the project. These meetings will help establish ties among team members and facilitate effective problem solving.

2. **Keep team members informed on how the overall project is going.** Use shareware or develop a central access point such as either a website or LAN account to

Carl A. Singer, a senior program manager at IBM Global Services, described how global time zones were used to complete a time intensive project. The project required subject matter experts (SMEs) to document existing best practices in maintenance domain and to port these into a knowledge management tool. The most proficient SMEs available were on opposite sides of the globe—Australia and Scotland. Review and control of the project was from the United States.

Management realized that just working harder and smarter was not going to meet the time and quality targets. For this project they used the dimension of time to their benefit. Applying sound management principles as well as taking advantage of electronic communication systems, the team was able to create a virtual 24-hour workday for quick responses and accelerated reviews.

Each team consisted of veteran professionals familiar with the rigors of time-pressured consulting projects. A local point person was identified for each team and mutually agreed-upon targets, terminology, and processes were established.

An all-hands kickoff meeting was organized in which participants were able to socialize, understand local and projectwide constraints, and finalize an agreed-upon plan. The meeting was held at a corporate hotel with dining accommodations. The facility was considered an "assisted living community for IBM consultants." This hastened recovery from jet lag and provided an interruption-free work environment.

Upon returning to their home bases, each team created the majority of their deliverables independently with periodic three-way conference calls to maintain coordination. A project control book was established electronically so that all participants had access to the latest project documents.

The final phase of the project required intense interfacing and reviews between the teams. These reviews necessitated changes to deal with concerns, differences among subprojects, and other issues. It was here that the worldwide nature of the project was leveraged. Using a "dry cleaning approach" (in by 5 P.M. out by 9 A.M.) team members in Australia and Scotland were able to address issues generated during the U.S.-based external reviews and provide concrete responses by the beginning of the next business day. Conference calls at 6:00 A.M. (U.S. EST) were used to coordinate responses and resolve issues. Conference calls at the end of the U.S. workday were used to finalize issues and assignments. Figure 11.6 depicts the 24-hour clock used to align communication schedules.

Telephone conferencing was used instead of videoconferencing due to the setup lead time and because it would force participants to leave their offices. E-mail was used extensively for general communication. An electronic repository of project work was used to coordinate global involvement. In practice, a participant could draft a document and deposit it electronically only to wake up the next day to find the document annotated with suggested revisions. Likewise, one could start the day by checking an in-basket populated with documents to review and issues to address. Over time, "G'day" and "Cheers" crept into the U.S. speech—a clear indicator of team cohesion.

Singer identified a number of lessons learned from the project. Among these included:

- The all-hands kickoff meeting was critical for establishing goals and procedures as well as "rules of courtesy."

- Loosen the reins—establish clear deliverables and then step out of the way and let the professionals do their work.

- Establish and enforce agreed-upon quality standards and deliverable templates.

- Maintain a regular schedule of conference calls, even if only to say "Hello, we have nothing to talk about today." Conference calls should be guided by pre-established agendas, note-taking procedures, and reviews.

*Carl A. Singer, "Leveraging a Worldwide Project Team," *PM Network*, April 2001, pp. 36–40.

provide members with updated project schedules. Team members need to know where they fit in the big picture.

3. **Don't let team members vanish.** Virtual teams often experience problems getting in touch with each other. Use an Internet scheduling software to store member's calendars.

4. **Establish a code of conduct to avoid delays.** Team members need to agree not only on what, when, and how information will be shared but also on how and when they will respond to it. Develop a priority system to distinguish messages that require immediate response from those with longer time frames.

5. **Establish clear norms and protocols for surfacing assumptions and conflicts.** Because most communication is nonvisual, project managers cannot watch body language and facial expressions to develop a sense of what is going on. They need to probe deeper when communicating to force members to explain their viewpoints, actions, and concerns more clearly; they must double-check comprehension.

FIGURE 11.6 24-Hour Global Clock

United States (East Coast)	Australia	Scotland	Comments
12 midnight	2 PM	5 AM	
1 AM	3 PM	6 AM	
2 AM	4 PM	7 AM	
3 AM	5 PM	8 AM	
4 AM	6 PM	9 AM	Australia handoff for off-shift review
5 AM	7 PM	10 AM	
6 AM	8 PM	11 AM	3-way conferencing window (primary)
7 AM	9 PM	12 noon	3-way conferencing window (primary)
8 AM	10 PM	1 PM	3-way conferencing window (primary)
9 AM	11 PM	2 PM	
10 AM	12 midnight	3 PM	
11AM	1 AM	4 PM	
12 noon	2 AM	5 PM	Scotland handoff for off-shift review
1 PM	3 AM	6 PM	
2 PM	4 AM	7 PM	
3 PM	5 AM	8 PM	
4 PM	6 AM	9 PM	3-way conferencing window (secondary)
5 PM	7 AM	10 PM	3-way conferencing window (secondary)
6 PM	8 AM	11 PM	U.S. handoff for off-shift review
7 PM	9 AM	12 midnight	
8 PM	10 AM	1 AM	
9 PM	11 AM	2 AM	
10 PM	12 noon	3 AM	
11 PM	1 PM	4 AM	
12 midnight	2PM	5 AM	

☐ Prime time   ☐ Secondary time   ☐ Downtime

To a large extent managing a virtual project team is no different from managing a regular project team. The key is working within the constraints of the situation to develop effective ways for team members to interact and combine their talents to complete the project.

Project Team Pitfalls

High-performance project teams can produce dramatic results. However, like any good thing, there is a dark side to project teams that managers need to be aware of. We referred to this phenomenon as *projectitis* in Chapter 3. In this section we examine in more detail some of the pathologies that high-performance project teams can succumb to and highlight what project managers can do to reduce the likelihood of these problems occurring.

Groupthink

Janis first identified *groupthink* as a factor that influenced the misguided 1961 Bay of Pigs invasion of Cuba. His term refers to the tendency of members in highly cohesive groups to lose their critical evaluative capabilities. This malady appears when pressures for conformity are combined with an illusion of invincibility to suspend critical discussion of decisions. As a result decisions are made quickly with little consideration of alternatives; often the practice leads to fiascoes that, after the fact, appear totally improbable. Some of the symptoms of groupthink include the following:

- *Illusion of invulnerability.* The team feels invincible. It is marked by a high degree of esprit de corps, an implicit faith in its own wisdom, and an inordinate optimism that allows group members to feel complacent about the quality of their decisions.
- *Whitewash of critical thinking.* The group members discuss only a few solutions, ignoring alternatives; they fail to examine the adverse consequences that could follow their preferred course of action; and they too quickly dismiss any alternatives that, on the surface, appear to be unsatisfactory.
- *Negative stereotypes of outsiders.* "Good guy/bad guy" stereotypes emerge in which the group considers any outsiders who oppose their decisions as the bad guys, who are perceived as incompetent and malicious and whose points are unworthy of serious consideration.
- *Direct pressure.* When a team member does speak out or question the direction in which the team is headed, direct pressure is applied to the dissenter. He or she is reminded that speed is important and that the aim is agreement, not argument.

Bureaucratic Bypass Syndrome

Project teams are often licensed to get things done without having to go through normal protocols of the parent organization. Bypassing bureaucratic channels is appealing and invigorating. However, if bypassing becomes a way of life, it results in the rejection of bureaucratic policies and procedures, which provide the glue for the overall organization. A team that operates outside the organization may alienate other workers who are constrained by the norms and procedures of the organization; eventually, these outside bureaucrats will find ways to put up roadblocks and thwart the project team.

Team Spirit Becomes Team Infatuation

High-performance project teams can be a tremendous source of personal satisfaction. The excitement, chaos, and joy generated by working on a challenging project can be an invigorating experience. Leavitt and Lipman-Blumen even go so far as to say that team members behave like people in love. They become infatuated with the challenge of the project and the talent around them. This total preoccupation with the project and the project team, while contributing greatly to the remarkable success of the project, can leave in its wake a string of broken professional and personal relationships that contribute to burnout and disorientation upon completion of the project.

Going Native

Going native is a phrase first used by the British Foreign Service during colonial times to describe agents who assumed the customs, values, and prerogatives of their foreign country assignment. They did so to the point that they were no longer representing the best interests of the British government but rather those of the natives. This same phenomenon can occur within project teams working abroad or in those who become closely identified with their customers. In essence, the customer's interests take precedence over the parent organization's interests. This change in viewpoint can lead to excessive scope creep and open defiance of corporate policy and interests.

Dealing with these maladies is problematic because, in most cases, they are a distortion of a good thing, rather than a simple evil. Awareness is the first step for prevention. The next step is to take preemptive action to reduce the likelihood of these pitfalls occurring. For example, managers can reduce the isolation of the project team by creating work-related connections outside the project team. These interactions naturally occur in a matrix environment where members work on multiple projects and maintain ties to their home department. Likewise, the isolation of dedicated project teams can be reduced by the timely involvement of external specialists. In either case, the active involvement of relevant members of the parent organization at project status meetings can help maintain the link between the project and the rest of the organization. If the team appears to be suffering from groupthink, then the project manager can encourage functional conflict by playing a devil's advocate role to encourage dissent or using a structured problem-solving approach like the nominal group technique (see Snapshot). Finally, formal team-building sessions may reveal dysfunctional norms and refocus the attention of the team on project objectives.

Summary

Project managers must often work under less-than-ideal conditions to develop a cohesive team committed to working together and completing the project to the best of their abilities. They have to recruit personnel from other departments and manage the temporary involvement of team members. They have to bring strangers together and quickly establish a set of operational procedures that unite their efforts and contributions. They have to be skilled at managing meetings so that they do not become a burden but rather a vehicle for progress. Project managers need to forge a team identity and a shared vision, which command the attention and allegiance of participants. They need to use group incentives to encourage teamwork while recognizing when it is appropriate to single out individuals for special recognition. Project managers have to encourage functional conflict that contributes to superior solutions while being on guard against dysfunctional conflict that can break a team apart. In doing these things, they have to be careful not to do too good a job and avoid the pitfalls of excessive group cohesion.

While agendas, charters, visions, rewards, and so forth, are important tools and techniques, it has been emphasized both in this chapter and in Chapter 10 that the most important tool a project manager has to build an effective project team is his or her own behavior. Just as the founding members of an organization shape the culture of the organization, the project manager shapes and influences the internal culture of the project team. A positive example can define how team members respond to changes, how they handle new tasks, and how they relate to one another and the rest of the organization. There is no easy way to lead by example. It requires personal conviction, discipline, sensitivity to team dynamics, and a constant awareness of how personal actions are perceived by others.

Key Terms

Brainstorming
Dysfunctional conflict
Functional conflict
Groupthink

Nominal group technique (NGT)
Positive synergy
Project kickoff meeting

Project vision
Team building
Team rituals
Virtual project team

Review Questions

1. What are the differences between the five stage model of team development and the punctuated equilibrium model?
2. What are the elements of an effective project vision? Why are they important?
3. Why should a project manager emphasize group rewards over individual rewards?
4. What is the difference between functional and dysfunctional conflict on a project?
5. When would it be appropriate to hold a formal team-building session on a project?
6. What are the unique challenges to managing a virtual project team?
7. What can a project manager do to avoid some of the pitfalls of a highly cohesive project team?

Exercises

1. The following activities are based on a recently completed group project that you have been involved in. This project may have been a student project, a work project, or an extracurricular project.
   a. Analyze the development of the team in terms of the five-phase model and the punctuated equilibrium model. Which model does the best job of describing how the team evolved?
   b. Analyze the group in terms of the nine situational factors that influence team development. What factors positively contributed to group performance? What factors negatively contributed to group performance? How did the group try to overcome the negative factors? What could you have done differently to overcome these negative factors?
   c. Analyze how effectively the group managed meetings. What did the group do well? What didn't the group do well? If the group were formed again, what specific recommendations would you make about how the group should manage meetings?
2. Assume that you have the following decision-making options: (1) make the decision on your own with available information, (2) consult others before making a decision, and (3) call a meeting and reach a consensus, seeking to arrive at a final

decision everyone can agree on. Which approach would you use to make each of the following decisions and why?

    a. You are the project leader for Casino Night on campus, a charitable event organized by your group to raise money for the homeless. The event was a big success, garnering a net profit of $3,500. Before the event your team researched nearby organizations that support the homeless and to whom the money could be given. You narrowed the choices to the "Chunk of Coal House" and "St. Mary's Soup Kitchen." Eventually your group decided that the funds be given to Chunk of Coal. You are about to write a check to its director when you read in the local newspaper that the Chunk of Coal House has terminated operations. What should you do with the money?

    b. You are a golf course designer hired by Trysting Tree Golf Club to renovate their golf course. You have worked closely with the board of directors of the club to develop a new layout that is both challenging and aesthetically pleasing. Everyone is excited about the changes. The project is nearly 75 percent complete when you encounter problems on the 13th hole. The 13th hole at Trysting Tree is a 125-yard par three in which golfers have to hit their tee shots over a lake to a modulated green. During the construction of the new tee box, workers discovered that an underground spring runs beneath the box to the lake. You inspected the site and agreed with the construction supervisor that this could create serious problems, especially during the rainy winter months. After surveying the area, you believe the only viable option would be to extend the hole to 170 yards and create elevated tees on the adjacent hillside.

    c. You are the leader of a new product development project. Your team has worked hard on developing a third-generation product that incorporates new technology and meets customer demands. The project is roughly 50 percent complete. You have just received a report from the marketing department detailing a similar product that is about to be released by a competitor. The product appears to utilize radical new design principles that expand the functionality of the product. This poses a serious threat to the success of your project. Top management is considering canceling your project and starting over again. They want you to make a recommendation.

3. The following activities are based on a current or recently completed group project that you have been involved in. This project may be a student project, a work project, or an extracurricular project.

    a. How strong is team identity on this project and why?

    b. What could participants do to strengthen team identity?

    c. What kind of informal activities could be used to rejuvenate the team? Why would these activities work?

References

Cleland, D. I., "Team Building: The New Strategic Weapon," *PM Network*, Vol. 11 (1) 1997.

Coutu, D. L., "Organization Trust in Virtual Teams," *Harvard Business Review*, Vol. 76 (3) 1998, pp. 20–21.

DeMarco, T., and T. Lister, *Peopleware: Productive Projects and Teams*, 2nd ed. (New York: Dorsett Housing, 1999).

Foti, R., "The Virtual Handshake," *PM Network*, March 2004, pp. 28–37.

Frame, J. D., *Managing Projects in Organizations* (San Francisco: Jossey-Bass, 1995).

Janis, I. L., *Groupthink* (Boston: Houghton Mifflin, 1982).

Johansen, R., D. Sibbet, S. Benson, A. Martin, R. Mittman, and P. Saffo, *Leading Business Teams: How Teams Can Use Technology and Group Process Tools to Enhance Performance* (Reading, MA: Addison-Wesley, 1991).

Katz, R., "How a Team at Digital Equipment Designed the 'Alpha' Chip," *The Human Side of Managing Technology Innovation,* 2nd ed. Ed. Ralph Katz (New York: Oxford Press, 2004), pp. 121–33.

Katzenbach, J. R., and D. K. Smith, *The Wisdom of Teams* (Boston: Harvard Business School Press, 1993).

Kidder, T., *The Soul of a New Machine* (New York: Avon Books, 1981).

Kirkman, B. L., B. Rosen, C.B. Gibson, P.E. Tesluk, and S.O. McPherson, "Five Challenges to Virtual Team Success: Lessons From Sabre, INC.," *Academy of Management Executive,* 16 (2) 2002, pp. 67–79.

Leavitt, H. J., and J. Lipman-Blumen, "Hot Groups," *Harvard Business Review,* Vol. 73 1995, pp. 109–16.

Linetz, B. P., and K. P. Rea, *Project Management for the 21st Century* (San Diego: Academic Press, 2001).

Maier, N. R. F., *Problem Solving and Creativity in Individuals and Groups* (Belmont, CA: Brooks-Cole, 1970).

Peters, T., *Thriving on Chaos: Handbook for a Management Revolution* (New York: Knopf, 1988).

Ritti, R. R., and S. Levy, *The Ropes to Skip and the Ropes to Know: Studies in Organizational Behavior,* 6th ed. (New York: Wiley, 2003).

Senge, P. M., *The Fifth Discipline* (New York: Doubleday, 1990).

Thamhain, H. J., and D. L. Wilemon, "Conflict Management in Project Life Cycle," *Sloan Management Review,* Vol. 16 (3) 1975, pp. 31–41.

Thoms, P., "Creating a Shared Vision With a Project Team," *PM Network,* January 1997, pp. 33–35.

Townsend, A. M., S. DeMarie, and A. R. Hendrickson, "Virtual Teams: Technology and the Workplace of the Future," *Academy of Management Executive,* Vol. 12 (3) 1998, pp. 17–29.

Tuchman, B. W., and M. C. Jensen, "Stages of Small Group Development Revisited," *Group and Organizational Studies,* Vol. 2 1997, pp. 419–27.

Vroom, V. H., and A. G. Jago, *The New Leadership* (Englewood Cliffs, NJ: Prentice Hall, 1988).

Zander, A., *Making Groups Effective* (San Francisco: Jossey-Bass, 1982).

Case

Kerzner Office Equipment

Amber Briggs looked nervously at her watch as she sat at the front of a large table in the cafeteria at Kerzner Office Equipment. It was now 10 minutes after 3:00 and only 10 of the 14 members had arrived for the first meeting of the Kerzner anniversary task force. Just then two more members hurriedly sat down and mumbled apologies for being late. Briggs cleared her throat and started the meeting.

KERZNER OFFICE EQUIPMENT

Kerzner Office Equipment is located in Charleston, South Carolina. It specializes in the manufacture and sales of high-end office furniture and equipment. Kerzner enjoyed steady growth during its first five years of existence with a high-water employment mark of more than 1,400 workers. Then a national recession struck, forcing Kerzner to lay off 25 percent of its employees. This was a traumatic period for the company. Justin Tubbs was brought in as the new CEO, and things began to slowly turn around. Tubbs was committed to employee participation and redesigned operations around the concept of self-managing teams. The company soon introduced an innovative line of ergonomic furniture designed to reduce back strain and carpal tunnel. This line of equipment proved to be a resounding success, and Kerzner became known as a leader in the industry. The company currently employs 1,100 workers and has just been selected for the second straight time by the *Charleston Post and Courier* as one of the 10 best local firms to work for in South Carolina.

AMBER BRIGGS

Amber Briggs is a 42-year-old human resource specialist who has worked for Kerzner for the past five years. During this time she has performed a variety of activities involving recruitment, training, compensation, and team building. David Brown, vice president of human resources, assigned Briggs the responsibility for organizing Kerzner's 10th anniversary celebration. She was excited about the project because she would report directly to top management.

CEO Tubbs briefed her as to the purpose and objectives of the celebration. Tubbs stressed that this should be a memorable event and that it was important to celebrate Kerzner's success since the dark days of the layoffs. Moreover, he confided that he had just read a book on corporate cultures and believed that such events were important for conveying the values at Kerzner. He went on to say that he wanted this to be an employee celebration—not a celebration conjured up by top management. As such, she would be assigned a task force of 14 employees from each of the major departments to organize and plan the event. Her team was to present a preliminary plan and budget for the event to top management within three months. When discussing budgets, Tubbs revealed that he felt the total cost should be somewhere in the $150,000 range. He concluded the meeting by offering to help Briggs in any way he could to make the event a success.

Soon thereafter Briggs received the list of the names of the task force members, and she contacted them either by phone or e-mail to arrange today's meeting. She had to scramble to find a meeting place. Her cubicle in human resources was too small to accommodate such a group, and all the meeting rooms at Kerzner were booked or being refurbished. She settled on the cafeteria because it was usually deserted in the late afternoon. Prior to the meeting she posted the agenda on a flipchart (see Figure C11.1) adjacent to the table. Given everyone's busy schedules, the meeting was limited to just one hour.

FIGURE C11.1
Celebration Task Force

Agenda

3:00	Introductions
3:15	Project overview
3:30	Ground rules
3:45	Meeting times
4:00	Adjourn

THE FIRST MEETING

Briggs began the meeting by saying, "Greetings. For those who don't know me, I'm Amber Briggs from human resources and I've been assigned to manage the 10th anniversary celebration at Kerzner. Top management wants this to be special event—at the same time they want it to be our event. This is why you are here. Each of you represents one of the major departments, and together our job is to plan and organize the celebration." She then reviewed the agenda and asked each member to introduce him/herself. The tall, red-haired woman to the right of Briggs broke the momentary silence by saying, "Hi, I'm Cara Miller from Plastics. I guess my boss picked me for this task force because I have a reputation for throwing great parties."

In turn each member followed suit. Below is a sampling of their introductions:

"Hi, I'm Mike Wales from maintenance. I'm not sure why I'm here. Things have been a little slow in our department, so my boss told me to come to this meeting."

"I'm Megan Plinski from domestic sales. I actually volunteered for this assignment. I think it will be a lot of fun to plan a big party."

"Yo, my name is Nick Psias from accounting. My boss said one of us had to join this task force, and I guess it was my turn."

"Hi, I'm Rick Fennah. I'm the only one from purchasing who has been here since the beginning. We've been through some rough times, and I think it is important to take time and celebrate what we've accomplished."

"Hi, I'm Ingrid Hedstrom from international sales. I think this is a great idea, but I should warn you that I will be out of the country for most of the next month."

"I'm Abby Bell from engineering. Sorry for being late, but things are a bit crazy in my department."

Briggs circled the names of the two people who were absent and circulated a roster so that everyone could check to see if their phone numbers and e-mail addresses were correct. She then summarized her meeting with Tubbs and told the group that he expected them to make a formal presentation to top management within 10 weeks. She acknowledged that they were all busy people and that it was her job to manage the project as efficiently as possible. At the same time, she reiterated the importance of the project and that this would be a very public event: "If we screw up everyone will know about it."

Briggs went over the ground rules and emphasized that from now on meetings would start on time and that she expected to be notified in advance if someone was going to be absent. She summarized the first part of the project as centering on five key questions: when, where, what, who, and how much? She created a stir in the group when she responded to a question about cost by informing them that top management was willing to pay up to $150,000 for the event. Megan quipped, "This is going to be one hell of a party."

Briggs then turned the group's attention to identifying a common meeting time. After jousting for 15 minutes, she terminated the discussion by requesting that each member submit a schedule of free time over the next month by Friday. She would use this information and a new planning software to identify optimal times. She ended the meeting by thanking the members for coming and asking them to begin soliciting ideas from co-workers about how this event should be celebrated. She announced that she would meet individually with each of them to discuss their role on the project. The meeting was adjourned at 4:00 P.M.

1. Critique Briggs's management of the first meeting. What, if anything, should she have done differently?
2. What barriers is she likely to encounter in completing this project?
3. What can she do to overcome these barriers?
4. What should she do between now and the next meeting?

Franklin Equipment, Ltd.*

Franklin Equipment, Ltd. (FEL), with headquarters and main fabrication facilities in Saint John, New Brunswick, was founded 75 years ago to fabricate custom-designed large machines for construction businesses in the Maritime Provinces. Over the years its product lines became strategically focused on creating rock-crushing equipment for dam and highway construction and for a few other markets that require the processing of aggregate. FEL now designs, fabricates, and assembles stationary and portable rock-crushing plants and services its own products and those of its competitors.

In the 1970s, FEL began to expand its market from the Maritime Provinces to the rest of Canada. FEL currently has several offices and fabrication facilities throughout the country. More recently, FEL has made a concerted effort to market its products internationally.

Last month, FEL signed a contract to design and fabricate a rock-crushing plant for a Middle East construction project, called Project Abu Dhabi. Charles Gatenby secured this contract and has been assigned as project manager. This project is viewed as a coup because FEL has wanted to open up markets in this area for a long time and has had difficulty getting prospective customers to realize that FEL is a Canadian firm and not from the United States. Somehow these customers view all North American vendors as the same and are reluctant to employ any of them because of international political considerations.

A project of this scope typically starts with the selection of a team of managers responsible for various aspects of the design, fabrication, delivery, and installation of the product. Manager selection is important because the product design and fabrication vary with the unique needs of each customer. For example, the terrain, rock characteristics, weather conditions, and logistical concerns create special problems for all phases of plant design and operations. In addition, environmental concerns and labor conditions vary from customer to customer and from region to region.

In addition to the project manager, all projects include a design engineer; an operations manager, who oversees fabrication and on-site assembly; and a cost accountant, who oversees all project financial and cost reporting matters. Each of these people must work closely together if a well-running plant is to be delivered on time and within cost constraints. Because international contracts often require FEL to employ host nationals for plant assembly and to train them for operations, a human resource manager is also assigned to the project team. In such cases, the human resource manager needs to understand the particulars of the plant specifications and then use this knowledge to design selection procedures and assess particular training needs. The human resource manager also needs to learn the relevant labor laws of the customer's country.

FEL assigns managers to project teams based on their expertise and their availability to work on a particular project given their other commitments. This typically means that managers without heavy current project commitments will be assigned to new projects. For instance, a manager finishing one project will likely be assigned a management position on a new project team. The project manager typically has little to say about who is assigned to his or her team.

* Courtesy of John A. Drexler, Jr.

Because he secured Project Abu Dhabi and has established positive working relationships with the Abu Dhabi customer, Gatenby was assigned to be project manager. Gatenby has successfully managed similar projects. The other managers assigned to Project Abu Dhabi are Bill Rankins, a brilliant design engineer, Rob Perry, operations manager with responsibility for fabrication and installation, Elaine Bruder, finance and cost accounting manager, and Sam Stonebreaker, human resource manager. Each of these managers has worked together on numerous past projects.

A few years ago, FEL began contracting for team facilitator services from several consulting firms to help new project teams operate effectively. Last month, FEL recruited Carl Jobe from one of these consulting firms to be a full-time internal consultant. A number of managers, including Gatenby, were so impressed with Jobe's skills that they convinced FEL top management of the need to hire a permanent internal facilitator; Jobe was the obvious choice.

Because Gatenby was instrumental in hiring Jobe at FEL, he was excited at the prospect of using Jobe to facilitate team building among Project Abu Dhabi team members. Gatenby was very proud of having secured this project and had expected to be appointed project manager. He knew that this project's success would be instrumental in advancing his own career.

Gatenby told Jobe, "This project is really important to FEL and to me personally. I really need for you to help us develop into a team that works well together to achieve the project's goals within budget. I've observed your success in developing teams on other projects, and I expect you'll do the same for Project Abu Dhabi. I'll take care of you if you help me make this work."

Jobe outlined for Gatenby how he would proceed. Jobe would begin by interviewing team members individually to learn their perceptions of each other and of the promises and pitfalls of being involved in this project. Meetings of the entire team would follow these interviews using the information he collected to help establish a team identity and a shared vision.

Jobe interviewed Bruder first. She expressed skepticism about whether the project could succeed. During the interview, Bruder appeared to be distant, and Jobe could not figure out why he had not established good rapport with her. Bruder intimated that she expected a lot of cost overruns and a lot of missed production deadlines. But not knowing Jobe well, Bruder was reluctant to identify any specific barriers to the project's success. While she would not directly say so, it was clear to Jobe that Bruder did not want to be a part of Project Abu Dhabi. Jobe left this interview confused and wondering what was going on.

Jobe's next interview was with Perry, the operations manager. Perry has worked at FEL for 15 years, and he immediately came to the point: "This project is not going to work. I cannot understand why upper management keeps assigning me to work on projects with Rankins. We simply cannot work together, and we don't get along. I've disliked him from day one. He keeps dropping the fact that he has earned all these advanced degrees from Purdue. And he keeps telling us how things are done there. I know he's better educated than I am, and he's really smart. But I'm smart too and am good at what I do. There's no need for Rankins to make me feel like an idiot because I don't have a degree. Jobe, I'll be honest with you. Rankins has only been here for five years, but I hold him personally responsible for my problem with alcohol, and for its resulting effect on my marriage. I got divorced last year, and it's Rankins's fault."

Jobe next talked with Rankins, who said, "I don't care what you do. Perry and I simply can't work closely together for the nine months it will take to get it done. One of us will kill the other. Ever since I arrived at FEL, Perry has hated my guts and does everything he can to sabotage my designs. We usually worry about customers creating change orders; here it's the fabrication and operations manager who is responsible for them. Perry second-guesses everything I do and makes design changes on his own, and these are always bad decisions. He is out of control. I swear he stays awake at nights thinking up ways to ruin my designs. I don't have this problem with any other manager."

Jobe left these interviews thoroughly discouraged and could not imagine what would come up in his interview with Stonebreaker. But Stonebreaker was quite positive: "I enjoy these international projects where I get to travel abroad and learn about different cultures. I can't wait to get started on this."

Jobe asked Stonebreaker about the ability of various team members to work together. Stonebreaker replied, "No problem! We've all worked together before and have had no problems. Sure, there have been ruffled feathers and hurt feelings between Rankins and Perry. Rankins can be arrogant and Perry stubborn, but it's never been anything that we can't work around. Besides, both of them are good at what they do—both professionals. They'll keep their heads on straight."

Jobe was even more bewildered. Gatenby says this project's success rides on Jobe's facilitation skills. The finance manager appears to want off this project team. The design engineer and operations manager admit they detest each other and cannot work together. And the human resources manager, having worked on projects with Perry and Rankins before, expects a rosy working relationship and anticipates no problems.

Jobe had a second meeting with Gatenby. Before discussing the design of the team building sessions, he asked questions to learn what Gatenby thought about the ability of team members to work together. Gatenby admitted that there has been very bad blood between Perry and Rankins, but added, "That's why we hired you. It's your job to make sure that the history between those two doesn't interfere with Project Abu Dhabi's success. It's your job to get them to work well together. Get it done."

Their dialogue toward the end of this meeting progressed as follows:

Jobe: "Why do you expect Rankins and Perry to work well together, given their history? What incentives do they have to do so?"

Gatenby: "As you should know, FEL requires formal goal setting between project managers and functional managers at the beginning of each project. I've already done this with Bruder, Stonebreaker, Perry, and Rankins. Perry and Rankins have explicit goals stating they must work well together and cooperate with each other."

Jobe: "What happens if they do not meet these goals?"

Gatenby: "I've already discussed this with top management. If it appears to me after two months that things are not working out between Perry and Rankins, FEL will fire Rankins."

Jobe: "Does Perry know this?"

Gatenby: "Yes."

1. Evaluate the criteria FEL uses to assign managers to project teams. What efficiencies do these criteria create? What are the resulting problems?
2. Why is it even more important that project team members work well together on international projects such as Project Abu Dhabi?
3. Discuss the dilemma that Jobe now faces.
4. What should Jobe recommend to Gatenby?

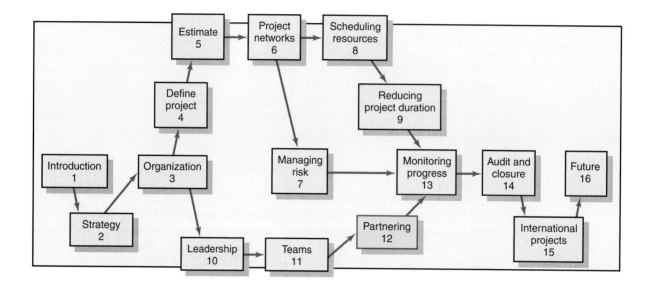

Partnering: Managing Interorganizational Relations

Introduction to Project Partnering

Preproject Activities—Setting the Stage for Successful Partnering

Project Implementation—Sustaining Collaborative Relationships

Project Completion—Celebrating Success

Why Project Partnering Efforts Fail

The Art of Negotiating

A Note on Managing Customer Relations

Summary

Appendix 12.1: Contract Management

CHAPTER TWELVE

Partnering: Managing Interorganizational Relations

. . . being a good partner has become a key corporate asset. I call it a company's collaborative advantage. In the global economy, a well-developed ability to create and sustain fruitful collaborations gives companies a significant competitive leg up.

—Rosabeth Moss Kanter, Harvard Business School professor

It is rare in today's downsized world to find significant projects that are being completed totally in-house. Outsourcing or contracting significant segments of project work to other companies is commonplace. For example, nine states attempting to unify the accounting of all their state agencies did not have the internal resources to implement such a large project. Hence, project teams were formed consisting of personnel from software, hardware, and accounting firms to implement the projects. Small high-tech firms outsource research to determine what features customers value in new products they are developing. Even industry giants such as Microsoft and Intel commonly hire independent firms to test new products they are developing.

Contracting project work has long been the norm in the construction industry, where firms hire general contractors who, in turn, hire and manage cadres of subcontractors to create new buildings and structures. For example, the Chunnel project, which created a transportation tunnel between France and England, involved more than 250 organizations. Contracting is not limited to large projects. For example, an insurance company worked with an outside contractor to develop an answering service that directs customers to specific departments and employees. The trend for the future suggests that more and more projects will involve working with people from different organizations.

This chapter extends the previous two chapters' discussion of building and managing relations by focusing specifically on issues surrounding working with people from other organizations to complete a project. The term *partnering* is used to describe this process. Partnering is a process for transforming contractual arrangements into a cohesive, collaborative team that deals with issues and problems encountered in implementing projects to meet a customer's need. First, the genesis of project partnering and its major assumptions are reviewed. This introduction is followed by a general description of the partnering process and the barriers to collaboration. The focus then shifts to the art of negotiating, which is at the heart of effective partnering. Negotiating skills and techniques for resolving disagreements and reaching optimal solutions are then presented. The chapter closes with a brief note on managing customer relations. In addition, an appendix on contract management is included to suggest some differences in the nature of partnering arrangements—given a particular type of contract.

Introduction to Project Partnering

The term *partnering,* as it relates to projects, emerged during the 1980s in the construction industry. During this period a report conducted by the Construction Industry Institute concluded that "the U.S. Construction Industry is ill." The report went on to document the general decline in productivity over the past two decades. Delays in construction were common and expensive, and litigation related to design and construction was rising at an exponential rate. As one building contractor put it, "The only people making money in construction are the lawyers." In addition, the U.S. construction industry experienced difficulty in securing overseas contracts. Representatives from several countries have stated, "U.S. construction companies were not even considered because of the fear of litigation during and after completion of the project."

The industry response was to test the concept of "partnering" by a few adventurous owners and construction firms. The intent was to keep the formal contract intact but change the way the owner and construction firms interact during project implementation. A variety of definitions of partnering are found in the literature. One of the more popular ones are noted here:

> Project partnering is a method of transforming contractual relationships into a cohesive, cooperative project team with a single set of goals and established procedures for resolving disputes in a timely manner. (Cowan, Gray, & Larson, 1992)

Partnering is more than a set of goals and procedures; it is a state of mind, a philosophy on how to conduct business with other organizations. Partnering represents a commitment from all the participants working on a project to respect, trust, and collaborate. Today, partnering is used across all industries because it makes good business sense.

Partnering is based on the assumption that the traditional adversarial relationship between owner and contractor(s) is ineffective and self-defeating. The basis for this adversarial posturing centers on the inherent conflict between the cost to the owner and the profit to the contractor. This is essentially a zero-sum game in which one party's gain is the other party's loss. The apparent conflict of interest predisposes owners and contractors to be suspicious of the motives and actions of each other. For the owners, this suspicion manifests itself by oppressively monitoring the contractor's performance, challenging each and every request to make an adjustment in plans or budget, and forcing compliance by withholding funds. Contractors respond by exploiting loopholes in the contract, withholding or manipulating information, or taking advantage of the owner's ignorance to inflate cost estimates and charging for unnecessary work.

Suspicion and mistrust prevent effective problem solving. Mistakes and problems are often hidden. When they surface, a game of "hot potato" is played as to who is responsible for correcting them. When conflicts emerge they are often deferred up the hierarchy. This creates costly delays as well as, at times, questionable responses because upper management is often too removed from the situation to make an effective decision. Many disputes end up in court as each side realizes that the only way to protect its interests is through litigation. To some extent litigation becomes a self-fulfilling prophecy. Managers spend almost as much time preparing a case as doing the work.

The tragedy is that often small problems mushroom into major obstacles because problems were not resolved at inception.

Partnering naturally emerged as people began to realize that the traditional win/lose adversarial relationship between owner and contractor degenerates into a costly lose/lose situation for all the parties. Furthermore, partnering assumes that the parties share sufficient common goals to warrant a more collaborative relationship. For example, both contractors and owners want projects completed on time and safely. Neither party wants rework. Both parties would prefer to avoid costly litigation. Each party would like to reduce costs while at the same time improve quality.

The existence of common goals, the prohibitive costs of the adversarial approach, and the benefits that can be shared provide an opportunity for transforming a competitive situation into a more collaborative relationship. The differences between the traditional approach and the partnering approach to managing contracted relationships are summarized in Table 12.1.

Major benefits can be enjoyed when partnering arrangements extend across multiple projects and are long term. For example, Corning and Toyota are among the many firms that have forged a network of long-term strategic partnerships with their suppliers. A recent study indicates that the average large corporation is involved in around thirty alliances today versus fewer than three in the early 1990s. Among the many advantages for establishing a long-term partnership are the following:

- **Reduced administrative costs**—The costs associated with bidding and selecting a contractor are eliminated. Contract administration costs are reduced as partners become knowledgeable of their counterpart's legal concerns.

TABLE 12.1 **Key Practices in Partnering Relationships versus Traditional Practices**	**Key Practices in Partnering Relationships**	**Traditional Practices**
	Mutual trust forms the basis for strong working relationships.	Suspicion and distrust; each party is wary of the motives for actions by the other.
	Shared goals and objectives ensure common direction.	Each party's goals and objectives, while similar, are geared to what is best for them.
	Joint project team exists with high level of interaction.	Independent project teams; teams are spatially separated with managed interactions.
	Open communications avoid misdirection and bolster effective working relationships.	Communications are structured and guarded.
	Long-term commitment provides the opportunity to attain continuous improvement.	Single project contracting is normal.
	Objective critique is geared to candid assessment of performance.	Objectivity is limited due to fear of reprisal and lack of continuous improvement opportunity.
	Access to each other's organization resources is available.	Access is limited with structured procedures and self-preservation taking priority over total optimization.
	Total company involvement requires commitment from CEO to team members.	Involvement is normally limited to project-level personnel.
	Integration of administrative systems equipment takes place.	Duplication and/or translation takes place with attendant costs and delays.
	Risk is shared jointly among the partners, which encourages innovation and continuous improvement.	Risk is transferred to the other party.

FIGURE 12.1
**Project Partnering
Framework**

- **More efficient utilization of resources**—Contractors have a known forecast of work while owners are able to concentrate their workforce on core businesses and avoid the demanding swings of project support.
- **Improved communication**—As partners gain experience with each other, they develop a common language and perspective, which reduces misunderstanding and enhances collaboration.
- **Improved innovation**—The partners are able to discuss innovation and associated risks in a more open manner and share risks and rewards fairly.
- **Improved performance**—Over time partners become more familiar with each other's standards and expectations and are able to apply lessons learned from previous projects to current projects.

Partnering requires more than a simple handshake. Partnering typically entails a considerable up-front investment in time and resources to forge a common team identity among participants from different organizations. It also involves the creation of mechanisms designed to sustain and expand collaboration over the course of the project. The actual partnering process can take many different shapes and forms, depending on the nature of the project and contract, the number of organizations involved, and their prior experience working together. Still, our experience suggests that there are several core elements associated with most first-time partnering endeavors. These elements are summarized in Figure 12.1.

Preproject Activities—Setting the Stage for Successful Partnering

Selecting a Partner(s)

Ideally contractors and even owners are selected based on an established track record of partnering on previous projects. Owners select only contractors with an interest and expertise in partnering. Contractors also screen potential work according to the owner's commitment to partnering principles. In some cases partnering provisions are explicitly stated in an advertised "invitation for bid" (IFB) and are a formal part of the contract. In other cases, the decision to pursue a partnering approach is made after the contract is awarded.

In either case, the first step is to get the commitment of the top management of all the firms involved to use the partnering process. For example, in the case of one public works contract, the owner arranged a meeting with the general contractor. At this meeting the owner congratulated the contractor for winning the contract and expressed a desire to manage the project according to partnering principles. The owner described in detail how this partnership would work and the benefits each would enjoy. The owner was careful to frame the proposal as an invitation and indicated that the contractor was free to choose whether to try partnering. Partnering will not work unless all sides freely commit themselves to implementation. Intimidation, shallow inducements, or halfhearted commitments on the part of either party will likely lead to failure.

Team Building: The Project Managers

Once top management from the major parties agree to try partnering, the next step is to begin to build a collaborative relationship among the key people from each organization who will actually be responsible for managing the project. This typically involves the lead representatives or project managers from the different organizations. For experienced managers this may simply involve meeting to review mutual objectives and outline the implementation of the partnering process. For less experienced managers this may involve more elaborate activities. For example, on one $34 million project, top management decided to send the managers to a weeklong leadership conference where they were exposed to principles of teamwork and effective communication. The training not only reinforced collaborative concepts but more importantly accelerated the evolution of their relationship from strangers to partners. The managers became bonded by a common, exhilarating experience and the development of a common set of project goals.

Team Building: The Stakeholders

Once the principal managers establish a personal commitment to partnering, the next step is to expand this commitment to the other key managers and specialists who will be working together on the project. Team-building workshops are held prior to project implementation that involve all the key players from the different firms, for example, engineers, architects, lawyers, specialists, and other staff. In many cases, firms find it useful to hire an outside consultant to design and facilitate the sessions. Such a consultant is typically well-versed in interorganizational team building and can provide an impartial perspective to the workshop. In other cases, the project managers jointly design and lead the sessions.

The length and design of the team-building sessions will depend on the experience, commitment, and skill level of the participants. For example, one project, in which the owner and the contractors were relatively inexperienced but committed to partnering, utilized a three-day workshop. The first day was devoted to ice-breaking activities and establishing the rationale behind partnering. The conceptual foundation was supported by exercises and minilectures on teamwork, synergy, win/win, and constructive feedback. The second day began by examining the problems and barriers that have prevented collaboration in the past. Representatives from the different organizations were separated and each asked the following:

• What actions do the other groups engage in that create problems for us?
• What actions do we engage in that we think create problems for them?
• What recommendations would we make to improve the situation?

Before starting a bond-financed school construction project, Ohio does what a theater company does before opening night—it holds a dress rehearsal. Led by Cleveland-based Project Management Consultants, state and local school officials, construction managers, and architects get together before building begins to figure out how to talk to each other and how to handle problems.

Just as a theatrical dress rehearsal can allow a company to find and fix glitches before they ruin a show, preconstruction partnering can find early solutions to problems before they become lawsuits.

"This works because traditionally everyone does their own work on a project, behind their own walls," said Jeffrey Applebaum, a construction lawyer and managing director of Project Management Consultants, a wholly owned subsidiary of the law firm of Thompson, Hine, & Flory. "We're taking down the walls. This is more efficient."

"We couldn't be more pleased with this process," said Randy Fischer, executive director of the Ohio School Facilities Commission, which distributes state money to school construction projects. "We are currently administering $3 billion of construction, and we don't have any major disputes."

Crystal Canan, chief of contract administration for the commission, offered a medical metaphor, comparing partnering to a "flu shot" that will prevent the debilitating effects of litigation, work stoppages, and communication breakdowns. "Every building construction project is a candidate for the flu," Canan said. "We see partnering as a vaccination."

*Mary Wisneiski, "Partnering Used to Curb Costs in Ohio School Construction," *Bond Buyer*, 11/22/2000, 334 (31023) 3/4p, 2bw.

The groups shared their responses and asked questions on points needing clarification. Agreements and disparities in the lists were noted and specific problems were identified. Once problem areas were noted, each group was assigned the task of identifying its specific interests and goals for the project. Goals were shared across groups, and special attention was devoted to establishing what goals they had in common. Recognition of shared goals is critical for transforming the different groups into a cohesive team.

Members from the different organizations were put into smaller mixed groups composed of their counterparts from the other organizations. For example, all of the lawyers were put in one group. These groups were assigned specific problems germane to their area of responsibility and asked to work out a recommended solution for each problem. The second day concluded with each group reporting their solutions to the entire group for review and agreement.

The final day of the workshop was devoted to consolidating the efforts of the previous day into a series of agreements and procedures to guide the partnering process. The session culminated with the creation of a project charter signed by all of the participants. This charter states their common goals for the project as well as the procedures that will be used to achieve these goals (see Figure 12.2 for an example of the first page of a project charter).

Carefully setting the stage for successful project implementation is imperative. Too often managers become preoccupied with the plans and technical challenges of the project and assume that people issues will work themselves out over time. Partnering recognizes that people issues are as important if not more important than technical issues. After all, who solves technical problems? Partnering accepts that one of the major barriers to effective collaboration is that participants come from different organizational cultures with different standards, habits, and priorities. The team-building sessions provide an opportunity for people to discuss differences and similarities and to begin to build a relationship with their counterparts before the project starts. At best, a common team culture begins to emerge that is based on successfully completing the project. At worst, participants develop a shared understanding so that cultural differences can coexist while jointly achieving the common objectives of the project.

FIGURE 12.2 Project Partnering Charter

Partnering Charter

Edwards AFB – F-22 Fighter Building 1870

**U.S. Air Force F-22 CTF, 411 FLTS • Edwards AFB Civil Engineers
Computer Science Corporation • Lockheed Martin • Telecom Solutions
U.S. Army Corps of Engineers • Valenzuela Engineering, Inc • VRR & Associates**

We, the partners of the F-22 design and construction team, recognizing the unique nature of this project, commit to creating an environment of trust and communication to design and build a quality project which meets or exceeds the customer's requirements. We commit to maintaining a positive and optimistic work environment in which all partners goals can be achieved.

- **Quality Project**
  - Meet program requirements for F-22 Support Systems.
  - Complete on schedule and within cost constraints.
  - Incorporate lessons learned from other F-22 projects.
  - Create an environment for a fair and reasonable profit.
  - Create an enjoyable work environment.

- **Safe Project**
  - Provide a safe environment.
  - With no lost-time accidents.

- **Maintain positive, cooperative relationships**
  - Clear and open communications through appropriate channels.
  - No surprises.
  - No hidden agendas.
  - Minimum delays of paperwork.
  - Resolve problems quickly at the lowest level.

The Partnering concept is a team relationship that promotes the achievement of mutually beneficial goals. This Partnering Charter does not create any legally enforceable rights or duties. Any changes to the contracts must be made by the contracting officers under the terms of the written contracts.

387

Project Implementation—Sustaining Collaborative Relationships

One of the objectives of the team-building sessions is to establish a "we" as opposed to "us and them" attitude among the different participants toward the project. Some companies reinforce this point by having the management teams from the different organizations work at the same location. Our experience tells us that co-location is critical and well worth the added expense and inconvenience. A second objective of the sessions is to establish in advance mechanisms designed to ensure that this collaborative spirit is able to withstand the problems and setbacks that will invariably occur on the project. These mechanisms require the unwavering, consistent, and fanatical support of senior management. Among the most significant mechanisms are problem resolution, continuous improvement, joint evaluation, and persistent leadership.

Problem Resolution

Escalation is the primary control mechanism for dealing with and resolving problems. The basic principle is that problems should be resolved at the lowest level within a set time limit (i.e., 24 hours), or they are "escalated" to the next level of management. If so, the principals have the same time limit to resolve the problem, or it gets passed on to the next higher level. No action is not an option. Nor can one participant force concessions from the other by simply delaying the decision. There is no shame in pushing significant problems up the hierarchy; at the same time, managers should be quick to point out to subordinates those problems or questions that they should have been able to resolve on their own.

Continuous Improvement

Partnering assumes that continuous improvement is a joint effort to eliminate waste and pursue opportunities for cost savings. Risks as well as benefits are typically shared 50/50 between the principals, with the owner adhering to a fast-track review to withstand the problems and setbacks that will invariably occur in the project/approval process. The Snapshot from Practice box on page 390 shows an alternative arrangement from a project involving two partners and an owner.

Joint Evaluation

All involved parties meet on a regular basis to review and evaluate the partnering process. Specific criteria relating to the effectiveness of the partnering process such as teamwork and timely problem resolution are evaluated. This provides a forum for identifying problems not only with the project but also with working relationships so that they can be resolved quickly and appropriately. Evaluation of the partnering process usually includes a periodic survey. Comparison of survey responses period by period identifies areas of improvement and potential problems. See Figure 12.3 for a partial example of a survey.

Persistent Leadership

Project managers and their subordinates must "walk the talk" and consistently display a collaborative as opposed to confrontational response to problem solving. This is especially true early in the project, where mutual trust will be tested by how the partners respond to the first disagreements or setbacks that emerge. Project managers have to reward those within their own organization who adhere to the principles of partnering as well as admonish those who resort to more adversarial practices. Finally, when it is time to celebrate a significant milestone, no matter who is responsible, all parties should gather to celebrate the success. This reinforces a common purpose.

FIGURE 12.3
Sample Partnering Evaluation

Evaluation of partnering process: attitudes, teamwork, process.
(Collected separately from owner and contractor participants, compared, and aggregated.)

1. Communications between the owner/contractor personnel are

1	2	3	4	5

Difficult,
guarded

Easy, open,
up front

2. Top management support of partnering process is

1	2	3	4	5

Not evident or
inconsistent

Obvious and
consistent

3. Problems, issues, or concerns are

1	2	3	4	5

Ignored

Attacked
promptly

4. Cooperation between owner and contractor personnel is

1	2	3	4	5

Cool, detached,
unresponsive,
removed

Genuine,
unreserved,
complete

5. Responses to problems, issues, or concerns frequently become

1	2	3	4	5

Personal issues

Treated as
project problems

Project Completion—Celebrating Success

Once the project is completed, management needs to jointly review accomplishments as well as disappointments and derive lessons to be applied to future projects. This formal review of project execution is typically accompanied by a more festive celebration (picnic or banquet) involving all the participants. Top management takes advantage of this social function to recognize special contributions. Such a festivity provides a sense of closure and reaffirms the collaborative nature of the project.

Why Project Partnering Efforts Fail

Organizational downsizing and concentration on utilizing core competencies has already increased the use of outside sources to assist or implement projects. The trend for the future suggests partnering will be more common. Partnering is critical to the emergence of virtual organizations and projects (see the Snapshot from Practice on page 368 for an example). The challenge is to get the project completed on time, within budget, and to customer specifications. Although the results achieved from successful partnering can be phenomenal, we have noticed three areas that lead to the breakdown of the partnering arrangement and one area that is frequently overlooked.

The first and most significant problem is with senior management—the owner and contractor. The owner and contractor must have compelling reasons to make the partnering relationship work. Although most partnering arrangements start out with good intentions, when senior management fails to keep on top of the project and partnership, the

The snapshot describes conversations with the project manager of the project.

The project was to design and build a high technology oil drilling ship for the North Sea. The ship would be capable of finding the selected location within less than one meter and hold the location for drilling. The project included the owner and two major partners. Early, precontract meetings indicated all three were interested in the benefits partnering could offer. All three wanted to complete the project on time, within budget, and to meet specifications.

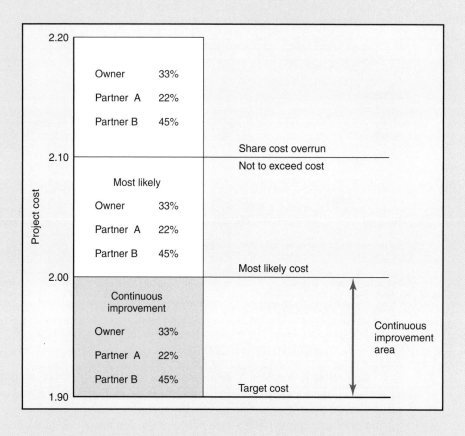

After several meetings, the owner and partners agreed to a simple incentive system to encourage continuous improvement during project implementation. The crux of the system centered on sharing *proportionally* any savings in total project cost or in cost overruns. The proportions for the project were determined by the money value each controlled—the owner, 33 percent, and 22 percent and 45 percent, respectively, for the partners.

The project manager used the above exhibit to explain the numbers and process to all stakeholders. The partners agreed to three cost levels—*not-to-exceed cost, most likely cost,* and *target cost.* The manager said, "Getting to these agreed costs was sticky, but we did it." The project manager related that everyone came out a winner! The project was on time, under target cost, and met specifications and expectations. He believed success can be attributed to primarily three factors:

1. The incentive system forced the owner to join the effort.
2. Sharing was proportional to cost responsibility.
3. The three project teams were joined, housed in one location. Responsibility for project implementation, control, and improvements was charged to the merged project team.

He suggested that the last factor of merging the three independent teams in one location seems to be the key that significantly increases the chances of partnering success.

SATT Control (SC) is a Swedish electronics firm that sells electronic products and control systems worldwide. It has 550 employees in Sweden and about the same number abroad. So how does SC successfully bid against such electronic giants as ABB, Siemens, and Hewlett-Packard on major contracts for equipment that the company has never sold before? In the words of Hedberg and his coauthors, SC does so by acting as system integrator. In this role SC recruits a contracting syndicate by preparing a system description and dividing the system into various subsystems with each potential partner bidding for a part of the system. SC's ability to describe the system and divide it into subsystems that can be outsourced are two of its core competencies.

Another core competence at SC is project management. After the company has received an order for a project, one of the first actions taken is to work with the customer to be develop clear specification of functions. While time consuming, this process is critical to be successful. The first step is to specify what the system is supposed to do, before deciding how it is to be done. This is commonly referred to as designing system architecture. It is crucial that the specifications are correct at the outset otherwise errors reappear all down the line. SC works hard at developing a common agreement among all the partners as to what the basic concept of the project is.

SC is also adroit at establishing a collaborative atmosphere among all the partners. The key is instilling a sense of "what is good for you is good for me." This comes from a history of treating each other with mutual respect and drafting contracts that share risks not isolate risks.

*B. Hedberg, G. Dahlgren, J. Hansson, and N-G. Olve, *Virtual Organizations and Beyond* (New York: Wiley, 1997), pp. 82–84.

seeds for failure are planted. The breakdown typically begins with a problem that needs resolution. A minor problem is escalated instead of solving the problem at the first level. Team members are hesitant to accept risk. The owner and contractor fail to return the problem to the first level where it should have been solved. Soon all problems are escalated and the relationship deteriorates as both sides hurl accusations and begin defensive posturing. Senior management must give clear signals that team members are empowered and encouraged to make decisions at the lowest possible level. The same problem occurs when senior management fails to resolve an escalated problem within the time limits set. Senior management is not leading the way. Senior management support of the partnering process cannot be ad hoc; leadership and commitment must be 100 percent and constant. Partnering will only be successful if senior management works at it!

A second major reason partnering arrangements break down is the failure to adequately deal with cultural differences among the contributing organizations. Differences in management styles, terminology, operating procedures, and perspectives of time can result in culture shock that frustrates the development and maintenance of good rapport between the participants. The key is to try to merge these cultural differences into a common team culture that is based on successfully completing the project. This process begins with the team-building sessions but must be a priority agenda item throughout the duration of the project. Much of the material on developing a high-performance team discussed in the previous chapter must be applied. Each organization must also be careful to select and place savvy professionals in key positions who are adept at forging relationships with people who do not necessarily share the same priorities, time orientation, or work habits.

A third reason for a partnering relationship to deteriorate is the absence or lack of use of a formal evaluation procedure. We estimate that fewer than 20 percent of partnering projects have a formal, effective procedure for evaluating the partnering process. Without regular evaluation, problems and deterioration of the process cannot be recognized until it is too late to correct things. Regardless of the procedure used (questionnaires, interviews by outsiders, weekly evaluation meetings), the procedure should regularly identify problems and opportunities at the operating level. In addition, the evaluation should measure and track the overall state of the partnering relationship. The "partnering report card" measures team performance and encourages team accountability. It measures if the relationship is improving or degenerating.

Photo by Sgt. Ken Hammond, U.S. Air Force.

As part of an effort to cut costs the United States Department of Defense (DoD) issues annual Value Engineering Awards. Value engineering is a systematic process to analyze functions to identify actions to reduce cost, increase quality, and improve mission capabilities across the entire spectrum of DoD systems, processes, and organizations. The Value Engineering Awards Program is an acknowledgement of outstanding achievements and encourages additional projects to improve in-house and contractor productivity.

In 2002 HBA Architecture, Engineering, and Interior Design, a Virginia Beach based firm, was selected as the Outstanding Navy Contractor. HBA's work on 3 projects was cited in the award:

- Design Maintenance and Operations Facility for the 2nd Marine Division Reconnaissance Battalion in Camp Lejeune, NC. Unique to the project was a curved glass wall designed to prevent infiltration by conventional listening devices and an 80 foot tall parachute drying tower that will double as a reppelling platform for training.

- Renovation of an aircraft maintenance hangar originally constructed in 1954 at Cherry Point, NC. A major portion of the work was devoted to the Under-Floor Aqueous Fire Fighting Foam (AFFF) Fire Suppression System throughout the hangar bays.

- Aircraft stripping facility addition at Naval Aviation Dept. in Cherry Point, NC. Designed a new PMB (Plastic Media Blasting) Hangar enclosure and training spaces to allow the Navy to strip aircraft as large as the V-22 (Ospry). PMB is a dry abrasive blasting process, designed to replace chemical stripping operations and conventional sand blasting.

HBA was recognized for using state-of-the art electronic technologies to produce functional design alternatives and communicate project value improvement that could be evaluated efficiently by the client. These efforts saved $20 million in design costs and $1.6 million in life-cycle costs.

During fiscal 2001, more than 2,100 in-house value engineer proposals and contractor-initiated value engineering change proposals were accepted by the Department of Defense with projected savings in excess of $768 million.

*http://www.defenselink.mil/news/Nov2002/b11222002_bt596-02.html

Finally, there is one opportunity a majority of partnering arrangements fail to exploit as fully as they should—continuous improvement. In many partnering projects lip service is given to continuous improvement, but that is the extent of it. In the words of one owner, "I expect that of any hired software contractor." The key, for those who have been successful, is setting up an incentive to encourage a contractor to seek improvements and innovation as the project is implemented. A procedure needs to be set up before the project begins. In essence there is little incentive for a contractor to strive for improvements, except for repeat business and reputation. All of the risk of innovation failure is on the contractor. An approach known as the "50/50 percent split" appears to work well and has resulted in savings of millions of dollars across a variety of projects—for example, R&D, construction, time to market. This procedure has the owner and contractor share the costs (risks) for any innovation and rewards on a 50/50 basis. How the U.S. Department of Defense reaps the benefits of continuous improvement through value engineering is highlighted in the adjacent Snapshot from Practice: Value Engineering Awards.

Partnering is a conscious effort on the part of management to form collaborative relationships with personnel from different organizations to complete a project. For partnering to work, the individuals involved need to be effective negotiators capable of merging interests and discovering solutions to problems that contribute to the ultimate success of the project and the partnership. The next section addresses some of the key skills and techniques associated with effective negotiation.

The Art of Negotiating

Effective negotiating is critical to successful partnering. All it takes is one key discussion to unravel a partnering arrangement. At the same time, negotiating is pervasive through all aspects of project management work. Project managers must negotiate support and funding from top management. They must negotiate staff and technical input from functional managers. They must coordinate with other project managers and negotiate project priorities and commitments. They must negotiate within their project team to determine assignments, deadlines, standards, and priorities. Project managers must negotiate prices and standards with vendors and suppliers. A firm understanding of the negotiating process, skills, and tactics is essential to project success.

Many people approach negotiating as if it is a competitive contest. Each negotiator is out to win as much as he or she can for his or her side. Success is measured by how much is gained compared with the other party. While this may be applicable when negotiating the sale of a house, it is not true for project management. *Project management is not a contest.* First, the people working on the project, whether they represent different companies or departments within the same organization, are not enemies or competitors but rather allies or partners. They have formed a temporary alliance to complete a project. For this alliance to work requires a certain degree of trust, cooperation, and honesty. Second, although the parties within this alliance may have different priorities and standards, they are bound by the success of the project. If conflicts escalate to the point where negotiations break down and the project comes to a halt, then everyone loses. Third, unlike bartering with a street vendor, the people involved on project work have to continue to work together. Therefore, it behooves them to resolve disagreements in a way that contributes to the long-term effectiveness of their working relationship. Finally, as pointed out in the previous chapter, conflict on a project can be good. When dealt with effectively it can lead to innovation, better decisions, and more creative problem solving.

Project managers accept this noncompetitive view of negotiation and realize that negotiation is essentially a two-part process: The first part deals with reaching an agreement; the second part is the implementation of that agreement. It is the implementation phase, not the agreement itself, that determines the success of negotiations. All too often, managers reach an agreement with someone only to find out later that they failed to do what they agreed to do or that their actual response fell far short of expectations. Experienced project managers recognize that implementation is based on satisfaction not only with the outcome but also with the process by which the agreement was

TABLE 12.2
Principled
Negotiation

1. Separate the people from the problem
2. Focus on interests, not positions
3. Invent options for mutual gain
4. When possible, use objective criteria

reached. If someone feels they have been bullied or tricked into doing something, this feeling will invariably be reflected by halfhearted compliance and passive resistance.

Veteran project managers do the best they can to merge individual interests with what is best for the project and come up with effective solutions to problems. Fisher and Ury from the Harvard Negotiation Project champion an approach to negotiating that embodies these goals. It emphasizes developing win/win solutions while protecting yourself against those who would take advantage of your forthrightness. Their approach is called *principled negotiation* and is based on four key points listed in Table 12.2 and discussed in the following sections.

Separate the People from the Problem

Too often personal relations become entangled with the substantive issues under consideration. Instead of attacking the problem(s), people attack each other. Once people feel attacked or threatened their energy naturally goes to defending themselves, and not to solving the problem. The key, then, to is to focus on the problem—not the other person—during the negotiation. Avoid personalizing the negotiation and framing the negotiation as a contest. Instead, try to keep the focus on the problem to be resolved. In Fisher and Ury's words: *Be hard on the problem, soft on the people.*

By keeping the focus on the issues and not the personalities, negotiators are better able to let the other person blow off steam. On important problems it is not uncommon for people to become upset, frustrated, and angry. However, one angry attack produces an angry counterattack, and the discussion quickly escalates into a heated argument, an emotional chain reaction. In some cases people use anger as a means of intimidating and forcing concessions because the other person wishes to preserve the relationship. When people become emotional, negotiators should keep a cool head and remember the old German proverb, "Let anger fly out the window." In other words, in the face of an emotional outburst, imagine opening a window and letting the heat of the anger out the window. Avoid taking things personally, and redirect personal attacks back to the question at hand. Don't react to the emotional outburst, but try to find the issues that triggered it. Skilled negotiators keep their cool under stressful times and, at the same time, build a bond with others by empathizing and acknowledging common sources of frustration and anger.

While it is important to separate the people from the problem during actual negotiations, it is beneficial to have a friendly rapport with the other person prior to negotiating. Friendly rapport is consistent with the social network tenet introduced in Chapter 10 of building a relationship before you need it. Reduce the likelihood of misunderstandings and getting off on the wrong foot by having a history of interacting in a friendly, responsive manner with the other person. If, in the past, the relationship has been marked by healthy give-and-take, in which both parties have demonstrated a willingness to accommodate the interests of the other, then neither individual is likely to adopt an immediate win/lose perspective. Furthermore, a positive relationship adds a common interest beyond the specific points of contention. Not only do both parties want to reach an agreement that suits their individual interests, but they also want to do so in a manner that preserves their relationship. Each is therefore more likely to seek solutions that are mutually beneficial.

Focus on Interests, not Positions

Negotiations often stall when people focus on positions:

> I'm willing to pay $10,000. No, it will cost $15,000.
>
> I need it done by Monday. That's impossible, we can't have it ready until Wednesday.

While such interchanges are common during preliminary discussions, managers must prevent this initial posturing from becoming polarized. When such positions are stated, attacked, and then defended, each party figuratively begins to draw a line he or she will not cross. This line creates a win/lose scenario in which someone has to lose by crossing the line in order to reach an agreement. As such, the negotiations can become a war of wills, with concessions being seen as a loss of face.

The key is to focus on the interests behind your positions (what you are trying to achieve) and separate these goals from your ego as best you can. Not only should you be driven by your interests, but you should try to identify the interests of the other party. Ask why it will cost so much or why it can't be done by Monday. At the same time, make your own interests come alive. Don't just say that it is critical that it be done by Monday; explain what will happen if it isn't done by Monday.

Sometimes when the true interests of both parties are revealed, there is no basis for conflict. Take, for example, the Monday versus Wednesday argument. This argument could apply to a scenario involving a project manager and the production manager of a small, local firm that was contracted to produce prototypes of a new generation of computer mouse. The project manager needs the prototypes on Monday to demonstrate to a users' focus group. The production manager said it would be impossible. The project manager said this would be embarrassing because marketing had spent a lot of time and effort setting up this demonstration. The production manager again denied the request and added that he already had to schedule overtime to meet the Wednesday delivery date. However, when the project manager revealed that the purpose of the focus group was to gauge consumers' reactions to the color and shape of the new devices, not the finished product, the conflict disappeared. The production manager told the project manager that she could pick up the samples today if she wanted because production had an excess supply of shells.

When focusing on interests, it is important to keep in mind that one of the habits of effective interpersonal communication is, *Seek first to understand, then to be understood*. This involves what Stephen Covey calls empathetic listening, which allows a person to fully understand another person's frame of reference—not only what they are saying but also how they feel. Covey asserts that people have an inherent need to be understood. He goes on to observe that satisfied needs do not motivate human behavior, only unsatisfied needs do. People try to go to sleep when they are tired, not when they are rested. The key point is that until the other party believes they are being understood, they will expend time and energy trying to bring about that understanding. They will repeat their points and reformulate their arguments. If, on the other hand, you satisfy this need by seeking first to understand, then the other party is free to understand your interests and focus directly on the issues at hand. Seeking to understand requires discipline and compassion. Instead of responding to the other person by asserting your agenda, respond by summarizing both the facts and feelings behind what the other person has said and checking the accuracy of comprehension.

Invent Options for Mutual Gain

Once the individuals involved have identified their interests, then they can explore options for mutual gain. This is not easy. Stressful negotiations inhibit creativity and free exchange. What is required is collaborative brainstorming in which people work together to solve the problem in a way that will lead to a win/win scenario. The key to brainstorming is separating the inventing from the deciding. Begin by taking 15 minutes to generate as many options as possible. No matter how outlandish any option is, it should not be subject to criticism or immediate rejection. People should feed off the ideas of others to generate new ideas. When all the possible options are exhausted, then sort through the ideas that were generated to focus on those with the greatest possibilities.

Clarifying interests and exploring mutual options creates the opportunity for dovetailing interests. Dovetailing means one person identifies options that are of low cost to them but of high interest to the other party. This is only possible if each party knows what the other's needs are. For example, in negotiating price with a parts supplier, a project manager learned from the discussion that the supplier was in a cash flow squeeze after purchasing a very expensive fabrication machine. Needed cash was the primary reason the supplier had taken such a rigid position on price. During the brainstorming session, one of the options presented was to prepay for the order instead of the usual payment on delivery arrangement. Both parties seized on this option and reached an amicable agreement in which the project manager would pay the supplier for the entire job in advance in exchange for a faster turnaround time and a significant price reduction. Such opportunities for win/win agreements are often overlooked because the negotiators become fixated on solving their problems and not on opportunities to solve the other person's problems.

When Possible, Use Objective Criteria

Most established industries and professions have developed standards and rules to help deal with common areas of dispute. Both buyers and sellers rely on the blue book to establish price parameters for a used car. The construction industry has building codes and fair practice policies to resolve proof of quality and safe work procedures. The legal profession uses precedents to adjudicate claims of wrongdoing.

Whenever possible, you should insist on using external, objective criteria to settle disagreements. For example, a disagreement arose between a regional airlines firm and the independent accounting team entrusted with preparing the annual financial statement. The airline firm had made a significant investment by leasing several used airplanes from a larger airline. The dispute involved whether this lease should be classified as an operating or capital lease. This was important to the airline because if the purchase was classified as an operating lease, then the associated debt would not have to be recorded in the financial statement. However, if the purchase was classified as a capital lease, then the debt would be factored into the financial statement and the debt/equity ratio would be much less attractive to stockholders and would-be investors. The two parties resolved this dispute by deferring to formulas established by the Financial Accounting Standards Board. As it turns out the accounting team was correct, but, by deferring to objective standards, they were able to deflect the disappointment of the airline managers away from the accounting team and preserve a professional relationship with that firm.

Dealing with Unreasonable People

Most people working on projects realize that in the long run it is beneficial to work toward mutually satisfying solutions. Still, occasionally you encounter someone who has a dominant win/lose attitude about life and will be difficult to deal with. Fisher and Ury recommend that you use negotiation jujitsu when dealing with such a person. That is, when the other person begins to push, don't push back. As in the martial arts, avoid pitting your strengths against theirs directly; instead use your skill to step aside and turn their strength to your ends. When someone adamantly sets forth a position, neither reject it nor accept it. Treat it as a possible option and then look for the interests behind it. Instead of defending your ideas, invite criticism and advice. Ask why it's a bad idea and discover the other's underlying interest.

Those who use negotiation jujitsu rely on two primary weapons. They ask questions instead of making statements. Questions allow for interests to surface and do not provide the opponent with something to attack. The second weapon is silence. If the other person makes an unreasonable proposal or attacks you personally, just sit there and don't say a word. Wait for the other party to break the stalemate by answering your question or coming up with a new suggestion.

The best defense against unreasonable, win/lose negotiators is having what Fisher and Ury call a strong BATNA (best alternative to a negotiated agreement). They point out that people try to reach an agreement to produce something better than the result of not negotiating with that person. What those results would be (BATNA) is the true benchmark for determining whether you should accept an agreement. A strong BATNA gives you the power to walk away and say, "No deal unless we work toward a win/win scenario."

Your BATNA reflects how dependent you are on the other party. If you are negotiating price and delivery dates and can choose from a number of reputable suppliers, then you have a strong BATNA. If on the other hand there is only one vendor who can supply you with specific, critical material on time, then you have a weak BATNA. Under these circumstances you may be forced to concede to the vendor's demands. At the same time, you should begin to explore ways of increasing your BATNA for future negotiations. This can be done by reducing your dependency on that supplier. Begin to find substitutable material or negotiate better lead times with other vendors.

Negotiating is an art. There are many intangibles involved. This section has reviewed some time-tested principles of effective negotiating based on the groundbreaking work of Fisher and Ury. Given the significance of negotiating, you are encouraged to read their book as well as others on negotiating. In addition, attending training workshops can provide an opportunity to practice these skills. You should also take advantage of day-to-day interactions to sharpen negotiating acumen.

A Note on Managing Customer Relations

In Chapter 4 it was emphasized that ultimate success is not determined by whether the project was completed on time, within budget, or according to specifications, but whether the customer is satisfied with what has been accomplished. Customer satisfaction is the bottom line. Bad news travels faster and farther than good news. For every happy customer who shares his satisfaction regarding a particular product or service with another person, a dissatisfied customer is likely to share her dissatisfaction with eight other people. Project managers need to cultivate positive working relations with clients to ensure success and preserve their reputations.

Customer satisfaction is a complex phenomenon. One simple but useful way of viewing customer satisfaction is in terms of met expectations. According to this model, customer satisfaction is a function of the extent to which perceived performance (or outcome) exceeds expectations. Mathematically, this relationship can be represented as the ratio between perceived performance and expected performance (see Figure 12.4). When performance falls short of expectations (ratio $<$ 1), the customer is dissatisfied. If the performance matches expectations (ratio $=$ 1), the customer is satisfied. If the performance exceeds expectations (ratio $>$ 1), the customer is very satisfied or even delighted.

FIGURE 12.4
The Met-Expectations Model of Customer Satisfaction

$$\underset{\text{Dissatisfied}}{0.90} = \frac{\text{Perceived performance}}{\text{Expected performance}} = \underset{\text{Very satisfied}}{1.10}$$

High customer satisfaction is the goal of most projects. However, profitability is another major concern. Exceeding expectations typically entails additional costs. For example, completing a construction project two weeks ahead of schedule may involve significant overtime expenses. Similarly, exceeding reliability requirements for a new electronic component may involve considerably more design and debugging effort. Under most circumstances, the most profitable arrangement occurs when the customer's expectations are only slightly exceeded. Returning to the mathematical model, with all other things being equal, one should strive for a satisfaction ratio of 1.05, not 1.5!

The met-expectations model of customer satisfaction highlights the point that whether a client is dissatisfied or delighted with a project is not based on hard facts and objective data but on perceptions and expectations. For example, a customer may be dissatisfied with a project that was completed ahead of schedule and under budget if he thought the work was poor quality and that his fears and concerns were not adequately addressed by the project team. Conversely, a customer may be very satisfied with a project that was over budget and behind schedule if she felt the project team protected her interests and did the best job possible under adverse circumstances.

Project managers must be skilled at managing customer expectations and perceptions. Too often they deal with these expectations after the fact when they try to alleviate a client's dissatisfaction by carefully explaining why the project cost more or took longer than planned. A more proactive approach is to begin to shape the proper expectations up front and accept that this is an ongoing process throughout the life of a project. Project managers need to direct their attention to both the customer's base expectations, the standard by which perceived performance will be evaluated, and to the customer's perceptions of actual performance. The ultimate goal is to educate clients so that they can make a valid judgment as to project performance as well as reduce chances for misunderstandings that can lead to disappointment and dissatisfaction.

Managing customer expectations begins during the preliminary project approval phase of negotiations. It is important to avoid the temptation to oversell the virtues of a project to win approval because this may create unrealistic expectations that may be too difficult, if not impossible, to achieve. At the same time, project proponents have been known to lower customer expectations by underselling projects. If the estimated completion time is 10 to 12 weeks, they will promise to have the project completed within 12 to 14 weeks, therefore increasing the chances of exceeding customer expectations by getting the project completed early.

Once the project is authorized, the project manager and team need to work closely with the client organization to develop a well-defined project scope statement that clearly states the objectives, parameters, and limits of the project work. The project scope statement is essential to establishing customer expectations regarding the project. It is critical that all parties are in agreement as to what is to be accomplished and that people are reading as best they can from the same page. It is also important to share significant risks that might disrupt project execution. Customers do not like surprises, and if they are aware in advance of potential problems they are much more likely to be accepting of the consequences.

Once the project is initiated it is important to keep customers abreast of project progress. The days when you would simply take orders from customers and tell them to return when the project is done are over. More and more organizations and their project managers are treating their customers as de facto members of the project team and are actively involving them in key aspects of project work. In the case of consulting assignments project managers sometimes *morph* into a member of the client organization (see Research Highlight: IT Project Managers).

Webber and Torti studied the multiple roles project managers play on IT projects. Based on a comprehensive set of interviews with project managers and clients in three different information-technology service organizations, they identified five key roles critical to successfully implement IT projects in client organizations: entrepreneur, politician, friend, marketer, and coach. They are described in part in Table 12.3.

TABLE 12.3
Project Roles, Challenges, and Strategies

Project Manager Roles	Challenges	Strategies
Entrepreneur	Navigate unfamiliar surroundings	Use persuasion to influence others
Politician	Understand two diverse cultures (parent and client organization)	Align with the powerful individuals
Friend	Determine the important relationships to build and sustain outside the team itself	Identify common interests and experiences to bridge a friendship with the client
Marketer	Understand the strategic objectives of the client organization	Align new ideas/proposals with the strategic objectives of the client organization
Coach	Motivate client team members without formal authority	Provide challenging tasks to build the skills of the team members

Webber and Torti observed that instead of maintaining a clearly defined relationship with the client, project managers become part of the client organization. They report that project managers attempt to "dress like the client, act like the client, and participate in the client organization's activities (i.e., social gatherings, blood drives, etc.)." They become such an integral part of their existence that many client employees, over the course of time, forget that the project manager is not an employee of the client organization. This helps establish a degree of trust essential to effective collaboration.

*S. S. Webber, and M. T. Torti, "Project Managers Doubling as Client Account Executives," *Academy of Management Executive,* Vol. 18, No. 1, pp. 60–71, 2004.

Project managers need to keep customers informed of project developments so that customers can make adjustments in their own plans. When circumstances dictate changing the scope or priorities of the project, project managers need to be quick to spell out as best they can the implications of these changes to the customers so that they can make an informed choice. Active customer involvement allows customers to naturally adjust their expectations in accordance with the decisions and events that transpire on a project, while at the same time, the customer's presence keeps the project team focused on the customer's objectives for the project.

Active customer involvement also provides a firmer basis for assessing project performance. The customer not only sees the results of the project but also acquires glimpses of the effort and actions that produced those results. Naturally project managers want to make sure these glimpses reflect favorably on their project teams, so they exercise extra care that customer interactions are handled in a competent and professional manner. In some respects, customer perceptions of performance are shaped more by how well the project team deals with adversity than by actual performance. Project managers can impress customers with how diligently they deal with unexpected problems and setbacks. Likewise, industry analysts have noted that customer dissatisfaction can be transformed into customer satisfaction by quickly correcting mistakes and being extremely responsive to customer concerns.

Managing customer relations on a project is a broad topic; we have only highlighted some of the central issues involved. This brief segment concludes with two words of advice passed on by veteran project managers:

Speak with one voice. Nothing erodes confidence in a project more than for a customer to receive conflicting messages from different project members. The project manager should remind team members of this fact and work with them to ensure that appropriate information is shared with customers.

Speak the language of the customer. Too often project members respond to customer inquiries with technical jargon that exceeds the customer's vocabulary. Project managers and members need to describe problems, trade-offs, and solutions in ways that the customer can understand.

Summary

More and more companies are seeking cooperative arrangements with each other to compete in today's business world. Project partnering represents a proactive response to many of the challenges associated with working with people from different organizations. Before the project is started, significant time and effort are invested up front to build relationships among stakeholders and develop agreed-upon procedures and provisions for dealing with problems and opportunities before they happen. These procedures typically include joint assessments of how well the partnering arrangement is working, escalation guidelines for resolving disputes in a timely and effective manner, and provisions for process improvement and risk sharing. Persistent leadership is required to make partnering work. Project managers must "walk the talk" and consistently display a collaborative response to problems. Similarly, top management must consistently and visibly champion the principles of openness, trust, and teamwork.

Partnering is not limited to contracted relationships. More and more companies are applying the partnering approach to managing internal projects involving different subsidiaries and departments. For example, in a large high-tech firm a team made up of 49 individuals from multiple disciplines used partnering to establish a more cohesive, cooperative relationship to implement their section of a project.

Effective negotiating skills are essential to making partnering work. People need to resolve differences at the lowest level possible in order to keep the project on track. Veteran project managers realize that negotiating is not a competitive game and work toward collaborative solutions to problems. They accomplish this by separating people from the problem, focusing on interests and not positions, inventing options for mutual gain, and relying on objective criteria whenever possible to resolve disagreements. They also recognize the importance of developing a strong BATNA, which provides them with the leverage necessary to seek collaborative solutions.

Customer satisfaction is the litmus test for project success. Project managers need to take a proactive approach to managing customer expectations and perceptions. They need to actively involve customers in key decisions and keep them abreast of important developments. Active customer involvement keeps the project team focused on the objectives of the project and reduces misunderstandings and dissatisfaction.

Key Terms

Best alternative to a negotiated agreement (BATNA)	Escalation	Partnering charter
	Joint evaluation	Principled negotiation
Co-location	Met-expectations model	Project partnering

Review Questions

1. Why should contractors and owners want to enter a partnering arrangement with each other?

2. Why do proponents of partnering claim that it is a proactive approach to managing projects?

3. What does the term "escalate" refer to, and why is it essential to project partnering success?

4. Why is the principle negotiation approach recommended for negotiating agreements on projects?

5. What does the acronym BATNA refer to, and why is it important to being a successful negotiator?

6. How can a project manager influence customer expectations and perceptions?

Exercises

1. Break into groups of four to five students. Assign half of the groups the role of Owner and the other half the role of Contractor.

   Owners: After saving for many years you are about to hire a contractor to build your "dream home." What are your objectives for this project? What concerns or issues do you have about working with a general contractor to build your home?

   Contractors: You specialize in building customized homes. You are about to meet with prospective owners to begin to negotiate a contract for building their "dream home." What are your objectives for this project? What concerns or issues do you have about working with the owners to build their home?

   Each Owner group meets with another Contractor group and shares their objectives, concerns, and issues.

   Identify what objectives, issues, and concerns you have in common and which ones are unique. Discuss how you could work together to realize your objectives. What would be the keys to working as partners on this project?

2. Enter "partnering" in an Internet search engine and browse different websites containing information on partnering (you may have to narrow your search to "project partnering" or "construction partnering"). Who appears to be interested in partnering? What kinds of projects is partnering being applied to? Does partnering mean the same thing to different people?

References

Charles Cowan, C., C. F. Gray, and E. Larson, "Project Partnering," *Project Management Journal,* Vol. 12, No. 4, December 1992, pp. 5–15.

Covey, S. R., *The Seven Habits of Highly Effective People* (New York: Simon and Schuster, 1990).

DiDonato, L. S., "Contract Disputes: Alternatives for Dispute Resolution (Part 1)," *PM Network,* May 1993, pp. 19–23.

Drexler, J. A. and E. Larson, "Partnering: Why Project Owner-Contractor Relationships Change," *Journal of Construction Engineering and Management,* 126 (4), July/August 2000, pp. 293–397.

Dyer, S., *Partner Your Project* (Warwickshire, UK: Pendulum Pub., 1997).

Economy, P., *Business Negotiating Basics* (Burr Ridge, IL: Irwin Professional Publishing, 1994).

Fisher R. and W. Ury, *Getting to Yes: Negotiating Agreement without Giving In,* 2nd ed. (New York: Penguin Books, 1991).

Kanter, R. M., "Collaborative Advantage: The Art of Alliances," *Harvard Business Review,* July–August 1994, pp. 92–113.

Kezsbom, D. S., D. L. Schilling, and K. A. Edward, *Dynamic Project Management* (New York: Wiley, 1989).

Larson, E., "Project Partnering: Results of a Study of 280 Construction Projects," *Journal of Management Engineering,* Vol. 11, No. 2, March/April 1995, pp. 30–35.

Larson, E., "Partnering on Construction Projects: A Study of the Relationship between Partnering Activities and Project Success," *IEEE Transactions in Engineering Management,* Vol. 44, No. 2, May 1997, pp. 188–95.

Larson, E. and J. A. Drexler, "Barriers to Project Partnering: Report from the Firing Line," *Project Management Journal,* Vol. 28, No. 1, March 1997, pp. 46–52.

Nambisan, S., "Designing Virtual Customer Environments for New Product Development: Toward a Theory," *Academy of Management Review,* 27 (3), 2002, pp. 392–413.

Quinn, R. E., S. R. Faerman, M. P. Thompson, and M. R. McGrath, *Becoming a Master Manager: A Competency Framework* (New York: Wiley, 1990).

Schultzel, H. J. and V. P. Unruh, *Successful Partnering: Fundamentals for Project Owners and Contractors* (New York: Wiley, 1996).

Shell, G. R., *Bargaining for Advantage: Negotiation Strategies for Reasonable People* (New York: Penguin, 2000).

Case

Partnering—The Accounting Software Installation Project

Sitting in her office, Karin Chung is reviewing the past four months of the large corporate accounting software installation project she has been managing. Everything seemed so well planned before the project started. Each company division had a task force that provided input into the proposed installation along with potential problems. All the different divisions had been trained and briefed on exactly how their division would interface and use the forthcoming accounting software. All six contractors, which included one of the Big Five consulting companies, assisted in developing the work breakdown structure—costs, specifications, time.

Karin hired a consultant to conduct a one-day partnering workshop attended by the major accounting heads, a member of each task force group, and key representatives from each of the contractors. During the workshop, several different team-building exercises were used to illustrate the importance of collaboration and effective communication. Everyone laughed when Karin fell into an imaginary acid pit during a human bridge-building exercise. The workshop ended on an upbeat note with everyone signing a partnering charter that expressed their commitment to working together as partners to complete the project.

TWO MONTHS LATER

One task force member came to Karin to complain that the contractor dealing with billing would not listen to his concerns about problems that could occur in the Virginia division when billings are consolidated. The contractor had told him, the task force member, he had bigger problems than consolidation of billing in the Virginia division. Karin replied, "You can settle the problem with the contractor. Go to her and explain how serious your problem is and that it will have to be settled before the project is completed."

Later in the week in the lunchroom she overheard one consulting contractor bad-mouthing the work of another— "never on time, interface coding not tested." In the hallway the same day an accounting department supervisor told her that tests showed the new software will never be compatible with the Georgia division's accounting practices.

While concerned, Karin considered these problems typical of the kind she had encountered on other smaller software projects.

FOUR MONTHS LATER

The project seemed to be falling apart. What happened to the positive attitude fostered at the prepartnering workshop? One contractor wrote a formal letter complaining that another contractor was sitting on a coding decision that was delaying their work. The letter went on: "We cannot be held responsible or liable for delays caused by others." The project was already two months behind, so problems were becoming very real and serious. Karin finally decided to call a meeting of all parties to the project and partnering agreement.

She began by asking for problems people were encountering while working on the project. Although participants were reluctant to be first for fear of being perceived as a complainer, it was not long before accusations and tempers flared out of control. It was always some group complaining about another group. Several participants complained that others were sitting on decisions that resulted in their work being held up. One consultant said, "It is impossible to tell who's in charge of what." Another participant complained that although the group met separately on small problems, it never met as a total group to assess new risk situations that developed.

Karin felt the meeting had degenerated into an unrecoverable situation. Commitment to the project and partnering appeared to be waning. She quickly decided to stop the meeting and cool things down. She spoke to the project stakeholders: "It is clear that we have some serious problems, and the project is in jeopardy. The project must get back on track, and the backbiting must stop. I want each of us to come to a meeting Friday morning with concrete suggestions of what it will take to get the project back on track and specific actions of how we can make it happen. We need to recognize our mutual interdependence and bring our relationships with each other back to a win/win environment. When we do get things back on track, we need to figure out how to stay on track."

1. Why does this attempt at project partnering appear to be failing?
2. If you were Karin, what would you do to get this project back on track?
3. What action would you take to keep the project on track?

Case

Goldrush Electronics Negotiation Exercise
OBJECTIVE

The purpose of this case is to provide you with an opportunity to practice negotiations.

PROCEDURE

STEP 1

The class is divided into four groups, each comprising the project management group for one of four projects at Goldrush Electronics.

STEP 2

Read the Goldrush Electronics, "Background Information" section given below. Then read the instructions for the project you represent. Soon you will meet with the management of the other projects to exchange personnel. Plan how you want to conduct those meetings.

BACKGROUND INFORMATION

Goldrush Electronics (GE) produces a range of electronic products. GE has a strong commitment to project management. GE operates as a projectized organization with each project organized as a fully dedicated team. The compensation system is based on a 40+30+30 formula. Forty percent is based on your base salary, 30 percent on your project performance, and 30 percent on overall performance of the firm.

Four new product development projects have been authorized. They are code named: Alpha, Beta, Theta, and Zeta. The preliminary assignment of personnel is listed below. You are assigned to represent the management of one of these projects.

The policy at GE is that once preliminary assignments are made project managers are free to exchange personnel as long as both parties agree to the transaction. You will have the opportunity to adjust your team by negotiating with other project managers.

Alpha Project		
Software Engineer	**Hardware Engineer**	**Design Engineer**
Jill	Cameron	Mitch
John	Chandra	Marsha

Beta Project		
Software Engineer	**Hardware Engineer**	**Design Engineer**
Jake	Casey	Mike
Jennifer	Craig	Maria

Theta Project		
Software Engineer	**Hardware Engineer**	**Design Engineer**
Jack	Chuck	Monika
Johan	Cheryl	Mark

Zeta Project		
Software Engineer	**Hardware Engineer**	**Design Engineer**
Jeff	Carlos	Max
Juwoo	Chad	Maile

Personnel may be traded for one or more other personnel.

STEP 3

Meet and negotiate with the other project managers.

STEP 4

Individual project scores are totaled and posted.

STEP 5

DISCUSSION QUESTIONS

1. What was your initial strategy before starting the actual negotiations? How did you view the other groups?
2. Did your initial strategy change once negotiations began? If so how and why?
3. What could top management at GE have done to make it easier to reach agreement with the other groups?

Appendix 12.1

Contract Management

Because most interorganizational work on projects is contractual in nature, this appendix discusses the different kinds of contracts that are used, their strengths and weaknesses, and how contracts shape the motives and expectations of different participants.

A contract is a formal agreement between two parties wherein one party (the contractor) obligates itself to perform a service and the other party (the client) obligates itself to do something in return, usually in the form of a payment to the contractor. For example, an insurance firm contracted with a consulting firm to reprogram segments of their information system to conform to the year 2000.

A contract is more than just an agreement between parties. A contract is a codification of the private law, which governs the relationship between the parties to it. It defines the responsibilities, spells out the conditions of its operations, defines the rights of the parties in relationship to each other, and grants remedies to a party if the other party breaches its obligations. A contract attempts to spell out in specific terms the transactional obligations of the parties involved as well as contingencies associated with the execution of the contract. An ambiguous or inconsistent contract is difficult to understand and enforce.

There are essentially two different kinds of contracts. The first is the "fixed-price" contract in which a price is agreed upon in advance and remains fixed as long as there are no changes to scope or provisions of the agreement. The second is a "cost-plus" contract in which the contractor is reimbursed for all or some of the expenses incurred during the performance of the contract. Unlike the fixed-price contract, the final price is not known until the project is completed. Within these two types of contracts, several variations exist.

FIXED-PRICE CONTRACTS

Under a fixed-price (FP) or lump-sum agreement, the contractor agrees to perform all work specified in the contract at a fixed price. Clients are able to get a minimum price by putting out the contract to competitive bid. Advertising an invitation for bid (IFB) that lists customer requirements usually results in low bids. Prospective contractors can obtain IFB notices through various channels. In the case of large business organizations and government agencies, potential contractors can request to be included on the bidder's list in the area of interest. In other cases, IFBs can be found by scanning appropriate industry media such as newspapers, trade journals, and web sites. In many cases, the owner can put restrictions on potential bidders, such as requiring that they be ISO 9000 certified.

With fixed-contract bids, the contractor has to be very careful in estimating target cost and completion schedule because once agreed upon, the price cannot be adjusted. If the contractor overestimates the target cost in the bidding stage, they may lose the contract to a lower-priced competitor; if the estimate it too low, they may win the job but make little or no profit.

Fixed-price contracts are preferred by both owners and contractors when the scope of the project is well defined with predictable costs and low implementation risks. Such might be the case for producing parts or components to specifications, executing training programs, or orchestrating a banquet. With fixed-price contracts, clients do not have to be concerned with project costs and can focus on monitoring work progress and performance specifications. Likewise, contractors prefer fixed-price contracts because the client is less likely to request changes or additions to the contract. Fewer potential changes reduce project uncertainty and allow the contractors to more efficiently manage their resources across multiple projects.

The disadvantage of a fixed-price contract for owners is that it is more difficult and more costly to prepare. To be effective, design specifications need to be spelled out in sufficient detail to leave little doubt as to what is to be achieved. Because the contractor's profit is determined by the difference between the bid and the actual costs, there is some incentive for contractors to use cheaper quality materials, perform marginal workmanship, or extend the completion date to reduce costs. The client can counteract these by stipulating rigid end-item specifications and completion date and by supervising work. In many cases, the client will hire a consultant who is an expert in the field to oversee the contractor's work and protect the client's interest.

The primary disadvantage of a fixed-price contract for contractors is that they run the risk of underestimating. If the project gets into serious trouble, cost overruns may make the project unprofitable, and, in some cases, may lead to bankruptcy. To avoid this, contractors have to invest significant time and money to ensure that their estimates are accurate.

Contracts with long lead times such as construction and production projects may include escalation provisions that protect the contractor against external cost increases in materials, labor rates, or overhead expenses. For example, the price may be tied to an inflation index, so it can be adjusted to sudden increases in labor and material prices, or it may be redetermined as costs become known. A variety of redetermination contracts are used: Some establish a ceiling price for a contract and permit only downward adjustments, others permit upward and downward adjustments; some establish one readjustment period at the end of the project, others use more than one period. Redetermination contracts are appropriate where engineering and design efforts are difficult to estimate or when final price cannot be estimated for lack of accurate cost data.

While, in principle, redetermination contracts are used to make appropriate adjustments in cost uncertainties, they are prone to abuse. A contractor may win an initial low bid contract, initiate the contracted work, and then "discover" that the costs are much higher than expected. The contractor can take advantage of redetermination provisions and a client's ignorance to justify increasing the actual cost of the contract. The contract evolves into a cost-plus contract.

Many question whether partnering arrangements can work on public works projects such as renovating a segment of a highway or building a new public school. Contracts for these projects tend to be mandated by law to be awarded on a competitive, low-bid basis. As a result, the government agencies do not get to screen potential contractors as to experience and willingness to work as partners. Critics also argue that the binding nature of the low-bid contractual arrangement prevents the necessary flexibility to work out optimal solutions when unexpected problems arise. Another drawback is that sustained business, which is one of the major incentives for adhering to partnering principles, is seldom possible because each contract must be awarded under open competition.

Despite these handicaps, the U.S. Army Corp of Engineers has been quite successful in creating partnering arrangements with contractors who were awarded contracts on a competitive, low-bid basis. For example, the Portland, Oregon, District of the Corp successfully partnered the completion of a $330 million Bonneville Lock project. Using a partnering process very similar to what is described in this chapter, the project was completed three months ahead of schedule, obtained more than $1.8 million in value in engineering savings, and encountered no litigation. Weston and Gibson compared the performance of 16 partnered Corp projects with 28 nonpartnered projects and reported that the partnered projects achieved superior cost savings. Col. Charles Cowan, who managed the Bonneville Lock project, said that while team building, joint evaluations, and the other partnering components were all important, the key to success was that the parties involved realized that partnering was a much more enjoyable way to work together.

*D. C. Weston and G. E. Gibson, "Partnering-Project Performance in U.S. Army Corps of Engineers," *Journal of Management Engineering*, Vol. 9, No. 4 (1993), pp. 410–25.

To alleviate some of the disadvantages of a fixed-price contract while maintaining some certainty as to final cost, many fixed-price contracts contain incentive clauses designed to motivate contractors to reduce costs and improve efficiency. For example, a contractor negotiates to perform the work for a target price based on target cost and a target profit. A maximum price and maximum profit are also established. If the total cost ends up being less than the target cost, the contractor makes a higher profit up to the profit maximum. If there is a cost overrun, the contractor absorbs some of the overrun until a profit floor is reached.

Profit is determined according to a formula based on a cost-sharing ratio (CSR). A CSR of 75/25, for example, indicates that for every dollar spent above target costs, the client pays 75 cents and the contractor pays 25 cents. This provision motivates contractors to keep costs low since they pay 25 cents on every dollar spent above the expected cost and earn 25 cents more on every dollar saved below the expected cost. Fixed-price incentive contracts tend to be used for long-duration projects with fairly predictable cost estimates. The key is being able to negotiate a reasonable target cost estimate. Unscrupulous contractors have been known to take advantage of the ignorance of the client to negotiate an unrealistically high target cost and use performance incentives to achieve excessive profits.

COST-PLUS CONTRACTS

Under a cost-plus contract the contractor is reimbursed for all direct allowable costs (materials, labor, travel) plus an additional fee to cover overhead and profit. This fee is negotiated in advance and usually involves a percentage of the total costs. On small projects this kind of contract comes under the rubric "time and materials contract" in which the client agrees to reimburse the contractor for labor cost and materials. Labor costs are based on an hourly or daily rate, which includes direct and indirect costs as well as profit. The contractor is responsible for documenting labor and materials costs.

Unlike fixed contracts, cost-plus contracts put the burden of risk on the client. The contract does not indicate what the project is going to cost until the end of the project. Contractors are supposed to make the best effort to fulfill the specific technical requirements of the contract but cannot be held liable, in spite of their best efforts, if the work is not produced within the estimated cost and time frame. These contracts are often criticized because there is little formal incentive for the contractors to control costs or finish on time because they get paid regardless of the final cost. The major factor motivating contractors to control costs and schedule is the effect overruns have on their reputation and their ability to secure future business. The government has curtailed use of cost-plus contracts in favor of incentive contracts in response to abuse by contractors.

The inherent weakness of cost-plus contracts has been compensated for by a variety of incentive clauses directed at providing incentives to contractors to control costs, maintain performance, and avoid schedule overruns. Contractors are reimbursed for costs, but instead of the fee being fixed, it is based on an incentive formula and subject to additional provisions. This is very similar to fixed-price incentive contracts, but instead of being based on a target cost, the fee is based on actual cost, using a cost-sharing formula.

Most contracts are concerned with the negotiated cost of the project. However, given the importance of speed and timing in today's business world, more and more contracts involve clauses concerning completion dates. To some extent schedule incentives provide some cost-control measures because schedule slippage typically but not always involves cost overruns. Schedule incentives/penalties are stipulated depending on the significance of time to completion for the owner. For example, the contract involving the construction of a new baseball stadium is likely to contain stiff penalties if the stadium is not ready for opening day of the season. Conversely, time-constrained projects in which the number one priority is getting the project completed as soon as possible are likely to include attractive incentives for completing the project early. For example, a software firm that is anxious to get a new product to market may offer a testing firm a sizable bonus for each day the tests are completed ahead of schedule.

CONTRACT CHANGE CONTROL SYSTEM

A contract change control system defines the process by which the contract may be modified. It includes the paperwork, tracking systems, dispute resolution procedures, and approval levels necessary for authorizing changes. There are a number of reasons a contract may need to be changed. Clients may wish to alter the original design or scope of the project once the project is initiated. This is quite common as the project moves from concept to reality. For example, an owner may wish to add windows after inspecting the partially completed homesite. Market changes may dictate adding new features or increasing the performance requirements of equipment. Declining financial resources may dictate that the owner cut back on the scope of the project. The contractor may initiate changes in the contract in response to unforeseen legitimate problems. A building contractor may need to renegotiate the contract in the face of excessive groundwater or the lack of availability of specified materials. In some cases, external forces may dictate contract changes, such as a need to comply with new safety standards mandated by the federal government.

There need to be formal, agreed-upon procedures for initiating changes in the original contract. Contract change orders are subject to abuse. Contractors sometimes take advantage of owners' ignorance to inflate the costs of changes to recoup profit lost from a low bid. Conversely, owners have been known to "get back" at contractors by delaying approval of contract changes, thus delaying project work and increasing the costs to the contractor. All parties need to agree upon the rules and procedures for initiating and making changes in the original terms of the contract in advance.

CONTRACT MANAGEMENT IN PERSPECTIVE

Contract management is not an exact science. For decades, the federal government has been trying to develop a more effective contract administration system. Despite their best efforts, abuses are repeatedly exposed in the news media. The situation is similar to trying to take a wrinkle out of an Oriental rug. Efforts to eliminate a wrinkle in one part of the rug invariably create a wrinkle in another part. Likewise, each new revision in government procurement procedures appears to generate a new loophole that can be exploited. There is no perfect contract management system. Given the inherent uncertainty involved in most project work, no contract can handle all the issues that emerge. Formal contracts cannot replace or eliminate the need to develop effective working relationships between the parties involved that are based on mutual goals, trust, and cooperation. For this reason, the earlier discussion of project partnering and effective negotiating is very important.

APPENDIX REVIEW QUESTIONS

1. What are the fundamental differences between fixed-price and cost-plus contracts?
2. For what kinds of projects would you recommend that a fixed-price contract be used? For what kinds of projects would you recommend that a cost-plus contract be used?

APPENDIX REFERENCES

Angus, R. B., N. A. Gundersen, and T. P. Cullinane, *Planning, Performing, and Controlling Projects* (Upper Saddle River, NJ: Prentice Hall, 2003).

Cavendish J. and M. Martin, *Negotiating and Contracting for Project Management* (Upper Darby, PA: Project Management Institute, 1982).

Fleming, Q. W., *Project Procurement Management: Contracting, Subcontracting, Teaming* (Tustin, CA: FMC Press, 2003).

Fraser, J., *Professional Project Proposals* (Aldershot, U.K.: Gower/Ashgate, 1995).

Worthington, M. M. and L. P. Goldsman, *Contracting with the Federal Government,* 4 Ed. (New York: Wiley, 1998).

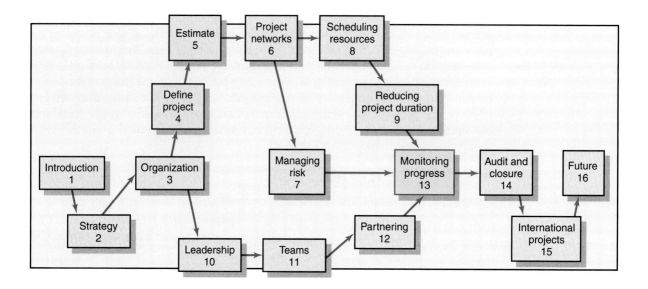

CHAPTER THIRTEEN

Progress and Performance Measurement and Evaluation

How does a project get one year late?

. . . One day at a time.

—*Frederick P. Brooks,* The Mythical Man Month, *p. 153*

Evaluation and control are part of every project manager's job. Control by "wandering around" and/or "involvement" can overcome most problems in small projects. But large projects need some form of formal control. Control holds people accountable, prevents small problems from mushrooming into large problems, and keeps focus. Except for accounting controls, project control is not performed well in most organizations. Control is one of the most neglected areas of project management. Unfortunately, it is not uncommon to find resistance to control processes. In essence, those who minimize the importance of control are passing up a great opportunity to be effective managers and, perhaps, allow the organization to gain a competitive edge. Neglecting control in organizations with multiple projects is even more serious. For effective control, the project manager needs a single information system to collect data and report progress on cost, schedule, and specifications. The general structure of such a system is discussed next.

Structure of a Project Monitoring Information System

A project monitoring system involves *determining what* data to collect; *how, when,* and *who* will collect the data; *analysis* of the data; and *reporting* current progress.

What Data Are Collected? Data collected are determined by *which* metrics will be used for project control. Typical key data collected are actual activity duration times, resource usage and rates, and actual costs, which are compared against planned times, resources, and costs. Since a major portion of the monitoring system focuses on cost/schedule concerns, it is crucial to provide the project manager and stakeholders with data to answer questions such as:

* What is the current status of the project in terms of schedule and cost?
* How much will it cost to complete the project?
* When will the project be completed?
* Are there potential problems that need to be addressed now?
* What, who, and where are the causes for cost or schedule overruns?
* What did we get for the dollars spent?
* If there is a cost overrun midway in the project, can we forecast the overrun at completion?

The performance metrics you need to collect should support answering these questions. Examples of specific metrics and tools for collecting data will be discussed in detail later in this chapter.

Collecting Data and Analysis With the determination of what data are collected, the next step is to establish who, when, and how the data will be assembled. Will the data be collected by the project team, contractor, independent cost engineers, project manager? Or, will the data be derived electronically from some form of surrogate data such as cash flow, machine hours, labor hours, or materials in place? Should the reporting period be one hour, one day, one week, or what? Is there a central repository for the data collected and is someone responsible for its dissemination?

Electronic means of collecting data have vastly improved data assembly, analysis, and dissemination. Numerous software vendors have programs and tools to analyze your customized collected data and present it in a form that facilitates monitoring the project, identifying sources of problems, and updating your plan.

Reports and Reporting First, who gets the progress reports? We have already suggested that different stakeholders and levels of management need different kinds of project information. Senior management's major interest is usually, "Are we on time and within budget? If not what corrective action is taking place?" Likewise, an IT manager working on the project is concerned primarily about her deliverable and specific work packages. The reports should be designed for the right audience.

Typically, project progress reports are designed and communicated in written or oral form. A common topic format for progress reports follows:

* Progress since last report
* Current status of project
  1. Schedule
  2. Cost
  3. Scope
* Cumulative trends
* Problems and issues since last report
  1. Actions and resolution of earlier problems
  2. New variances and problems identified
* Corrective action planned

Given the structure of your information system and the nature of its outputs, we can use the system to interface and facilitate the project control process. These interfaces need to be relevant and seamless if control is to be effective.

The Project Control Process

Control is the process of comparing actual performance against plan to identify deviations, evaluate possible alternative courses of actions, and take appropriate corrective action. The project control steps for measuring and evaluating project performance are presented below.

1. Setting a baseline plan.
2. Measuring progress and performance.
3. Comparing plan against actual.
4. Taking action.

Each of the control steps is described in the following paragraphs.

Step 1: Setting a Baseline Plan

The baseline plan provides us with the elements for measuring performance. The baseline is derived from the cost and duration information found in the work breakdown structure (WBS) database and time-sequence data from the network and resource scheduling decisions. The WBS defines the work in discrete work packages that are tied to deliverables and organization units. In addition, each work package defines the work, duration, and budget. From the WBS the project network schedule is used to time-phase all work, resources, and budgets into a baseline plan.

Step 2: Measuring Progress and Performance

Time and budgets are quantitative measures of performance that readily fit into the integrated information system. Qualitative measures such as meeting customer technical specifications and product function are most frequently determined by on-site inspection or actual use. This chapter is limited to quantitative measures of time and budget. Measurement of time performance is relatively easy and obvious. That is, is the critical path early, on schedule, or late; is the slack of near-critical paths decreasing to cause new critical activities? Measuring performance against budget (e.g., money, units in place, labor hours) is more difficult and is *not* simply a case of comparing actual versus budget. Earned value is necessary to provide a realistic estimate of performance against a time-phased budget. Earned value will be defined as the budgeted cost of the work performed (EV).

Step 3: Comparing Plan against Actual

Because plans seldom materialize as expected, it becomes imperative to measure deviations from plan to determine if action is necessary. Periodic monitoring and measuring the status of the project allow for comparisons of actual versus expected plans. It is crucial that the timing of status reports be frequent enough to allow for early detection of variations from plan and early correction of causes. Usually status reports should take place every one to four weeks to be useful and allow for proactive correction.

Step 4: Taking Action

If deviations from plans are significant, corrective action will be needed to bring the project back in line with the original or revised plan. In some cases, conditions or scope can change, which, in turn, will require a change in the baseline plan to recognize new information.

The remainder of this chapter describes and illustrates monitoring systems, tools, and components to support managing and controlling projects. Several of the tools you developed in the planning and scheduling chapters now serve as input to your information system for monitoring performance. Monitoring time performance is discussed first, followed by cost performance.

Monitoring Time Performance

A major goal of progress reporting is to catch any negative variances from plan as early as possible to determine if corrective action is necessary. Fortunately, monitoring schedule performance is relatively easy. The project network schedule, derived from the WBS/OBS, serves as the baseline to compare against actual performance.

Gantt charts (bar charts) and control charts are the typical tools used for communicating project schedule status. As suggested in Chapter 6, the Gantt chart is the most favored, used, and understandable. This kind of chart is commonly referred to as a tracking Gantt chart. Gantt and control charts serve well as a means for tracking and trending schedule performance. Their easy-to-understand visual formats make them favorite tools for communicating project schedule status—especially to top management who do not usually have time for details. Adding actual and revised time estimates to the Gantt chart gives a quick overview of project status on the report date.

Tracking Gantt Chart

Figure 13.1 presents a baseline Gantt chart and a tracking Gantt chart for a project at the end of period 6. The solid bar below the original schedule bar represents the actual start and finish times for completed activities or any portion of an activity completed (see activities A, B, C, D, and E). For example, the actual start time for activity C is period 2; the actual finish time is period 5; the actual duration is three time units, rather

FIGURE 13.1
Baseline Gantt Chart

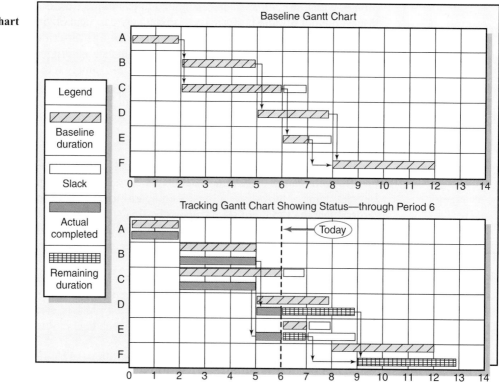

than four scheduled time periods. Activities in process show the actual start time until the present; the extended bar represents the remaining scheduled duration (see activities D and E). The remaining expected duration for activities D and E are shown with the hatched bar. Activity F, which has not started, shows a revised estimated actual start (9) and finish time (13).

Note how activities can have durations that differ from the original schedule, as in activities D and E. Either the activity is complete and the actual is known, or new information suggests the estimate of time be revised and reflected in the status report. In activity D the revised duration is expected to be four time units, which is one time period longer than the original schedule. Although sometimes the Gantt chart does not show dependencies, when it is used with a network, the dependencies are easily identified if tracing is needed.

Control Chart

This chart is another tool used to monitor past project schedule performance and current performance and to estimate future schedule trends. Figure 13.2 depicts a project control chart. The chart is used to plot the difference between the scheduled time on the critical path at the report date with the actual point on the critical path. Although Figure 13.2 shows the project was behind early in the project, the plot suggests corrective action brought the project back on track. If the trend is sustained, the project will come in ahead of schedule. Because the activity scheduled times represent average durations, four observations trending in one direction indicate there is a very high probability that there is an identifiable cause. The cause should be located and action taken if necessary. Control chart trends are very useful for giving warning of potential problems so appropriate action can be taken if necessary.

Control charts are also frequently used to monitor progress toward milestones, which mark events and as such have zero duration. Milestones are significant project events that mark major accomplishments. To be effective, milestones need to be concrete, specific, measurable events. Milestones must be easily identifiable by all project stakeholders—for example, product testing complete. Critical merge activities are good

FIGURE 13.2
**Project Schedule
Control Chart**

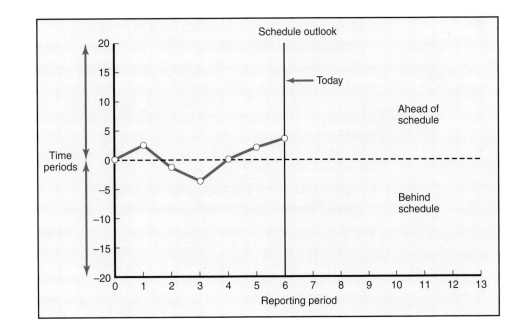

candidates for milestones. Control charts very similar to the example shown in Figure 13.2 are often used to record and communicate project progress toward a milestone.

Schedule slippage of one day seldom receives a great deal of attention. However, one day here and another there soon add up to large delay problems. It is well known that once work gets behind, it has a tendency to stay behind because it is difficult to make up. Examples of causes of schedule slippage are unreliable time estimates, minor redesign, scope creep, and unavailable resources. Using slack early in a path may create a problem for someone responsible for a later activity; flexibility and potential opportunities are reduced. For these reasons, having frequent and clearly defined monitoring points for work packages can significantly improve the chances of catching schedule slippage early. Early detection reduces the chance of small delays growing to large ones and thereby reducing opportunities for corrective action to get back on schedule. See Snapshot from Practice: Status Reports at Microsoft.

The Need for An Integrated Information System

There are many customized monitoring and control systems used in practice. Generally, their form and formats are very similar; however, in too many cases there is a small but crucial missing piece on the cost side that renders many of the systems useless to the point of actually giving wrong cost information. The disparity among monitoring systems is usually found in the lack of connections to a time-phased baseline plan.

Such systems fail to compare actual work completed for any time period against budgeted scheduled costs for the same time period. Without matching time-phased budgets to actual cost of work completed, we shall see it is impossible to reliably measure cost performance. An example of a hypothetical project will demonstrate the need for time-phasing the project budget to the project schedule.

A high-tech firm is implementing an R&D project. The original plan calls for completion of the project in 10 months at a cost of $200,000 per month for a total cost of $2.0 million. After five months, top management wishes to assess the status of the project. The following information is available:

- Actual costs for the first five months are $1.3 million.
- Planned budget costs for the first five months are $1.0 million.

Management might draw the conclusion the project has a $300,000 cost overrun. This could be a correct conclusion, but it may not be. It is possible the project is way ahead of schedule and the $300,000 represents payments to labor working ahead of schedule. It is possible we may have both a cost overrun and be behind schedule. These data do not tell the full story.

Using the same high-tech example with another set of outcome data, we again see the data are inadequate to draw accurate conclusions five months into the project:

- Actual costs for the first five months are $800,000.
- Planned costs for the first five months are $1.0 million.

These data can lead to the conclusion the project is costing less than expected by $200,000. Is this true? If the project is behind schedule, the $200,000 may represent planned work that has not started. It is possible the project is behind schedule and also over in cost.

From the data in these two examples, it is easy to understand why real-world systems using only actual and planned costs can mislead management and customers in evaluating project progress and performance. Cost variance of budget-to-actual alone is inadequate. It does not measure how much work was accomplished for the money spent.

We have firmly noted conventional systems miss the point. *Without time-phasing of costs to match scheduled activities, cost control cannot yield information that is reliable for control purposes.*

A system that attempts to overcome these issues is known as the earned value system. Earned value is not new; although its initial use was in military contracts, in recent years the private sector has come to depend on the system for managing multiple and large projects.

The original earned value cost/schedule system was pioneered by the U.S. Department of Defense (DOD) in the 1960s. Cost overruns and the lack of consistency among contractors served as a major motivation for the DOD to search for a system to track schedule and cost in large project contracts. Basically, the system brings discipline to the process of measuring project progress. The private sector was quick to recognize the worth of the system as a totally integrated project management system. It is probably safe to say project managers in every major country are using some form of the system. It is not limited to construction or contracts. The system is being used on internal projects in the manufacturing, pharmaceutical, and high-tech industries. For example, organizations such as EDS, NCR, Levi Strauss, Tektronics, and Disney have used earned-value systems to track projects. The basic framework of the EV system is withstanding the test of time. Most project management software includes the original framework; many systems have added industry-specific variations to more precisely track progress and costs. This chapter presents the "generic" core of an integrated cost/schedule information system.

The earned value system starts with the time-phased costs that provide the project budget *baseline,* which is called the planned budgeted value of the work scheduled (PV). Given this time-phased baseline, comparisons can be made with actual and planned schedule and costs using a concept called earned value. The earned value system uses data developed from the work breakdown structure, the project network, and schedule. This integrated cost/schedule system provides schedule and cost variance and can also be used to forecast the remaining costs for the in-process project. The earned-value approach provides the missing links not found in conventional

417

cost-budget systems. At any point in time, a status report can be developed for the project. The development of an integrated cost/schedule system is discussed next.

Development of An Integrated Cost/Schedule System

The earned value cost/schedule system uses several acronyms and equations for analysis. Table 13.1 presents a glossary of these acronyms. You will need this glossary as a reference. In recent years acronyms have been shortened to be more phonetically friendly. This movement is reflected in material from the Project Management Institute, in project management software, and by practitioners. This text edition follows the recent trend. The acronyms found in brackets represent the older acronyms. To the uninitiated, the terms used in practice appear horrendous and intimidating. However, once a few basic terms are understood, the intimidation index will evaporate.

Following five careful steps ensures that the cost/schedule system is integrated. These steps are outlined here. Steps 1, 2, and 3 are accomplished in the planning stage. Steps 4 and 5 are sequentially accomplished during the execution stage of the project.

1. Define the work using a WBS. This step involves developing documents that include the following information:
   a. Scope.
   b. Work packages.
   c. Deliverables.
   d. Organization units.
   e. Resources.
   f. Budgets for each work package.
2. Develop work and resource schedules.
   a. Schedule resources to activities.
   b. Time-phase work packages into a network.

TABLE 13.1
Glossary of Terms

EV	Earned value (EV) for a task is simply the percent complete times its original budget. Stated differently, EV is the percent of the original budget that has been earned by actual work completed. [The older acronym for this value was BCWP—budgeted cost of the work performed.]
PV	The planned time-phased baseline of the value of the work scheduled. An approved cost estimate of the resources scheduled in a time-phased cumulative baseline [BCWS—budgeted cost of the work scheduled].
AC	Actual cost of the work completed. The sum of the costs incurred in accomplishing work. [ACWP—actual cost of the work performed].
CV	Cost variance is the difference between the earned value and the actual costs for the work completed to date where $CV = EV - AC$.
SV	Schedule variance (SV) is the difference between the earned value and the baseline line to date where $SV = EV - PV$.
BAC	Budgeted cost at completion. The total budgeted cost of the baseline or project cost accounts.
EAC	Estimated costs at completion. Includes costs to-date plus revised estimated costs for the work remaining.
ETC	Estimate to complete.
VAC	Cost variance at completion ($BAC - EAC_e$), where EAC_e is derived by estimators in the field. Or, alternatively, cost variance at completion ($BAC - EAC_f$), where EAC_f is derived from a formula using actual and earned value costs. VAC indicates expected actual over- or underrun cost at completion.

3. Develop a time-phased budget using work packages included in an activity. The cumulative values of these budgets will become the baseline and will be called the planned budgeted cost of the work scheduled (PV). The sum should equal the budgeted amounts for all the work packages in the cost accounts.

4. At the work package level, collect the actual costs for the work performed. These costs will be called the actual cost of the work completed (AC). Collect percent complete and multiply this times the original budget amount for the value of the work actually completed. These values will be called earned value (EV).

5. Compute the schedule variance (SV = EV − PV) and cost variance (CV = EV − AC). Prepare hierarchical status reports for each level of management—from work package manager to customer or project manager. The reports should also include project rollups by organization unit and deliverables. In addition, actual time performance should be checked against the project network schedule.

Figure 13.3 presents a schematic overview of the integrated information system, which includes the techniques and systems presented in earlier chapters. Those who have tenaciously labored through the early chapters can smile! Steps 1 and 2 are already carefully developed. Observe that control data can be traced backward to specific deliverables and organization unit responsible.

Development of Project Baselines

The baseline (PV) serves as an anchor point for measuring performance. The baseline is a concrete document and commitment; it is the planned cost and expected schedule performance against which actual cost and schedule are measured. It can also serve as a basis for developing cash flows and awarding progress payments. Development of the project baseline is properly part of the planning process. The baseline is included in this chapter because it is the major input to the cost/schedule system to be described. The building blocks or data for development of the baseline have already been set in

FIGURE 13.3
Project Management Information System Overview

place. The placement of work packages in the activities of the network essentially assigns start times for those work packages; it also *time-phases the budgets* that are tied to the work packages. Budgets are ultimately expressed in monetary units—for example, dollars, yen, marks, pounds. These time-phased budgets are added along a project timeline to create the project baseline. The cumulative sum of all these time-phased budgets should equal the sum of all the work packages found in the cost accounts. Figure 13.4 depicts the relationship of the data used to create the baseline.

What Costs Are Included in Baselines?

The baseline PV is the sum of the cost accounts, and each cost account is the sum of the work packages in the cost account. Three costs are typically included in baselines—labor, equipment, and materials. Sometimes project direct overhead costs are included.

Direct overhead costs (DOC) represent time-related activities. These activities, such as administrative support, computer support, legal, public relations, etc., exist for a work package, segment of the project, or the duration of the project and represent direct project overhead. Because these DOC costs are very different, it is common to separate DOC costs from costs for labor, materials, and equipment and to compute separate variances for them. The ability to control DOC costs is minimal, which is the reason they are included in direct project overhead costs. DOC costs can also be tied to a hammock activity that covers a segment of a project. When DOC costs are tied to work packages that have no measurable outputs, their costs are budgeted as a rate per unit of time (e.g., $200 per day). DOC work packages should represent a very small portion of project costs (1 to 10 percent). There are a few rare circumstances that warrant high DOC costs. For example, the cost of having a crew on-site on the Alaskan pipeline exceeds the direct cost of their actual work. This cost of providing housing, food, and 10 days' leave for every 23 days of work was counted as DOC cost and exceeded the 10 percent level. The nuclear industry faces a similar situation with crews working in "hot spots." After workers are exposed to a fixed number of REMs (Roentgen equivalent man), they are required to stop working until the number decreases to a safe level. During this waiting period, the individuals are paid; this waiting cost is considered an DOC cost. These examples are extreme and under normal circumstances DOC costs should be minimized as much as possible.

Most work packages should be discrete, of short time span, and have measurable outputs. Usually the major costs are labor, machines, and/or materials. If materials are a significant portion of the cost of work packages, they can be budgeted in separate work packages and cost accounts.

FIGURE 13.4
Baseline Data Relationships

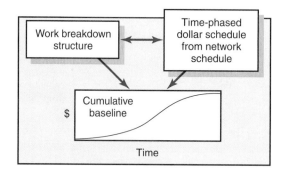

Rules for Placing Costs in Baselines

The major reasons for creating a baseline are to monitor and report progress and to estimate cash flow. Therefore, it is crucial to integrate the baseline with the performance measurement system. Costs are placed (time-phased) in the baseline exactly as managers expect them to be "earned." This approach facilitates tracking costs to their point of origin. In practice, the integration is accomplished by using the same rules in assigning costs to the baseline as those used to measure progress using earned value. You may find several rules in practice, but percent complete is the workhorse most commonly used. Someone familiar with each task estimates what percent of the task has been completed or how much of the task remains.

Percent Complete Rule

This rule is the heart of any earned value system. The best method for assigning costs to the baseline under this rule is to establish frequent checkpoints over the duration of the work package and assign completion percentages in dollar terms. For example, units completed could be used to assign baseline costs and later to measure progress. Units might be lines of code, hours, drawings completed, cubic yards of concrete in place, workdays, prototypes complete, etc. This approach to percent complete adds "objectivity" to the subjective observation approaches often used. When measuring percent complete in the monitoring phase of the project, it is common to limit the amount earned to 80 or 90 percent until the work package is 100 percent complete.

Methods of Variance Analysis

Generally the method for measuring accomplishments centers on two key computations:

1. Comparing earned value with the expected schedule value.
2. Comparing earned value with the actual costs.

These comparisons can be made at the project level or down to the cost account level. Project status can be determined for the latest period, all periods to date, and estimated to the end of the project.

Assessing the current status of a project using the earned-value cost/schedule system requires three data elements—planned cost of the work scheduled (PV), budgeted cost of the work completed (EV), and actual cost of the work completed (AC). From these data the schedule variance (SV) and cost variance (CV) are computed each reporting period. *A positive variance indicates a desirable condition, while a negative variance suggests problems or changes that have taken place.*

Cost variance tells us if the work accomplished costs more or less than was planned at any point over the life of the project. If labor and materials have not been separated, cost variance should be reviewed carefully to isolate the cause to either labor or materials—or to both.

Schedule variance presents an overall assessment of *all* work packages in the project scheduled to date. It is important to note schedule variance contains *no* critical path information. Schedule variance measures progress in dollars rather than time units. Therefore, it is unlikely that any translation of dollars to time will yield accurate information telling if any milestone or critical path is early, on time, or late (even if the project occurs exactly as planned). *The only accurate method for determining the true time progress of the project is to compare the project network schedule against the actual network schedule to measure if the project is on time* (refer to Figure 13.1). However, SV is very useful in assessing the direction all the work in the project is taking—after 20 or more percent of the project has been completed.

FIGURE 13.5

Cost/Schedule Graph

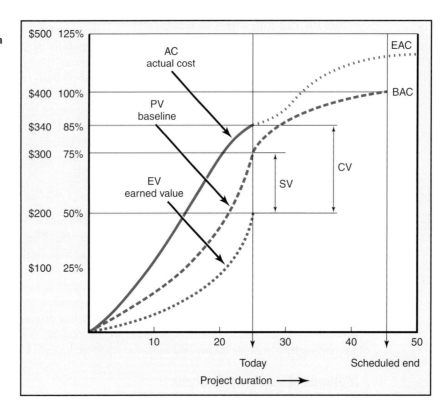

Figure 13.5 presents a sample cost/schedule graph with variances identified for a project at the current status report date. Note the graph also focuses on what remains to be accomplished and any favorable or unfavorable trends. The "today" label marks the report date (time period 25) of where the project has been and where it is going. Because our system is hierarchical, graphs of the same form can be developed for different levels of management. In Figure 13.5 the top line represents the actual costs (AC) incurred for the project work to date. The middle line is the baseline (PV) and ends at the scheduled project duration (45). The bottom line is the budgeted value of the work actually completed to date (EV) or the earned value. The dotted line extending the actual costs from the report date to the new estimated completion date represents revised estimates of *expected* actual costs; that is, additional information suggests the costs at completion of the project will differ from what was planned. Note that the project duration has been extended and the variance at completion (VAC) is negative (BAC − EAC).

Another interpretation of the graph uses percentages. At the end of period 25, 75 percent of the work was scheduled to be accomplished. At the end of period 25, the value of the work accomplished is 50 percent. The actual cost of the work completed to date is $340, or 85 percent of the total project budget. The graph suggests the project will have about a 12 percent cost overrun and be five time units late. The current status of the project shows the cost variance (CV) to be over budget by $140 (EV − AC = 200 − 340 = −140). The schedule variance (SV) is negative $100 (EV − PV = 200 − 300 = −100), which suggests the project is behind schedule. Before moving to an example, consult Figure 13.6 to practice interpreting the outcomes of cost/schedule graphs. Remember, PV is your baseline and anchor point.

FIGURE 13.6
Earned-Value
Review Exercise

Developing a Status Report: A Hypothetical Example

Working through an example demonstrates how the baseline serves as the anchor from which the project can be monitored using earned-value techniques.

Assumptions

Because the process becomes geometrically complex with the addition of project detail, some simplifying assumptions are made in the example to more easily demonstrate the process:

1. Assume each cost account has only one work package, and each cost account will be represented as an activity on the network.
2. The project network early start times will serve as the basis for assigning the baseline values.
3. From the moment work on an activity task begins, some actual costs will be incurred each period until the activity is completed.

Baseline Development

Review Chapter 4, "Project Rollup" and Figure 4.7. Figure 13.7 (Work Breakdown Structure with Cost Accounts) depicts a simple work breakdown structure (WBS/OBS) for the Digital Camera example. There are six deliverables (Design Specifications, Shell & Power, Memory/Software, Zoom System, Assemble, and Test), and five responsible departments (Design, Shell, Storage, Zoom and Assembly). The total for all the cost accounts (CA) is $320,000, which represents the total project cost. Figure 13.8, derived from the WBS, presents a planning Gantt chart for the Digital Camera project. The planned project duration is 11 time units. This project information is used to time-phase the project budget baseline. Figure 13.9 (Project Baseline Budget) presents a worksheet with an early start baseline developed with costs assigned. They are assigned "exactly" as managers plan to monitor and measure schedule and cost performance.

FIGURE 13.7 **Work Breakdown Structure with Cost Accounts**

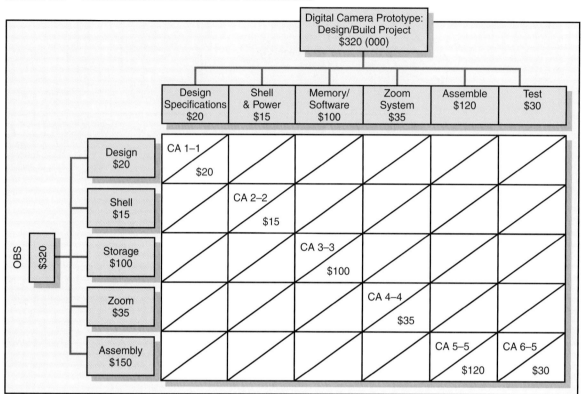

Development of the Status Report

A status report is analogous to a camera snapshot of a project at a specific point in time. The status report uses earned value to measure schedule and cost performance. Measuring earned value begins at the work package level. Work packages are in one of three conditions on a report date:

1. Not yet started.
2. Finished.
3. In-process or partially complete.

FIGURE 13.8
Digital Camera Prototype Project Baseline Gantt Chart

FIGURE 13.9
Digital Camera Prototype Project Baseline (000)

ACT/WP	DUR	ES	LF	SLK	Total PV	0	1	2	3	4	5	6	7	8	9	10	11
		Schedule information							Baseline budget needs — Time period								
A	2	0	2	0	20	10	10										
B	2	2	6	2	15			5	10								
C	4	2	6	0	100			20	30	30	20						
D	3	2	6	1	35			15	10	10							
E	3	6	9	0	120							30	40	50			
F	2	9	11	0	30											10	20
Total PV by period						10	10	40	50	40	20	30	40	50	10	20	
Cumulative PV by period						10	20	60	110	150	170	200	240	290	300	320	

Earned values for the first two conditions present no difficulties. Work packages that are not yet started earn zero percent of the PV (budget). Packages that are completed earn 100 percent of their PV. In-process packages apply the percent complete rule to the PV baseline to measure earned value (EV). In our camera example we will only use the percent complete rule to measure progress.

Table 13.2 presents the completed, separate status reports of the Digital Camera Prototype project for periods one through seven. Each period percent complete and actual cost were gathered for each task from staff in the field. The schedule and cost variance are computed for each task and the project to-date. For example, the status in period 1 shows only Task A (Design Specifications) is in process and it is 50 percent complete and actual cost for the task is 10. The planned value at the end of period 1 for Task A is 10 (See Figure 13.9). The cost and schedule variance are both zero, which indicates the project is on budget and schedule. By the end of period 3, Task A is finished. Task B (Shell and Power) is 33 percent complete and AC is 10; Task C is 20 percent complete and AC is 30; and D is 60 percent complete and AC is 20. Again, from Figure 13.9 *at the end of period 3,* we can see that the PV for Task A is 20 (10 + 10 = 20), for task B is 5, for Task C is 20, and for Task D is 15. At the end of period 3 it is becoming clear the actual cost (AC) is exceeding the value of the work completed (EV). The cost variance for the project at the end of period 3 is negative 24. Schedule variance is positive 6, which suggests the project may be ahead of schedule.

It is important to note that since earned values are computed from costs (or sometimes labor hours or other metrics), the relationship of costs to time is not one-for-one. For example, it is possible to have a negative SV variance when the project is actually ahead on the critical path. Therefore, it is important to remember, SV is in dollars and is not an accurate measure of time; however, it is a fairly good indicator of the status of the whole project in terms of being ahead or behind schedule after the project is over 20 percent complete. Only the project network, or tracking Gantt chart, and actual work completed can give an accurate assessment of schedule performance down to the work package level.

By studying the separate status reports for periods 5 through 7, you can see the project will be over budget and behind schedule. By period 7 tasks A, B, and D are finished, but all are over budget—negative 10, 5, and 25. Task C (Memory/Software) is 90 percent complete. Task E is late and hasn't started because Task C is not yet completed. The result is that, at the end of period 7, the digital camera project is over budget $70, with a schedule budget over $40.

TABLE 13.2
Digital Camera Prototype Status Reports: Periods 1–7

Cost Variance		CV = EV − AC			
Schedule Variance		SV = EV − PV			

Status Report: Ending Period 1

Task	%Complete	EV	AC	PV	CV	SV
A	50%	10	10	10	0	0
Cumulative Totals		**10**	**10**	**10**	**0**	**0**

Status Report: Ending Period 2

Task	%Complete	EV	AC	PV	CV	SV
A	Finished	20	30	20	−10	0
Cumulative Totals		**20**	**30**	**20**	**−10**	**0**

Status Report: Ending Period 3

Task	%Complete	EV	AC	PV	CV	SV
A	Finished	20	30	20	−10	0
B	33%	5	10	5	−5	0
C	20%	20	30	20	−10	0
D	60%	21	20	15	+1	+6
Cumulative Totals		**66**	**90**	**60**	**−24**	**+6**

Status Report: Ending Period 4

Task	%Complete	EV	AC	PV	CV	SV
A	Finished	20	30	20	−10	0
B	Finished	15	20	15	−5	0
C	50%	50	70	50	−20	0
D	80%	28	30	25	−2	+3
Cumulative Totals		**113**	**150**	**110**	**−37**	**+3**

Status Report: Ending Period 5

Task	%Complete	EV	AC	PV	CV	SV
A	Finished	20	30	20	−10	0
B	Finished	15	20	15	−5	0
C	60%	60	100	80	−40	−20
D	80%	28	50	35	−22	−7
Cumulative Totals		**123**	**200**	**150**	**−77**	**−27**

Status Report: Ending Period 6

Task	%Complete	EV	AC	PV	CV	SV
A	Finished	20	30	20	−10	0
B	Finished	15	20	15	−5	0
C	80%	80	110	100	−30	−20
D	Finished	35	60	35	−25	0
Cumulative Totals		**150**	**220**	**170**	**−70**	**−20**

Status Report: Ending Period 7

Task	%Complete	EV	AC	PV	CV	SV
A	Finished	20	30	20	−10	0
B	Finished	15	20	15	−5	0
C	90%	90	120	100	−30	−10
D	Finished	35	60	35	−25	0
E	0%	0	0	30	0	−30
F	0%	0	0	0	0	0
Cumulative Totals		**160**	**230**	**200**	**−70**	**−40**

FIGURE 13.10
Digital Camera
Prototype Summary
Graph (000)

Figure 13.10 shows the graphed results of all the status reports through period 7. This graph represents the data from Table 13.2. The cumulative actual costs (AC) to date and the earned value budgeted costs to date (EV) are plotted against the original project baseline (PV). The cumulative AC to date is $230; the cumulative EV to date is $160. Given these cumulative values, the cost variance (CV = EV − AC) is negative $70 (160 − 230 = −70). The schedule variance (SV = EV − PV) is negative $40 (160 − 200 = −40). Again, recall that only the project network or Gantt tracking chart can give an accurate assessment of schedule performance down to the work package level.

A Gantt tracking bar chart for the Digital Camera Prototype is shown in Figure 13.11. From this figure you can see Task C (Memory/Software), which had an original duration of 4 time units, now is expected to require 6 time units. This delay of 2 time units for Task C will also delay Tasks E and F two time units and result in the project being late 2 time periods.

FIGURE 13.11
Digital Camera
Project-Tracking
Gantt Chart Showing
Status—Through
Period 7

FIGURE 13.12 **Project Rollup End Period 7 (000)**

Figure 13.12 shows an oversimplified project rollup at the end of period 7. The rollup is by deliverables and organization units. For example, the Memory/Software deliverable has an SV of $ −10 and a CV of −30. The responsible "Storage" department should have an explanation for these variances. Similarly, the assembly department, which is responsible for the Assemble and Test deliverables, has an SV of $ −30 due to the delay of Task C (See Figure 13.11). Most deliverables look unfavorable on schedule and cost variance.

In more complex projects, the crosstabs of cost accounts by deliverables and organization units can be very revealing and more profound. This example contains the basics for developing a status report, baseline development, and measuring schedule and cost variance. In our example, performance analysis had only one level above the cost account level. Because all data are derived from the detailed database, it is relatively easy to determine progress status at all levels of the work and organization breakdown structures. Fortunately, this same current database can provide additional views of the current status of the project and forecast costs at the completion of the project. Approaches for deriving additional information from the database are presented next.

To the uninitiated, a caveat is in order. In practice budgets may not be expressed in total dollars for an activity. Frequently, budgets are time-phased for materials and labor separately for more effective control over costs. Another common approach used in practice is to use labor hours in place of dollars in the earned-value system. Later labor hours are converted to dollars. The use of labor hours in the earned-value system is the *modus operandi* for most construction work. Labor hours are easy to understand and are often the way many time and cost estimates are developed. Most earned-value software easily accommodates the use of labor hours for development of cost estimates.

Indexes to Monitor Progress

Practitioners sometimes prefer to use schedule and cost indexes over the absolute values of SV and CV, because indexes can be considered efficiency ratios. Graphed indexes over the project life cycle can be very illuminating and useful. The trends are easily identified for deliverables and the whole project.

Indexes are typically used at the cost account level and above. In practice, the database is also used to develop indexes that allow the project manager and customer to view progress from several angles. An index of 1.00 (100 percent) indicates progress is as planned. An index greater than 1.00 shows progress is better than expected. An index less than 1.00 suggests progress is poorer than planned and deserves attention. Table 13.3 presents the interpretation of the indexes.

Performance Indexes

There are two indexes of performance efficiency. The first index measures *cost* efficiency of the work accomplished to date:

$$\text{Cost performance index (CPI)} = EV/AC = 160/230 = .696 \text{ or } .70$$

The CPI of .696 shows that $.70 worth of work planned to date has been completed for each $1.00 actually spent—an unfavorable situation indeed. The CPI is the most accepted and used index. It has been tested over time and found to be the most accurate, reliable, and stable.

The second index is a measure of scheduling efficiency to date:

$$\text{Scheduling performance index (SPI)} = EV/PV = 160/200 = .80$$

The schedule index indicates $.80 worth of work has been accomplished for each $1.00 worth of scheduled work to-date. Table 13.2 presents the interpretation of the indexes. Figure 13.13 shows the indexes plotted for our example project through period 7. This figure is another example of graphs used in practice.

Project Percent Complete Index

Two project percent complete indexes are used, depending on your judgment of which one is most representative of your project. The first index assumes the original budget of work complete is the most reliable information to measure project percent complete. The second index assumes the actual costs-to-date and expected cost at completion are the most reliable for measuring project percent complete. These indexes compare the to-date progress to the end of the project. The implications underlying use of these

TABLE 13.3
Interpretation of Indexes

Index	Cost (CPI)	Schedule (SPI)
>1.00	Under cost	Ahead of schedule
=1.00	On cost	On schedule
<1.00	Over cost	Behind schedule

FIGURE 13.13
Indexes Periods 1–7

indexes are that conditions will not change, no improvement or action will be taken, and the information in the database is accurate. The first index looks at percent complete in terms of *budget* amounts:

$$\text{Percent complete index PCIB} = \text{EV/BAC} = 160/320 = 0.50\ (50\%)$$

This PCIB indicates the work accomplished represents 50 percent of the total budgeted (BAC) dollars to date. Observe that this calculation does not include actual costs incurred. Because actual dollars spent do not guarantee project progress, this index is favored by many project managers when there is a high level of confidence in the original budget estimates.

The second index views percent complete in terms of *actual* dollars spent to accomplish the work to date and the actual expected dollars for the completed project (EAC). For example, at the end of period 7 the staff re-estimates that the EAC will be 575 instead of 320. The application of this view is written as

$$\text{Percent complete index PCIC} = \text{AC/EAC} = 230/575 = .40\ (40\%)$$

Some managers favor this index because it contains actual and revised estimates that include newer, more complete information.

These two views of percent complete present alternative views of the "real" percent complete. These percents may be quite different as shown above. (Note: The PCIC index was not plotted in Figure 13.13. The new figures for EAC would be derived each period by estimators in the field.)

Technical Performance Measurement

Measuring technical performance is as important as measuring schedule and cost performance. Although technical performance is often assumed, the opposite can be true. The ramifications of poor technical performance frequently are more profound—something works or it doesn't if technical specifications are not adhered to. Assessing technical performance of a system, facility, or product is often accomplished by examining the documents found in the scope statement and/or work package documentation. These documents should specify criteria and tolerance limits against which performance can be measured. For example, the technical performance of a software project suffered because the feature of "drag and drop" was deleted in the final product. Conversely, the prototype of an experimental car exceeded the miles per gallon technical specification and, thus, its technical performance. It is very difficult to specify how to measure technical performance because it depends on the nature of the project. Suffice it to say, measuring technical performance must be done. Technical performance is frequently where quality control processes are needed and used. Project managers must be creative in finding ways to control this very important area.

Software for Project Cost/Schedule Systems

Software developers have created sophisticated schedule/cost systems for projects that track and report budget, actual, earned, committed, and index values. These values can be labor hours, materials, and/or dollars. This information supports cost and schedule progress, performance measurements, and cash flow management. Recall from Chapter 5 that budget, actual, and committed dollars usually run in different time frames (see Figure 5.5). A typical computer-generated status report includes the following information outputs:

1. Schedule variance (EV − PV) by cost account and WBS and OBS.
2. Cost variance (EV − AC) by cost account and WBS and OBS.
3. Indexes—total percent complete and performance index.
4. Cumulative actual total cost to-date (AC).
5. Expected costs at completion (EAC).
6. Paid and unpaid commitments.

The variety of software packages, with their features and constant updating, is too extensive for inclusion in this text. Software developers and vendors have done a superb job of providing software to meet the information needs of most project managers. Differences among software in the last decade have centered on improving "friendliness" and output that is clear and easy to understand. Anyone who understands the concepts and tools presented in Chapters 4, 5, 6, 8, and 13 has little trouble understanding the output of any of the popular project management software packages.

Additional Earned-Value Rules

Although the percent complete rule is the most-used method of assigning budgets to baselines and for cost control, there are two additional rules that are very useful for reducing the overhead costs of collecting detailed data on percent complete of individual work packages. (An additional advantage of these rules, of course, is that they remove the often subjective judgments of the contractors as to how much has actually been completed.) These rules are the 0/100 percent rule and the 50/50 rule. These two rules are typically used for short-duration activities and/or small-cost activities.

- **0/100 percent rule.** This rule assumes credit is earned for having performed the work once it is completed. Hence, 100 percent of the budget is earned when the work package is completed. This rule is used for work packages having very short durations.
- **50/50 rule.** This approach allows 50 percent of the value of the work package budget to be earned when it is started and 50 percent to be earned when the package is completed. This rule is popular for work packages of short duration and small total costs.

Again, notice the only information needed is that the work package has started and the package has been completed. These two rules are very popular with project managers, but contractors are not enthusiastic about their use on larger work packages or where the contractor has cash flow problems. For those who wish to explore the application of these rules, or who are studying for certification, Appendix 13.1 presents two exercises that apply these rules along with the percent complete rule.

Forecasting Final Project Cost

There are basically two methods used to revise estimates of future project costs. In many cases both methods are used on specific segments of the project. The result is confusion of terms in texts, in software, and among practitioners in the field. We have chosen to note the differences between the methods. The first method allows experts in the field to change original baseline durations and costs because new information tells them the original estimates are not accurate. We have used EAC_e to represent revisions made by experts and practitioners associated with the project. The revisions from project experts are almost always used on smaller projects.

A second method is used in large projects where the original budget is less reliable. This method uses the actual costs to date plus an efficiency index, (CPI = EV/AC) applied to the remaining project work. When the estimate for completion uses the CPI as the basis for forecasting cost at completion, we use the acronym, EAC_f. The equation is presented here.

The equation for this forecasting model (EAC_f) is as follows:

$$ETC = \frac{\text{Work remaining}}{CPI} = \frac{BAC - EV}{EV/AC}$$

$$EAC_f = ETC + AC$$

where   ETC = estimated cost to complete remaining work.

CPI = cumulative cost index to date.

EV = cumulative budgeted cost of work completed to date.

AC = cumulative actual cost of work completed to date.

BAC = total budget of the baseline.

EAC_f = estimated total cost at completion.

The following information is available from our earlier example; the estimate cost at completion (EAC_f) is computed as follows:

Total baseline budget (BAC) for the project	$320
Cumulative earned value (EV) to date	$160
Cumulative actual cost (AC) to date	$230

$$EAC_f = \frac{320 - 160}{160/230} + 230 = \frac{160}{.7} + 230 = 229 + 230$$

$$EAC_f = \$459$$

The final project projected cost forecast is $459 versus $320 originally planned.

Another popular index is the To Complete Performance Index (TCPI), which is useful as a supplement to the estimate at complete (EAC_f) computation. This ratio measures the amount of value each *remaining* dollar in the budget must earn to stay within the budget. The index is computed for the Digital Camera project at the end of period 7.

$$\text{TCPI} = \frac{\text{BAC} - \text{EV}}{\text{BAC} - \text{AC}} = \frac{320 - 160}{320 - 230} = \frac{160}{90} = 1.78$$

The index of 1.78 indicates that each remaining dollar in the budget must earn $1.78 in value. There is more work to be done than there is budget left. Clearly, it would be tough to increase productivity that much to make budget. The work to be done will have to be reduced or accept running over budget. If the TCPI is less than 1.00, you should be able to complete the project without using all of the remaining budget. A ratio of less than 1.00 opens the possibility of other opportunities such as improving quality, increasing profit, or expanding scope.

Research data indicate that on large projects that are more than 15 percent complete, the model performs well with an error of less than 10 percent. This model can also be used for WBS and OBS cost accounts that have been used to forecast remaining and total costs. It is important to note that this model assumes conditions will not change, the cost database is reliable, EV and AC are cumulative, and past project progress is representative of future progress. This objective forecast represents a good starting point or benchmark that management can use to compare other forecasts that include other conditions and subjective judgments.

Exhibit 13.1 presents an abridged monthly status report similar to one used by a project organization. The form is used for all projects in their project portfolio. (Note

EXHIBIT 13.1
Monthly Status Report

Project number: 163					Project manager: Connor Gage
Project priority now: 4					
Status as of: April 1, 2002					
Earned value figures:					
PV	**EV**	**AC**	**SV**	**CV**	**BAC**
588,240	566,064	596,800	(22,176)	(30,736)	1,051,200
EAC	**VAC**	**EAC$_f$**	**CPI**	**CPIB**	**CPIC**
1,090,640	(−39,440)	1,108,278	.95	.538	.547

Project description: A computer-controlled conveyor belt that will move and position items on the belt with accuracy of less than one millimeter.

Status summary: The project is approximately 25 days behind schedule. The project has a cost variance of ($30,736).

Explanations: The schedule variance has moved from noncritical activities to those on the critical path. Integration first phase, scheduled to start 3/26, is now expected to start 4/19, which means it is approximately 25 days behind schedule. This delay is traced to the loss of the second design team which made it impossible to start utilities documentation on 2/27 as planned. This loss illustrates the effect of losing valuable resources on the project. The cost variance to date is largely due to a design change that cost $21,000.

Major changes since last report: The major change was loss of one design team to the project.

Total cost of approved design changes: $21,000. Most of this amount is attributed to the improved design of the serial/IO drivers.

Projected cost at completion: EAC$_f$ is estimated to be $1,108,278. This represents an overrun of $57,078, given a CPI of .95. The CPI of .95 causes the forecast to be greater than the VAC (−$39,440).

Risk watch: Nothing suggests the risk level of any segments has changed.

Brendan McDermid/EPA/Landov.

Portland General Electric Company has been charged with decommissioning the Trojan Nuclear Plant. This is a long and complex project extending over two decades. The first segment of the project of moving the used reactors to a storage location is complete and was awarded the Project of the Year, 2000, by the Project Management Institute (PMI). The remainder of the project—decontamination of the remaining structures and waste—is ongoing.

The figure on page 435 shows their earned-value status report through December 2000. This report measures schedule and cost performance for monitoring the project. TDF represents the original EV for 1/1/00. The current BCWS is modified by scope changes

($) or baseline schedule changes. (Notice SI is measured against TDF.) The report also serves as a basis for funding for rate filings with the Public Utilities Commission.

The SI (0.88) suggests the project schedule is falling behind. Resolving issues with a major vendor and solutions for technical problems should solve these delay problems. The CI (1.14) for the project is positive. Some of this good cost performance is attributed to partnering and incentive arrangements with vendors and labor unions.

Interview with Michael B. Lackey, general manager, Trojan, PGE (September 2001).

that the schedule variance of $-\$22,176$ does not translate directly to days. The 25 days were derived from the network schedule.)

Another summary report is shown in the Snapshot from Practice: Trojan Decommissioning Project. Compare the differences in format.

Other Control Issues

Baseline Changes

Changes during the life cycle of projects are inevitable and will occur. Some changes can be very beneficial to project outcomes; changes having a negative impact are the ones we wish to avoid. Careful project definition can minimize the need for changes. The price for poor project definition can be changes that result in cost overruns, late schedules, low morale, and loss of control. Change comes from external sources or from within. Externally, for example, the customer may request changes that were not

Cost/Budget Performance (EV and TDF)

Decommissioning Cumulative Costs   **Nominal Year Dollars**

Portland General Electric Co.-Trojan Nuclear Plant

Report Run: 23-Jan-01 8:13 A.M.   Report Number: DECT005

Description	Dec 2000 PV	Dec 2000 EV	Dec 2000 AC	YTD PV	YTD EV	YTD AC	YTD Variance BCP/ACP	2000 PV	2000 TDF	CPI EV/AC	SPI EV/PV
ISFSI	193,014	182,573	162,579	3,655,677	3,586,411	3,263,995	322,416	3,855,877	4,348,754	1.10	0.83
RVAIR	0	0	0	0	0	399	(399)	0	0	0.00	0.00
Equip removal—AB/FB	79,083	79,649	73,899	497,197	504,975	308,461	196,514	497,197	479,534	1.64	1.05
Equip removal—other	0	0	0	0	(36,822)	519	(37,341)	0	0	0.00	0.00
Embed piping—AB/FB	3,884	0	2,118	532,275	540,232	515,235	24,997	532,275	763,579	1.05	0.71
Embed piping—other	0	0	3,439	175,401	210,875	79,235	131,640	175,401	195,405	2.86	1.08
Surface decon—AB/FB	29,935	23,274	21,456	1,266,685	1,293,315	1,171,712	121,603	1,266,665	1,453,029	1.10	0.90
Surface decon—other	2,875	2	11,005	308,085	199,853	251,265	(51,413)	308,085	141,183	0.80	1.24
Surface decon—containment	680,502	435,657	474,427	5,271,889	4,950,528	4,823,338	127,190	5,271,889	4,693,551	1.03	0.96
Radwaste disposal	884,873	453,032	(28,675)	10,680,118	8,276,616	10,807,916	(2,531,300)	10,880,118	10,645,292	0.77	0.78
Final survey	58,238	57,985	27,091	780,990	780,990	700,942	80,048	780,990	1,568,600	1.11	0.50
Nonradiological areas	92,837	91,956	58,538	2,471,281	2,376,123	834,643	1,541,480	2,471,281	3,579,292	2.85	0.66
Staffing	714,806	714,509	468,858	9,947,775	9,947,775	8,241,383	1,706,392	9,947,775	9,772,793	1.21	1.02
ISFSI—Long-term ops	85,026	85,028	19,173	2,004,398	2,004,398	337,206	1,667,192	2,004,398	2,707,316	5.94	0.74
Labor loadings	258,289	258,289	240,229	3,216,194	3,216,194	2,755,604	460,590	3,216,194	3,216,194	1.17	1.00
Material loadings	17,910	17,910	(95,128)	211,454	211,454	136,973	74,481	211,454	211,454	1.54	1.00
Corporate governance	153,689	228,499	228,521	1,814,523	1,814,523	1,814,520	3	1,814,523	2,277,711	1.00	1.00
Undistributable costs	431,840	401,720	242,724	5,541,679	5,575,879	4,007,732	1,567,947	5,541,679	5,455,764	1.39	0.80
Total decommissioning	3,688,481	3,008,081	1,905,084	48,375,399	45,453,119	40,051,079	5,402,040	48,375,399	51,507,451	1.13	0.87
Total (less ISFSI and RVAIR)	3,493,467	2,845,508	1,743,485	44,719,720	41,886,710	36,788,680	5,080,024	44,719,720	47,160,700	1.14	0.88

included in the original scope statement and that will require significant changes to the project and thus to the baseline. Or the government may render requirements that were not a part of the original plan and that require a revision of the project scope. Internally, stakeholders may identify unforeseen problems or improvements that change the scope of the project. In rare cases scope changes can come from several sources. For example, the Denver International Airport automatic baggage handling system was an afterthought supported by several project stakeholders that included the Denver city government, consultants, and at least one airline customer. The additional $2 billion in costs were staggering, and the airport opening was delayed 16 months. If this automatic baggage scope change had been in the original plan, costs would have been only a fraction of the overrun costs, and delays would have been reduced significantly. Any changes in scope or the baseline should be recorded by the change control system that was set in place during risk control planning. (See Chapter 7.)

Generally, project managers monitor scope changes very carefully. They should allow scope changes only if it is clear that the project will fail without the change, the project will be improved significantly with the change, or the customer wants it and will pay for it. This statement is an exaggeration, but it sets the tone for approaching baseline changes. The effect of the change on the scope and baseline should be accepted and signed off by the project customer. Figure 13.14 depicts the cost impact of a scope change on the baseline at a point in time—"today." Line A represents a scope change that results in an increase in cost. Line B represents a scope change that decreases cost. Quickly recording scope changes to the baseline keeps the computed earned values valid. Failure to do so results in misleading cost and schedule variances.

Care should be taken to not use baseline changes to disguise poor performance on past or current work. A common signal of this type of baseline change is a constantly revised baseline that seems to match results. Practitioners call this a "rubber baseline" because it stretches to match results. Most changes will not result in serious scope changes and should be absorbed as positive or negative variances. Retroactive changes for work already accomplished should not be allowed. Transfer of money among cost accounts should not be allowed after the work is complete. Unforeseen changes can be

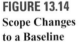

FIGURE 13.14
Scope Changes to a Baseline

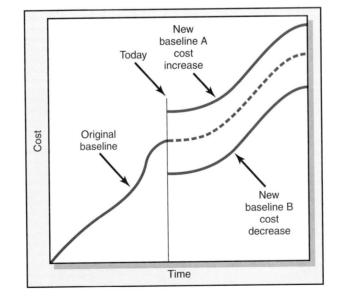

handled through the contingency reserve. The project manager typically makes this decision. In some large projects, a partnering "change review team," made up of members of the project and customer teams, makes all decisions on project changes.

Contingency Reserve

Plans seldom materialize in every detail as estimated—identified and unidentified risks occur, estimates are wrong, the customer wants changes, technology changes. Because perfect planning doesn't exist, some contingency funds should be agreed upon before the project commences to cover the unexpected. The size of the contingency reserve should be related to the uncertainty and risk of schedule and cost estimate inaccuracies. For example, if the project represents little that is new to the project team, the contingency reserve might be 1 to 2 percent of the total cost of the project. Conversely, if the project represents something that is new to all team members, the reserve might be 5 to 20 percent of the total cost. A rule of thumb used by a construction management firm centers around the percent of design complete when the project begins. For example, if 30 percent of design is completed when the project begins, a contingency reserve of 25 percent is included as a hedge against uncertainty; if 60 percent of design is complete, the reserve is 15 percent; if design is 95 percent complete, a 10 percent reserve is included. Contingency reserve funds represent flexibility for the project manager so he or she can move the project forward.

Contingency reserve is not a free lunch for all who come. Reserve funds should only be released by the project manager on a very formal and documented basis. Recall that *budget reserve* contingency funds are not for scope changes. Scope changes are covered by *management reserve* funds. Chapter 7 provides a detailed description of budget and management contingency reserves. The trend today is to allow all stakeholders to know the size of the contingency reserve (even subcontractors). This approach is built on trust, openness, and the self-discipline of the project stakeholders who are all focused on one set of goals.

The Costs and Problems of Data Acquisition

The Snapshot from Practice: A Pseudo-Earned Value Percent Complete Approach captures some of the frequent issues surrounding resistance to data collection of percent complete for earned value systems. Similar pseudo-percent complete systems have been used by others. Such pseudo-percent complete approaches appear to work well in multiproject environments that include several small and medium-sized projects. Assuming a one-week reporting period, care needs to be taken to develop work packages with a duration of about one week long so problems are identified quickly. For large projects, there is no substitute for using a percent complete system that depends on data collected through observation at clearly defined monitoring points.

Scope Creep

Large changes in scope are easily identified. It is the "minor refinements" that eventually build to be major scope changes that can cause problems. These small refinements are known in the field as *scope creep*. For example, the customer of a software developer requested small changes in the development of a custom accounting software package. After several minor refinements, it became apparent the changes represented a significant enlargement of the original project scope. The result was an unhappy customer and a development firm that lost money and reputation.

A consultant for the U.S. Forest Service suggested the use of earned value to monitor the 50-plus timber sale projects taking place concurrently in the district. As projects were completed, new ones were started. Earned value was tried for approximately nine months. After a nine-month trial, the process was to be reviewed by a task force. The task force concluded the earned-value system provided good information for monitoring and forecasting project progress; however, the costs and problems of collecting timely percent complete data were unacceptable because there were no funds available to collect such data.

The level of detail dilemma was discussed, but no suggestions satisfied the problem. The discussion recognized that too little data fail to offer good control, while excessive reporting requires paperwork and people, which are costly. The task force concluded progress and performance could be measured using a pseudo-version of percent complete while not giving up much

accuracy for the total project. This modified approach to percent complete required that very large work packages (about 3 to 5 percent of all work packages in a project) be divided into smaller work packages for closer control and identification of problems sooner. It was decided work packages of about a week's duration would be ideal. The pseudo-version required only a telephone call and "yes/no" answers to one of the following questions to assign percent complete:

Has work on the work package started?	No = 0%
Working on the package?	Yes = 50%
Is the work package completed?	Yes = 100%

Data for the pseudo-earned value percent complete system was collected for all 50-plus projects by an intern working fewer than eight hours each week.

Although scope changes are usually viewed negatively, there are situations when scope changes result in positive rewards. Scope changes can represent significant opportunities. In product development environments, adding a small feature to a product can result in a huge competitive advantage. A small change in the production process may get the product to market one month early or reduce product cost.

Scope creep is common early in projects—especially in new-product development projects. Customer requirements for additional features, new technology, poor design assumptions, etc., all manifest pressures for scope changes. Frequently these changes are small and go unnoticed until time delays or cost overruns are observed. Scope creep affects the organization, project team, and project suppliers. Scope changes alter the organization's cash flow requirements in the form of fewer or additional resources, which may also affect other projects. Frequent changes eventually wear down team motivation and cohesiveness. Clear team goals are altered, become less focused, and cease being the focal point for team action. Starting over again is annoying and demoralizing to the project team because it disrupts project rhythm and lowers productivity. Project suppliers resent frequent changes because they represent higher costs and have the same effect on their team as on the project team.

The key to managing scope creep is change management. One project manager of an architectural firm related that scope creep was the biggest risk his firm faced in projects. The best defense against scope creep is a well-defined scope statement. Poor scope statements are one of the major causes of scope creep.

A second defense against scope creep is stating what the project is not, which can avoid misinterpretations later. (Chapter 7 discusses the process. See Figure 7.8 to review key variables to document in project changes.) First, the original baseline must be well defined and agreed upon with the project customer. Before the project begins, it is imperative that clear procedures be in place for authorizing and documenting scope changes by the customer or project team. If a scope change is necessary, the impact on the baseline should be clearly documented—for example, cost, time, dependencies, specifications, responsibilities, etc. Finally, the scope change must be quickly added to the original baseline to reflect the change in budget and schedule; these changes and their impacts need to be communicated to all project stakeholders.

Summary

The best information system does not result in good control. Control requires the project manager to *use* information to steer the project through rough waters. Control and Gantt charts are useful vehicles for monitoring time performance. The cost/schedule system allows the manager to have a positive influence on cost and schedule in a timely manner. The ability to influence cost decreases with time; therefore, timely reports identifying adverse cost trends can greatly assist the project manager in getting back on budget and schedule. The integrated cost/schedule model provides the project manager and other stakeholders with a snapshot of the current and future status of the project. The benefits of the cost/schedule model are as follows:

1. Measures accomplishments against plan and deliverables.
2. Provides a method for tracking directly to a problem work package and organization unit responsible.
3. Alerts all stakeholders to early identification of problems, and allows for quick, proactive corrective action.
4. Improves communication because all stakeholders are using the same database.
5. Keeps customer informed of progress, and encourages customer confidence that the money spent is resulting in the expected progress.
6. Provides for accountability over individual portions of the overall budget for each organizational unit.

Key Terms

Baseline budget	Estimate at completion	Time phasing
Cost performance index (CPI)	(EAC)	Variance at completion (VAC)
Cost variance (CV)	Schedule variance (SV)	
Earned value		

Review Questions

1. How does earned value give a clearer picture of project schedule and cost status than a simple plan versus actual system?
2. How does a baseline facilitate integrating the planning and controlling of projects?
3. Why is it important for project managers to resist changes to the project baseline? Under what conditions would a project manager make changes to a baseline? When would a project manager not allow changes to a baseline?
4. How does a project rollup help identify project cost and schedule problems?
5. Costs can be aggregated or disaggregated horizontally and vertically. What are the advantages of this system?
6. What are the differences between BAC and EAC?

Exercises

1. In month 9 the following project information is available: actual cost is $2,000, earned value is $2,100, and planned cost is $2,400. Compute the SV and CV for the project.
2. On day 51 a project has an earned value of $600, an actual cost of $650, and a planned cost of $560. Compute the SV, CV, and CPI for the project. What is your assessment of the project on day 51?

3. Given the project network and baseline information below, complete the form to develop a status report for the project at the end of period 4 and the end of period 8. From the data you have collected and computed for periods 4 and 8, what information are you prepared to tell the customer about the status of the project at the end of period 8?

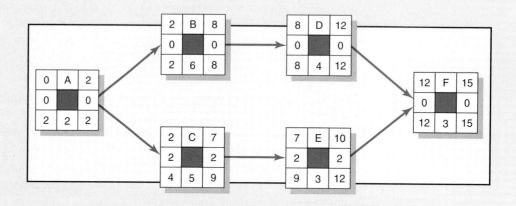

Task	Dur.	ES	LF	Slack	Budget (PV)	0	1	2	3	4	5	6	7	8	9	10	11	12	13	14	15
A	2	0	4	0	400	200	200														
B	6	2	8	0	2400			200	600	200	600	200	600								
C	9	2	9	2	1500			200	400	500	100	300									
D	4	8	12	0	1600											400	400	400	400		
E	3	7	12	2	900									300	400	200					
F	3	12	15	0	600														200	100	300
Period PV total						200	200	400	1000	700	700	500	900	800	600	400	400	200	100	300	
Cumulative PV total						200	400	800	1800	2500	3200	3700	4600	5400	6000	6400	6800	7000	7100	7400	

Project baseline (PV) (in $)

End of Period 4

Task	Actual % Complete	EV	AC	PV	CV	SV
A	Finished	———	300	400	———	———
B	50%	———	1000	800	———	———
C	33%	———	500	600	———	———
D	0	———	0	———	———	———
E	0	———	0	———	———	———
Cumulative Totals		———	———	———	———	———

End of Period 8

Task	Actual % Complete	EV	AC	PV	CV	SV
A	Finished	_____	300	400	_____	_____
B	Finished	_____	2200	2400	_____	_____
C	Finished	_____	1500	1500	_____	_____
D	25%	_____	300	0	_____	_____
E	33%	_____	300		_____	_____
F	0	_____	0		_____	_____
Cumulative Totals		_____	_____	_____	_____	_____

4. Given the following project network, baseline, and status information, develop status reports for periods 1–4 and complete the project summary graph (or a similar one). Report the final SV, CV, CPI, and PCIB. Based on your data, what is your assessment of the current status of the project? At completion?

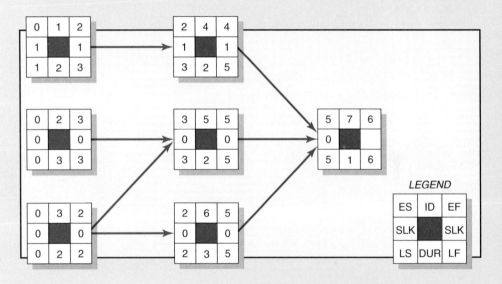

Schedule information					Baseline budget needs ($ 000)							
ACT/WP	DUR	ES	LF	SLK	Total PV	Time period						
						0	1	2	3	4	5	6
1	2	0	3	1	12	4	8					
2	3	0	3	0	15	3	7	5				
3	2	0	3	1	8	4	4					
4	2	2	5	1	6			3	3			
5	2	3	5	0	10				6	4		
6	3	2	5	2	9			3	3	3		
7	1	5	6	0	5							5
Total PV by period						11	19	11	12	7	5	
Cumulative PV by period						11	30	41	53	60	65	

Status Report: Ending Period 1

Task	%Complete	EV	AC	PV	CV	SV
1	50%	_____	6	4	_____	_____
2	40%	_____	8	3		
3	25%	_____	3			
Cumulative Totals		_____	**17**	_____	_____	_____

Status Report: Ending Period 2

Task	%Complete	EV	AC	PV	CV	SV
1	Finished	_____	13	_____	_____	_____
2	80%	_____	14	_____	_____	_____
3	75%	_____	8	_____	_____	_____
Cumulative Totals		_____	**35**	_____	_____	_____

Status Report: Ending Period 3

Task	%Complete	EV	AC	PV	CV	SV
1	Finished	12	13	_____	_____	_____
2	80%	_____	15	_____	_____	_____
3	Finished	_____	10	_____	_____	_____
4	50%	_____	4	_____	_____	_____
5	0%	_____	0	_____	_____	_____
6	33.3%	_____	4	_____	_____	_____
Cumulative Totals		_____	_____	_____	_____	_____

Status Report: Ending Period 4

Task	%Complete	EV	AC	PV	CV	SV
1	Finished	12	13	_____	_____	_____
2	Finished	15	18	_____	_____	_____
3	Finished	_____	10	_____	_____	_____
4	Finished	_____	8	_____	_____	_____
5	30%	_____	3	_____	_____	_____
6	66.7%	_____	8	_____	_____	_____
7	0	_____	0	_____	_____	_____
Cumulative Totals		_____	_____	_____	_____	_____

Summary Graph

5. The following labor hours data have been collected for a nanotechnology project for periods 1 through 6. Compute the SV, CV, SPI, and CPI for each period. Plot the EV and the AC on the summary graph provided (or a similar one). Plot the SPI, CPI, and PCIB on the index graph provided (or a similar one). What is your assessment of the project at the end of period 6?

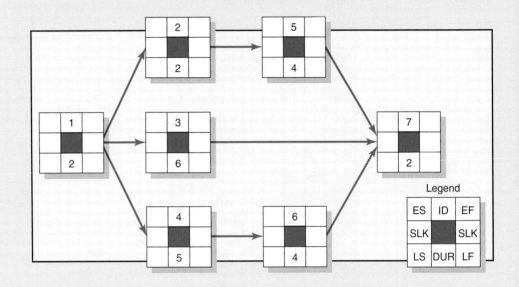

	Schedule information					Baseline budget needs–labor hours (00)														
ACT/ WP	DUR	ES	LF	TF	Total PV	Time period														
						0	1	2	3	4	5	6	7	8	9	10	11	12	13	14
1	2	0	2	0	20	10	10													
2	2	2	7	3	24			16	8											
3	6	2	11	3	30			5	5	10	3	2	5							
4	5	2	7	0	25			10	10	2	2	1								
5	4	4	11	3	16					4	4	4	4							
6	4	7	11	0	20								5	5	6	4				
7	2	11	13	0	10													5	5	
Total PV by period						10	10	31	23	16	9	7	14	5	6	4	5	5		
Cumulative PV by period						10	20	51	74	90	99	106	120	125	131	135	140	145		

Status Report: Ending Period 1

Task	%Complete	EV	AC	PV	CV	SV
1	50%	____	500	1000	____	____
Cumulative Totals		____	**500**	**1000**	____	____

Status Report: Ending Period 2

Task	%Complete	EV	AC	PV	CV	SV
1	Finished	____	1500	2000	____	____
Cumulative Totals		____	**1500**	**2000**	____	____

Status Report: Ending Period 3

Task	%Complete	EV	AC	PV	CV	SV
1	Finished	2000	1500	2000	____	____
2	0	____	0	____	____	____
3	10%	____	200	____	____	____
4	20%	____	500	____	____	____
Cumulative Totals		____	**2200**	____	____	____

Status Report: Ending Period 4

Task	%Complete	EV	AC	PV	CV	SV
1	Finished	2000	1500	2000	____	____
2	50%	____	1000	____	____	____
3	30%	____	800	____	____	____
4	40%	____	1500	____	____	____
Cumulative Totals		____	**4800**	____	____	____

Status Report: Ending Period 5

Task	%Complete	EV	AC	PV	CV	SV
1	Finished	2000	1500	2000	____	____
2	Finished	____	2000	____	____	____
3	50%	____	800	____	____	____
4	60%	____	1500	____	____	____
5	25%	____	400	____	____	____
Cumulative Totals		____	**6200**	____	____	____

Status Report: Ending Period 6

Task	%Complete	EV	AC	PV	CV	SV
1	Finished	2000	1500	2000	____	____
2	Finished	____	2000	____	____	____
3	80%	____	2100	____	____	____
4	80%	____	1800	____	____	____
5	50%	____	600	____	____	____
Cumulative Totals		____	**8000**	____	____	____

Period	SPI	CPI	PCIB
1	————	————	————
2	————	————	————
3	————	————	————
4	————	————	————
5	————	————	————
6	————	————	————

SPI = EV/PV
CPI = EV/AC
PCIB = EV/BAC

Summary Graph

Indexes Periods 1–7

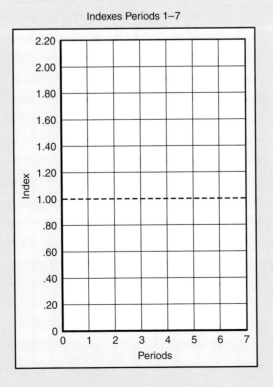

6. The following data have been collected for a British health care IT project for two-week reporting periods 2 through 12. Compute the SV, CV, SPI, and CPI for each period. Plot the EV and the AC on the summary graph provided. Plot the SPI, CPI, and PCIB on the index graph provided. (You may use your own graphs.) What is your assessment of the project at the end of period 12?

Baseline (PV) (00 $)																
Task	Dur.	ES	LF	Slack	PV (00 $)	0	2	4	6	8	10	12	14	16	18	20	22
1	4	0	4	0	8	4	4									
2	8	4	14	2	40			10	10	10	10					
3	6	4	10	0	30			10	15	5						
4	4	4	10	2	20			10	10							
5	4	10	14	0	40							20	20			
6	8	8	18	2	60						20	20	10	10		
7	4	14	18	0	20								10	10		
8	4	18	22	0	30											20	10
Period PV total						4	4	30	35	35	50	30	20	10	20	10
Cumulative PV total						4	8	38	73	108	158	188	208	218	238	248

Status Report: Ending Period 2

Task	%Complete	EV	AC	PV	CV	SV
1	50%	___	4	___	___	___
Cumulative Totals		___	**4**	___	___	___

Status Report: Ending Period 4

Task	%Complete	EV	AC	PV	CV	SV
1	Finished	___	10	___	___	___
Cumulative Totals		___	**10**	___	___	___

Status Report: Ending Period 6

Task	%Complete	EV	AC	PV	CV	SV
1	Finished	___	10	___	___	___
2	.25%	___	15	___	___	___
3	.33%	___	12	___	___	___
4	0%	___	0	___	___	___
Cumulative Totals		___	**37**	___	___	___

Status Report: Ending Period 8

Task	%Complete	EV	AC	PV	CV	SV
1	Finished	___	10	___	___	___
2	30%	___	20	___	___	___
3	60%	___	25	___	___	___
4	0%	___	0	___	___	___
Cumulative Totals		___	**55**	___	___	___

Status Report: Ending Period 10

Task	%Complete	EV	AC	PV	CV	SV
1	Finished	___	10	___	___	___
2	60%	___	30	___	___	___
3	Finished	___	40	___	___	___
4	50%	___	20	___	___	___
5	0%	___	0	___	___	___
6	30%	___	24	___	___	___
Cumulative Totals		___	**124**	___	___	___

Status Report: Ending Period 12

Task	%Complete	BCWP	ACWP	BCWS	CV	SV
1	Finished	___	10	___	___	___
2	Finished	___	50	___	___	___
3	Finished	___	40	___	___	___
4	Finished	___	40	___	___	___
5	50%	___	30	___	___	___
6	50%	___	40	___	___	___
Cumulative Totals		___	**210**	___	___	___

Indexes

Period	SPI	CPI	PCIB
2	___	___	___
4	___	___	___
6	___	___	___
8	___	___	___
10	___	___	___
12	___	___	___

SPI = EV/PV
CPI = EV/AC
PCIB = EV/BAC

Summary Graph

Indexes Periods 2–12

References

Abramovici, Adrian, "Controlling Scope Creep," *PM Network,* Vol. 14, No. 1, January 2000, pp. 44–48.

Anbari, Frank T. "Earned Value Project Management Method and Extensions," *Project Management Journal,* Vol. 34, No. 4, December 2003, pp. 12–22.

Brandon, Daniel M. Jr., "Implementing Earned Value Easily and Effectively," *Project Management Journal,* Vol. 29, No. 3, June, 1998, pp. 11–17.

Fleming, Quentin, and Joel M. Koppelman, *Earned Value Project Management,* 2nd ed. Project Management Institute, Newton Square, PA, 2000.

Kerzner, Harold, "Strategic Planning for A Project Office," *Project Management Journal,* Vol. 34, No. 2, June 2003, pp. 13–25.

Webb, Alan, *Using Earned Value: A Project Manager's Guide,* Gower Publishing Co., Aldershot, UK, 2003.

Case

Scanner Project

You have been serving as Electroscan's project manager and are now well along in the project. Develop a narrative status report for the board of directors of the chain store that discusses the status of the project to date and at completion. Be as specific as you can using numbers given and those you might develop. Remember, your audience is not familiar with the jargon used by project managers and computer software personnel; therefore, some explanation may be necessary. Your report will be evaluated on your detailed use of the data, your total perspective of the current status and future status of the project, and your recommended changes (if any).

Electroscan, Inc.
555 Acorn Street, Suite 5
Boston, Massachusetts

29 In-store Scanner Project
(thousands of dollars)
Actual Progress as of January 1

Name	PV	EV	AC	SV	CV	BAC	EAC$_f$
Scanner project	420	395	476	-25	-81	915	1103
H 1.0 Hardware	92	88	72	-4	16	260	213
H 1.1 Hardware specifications (DS)	20	20	15	0	5	20	15
H 1.2 Hardware design (DS)	30	30	25	0	5	30	25
H 1.3 Hardware documentation (DOC)	10	6	5	-4	1	10	8
H 1.4 Prototypes (PD)	2	2	2	0	0	40	40
H 1.5 Test Prototypes (T)	0	0	0	0	0	30	30
H 1.6 Order circuit boards (PD)	30	30	25	0	5	30	25
H 1.7 Preproduction models (PD)	0	0	0	0	0	100	100
OP 1.0 Operating system	195	150	196	-45	-46	330	431
OP 1.1 Kernel specifications (DS)	20	20	15	0	5	20	15
OP 1.2 Drivers	45	55	76	10	-21	70	97
OP 1.2.1 Disk drivers (DEV)	25	30	45	5	-15	40	60
OP 1.2.2 I/O drivers (DEV)	20	25	31	5	-6	30	37
OP 1.3 Code software	130	75	105	-55	-30	240	336
OP 1.3.1 Code software (C)	30	20	40	-10	-20	100	200
OP 1.3.2 Document software (DOC)	45	30	25	-15	5	50	42
OP 1.3.3 Code interfaces (C)	55	25	40	-30	-15	60	96
OP 1.3.4 Beta test software (T)	0	0	0	0	0	30	30
U 1.0 utilities	87	108	148	21	-40	200	274
U 1.1 Utilities specifications (DS)	20	20	15	0	5	20	15
U 1.2 Routine utilities (DEV)	20	20	35	0	-15	20	35
U 1.3 Complex utilities (DEV)	30	60	90	30	-30	100	150
U 1.4 Utilities documentation (DOC)	17	8	8	-9	0	20	20
U 1.5 Beta test utilities (T)	0	0	0	0	0	40	40
S 1.0 System integration	46	49	60	3	-11	125	153
S 1.1 Architecture decisions (DS)	9	9	7	0	2	10	8
S 1.2 Integration hard/soft (DEV)	25	30	45	5	-15	50	75
S 1.3 System hard/software test (T)	0	0	0	0	0	20	20
S 1.4 Project documentation (DOC)	12	10	8	-2	2	15	12
S 1.5 Integration acceptance testing (T)	0	0	0	0	0	30	30

Appendix 13.1

The Application of Additional Earned-Value Rules

The following example and exercises are designed to provide practice in applying the following three earned-value rules:

- Percent complete rule
- 0/100% rule
- 50/50 rule

See the chapter for an explanation of each of these rules.

SIMPLIFYING ASSUMPTIONS

The same simplifying assumptions used for the chapter example and exercises will be also used here.

1. Assume each cost account has only one work package, and each cost account will be represented as an activity on the network.
2. The project network early start times will serve as the basis for assigning the baseline values.
3. Except when the 0/100 rule or 50/50 rule is used, baseline values will be assigned linearly, unless stated differently. (Note: In practice estimated costs should be applied "exactly" as they are expected to occur so measures of schedule and cost performance are useful and reliable.)
4. For purposes of demonstrating the examples, from the moment work on an activity begins, some actual costs will be incurred each period until the activity is completed.
5. When the 0/100 rule is used, the total cost for the activity is placed in the baseline on the early finish date.
6. When the 50/50 rule is used, 50 percent of the total cost is placed in the baseline on the early start date and 50 percent on the early finish date.

APPENDIX EXERCISES

1. Given the information provided for development of a product warranty project for periods 1 through 7, compute the SV, CV, SPI, and CPI for each period. Plot the EV and the AC on the PV graph provided. Explain to the owner your assessment of the project at the end of period 7 and the future expected status of the project at completion. Figure A13.1a presents the project network. Figure A13.1b presents the project baseline noting those activities using the 0/100 (rule 3) and 50/50 (rule 2) rules. For example, activity 1 uses rule 3, the 0/100 rule. Although the early start time is period 0, the budget is not placed in the time-phased baseline until period 2 when the activity is planned to be finished (EF). This same procedure has been used to assign costs for activities 2 and 7. Activities 2 and 7 use the 50/50 rule. Thus, 50 percent of the budget for each activity is assigned on its respective early start date (time period 2 for activity 2 and period 11 for activity 7) and 50 percent for their respective finish dates. Remember, when assigning earned value as the project is being implemented, if an activity actually starts early or late, the earned values must shift with the actual times. For example, if activity 7 actually starts in period 12 rather than 11, the 50 percent is not earned until period 12.

FIGURE A13.1A

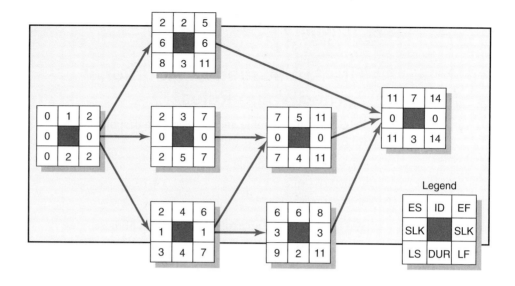

FIGURE A13.1B

EV Rule	ACT/ WP	DUR	ES	LF	TF	Total PV	0	1	2	3	4	5	6	7	8	9	10	11	12	13	14
③	1	2	0	2	0	6		6													
②	2	3	2	11	6	20			10		10										
①	3	5	2	7	2	30			9	6	6	6	3								
①	4	4	2	7	0	20			8	2	5	5									
①	5	4	7	11	0	16									4	4	4	4			
①	6	2	6	11	3	18								9	9						
②	7	3	11	14	0	8													4		4
Total PV by period							0	6	27	8	21	11	12	13	4	4	4	4	0	4	
Cumulative PV by period							0	6	33	41	62	73	85	98	102	106	110	114	114	118	

Schedule information | Baseline budget needs (000)

Rule
1 = %complete
2 = 50/50
3 = 0/100

Status Report: Ending Period 1

Task	%Complete	EV	AC	PV	CV	SV
1	0%	_____	3	0	_____	_____
Cumulative Totals		_____	3	0	_____	_____

Status Report: Ending Period 2

Task	%Complete	EV	AC	PV	CV	SV
1	Finished	6	5	_____	_____	_____
Cumulative Totals		**6**	**5**	_____	_____	_____

Status Report: Ending Period 3

Task	%Complete	EV	AC	PV	CV	SV
1	Finished	6	5	___	___	___
2	0%	___	5	___	___	___
3	.30%	___	7	___	___	___
4	25%	___	5	___	___	___
Cumulative Totals		___	**22**	___	___	___

Status Report: Ending Period 4

Task	%Complete	EV	AC	PV	CV	SV
1	Finished	6	5	___	___	___
2	0%	___	7	___	___	___
3	50%	___	10	___	___	___
4	50%	___	8	___	___	___
Cumulative Totals		___	**30**	___	___	___

Status Report: Ending Period 5

Task	%Complete	EV	AC	PV	CV	SV
1	Finished	6	5	___	___	___
2	50%	___	8	___	___	___
3	60%	___	12	___	___	___
4	70%	___	10	___	___	___
Cumulative Totals		___	**35**	___	___	___

Status Report: Ending Period 6

Task	%Complete	EV	AC	PV	CV	SV
1	Finished	6	5	___	___	___
2	50%	___	10	___	___	___
3	80%	___	16	___	___	___
4	Finished	___	15	___	___	___
Cumulative Totals		___	**46**	___	___	___

Status Report: Ending Period 7

Task	%Complete	EV	AC	PV	CV	SV
1	Finished	6	5	___	___	___
2	Finished	___	14	___	___	___
3	Finished	___	20	___	___	___
4	Finished	___	15	___	___	___
5	0%	___	0	___	___	___
6	50%	___	9	___	___	___
Cumulative Totals		___	**63**	___	___	___

Period	SPI	CPI	PCIB
1	___	___	___
2	___	___	___
3	___	___	___
4	___	___	___
5	___	___	___
6	___	___	___
7	___	___	___

SPI = EV/PV
CPI = EV/AC
PCIB = EV/BAC

FIGURE A13.1D

FIGURE A13.1E

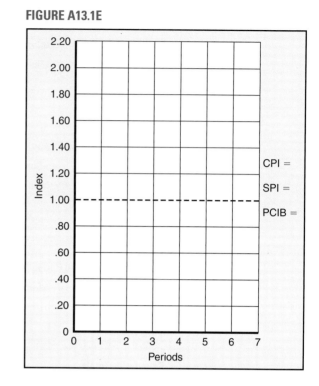

2. Given the information provided for development of a catalog product return process for periods 1 through 5, assign the PV values (using the rules) to develop a baseline for the project. Compute the SV, CV, SPI, and CPI for each period. Explain to the owner your assessment of the project at the end of period 5 and the future expected status of the project at the completion.

FIGURE A13.2A

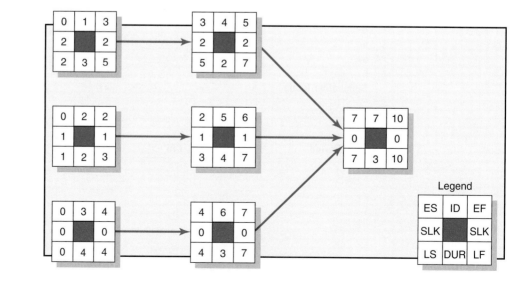

FIGURE A13.2B

Schedule information							Baseline budget needs (000)												
EV Rule	ACT/ WP	DUR	ES	LF	TF	Total PV	0	Time period											
								1	2	3	4	5	6	7	8	9	10		
②	1	3	0	5	2	30													
③	2	2	0	3	1	20													
②	3	4	0	4	0	30													
③	4	2	3	7	2	10													
②	5	4	2	7	1	40													
①	6	3	4	7	0	30													
①	7	3	7	10	0	60													
Total PV by period																			
Cumulative PV by period																			

Rule
1 = %complete
2 = 50/50
3 = 0/100

Status Report: Ending Period 1

Task	%Complete	EV	AC	PV	CV	SV
1	40%	___	8			
2	0%	___	12			
3	30%	___	10			
Cumulative Totals		___	**30**			

Status Report: Ending Period 2

Task	%Complete	EV	AC	PV	CV	SV
1	80%	___	20			
2	100%	20	18			
3	50%	___	12			
Cumulative Totals		___	**50**			

Status Report: Ending Period 3

Task	%Complete	EV	AC	PV	CV	SV
1	100%	___	27			
2	100%	___	18			
3	70%	___	15			
4	0%	___	5			
5	30%	___	8			
Cumulative Totals		___	**73**			

Status Report: Ending Period 4

Task	%Complete	EV	AC	PV	CV	SV
1	100%	___	27			
2	100%	___	18			
3	100%	___	22			
4	0%	___	7			
5	60%	___	22			
Cumulative Totals		___	**96**			

Status Report: Ending Period 5

Task	%Complete	EV	AC	PV	CV	SV
1	100%	_____	27	_____	_____	_____
2	100%	_____	18	_____	_____	_____
3	100%	_____	22	_____	_____	_____
4	100%	_____	8	_____	_____	_____
5	70%	_____	24	_____	_____	_____
6	30%	_____	10	_____	_____	_____
Cumulative Totals		_____	**109**	_____	_____	_____

Period	SPI	CPI	PCIB
1	_____	_____	_____
2	_____	_____	_____
3	_____	_____	_____
4	_____	_____	_____
5	_____	_____	_____

$$SPI = EV/PV$$
$$CPI = EV/AC$$
$$PCI\text{-}B = EV/BAC$$

FIGURE A13.2D

Appendix 13.2

Obtaining Project Performance Information from MS Project

The objective of this appendix is to illustrate how one can obtain the performance information discussed in Chapter 13 from MS Project 2002. One of the great strengths of MS Project is its flexibility. The software provides numerous options for entering, calculating, and presenting project information. Flexibility is also the software's greatest weakness in that there are so many options that working with the software can be frustrating and confusing. The intent here is to keep it simple and present basic steps for obtaining performance information. Students with more ambitious agendas are advised to work with the software tutorial or consult one of many instructional books on the market.

For purposes of this exercise we will use the Digital Camera project, which was introduced in Chapter 13. In this scenario the project started as planned on March 1, 2005 and today's date is March 6, 2005. We have received the following information on the work completed to date:

Design Spec.s took 2 days to complete at a total cost of $20.

Shell & Power took 3 days to complete at a total cost of $25.

Memory/Software is in progress with 4 days completed and two days remaining. Cost to date is $100.

Zoom System took 2 days to complete at a cost of $25.

All tasks started on time.

STEP 1 ENTERING PROGRESS INFORMATION

We enter this progress information in the TRACKING TABLE from the GANTT VIEW ▶ TABLE:

TABLE A13.2A   Tracking Table

ID	Task Name	Act. Start	Act. Finish	% Comp.	Act. Dur.	Rem. Dur.	Act. Cost	Act. Work
1	**Digital Camera Prototype**	**Tue 3/1/05**	**NA**	**61%**	**6.72 days**	**4.28 days**	**$170.00**	**272 hrs**
2	Design Spec.s	Tue 3/1/05	Wed 3/2/05	100%	2 days	0 days	$20.00	32 hrs
3	Shell & Power	Thu 3/3/05	Mon 3/7/05	100%	3 days	0 days	$25.00	40 hrs
4	Memory/Software	Thu 3/3/05	NA	67%	4 days	2 days	$100.00	160 hrs
5	Zoom System	Thu 3/3/05	Fri 3/4/05	100%	2 days	0 days	$25.00	40 hrs
6	Assemble	NA	NA	0%	0 days	3 days	$0.00	0 hrs
7	Test	NA	NA	0%	0 days	2 days	$0.00	0 hrs

Note that the software automatically calculates the percent complete and actual finish, cost, and work. In some cases you will have to override these calculations if they are inconsistent with what actually happened. **Be sure to check** to make sure the information in this table is displayed the way you want it to be.

The final step is to enter the current status date (March 6, 2005). You do so by clicking PROJECT ▶ PROJECT INFORMATION and inserting the date into the status date window.

STEP 2 ACCESSING PROGRESS INFORMATION

MS project provides a number of different options for obtaining progress information. The most basic information can be obtained from VIEW ▶ REPORT ▶ COST ▶ EARNED VALUE.

TABLE A13.2B   Earned Value Table

ID	Task Name	BCWS	BCWP	ACWP	SV	CV	EAC	BAC	VAC
2	Design Spec.s	$20.00	$20.00	$20.00	$0.00	$0.00	$20.00	$20.00	$0.00
3	Shell & Power	$15.00	$15.00	$25.00	$0.00	($10.00)	$25.00	$15.00	($10.00)
4	Memory/Software	$100.00	$65.00	$100.00	($35.00)	($35.00)	$100.00	$100.00	($53.85)
5	Zoom System	$35.00	$35.00	$25.00	$0.00	$10.00	$25.00	$35.00	$10.00
6	Assemble	$0.00	$0.00	$0.00	$0.00	$0.00	$120.00	$120.00	$0.00
7	Test	$0.00	$0.00	$0.00	$0.00	$0.00	$30.00	$30.00	$0.00
		$170.00	$135.00	$170.00	$35.00	($35.00)	$320.00	$320.00	($53.85)

When you scale this table to 80 percent you can obtain all the basic CV, SV and VAC information on one convenient page.

Note: MS Project uses the old acronyms:

BCWS = PV

BCWP = EV

ACWP = AC

STEP 3 ACCESSING CPI INFORMATION

To obtain additional cost information such as CPI and TCPI click from the GANTT CHART view click TABLE ► MORE TABLES ► EARNED VALUE COST INDI-CATORS which will display the following information:

TABLE 13.2C   **Earned Value Cost Indicators Table**

ID	Task Name	BCWS	BCWP	CV	CV%	CPI	BAC	EAC	VAC	TCPI
1	**Digital Camera Prototype**	$240.00	$140.00	($30.00)	−21%	0.82	$320.00	$388.57	($68.57)	1.2
2	Design Spec.s	$20.00	$20.00	$0.00	0%	1	$20.00	$20.00	$0.00	4294967295
3	Shell & Power	$15.00	$15.00	($10.00)	−66%	0.6	$15.00	$25.00	($10.00)	0
4	Memory/Software	$100.00	$70.00	($30.00)	−42%	0.7	$100.00	$142.86	($42.86)	4294967295
5	Zoom System	$35.00	$35.00	$10.00	28%	1.4	$35.00	$25.00	$10.00	0
6	Assemble	$70.00	$0.00	$0.00	0%	0	$120.00	$120.00	$0.00	1
7	Test	$0.00	$0.00	$0.00	0%	0	$30.00	$30.00	$0.00	1

Note: The EAC (388.57) is different than what appeared in the earned value table in Step 2 because it is the **EAC$_f$!**

Note: The number that appears in the TCPI cell for Design Spec.s and Memory/Software is a recurring anomaly in the software and should be ignored.

STEP 4 ACCESSING SPI INFORMATION

To obtain additional schedule information such as SPI from the GANTT CHART view, click TABLE ► MORE TABLES ► EARNED VALUE SCHEDULE INDICATORS which will display the following information:

TABLE 13.2D Earned Value Schedule Indicators Table

ID	Task Name	BCWS	BCWP	SV	SV%	SPI
1	**Digital Camera Prototype**	$170.00	$140.00	($30.00)	−17%	0.82
2	Design Spec.s	$20.00	$20.00	$0.00	0%	1
3	Shell & Power	$15.00	$15.00	$0.00	0%	1
4	Memory/Software	$100.00	$70.00	($30.00)	−29%	0.7
5	Zoom System	$35.00	$35.00	$0.00	0%	1
6	Assemble	$0.00	$0.00	$0.00	0%	0
7	Test	$0.00	$0.00	$0.00	0%	0

STEP 5 CREATING A TRACKING GANTT CHART

You can create a Tracking Gantt Chart like the one presented on page 459 by simply clicking VIEW ► TRACKING GANTT

FIGURE 13.2A   Tracking Gantt Chart

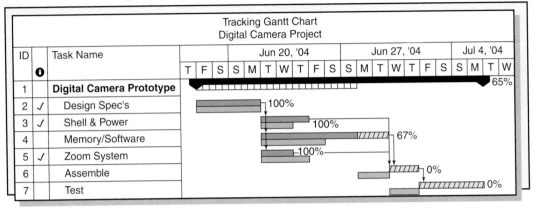

STEP 6 OBTAINING PCIB AND PCIC

The current version of MS Project does not generate these indexes. You will have to calculate these based on the formulas presented in this chapter.

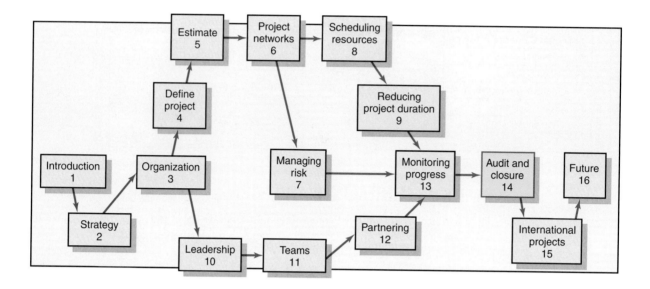

Project Audit and Closure

Project Audits

The Project Audit Process

Project Audits: The Bigger Picture

Project Closure

Team, Team Member, and Project Manager Evaluations

Summary

Appendix 14.1: Project Closeout Checklist

Project Audit and Closure

Those who cannot remember the past are condemned to relive it.
—*George Santayana, 1863–1952*

Mistakes are made; the unexpected happens; conditions change. In organizations that have several projects going on concurrently, it is prudent to have periodic reality checks on current and recently completed projects and their role in the organization's future. The project audit includes three major tasks:

1. Evaluate if the project delivered the expected benefits to all stakeholders. Was the project managed well? Was the customer satisfied?
2. Assess what was done wrong and what contributed to successes.
3. Identify changes to improve the delivery of future projects.

The project audit and report are instruments for supporting continuous improvement and quality management. We learn from past mistakes and what we did right.

Unfortunately, it is estimated that about 90 percent of all projects are not seriously reviewed or audited. The most common reason given is "we're too busy to stop and assess how well we manage projects." This is a big mistake. Without reflective assessment, valuable lessons learned are forgotten and mistakes are repeated. Sadly, those projects that are audited tend to be major failures or disasters. This is another big mistake. One tends to learn only what *not* to do from failures, not what to do. By examining both successes and failures, better practices can be incorporated into the project management system of an organization.

We have observed that organizations that seriously audit their projects are leaders in their fields. These organizations are vigorously committed to continuous improvement and organizational learning.

This chapter begins by discussing different kinds of project audits as well as the audit process. The emergence of maturity models to benchmark the evolution of project management practices is addressed next, followed by issues related to project closure. The chapter concludes by discussing the evaluation of team and individual performance on a project.

Project Audits

Project audits are more than the status reports suggested in Chapter 13, which check on project performance. Project audits do use performance measures and forecast data. But project audits are more inclusive. Project audits review why the project was selected. Project audits include a reassessment of the project's role in the organization's priorities.

Project audits include a check on the organizational culture to ensure it facilitates the type of project being implemented. Project audits assess if the project team is functioning well and is appropriately staffed. Audits of projects in process should include a check on external factors that might change where the project is heading or its importance—for example, technology, government laws, competitive products. Project audits include a review of all factors relevant to the project and to managing future projects.

Project audits can be performed while a project is in process and after a project is completed. There are only a few minor differences between these audits.

- **In-process project audits.** Project audits early in projects allow for corrective changes, if they are needed, on the audited project or others in progress. In-process project audits concentrate on project progress and performance and check if conditions have changed. For example, have priorities changed? Is the project mission still relevant? In rare cases, the audit report may recommend closure of a project that is in process.

- **Postproject audits.** These audits tend to include more detail and depth than in-process project audits. Project audits of completed projects emphasize improving the management of future projects. These audits are more long-term oriented than in-process audits. Postproject audits do check on project performance, but the audit represents a broader view of the project's role in the organization; for example, were the strategic benefits claimed actually delivered?

TABLE 14.1
Factors Influencing Audit Depth and Detail

- Organization size
- Project importance
- Project type
- Project risk
- Project size
- Project problems

The depth and detail of the project audit depend on many factors. Some are listed in Table 14.1. Because audits cost time and money, they should include no more time or resources than are necessary and sufficient. Early in-process project audits tend to be perfunctory unless serious problems or concerns are identified. Then, of course, the audit would be carried out in more detail. Because in-process project audits can be worrisome and destructive to the project team, care needs to be taken to protect project team morale. The audit should be carried out quickly, and the report should be as positive and constructive as possible. Postproject audits are more detailed and inclusive and contain more project team input.

In summary, plan the audit, and limit the time for the audit. For example, in postproject audits, for all but very large projects, a one-week limit is a good benchmark. Beyond this time, the marginal return of additional information diminishes quickly. Small projects may require only one or two days and one or two people to conduct an audit.

The priority team functions well in selecting projects and monitoring performance—cost and time. However, reviewing and evaluating projects and the process of managing projects is usually delegated to independent audit groups. Each audit group is charged with evaluating and reviewing *all* factors relevant to the project and to managing future projects. The outcome of the project audit is a report.

The Project Audit Process

Below are guidelines that should be noted before you conduct a project audit. The guidelines below will improve your chances for a successful audit.

Guidelines for Conducting a Project Audit

1. First and foremost, the philosophy must be that the project audit is not a witch hunt.
2. Comments about individuals or groups participating in the project are no-nos. Keep to project issues, not what happened or by whom.

3. Audit activities should be intensely sensitive to human emotions and reactions. The inherent threat to those being evaluated should be reduced as much as possible.

4. Accuracy of data should be verifiable or noted as subjective, judgmental, or hearsay.

5. Senior management should announce support for the project audit and see that the audit group has access to all information, project participants, and (in most cases) project customers.

6. The attitude toward a project audit and its aftermath depends on the modus operandi of the audit leadership and group. The objective is not to prosecute. The objective is to learn and conserve valuable organization resources where mistakes have been made. Friendliness, empathy, and objectivity encourage cooperation and reduce anxiety.

7. The audit should be completed as quickly as is reasonable.

8. The audit leader should be given access to senior management above the project manager.

With these guidelines in mind, the process of the project audit is conveniently divided into three steps: initiation and staffing, data collection and analysis, and reporting. Each step is discussed next.

Step 1: Initiation and Staffing

Initiation of the audit process depends primarily on organization size and project size along with other factors. However, every effort should be made to make the project audit a normal process rather than a surprise notice. In small organizations and projects where face-to-face contact at all levels is prevalent, an audit may be informal and only represent another staff meeting. But even in these environments the content of a formal project audit should be examined and covered with notes made of the lessons learned. In medium-sized organizations that have several projects occurring simultaneously, initiation can come from a formal project review group, from the project priority team, or be automatic. For example, in the latter case, all projects are audited at specific stages in the project life cycle—perhaps when a project is 10 to 20 percent complete in time or money, 50 percent complete, and after completion. The automatic process works well because it removes the perceptions that a project has been singled out for evaluation and that someone might be on a witch hunt. In large projects, the audit may be planned for major milestones.

There are rare circumstances that require an unplanned project audit, but they should be few and far between. For example, in a project that involved the development of a very large computer accounting system for multiple locations, one major consulting firm (of many) gave notice of withdrawal from the project, with no apparent reason. The project customer became alarmed that perhaps there was a serious fundamental problem in the project that caused the large consulting firm to drop out. A project audit identified the problem. The problem was one of sexual harassment by members of a small consulting firm toward members of the larger consulting firm. The small consulting firm engagement was terminated and replaced with a firm of similar expertise. The larger firm agreed to remain with the project. There are many other avenues to identify and solve such problems, but this example occurred as reported. Other circumstances, internal and external to the project, can cause an unplanned audit—for example, large cost or time overruns, change in project managers, or coverups. Regardless, unplanned audits should be avoided except in unusual circumstances.

A major tenet of the project audit is that the outcome must represent an independent, outside view of the project. Maintaining independence and an objective view is difficult, given that audits are frequently viewed as negative by project stakeholders. Careers and reputations can be tarnished even in organizations that tolerate mistakes.

In less forgiving organizations, mistakes can lead to termination or exile to less significant regions of an organization. Of course, if the result of an audit is favorable, careers and reputations can be enhanced. Given that project audits are susceptible to internal politics, some organizations rely on outside consulting firms to conduct the audits. Regardless, it is imperative the audit leader possess the following characteristics:

1. No direct involvement or direct interest in the project.
2. Respect (perceived as impartial and fair) of senior management and other project stakeholders.
3. Willingness to listen.
4. Independence and authority to report audit results without fear of recriminations from special interests.
5. Perceived as having the best interests of the organization in making decisions.
6. Broad-based experience in the organization or industry.

Other audit members should have similar characteristics even if they are selected for their special expertise. Some project team members will need to be included in the audit evaluation. Postproject audits have a stronger representation of project team members than in-process project audits because of the slightly different orientation. The concern that team members will come to the audit with strong biases is usually overstated. In general, project team members are genuinely interested in improving the future project management process; they make every attempt to be objective.

Step 2: Data Collection and Analysis

The traditional content model for a project audit presents two perspectives. One evaluates the project from the view of the organization. The second perspective represents the project team's evaluative view. The organization perspective is developed by a small group primarily made up of persons not having a direct interest in the project. The project team perspective is developed by a group composed primarily of team members along with persons independent of the project to ensure the evaluation is objective.

Each organization and project is unique. Therefore, many factors need to be considered. For example, the industry, project size, newness of technology, and project experience can influence the nature of the audit. However, information and data are gathered to answer questions similar to those suggested next.

Organization View

1. Was the organizational culture supportive and correct for this type of project? Why? Why not?
2. Was senior management's support adequate?
3. Did the project accomplish its intended purpose?
   a. Is there a clear link to organizational strategy and objectives?
   b. Does the priority system reflect importance to the future of the organization?
   c. Has the environment (internal or external) changed the need for the project's completion (if project is still in process)?
4. Were the risks for the project appropriately identified and assessed? Were contingency plans used? Were they realistic? Have risk events occurred that have an impact greater than anticipated?
5. Were the right people and talents assigned to this project?
6. If the project was completed, have staff been fairly assigned to new projects?

7. What does evaluation from outside contractors suggest?
8. Were the project start-up and hand-off successful? Why? Is the customer satisfied?

Project Team View

1. Were the project planning and control systems appropriate for this type of project? Should all similar size and type of projects use these systems? Why/why not?
2. Did the project conform to plan? Is the project over or under budget and schedule? Why?
3. Were interfaces and communications with project stakeholders adequate and effective?
4. If the project is completed, have staff been fairly assigned to new projects?
5. Did the team have adequate access to organizational resources—people, budget, support groups, equipment? Were there resource conflicts with other ongoing projects? Was the team managed well?
6. What does evaluation from outside contractors suggest?

The audit group should not be limited to these questions. The audit group should include other questions related to their organization and project type—e.g., research and development, marketing, information systems, construction, facilities. The generic questions above, although overlapping, represent a good starting point and will go a long way toward identifying project problem and success patterns.

Step 3: Reporting

The major goal of the audit report is to improve the way future projects are managed. Succinctly, the report attempts to capture needed changes and lessons learned from a current or finished project. The report serves as a training instrument for project managers of future projects.

Audit reports need to be tailored to the specific project and organizational environment. Nevertheless, a generic format for all audits facilitates development of an audit database and a common outline for those who prepare audit reports and the managers who read and act on their content. A very general outline common to those found in practice is as follows:

1. Classification of project.
2. Analysis of information gathered.
3. Recommendations.
4. Lessons learned.
5. Appendix.

Classification

Each project audit is categorized because there are differences in the way projects with different characteristics are managed and handled in an organization. A prospective project manager of a software coding project will have little interest in the construction of a clean room or recycling of inkjet reservoirs for printers. A prospective project manager of a small project will not be as interested in a computer project planning and control system as a project manager who is going to manage a very large project. The classification of projects by characteristics allows prospective readers and project managers to be selective in the use of the report content. Typical classification categories include the following:

- Project type—e.g., development, marketing, systems, construction.
- Size—monetary.

- Number of staff.
- Technology level—low, medium, high, new.
- Strategic or support.

Other classifications relevant to the organization should be included.

Analysis

The analysis section includes succinct, factual review statements of the project. For example,

- Project mission and objectives.
- Procedures and systems used.
- Organization resources used.

Recommendations

Usually audit recommendations represent major corrective actions that should take place. However, it is equally important to recommend positive successes that should be continued and used in future projects. Postproject audits may be the place to give credit to the project team for an outstanding contribution.

Lessons Learned

These do not have to be in the form of recommendations. Lessons learned serve as reminders of mistakes easily avoided and actions easily taken to ensure success. In practice, new project teams reviewing audits of past projects similar to the one they are about to start have found audit reports very useful. Team members will frequently remark later, "The recommendations were good, but the 'lessons learned' section really helped us avoid many pitfalls and made our project implementation smoother." See Snapshot from Practice: Operation Eagle Claw.

Appendix

The appendix may include backup data or details of analysis that would allow others to follow up if they wished. It should not be a dumping ground used for filler; only critical pertinent information should be attached.

Summary Booklet

Finally, it is good to keep a small summary booklet of major lessons learned. Give references to archived audit reports if additional information is desired. This process may appear a bit formal, but people use these summaries and archives when they are available—more frequently than most would believe.

Project Audits: The Bigger Picture

Individual audits or post project reviews can yield valuable lessons that team members can apply to future project work. When done on a consistent basis, audits can lead to significant improvements in the processes and techniques that organizations use to complete projects. A more encompassing look from an organizationwide point of view is to use a project maturity model. The purposes of all maturity models, and there are many available, are to enable organizations to assess their progress in implementing the best practices in their industry and move to improvement. It is important to understand

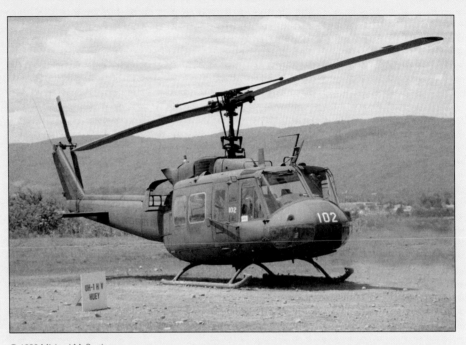

© 1999 Michael McGrath.

On November 4, 1979, a mob in Iran stormed the U.S. Embassy and took 52 Americans hostage. After six months of failed negotiation, the decision was made to execute Operation Eagle Claw, a joint military effort to free the U.S. hostages.

The plan called for eight Navy RH-53D helicopters to fly 600 miles to a remote site in Iran, code named Desert One. Under the cover of darkness, the helicopters would be refueled by KC-130 tankers. The helicopters would then fly the assault force to a spot near the outskirts of Tehran where they would meet up with special agents already in the country. The agents would lead them to a safe house to await the assault on the embassy the next night. Upon rescuing the hostages, the assault team would escort the hostages to a nearby airfield that had been secured by a second attack team where they would be flown to safety.

What actually happened was far different from what was planned.

The helicopter pilots were ordered to fly at or below 200 feet to avoid radar. This caused them to run into "haboobs" or dust storms. Two helicopters malfunctioned and turned back. The remainder battled the dust storms and arrived at Desert One an hour late. The rescue attempt was dealt its final blow when it was discovered that a third helicopter had a hydraulic leak and was inoperable. Only five aircraft were serviceable and six were needed, so the mission was aborted. Things got worse, though, when one of the helicopters moved into position to refuel and collided with a KC-130 plane. Both aircraft burst into flames. All told, eight soldiers died and dozens were injured. The Iranians scattered the hostages around the country afterward, making any further rescue attempts impossible.

The Armed Services routinely conduct audits of every exercise and operation. Given the gravity of the situation, a special six-member commission was appointed by the Joint Chiefs of Staff to investigate the failed operation. They discovered a number of issues that contributed to the failure. One issue was the selection of air crew. Navy and Marine pilots with little experience in long-range overland navigation or refueling were selected though more than a hundred qualified Air Force pilots were available. Another issue was the lack of a comprehensive mission rehearsal program. From the beginning, training was not conducted in a truly joint manner; it was compartmentalized by service and held in scattered locations across the United States. The limited rehearsals that were conducted assessed only portions of the total mission.

The number of helicopters used was also an issue. The commission concluded that 10 and perhaps 12 helicopters should have been launched to guarantee the minimum six required for completion of the mission. Finally, the hopscotch method of ground refueling was criticized. If the planners had chosen to use enroute air fueling, the entire Desert One scenario could have been avoided. The final report of the commission contained several important recommendations designed to prevent such a tragedy from occurring again.

*D. M. Giangreco and Terry A. Griswold, *Delta: America's Elite Counterterrorist Force* (New York: Motorbooks International, 1992).

that the model does not ensure success; it only serves as a measuring stick and an indicator of progress.

The term *maturity model* was coined in the late 1980s from a research study by the United States government and the Software Engineering Institute (SEI) at Carnegie-Mellon University. The government wanted a tool to predict successful software development by contractors. The outcome of this research was the Capability Maturity Model (CMM). The model focuses on guiding and assessing organizations in implementing concrete best practices of managing software development projects. Since its development, the model is now used across all industries. Currently, over 2,400 organizations around the world report their maturity progress to the Software Engineering Institute. (See website at http://www.sei.cmu.edu/activities/sema/profile.html.)

One newer model has received a great deal of publicity. In January of 2004, after eight years of development, the Project Management Institute rolled out its second version of the "Organizational Project Maturity Model." The latest version is called *OPM3*™. (See www.pmi.org/opm3.) Typically, these models are divided into a continuum of growth levels: Initial, Repeatable, Defined, Managed, and Optimized. Figure 14.1 presents our version, which borrows liberally from other models. What we have tried to do is focus less on a process and more on the state an organization has evolved to in managing projects.

Level 1: Ad Hoc Project Management   No consistent project management process is in place. How a project is managed depends upon the individuals involved. Characteristics of this level include

- No formal project selection system exists—projects are done because people decide to do them or because a high-ranking manager orders it done.
- How any one project is managed varies by individual—unpredictability.
- No investment in project management training is made.
- Working on projects is a struggle because it goes against the grain of established policies and procedures.

FIGURE 14.1
Project Management Maturity Model

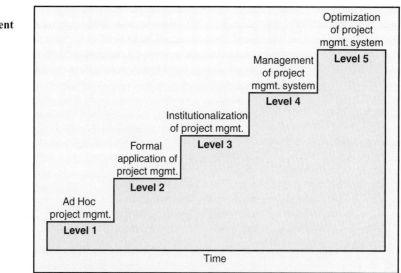

Level 2: Formal Application of Project Management The organization applies established project management procedures and techniques. This level is often marked by tension between project managers and line managers, who need to redefine their roles. Features of this level include

* Standard approaches to managing projects including scope statements, WBS, activity lists are used.
* Quality emphasis is on the product or outcome of the project and is inspected instead of built in.
* The organization is moving in the direction of stronger matrix with project managers and line managers working out their respective roles.
* Growing recognition of need for cost control, not just scope and time management, exists.
* There is no formal project priority system established.
* Limited training in project management is provided.

Level 3: Institutionalization of Project Management An organizationwide project management system, tailored to specific needs of the organization with the flexibility to adapt the process to unique characteristics of the project, is established. Characteristics of this level include

* An established process for managing projects is evident by planning templates, status report systems, and checklists for each stage of project life cycle.
* Formal criteria are used to select projects.
* Project management is integrated with quality management and concurrent engineering.
* Project teams try to build in quality not simply inspect it.
* The organization is moving toward a team-based reward system to recognize project execution.
* Risk assessment derived from WBS and technical analyses and customer input is in place.
* The organization offers expanded training in project management.
* Time-phased budgets are used to measure and monitor performance based on earned value analysis.
* A specific change control system for requirements, cost, and schedule is developed for each project, and a work authorization system is in place.
* Project audits tend to be performed only when a project fails.

Level 4: Management of Project Management System The organization develops a system for managing multiple projects that are aligned with strategic goals of the organization. Characteristics of this level include

* Portfolio project management is practiced; projects are selected based on resource capacity and contribution to strategic goals.
* A project priority system is established.
* Project work is integrated with ongoing operations.
* Quality improvement initiatives are designed to improve both the quality of the project management process and the quality of specific products and services.

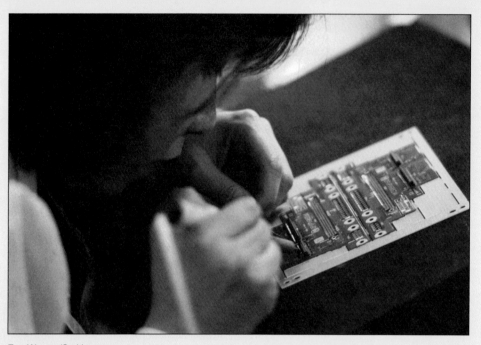

Tom Wagner/Corbis.

In today's rapidly changing world, the risk of failing to develop new products for the market on time is the difference between success and failure. The Mobile Systems Unit (MSU) of Taiwan computer maker Acer, which produces computer notebooks, operates under extreme time-to-market pressures. By 1998 MSU development cycles had shrunk to eight months. Still, missing the market introduction window by only one month on any given model eliminated the unit's profit potential for that model.

MSU did a companywide analysis into the causes of costly delays in their projects. They discovered that schedule variance was a function of multiple causes. Vendors would occasionally not deliver sufficient volumes of a promised new component on time. Major customers such as IBM would change their requirements. Design problems with the motherboard would cause additional design loops. Negotiations among multiple parties might change internal specifications. Administrative pressure on engineers and insufficiently documented procedures led to shortcuts in testing, causing major rework at a more costly stage.

Acer attacked the multiple causes on multiple fronts. First, MSU management created resource buffers in the form of slack capacity by canceling two projects that were already delayed. This wasn't easy, because one was to be a showpiece, top-of-the-line model, and the decision to kill it was hotly contested. MSU then concentrated on improving documentation of operating procedures in order to increase testing coverage and facilitate the training of young engineers. Those steps reduced the number of correction loops during product development and improved the quality of the company's manufacturing ramp-up. Acer also concentrated the responsibility of product specifications in one group, thereby reducing negotiation loops and internally-caused specification changes. Over the next two years, MSU more than doubled its sales and gained significant market share.

*Einhorn, B. "Acer's About Face," *BusinessWeek (International Edition)*, April 23, 2000.

- Benchmarking is used to identify opportunities for improvement.
- The organization has established a Project Management Office or Center for Excellence.
- Project audits are performed on all significant projects; lessons learned are recorded and used on subsequent projects.

- An integrative information system is established for tracking resource usage and performance of all significant projects. See Snapshot from Practice: Acer Attacks Costly Delays.

Level 5: Optimization of Project Management System   The focus is on continuous improvement through incremental advancements of existing practices and by innovations using new technologies and methods. Features include

- A project management information system is fine-tuned; specific and aggregate information is provided to different stakeholders.
- An informal culture that values improvement drives the organization, not policies and procedures.
- There is greater flexibility in adapting the project management process to demands of a specific project.

Progress from one level to the next will not occur overnight. The Software Engineering Institute estimates the following median times for movement:

> Maturity level 1 to 2 is 22 months.
> Maturity level 2 to 3 is 19 months.
> Maturity level 3 to 4 is 25 months.
> Maturity level 4 to 5 is 13 months.

Why does it take so long? One reason is simply organizational inertia. It is difficult for complex social organizations to institute significant changes while at the same time maintaining business efficacy. "How do we find time to change when we are so busy just keeping our heads above water?"

A second significant reason is that one cannot leapfrog past any one level. Just as a child cannot avoid the trials and tribulations of being a teenager by adopting all the lessons learned by his or her parents, people within the organization have to work through the unique challenges and problems of each level to get to the next level. Learning of this magnitude naturally takes time and cannot be avoided by using quick fixes or simple remedies.

Our best-guess estimates are that most companies are in the throes of moving from level 2 to level 3 and that fewer than 10 percent of those firms that actively practice project management are at level 4 or 5.

Project Closure

Every project comes to an end, eventually. On some projects the end may not be as clear as would be hoped. Although the scope statement may define a clear ending for a project, the actual ending may or may not correspond. Fortunately, a majority of projects are blessed with a well-defined ending. Regular project audits and a priority team will identify those projects that should have endings different from those planned.

Conditions for Project Closure

Normal

The most common circumstance for project closure is simply a completed project. In the case of "turnkey" projects, such as building a new manufacturing facility or creating a customized information system, the finish is marked by the transfer of ownership to the customer. For many development projects, the end involves handing off the final design to production and the creation of a new product or service line. For other internal projects, such as system upgrades or creation of new inventory control systems, the end occurs when the output is incorporated into ongoing operations. Some modifications in scope, cost, and schedule probably occurred during implementation.

Premature

For a few projects, the project may be completed early with some parts of the project eliminated. For example, in a new-product development project, a marketing manager may insist on production models before testing:

> Give the new product to me now, the way it is. Early entry into the market will mean big profits! I know we can sell a bizzillion of these. If we don't do it now, the opportunity is lost!

The pressure is on to finish the project and send it to production. Before succumbing to this form of pressure, the implications and risks associated with this decision should be carefully reviewed and assessed by senior management and all stakeholders. Too frequently, the benefits are illusory, dangerous, and carry large risks. Why have the original project scope and objectives changed? If early project closure occurs, it should have the support of all project stakeholders. This decision should be left to the audit group, project priority team, or senior management.

Perpetual

Some projects never seem to end. That is, the project appears to develop a life of its own. Although these projects are plagued with delays, they are viewed as desirable when they finally are completed. The major characteristic of this kind of project is constant "add-ons." The owner or others continuously require more small changes that will improve the project outcome—product or service. These changes typically represent "extras" perceived as being part of the original project intent. Examples are adding features to software, to product design, to systems, or to construction projects. Constant add-on changes suggest a poorly conceived project scope. More care in upfront definition of the project scope and limitations will reduce the add-on phenomenon.

At some point the project manager or audit group needs to call the project design locked to bring closure. Although these projects are exhibiting scope, cost, and schedule creep, facing the fact that the project should be brought to an end is not an easy chore. An interesting study by Isabelle Royer chronicles "perpetual" projects of two French companies that lasted well over a decade. Essilor, maker of "progressive" lenses that correct for nearsightedness, and Lafarge, maker of building materials, each had projects that started with much fanfare only to fail to make significant progress. Signs of problems were ignored and allowed the doomed projects to drag on for over 10 years before being killed. Both companies absorbed millions of dollars of lost investment.

Project managers or audit/priority groups have several alternatives available for projects displaying characteristics of being perpetual. They can redefine the project end or scope so that closure is forced. They can limit budget or resources. They can set a time limit. All alternatives should be designed to bring the project to an end as quickly as possible to limit additional costs and still gain the positive benefits of a completed project. The audit group should recommend methods for bringing final closure to this type of project. Failed projects are usually easy to identify and easy for an audit group to close down. However, every effort should be made to communicate the technical

Germany is the major crossroad for Europe's international commercial trucks. The German government felt the need to have international trucks (over 12 tons) using their road infrastructure assist in paying for the road maintenance and additional new infrastructure. The project objectives were clear—a new electronic truck toll-collection system that ensures accurate charges and easy fee collection across German, Swiss, and Austrian highways by August 31, 2003. The technology relied on global positioning systems (GPS), telecommunications, and software to record miles and charges, without using toll booths along the highways.

Several problems sabotaged the project. Time-to-market deadlines were impossible to meet. Delayed launch dates were caused by technical problems with truck tracking units and software that failed to function as expected. Interface communication with public and private stakeholders failed. As a result, the August 2003 deadline was never met. The revised November 2003 deadline was not met. Finally, in March 2004 the German government pulled the plug and cancelled the project.

The cancellation of the project had serious impacts on other governmental programs. The shortfall of not receiving the revenue from the new toll system is estimated at $1.6 billion. Some of those revenues were destined for a high-speed maglev train in Munich and other infrastructure projects.

Lessons learned reveal that lack of project management knowledge was evident. More importantly, failure to identify and assess the impact of schedule and complex technology risks resulted in the death of the project. Perhaps a simpler, cheaper microwave system recommended by the Swiss and Austrians to be operational by 2005 would have sufficed.

*"Case Analysis: Taking a Toll," *PM Network,* Vol. 18, No. 3, March, 2004, p. 1.

reasons for termination of the project; project participants should not be left with an embarrassing stigma of working on a project that failed.

Failed Project

In rare circumstances projects simply fail—for a variety of reasons. For example, developing a prototype of a new technology product may show the original concept to be unworkable. Or in the development of a new pharmaceutical drug, the project may need to be abandoned because side effects of the drug are deemed unacceptable. See Snapshot from Practice: Project Cancelled.

Changed Priority

The priority team continuously revises project selection priorities to reflect changes in organizational direction. Normally these changes are small over a period of time, but periodically major shifts in organization require dramatic shifts in priorities. In this transition period, projects in process may need to be altered or canceled. Thus, a project may start with a high priority but see its rank erode or crash during its project life cycle as conditions change. For example, a computer game company found their major competitor placed a 64-bit, 3-D game on the market while their product development projects still centered on 32-bit games. From that moment on, 32-bit game projects were considered obsolete and met sudden deaths. The priority team of this company revised organization priorities. Audit groups found it easy to recommend closure for many projects, but those on the margin or in "gray areas" still presented formidable analysis and difficult decisions.

In some cases the original importance of the project was misjudged; in some the needs have changed. In other situations implementation of the project is impractical or impossible. Because the audit group and priority team are periodically reviewing a project, the changed perception of the project's role (priority) in the total scheme of things becomes apparent quickly. If the project no longer contributes significantly to organization strategy, the audit group or priority team needs to recommend the project be terminated. In many termination situations, these projects are integrated into related projects or routine daily operations.

Termination of "changed priority" projects is no easy task. The project team's perception may be that the project priority is still high in relation to other projects. Egos and, in some cases perhaps, jobs are on the line. Individuals or teams feel success is just over the horizon. Giving up is tantamount to failure. Normally, rewards are given for staying with a project when the chips are down, not giving up. Such emotional issues make project termination difficult.

There is little advantage to placing blame on individuals. Other modes should be used to "justify" early project closure or to identify a project problem—for example, customer needs or tastes have changed, technology is ahead of this project, or competition has a better, more advanced product or service. These examples are external to the organization and perceived as beyond anyone's control. Another approach that weakens close team loyalty is changing team members or the project manager. This approach tends to minimize team commitment and makes closing the project easier, but it should only be used as a last resort. Minimizing embarrassment should be a primary goal for a project review group closing down an unfinished project.

Signals for Continuing or Early Project Closure

Persons who are preparing to join a project audit group for the first time would find it rewarding to read a few studies that identify barriers to project success and the antithesis, factors that contribute to success. Knowledge of these factors will suggest areas to review in an audit. These factors signal where problems or success patterns might exist.

TABLE 14.2
Barriers to Project Success

Activity*	Barrier	Incidence (%)
Planning 32%	Unclear definition	16%
	Poor decision making	9
	Bad information	3
	Changes	4
Scheduling 12%	Tight schedule	4
	Not meeting schedule	5
	Not managing schedule	3
Organizing 11%	Lack of responsibility or accountability	5
	Weak project manager	5
	Top management interference	1
Staffing 12%	Inadequate personnel	5
	Incompetent project manager	4
	Project member turnover	2
	Poor staffing process	1
Directing 26%	Poor coordination	9
	Poor communication	6
	Poor leadership	5
	Low commitment	6
Controlling 7%	Poor follow-up	3
	Poor monitoring	2
	No control system	1
	No recognition of problems	1

*To interpret the table, note that 32 percent of the 1,654 participants reported the barriers under "Planning," 12 percent reported the barriers under "Scheduling," and so on.

The Standish Group International is a market research and advisory firm specializing in mission-critical software and electronic commerce. They have conducted and published extensive research on the success and failure of software development/application projects. Their research, code name "Chaos," shows that a staggering 31 percent of software projects will be canceled before they are ever completed. In addition, 53 percent of projects will cost 189 percent of their original estimates. In terms of success, on the average only 16 percent of software projects are completed on time and within budget. In larger companies, the success rate is much worse—9 percent. The Standish Group estimated that in 1995 American companies and government agencies spent $81 billion for canceled software projects.

The Chaos research is based on "key findings" from research surveys and personal interviews. The respondents were information technology (IT) executive managers. The sample included large, medium, and small companies across major industry segments, for example, banking; securities; manufacturing; retail; wholesale; health care; insurance service; and local, state, and federal organizations. The total sample size was 365 respondents and represented 8,380 projects.

Based on an in-depth comparison of successful versus unsuccessful software projects, the Standish Group created a success potential chart that identifies key factors associated with project success. The success criteria were weighted based on the input from the surveyed IT managers. The most important criterion, "user involvement," was given 19 success points, while the least important, "hard-working, focused staff," was given 3 success points. The following chart lists the criteria in order of importance:

Success Criteria	Points
1. User involvement	19
2. Executive management support	16
3. Clear statement of requirements	15
4. Proper planning	11
5. Realistic expectations	10
6. Smaller project milestones	9
7. Competent staff	8
8. Project team ownership	6
9. Clear vision and objectives	3
10. Hard-working, focused staff	3
Total	100

*Used by permission of the Standish Group International, Inc., 196 Old Town House Rd., West Yarmouth, MA 02673. The CHAOS report was updated in 2001. Although improvement was noted (e.g., cost over runs were reduced to 145 percent), the magnitude of the core problems remains the same.

In rare cases their existence may signal problems and the need for an in-process project to be terminated early.

A number of studies have examined this area. There is surprising conformity among these studies. For example, all of these studies (and others) rank poor project definition (scope) as a major barrier to project success. There is no evidence these factors have changed over the years, although some differences in relative importance have been noted in different industries. See Research Highlight—Chaos: Software Projects. Table 14.2 presents the barriers identified by 1,654 participating project managers in a survey by Gobeli and Larson. The signals noted in Table 14.2 can be useful to audit groups in their preliminary review of in-process projects or even in postproject audits.

The Closure Decision

For an incomplete project, the decision to continue or close down the project is fundamentally an organizational resource allocation decision. Should the organization commit additional resources to complete the project and realize the project objectives? This is a complex decision. The rationale for closing or proceeding is often based on many cost factors that are primarily subjective and judgmental. Thus, care needs to be taken to avoid inferences concerning groups or individuals. The audit report needs to focus on organizational goals, changing conditions, and changing priorities requiring reallocation of scarce organizational resources.

When the audit group or priority team suggests closure, the announcement may need to come from a CEO position if the effect is large or if key egos are involved. But, in most cases, the closure decision is left to the audit group or priority team. Prior to announcement of closure, a plan for future assignment of the project team members should be in place.

Project Closure Process

As the project nears the end of its life cycle, people and equipment are directed to other activities or projects. Carefully managing the closure phase is as important as any other phase of the project. The major challenges for the project manager and team members are over. Getting the project manager and team members to wrap up the odds and ends of closing down the project is sometimes difficult. For example, accounting for equipment and completing final reports are perceived as boring by project professionals who are action-oriented individuals. They are looking forward to new opportunities and challenges. The major activities found in project terminations are developing a plan, staffing, communicating the plan, and implementing the plan.

The typical close-out plan includes answers to questions similar to these:

* What tasks are required to close the project?
* Who will be responsible for these tasks?
* When will closure begin and end?
* How will the project be delivered?

Staffing is usually not a significant issue if the termination is not a sudden hatchet job. If the project is suddenly canceled early, before completion, it may be judicious to seek someone other than the project manager to close out the project. In successful, completed projects, the project manager is the likely choice for closing down the project. In this case it is best to have the project manager's next assignment known; this will serve as an inducement to terminate the project as quickly as possible and move on to new challenges.

Communicating the termination plan and schedule early allows the project team to (1) accept the psychological fact the project will end and (2) prepare to move on. The ideal scenario is to have the team member's next assignment ready when the termination is announced. Conversely, a major dilemma in the termination phase is that project participants are looking forward to future projects or other opportunities. The project manager's challenge is to keep the project team focused on the project activities and delivery to the customer until the project is complete. Project managers need to be careful to maintain their enthusiasm for completing the project and hold people accountable to deadlines, which are prone to slip during the waning stages of the project.

Implementing the closedown plan includes several wrap-up activities. Many organizations develop lengthy lists for closing projects as they gain experience. These are very helpful and ensure nothing is overlooked. Implementing closedown includes the following five major activities:

1. Getting delivery acceptance from the customer.
2. Shutting down resources and releasing to new uses.
3. Reassigning project team members.
4. Closing accounts and seeing all bills are paid.
5. Evaluating the project team, project team members, and the project manager.

Figure 14.2 depicts a partial closedown checklist for the Euro conversion project for a space company. See Appendix 14.1 for another example used by the state of Virginia.

FIGURE 14.2   **European Space Launch, AG—Project Closure Checklist**

Project _____ Euro Conversion _____   Customer _____ Finance Department _____

Project manager _____ Hans Kramer _____   Completion date _____ 12 December XX _____

	Due date	Person responsible	Notes
1. Document finance department acceptance	16/12	Hans	
2. Customer training in Euro software	28/12	Joan	Train all departments before conversion
3. Archive all			
Schedules/actuals	31/12	Maeyke	
Budgets/actual costs	31/12	Maeyke	
Changes	31/12	Maeyke	
4. Close out all accounts with vendors	31/12	Guido	
5. Close out all work orders	31/12	Mayo	
6. Close out partner accounts	31/12	Guido	
7. Reassign project staff	16/12	Sophie	
8. Evaluation of			
Vendors	31/12	Mayo	Use standard questionnaire for vendors
Staff members	31/12	Sophie	Have HR department develop and administer
9. Final report and lessons learned meeting	4/1	Hans	Send notice to all stakeholders
10. Lessons learned archive to database	10/1	Maeyke	Contact IS department
tribute awards		Sophie	Notify all stakeholders

If team evaluation is not done well in practice, how bad is it? Joseph Fusco surveyed 1,667 project managers representing 134 different projects. Fifty-two percent of the respondents indicated their team received no collective evaluation of their team performance. Of the 22 percent who indicated their team was evaluated, further probing found their evaluation was informal, lasting little more than 20 minutes. This apparent lack of team evaluation practices may be sending the wrong signal. Individual team members can slough off poor team performance by relying on the old saying, "I did my job." Strong team evaluation practices need to emphasize team members are "in this together," while minimizing individual performance. Nearly every company in Fusco's survey lacked an effective project management reward system.

*Joseph Fusco, "Better Policies Provide the Key to Implementing Project Management," *Project Management Journal*, Vol. 28, No. 3, September 1997, p. 38.

Orchestrating the closure of a project can be a difficult task and a challenge to the manager's leadership ability. Implementing closure usually takes place in an emotionally charged web of happiness from successful completion of the project and sadness that newly forged friendships are now being severed as individuals go their separate ways. It is customary in organizations to arrange a celebration of the completion of the project; this could range from an informal pizza party after work to a more formal banquet including speeches and awards or certificates of recognition for participants. Such a festivity provides a sense of closure and emotional release for the participants as they bid farewell to each other. For less successful projects, this ending can take the form of a ceremonial wake; even though the atmosphere may be less than festive, such an event can also provide a sense of closure and help people move on with their lives.

It is important to remember that dragging out the project closure process can also drag out costs that continue for the life of the project. If the project is not completed and earning the benefits promised, the interest costs of the money spent for the project continue, along with other continuing costs. Not only that, but for contracted projects final payment is not received until after the closeout.

Team, Team Member, and Project Manager Evaluations

Auditing includes performance evaluations of the project team, individual team members, and the project manager. See Research Highlight: Measures of Team Performance. Evaluation of performance is essential to encourage changes in behavior and to support individual career development and continuous improvement through organization learning. Evaluation implies measurement against specific criteria. Experience corroborates that before commencement of the project the stage must be set so all expectations, standards, supportive organization culture, and constraints are in place; if not, the effectiveness of the evaluation process will suffer.

In a macro sense, the evidence today suggests that performance evaluation in each of these realms is not done well. The major reasons cited by practitioners are twofold:

1. Evaluations of individuals are still left to supervisors of the team member's home department.
2. Typical measures of team performance center on time, cost, and specifications.

Most organizations do not go beyond these measures, although they are important and critical. Organizations should consider evaluating the team-building process, effectiveness of group decision and problem-solving processes, group cohesion, trust among team members, and quality of information exchanged. Addressing evaluation of teams, team members, and project managers is extremely complex and project dependent. The discussion that follows touches on some of the major issues and approaches found in practice.

Team Evaluation

Before an auditing of the project team can be effective and useful, a minimum core of conditions needs to be in place before the project begins (see Chapter 11). Some conditions are listed here in the form of questions:

1. Do standards for measuring performance exist? (You can't manage what you can't measure.) Are the goals clear for the team and individuals? Challenging? Attainable? Lead to positive consequences?
2. Are individual and team responsibilities and performance standards known by all team members?
3. Are team rewards adequate? Do they send a clear signal that senior management believes the synergy of teams is important?
4. Is a clear career path for successful project managers in place?
5. Does the team have discretionary authority to manage short-term difficulties?
6. Is there a relatively high level of trust emanating from the organization culture?
7. Team evaluation should go beyond time, cost, and specifications. Are there criteria beyond these triple threat criteria? The "characteristics of highly effective teams" from Chapter 11 can easily be adapted as measurements of team effectiveness.

These "in-place conditions" will support any evaluation approach for teams and their members.

In practice, the actual team evaluation process takes many forms—especially when evaluation goes beyond time, budget, and specifications. The typical mechanism for evaluation of teams is a survey administered by a consultant, a staff member from the human resources department, or through computer e-mail. The survey is normally restricted to team members, but, in some cases, other project stakeholders interacting with the team may be included in the survey. When the results are tabulated, the team meets with senior management, and the results are reviewed. An example of a partial survey is found in Table 14.3.

This session is comparable to the team-building sessions described in Chapter 11 except that the focus is on using the survey results to assess the development of the

TABLE 14.3
Sample Team Evaluation and Feedback Survey

Using the scale below, assess each statement.					
	Disagree				**Agree**
1. The team shared a sense of common purpose, and each member was willing to work toward achieving project objectives.	1	2	3	4	5
2. Respect was shown for other points of view. Differences of opinion were encouraged and freely expressed.	1	2	3	4	5
3. All interaction among team members occurred in a comfortable, supportive atmosphere.	1	2	3	4	5

team, its strengths and weaknesses, and the lessons that can be applied to future project work. The results of team evaluation surveys are helpful in changing behavior, stressing the importance of supporting the team approach, and continuous improvement.

Individual Team Member and Project Manager Evaluation

Team evaluation is crucial, but at some point a project manager is likely to be asked to evaluate the performance of individual members. Such an evaluation will typically be required as part of the closure process and will then be incorporated in the annual performance appraisal system of the organization. These evaluations constitute a major element of an individual's personnel file and often form the basis for making decisions about promotions, future job assignments, merit pay increases, and other rewards.

Organizations vary in the extent to which project managers are actively involved in performing the appraisal process. In organizations where projects are managed within a functional organization or functional matrix, the individual's area manager, not the project manager, is responsible for assessing performance. The area manager may solicit the project manager's opinion of the individual's performance on a specific project; this will be factored into the individual's overall performance. In a balanced matrix, the project manager and the area manager jointly evaluate an individual's performance. In project matrix and project organizations in which the lion's share of the individual's work is project related, the project manager is responsible for appraising individual performance. One new process, which appears to be gaining wider acceptance, is the multirater appraisal or "360-degree feedback," which involves soliciting feedback concerning team members' performance from all the people their work affects. This would include not only project and area managers, but also peers, subordinates, and even customers. See Snapshot from Practice: The 360-Degree Feedback.

Performance appraisals generally fulfill two important functions. The first is developmental in nature; the focus is on identifying individual strengths and weaknesses and developing action plans for improving performance. The second is evaluative and involves assessing how well the person has performed in order to determine salary or merit adjustments. These two functions are not compatible. Employees, in their eagerness to find out how much pay they will receive, tend to tune out constructive feedback on how they can improve their performance. Likewise, managers tend to be more concerned with justifying their decision than engaging in a meaningful discussion on how the employee can improve his or her performance. It is difficult to be both a coach and a judge. As a result, several experts on performance appraisal systems recommend that organizations separate performance reviews, which focus on individual improvement, and pay reviews, which allocate the distribution of rewards.

In some matrix organizations, project managers conduct the performance reviews, while area managers are responsible for pay reviews. In other cases, performance reviews are part of the project closure process, and pay reviews are the primary objective of the annual performance appraisal. Other organizations avoid this dilemma by allocating only group rewards for project work. The remaining discussion is directed at reviews designed to improve performance because pay reviews are often outside the jurisdiction of the project manager.

Performance Reviews

Organizations employ a wide range of methods to review individual performance on a project. In general, all review methods of individual performance center on the technical and social skills brought to the project and team. Some organizations rely simply on

More and more companies are discarding the traditional superior-subordinate performance feedback process and replacing it with 360-degree feedback systems. The 360-degree feedback approach gathers behavioral observations from many sources within the organization and includes employee self-assessment. The individual completes the same structured evaluation process that superiors, project team members, peers and, in many cases, external customers use to evaluate a performance. Survey questionnaires, augmented by a few open-ended questions, are typically used to gather information.

Summary results are compared against organizational strategies, values, and business objectives. The feedback is communicated to the individual with the assistance of the company's human resource department or an outside consultant. The technique is used by a growing number of firms including General Electric, AT&T, Mobil Oil, Nabisco, Hewlett-Packard, and Warner-Lambert.

The objective of the 360-degree process is to identify areas for individual improvement. When anonymous feedback solicited from others is compared with the individual's self-evaluations, the individual may form a more realistic picture of her strengths and weaknesses. This may prompt behavioral change if the weaknesses identified were previously unknown to the individual. Such appears

to be the case for Jerry Wallace, an up-and-coming manager at General Motors. "The strongest message I got was that I need to delegate more," he says, "I thought I'd been doing it. But I need to do it more and sooner. My people are saying, 'Turn me loose.'"

Many firms obtain feedback from internal and external project customers. For example, a client may evaluate a project manager or member of the project team according to, "How effectively does the individual get things done without creating unnecessary adversarial relationships?" Incorporating customer feedback in the evaluation process underscores collaboration and the importance of client expectations in determining project success.

William J. Miller, a program director at Du Pont, helped install a 360-degree feedback system for 80 scientists and support people. "A high or low score didn't predict a scientist's ability to invent Teflon," says Miller. "But what feedback did was really improve the ability of people to work in teams. Their regard for others and behaviors that were damaging and self-centered are what changed."

*Brian O'Reilly, "360 Feedback Can Change Your Life," *Fortune,* October, 17, 1994, pp. 93–100; and Robert Hoffman, "Ten Reasons You Should Be Using 360 Degree Feedback," *HR Magazine,* April 1995, pp. 82–85; Dick Cochran, "Finally, a Way to Completely Measure Project Manager Performance," *PM Network,* September 2000, pp. 75–80.

an informal discussion between the project manager and the project member. Other organizations require project managers to submit written essays that describe and assess an individual's performance on a project. Many organizations use rating scales similar to the team evaluation survey in which the project manager rates the individual according to a certain scale (i.e., from 1 to 5) on a number of relevant performance dimensions (i.e., teamwork, customer relations). Some organizations augment these rating schemes with behaviorally anchored descriptions of what constitutes a 1 rating, a 2 rating, and so forth. Each method has its strengths and weaknesses, and, unfortunately, in many organizations the appraisal systems were designed to support mainstream operations and not unique project work. The bottom line is that project managers have to use the performance review system mandated by their organization as best they can.

Regardless of the method, the project manager needs to sit down with each team member and discuss his or her performance. Here are some general tips for conducting performance reviews:

- Always begin the process by asking the individual to evaluate his or her own performance. First, this approach may yield valuable information that you were not aware of. Second, the approach may provide an early warning for situations in which there is disparity in assessments. Finally, this method reduces the judgmental nature of the discussion.

- Avoid, when possible, drawing comparisons with other team members; rather, assess the individual in terms of established standards and expectations. Comparisons tend to undermine cohesion and divert attention away from what the individual needs to do to improve performance.

- When you have to be critical, focus the criticism on specific examples of behavior rather than on the individual personally. Describe in specific terms how the behavior affected the project.
- Be consistent and fair in your treatment of all team members. Nothing breeds resentment more than if, through the grapevine, individuals feel that they are being held to a different standard than are other project members.
- Treat the review as only one point in an ongoing process. Use it to reach an agreement as to how the individual can improve his or her performance.

Both managers and subordinates may dread a formal performance review. Neither side feels comfortable with the evaluative nature of the discussion and the potential for misunderstanding and hurt feelings. Much of this anxiety can be alleviated if the project manager is doing her job well. Project managers should be constantly giving team members feedback throughout the project so that individual team members can have a pretty good idea how well they have performed and how the manager feels before the formal meeting.

While in many cases the same process that is applied to reviewing the performance of team members is applied to evaluating the project manager, many organizations augment this process, given the importance of the position to their organization. This is where conducting the 360-degree review is becoming more popular. In project-driven organizations, directors or vice presidents of project management will be responsible for collecting information on a specific project manager from customers, vendors, team members, peers, and other managers. This approach has tremendous promise for developing more effective project managers.

Summary

Project audits enhance individual and organizational change and improvement. In this chapter processes for conducting project audits and developing the report were examined. Project closures and the importance of conducting team and individual evaluations were also reviewed. Key points of the chapter include the following:

- It is better to have automatic times or points when audits will take place. Surprises should be avoided.
- Audits of projects (especially those in process) need to be conducted carefully and with sensitivity to human reactions. The audit should focus on issues, problems, and successes and avoid references to groups or individuals.
- The audit is best staffed with individuals independent of the project.
- Audit reports need to be used and accessible.
- Audits support an organizational culture that vigorously promotes continuous improvement and organizational learning.
- Project closures should be planned and orderly regardless of the type of closure.
- Certain "core conditions" should be in place to support team and individual evaluation.
- Both individual and team evaluations should be conducted, and performance reviews should be separated from pay or merit reviews.

Competitive conditions appear to be forcing more organizations to adopt continuous improvement and organizational learning. Regular use of project audits has yielded dramatic improvements in the way projects are managed. As more members of these organizations are learning from project mistakes and what is contributing to project successes, the process of managing projects is continuously improving in their respective organizations. The major instrument for implementing this philosophy will be the project audit and report.

Since the purpose of the audit it to improve performance, the project maturity model is a good approach for checking project management performance and improvement for the organization over the long haul. Using the model as a starting benchmark, improvements can easily be tracked to higher levels.

Key Terms

In-process project audit	Postproject audit	Three hundred and sixty degree feedback
Maturity model	Project audit report	
Performance review	Project closure	
	Team evaluation	

Review Questions

1. How does the project audit differ from the performance measurement control system discussed in Chapter 13?
2. What major information would you expect to find in a project audit?
3. Why is it difficult to perform a truly independent, objective audit?
4. What personal characteristics and skills would you look for in selecting a project audit leader?
5. Comment on the following statement: "We cannot afford to terminate the project now. We have already spent more than 50 percent of the project budget."
6. Why should you separate performance reviews from pay reviews? How?
7. What are three major advantages to an organization for using a maturity model?

Exercises

1. Consider a course that you recently completed. Perform an audit of the course (the course represents a project and the course syllabus represents the project plan). Summarize the results of the audit as a report organized in accordance with the outline on page 465.
2. Imagine you are conducting an audit of the International Space Station project. Research press coverage and the Internet to collect information on the current status of the project. What are the successes and failures to date? What forecasts would you make about the completion of the project, and why? What recommendations would you make to top management of the program, and why?
3. Conduct an Internet search for information on Operation Eagle Claw. What further insights are obtained about the value of project audits and lessons to be learned from this failed project?
4. Interview a project manager who works for an organization that implements multiple projects. Using the maturity levels presented in this chapter, ask the manager to evaluate their organization's project maturity level and explain why this level was selected. Report the results.

References

Cochran, D., "Finally, a Way to Completely Measure Project Manager Performance," *PM Network,* September 2000, pp. 75–80.

Fincher, A. and G. Levin, "Project Management Maturity Model," *Proceedings of the 28th Annual PMI Symposium* (Newtown Square, PA: PMI, 1997), pp. 1028–35.

Gobeli, D. and E. Larson, "Barriers Affecting Project Success," in *1986 Proceedings Project Management Institute: Measuring Success* (Upper Darby, PA: Project Management Institute, 1986), pp. 22–29.

Hoffman, R., "Ten Reasons You Should Be Using 360 Degree Feedback," *HRMagazine,* April 1995, pp. 82–85.

Ibbs, W. C. and Y. H. Kwak, "Assessing Project Maturity," *Project Management Journal,* Vol. 31, No. 1, March 2000, pp. 32–43.

Kwak, Y. H. and W. C. Ibbs, "Calculating Project Management's Return on Investment," *Project Management Journal,* Vol. 31, No. 2, March 2000, pp. 38–47.

Pippett D. D. and J. F. Peters, "Team Building and Project Management: How Are We Doing?" *Project Management Journal,* Vol. 26, No. 4, December 1995, pp. 29–37.

Royer, I., "Why Bad Projects are so Hard to Kill," *Harvard Business Review,* February 2003, pp. 49–56.

Software Engineering Institute (SEI). (See website at http://www.sei.cmu/edu/activities/sema/profile.html.)

Stewart, W. E., "Balanced Scorecard for Projects," (2000 International Student Paper Award Winner) *Project Management Journal,* Vol. 32, No. 1, March 2001, pp. 38–47.

Wheatly, M., "Over the Bar," *PM Network,* Vol. 17, No. 1, January, 2003, pp. 40–45.

Yates, J. K. and S. Aniftos, "ISO 9000 Series of Quality Standards and the E/C Industry," *Project Management Journal,* Vol. 28, No. 2, June 1997, pp. 21–31.

Appendix 14.1

Project Closeout Checklist

Section 5: Project Closeout

Project Closeout Transition Checklist

Provide basic information about the project including: Project Title—The proper name used to identify this project; Project Working Title—The working name or acronym that will be used for the project; Proponent Secretary—The Secretary to whom the proponent agency is assigned or the Secretary that is sponsoring an enterprise project; Proponent Agency—The agency that will be responsible for the management of the project; Prepared by—The person(s) preparing this document; Date/Control Number—The date the checklist is finalized and the change or configuration item control number assigned.

Project Title:	_____	**Project Working Title:**	_____
Proponent Secretary:	_____	**Proponent Agency:**	_____
Prepared by:	_____	**Date/Control Number:**	_____

Complete the Status and Comments columns. In the Status column indicate: Yes, if the item has been addressed and completed; No, if item has not been addressed, or is incomplete; N/A, if the item is not applicable to this project. Provide comments or describe the plan to resolve the item in the last column.

Section 5: Project Closeout

	Item	Status	Comments/ Plan to Resolve
1	Have all the product or service deliverables been accepted by the customer?		
1.1	Are there contingencies or conditions related to the acceptance? If so, describe in the Comments.		
2	Has the project been evaluated against each performance goal established in the project performance plan?		
3	Has the actual cost of the project been tallied and compared to the approved cost baseline?		
3.1	Have all approved changes to the cost baseline been identified and their impact on the project documented?		
4	Have the actual milestone completion dates been compared to the approved schedule?		
4.1	Have all approved changes to the schedule baseline been identified and their impact on the project documented?		
5	Have all approved changes to the project scope been identified and their impact on the performance, cost, and schedule baselines documented?		
6	Has operations management formally accepted responsibility for operating and maintaining the product(s) or service(s) delivered by the project?		
6.1	Has the documentation relating to operation and maintenance of the product(s) or service(s) been delivered to, and accepted by, operations management?		
6.2	Has training and knowledge transfer of the operations organization been completed?		

(continued)

Section 5: Project Closeout (*Continued*)

	Item	Status	Comments/ Plan to Resolve
6.3	Does the projected annual cost to operate and maintain the product(s) or service(s) differ from the estimate provided in the project proposal? If so, note and explain the difference in the Comments column.		
7	Have the resources used by the project been transferred to other units within the organization?		
8	Has the project documentation been archived or otherwise disposed as described in the project plan?		
9	Have the lessons learned been documented in accordance with the Commonwealth Project Management guideline?		
10	Has the date for the postimplementation review been set?		
10.1	Has the person or unit responsible for conducting the postimplementation review been identified?		

Signatures

The Signatures of the people below relay an understanding that the key elements within the Closeout Phase section are complete and the project has been formally closed.

Position/Title	Name	Date	Phone Number

Source: http://www.vita.virginia.gov/projects/cpm/cpmDocs/CPMG-SEC5-Final.pdf

Case

Maximum Megahertz Project

Olaf Gundersen, the CEO of Wireless Telecom Company, is in a quandary. Last year he accepted the Maximum Megahertz Project suggested by six up-and-coming young R&D corporate stars. Although Olaf did not truly understand the technical importance of the project, the creators of the project needed only $600,000, so it seemed like a good risk. Now the group is asking for $800,000 more and a six-month extension on a project that is already four months behind. However, the team feels confident they can turn things around. The project manager and project team feel that if they hang in there a little longer they will be able to overcome the roadblocks they are encountering—especially those that reduce power, increase speed, and use a new technology battery. Other managers familiar with the project hint that the power pack problem might be solved, but "the battery problem will never be solved." Olaf believes he is locked into this project; his gut feeling tells him the project will never materialize, and he should get out. John, his human resource manager, suggested bringing in a consultant to axe the project. Olaf is thinking maybe he should do that on this project if it needs to be terminated.

Olaf decided to call his friend, Dawn O'Connor, the CEO of an accounting software company. He asked her, "What do you do when project costs and deadlines escalate drastically? How do you handle doubtful projects?" Her response was, "Let another project manager look at the project. Ask: 'If you took over this project tomorrow, could you bring the project in on time and within budget with the extended time and additional money?' If the answer is no, I call my top management team together and have them review the doubtful project in relation to other projects in our project portfolio." Olaf feels this is good advice.

Unfortunately, the Maximum Megahertz Project is not an isolated example. Over the last five years there have been three projects that were never completed. "We just seemed to pour more money into them, even though we had a pretty good idea the projects were dying. The cost of those projects was high; those resources could have been better used on other projects." Olaf wonders, "Do we ever learn from our mistakes? How can we develop a process that catches errant projects early? More importantly, how do we ease a project manager and team off an errant project without embarrassment?" Olaf certainly does not want to lose the six bright stars on the Maximum Megahertz Project.

Olaf is contemplating how his growing telecommunications company should deal with the problem of identifying projects that should be terminated early, how to allow good managers to make mistakes without public embarrassment, and how they all can learn from their mistakes.

Give Olaf a plan of action for the future that attacks the problem. Be specific and provide examples that relate to Wireless Telecom Company.

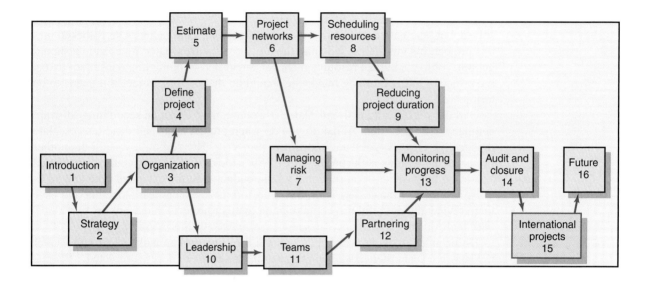

International Projects
International Projects
Environmental Factors
Project Site Selection
Cross-Cultural Considerations: A Closer Look
Selection and Training for International Projects
Summary

CHAPTER FIFTEEN

International Projects

The principal benefit of living abroad is that it enables us to get glimpses of ourselves as others see us and to realize that others' views are more accurate than ours. Progress begins with grasping the truth about ourselves, however unpleasant it may be.

—Russel Ackoff, The Wharton School, University of Pennsylvania

Projects are frequently classified as domestic, overseas, foreign, or global. A domestic project is one performed in its native country for a resident firm (a construction firm building a bridge in its state). An overseas project is one executed in a foreign country for a native firm (a Swedish company building a truck factory in the United States for their native company). A foreign project is executed in a foreign country for a foreign firm (a U.S. firm developing an information system in Malaysia for Malaysian banks). A global project consists of teams formed from professionals spanning multiple countries, continents, and cultures with their work integrated for the entire enterprise (e.g., multinational enterprise developing a global distribution system). Global teams are a crisscross of functions, work locale, markets, culture, and products. Today, these distinctions become blurred as the world economy and organizations become more integrated.

This chapter targets the international project manager who must resettle in a foreign environment to manage the project. The chapter also includes useful information for project professionals working overseas as well as those working on virtual projects involving colleagues from different countries.

There is no generally accepted framework or road map for project managers given international assignments. These project managers typically face a difficult set of problems—for example, absence from home, friends, and sometimes family; personal risks; missed career opportunities; foreign language, culture, and laws; adverse conditions. Of course there are positives—for example, increased income, increased responsibilities, career opportunities, foreign travel, new lifetime friends. How the international project manager adapts and approaches problems encountered in the host country often determines the success or failure of a project.

This chapter focuses on four major issues surrounding the management of international projects. First, major environmental factors that impact project selection and implementation are briefly highlighted. Second, an example of how organizations decide where to expand globally is provided. Third, the challenge of working in a strange and foreign culture is addressed. Finally, how companies select and train professionals for international projects is discussed. Although by no means comprehensive, this chapter attempts to provide a solid understanding of the major issues and challenges confronting the international project manager.

Environmental Factors

The major challenge international project managers face is the reality that what works at home may not work in a foreign environment. Too often project managers impose practices, assumed to be superior, from their home country on host-country nationals without questioning applicability to the new environment. Although there are similarities between domestic and international projects, it is a fact that good management practices vary across nations and cultures. It is these differences that can turn an international project into a nightmare. If potential international project managers have a keen awareness of differences in the host country's environment from their own domestic environment, dangers and obstacles of the global project can be reduced or avoided. There are several basic factors in the host country's environment that may alter how projects will be implemented: legal/political, security, geographical, economic, infrastructure, and culture (see Figure 15.1).

Legal/Political

Expatriate project managers should operate within the laws and regulations of the host country. Political stability and local laws strongly influence how projects will be implemented. Typically, these laws favor protection of local workers, suppliers, and environment. For example, how much control will be imposed from government agencies? What is the attitude of federal and state bureaucracies toward regulations and approval policies that can cause project delays? How much government interference or support can one expect? For example, an expatriate project manager based in Ho Chi Minh City observed:

> There is a common saying among the barflies about doing business in Vietnam: "The government interprets the law for its friends, and applies the law to strangers." Vietnam is no place for strangers to do business. The foreign investment law is tailored to approve investments based on the government's view of how a company and its project will further certain economic and social objectives.

The constraints imposed by national and local laws need to be identified and adhered to. Are local ecological laws restrictive? Will manufacturing a new product in a computer chip plant require exporting toxic waste materials? What are the pollution standards? How will labor laws affect the use of indigenous workers to complete the

FIGURE 15.1
Environmental Factors Affecting International Projects

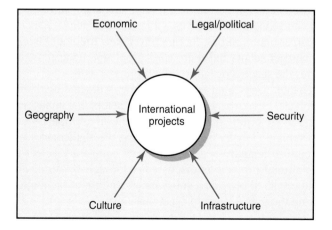

project? Given laws that affect business vary widely across countries, qualified legal assistance is essential.

Government corruption is a very real part of international business. In China various forms of obligatory "profit sharing" with city officials in the Hainan province have been reported. Employment of relatives, donations, and other "favors" are an expected cost of doing business in that region. The *Wall Street Journal* reports that Russia has become a nation in which corruption is both pervasive and arbitrary: "Without the structure the Communist Party provided, people did not know whom to pay and many anarchistic bribe collectors stepped up with their hands out."

Political stability is another key factor in deciding to implement a project in a foreign country. What are the chances that there will be a change in the party in power during the project? Are the tax provisions and government regulations stable or subject to change with the winds of political change? How are laws made, and what is the past record of fairness? How are labor unions treated in the political realm? Does labor unrest exist? Is there a chance for a coup d'état? Contingency plans need to be established to respond to emergencies.

Security

International terrorism is a fact of life in today's world. Tim Daniel, chief operating officer of International SOS Assistance, Inc., reported that the number of his firm's clients doubled after September 11th. SOS is a security firm that specializes in evacuating expatriates from dangerous situations around the world. The company cites Pricewaterhouse Coopers, Nortel Networks Corp., and Citigroup among its clients.

While the 9/11 attacks magnified the fact that Americans are vulnerable to terrorism at home, they also heightened security concerns for working abroad. For example, after September 11th, several American firms canceled or scaled back projects in potential hotspots such as Pakistan and the Philippines. Others reported increased pressures from expatriates who wanted to return home with their families. On June 3, 2004, the Nobel Peace Prize-winning relief agency *Medecins Sans Frontieres* (Doctors Without Borders) suspended all Afghan projects after five of its aid workers were killed in an ambush claimed by the former Taliban regime.

Crime is another factor. The growing presence of the Russian Mafia has discouraged many foreign firms from setting up operations in the former Soviet Union. Kidnapping of American professionals is also a very real threat in many parts of the world.

Security nationally involves the capacity of a country's military and police forces to prevent and respond to attacks. In many foreign countries, American firms will have to augment the countries' security system. For example, it is common practice to hire tribal bodyguards in such places as Angola and Uzbekistan.

Another real cost associated with international terrorism is the ease of commerce across borders. Heightened security measures have created border congestions that have expanded the time and cost of moving personnel, materials, and equipment across countries. These constraints need to be factored into the budget and schedule of projects.

Risk management is always a vital part of project management. It plays an even bigger role in managing projects overseas. For example, Strohl Systems Group, a global leader in recovery-planning software and services, includes the following among the questions it uses to evaluate vulnerability to terrorism: Have you included possible terrorist targets (facilities and personnel) in your hazard and vulnerability analysis? Have you conducted a counterterrorism exercise complete with law enforcement, fire, medical, and emergency management participation? What should your organization's policy be on negotiating with a person threatening a terrorist act?

Managing projects in a dangerous world is a tough assignment. Security precautions are major cost considerations not only in dollars and cents, but also in the psychological well-being of personnel sent abroad. Effective risk management is critical to success.

Geography

One factor that is often underestimated until project personnel actually arrive at a foreign destination is the geography of the country. Imagine what it is like to deplane from a modern aircraft and encounter the 105-degree heat and 90 percent humidity of Jakarta, Indonesia, or three feet of fresh snow and −25-degree temperatures in Kokkla, Finland. Whether it is the wind, the rain, the heat, the jungle, or the desert, more than one project manager has asserted that their greatest challenge was overcoming the "elements." Mother Nature cannot be ignored.

The planning and implementation of a project must take into account the impact the country's geography will have on the project. For example, a salvage operation off the coast of Greenland can only be scheduled one month out of the year because the waterway is frozen over during the remainder of the year. Construction projects in Southeast Asia have to accommodate the monsoon season when rainfall can be as high as 50 inches per month. Geography does not just affect outdoor projects. It can have an indirect effect on "indoor" projects. For example, one information systems specialist reported that his performance on a project in northern Sweden declined due to sleep deprivation. He attributed his problems to the 20 hours of daylight this part of the world experiences during summer months. Finally, extreme weather conditions can make extraordinary demands on equipment. Projects can grind to a halt because of equipment breakdown under the brunt of the elements. Working under extreme conditions typically requires special equipment, which increases the costs and complexity of the project.

Before beginning a project in a foreign land, project planners and managers need to study carefully the unique characteristics of the geography of that country. They need to factor into project plans and schedules such items as climate, seasons, altitude, and natural geographical obstacles.

Economic

How business is conducted in the host country can influence project success. Basic economic factors in foreign countries and regions influence choices of site selection and how business will be conducted for potential projects. The gross domestic product (GDP) of a country suggests the level of development of a country. A faltering economy may indicate fewer sources of capital funding. For example, changes in protectionist strategies of a host country, such as import quotas and tariffs, can quickly alter the viability of projects. Other factors such as balance of payments, currency fluctuations, hyperinflation, population growth, education level of workforce, and market size can influence project choices and operations. For example, the economic downturn in Southeast Asia during the late 1990s saw local economies in Thailand, Malaysia, and Indonesia being devastated by inflation rates in excess of 60 percent. A company can protect against currency fluctuations by hedging or tying costs to a strong currency such as the U.S. dollar, British pound, or Euro. Still, the social upheaval caused by such dramatic economic events cannot be underestimated.

Bartering is a form of compensation that is still used by some countries and organizations. For example, one project in Africa was paid in goat skins. The goat skins were eventually sold to an Italian manufacturer of gloves. Another project along the Caspian

In February 1976, Francis Ford Coppola took his Hollywood film crew to the Philippines to shoot *Apocalypse Now,* a film adaptation of Joseph Conrad's *Heart of Darkness* within the context of the Vietnam conflict. The Philippines was chosen because the terrain was similar to Vietnam's, and the government was willing to rent its helicopter force for the movie. At the time, the U.S. military was unwilling to cooperate on a film about Vietnam. An additional advantage was cheap labor. Coppola was able to hire more than 300 laborers at $1 to $3 per day to construct elaborate production sets, including an impressive Cambodian temple. *Apocalypse Now* was scheduled for 16 weeks of shooting at a budget of $12 to $14 million.

Months earlier, George Lucas, of *Star Wars* fame, warned Coppola against filming the movie in the Philippines. He said, "It's one thing to go over there for three weeks with five people and scrounge some footage with the Filipino Army, but if you go over there with a big Hollywood production, the longer you stay the more in danger you are of getting sucked into the swamp." His words turned out to be prophetic.

A civil war was going on between government forces and communist rebels. Shooting was repeatedly interrupted because the Philippine military ordered their helicopter pilots to leave the set and fly to the mountains to fight the rebels.

In May 1976, a typhoon struck the Philippine Islands, destroying most of the movie sets. The film team was forced to shut down production and returned to the United States for two months.

The lead character was played by Martin Sheen, who suffered a serious heart attack under the stress and heat of the filming and had to return to the United States. Coppola scrambled to film the scenes that did not require Sheen, but eventually production came to a standstill until Sheen's return nine weeks later.

The entire project proved to be a traumatic experience for Coppola, who had enjoyed Academy Award success with his previous *Godfather* movies, "There were times when I thought I was going to die, literally, from the inability to move the problems I had. I would go to bed at four in the morning in a cold sweat."

Film production ended in May 1977 after more than 200 days of shooting. The final cost was about $30 million. To date, *Apocalypse Now* has earned more than $150 million throughout the world.

* Hearts of Darkness: A Filmmaker's Apocalypse (Paramount Pictures, 1991).

Sea was paid for in oil. There is a small group of firms that specialize in bartering for project contractors. These intermediaries charge a commission to sell the bartered goods (e.g., oil) for the contractor. However, dealing with commodities can be a risky enterprise.

Skills, educational level, and labor supply prevalent in a host country can determine the choice of a project site. Is project selection driven by low wage levels or availability of technically skilled talent? For example, you can hire three computer programmers in India for the price of one programmer in the United States. Conversely, many high-tech companies are willing to endure the additional expense of setting up joint projects in Switzerland and Germany to take advantage of their engineering prowess.

Infrastructure

Infrastructure refers to a country or community's ability to provide the services required for a project. Infrastructure needs for a project could be communication, transportation, power, technology, and education systems. For example, developing an electric steel plant to be near a major market requires a reliable supply of electric power. If reliable power is not sufficient, other alternatives need to be considered. Software projects across borders are common today; however, they depend on reliable telecommunication networks. These networks simplify and facilitate project coordination and management among project stakeholders in different locations. If the project depends on a high ratio of vendor suppliers, good roads, and other transportation modes such as air and seaports, a good infrastructure will be imperative.

An example of a project that failed to take into account the needs and infrastructure of the host nation involved a U.S. company that was awarded the contract for building a hospital in an African nation. The local African officials wanted a "low-tech" health care facility that would take local traditions into consideration. Because their relatives generally accompanied patients, space had to be provided for them, too. Electricity was not reliably supplied, and it was doubtful whether well-educated doctors would want to spend careers away from the city. Therefore, the locals wanted a hospital for basic care with minimum technology. The construction company doing the building, on the other hand, had a preconceived notion of what a hospital should be and was not going to be accused of building a second-rate facility. It built a modern hospital that could have stood in any U.S. city. The building was completed; however, even after several years it was not used because the electricity was not sufficient, the air-conditioning could not be used, and doctors refused to live in the rural area.

Organizations need to consider the needs of the families of personnel they send overseas. Will the facilities and living conditions for the expatriate families place an undue hardship on families? Will schooling for children be available? The welfare and comfort of expatriate families play an important role in retaining good project managers and promoting their peak performance.

Culture

Visiting project managers must accept and respect the customs, values, philosophies, and social standards of their host country. Global managers recognize that if the customs and social cultural dimensions of the host country are not accommodated, projects will not succeed. Too many project audits and final reports of international projects reflect challenges and problems linked to cultural differences.

For most project managers, the biggest difference in managing an international project is operating in a national culture where things are done differently. For example, most developed nations use the same project management techniques (CPM, risk analysis, trade-off analysis). However, how activity work is performed can be very different in the host country.

Will English be the operating language, or will the project manager need to be fluent in the foreign language? Will translation services be available and sufficient? Communication problems—because of language differences—often become a major problem in carrying out even simple tasks. Although the use of translators can help tremendously, their use does not solve the communication problem completely because something is lost in translation.

Will religious factors influence the project? For example, religious factors touched the spouse of a Scandinavian project manager responsible for building a water desalination plant from sea water in a Middle East country. She was restricted to the living compound for families of foreign guest workers. Going outside the compound to a nearby city meant covering her head, arms, and legs and being accompanied by another woman or, preferably, a man. A physical altercation in the city concerning her clothing was traumatic for her. She left the country and returned home. Her husband requested a transfer back home three months later. The loss of the original project manager from the project required the assigned project manager to establish relationships with the project team and host country's nationals to get the project moving smoothly again.

Not only do project managers have to adapt to the culture of the host country, but oftentimes overseas projects require working with people from different countries. For example, on a light rail project in the Philippines, an American firm was hired to oversee the interests of local real estate companies who were funding the project. The American project manager had to work with Czech representatives who were providing the rail equipment, Japanese engineers responsible for building the rail, Australian bankers who were providing additional financing, an Indian firm that were the principal architects, as well as the native Filipinos.

Of all the factors, working within a multicultural environment is most often the greatest challenge for project managers. It will be dealt with in detail later in this chapter.

Project Site Selection

As the project manager studies the factors contributing to site selection, he will see that inherent in all of these factors is the risk level senior management and directors are willing to accept for the potential rewards of a successful international project. One approach for the project manager to digest, clarify, and understand the factors leading to the selection of a specific project is to use a risk matrix similar to those found in Chapter 7. The major difference lies in the selection of the risk factors for different project sites.

Figure 15.2 presents a truncated matrix for project site selection of the construction of a laser printer factory in Singapore, India, or Ireland. In this example, political stability, worker skill and supply, culture compatibility, infrastructure, government support, and product-to-market advantage were the major assessment factors. Each project site is compared against each factor. Figure 15.3 depicts a further breakdown of the infrastructure evaluation factor. In this example, transportation, educated workforce, utilities, telecommunications, and vendor suppliers are considered important to evaluating the infrastructure for each site. The scores given in Figure 15.3 are used to assign values to the infrastructure factor of the assessment matrix, Figure 15.2. In this project, Ireland was the choice. Clearly, Singapore and Ireland were very close in terms

FIGURE 15.2
Assessment Matrix Project Site Selection

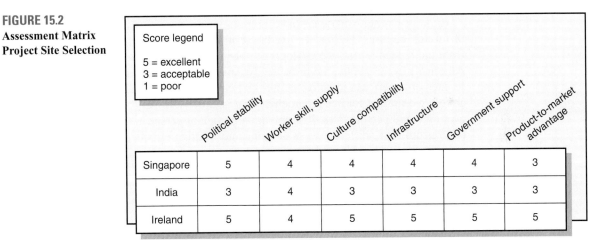

Score legend

5 = excellent
3 = acceptable
1 = poor

	Political stability	Worker skill, supply	Culture compatibility	Infrastructure	Government support	Product-to-market advantage
Singapore	5	4	4	4	4	3
India	3	4	3	3	3	3
Ireland	5	4	5	5	5	5

FIGURE 15.3
Evaluation Matrix Breakdown for Infrastructure

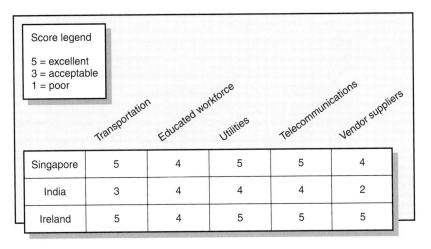

Score legend

5 = excellent
3 = acceptable
1 = poor

	Transportation	Educated workforce	Utilities	Telecommunications	Vendor suppliers
Singapore	5	4	5	5	4
India	3	4	4	4	2
Ireland	5	4	5	5	5

of infrastructure and several other factors. However, the major assessment factor of using Ireland to access the EEC (product-to-market advantage) turned the decision.

Given the macro economic factors, the firm's strategic posture toward global projects, and the major considerations for selecting this project, it is imperative the project manager quickly become sensitized to the foreign cultural factors that can spell project success or failure.

Cross-Cultural Considerations: A Closer Look

The concept of culture was introduced in Chapter 3 as referring to the unique personality of a particular firm. More specifically, culture was defined as a system of shared norms, beliefs, values, and customs that bind people together, creating shared meaning and a unique identity. *Culture* is a concept created for descriptive purposes and depends on the group that is the focus of attention. For example, within a global context culture can refer to certain regions (i.e., Europeans, Arabs), to specific nations (i.e., French, Thai), or to certain ethnic or religious groups (i.e., Kurds, African-Americans). This chapter looks at national cultures; we freely recognize that many cultural characteristics are borderless and that there is considerable variation within any one country. Still, national cultures provide a useful anchor for understanding different habits, customs, and values around the world.

Right or wrong, Americans have a reputation for not being able to work effectively in foreign cultures. (When we use the term "American," we are referring to people from the United States; we apologize to our friends in Canada and Central and South America.) In the 1960s, the term "Ugly American" encapsulated the apparent indifference of Americans to native cultures when working or traveling abroad. Americans are often criticized for being parochial; that is, they view the world solely through their own eyes and perspectives. People with a parochial perspective do not recognize that other people have different ways of living and working effectively. American parochial attitudes probably reflect the huge domestic market of the United States, the geographic isolation of the United States, and the reality that English is becoming the international business language in many parts of the world.

It is important that Americans working on international projects anticipate cultural differences. Take, for example, a project manager from a large North American construction company who was given responsibility to select a site for the design and construction of a large fish-processing plant in a West African country. The manager assessed potential sites according to the availability of reliable power, closeness to transportation, nearness to the river for access of fishing boats from the Atlantic Ocean, proximity to main markets, and availability of housing and people for employment. After evaluating alternative sites, the project manager chose the optimum location. Just prior to requesting bids from local contractors for some of the site preparation, the manager discovered, in talking to the contractors, that the site was located on ground considered sacred by the local people, who believed this site was the place where their gods resided. None of the local people upon whom the project manager was depending for staff would ever consider working there! The project manager quickly revised his choice and relocated the site. In this case, he was lucky that the cultural gaffe was discovered prior to construction. Too often these errors are realized only after a project is completed.

Some argue that Americans have become less parochial. International travel, immigration, movies, and the popularity of such international events as the Olympics have made more Americans sensitive to cultural differences. While Americans may be more worldly, there is still a tendency for them to believe that American cultural values and ways of doing things are superior to all others. This ethnocentric perspective is reflected in wanting to conduct business only on their terms and stereotyping other countries as lazy, corrupt, or inefficient. Americans need to make a serious effort to appreciate other ways of approaching work and problems in other countries.

Finally, American project managers have earned a reputation abroad for being very good at understanding technology but not good at understanding people. As one Indonesian engineer put it, "Americans are great at solving technical problems, but they tend to ignore the people factor." For example, Americans tend to underestimate the importance that relationship building plays in conducting business in other countries. Americans have a tendency to want to get down to work and let friendships evolve in the course of their work. In most other cultures just the opposite is true. Before a foreigner works with you, they want to get to know you as a person. Trust is not established by credentials but rather evolves from personal interaction. Business deals often require a lengthy and elaborate courtship. For example, it may take five to eight meetings before Arab managers are even willing to discuss business details.

Adjustments

Two of the biggest adjustments Americans typically have to make in working abroad are adapting to the general pace of life and the punctuality of people. In America "time is money," and a premium is placed on working quickly. Other cultures do not share Americans' sense of urgency and are accustomed to a much slower pace of life. They can't understand why Americans are always in such a hurry. Punctuality varies across cultures. For example, Americans will generally tolerate someone being 5 to 10 minutes late. In contrast, among Peruvians, the period before an apology or explanation for being late is expected might be 45 minutes to an hour!

While working on multicultural projects, managers sometimes encounter ethical dilemmas that are culturally bound. For example, the 1999 Olympic site selection scandal featured the sordid details of committee members peddling their votes for a wide range of gifts (i.e., university scholarships for their children, extravagant trips). In many societies such "bribes" or "tributes" are expected and the only way to conduct meaningful business. Moreover, many cultures will not grant a female project manager the same respect they will a male project manager. Should U.S. management increase project risk or violate its own sex-discrimination policy?

These cultural differences are just the tip of the iceberg. There are numerous "How to Do Business in . . ." books written by people who have traveled and worked abroad. Although these books may lack rigor, they typically do a good job of identifying local customs and common mistakes made by outsiders. On the other hand, anthropologists have made significant contributions to our understanding of why and how the cultures of societies are different (see the accompanying Research Highlights). Students of international project management are encouraged to study these works to gain a deeper understanding of the root causes of cultural diversity.

So what can be said to prepare people to work on international projects? The world is too diverse to do justice in one chapter to all the cultural variations managers are likely to encounter when working on international projects. Instead, a sample of some of these differences will be highlighted by discussing working on projects in four different countries: Mexico, France, Saudi Arabia, and China. We apologize to our readers outside the United States because briefings are presented from the viewpoint of a U.S. project manager working in these countries. Still, in an effort not to be too ethnocentric, we present a fifth scenario for foreign project managers assigned to working in the United States. Although by no means exhaustive, these briefings provide a taste of what it is like to work in and with people from these countries.

Anthropologists Kluckhohn and Strodtbeck assert that cultural variations reflect how different societies have responded to common issues or problems throughout time (see Figure 15.4). Five of the issues featured in their comparative framework are discussed here.

- *Relation to nature*—This issue reflects how people relate to the natural world around them and to the supernatural. Should people dominate their environment, live in harmony with it, or be subjugated to it? North Americans generally strive to harness nature's forces and change them as they need. Other societies, as in India, strive to live in harmony with nature. Still other societies see themselves at the mercy of physical forces and/or subject to the will of a supreme being. Life in this context is viewed as predetermined, preordained, or an exercise in chance.

- *Time orientation*—Does the culture focus on the past, present, or future? For example, many European countries focus on the past and emphasize maintaining tradition. North Americans, on the other hand, are less concerned with tradition and tend to focus on the present and near future. Paradoxically, Japanese society, while rich with tradition, has a much longer time horizon.

- *Activity orientation*—This issue refers to a desirable focus of behavior. Some cultures emphasize "being" or living in the moment. This orientation stresses experiencing life and seeking immediate gratification. Other cultures emphasize "doing" and emphasize postponing immediate gratification for greater accomplishment. A third alternative is the "control" orientation, where people restrain their desires by detaching themselves from objects. The activity dimension affects how people approach work and leisure and the extent to which work-related concerns pervade their lives. It is reflected in the age-old question, "Do we live to work or work to live?"

- *Basic nature of people*—Does a culture view people as good, evil, or some mix of these two? In many Third World countries, people see themselves as basically honest and trustworthy. Conversely, some Mediterranean cultures have been characterized as taking a rather evil view of human nature. North Americans are somewhere in between. They see people as basically good but stay on guard so as not to be taken advantage of.

- *Relationships among people*—This issue concerns the responsibility one has for others. Americans, for instance, tend to be highly individualistic and believe everyone should take care of him- or herself. In contrast, many Asian societies emphasize concern for the group or community he or she is a member of. A third variation is hierarchical, which is similar to the group except that in these societies groups are hierarchically ranked, and membership is essentially stable over time. This is a characteristic of aristocratic societies and caste systems.

The Kluckhohn and Strodtbeck framework provides a basis for a deeper understanding of cultural differences. At the same time, they warn that not all members of a culture practice the same behavior all the time, and, as in the United States, there is likely to be considerable variation within a given culture.

*F. Kluckhohn and F. L. Strodtbeck, *Variations in Value Orientations* (Evanston, IL: Row, Peterson, 1961).

FIGURE 15.4
Kluckhohn-Strodtbeck's Cross-Cultural Framework
Note: The line indicates where the United States tends to fall along these issues.

Cultural issue	Variations		
Relationship to nature	Domination	Harmony	Subjugation
Time orientation	Past	Present	Future
Activity orientation	Being	Doing	Controlling
Nature of people	Good	Evil	Mixed
Relationships among people	Individualist	Group	Hierarchical

The Hofstede framework grew from a study of 88,000 people working in IBM subsidiaries in 50 countries and 3 multicountry regions. Based on responses to a 32-item questionnaire, Dutch social scientist Geert Hofstede developed different dimensions for examining cultures:

1. Individualism versus collectivism. Identifies whether a culture holds individuals or the group responsible for each member's welfare.

2. Power distance. Describes degree to which a culture accepts status and power differences among its members.

3. Uncertainty avoidance. Identifies a culture's willingness to accept uncertainty and ambiguity about the future.

4. Masculinity-femininity. Describes the degree to which the culture emphasizes competitive and achievement-oriented behavior or displays concerns for relationships.

Figure 15.5 shows how he ranked selected countries according to collectivism-individualism and power distance. Wealth appears to influence both factors. Power distance is correlated with income inequality in a country while individualism is correlated with national wealth (Per Capita Gross National Product). As a result high power distance and collectivism are often found together, as are low power distance and individualism. This can affect decision making on project teams. For example, while the high collectivism may lead a project team in Thailand to operate consensually, the high power distance may cause decisions to be heavily influenced by the desires of the project manager. Conversely, a similar team operating in more individualistic and low power distance such as Great Britain or America might make decisions with more open debate including challenging the preferences of the project manager.

*Culture's Consequences: Comparing Values, Behaviors, Institutions and Organizations Across Nations, 2nd Edition. (Thousand Oaks, CA: Sage Publications, 2001). http://www.geerthofstede.nl

FIGURE 15.5
Sample Country Clusters on Hofstede's Dimensions of Individualism-Collectivism and Power Distance

Collectivism		Columbia, Peru, Thailand, Singapore, Mexico, Turkey, Indonesia
Individualism	Israel, Finland, Germany, Ireland, New Zealand, Canada, Great Britain, United States	Spain, South Africa, France, Italy, Belgium
	Low power distance	High power distance

Working in Mexico

America developed historically in an environment where it was important for strangers to be able to get along, interact, and do business. On the American frontier almost everyone was a stranger, and people had to both cooperate and keep their distance. The New England Yankee sentiment that "Good fences make good neighbors" expresses this American cultural value well. Conversely, Mexico developed historically in an environment where the only people to trust were family and close friends—and by extension, people who were known to those whom you knew well. As a consequence, personal relationships dominate all aspects of Mexican business. While Americans are generally taught not to do business with friends, Mexicans and other Latin Americans are taught to do business with no one but friends.

The significance of personal relationships has created a *compadre* system in which Mexicans are obligated to give preference to relatives and friends when hiring, contracting,

Americans tend to discount the significance of luck and believe that good fortune is generally a result of hard work. In other cultures, luck takes on greater significance and has supernatural ramifications. For example, in many Asian cultures certain numbers are considered lucky, while others are unlucky. In Hong Kong the numbers 7, 3, and especially 8 (which sounds like the word for prosperity) are considered lucky, while the number 4 is considered unlucky (because it is pronounced like the word "death"). Hong Kong businesspeople go to great lengths to avoid the number 4. For example, there is no fourth floor in office and hotel buildings. Business executives have been known to reject ideal sites in heavily congested Hong Kong because the address would contain the number 4. They pay premium prices for suitable sites containing addresses with the lucky numbers. Likewise, Hong Kong business managers avoid scheduling important events on the fourth day of each month and prefer to arrange critical meetings on the eighth day.

Hong Kong is also a place where the ancient art of *Feng shui* (literally "wind water") is practiced. This involves making sure a site and buildings are aligned in harmony with the earth's energy forces so that the location will be propitious. Feng shui practitioners are often called in on construction projects to make sure that the building is aligned correctly on the site. In some cases, the technical design of the building is changed to conform to the recommendations of such experts. Similarly, Feng shui experts have been known to be called in when projects are experiencing problems. Their recommendations may include repositioning the project manager's desk or hanging up mirrors to deflect the flow of unharmonious influences away from the building or site of the project.

Taxi/Getty Images.

In cultures where luck is believed to play a role in business, people who discount luck may not only insult the luck seekers, they may risk being thought negligent in not paying enough attention to what is viewed as a legitimate business concern.

procuring, and sharing business opportunities. North Americans often complain that such practices contribute to inefficiency in Mexican firms. While this may or may not be the case, efficiency is prized by Americans, while Mexicans place a higher value on friendship.

Mexicans tend to perceive Americans as being "cold." They also believe that most Americans look down on them. Among the most effective things an American can do to prevent being seen as a typical *Gringo* is to take the time and effort in the beginning of a working relationship to really get to know Mexican counterparts. Because family is all-important to Mexicans, a good way for developing a personal relationship is exchanging information about each other's family. Mexicans will often gauge people's trustworthiness by the loyalty and attention they devote to their family.

The *mañana* syndrome reflects another cultural difference between Americans and Mexicans. Mexicans have a different concept of time than Americans do. Mexicans feel confined and pressured when given deadlines; they prefer open-ended schedules. They generally consider individuals to be more important than sticking to a schedule. If a friend drops in at work, most Mexicans will stop and talk, regardless of how long it takes, and even if chatting makes their work late.

Finally, as in many other cultures, Mexicans do not share Americans' confidence that they control their own destiny. While Americans are taught, "When the going gets tough, the tough get going," Mexicans are taught, "Taking action without knowing what is expected or wanted can have dangerous consequences." Mexicans tend to be more cautious and want to spend more time discussing risks and potential problems that Americans might dismiss as improbable or irrelevant.

Other useful guidelines for working with Mexicans on projects include the following:

1. Americans tend to be impersonal and practical when making arguments; Mexicans can be very passionate and emotional when arguing. They enjoy a lively debate.
2. Where Americans tend to use meetings as the place to work things out publicly, Mexicans tend to see meetings as the place where persons with authority ratify what has been decided during informal private discussions.
3. While Mexicans can be emotional, they tend to shy away from any sort of direct confrontation or criticism. A long silence often indicates displeasure or disagreement.
4. Although Mexicans tend to prefer a more distant relationship between workers and managers than Americans do, they still value managers who treat them in a friendly but dignified manner.
5. Titles are extremely important in Mexico and are always used when a person is introducing him- or herself or being introduced. Pay as much attention to remembering a person's title as to remembering his or her name.

Today, with NAFTA and increased international business activity in Mexico, old traditions are disappearing. American managers report that cultural differences are less evident in northern Mexico where many multinational firms operate. Project managers should devote up-front effort to understanding how much older mores of Mexican culture apply to their project.

Working in France

Some Americans consider the French the most difficult to work with among Europeans. This feeling probably stems from a reflection of the French culture, which is quite different from that in the United States.

In France, one's social class is very important. Social interactions are constrained by class standing, and during their lifetimes most French people do not encounter much change in social status. Unlike an American, who through hard work and success can move from the lowest economic stratum to the highest, a successful French person might, at best, climb one or two rungs up the social ladder. Additionally, the French are very status conscious and like to provide signs of this status, such as knowledge of literature and arts; a well-designed, tastefully decorated house; and a high level of education.

The French tend to admire or be fascinated with people who disagree with them; in contrast, Americans are more attracted to those who agree with them. As a result, the French are accustomed to conflict and, during negotiations, accept the fact that some positions are irreconcilable and must be accepted as such. Americans, on the other hand, tend to believe that conflicts can be resolved if both parties make an extra effort and are willing to compromise. Also, the French often determine a person's trustworthiness based on their firsthand, personal evaluation of the individual's character. Americans, in contrast, tend to evaluate a person's trustworthiness on the basis of past achievements and other people's evaluations.

The French are often accused of lacking an intense work ethic. For example, many French workers frown on overtime and on average they have one of the longest vacations in the world (four to five weeks annually). On the other hand, the French enjoy a reputation for productive work, a result of the French tradition of craftsmanship. This tradition places a greater premium on quality rather than on getting things accomplished quickly.

Most French organizations tend to be highly centralized with rigid structures. As a result, it usually takes longer to carry out decisions. Because this arrangement is quite different from the more decentralized organizations in the United States, many U.S. project managers find the bureaucratic red tape a source of considerable frustration.

In countries like the United States, a great deal of motivation is derived from professional accomplishments. The French do not tend to share this same view of work. While they admire American industriousness, they believe that quality of life is what really matters. As a result they attach much greater importance to leisure time, and many are unwilling to sacrifice the enjoyment of life for a dedication to project work.

Cautions to remember with the French include these:

1. The French value punctuality. It is very important to be on time for meetings and social occasions.

2. Great importance is placed on neatness and taste. When interacting with French businesspeople, pay close attention to your own professional appearance and appear cultured and sophisticated.

3. The French can be very difficult to negotiate with. Often, they ignore facts, no matter how convincing they may be. They can be quite secretive about their position. It is difficult to obtain information from them, even in support for their position. Patience is essential for negotiating with them.

4. French managers tend to see their work as an intellectual exercise. They do not share the American view of management as an interpersonally demanding exercise, where plans have to be constantly "sold" upward and downward using personal skills.

5. The French generally consider managers to be experts. They expect managers to give precise answers to work-related questions. To preserve their reputation, some French managers act as if they know the answers to questions even when they don't.

Working in Saudi Arabia

Project management has a long tradition in Saudi Arabia and other Arab countries. Financed by oil money, European and American firms have contributed greatly to the modernization of Arab countries. Despite this tradition, foreigners often find it very hard to work on projects in Saudi Arabia. A number of cultural differences can be cited for this difficulty.

One is the Arabian view of time. In North America, it is common to use the cliché, "The early bird gets the worm." In Saudi Arabia, a favorite expression is, "Bukra insha Allah," which means, "Tomorrow if God wills," an expression that reflects the Saudis' approach to time. Unlike Westerners, who believe they control their own time, Arabs believe that Allah controls time. As a result, when Saudis commit themselves to a date in the future and fail to show up, there is no guilt or concern on their part because they have no control over time in the first place. In planning future events with Arabs, it pays to hold lead time to a week or less, because other factors may intervene or take precedence.

An associated cultural belief is that destiny depends more on the will of a supreme being than on the behavior of individuals. A higher power dictates the outcome of important events, so individual action is of little consequence. As a result, progress or the lack of progress on a project is considered more a question of fate than effort. This leads Saudis to rely less on detailed plans and schedules to complete projects than Americans do.

Another important cultural contrast between Saudi Arabians and Americans is emotion and logic. Saudis often act on the basis of emotion; in contrast, those in an Anglo culture are taught to act on logic. During negotiations, it is important not only to share the facts but also to make emotional appeals that demonstrate your suggestion is the right thing to do.

Saudis also make use of elaborate and ritualized forms of greetings and leave-takings. A businessperson may wait far past the assigned meeting time before being admitted to a Saudi office. Once there, the individual may find a host of others present; one-on-one meetings are rare. Moreover, during the meeting there may be continuous interruptions. Visitors arrive and begin talking to the host, and messengers may come in and go out on a regular basis. The businessperson is expected to take all this activity as perfectly normal and to remain composed and ready to continue discussions as soon as the host is prepared to do so.

Initial meetings are typically used to get to know the other party. Business-related discussions may not occur until the third or fourth meeting. Business meetings typically conclude with an offer of coffee or tea. This is a sign that the meeting is over and that future meetings, if there are to be any, should now be arranged.

Saudis attach a great deal of importance to status and rank. When meeting with them, defer to the senior person. It is also important never to criticize or berate anyone publicly. This causes the individual to lose face; the same is true for the person who makes these comments. Mutual respect is expected at all times.

Other useful guidelines for working in an Arab culture such as Saudi Arabia include the following:

1. It is important never to display feelings of superiority because this makes the other party feel inferior. No matter how well someone does something, the individual should let the action speak for itself and not brag or draw attention to himself.

2. A lot of what gets done is a result of going through administrative channels in the country. It is often difficult to sidestep a lot of this red tape, and efforts to do so can be regarded as disrespect for legal and governmental institutions.

3. Connections are extremely important in conducting business. More important people get fast service from less important people. Close relatives take absolute priority; nonrelatives are kept waiting.

4. Patience is critical to the success of business negotiations. Time for deliberations should be built into all negotiations to prevent a person from giving away too much in an effort to reach a quick settlement.

5. Important decisions are usually made in person and not by correspondence or telephone. While Saudis seek counsel from many people, the ultimate power to make a decision rests with the person at the top, and this individual relies heavily on personal impressions, trust, and rapport.

Working in China

In recent years the People's Republic of China (PRC, or China, for short) has slowly moved away from isolation to encourage more business with the rest of the world. While China holds tremendous promise, many Western firms have found working on projects in China to be a long, grueling process that often results in failure. One of the primary reasons for problems is the failure to appreciate Chinese culture.

Chinese society, like those of Japan and Korea, is influenced by the teachings of Confucius (551–478 B.C.). Unlike America, which relies on legal institutions to regulate behavior, in Confucian societies the primary deterrent against improper or illegal behavior is shame or loss of face. Face is more than simply reputation. There is a Chinese saying that, "Face is like the bark of a tree; without its bark, the tree dies."

Loss of face not only brings shame to individuals but also to family members. A member's actions can cause shame for the entire family, hampering that family from working effectively in Chinese society.

In China, "whom you know is more important than what you know." The term *guanxi* refers to personal connections with appropriate authorities or individuals. China observers argue that *guanxi* is critical for working with the Chinese. Chinese are raised to distrust strangers, especially foreigners. Trust is transmitted via guanxi. That is, a trusted business associate of yours must pass you along to his trusted business associates. Many outsiders criticize *guanxi,* considering it to be like nepotism where decisions are made regarding contracts or problems based on family ties or connections instead of an objective assessment of ability.

Many believe that the quickest way to build *guanxi* relationships is through tendering favors. Gift-giving, entertainment at lavish banquets, questionable payments, and overseas trips are common. While Westerners see this as nothing short of bribery, the Chinese consider it essential for good business. Another common method for outsiders to acquire *guanxi* is by hiring local intermediaries, who use their connections to create contacts with Chinese officials and businesspeople.

In dealing with the Chinese, you must realize they are a collective society in which people pride themselves on being a member of a group. For this reason, you should never single out a Chinese for specific praise because this is likely to embarrass the individual in front of his peers. At the same time, you should avoid the use of "I" because it conveys that the speaker is drawing attention to himself or herself.

Chinese do not appreciate loud, boisterous behavior, and when speaking to each other they maintain a greater physical distance than is typical in America. Other cautions include the following:

1. Once the Chinese decide who and what is best, they tend to stick to their decisions. So while they may be slow in formulating a plan, once they get started they make good progress.
2. Reciprocity is important in negotiations. If Chinese give concessions, they expect some in return.
3. The Chinese tend to be less animated than Americans. They avoid open displays of affection and physical contact; they are more reticent and reserved than Americans.
4. The Chinese place less value on the significance of time and often get Americans to concede concessions by stalling.
5. In Confucian societies those in position of power and authority are obligated to assist the disadvantaged. In return they gain face and a good reputation.

Working in the United States

In the world of international projects, professionals from other countries will come to the United States to manage projects. To them, the United States is a foreign assignment. They will have to adapt their management style to the new environment they find in the States.

Immigration has made the United States a melting pot of diverse cultures. While many are quick to point out the differences between North and South, Silicon Valley and Wall Street, social anthropologists have identified certain cultural characteristics that shape how many Americans conduct business and manage projects.

Mainstream Americans are motivated by achievement and accomplishment. Their identity and, to a certain extent, their self-worth are measured by what they have achieved. Foreigners are often astounded by the material wealth accumulated by

Americans and the modern conveniences most Americans enjoy. They are also quick to point out that Americans appear too busy to truly enjoy what they have achieved.

Americans tend to idolize the self-made person who rises from poverty and adversity to become rich and successful. Most Americans have a strong belief that they can influence and create their future, that with hard work and initiative, they can achieve whatever they set out to do. Self-determination and pragmatism dominate their approach to business.

Although Americans like to set precise objectives, they view planning as a means and not an end. They value flexibility and are willing to deviate from plans and improvise if they believe change will lead to accomplishment. Obstacles on a project are to be overcome, not worked around. Americans think they can accomplish just about anything, given time, money, and technology.

Americans fought a revolution and subsequent wars to preserve their concept of democracy, so they resent too much control or interference, especially by governments. While more an ideal than practice, there is deep-rooted belief in American management philosophy that those people who will be affected by decisions should be involved in making decisions. Many foreign businesspeople are surprised at the amount of autonomy and decision-making authority granted to subordinates. Foreign personnel have to learn to interact with American professionals below their rank in their own organizations.

Businesspeople from different African, Asian, and Latin American countries are amazed and often somewhat distressed at the rapid pace of America. "Getting things done" is an American characteristic. Americans are very time-conscious and efficient. They expect meetings to start on time. They tinker with gadgets and technological systems, always searching for easier, better, more efficient ways of accomplishing things. American professionals are often relentless in pursuing project objectives and expect that behavior of others also.

Americans in play or business generally are quite competitive, reflecting their desire to achieve and succeed. Although the American culture contains contradictory messages about the importance of success (i.e., "It's not whether you win or lose but how you play the game" versus "nice guys finish last"), winning and being number one are clearly valued in American society. Foreigners are often surprised at how aggressively Americans approach business with adversarial attitudes toward competitors and a desire to not just meet but to exceed project goals and objectives.

Other guidelines and cautions for working with Americans on projects include:

1. More than half of U.S. women work outside the home; females have considerable opportunity for personal and professional growth, guaranteed by law. It is not uncommon to find women in key project positions. Female professionals expect to be treated as equals. Behavior tolerated in other countries would be subject to harassment laws in the States.

2. In the United States, gifts are rarely brought by visitors in a business situation.

3. Americans tend to be quite friendly and open when first meeting someone. Foreigners often mistake this strong "come-on" for the beginning of a strong reciprocal friendship. This is in contrast to many other cultures where there is more initial reserve in interpersonal relations, especially with strangers. For many foreigners, the American comes on too strong, too soon, and then fails to follow up with the implicitly promised friendship.

4. Although in comparison to the rest of the world Americans tend to be informal in greeting and dress, they are a noncontact culture (e.g., they avoid embracing in public usually) and Americans maintain certain physical/psychological distance with others (e.g., about two feet) in conversations.

Will corruption influence the project? Bribes are illegal in the United States, but in some countries they are the usual way to do business. For example, one American project manager in a foreign country requested that a shipment of critical project equipment be sent "overnight rush." Two days later, inquiries to the sender confirmed the materials had been delivered to the nearby airport. Further inquiries to the port found the shipment "waiting to pass customs." Locals quickly informed the American that money paid to the chief customs inspector would expedite clearance. The American project manager's response was, "I will not be held hostage. Bribes are illegal!" Two more days of calling government officials did not move the shipment from customs. The manager related his problem to a friendly businessman of the host nation at a social affair. The local businessman said he would see if he could help. The shipment arrived the next morning at 10:00 A.M. The American called his local business friend and thanked him profusely. "I owe you one." "No," replied the local. "You owe me a $50 dinner when I visit you in the States." The use of an intermediary in such situations may be the only avenue available to a manager to reduce the stress and personal conflict with the U.S. value system.

5. American decision making is results oriented. Decisions tend to be based on facts and expected outcomes, not social impact.

Summary Comments about Working in Different Cultures

These briefings underscore the complexity of working on international projects. It is common practice to rely on intermediaries—often natives who are foreign educated—to bridge the gap between cultures. These intermediaries perform a variety of functions. They act as translators. They use their social connections to expedite transactions and protect the project against undue interference. They are used to sidestep the touchy bribery/gift dilemma (see the accompanying Snapshot from Practice). They serve as cultural guides, helping outsiders understand and interpret the foreign culture. In today's world, there are a growing number of consulting firms that perform these functions by helping foreign clients work on projects in their country.

The international briefings also highlight the importance of project managers doing their homework and becoming familiar with the customs and habits of the host country they are going to be working in. As far as possible, the project should be managed in such a way that local-country norms and customs are honored. However, there are limits to the extent to which you should accommodate foreign cultures. *Going native* is generally not an alternative. After all, it took a Russian his entire life to learn how to be a Russian. It would be foolish to think an outsider could learn to be one in six months, two years, or perhaps ever.

The remainder of this chapter focuses on the selection and training of project personnel for international projects. But before these issues are discussed, this section concludes with a discussion of the phenomenon of culture shock, which can have a profound effect on a foreigner's performance on a project in a strange culture.

Culture Shock

My first few weeks in Chiang Mai [Thailand] were filled with excitement. I was excited about the challenge of building a waste treatment plant in a foreign country. I was fascinated with Thai customs and traditions, the smells and sights of the night market. Soon I noticed a distinct change in my attitude and behavior. I started having problems sleeping and lacked energy. I became irritable at work, frustrated by how long things took to accomplish, and how I couldn't seem to get anything accomplished. I started staying up late at night watching CNN in my hotel room.

This engineer is experiencing what many would call "culture shock." *Culture shock* is a natural psychological disorientation that most people suffer when they move into a culture different from their own. The culture shock cycle has four stages (see Figure 15.6):

1. *Honeymoon*—You start your overseas assignment with a sense of excitement. The new and the unusual are welcomed. At first it is amusing not to understand or be understood. Soon a sense of frustration begins to set in.

2. *Irritability and hostility*—Your initial enthusiasm is exhausted, and you begin to notice that differences are greater than you first imagined. You become frustrated by your inability to get things done as you are accustomed to. You begin to lose confidence in your abilities to communicate and work effectively in the different culture.

3. *Gradual adjustment*—You begin to overcome your sense of isolation and figure out how to get things done in the new culture. You acquire a new perspective of what is possible and regain confidence in your ability to work in the culture.

4. *Adaptation*—You recover from your sense of psychological disorientation and begin to function and communicate in the new culture.

Culture shock is not a disease but a natural response to immersing yourself in a new environment. Culture shock results from a breakdown in your selective perception and effective interpretation system. At a subliminal level, your senses are being bombarded by a wide variety of strange sounds, sights, and smells. At the same time, the normal assumptions you are accustomed to using in your home culture to interpret perceptions and to communicate intentions no longer apply. When this happens, whether in a business context or in normal attempts to socialize, confusion and frustration set in. The natives' behavior does not seem to make sense, and, even more importantly, your behavior does not produce expected results. Frustration occurs because you are used to being competent in such situations and now find you are unable to operate effectively.

Culture shock is generally considered a positive sign that the professional is becoming involved in the new culture instead of remaining isolated in an expatriate ghetto. The significant question is how best to manage culture shock, not how to avoid it. The key appears to be managing the stress associated with culture shock.

Stress-related culture shock takes many forms: disappointment, frustration, withdrawal, anxiety, and physiological responses such as fatigue, sleeplessness, and headaches. Stress is induced by the senses being overwhelmed by foreign stimuli and the inability to function effectively in a strange land. Stress is exacerbated when one

FIGURE 15.6
Culture Shock Cycle

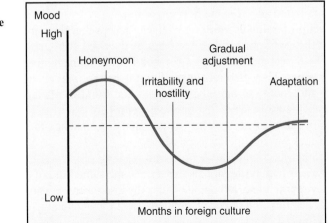

encounters disturbing situations that, as a foreigner, are neither understood nor condoned. For example, many North Americans are appalled by the poverty and hunger in many underdeveloped countries.

Coping with Culture Shock

There are a wide range of stress management techniques for coping with culture shock. One method does not necessarily work any better than another; success depends on the particular individual and situation involved. Some people engage in regular physical exercise programs, some practice meditation and relaxation exercises, and others find it healthy to keep a journal.

Many effective international managers create "stability zones." They spend most of their time immersed in the foreign culture but then briefly retreat into an environment—a stability zone—that closely recreates home. For example, when one of the authors was living in Kraków, Poland, with his family, they would routinely go to the Polish movie houses to see American movies with Polish subtitles. The two hours spent hearing English and seeing a familiar environment on the screen had a soothing effect on everyone.

On the project, managers can reduce the stress caused by culture shock by recognizing it and modifying their expectations and behavior accordingly. They can redefine priorities and develop more realistic expectations as to what is possible. They can focus their limited energy on only the most important tasks and relish small accomplishments.

After three to six months, depending on the individual and assignment, most people come up from their culture shock "low" and begin living a more normal life in the foreign country. They talk to acquaintances from the host country and experienced outsiders from their own culture to find out how to behave and what to expect. Little by little they learn how to make sense of the new environment. They figure out when "yes" means "yes" and when it means "maybe" and when it means "no." They begin to master the language so that they can make themselves understood in day-to-day conversations.

The vast majority of people eventually make the adjustment, although for some people it can take much longer than three to six months. A smaller number never recover, and their international experience turns into a nightmare. Some exhibit severe stress symptoms (e.g., alcoholism, drug abuse, nervous breakdown) and must return home before finishing their assignment.

Professionals can use project work as a bridge until they adjust to their new environment. Unfortunately, spouses who do not work do not have this advantage. When spouses are left to cope with the strange environment on their own, they often have a much more difficult time overcoming culture shock. The effect on spouses cannot be underestimated. The number one reason expatriate managers return home is that their spouses failed to adjust to the new environment.

Project professionals working overseas accept that they are in a difficult situation and that they will not act as effectively as they did at home, especially in the initial stages. They recognize the need for good stress management techniques, including stability zones. They also recognize that it is not an individual problem and invest extra time and energy to help their spouses and families manage the transition. At the same time, they appreciate that their colleagues are experiencing similar problems and are sensitive to their needs. They work together to manage the stress and pull out of a culture shock low as quickly as possible.

It is somewhat ironic, but people who work on projects overseas experience culture shock twice. Many professionals experience the same kind of disorientation and stress when they return home, although it is usually less severe. For some, their current job has less responsibility and is boring compared with the challenge of their overseas assignment. For others, they have problems adjusting to changes made in the home organization while they were gone. This can be compounded by financial shock when the salary and fringe benefits they became accustomed to in the foreign assignment are now lost, and adjusting to a lower standard of living is difficult. It typically takes six months to a year before managers operate again at full effectiveness after a lengthy foreign assignment.

Selection and Training for International Projects

When professionals are selected for overseas projects and they do not work out, the overall costs can be staggering. Not only does the project experience a serious setback, but the reputation of the firm is damaged in the region. This is why many firms have developed formal screening procedures to help ensure the careful selection of personnel for international projects. Organizations examine a number of characteristics to determine whether an individual is suitable for overseas work. They may look for work experience with cultures other than one's own, previous overseas travel, good physical and emotional health, a knowledge of a host nation's language, and even recent immigration background or heritage. Prospective candidates and their family members are often interviewed by trained psychologists, who assess their ability to adapt and function in the new culture.

While there is growing appreciation for screening people for foreign assignments, the number one reason for selection is that the personnel assigned are the best people available for the technical challenges of the project. Technical know-how takes precedence over cross-cultural sensitivity or experience. As a consequence, training is critical to fill in the cultural gaps and prepare individuals to work in a foreign land.

Training varies widely, depending on the individual, company, nature of the project, and cultures to work with. Project professionals assigned to foreign countries should have a minimal understanding of the following areas:

- Religion.
- Dress codes.
- Education system.
- Holidays—national and religious.
- Daily eating patterns.
- Family life.
- Business protocols.
- Social etiquette.
- Equal opportunity.

An example of a short-term training program is the one developed by Underwriter Laboratories, Inc., to train staff who travel to Japan to work with clients on projects. The program is designed around a series of mini-lectures that cover topics ranging from how to handle introductions to the proper way to exchange gifts to the correct way of interpreting Japanese social and business behavior. The two-day program consists of lectures, case studies, role plays, language practice, and a short test on cultural terminology; it concludes with a 90-minute question-and-answer period. At the end of the program, participants have a fundamental understanding of how to communicate with the Japanese. More importantly, they know the types of information they lack and how to go about learning more to become effective intercultural communicators.

Other training programs are more extensive. For example, Peace Corps volunteers undergo an intense two- to four-month training program in their country of service. The training includes classes on the history and traditions of the country, intensive language instruction, and cross-cultural training as well as home-stays with local families.

Many companies outsource training to one of the many firms specializing in overseas and intercultural training.

Figure 15.7 attempts to link the length and type of training with the cultural fluency required to successfully complete the project. Three different learning approaches are highlighted:

1. The "information-giving" approach—the learning of information or skills from a lecture-type orientation.
2. The "affective approach"—the learning of information/skills that raise the affective responses on the part of the trainee and result in cultural insights.
3. The "behavioral/experiential" approach—variant of the affective approach technique that provides the trainee with realistic simulations or scenarios.

According to this framework, the length and level of training would depend on the degree of cultural fluency required to be successful. In general, the longer the person is expected to work in the foreign country, the more intensive the training should be. Length of stay should not be the only consideration; high levels of cultural fluency, and therefore more extensive training, may be required to perform short-term, intense projects. In addition, location is important. Working in Australia will likely require less cultural fluency than working on a project in Pakistan.

While English is rapidly becoming the international language for business in many parts of the world, you should not underestimate the value of being able to speak the language of the host country. At a minimum you should be able to exchange basic pleasantries in the native tongue. Most foreigners consider this a sign of respect, and even if you stumble they appreciate the effort.

FIGURE 15.7   Relationship between Length and Rigor of Training and Cultural Fluency Required

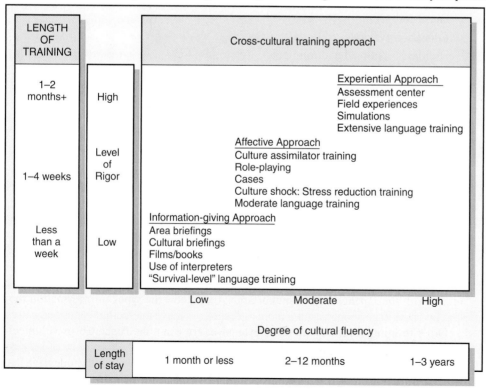

In many situations translators are used to facilitate communication. While time-consuming, this is the only way to communicate with non-English-speaking personnel. Be careful in the selection of translators, and do not just assume they are competent. For example, one of the authors enlisted the help of a Polish translator to conduct a meeting with some Polish managers. After the meeting the translator, who taught English at a local university, asked if the author "had good time." I responded that I felt things went well. The translator repeated her question. Puzzled, I reaffirmed that I felt things went well. After the interchange was repeated several times, the translator finally grabbed my wrist, pointed at my watch, and asked again if I "had good time?" Doubts arose concerning the accuracy of the meeting translation!

Summary

The number of international projects continues to increase, and nothing on the horizon suggests things will change in the new millennium. More and more project managers will be needed to implement international projects. There are few guidelines for the fledgling international project manager. Preparing for international projects can be enhanced through training. As a general background, potential international project managers can benefit from a basic international business course that sensitizes them to the forces of change in the global economy and to cultural differences. Learning a foreign language is also strongly recommended.

Further training specific to the host country is a very useful preproject endeavor. The length and type of training usually depend on the duration of the project manager's assignment. Review Figure 15.7. Still, self-learning, on-the-job training, and experience are the best teachers for international project managers.

Preparing for a specific international project requires serious preproject homework. Understanding the motivation of the firm in selecting the project and its site provides important insights. What basic political, geographic, economic, and infrastructure factors were key considerations? How will they impact the implementation of the project?

Finally, preparation and understanding the cultural differences of the host country go a long way toward making positive first impressions with the nationals and managing the project. International projects have distinct personalities. All people are not the same. Differences within and among countries and cultures are numerous and complex. Project managers need to accept these differences and treat them as real—or live with the consequences. What works at home may not work in the foreign country. Americans are regarded as friendly by our neighbors in the global village, but Americans are also noted to be insensitive to differences in local cultures and customs and awkward in our use of languages other than English. Although most attention in foreign projects is focused on technical efforts and their cost, the project must be carried out within the environment of the country's social customs, work practices, government controls, and religious beliefs. In most cultures, sincerity and flexibility will pay off.

Key Terms

Cross-cultural orientations	Culture	Infrastructure
	Culture shock	International projects

Review Questions

1. How do environmental factors affect project implementation?
2. What role do local intermediaries play in helping an outsider complete a project?
3. Why is it important to honor the customs and traditions of a country when working on an international project?

4. What is culture shock? What can you do to reduce the negative effects of culture shock?

5. How should you go about preparing yourself for an international project?

Exercises

1. Interview someone who has worked or lived in a foreign country for more than six months.

   a. What was their experience with culture shock?

   b. What did they learn about the culture of the country they lived in?

   c. What advice would they give to someone who would be working on a project in that country?

2. Try as best you can to apply the Kluckhohn-Strodtbeck cross-cultural framework to the four countries discussed in this chapter: Mexico, France, Saudi Arabia, and China. Where do you think these countries lie on each of the cultural issues?

3. Place in order the following countries in terms of what you would think would be the least to most corrupt:

   United States, Finland, Saudi Arabia, Russia, Australia, Hong Kong, Brazil, China, Kenya, Indonesia, Germany, Chile.

   Use an internet search engine to find the most recent International Corruptions Perceptions Index (CPI) released by the Berlin-based organization Transparency International.

   a. Check your predictions with the Index.

   b. How well did you do? What countries surprised you? Why?

References

Ackoff, R. L., *Ackoff's Fables: Irreverent Reflections on Business and Bureaucracy* (New York: Wiley, 1991), p. 221.

Alder, N., *International Dimensions of Organizational Behavior, 2nd ed.* (Boston: PWS-Kent Publishing, 1991).

Borsuk, R., "In Indonesia, a twist on spreading the wealth: Decentralization of power multiplies opportunities for bribery, corruption," *The Wall Street Journal,* 29, January 2003, p. A16.

Contingency Planning and Management.com, "Strohl Systems Offers Terrorism Readiness Questionnaire," September 24, 2001.

Deneire, M. and M. Segalla, "Mr. Christian Pierret, Secretary of State for Industry (1997–2002), on French perspectives on organizational leadership and management," *The Academy of Management Executive,* 16 (4), November 2002, pp. 25–30.

Doh, J. P., P. Rodriguez, K. Uhlenbruck, J. Collins and L. Eden, "Coping with corruption in foreign markets," *Academy of Management Executive,* 17 (3) August 2003, pp. 114–127.

Graham, J. L. and N. M. Lam, "The Chinese Negotiation," *Harvard Business Review,* October 1, 2003, pp. 82–91.

Graham, S., "Relief Agency Suspends Afghan Operations," *www.guardian.co.uk,* June 3, 2004.

Hallowell, R., D. Bowen, and C-I. Knoop, "Four Seasons Goes to Paris," *The Academy of Management Executive,* 16 (4), November 2002, pp. 7–24.

Henry W. L. and J. J. DiStefano, *International Project Management,* 2nd ed. (Boston: PWS-Kent Publishing, 1992).

Hodgetts, R. M. and F. Luthans, *International Management: Culture, Strategy, and Behavior,* fifth ed. (Boston: McGraw-Hill/Irwin, 2003).

Hofstede, G., *Cultures Consequences: International Difference in Work-Related Values* (Beverly Hills, CA: Sage Publishing, 1980).

International Straight Talk on Mexico, video (Waxahachie, TX: William Drake, 1996).

Kluckhohn F. and F. L. Strodtbeck, *Variations in Value Orientations* (Evanston, IL: Row, Peterson, 1961).

Krane, J., "Intelligence Companies Help Overseas Business Travelers," *The Cincinnati Enquirer,* April 2, 2002, website.

Kras, E., *Management in Two Cultures: Bridging the Gap between U.S. and Mexican Managers,* rev. ed. (Yarmouth, ME: Intercultural Press, 1995).

Lieberthal, K. and G. Lieberthal, "The Great Transition," *Harvard Business Review,* October 1, 2003, pp. 71–81.

Mendenhall, M. E., E. Dunbar, and G. R. Oddou, "Expatriate Selection, Training, and Career-Pathing: A Review and Critique," *Human Resource Management,* Vol. 26, No. 3, Fall 1987, pp. 331–45.

Milosevic, D. Z., "Echoes of the Silent Language of Project Management," *Project Management Journal,* Vol. 30, No. 1, March 1999, pp. 27–39.

Ricks, D. and D. A. Ricks, *Blunders in International Business* (London: Blackwell, 2000).

Scown, M. J., "Managers Journal: Barstool Advice for the Vietnam Investor," *Asian Wall Street Journal,* July 15, 1993.

Tung, R. L., "Expatriate Assignments: Enhancing Success and Minimizing Failure," *The Academy of Management Executive,* Vol. 1, No. 2 (1987), pp. 117–26.

Yeung I. and R. L. Tung, "Achieving Business Success in Confucian Societies: The Importance of Guanxi (Connections)," *Organizational Dynamics,* Vol. 25, No. 2, Autumn 1996, pp. 54–65.

Case

AMEX, Hungary

Michael Thomas shouted, "Sasha, Tor-Tor, we've got to go! Our driver is waiting for us." Thomas's two daughters were fighting over who would get the last orange for lunch that day. Victoria ("Tor-Tor") prevailed as she grabbed the orange and ran out the door to the Mercedes Benz waiting for them. The fighting continued in the back seat as they drove toward the city of Budapest, Hungary. Thomas finally turned around and grabbed the orange and proclaimed that he would have it for lunch. The back seat became deadly silent as they made their way to the American International School of Budapest.

After dropping the girls off at the school, Thomas was driven to his office in the Belváros area of Budapest. Thomas worked for AMEX Petroleum and had been sent to Budapest four months earlier to set up business operations in central Hungary. His job was to establish 10 to 14 gas stations in the region by purchasing existing stations, building new ones, or negotiating franchise arrangements with existing owners of stations. Thomas jumped at this project. He realized that his career at AMEX was going nowhere in the United States, and if he were going to realize his ambitions, it would be in the "wild, wild east" of the former Soviet empire. Besides, Thomas's mother was Hungarian, and he could speak the language. At least he thought he could until he arrived in Budapest and realized that he had greatly exaggerated his competence.

As he entered the partially refurbished offices of AMEX, he noticed that only three of his staff were present. No one knew where Miklos was, while Margit reported that she would not be at work today because she had to stay at home to take care of her sick mother. Thomas asked Béla why the workmen weren't present to work on finishing the office. Béla informed him that the work had to be halted until they received approval from the city historian. Budapest, anxious to preserve its historical heritage, required that all building renovations be approved by the city historian. When Thomas asked Béla how long it would take, Béla responded, "Who knows—days, weeks, maybe even months." Thomas muttered "great" to himself and turned his attention to the morning business. He was scheduled to interview prospective employees who would act as station managers and staff personnel.

The interview with Ferenc Erkel was typical of the many interviews he held that morning. Erkel was a neatly dressed, 42-year-old, unemployed professional who could speak limited English. He had a masters degree in international economics and had worked for 12 years in the state-owned Institute for Foreign Trade. Since being laid off two years ago, he has been working as a taxicab driver. When asked about his work at the Institute, Erkel smiled sheepishly and said that he pushed paper and spent most of the time playing cards with his colleagues.

To date Thomas had hired 16 employees. Four quit within three days on the job, and six were let go after a trial period for being absent from work, failing to perform duties, or showing a lack of initiative. Thomas thought that at this rate it would take him over a year just to hire his staff.

Thomas took a break from the interview schedule to scan the *Budapest Business Journal,* an English newspaper that covered business news in Hungary. Two items caught his eye. One article was on the growing threat of the Ukrainian Mafia in Hungary, which detailed extortion attempts in Budapest. The second story was that inflation had risen to 32 percent. This last item disturbed Thomas because at the time only one out of every five Hungarian families owned a car. AMEX's strategy in Hungary depended on a boom in first-time car owners.

Thomas collected his things and popped a few aspirin for the headache he was developing. He walked several blocks to the Kispipa restaurant where he had a supper meeting with Hungarian businessman Zoltán Kodaly. He had met Kodaly briefly at a reception sponsored by the U.S. consulate for American and Hungarian businesspeople. Kodaly reportedly owned three gas stations that Thomas was interested in.

Thomas waited, sipping bottled water for 25 minutes. Kodaly appeared with a young lady who could not have been older than 19. As it turned out Kodaly had brought his daughter Annia, who was a university student, to act as translator. While Thomas made an attempt to speak in Hungarian at first, Kodaly insisted that they use Annia to translate.

After ordering the house specialty, *szekelygulas,* Thomas immediately got down to business. He told Kodaly that AMEX was willing to make two offers to him. They would like to either purchase two of his stations at a price of $150,000 each, or they could work out a franchise agreement. Thomas said AMEX was not interested in the third station located near Klinikak because it would be too expensive to modernize the equipment. Annia translated, and as far as Thomas could tell she was doing a pretty good job. At first Kodaly did not respond and simply engaged in side conversations with Annia and exchanged pleasantries with people who came by. Thomas became frustrated and reiterated his offer. Eventually Kodaly asked what he meant by franchising, and Thomas tried to use the local McDonald's as an example of how it worked. He mentioned that Kodaly would still own the stations, but he would have to pay a franchisee fee, share profits with AMEX, and adhere to AMEX procedures and practices. In exchange, AMEX would provide petroleum and funds to renovate the stations to meet AMEX standards.

Toward the end of the meal Kodaly asked what would happen to the people who worked at the stations. Thomas asserted that according to his calculation the stations were overstaffed by 70 percent and that to make a profit, at least 15 workers would have to be let go. This statement was greeted with silence. Kodaly then turned the conversation to soccer and asked Thomas if it was true that in America girls play "football." Thomas said that both of his daughters played AYSO soccer in America and hoped to play in Hungary. Kodaly said girls don't play football in Hungary and that Annia was an accomplished volleyball player. Thomas pressed Kodaly for a response to his offer, but Kodaly rose and thanked Thomas for the meal. He said he would think about his offer and get back in touch with him.

Thomas left the Kispipa wondering if he would ever see Kodaly again. He returned to his office where an urgent message was waiting from Tibor. Tibor was responsible for retrofitting the first station Thomas had purchased for AMEX. The new tanks had not arrived from Vienna, and the construction crew had spent the day doing nothing. After several phone calls he found out that the tanks were being held at the border by customs. This irritated him because he had been assured by local officials that everything had been taken care of. He asked his secretary to schedule an appointment with the Hungarian trade office as soon as possible.

At the end of the day he checked his e-mail from the States. There was a message from headquarters asking about the status of the project. By this time he had hoped to have his office staffed and up and running and at least three stations secured. So far he had only one-third of his staff, his office was in shambles, and only one station was being retrofitted. Thomas decided to wait until tomorrow to respond to the e-mail.

Before returning home Thomas stopped off at the English Pub, a favorite hangout for expats in Budapest. There he met Jan Krovert, who worked for a Dutch company that was building a large discount retail store on the outskirts of Badapest. Thomas and Krovert often talked about being "strangers in a strange land" at the pub. Thomas talked about the interviews and how he could just see in their eyes that they didn't have the drive or initiative to be successful. Krovert responded that Hungary has high unemployment but a shortage of motivated workers. Krovert confided that he no longer interviewed anyone over the age of 30, claiming that what fire they had in their bellies was burned out after years of working in state-run companies.

1. What are the issues confronting Thomas in this case?
2. How well is Thomas dealing with these issues?
3. What suggestions would you have for Thomas in managing this project?

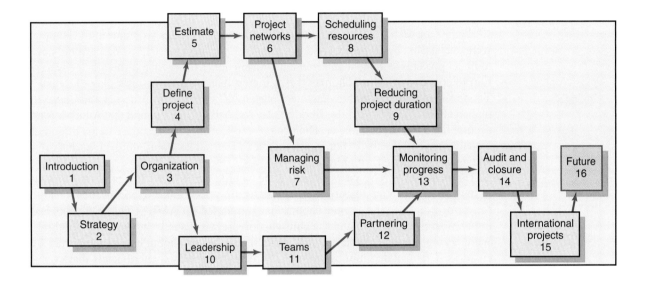

Estimate 5	Project networks 6	Scheduling resources 8
Define project 4		Reducing project duration 9
Introduction 1	Organization 3	Managing risk 7	Monitoring progress 13	Audit and closure 14	Future 16
Strategy 2		Partnering 12	International projects 15
Leadership 10	Teams 11	

Project Management and the Future

Current and Future Trends in Project Management

Unresolved Issues

Project Management Career Issues

Summary

Conclusions

CHAPTER SIXTEEN

Project Management and the Future

A great wind is blowing and that gives you either imagination or a headache.
—Catherine the Great, Empress of Russia, 1726–1796

The chapter identifies some emerging trends and speculates on what the process of managing projects will be like in the next decade. Unresolved issues confronting the field are also identified and discussed. Because the premise is that project management has a bright future, it is appropriate to conclude with some suggestions on how to pursue a career in project management.

Current and Future Trends in Project Management

Overview

Project management is thousands of years old. But project management as we know it today started in the early 1960s with network planning and the critical path technique. The introduction of microcomputer software in the 1980s made computerized project planning and control tools available to all kinds of projects and organizations. The 1990s saw an expansion of project management into mainstream business. During this period, the need to balance the technical and human side of managing projects became obvious. Although project planning and control methods still dominate the discipline, the human/social side to managing projects is finally taking on greater and greater importance.

Concurrently, during the 60s through the 90s and into the new millennium, the forces of global competition, knowledge explosion, innovation, time to market, and shortened product life cycles resulted in intensified industry consolidation. Organizations became more project driven and operate in a multiproject environment, bringing the challenges of managing projects across differing organization cultures and borders. Two major outcomes for the 21st century are

- an increase in the scope of project management and system integration.
- an accompanying discipline in the way projects are managed.

These trends carry with them many more specific developments that are identified next.

Increasing Scope of Project Management and System Integration

The scope of project management has expanded to touch every fiber of the organization. The focus of projects has shifted *from tactical to strategic.* In place of an independent project to solve a single problem, the emphasis has shifted to projects as the vehicle to deliver strategic initiatives. As organizations found themselves managing more and more projects, some effort to centralize these efforts was inevitable. Bringing all the projects and processes under a single, integrated system has been and continues to be a major thrust in project-driven organizations. Enterprise project management and the project office are two of the outcomes of this effort.

Enterprise Project Management When project effort moves from tactical to strategic, all project processes and resources are brought under one umbrella known as Enterprise Project Management (EPM). A representative definition of EPM is shown here:

> **EPM** (Enterprise project management): Centralized management of a portfolio of projects to ensure that the allocation of resources to projects is directed and balanced toward the strategic focus of the organization.

The major justification for EPM lies in the need to allocate and control resources to a portfolio of projects that clearly align with the strategic goals of the organization. The major benefit of EPM is managing multiple projects in a coordinated way to obtain the benefits not available from managing them individually. The Meta Stamford Group (a research and consultant firm) estimates that 40 percent of over 2000 leading global businesses utilize EPM today. Accompanying the movement to enterprise project management is the movement to use project management offices.

Project Management Office (PMO) Project offices are frequently used and needed to support enterprise project management efforts. Project management office is defined as:

> **PMO** (Project management office): the unit responsible for continued support of standards, processes, and an information system that defines project management for the organization.

It is not clear which came first, or should come first—EPM or the PMO. What is clear is that both perform an integration function for planning and control. The EPM approach integrates projects with current priorities, the organization strategic focus, and overall resource allocation. The PMO supports the integration of the technical processes of managing projects within the social/cultural environment of the organization.

Figures 16.1 and 16.2 provide an example of a report the project office provides senior management of an international organization. Note that such a report requires a standard format for all projects. Figure 16.1 depicts a project portfolio cost summary report developed for top management. Figure 16.2 presents the same summary for project schedules. Additional detailed information for any specific highlighted project—such as the project schedule, cost status report, project team—is only a double click away. For example, the Smart Card project in the EEC appears to be behind schedule. It is possible to "drill down" to the project schedule, WBS, resources, or issues to identify the cause. Standard project formats such as these provide a wealth of information in multiproject organizations.

Establishing EPM and a PMO represent radical changes in the balance of power and authority and the organization culture; both need strong support and signals from top management. EPM and PMOs are ideally suited to bring about the integration stressed in this text. The necessity and growth in the application of EPM and PMO will continue. We know ever-increasing advances in science and technology will generate dramatic breakthroughs and increase the number of organizations managing multiple projects.

FIGURE 16.1 **Project Portfolio Cost Summary Report for Top Management**

Location	Project ID	Description	PV	EV	AC	CPI	SPI	PCIB	BAC	EAC	VAC
Summary All		Portfolio							$18,120		
United States									$10500		
○ 01-003		Digitize Fingerprints-FBI	3,000	3,500	3,230	1.08	1.17	97.2%	3,600	3322	278
○ 01-011		Encryption	270	250	250	1.00	0.93	71.4%	350	350	0
○ 01-002		Internet Protocol--CIA						0.0%	950		
○ 01-009		Supply Chain Partners	90	90	90	1.00	1.00	16.7%	540	540	0
01-012		Bonus Mileage Awards						0.0%	630		
● 01-005		E-sales Claims	150	140	150	0.93	0.93	35.0%	400	429	-29
● 01-011		Procurement Net	400	340	380	0.89	0.85	27.6%	1,230	1,375	-145
○ 01-008		Smart Tag Tracking	850	900	900	1.00	1.06	32.1%	2,800	2,800	0
Asia/Pacific									$2,800		
○ 02-007		Currency Conversion	125	120	120	1.00	0.96	80.0%	150	150	0
○ 02-002		Billing System	280	280	280	1.00	1.00	70.0%	400	400	0
○ 02-005		Web-Based Cash Flow	210	220	200	1.00	1.05	73.3	300	273	27
02-004		Olympic Simulation						0.0%	1950		
EEC									$4,820		
● 03-008		Smart Card	145	110	140	0.79	0.76	18.3%	600	764	-164
03-003		Warranty						0.0%	70		
03-004		Simulation--ESA						0.0%	800		
● 03-005		Air Reservation Net	510	490	520	0.94	0.96	35.0%	1,400	1,486	-86
● 03-007		Pilot Internet Log Syst.	540	490	550	0.89	0.91	57.6%	850	954	-104
○ 03-006		Internet Telephone Syst.	850	850	860	0.99	1.00	77.3%	1,100	1,113	-13

Net Services, Inc. View Cost ▼ Project Portfolio Cost Summary ($ 000) Date:

Left sidebar icons: Gantt, Network, Resource, Status, WBS, Sponsor, Team, Priority, Issues

LEGEND
○ Under Budget
◑ On Budget
● Over Budget

Increasing Discipline in the Way Projects Are Managed

Training One of the major outcomes of applying portfolio management is the necessity to standardize the language and processes across all projects in a portfolio of projects. Recall, both EPM and PMO approaches have one major requirement: standardization across all projects! The forms of process standardization are almost always similar to the content found in Chapters 2, 4, 5, 6, 7, 8, 13, and 14. Standardization demands discipline and cooperation. Efforts to support standardization are usually accomplished through intensive training and heavy use of templates and checklists. For example, IBM, Hewlett-Packard, and many others have worldwide training centers to ensure consistent best practices are used on projects in all locations. Training is not limited to technical processes for managing projects. Training extends to team makeup, team culture, outside partners, and organization support. Your authors continue to be amazed at the results of uniform training. In one global company, regardless of the

FIGURE 16.2 **Project Portfolio Cost Summary Report for Project Schedules**

Location	Project ID	Description	Project Manager	Start Date	Finish Date	SPI	2005 / 2006
Summary / All		Portfolio					
United States							
○ 01-003		Digitize Fingerprints-FBI	Beth Gage	11/15/03	8/15/05	1.17	
● 01-011		Encryption	Alfonso Buco	1/1/04	9/25/05	0.93	
○ 01-002		Internet Protocol--CIA		10/1/05	6/1/06		
○ 01-009		Supply chain partners	Mike Chow	6/5/05	11/16/05	1.00	
○ 01-012		Bonus Mileage Awards	Sally Peters	8/1/05	2/12/06		
● 01-005		E-sales Claims	Kevin Lee	2/4/05	11/15/05	0.93	
● 01-011		Procurement Net	Tzvi Jafarri	5/5/05	12/30/05	0.85	
○ 01-008		Smart Tag Tracking	Jan Snyder	3/1/05	12/4/05	1.06	
Asia/Pacific							
○ 02-007		Currency Conversion	Jeff Bush	2/1/05	7/10/05	0.96	
○ 02-002		Billing System	Kia Wong	10/7/04	10/5/05	1.00	
○ 02-005		Web-Based Cash Flow	Naoki Oshima	2/15/05	9/15/05	1.05	
○ 02-004		Olympic Simulation		7/12/05	2/10/06		
EEC							
● 03-008		Smart Card	Ido Alons	4/16/05	9/15/05	0.76	
○ 03-003		Warranty	Connor Gage	8/11/05	12/12/05		
○ 03-004		Simulation--ESA	Ib Ericson	9/15/05	2/13/06		
○ 03-005		Air Reservation Net	Dragan Milosovik	3/22/05	1/12/06	0.96	
● 03-007		Pilot Internet Log Syst.	Ken Thompson	3/1/05	10/3/05	0.91	
○ 03-006		Internet Telephone Syst	Ann McGraddy	8/10/04	9/29/05	1.00	

Net Services, Inc. | View: Schedule | Project Portfolio Schedule Summary | Date:

Side panel icons: Gantt, Network, Resource, Status, WBS, Sponsor, Team, Priority, Issues

LEGEND
○ Ahead of schedule
○ On schedule
● Behind schedule

country or language, everyone approaches projects similarly and uses the same processes where applicable, being careful not to push standardization too far, which can result in a bureaucratic quagmire.

The maturity model discussed in Chapter 14 also supports standard processes and language. The maturity model serves as a benchmark and goal for which to strive. Training and lessons learned support the model and moving up to a higher maturity level.

Organization Culture In today's ever-changing, fast-moving global economy, organization flexibility in adapting to change is critical. What system of shared beliefs, norms, social structure, and values best supports this needed flexibility? We have noted that organizations that have flat structures, strongly support innovation, allow managers to make mistakes without persecution, and delegate power and control to project managers who exhibit the flexibility to manage change and projects. 3M emulates this flexibility. It encourages technical people to spend up to 15 percent of their time on projects of their own choice. No wonder 3M is a leader in the development of new products. Organization cultures of project-driven organizations allow the freedom to adapt to a rapidly shifting environment.

Begun in 1990, the Human Genome Project (HGP) is a 15-year, $3 billion effort coordinated by the U.S. Department of Energy and the National Institutes of Health. The project goals are to:

- Identify all the approximately 30,000 genes in human DNA.
- Determine the sequences of the 3 billion chemical base pairs that make up human DNA.
- Store this information in databases.
- Improve tools for data analysis.
- Transfer related technologies to the private sector.
- Address the ethical, legal, and social issues that may arise from the project.

The project involves the active partnership of medical, government, and business communities. All totaled, over 43 different institutes, medical schools, pharmaceutical firms, and research centers are involved in completing the project.

In June 2000, HGP leaders announced that the rough draft of the human genome had been completed a year ahead of schedule. The draft sequence will provide a scaffold of sequence across about 90 percent of the human genome.

Remaining gaps will be closed and accuracy will improve over the following three years to achieve a complete high-quality DNA reference sequence by 2003, two years earlier than originally planned.

The completion of the human DNA sequence in 2003 will coincide with the 50th anniversary of Watson and Crick's description of the fundamental structure of DNA. Current and potential applications of genome research address international needs in molecular medicine, waste control and environmental cleanup, biotechnology, energy sources, and risk assessment. The analytical power arising from the reference DNA sequences of entire genomes and other genomics resources is anticipated to jump-start what has been predicted to be the "biology century."

*www.ornl.gov/TechResources/Human_Genome/home.html

Multicultural Projects   Transcultural projects are becoming commonplace. Cultural differences need to be addressed early. Merging people from different cultures into one project team that works together for a common goal is no simple endeavor. In the words of one global manager, "Language is not the problem. Overcoming cultural differences and gaining trust among team members are major hurdles to overcome." This manager's company refuses to start an international project until all major team members have spent several days together in a workshop designed to build trust and agreeing on mutual project objectives that will improve chances of success. Multinational companies are searching diligently to discover ways to improve multicultural team trust and minimize cultural differences and agendas. See Snapshot from Practice: The International Space Station Project.

Information Technology   Web-based management of projects continues to increase. As outsourcing increases, so does the use of Web-based project management systems. New software for international projects is developed rapidly. Virtual teams continue to increase and depend on Web-based systems for communication. Advances in information technology, such as wireless communication, will provide new avenues for managing projects.

Another area gaining attention is the establishment of databases, sometimes call "data mining." See Snapshot from Practice: Human Genome Project. Organizations are establishing Web-based databases for recording estimates and actual task times and costs on past projects. These data can be used for improving estimates on future projects. Similarly, data libraries of lessons learned are being created to avoid making the same mistakes again.

Risk Management   With the acceptance of portfolio management and system integration, more attention is turning to risk management. Organizations need to balance the choice of projects with a variety of low, medium, and high risk projects. If managers select only those projects with the highest rate of return, they are failing to remember that high returns usually carry higher risks. Selecting only high-rate-of-return projects is a dangerous strategy for an organization.

Courtesy of NASA.

Hopefully, by 2006 the space station assembly will be complete and functional 220 miles above the earth at a cost of more than $40 billion. The station will cover an area of approximately two football fields and have a housing unit the size of a jumbo jet. This space station will conduct research concerning human life and production of products in space. The complexity of the space station and the coordination required among 16 partner nations is daunting.

Russia launched the first piece of the space station on November 20, 1998. This module provides power for future assembly operations. On December 3 of the same year, the United States launched the first space component hub, which serves as the connector for other pieces of the station. This hub also serves as housing for up to seven astronauts. In total it is planned that 34 space deliveries will transport more than 900,000 pounds of materials needed to assemble the completed station. It is estimated that 144 to 160 two-person space walks and 1,800 hours of construction will be needed to assemble the station.

The project has had a bumpy ride to date, and more problems are expected before the project is complete. The project is billions of dollars over budget; the total cost could reach $96 billion. The collapse of the Russian economy has caused delays on their development of a major module of the station. Financial support has been needed to get the Russian effort back on track. Redesign has been continual because of the multiple needs of the partners of

the 16 nations; these changes have resulted in costly delays. Some of the risks have been underestimated, and reassessment has suggested failures along the way are inevitable—delivery vehicles blowing up, docking problems, even someone killed during construction. There have been calls to "pull the plug" on the project. Nevertheless, the project moves forward.

The ESA (European Space Agency) is coordinating several ISS projects linked to the development of an ATV (automatic transfer vehicle—not related to all-terrain vehicles), which will supply nine tons of cargo and fuel to the space station. These projects, which include countries and companies from France, Germany, Russia, Italy, will take place in their respective countries under the guidance of ESA. DaimlerChrysler will produce the estimated 15 ATVs scheduled for delivery between 2003 and 2013. Standard penalty clauses for late delivery are in place. Incentive provisions for continuous improvement of mission success and payload mass are included in this multination endeavor.

Problems are deemed surmountable, and plans to complete the assembly by 2006 are in place. It is expected that the world-class laboratory will lead to discoveries that will touch the lives of everyone in the world. Perhaps the lessons learned will be as valuable as the discoveries.

*Michael A. Taverna, "Europe Advances ATV Development for ISS," *Aviation Week and Space Technology,* November 30, 1998, p. 29.

We can expect the processes of risk management at the project task level to receive more consideration in the next decade. At this time, rudimentary processes are used to identify, assess, and respond in a general way. There is a need to develop a complete methodology that details processes to catch and handle all project risks at the task level. Consultants, organizations, and academics are already at work.

Outsourcing   Outsourcing segments of a project is growing in project-driven organizations. A common strategy is to outsource standard work or parts and reserve inside work that is complex and deemed proprietary. Of course, some organizations will need to bring in expertise if it is not available in their organization. Outsourcing brings with it many areas that need to be managed such as contract management, RFPs, change control, partnering. The outsourcing trend will continue to grow, and ways to manage this function should stabilize in the future.

Summary   Today we see a major emphasis on the development of an integrated project management process that focuses all effort toward the organization's strategic plan, development of an organization culture that supports a multiproject environment, and mastery of *both* project management tools/techniques and interpersonal skills necessary to manage a project to successful completion. Project management continues to evolve and is ideally positioned to meet the challenges confronting global business enterprises in this twenty-first century.

Unresolved Issues

While we are fairly confident in our observations and resulting inferences, there are still some unresolved issues confronting project management. Two of these are virtual project management and the management of projects under high levels of uncertainty:

• How far can virtual project management evolve?

In Chapter 11 we introduced the subject of virtual project teams in which members primarily interact electronically. Today, most project communication is limited to e-mail, teleconferencing, faxes, and, in some cases, videoconferencing. As telecommunication systems become more reliable worldwide and videoconferencing with high-definition resolution becomes readily available, project teams will be able to hold meetings in which geographically separated members visually interact with each other; e-mail will be augmented by video messages. Similarly, telephone conversations will be replaced by direct video interaction using PCs.

Some companies with access to the latest technology are experimenting with 24-hour product design teams. These teams have members scattered across the time zones so that work on a project is nonstop. For example, team members work on the project during normal hours in New York and then electronically pass their work to members in Hawaii, who are beginning their workday when the New York team is about to go home. The Hawaiian team passes their work to a team in Bangkok, Thailand, which, in turn, passes their work to a team situated in Copenhagen, Denmark. The Danish team passes their work to the New York team, and the cycle is repeated. Although it is too early to say how successful this tag-team approach to project management will be, it exemplifies the potential that exists given the information technology that is available today.

Clearly in the world of the future, project professionals will have access to technology to reduce the barriers of distance and time and improve their ability to interact in a virtual domain. The question is, what are the limits to virtual project management? What kinds of projects and under what circumstances will virtual project management best work? Or not work? Will different skill sets and personal characteristics be required to work in a virtual environment? What protocols, habits, and procedures need to be developed to successfully manage a virtual project team? Will visual, video interaction enhance the development of trust among physically separated team members? Conversely, new technology often produces unintended side effects (smog in the case of the gasoline engine; carpal tunnel in the case of PCs). What are the potential negative physical and psychological side effects of working in a virtual environment? How will workers respond if their sleep is periodically interrupted by urgent calls from Krakow, Poland, or if they have to make sure they are home from the movies at 11:00 P.M. so they can participate in a video project meeting?

Answers to these questions and others will emerge as organizations experiment with virtual project management.

- How do we manage projects under high levels of uncertainty?

Research on project success and failure consistently points to poor planning as a major reason behind project failures. The general recommendation is that more time and attention should be devoted to clearly defining the scope of the project and developing the project plan. However, poor planning may not simply be a result of a lack of effort but rather due to the inherent difficulty of planning a project under conditions of high uncertainty. For example, software development projects are notorious for being completed way over budget and behind schedule. Is this a result of poor planning? Or an innate characteristic of project work that involves tightly coupled activities, trial-and-error problem solving, and shifting design parameters?

Modern project management planning tools and techniques are well suited to accomplish projects in which the scope is well defined. They are less well suited to manage projects with vaguely defined or unstable scope. Purists would argue that this is a moot point because, by definition, project management involves only endeavors with well-defined objectives. While this is a neat "academic" solution to the problem, it does not mirror the reality of project management today. More and more people are engaged in projects in which, by intent, the initial scope is broadly defined or subject to significant change. Customers' needs change. Top management strategies and priorities change. Innovations create the impossible. Competitors change the playing field. In today's business world, certainty is a luxury, and a premium is placed on flexibility.

The key question is how to effectively manage projects with loosely defined or *unstable scope* accompanied by high levels of *uncertainty*. How do managers plan a project for which they are not sure what the final outcome will be? How do they develop a project control system that is both flexible and responsive yet, at the same time, ensures accountability and yields reliable projections? How do they avoid paralysis through overanalysis yet, at the same time, engage in prudent risk management? How do they know when it is appropriate to freeze the scope or design of the project and begin formal implementation? Conversely, using uncertainty as an excuse for not planning and flying into the wind by the seat of the pants is an invitation for disaster.

The next decade should see a whirlwind of attention to the problem of managing projects with ill-defined project scopes and project uncertainties. Answers to the problem are not obvious. Some of the ideas and techniques will be short-term fads. Others will withstand the test of time and make significant contributions to the project management body of knowledge.

Executives "don't have a clue about how to grow project managers," says Gopal Kapur, president of the Center for Project Management, a consulting agency in San Ramon, California. "Project managers do not grow on trees. You have to understand the process of gardening before you can grow something." Kapur advocates that corporations develop internal programs to develop project managers.

The Federal Reserve Bank of St. Louis has had such a program for more than a year, and it's helped the bank grow 45 new project managers. It combines hands-on work in medium-to low-risk projects with classroom training. A new project manager is guided by a veteran leader, who acts as a coach or mentor. Gary Arnold, manager of learning and development services, calls that a very critical piece of the program. The coach/mentor can offer advice based on experience.

Typically, Arnold says, project manager wannabes are sent to the classroom for a few days before they apply some skills. But the Federal Reserve Bank found that the opposite works better and starts them off in the trenches. This way they experience firsthand the need to master key project management tools and concepts.

*Rick Saia, "Harvesting Project Leaders," *Computerworld,* Vol. 31, No. 29, July 21, 1997, p. 1.

Project Management Career Issues

Career Paths

There is no set career path for becoming a project manager. Career avenues vary from industry to industry, organization to organization, and from profession to profession. What can be said is that advancement occurs incrementally. You don't simply graduate and become a project manager. As in other careers you have to work your way up to the position. For example, in project-based organizations such as construction firms, you may begin by working on several projects as an assistant engineer, then take an assignment as a project analyst. From there you are promoted to principal engineer, advance to assistant project manager, assume the role of project manager over a small project, and then continue to bigger, riskier projects. In other organizations, project management careers run parallel with functional advancement with many crossovers. For example, at Intel a management information systems (MIS) specialist might start his career as a designer, then take an assignment as a project specialist, later work as a project manager, and then return to a functional position as head of a department or as a product manager.

Other people find that their project management responsibilities expand as they move up the organization's hierarchy. For example, a former marketing student began her career as an assistant buyer for a large retail company. She then became area sales manager at a specific store and became involved on a part-time basis in a series of projects acting as a facilitator of focus groups. She was promoted to buyer and eventually became a store manager. In her current position she coordinates a variety of projects ranging from improving the sales acumen of her salesforce to altering the physical layout of the store. Although the title of project manager does not appear in her job description, more than 50 percent of her work involves managing projects.

Temporary Assignments

One aspect of project managing that is unique is the temporary nature of assignments. With line appointments, promotions are for the most part permanent and there is a natural, hierarchical progression to positions with greater authority and responsibility. In the example of the former marketing student, she progressed from assistant buyer to sales manager to buyer to store manager. Only under very unusual circumstances would she regress to being a buyer. Conversely, tenure is rarely granted to project managers. Once the project is completed, the manager may return to his previous department, even to a lesser position. Or, depending on the projects available, he may be assigned to manage a more or less significant project. Future work depends on what projects are available at the time the individual is available and how well the last project went. A promising career can be derailed by one unsuccessful project.

Pursuing a Career

If you are considering pursuing a career in project management, you should first find out what specific project job opportunities exist in your company. You should talk to people in project management positions and find out how they got to where they are and what advice they can give you. Because career paths, as noted earlier, vary from organization to organization, you need to be attuned to the unique pathways within your company. For example, retail companies naturally assign marketing managers to projects.

Once you have concluded that you wish to pursue a career in project management, or see project management as an avenue for advancement, you need to share your aspirations with your immediate superior. Your superior can champion your ambitions, sanction additional training in project management, and assign immediate work that will contribute to your project skill base.

Professional Training and Certification

Most project managers have never received formal training in project management. They mastered the job through on-the-job training, buttressed by occasional workshops on specific project topics such as project scheduling or negotiating contracts. It wasn't until recently that universities started offering courses on project management outside of schools of engineering; to date there are only a handful of degree programs in project management. Regardless of your level of training you will likely need to supplement your education. Many large companies have in-house training programs on project management. For example, Hewlett-Packard has more than 32 training modules in its project management curriculum, which is organized around five levels of experience: project team, new project manager, project manager, experienced project manager, and manager of project managers. Take advantage of professional workshops, which can cover a range of specific project management tools and topics. Continued education should not be restricted to project management. Many technical professionals return to universities to complete an MBA or take night classes in management to expand their general business background.

Many professionals find it beneficial to join the Project Management Institute (PMI). Membership entitles you to subscriptions to PMI publications including the academic *Project Management Journal* and the *PM Network,* a trade magazine. PMI sponsors workshops and national forums on project management. When you join PMI you also become a member of one of the more than 200 local chapters across North America. These chapters meet on a monthly basis and provide project managers with opportunities to network and learn from each other. In addition, PMI, as part of its effort to advance the profession, certifies mastery of project manager competency through a formal examination that covers the entire body of knowledge of project management. Passing the exam and being certified as a project management professional (PMP) is a clearly visible way to signal your competence and interest.

Gaining Visibility

As you accumulate knowledge and techniques, you need to apply them to your immediate job situation. Most people's jobs entail some form of project, whether realizing a mandated objective or simply figuring out ways to improve the quality of performance. Gantt charts, responsibility matrixes, CPM networks, and other project management tools can be used to plan and implement these endeavors. It may also be wise to look outside the workplace for opportunities to develop project management skills. Active involvement in your local community can provide numerous opportunities to manage projects. Organizing a local soccer tournament, managing a charitable fund-raising event, or coordinating the renovation of the neighborhood park can allow you to practice project management. Furthermore, given the volunteer nature of most of these projects, they can provide you with an excellent training ground to sharpen your ability to exercise influence without formal authority.

Regardless of how competent and worthy you are, your project management skills must be visible to others for them to be recognized. Many project managers' careers began by volunteering for task forces and small projects. Ideally you should select task forces and projects that allow you access to higher-ups and other departments within your organization, providing you with opportunities to develop contacts.

This was certainly true for a former student of ours named Bob who escaped the trenches of a large corporation by volunteering to lead the organization's annual United Way campaign. While an important cause, directing the United Way campaign was generally given to someone who was expendable. This was true for Bob whose career had bottomed out. Bob took advantage of the United Way task force to show off his project management skills. Through recruiting key participants, establishing a shared vision, managing milestones, and contagious enthusiasm the campaign was a resounding success shattering previous records. Bob's efforts caught the attention of top management and he was rewarded with more project work.

Mentors

In pursuing your ambition you should continually be on the lookout for a mentor. Most fast-track managers acknowledge that mentors played a significant role in their advancement. Mentors are typically superiors who take a special interest in you and your career. They use their clout to champion your ambitions and act as a personal coach, teaching you "the ropes to skip and the ropes to know." This special treatment does not come without a price. Mentors typically require fervent loyalty and superior performance; after all, the mentor's reputation rests on your performance. How do you find a mentor? Most people say it just happens. But it doesn't happen to everyone. Mentors typically seek A+ workers, not C workers, and you must make your abilities known to others.

Many organizations have instituted formal mentoring programs in which experienced project managers are assigned to promising young managers. Although the relationship may not evolve to the personal level experienced with an informal mentor, designated mentors play a very similar role in coaching and championing one's professional progress. You should take advantage of this opportunity to learn as much as you can from these seasoned veterans.

Since much project work is temporary and contractual in nature, it is important to develop professional contacts that may lead to future work. Attending conferences, trade fairs, and workshops provides good opportunities to "network" and develop social connections that might precipitate project assignments. These social/professional networks can provide a safety net for project work during times of downsizing and layoffs.

Success in Key Projects

Ultimately your goal is to accumulate a portfolio of project management experiences that broaden your skill base and reputation. Early on you should choose, when possible, projects with the greatest learning opportunities. Pick projects more for the quality of the people working on them than for the scope of the projects. There is no better way to learn how to be an effective project manager than by watching one at work. Keep a diary of your observations and review and refine lessons learned. Later, as your confidence and competency grow, you should try to get involved in projects that will enhance your reputation within the firm. Remember the comments about customer satisfaction. You want to exceed your superior's expectations. Avoid run-of-the-mill projects or assignments. Seek high-profile projects that have some risks and tangible payoffs. At the same time, be careful to be involved in projects commensurate with your abilities.

Finally, despite your efforts you may find that you are not making satisfactory progress toward your career goals. If this is your appraisal, you may wish to seriously consider moving to a different company or even a different industry that might provide more project management opportunities. Hopefully you have managed to accumulate sufficient project management experience to aid in your job search. One advantage of project work over general management is that it is typically easier to highlight and "sell" your accomplishments.

Summary

The twenty-first century should be the Golden Age for project management. Not only will there be an increased demand for project management skills and know-how, but organizations will evolve and change to support more effective project management. Instead of trying to get projects done despite everything else, the organization's culture, structure, reward system, and administrative systems will be reengineered to support successful project management. Mastery of the process of managing projects will be critical to business growth and survival.

The project manager of the new millennium will be a businessperson with responsibilities that encompass the total organization. The past 30 years have seen the transition from a technically oriented project manager to one skilled in all aspects of business. Worldwide competition will direct projects toward technology transfer, infrastructure, consumer goods, environment/ecological recovery, defense, and fundamental needs. The future project manager will be comfortable in foreign or domestic settings and will understand the needs of people in all social settings. The project-driven organization will recognize the project manager as an agent of change and, from their ranks, select the senior managers of tomorrow.

Twenty years from now career paths in project management should be more clearly defined. Until then, people wishing to pursue a career in project management should take advantage of the transition and improvise within the constraints of their situation to develop their project management skills. They should volunteer to work on task forces, take advantage of training opportunities, and apply project management tools and techniques to their work. They should signal to their superiors their interest in project management and garner project assignments. Over time they should accumulate a portfolio of project management experiences that establishes their skill base and reputation as someone who gets things done quickly and done right.

Conclusions

By studying this text you have been exposed to the major elements of the process of managing projects. When you apply these ideas and techniques to real project situations, we offer three suggestions.

1. Maintain a sense of the big picture. Engage regularly in what some have called "helicopter management," which means expand your perspective beyond immediate concerns and assess how the project fits in the larger scheme of things. Project managers need to constantly assess how the project fulfills the mission and strategy of the firm, how the project is affecting the rest of the organization, whether the expectations of stakeholders are changing, and what key project interfaces have to be managed.

2. Remember that successful project management is essentially a balancing act. Project managers need to balance the soft (people) side of project management with the hard (technical) side, the demands of top management with the needs of team members, short-term gain with long-term need, and so forth.

3. Project management is the wave of the future. Change produces career opportunities that are often not available during normal times. We encourage you to take advantage of these opportunities by developing your project management skills and knowledge. It is not too late to catch the first wave.

Key Terms

Enterprise project management
Mentor

Project management office

Exercises

1. Reread the "Day in a Life" case in Chapter 1. How would you assess her effectiveness now that you have studied project management? What part of Rachel's experience contributes to her success?

2. Access the Project Management Institute's home page at *www.pmi.org*. Review the qualifications necessary to earn certification as a project management professional. Take the practice exam. How well did you do?

References

Baker, B., "The Nominees are . . . ," *PM Network,* Vol. 18, No. 6, June 2004, p. 23.

Dinsmore, P. C., "Toward a Corporate Project Management Culture: Fast Tracking into the Future," *Proceedings of the Project Management Institute 28th Annual Seminars and Symposium* (Newton Square, PA: Project Management Institute, 1997).

Lientz, B. P. and K. P. Rea, *Project Management for the 21st Century* (San Diego Academic Press, 1995).

Mackay, H., *Dig Your Well Before You're Thirsty* (New York: Doubleday, 1997).

Martin, P. and K. Tate, *Getting Started in Project Management* (New York: Wiley & Sons, 2004).

SimProject Case*

A special feature of this text, the SimProject case, is introduced in this section. The case will be different for every class and uses the software to generate a different scenario for each class. The use of a computer simulation, specifically SimProject, in your class is a unique method of learning both the fundamentals as well as the intricacies of project management.

Simulation is not a new pedagogy but one that has been in existence for many years. Both you as well as your instructor may use a simulation either passively or actively. The Simulation Experiential Exercises in this section allow you to use SimProject actively by getting you involved in the actual operation of a project from the acquisition of people to the management of a team's process and content throughout the project.

The Simulation Experiential Exercises (SEE) that follow are designed to coordinate with your textbook and are numbered by chapter for you to follow along easily. The computer simulation will provide specific details about the actual scenario in which you find yourself. SEE's may give you additional information from the chapter and the simulation that will help you to do the experiential exercise.

There are effectively two teams involved in this project: the *project* team and your *class* team. The *project* team consists of the hypothetical set of individuals selected from the "pool" of resources available to you in the simulation. The simulation will give descriptions. The decisions you and your *class* team make in the simulation are made on behalf of the *project* team and the *simulated* project. Your *class* team will consist of real people within your class with whom you form your team.

The instructor will select SEE's and will be specific as to whether you should perform the exercise using the *project* team or your *class* team.

After reading the text, applying the principles to the *simulation project* through the Simulation Experiential Exercises, and participating in SimProject, you should be prepared to apply your skills to a real world situation.

Simulation Experiential Exercises

Simulation Experiential Exercise 1-1: Defining a Project

Purpose

To provide the opportunity to begin to identify how the simulation project exercise qualifies as a project. *{Project Team}*

Instructions

Use the description of the project provided by the simulation setup and identify the five (5) major characteristics of this project.

* Prepared by Diane Parente, Penn State University—Erie.

Deliverable

Short description of your project, followed by the details of the five major characteristics of this project.

Simulation Experiential Exercise 1-2: Project Life Cycle

Purpose

To provide the vehicle for the team to look ahead and anticipate some of the activities in the various stages of the project life cycle (PLC). *{Project Team}*

Instructions

Review the four stages of the Project Life Cycle. Adapt the tasks in each stage to reflect your simulation project. Identify the category of resource (i.e., engineer, programmer, or carpenter) that is appropriate for each of the major activities.

Deliverable

The document should reflect the PLC stages, component activities, and the resource type that is planned.

Simulation Experiential Exercise 2-1: Project Fit

Purpose

The intent of this exercise is to describe the project "fit" with the organization's mission. *{Project Team}*

Instructions

Step 1: Identify the project stakeholders and describe the interests of each stakeholder group. (i.e., what are the project team members' interests in the success of the project?)

Step 2: Use the organization's mission provided in the description of your simulation scenario and discuss the consistencies and inconsistencies between the organization's mission and the stakeholders' interests.

Deliverable

Short narrative including mission statement, list of stakeholders and corresponding stakeholder interests, and discussion of consistencies and inconsistencies.

Simulation Experiential Exercise 2-2: Writing Goals

Purpose

To practice writing "good" goals. *{Project Team or Class Team}*

Instructions

Write three goals for either your *Project Team* or *Class Team* (as directed by your instructor). Be sure that the goals are in SMARTc3 format.

> Note: Specific, Measurable, Achievable, Relevant, Timed, caveat or limitation, 3 levels Eg. Increase sales by 10% within the next year without decreasing price. (satisfactory = 10%; good = 13%; outstanding = 15%)

Deliverable

Three goals in SMARTc3 format.

Simulation Experiential Exercise 2-3: Cost Benefit Analysis

Purpose

To develop the payback period and internal rate of return for your project. *{Project Team}*

Instructions

Identify the costs and benefits of your simulated project over the life of the project. Calculate the net cash flow, the internal rate of return and the payback period. Is this an acceptable project? What are the criteria for determining feasibility?

Deliverable

Costs, benefits, cash flow, IRR, and payback calculation.

Simulation Experiential Exercise 2-4:

Purpose

To link strategic alternatives to SWOT analysis. *{Class Team}*

Instructions

Develop an objective for the completion of the project or use one of the objectives developed in SEE 2-2. Do a SWOT analysis for your Class Team and the class environment in which you will work. Identify a minimum of three (3) each strengths, weaknesses, opportunities, and threats. Then develop at least four strategic alternatives from the SWOT analysis that will help you achieve your objective. Be sure to explain how your SWOT analysis leads you to your objective.

Deliverable

One to two page document including the team objective, SWOT analysis, and four strategic alternatives.

Simulation Experiential Exercise 2-4: Strategic Alternative Selection

Purpose

To make a qualitative determination of the best strategic alternative. *{Class Team}*

Instructions

Discuss the advantages and disadvantages of each strategic alternative developed in SEE 2-3. Make a recommendation of one (1) strategic alternative that will help you achieve your objective.

Deliverable

One to two page writeup of four alternatives and justification for the choice of one alternative.

Simulation Experiential Exercise 2-5: Project Proposal

Purpose

To learn to prepare a project proposal. *{Project Team}*

Instructions

Prepare a major project proposal (Figure 2.4) and the risk analysis (Figure 2.5) for your project.

Deliverable

Two page output that is in the exact format of the figures named on page 533.

Simulation Experiential Exercise 3-1: Project Organization Structure

Purpose

To analyze the project organization structure. *{Project Team}*

Instructions

Based on the information available from SimProject, prepare a recommendation to management on the most appropriate organizational structure for your *project team.* Diagram your proposed structure and discuss the strengths and weaknesses and potential issues with your recommended structure.

Deliverable

Formal recommendation to management regarding project organization structure including cover letter, project structure diagram, and explanation.

Simulation Experiential Exercise 3-2: Project Organizational Culture

Purpose

To understand the elements of organizational culture in a project team. *{Class Team}*

Instructions

Using the primary characteristics of organizational culture described in your text, assess your *Class Team* on each of the dimensions. Your text also gives you ideas on how to identify these cultural characteristics. Chart the results of your cultural assessment and compare to the chart in Figure 3.9 for an organization supportive of project management. Discuss the differences and potential adjustments that your team might make.

Deliverable

Assessment of cultural dimensions, bar chart, and comparison discussion—all based on *Class Team.* Be sure to discuss the implications of your assessment.

Simulation Experiential Exercise 4-1: Project Scope

Purpose

To write a project scope statement. *{Project Team}*

Instructions

Using the instructions and the examples in your text, write a Project Scope Statement using the information given in your simulation. As in a real project, you will need to extrapolate some of the information (i.e., requirements and limitations) and use the project scope statement to obtain clarification from the customer and pre-project approval.

Deliverable

Project Scope Statement including objectives, deliverables, milestones, technical requirements, limits and exclusions, and customer review as appropriate.

Simulation Experiential Exercise 4-2: Project Costs

Purpose

To identify the cost of project deliverables and the total project. *{Project Team}*

Instructions

Identify each of the project deliverables and develop the total cost for each one. Compute the total project cost and compare to your budget. Identify actions that you might take to correct any problems identified.

Deliverable

Budgeted vs. outlook cost comparison by deliverable. Action plan for deficiencies. (Note: Outlook costs are those that will be incurred given the current plan. This typically includes project to date plus anticipated expenses to project completion.)

Simulation Experiential Exercise 4-3: Project Responsibility Matrix

Purpose

To create a Project Responsibility Matrix. *{Class Team}*

Instructions

Identify the project tasks for your *Class Team.* Create a Responsibility Matrix for your project for the semester. Be sure to assign primary and supporting responsibilities.

Deliverable

Project Responsibility Matrix for your *Class Project.*

Simulation Experiential Exercise 4-4: Project Priority Matrix

Purpose

To understand the relative priorities of a project. *{Project Team}*

Instructions

Project success in your simulated organization will be based on competing priorities. Based on the information available to you concerning your project to date, how would you rate the relative importance of time, cost, functionality, and quality (stakeholder satisfaction).

Complete a Project Priority Matrix for your simulation project. Divide 100 points between the above four competing priorities. Briefly discuss the rationale for your point assignment.

Deliverable

Project Priority Matrix. Also, each of the four components (time, cost, functionality, and stakeholder satisfaction) will have a point assignment and a brief statement of the reason for the assignment.

Simulation Experiential Exercise 4-5: Project Tasks and WBS

Purpose

To evaluate the WBS.

Instructions

Evaluate the project tasks and create a WBS complete with time and budget estimates and responsibilities. Use the tasks beginning on page 106 as a guide.

Deliverable

Complete annotated WBS.

Simulation Experiential Exercise 5-1: Project Budget

Purpose

To create a detailed project budget and compare to the macro-level budget. *{Project Team}*

Instructions

Based on the information in your simulation scenario, create a detailed project budget. Compare to the deliverable from SEE 4-2 and reconcile the differences. Define your action plan to resolve the top-down vs. bottom-up approaches to project estimation. Which is better? (Please note that you may need to be somewhat creative if the costs or benefits are not available to you in specific instances. Make reasonable and justified assumptions.)

Deliverable

Bottom-up project estimate and comparison to top-down approach. Action plan to resolve differences and short discussion of choice of approaches.

Simulation Experiential Exercise 5-2: Cost vs. Time Comparison

Purpose

To estimate the cost vs. time expenditures. *{Project Team}*

Instructions

Build a graph of the budgeted cost of work scheduled (BCWS) vs. the project periods. Discuss any obvious issues with the project as it is planned.

Deliverable

BCWS vs. time chart and short discussion of issues.

Simulation Experiential Exercise 5-3: Net Present Value Calculation

Purpose

To calculate the project NPV. *{Project Team}*

Instructions

Using the data from SEE 2-3, 5-1, and 5-2, calculate the net present value for the project. Identify the appropriate discount rate and justify.

Deliverable

Net present value for the project with explanation of whether to proceed or not.

Simulation Experiential Exercise 5-4: Estimating Guidelines

Purpose

To prepare a set of estimating guidelines for the project. *{Project Team}*

Instructions

Prepare a set of estimating guidelines for the simulated project. Be sure to incorporate and identify each of the seven areas on pages 127–129.

Deliverable

Estimating guidelines for the simulated projects. Be sure to include a sample work package estimate.

Simulation Experiential Exercise 5-5: Estimating Accuracy

Purpose

To compare estimates and actual performance for the project. *{Project Team}*

Instructions

Prepare a set of estimates for the project. Compare the results at the end of the project and explain the variances.

Deliverable

Budget vs. actual performance with variance analysis and explanation.

Simulation Experiential Exercise 6-1: Project Network Analysis

Purpose

To prepare and analyze the project network. *{Project Team}*

Instructions

After assigning personnel and estimating the task times, develop and printout the project network for your simulation project. Identify areas of potential problems that you can see as a result of examining the project network.

Deliverable

Project network diagram and list of issues regarding the plan.

Simulation Experiential Exercise 6-2: Project Network vs. Gantt Comparison

Purpose

To compare the value of the Gantt chart and the project network. *{Project Team}*

Instructions

Prepare a Gantt chart for your simulation project. Compare it with the output from SEE 6-1 and discuss the advantages and disadvantages of each.

Deliverable

Gantt chart and discussion of comparison between Gantt and project network.

Simulation Experiential Exercise 7-1: Risk and Risk Response

Purpose

To appropriately identify risk and develop plans for response. *{Project Team}*

Instructions

Identify the sources of possible risk for your simulation project. Use the technique shown in Figure 7.5 in your text to develop a Risk Assessment Matrix and a response to Risk Matrix.

Deliverable

Risk Assessment Matrix and Response to Risk Matrix.

Simulation Experiential Exercise 7-2: Change Control Management

Purpose

To reinforce the importance of change control management. *{Project Team}*

Instructions

Design a process and the appropriate documentation for Change Control in your simulation project.

Deliverable

Procedure for Change Control including forms, screens, responsibilities, and step-by-step directions for how change is initiated, approved, and implemented.

Simulation Experiential Exercise 7-3: Failure Mode Analysis

Purpose

To learn and practice Failure Mode Analysis. *{Project Team}*

Instructions

Prepare a Risk Assessment for your Project Team or use the one developed in SEE 7-1. Do a Failure Mode & Effects Analysis (FMEA). Stratify the risks into three (3) categories. Explain the rationale for your stratification.

Deliverable

FMEA Analysis including three (3) strata for risks.

Simulation Experiential Exercise 8-1: Resource Limitations

Purpose

To understand resource limitations. *{Project Team}*

Instructions

Once you have reviewed the Resource Pool and bid for services initially, you will find that you have accomplished the "hiring" of the resource in some cases and not "hired" them in others.

   Answer the following questions about the process:

1. What was your strategy for resource selection?
2. What are the implications of not achieving your hiring objectives in terms of time, cost, functionality, and stakeholder satisfaction?
3. What are your contingency plans?

Deliverable

A written evaluation of the resource selection process.

Simulation Experiential Exercise 8-2: Unplanned Time Constraints

Purpose

To evaluate how to respond to an unplanned time constraint. *{Project Team}*

Instructions

Your simulation has demonstrated a special event in which there is now a time constraint. Identify and implement your action plan to deal with this constraint.

Deliverable

Description of the time impact on the simulated project and a plan to address the issue.

Simulation Experiential Exercise 8-3: Unplanned Resource Constraints

Purpose

To evaluate how to respond to an unplanned resource constraint. *{Project Team}*

Instructions

Your simulation has demonstrated that there is a resource constraint. Identify and implement your action plan to deal with this constraint.

Deliverable

Description of the resource impact on the simulated project and a plan to address the issue.

Simulation Experiential Exercise 8-4: Unplanned Constraints

Purpose

To identify non-resource and time constraints. *{Project Team}*

Instructions

Identify additional constraints for your simulated project, to include but not be limited by materials, equipment, or working capital.

Deliverable

Description of the alternate resource constraints including a short description of a contingency plan for each resource constraint.

Simulation Experiential Exercise 9-1: Crashing the Project

Purpose

To understand the impact of "crashing." *{Project Team}*

Instructions

Your simulation due date has been moved forward. Make the appropriate changes in your project plan to accomplish the required schedule reduction. Discuss the areas of the project that are most likely to be impacted by the "crashing."

Deliverable

New project plan and list of actions taken. Assessment of the potential results of actions.

Simulation Experiential Exercise 9-2: Results of Project Crashing

Purpose

To evaluate the results of project crashing. *{Project Team}*

Instructions

As a result of the time reduction in SEE 9-1, there have been several outcomes. Evaluate the various project issues that have arisen as a result of your actions. Include time, cost, money, team cohesiveness, stakeholder satisfaction, and functionality.

Deliverable

Written review of the impact of project crashing.

Simulation Experiential Exercise 10-1: Project Stakeholders

Purpose

To understand the relationship between the various stakeholders on the project. *{Project Team}*

Instructions

Draw the network of stakeholders for your simulation project. Identify whether the potential impact of the stakeholder on the project success is direct or indirect.

Deliverable

Diagram of network with stakeholders identified as direct or indirect impact to the project.

Simulation Experiential Exercise 10-2: Project Currencies

Purpose

To understand various project currencies in the implementation of a project. *{Project Team}*

Instructions

Identify and explain which of the project currencies are appropriately being used or will be used in your project.

Deliverable

Listing and explanation of project-related currencies.

Simulation Experiential Exercise 11-1: Team Development Model

Purpose

To apply the Five-Stage Team Development Model. *{Class Team}*

Instructions

Discuss your class team within the framework of the Five-Stage Model. Be specific in identifying the characteristics and timing of each stage through which the team passed as well the final performance of the team on the project. Discuss where improvements should have been made to facilitate the team-building process.

Deliverable

Written review of the Team Development.

Simulation Experiential Exercise 11-2: Conflict

Purpose

To debrief conflict in the team. *{Class Team}*

Instructions

Discuss an instance of functional and dysfunctional conflict within your team. Identify your method of dealing with each type of conflict within your team.

Deliverable

Short written report debriefing the conflict.

Simulation Experiential Exercise 11-3: Virtual Team Assessment

Purpose

To debrief the operation of a virtual class team. *{Class Team}*

Instructions

If your class team has been a virtual one, review the mechanisms used for effectively (or ineffectively) managing your class team.

Deliverable

Short written report debriefing the operation of the virtual class team.

Simulation Experiential Exercise 11-4: High Performance Teams

Purpose

To construct and understand high performance teams. *{Class or Project Team}*

Instructions

Refer to Building High Performance Teams on page 347. Develop a strategy for hiring people on your team. Identify the attributes that will be important to your project team's success. Prepare an action plan for acquiring resources with the appropriate skills.

Deliverable

Short written report of constructing a high performance team.

Simulation Experiential Exercise 11-5: Behavioral Guidelines

Purpose

To construct team guidelines. *{Class Team}*

Instructions

Prepare a list of guidelines for your class team. Consider the areas and questions in the section on page 350. Your team should agree on a minimum of ten guidelines and include consequences for a minimum of ten guidelines. All members should sign and date the final documents.

Deliverable

Minimum list of ten students working at summer homes. Short written report of constructing a high performance team.

Simulation Experiential Exercise 12-1: Project Partnering

Purpose

To assess potential project partnering. *{Class or Project Team}*

Instructions

Identify areas of your simulation project in which you could have partnered with another organization. Write a formal proposal to management requesting approval for the partnering arrangement. Discuss the terms that you propose for the arrangement and assess the benefits and risks of your proposal.

Deliverable

Formal business proposal including memo to management and cost benefit analysis of the proposal.

Simulation Experiential Exercise 13-1: Project Status Report

Purpose

To create a project status report. *{Project Team}*

Instructions

Develop a project status report for your simulation project such as the one that is in Figure 13.10. Include an earned value chart and a tracking Gantt. Be sure to include a report that reports on actual costs, variance from budget, and explanations for the variances.

Deliverable

Complete formal project status report.

Simulation Experiential Exercise 13-2: Monthly Status Report

Purpose

To learn how to do a monthly status report. *{Project Team}*

Instructions

Develop the monthly status report for your simulation project as shown in Exhibit 13.1. Be sure to forecast remaining costs and time as well as to provide explanations and plans for getting back on budget in either time or cost or both.

Deliverable

Formal monthly status report including variance analysis and explanations.

Simulation Experiential Exercise 14-1: Project Audit Report

Purpose

To prepare a project audit report. *{Class Team or Project Team}*

Instructions

Your instructor will determine whether you will use your *class team* or the *project team* in the simulation to complete this exercise. Using the guidelines in the chapter, prepare a project audit report. Be sure to include project classification, analysis of information gathered, recommendations, and lessons learned. You may also include an appendix of appropriate documentation.

Deliverable

Final project report discussing all phases of the project.

Simulation Experiential Exercise 14-2: Individual Performance Appraisal System

Purpose

To implement a performance appraisal process. *{Class Team}*

Instructions

Using the process developed in SEE 2-3, conduct individual performance appraisals on all team members. Write a short debrief on the effectiveness of the process.

Deliverable

Individual performance appraisals for each team member and brief evaluation of the process.

Computer Project Exercises

In developing the exercises, trade-offs had to be made to enrich the learning experience. One of the major problems students initially encounter is data and detail overload. This reduces their ability to identify project and data problems and to compare alternatives. Although the project found in the exercises is real, it has been reduced and detail has been eliminated many times to concentrate on applying project management principles and understanding linkages. In addition, other simplifying assumptions have been made so that students and instructors can trace problems and discuss outcomes. These assumptions detract from reality, but they keep the focus on the objectives of the exercises and reduce student frustration with software intricacies. Moving from these exercises to real projects is primarily one of increasing detail. The simplifying assumptions are given below (make sure they are included in "default," "preferences," and/or "options" sections of the software used):

Silver Zuma Project

The ARC Company specializes in developing and selling a wide range of high-quality scooters. Sales representatives report that there is a growing demand for racing scooters. ARC's president, Robin Lane, is excited about the possibilities and predicts that one day these kinds of razor scooters will be featured in X-Game events. ARC is a small company and uses a strong matrix to optimally utilize limited manpower.

The Project Priority Matrix for the Silver Zuma Project is:

	Time	Scope	Cost
Constrain		X	
Enhance	X		
Accept			X

Part 1

You are a member of a project team assigned to develop the new razor scooter code named "Silver Zuma." Table A2.1 contains the information necessary to create a project schedule. For the purpose of this case assume the following:

1. The project begins January 1, 2006.
2. The following holidays are observed: January 1, Memorial Day (last Monday in May), July 4th, Labor Day (first Monday in September), Thanksgiving Day (4th Thursday in November), December 25 and 26.

TABLE A2.1 **Silver Zuma Project**

ID	Task Name	Duration	Predecessors	Resources
1	Product development project			
2	Market analysis	25 days		Marketing (4) Design (1)
3	Product design	40 days	2	Marketing (1) Design (4) Development (1) Industrial (1)
4	Manufacturing study	20 days	2	Industrial (4) Development (2)
5	Product design selection	10 days	3,4	Marketing (2) Design (3) Development (2) Industrial (2) Purchasing (.25)
6	Detailed marketing plans	15 days	5	Marketing (4)
7	Manufacturing process	30 days	5	Design (1) Development (2) Industrial (4)
8	Detailed product design	50 days	5	Marketing (1) Design (4) Development (2) Industrial (1)
9	Test prototype	10 days	8	Design (3) Development (2)
10	Finalized product design	25 days	7,9	Marketing (1) Design (3) Development (3) Industrial (2)
11	Order components	7 days	10	Purchasing (1)
12	Order production equipment	14 days	10	Purchasing (1)
13	Install production equipment	25 days	11FS+20 days, 12FS+40 days	Development (3) Industrial (4)
14	Celebrate	1 day	13	Development (4) Industrial (4) Design (4) Marketing (4) Purchasing (1)

3. If a holiday falls on a Saturday then Friday will be given as an extra day off, and if it falls on a Sunday, then Monday will be given as a day off.

4. The project team works eight-hour days, Monday through Friday.

Construct a network schedule for this project and prepare a memo that answers the following questions:

1. When is the project estimated to be completed? How long will the project take?
2. What is the critical path for the project?
3. Which activity has the greatest amount of slack?
4. How sensitive is this network?
5. Identify two sensible milestones and explain your choices.
6. Compare the advantages/disadvantages of displaying the schedule as a network versus a Gantt chart.

Include the following printouts:

- A Gantt chart.
- A network diagram highlighting the critical path.
- A schedule table reporting ES, LS, EF, LF, and slack for each activity.

Part 2

The following personnel have been assigned to the Silver Zuma project team:

4 marketing specialists

4 design engineers

TABLE A2.2
Zuma Project
Resources

Resource	$/hour	Number Available
Marketing specialist	$60	4
Design engineer	$90	4
Development engineer	$80	4
Industrial engineer	$70	4
Purchasing agent	$50	1

4 development engineers

4 industrial engineers

1 purchasing agent

Use the file from Part 1 and the information contained in Tables A2.1 and A2.2 to assign resources to the project schedule.

Part A

Prepare a memo that addresses the following questions:

1. Which if any of the resources are overallocated?
2. Which activities involve overallocated resources?
3. Assume that the project is time constrained and try to resolve any overallocation problems by leveling within slack. What happens?
4. What is the impact of leveling within slack on the sensitivity of the network?

Include: a Gantt chart with the schedule table after leveling within slack.

Part B

Prepare a memo that addresses the following questions:

1. Assume that the project is resource constrained and no additional personnel are available. How long will the project take given the resources assigned? (Hint: Undo leveling performed in Part A before answering this question.)

Note: No splitting of activities is allowed.

2. How does the new duration compare with the estimated completion date generated from Part 1? What does this tell you about the impact resources can have on a schedule?

Include a Gantt chart with a schedule table depicting the resource-constrained schedule.

Part 3

Top management is not happy with the resource-constrained schedule generated at the end of Part 2. Robin Lane, the president, has promised retailers that production of the new scooters would start on January 2nd. This means the project must be completed before the new year.

1. What options are available to meet this new deadline if the project is not resource constrained?
2. What options are available to meet this deadline if the project is resource constrained?

Dewey Martin, director of product development, has managed to make the following personnel available to work on specific activities on the project. Since there is an acute shortage of personnel at ARC he requests that you only use additional manpower that

TABLE A2.3
Zuma Project
Crashing Options

Activity	Additional Resource	Revised Duration Estimates
Product design	Design (1) Development (1)	25 days
Manufacturing study	Industrial (1)	12 days
Detailed marketing plan	Marketing (1)	12 days
Manufacturing process	Industrial (1)	20 days
Finalize product design	Design (1) Development (1)	20 days
Install production equipment	Industrial (1) Development (1)	18 days

will help meet the new deadline. Your objective is to develop a schedule which will satisfy the deadline with minimum additional resource usage. The available personnel and impact on activity duration are presented in Table A2.3.

Prepare a memo that addresses the following questions:

1. Which additional personnel assignments would you choose to complete the project within the original deadline? Explain your choices as well as the reasons for not choosing other options.
2. How have these changes affected the sensitivity of the network?

Include a Gantt chart with a schedule table presenting the new schedule.

Note: You can not go back and relevel resources. These new resources are only available for the stated specific tasks according to the schedule created at the end of Part 2.

Part 4

Robin Lane and top management have approved the schedule generated at the end of Part 3. Save the file containing this schedule as a baseline schedule.

Prepare a memo that addresses the following questions:

1. How much is the project estimated to cost?
2. What activity is estimated to cost the most to complete?
3. What resource commands the greatest total cost?
4. During which month of the project are the highest and lowest costs expected to occur? What are those costs?
5. What likely costs are not contained in this budget?

Include a table containing the estimated costs for each activity and a cash flow schedule for each month of the project.

Part 5

Today's date is July 28, 2006. Table A2.4 summarizes the information regarding activities accomplished to date.

TABLE A2.4
Silver Zuma Update

Activity	Start Date	Finish Date	Actual Duration	Remaining Duration
Market analysis	1/3/06	2/3/06	24	
Product design	2/6/06	3/17/06	30	
Manufacturing study	4/3/06	4/14/06	10	
Product design selection	4/17/06	4/28/06	10	
Manufacturing process	7/14/06		10	10
Detailed product design	5/1/06	7/25/06	60	
Test prototype	7/26/06		2	8

Robin Lane has requested a written status report for the Zuma project.

1. Your status report should include a table containing the PV, EV, AC, BAC, EAC, SV, CV, and CPI for each activity and the whole project. The report should also address the following questions:
   a. How is the project progressing in terms of cost and schedule?
   b. What activities have gone well? What activities have not gone well?
   c. What do the PCIB and PCIC indicate in terms of how much of the project has been accomplished to date?
   d. What is the forecasted cost at completion (FAC)? What is the predicted VAC_f?
   e. Report and interpret the TCIP for the project at this point in time.
   f. What is the estimated date of completion?
   g. How well is the project doing in terms of its priorities?

Try to present the above information in a form worthy of consideration by top management.

Include a Tracking Gantt Chart with your report.

Note: Enter July 27th as the status report date since you are preparing your report on the 28th.

2. While preparing your report you receive a phone call from Jim Keltner, a fellow project manager. He is calling to see if one of the industrial engineers assigned to your project would be available to work on his project from August 10–15, 2006. What would you tell him?

Part 6

Robin Lane has asked you to update completion and cost estimates for the Zuma project. Table A2.5 presents the revised estimates generated by the Zuma project team.

Based on this new information prepare a memo that answers the following questions:

1. When will the project be completed? How does this compare with the baseline completion date?
2. What is the new estimated cost at completion (EAC)? What is the new VAC? How does this compare with VAC based on the FAC generated in Part 5? Which of the two VACs would you have the greatest confidence in and why?
3. How do you think Robin will react given the priorities for this project?

Include a Tracking Gantt with a cost table for the estimated completion schedule.

TABLE A2.5
Silver Zuma Estimate to Completion

Activity	Start Date	Finish Date	Actual Duration
Market analysis	1/3/06	2/3/06	24
Product design	2/6/06	3/17/06	30
Manufacturing study	4/3/06	4/14/06	10
Product design selection	4/17/06	4/28/06	10
Detailed MRKT plan	9/8/06	9/26/06	13
Manufacturing process	7/14/06	8/10/06	18
Detailed product design	5/1/06	7/25/06	60
Test prototype	7/26/06	8/7/06	9
Finalized product design	8/11/06	9/1/06	16
Order components	9/25/06	10/7/06	10
Order production equip.	9/5/06	9/22/06	14
Install production equip.	11/20/06	12/18/06	20
Celebrate	12/19/06	12/19/06	1

Conveyor Belt Project

Part 1

Project Description

The new computer-controlled conveyor belt is an exciting project that moves and positions items on the conveyor belt within <1 millimeter. The proposed project will produce a new system for future installations, and for replacement of those in the field, at a low cost. The computer-controlled conveyor belt has the potential to be a critical unit in 30 percent of the systems installed in factories. The new system is also easier to update with future technologies.

The Project Priority Matrix for the Conveyor Belt Project (CBP) is:

	Time	Scope	Cost
Constrain	X		
Enhance		X	
Accept			X

Table A2.6 has been developed for you to use in completing the project exercises.

Assignment

Develop the WBS outline using the software available to you.

TABLE A2.6
Conveyor Belt Project; WBS

Conveyor Belt Project	
Hardware	Hardware specifications
	Hardware design
	Hardware documentation
	Prototypes
	Order circuit boards
	Assemble preproduction models
Operating system	Kernel specifications
	Drivers
	Disk drivers
	Serial I/O drivers
	Memory management
	Operating system documentation
	Network interface
Utilities	Utilities specifications
	Routine utilities
	Complex utilities
	Utilities documentation
	Shell
System integration	Architectural decisions
	Integration first phase
	System hard/software test
	Project documentation
	Integration acceptance testing

Question

Does this information (WBS) allow you to define any milestones of the project? Why or why not? What are they?

Remember: Save your file for future exercises!

Part 2

Use your file from Part 1 and the information provided below to complete this exercise. (See Table A2.7.)

1. Each work package will represent an activity.
2. The project begins January 3, 2006.
3. The following holidays are observed: January 1, Memorial Day (last Monday in May), July 4th, Labor Day (first Monday in September), Thanksgiving Day (4th Thursday in November), December 25 and 26.
4. If a holiday falls on a Saturday then Friday will be given as an extra day off, and if it falls on a Sunday, then Monday will be given as a day off.
5. The project team work eight-hour days, Monday through Friday.

Warning: Experience has taught students to frequently make separate backup files for each exercise. The software is never as friendly as users expect!

Construct a network schedule for the conveyor belt project and prepare a memo that addresses the following questions:

1. When is the project estimated to be completed? How long will the project take?
2. What is the critical path(s) for the project?
3. Which activity has the greatest amount of slack?

TABLE A2.7   Conveyor Belt Project; Schedule

Activity	Description	Resource	Duration (days)	Preceding Activity
1	Architectural designs	Design	25	—
2	Hardware specifications	Development, design	50	1
3	Kernel specifications	Design	20	1
4	Utilities specifications	Development, design	15	1
5	Hardware design	Design, development	70	2
6	Disk drivers	Assembly, development	100	3
7	Memory management	Development	90	3
8	Operating system documentation	Design, documentation	25	3
9	Routine utilities	Development	60	4
10	Complex utilities	Development	80	4
11	Utilities documentation	Documentation, design	20	4
12	Hardware documentation	Documentation, design	30	5
13	Integration first phase	Assembly, development	50	6,7,8,9,10,11,12
14	Prototypes	Assembly development	80	13
15	Serial I/O drivers	Development	130	13
16	System hard/software test	Assembly	25	14,15
17	Order printed circuit boards	Purchasing	5	16
18	Network interface	Development	90	16
19	Shell	Development	60	16
20	Project documentation	Documentation, development	50	16
21	Assemble preproduction	Assembly, development	30	17F-S, lag 50 days
22	Integrated acceptance test	Assembly, development	60	18,19,20,21

4. How sensitive is this network?
5. Identify two sensible milestones and explain your choices.
6. Compare the advantages/disadvantages of displaying the schedule as a network versus a Gantt chart.

Include the following printouts:

- A Gantt chart.
- A network diagram highlighting the critical path.
- A schedule table reporting ES, LS, EF, LF, and slack for each activity.

Hint: the project should be completed in 530 days.
Remember: Save your file for future exercises!

Part 3

Remember the old saying, "A project plan is not a schedule until resources are committed." This exercise illustrates this subtle, but very important, difference.

Part A

Using your files from Part 2 input resources and their costs if you have not already done so. All information is found in Tables A2.7 and A2.8
Prepare a memo that addresses the following questions:

1. Which if any of the resources are overallocated?
2. Assume that the project is time constrained and try to resolve any overallocation problems by leveling within slack. What happens?
3. What is the impact of leveling within slack on the sensitivity of the network?

Include a Gantt chart with the schedule table after leveling within slack.

4. Assume the project is resource constrained and resolve any overallocation problems by leveling outside of slack. What happens? What are the managerial implications?
5. What options are available at this point in time?

Include a Gantt chart with the schedule table after leveling outside of slack.

Note: No splitting of activities is allowed.
Note: No partial assignments (i.e., 50 percent). All resources must be assigned 100 percent.

Part B

When you show the resource-constrained network to top management, they are visibly shaken. After some explanation and negotiation they make the following compromise with you:

- The project must be completed no later than February 1, 2008 (530 days).
- You may assign two additional development teams.

TABLE A2.8
**Organization
Resources**

Name	Group	Cost ($/hr)
Research and development design	R&D (2 teams)	$100
Development	R&D (2 teams)	70
Documentation	R&D	60
Assembly/test	R&D	70
Purchasing		40

- If this does not suffice, you may hire other development teams from the outside. Hire as few external teams as possible because they cost $50 more per hour than your inside development people.

Internal Development

Add as many development units (teams) as needed to stay within the 530 days. If you need more than the two units, examine all possibilities. Select the cheapest possibilities! Change as few activities as possible. It is recommended you keep work packages which require cooperation of several organizational units inside your company. You decide how best to do this.

   Hint: Undo leveling prior to adding new resources.

   Once you have obtained a schedule that meets the time and resource constraints, prepare a memo that addresses the following questions:

A. What changes did you make and why?
B. How long will the project take?
C. How did these changes affect the sensitivity of the network?

Include a Gantt chart with a schedule table presenting the new schedule.

Conveyor Belt Project—Part 4

Based on the file created at the end of Part 3, prepare a memo that addresses the following questions:

A. How much will the project cost?
B. What does the cash flow statement tell you about how costs are distributed over the lifespan of the project?

Include a monthly cash flow and a cost table for the project.

   Once you are confident that you have the final schedule, save the file as a baseline. (**Hint:** Save a backup file just in case without baseline!)

Conveyor Belt Project—Part 5

Prepare status reports for each of the first four quarters of the project given the information provided here. This requires saving your resource schedule as a baseline and inserting the appropriate status report date in the program. Assume that no work has been completed on the day of the status report.

   Your status report should include a table containing the PV, EV, AC, BAC, EAC, SV, CV, and CPI for each activity and the whole project. The report should also address the following questions:

A. How is the project progressing in terms of cost and schedule?
B. What activities have gone well? What activities have not gone well?
C. What do the PCIB and PCIC indicate in terms of how much of the project has been accomplished to date?
D. What is the forecasted cost at completion (FAC)? What is the predicted VAC_f?
E. Report and interpret the TCIP for the project at this point in time.

F. What is the estimated date of completion?

G. How well is the project doing in terms of its priorities?

Try to present the above information in a form worthy of consideration by top management.

Include a Tracking Gantt Chart with each report.

First Quarter, April 1

Table A2.9 summarizes the information regarding activities accomplished to date.

Be sure to save your file after each quarterly report and use it to build the next report!

Second Quarter, July 1

Table A2.10 summarizes the information regarding activities accomplished since the last report.

Third Quarter, October 1

Table A2.11 summarizes the information regarding activities accomplished since the last report.

Fourth Quarter, January 1, 2007

Table A2.12 summarizes the information regarding activities accomplished since the last report.

TABLE A2.9
April 1, 2006

Activity	Start Date	Finish Date	Actual Duration	Remaining Duration
Hardware specifications	2/8/06		38	7
Kernel specifications	2/7/06	3/13/06	25	0
Disk drivers	3/14/06		14	86
Memory management	3/14/06		14	76
Op. systems documentation	3/14/06		14	6
Utilities specifications	3/7/06	3/28/06	16	0
Complex utilities	3/29/06		3	84
Architectural decisions	1/3/06	2/6/06	25	0

TABLE A2.10
July 1, 2006

Activity	Start Date	Finish Date	Actual Duration	Remaining Duration
Hardware specifications	2/8/06	4/11/06	45	0
Hardware design	4/12/06		58	9
Kernel specifications	2/7/06	3/13/06	25	0
Disk drivers	3/14/06		79	31
Memory management	3/14/06		79	17
Op. systems documentation	3/14/06	4/17/06	25	0
Utilities specifications	3/7/06	3/28/06	16	0
Routine utilities*	4/26/06		48	17
Complex utilities	3/29/06		65	26
Utilities documentation	5/3/06	6/2/06	22	0
Architectural decisions	1/3/06	2/6/06	25	0

*The project manager for the external development team that was hired to perform routine utilities reported that due to commitments to other clients they would be able to start on that activity 4/26/06.

TABLE A2.11
October 1, 2006

Activity	Start Date	Finish Date	Actual Duration	Remaining Duration
Hardware specifications	2/8/06	4/11/06	45	0
Hardware design	4/12/06	7/17/06	67	0
Hardware documentation	7/18/06	8/23/06	27	0
Kernel specifications	2/7/06	3/13/06	25	0
Disk drivers	3/14/06	8/16/06	110	0
Memory management	3/14/06	7/31/06	98	0
Op. systems documentation	3/14/06	4/17/06	25	0
Utilities specifications	3/7/06	3/28/06	16	0
Routine utilities	4/26/06	7/27/06	65	0
Complex utilities	3/29/06	8/10/06	95	0
Utilities documentation	5/3/06	6/2/06	22	0
Architectural decisions	1/3/06	2/6/06	25	0
Integration 1st phase	8/24/06		27	23

TABLE A2.12
January 1, 2007

Activity	Start Date	Finish Date	Actual Duration	Remaining Duration
Hardware specifications	2/8/06	4/11/06	45	0
Hardware design	4/12/06	7/17/06	67	0
Hardware documentation	7/18/06	8/23/06	27	0
Prototypes	11/10/06		33	45
Kernel specifications	2/7/06	3/13/06	25	0
Disk drivers	3/14/06	8/16/06	110	0
Serial I/O drivers	11/10/06		33	120
Memory management	3/14/06	7/31/06	98	0
Op. systems documentation	3/14/06	4/17/06	25	0
Utilities specifications	3/7/06	3/28/06	16	0
Routine utilities	4/26/06	7/27/06	65	0
Complex utilities	3/29/06	8/10/06	95	0
Utilities documentation	5/3/06	6/2/06	22	0
Architectural decisions	1/3/06	2/6/06	25	0
Integration 1st phase	8/24/06	11/9/06	55	0

Conveyor Belt Project—Part 6

A

You have received revised estimates for the remaining activities at the end of the fourth quarter:

- Prototypes will be completed on 3/5/07.
- Serial I/O drivers will be completed on 6/28/07.
- System hardware/software tests will start on 6/29/07 and take 25 days.
- Order circuit boards will start on 7/26/07 and take 5 days.
- Assemble preproduction model will begin on 10/12/07 and take 18 days.
- Project documentation is expected to start on 8/6/07 and will take 55 days.
- Network interface is expected to start on 8/6/07 and will take 100 days.

- Shell is expected to start on 8/6/07 and will take 55 days.
- Integrated acceptance test is expected to start on 12/28/07 and will take 54 days.

Prepare a memo that addresses the following questions:

A. What is the new EAC for the project? How long should the project take given these revised estimates?

Include a cost table and Tracking Gantt chart with your memo.

B

Management is insisting that the project be done no later than February 1, 2008 or else. They are willing to add additional manpower to development teams to speed up completion of the project. The cost will be an additional $150 per hour for each development team. You have forecasted the impact of adding development manpower on the remaining activities:

- System hardware/software tests will take 22 days to complete.
- Assemble preproduction model will take 15 days to complete.
- Project documentation will take 50 days.
- Network interface will take 85 days.
- Shell will take 50 days.
- Integrated acceptance test will take 50 days.

Decide which activities you would add the additional development manpower to (at a cost of +$150 an hour) in order to meet the February 1st deadline. (Note: A development team would be added to the assembly team in order to expedite the system hardware/software tests.)

Prepare a memo justifying your decision and that addresses the following questions:

A. How long will the project take?
B. How much will the project cost?
C. How happy will be top management with these forecasts given the priorities of the project?

Include a revised schedule and cost table with your memo.

GLOSSARY

A

activity Task(s) of the project that consumes time while people/equipment either work or wait.

activity duration Estimate of time (hours, days, weeks, months, etc.) necessary to complete a project task.

actual cost of the work completed (AC) The sum of the cost incurred in accomplishing work. Previously this was called the actual cost of the work performed (ACWP).

actual cost of the work performed (ACWP) Actual cost of the work performed in a given time period. The sum of the costs incurred in accomplishing work.

AOA Activity-on-arrow method for drawing project networks. The activity is shown as an arrow.

AON Activity-on-node method for drawing project networks. The activity is on the node (rectangle).

apportionment method Costs allocated to a specific segment of a project by using a percent of planned total cost—for example, framing a house might use 25 percent of the total cost, or coding a teaching module 40 percent of total cost.

B

backward pass The method used to compute the late start and finish times for each activity in the project network.

balanced matrix A matrix structure in which the project manager and functional managers share roughly equal authority over the project. The project manager decides what needs to be done; functional managers are concerned with how it will be accomplished.

balanced scorecard method Model that measures the long-run results of major program activities in four areas—customer, internal, innovation and learning, and financial.

bar chart A graphic presentation of project activities depicted as a time-scaled bar line (also called a Gantt chart).

baseline A concrete document and commitment; it represents the first real plan with cost, schedule, and resource allocation. The planned cost and schedule performance are used to measure actual cost and schedule performance. Serves as an anchor point for measuring performance.

brainstorming Generating as many ideas/solutions as possible without critical judgment.

budget at completion (BAC) Budgeted cost at completion. The total budgeted cost of the baseline or project cost accounts.

budget reserve Reserves set up to cover identified risks that may occur and influence baseline tasks or costs. These reserves are typically controlled by the project manager and the project team. See management reserve.

budgeted cost of the work performed (BCWP) The value for completed work measured in terms of the planned budget for the work. The earned value or original budgeted cost for work actually completed.

burst activity An activity that has more than one activity immediately following it.

C

capability maturity model (CMM) A framework which describes the evolutionary stages of project management systems.

change management system A defined process for authorizing and documenting changes in the scope of a project.

chart of accounts A hierarchical numbering system used to identify tasks, deliverables, and organizational responsibility in the work breakdown structure.

co-location A situation in which project members including those from different organizations work together in the same location.

concurrent engineering or simultaneous engineering Cross-functional teamwork in new-product development projects that provides product design, quality engineering, and manufacturing process engineering all at the same time.

consensus decision making Reaching a decision that all involved parties basically agree with and support.

contingency plan A plan that covers possible identified project risks that may materialize over the life of the project.

contingency reserves Usually an amount of money or time set aside to cover identified and unforeseen project risks.

contract A formal agreement between two parties wherein one party (the contractor) obligates itself to perform a service and the other party (the client) obligates itself to do something in return, usually in the form of a payment to the contractor.

cost account A control point of one or more work packages used to plan, schedule, and control the project. The sum of all the project cost accounts represents the total cost of the project.

cost performance index (CPI) The ratio of budgeted costs to actual costs (BCWP/ACWP).

cost-plus contract A contract in which the contractor is reimbursed for all direct allowable costs (materials, labor, travel) plus an additional fee to cover overhead and profit.

cost variance (CV) The difference between BCWP and ACWP (CV = BCWP − ACWP). Tells if the work accomplished cost more or less than was planned at any point over the life of the project.

crash point The most a project activity time can realistically be compressed with the resources available to the organization.

crash time The shortest time an activity can be completed (assuming a reasonable level of resources).

critical path The longest activity path(s) through the network. The critical path can be distinguished by identifying the collection of activities that all have the same minimum slack.

critical path method (CPM) A scheduling method based on the estimates of time required to complete activities on the critical path. The method computes early, late, and slack times for each activity in the network. It establishes a planned project duration, if one is not imposed on the project.

culture The totality of socially transmitted behavior patterns, beliefs, institutions, and all other products of human work and thought characteristic of a community or country.

culture shock A natural psychological disorientation that most people suffer when they move to a culture different from their own.

D

dedicated project team An organizational structure in which all of the resources needed to accomplish a project are assigned full time to the project.

direct costs Costs that are clearly charged to a specific work package—usually labor, materials, or equipment.

dummy activity An activity that does not consume time; it is represented on the AOA network as a dashed line. A dummy activity is used to ensure a unique identification number for parallel activities and used to maintain dependencies among activities on the project network.

duration (DUR) The time needed to complete an activity, a path, or a project.

dysfunctional conflict Disagreement that does not improve project performance.

E

early finish The earliest an activity can finish if all its preceding activities are finished by their early finish times (EF = ES + DUR).

early start The earliest an activity can start. It is the largest early finish of all its immediate predecessors (ES = EF − DUR).

earned value (EV) The physical work accomplished plus the authorized budget for this work. Previously this was called the budgeted cost of work performed (BCWP).

enterprise project management (EPM) Centralized selection and management of a portfolio of projects to ensure the allocation of resources to projects are directed and balanced toward the strategic focus of the organization.

escalation A control mechanism for resolving problems in which people at the lowest appropriate level attempt to resolve a problem within a set time limit or the problem is "escalated" to the next level of management.

estimated cost at completion (EAC) The sum of actual costs to date plus revised estimated costs for the work remaining in the WBS.

event A point in time when an activity(s) is started or completed. It does not consume time.

F

failure mode and effects analysis (FEMA) Each potential risk is assessed in terms of severity of impact, probability of the event occurring, and ease of detection.

fast-tracking Accelerating project completion typically by rearranging the network schedule and using start-to-start lags.

fixed-price or "lump sum" contract A contract in which the contractor agrees to perform all the work specified in the contract at a predetermined, fixed price.

float See slack.

forecast at completion (FAC) The forecasted cost at completion—using forecast equation.

forward pass   The method for determining the early start and finish times for each activity in the project network.

free slack   The maximum amount of time an activity can be delayed from its early start (ES) without affecting the early start (ES) of any activity immediately following it.

function points   Points derived from past software projects to estimate project time and cost, given specific features of the project.

functional conflict   Disagreement that contributes to the objectives of the project.

functional manager   A manager responsible for activities in a specialized department or function (e.g., engineering, marketing, finance).

functional organization   A hierarchical organizational structure in which departments represent individual disciplines such as engineering, marketing, purchasing.

G

Gantt chart   See bar chart.

going native   Adopting the customs, values, and prerogatives of a foreign culture.

Golden Rule   Do unto others as you would wish them to do unto you.

groupthink   A tendency of members in highly cohesive groups to lose their critical evaluative capabilities.

H

hammock activity   A special-purpose, aggregate activity that identifies the use of fixed resources or costs over a segment of the project—e.g., a consultant. Derives its duration from the time span between other activities.

I

implementation gap   The lack of consensus between the goals set by top management and those independently set by lower levels of management. This lack of consensus leads to confusion and poor allocation of organization resources.

indirect costs   Costs that cannot be traced to a particular project or work package.

infrastructure   Basic services (i.e., communication, transportation, power) needed to support project completion.

in-process project audit   Project audits early in projects that allow for corrective changes if they are needed on the audited project or others in progress.

insensitive network   A network in which the critical path is likely to remain stable during the life of the project.

ISO 900   A set of standards governing the requirements for documentation of a quality program.

J

joint evaluation   A process in which different parties involved in a project evaluate how well they work together.

L

lag   The amount of time between the end of one activity and the start of another. A duration assigned to the activity dependency. The minimum amount of time a dependent activity must be delayed to begin or end.

lag relationship   The relationship between the start and/or finish of a project activity and the start and/or finish of another activity. The most common lag relationships are (1) finish-to-start, (2) finish-to-finish, (3) start-to-start, and (4) start-to-finish.

late finish   The latest an activity can finish and not delay a following activity (LF = LS + DUR).

late start   The latest an activity can start and not delay a following activity. It is the largest late finish (LF) of all activities immediately preceding it (LS = LF − DUR).

law of reciprocity   People are obligated to grant a favor comparable to the one they received.

leading by example   Exhibiting the behaviors you want to see in others.

learning curves   A mathematical curve used to predict a pattern of time reduction as a task is performed over and over.

level of effort (LOE)   Work packages that represent time-related activities. These activities, such as administrative support, computer support, legal, public relations, etc., exist for a segment or the duration of the project. LOE work packages have no measurable outputs.

M

macro and micro estimating   Macro estimates are top-down, rough estimates that use surrogates to estimate project time and cost and are used to determine project selection or go-ahead decisions. Bottom-up micro estimates are detailed estimates of work packages usually made by those who are most familiar with the task.

management by wandering around (MBWA)   A management style in which managers spend the majority of their time outside their offices interacting with key people.

management reserve A percentage of the total project budget reserved for contingencies. The fund exists to cover unforeseen, new problems—not unnecessary overruns. The reserve is designed to reduce the risk of project delays. Management reserves are typically controlled by the project owner or project manager. See budget reserve.

matrix Any organizational structure in which the project manager shares responsibility with the functional managers for assigning priorities and for directing the work of individuals assigned to the project.

mentor Typically a more experienced manager who acts as a personal coach and champions a person's ambitions.

merge activity An activity that has more than one activity immediately preceding it.

met-expectations model Customer satisfaction is a function of the extent to which perceived performance exceeds expectations.

milestone An event that represents significant, identifiable accomplishment toward the project's completion.

mitigating risk Action taken to either reduce the likelihood that a risk will occur and/or the impact the risk will have on the project.

Monte Carlo simulation A method of simulating project activity durations using probabilities. The method identifies the percentage of times activities and paths are critical over thousands of simulations.

N

negative reinforcement A motivational technique in which negative stimuli are removed once desired behavior is exhibited.

net present value (NPV) A minimum desired rate of return discount (e.g., 15 percent) is used to compute present value of all future cash inflows and outflows.

network A logic diagram arranged in a prescribed format (e.g., AOA or AON) consisting of activities, sequences, interrelationships, and dependencies.

network organization An alliance of several organizations created for the purpose of creating products and services for customers.

network sensitivity The likelihood that the critical path will change on a project.

nominal group technique (NGT) A structured problem-solving process in which members privately rank-order preferred solutions.

O

objective An end you seek to create or acquire. Should be specific, measurable, realistic, assignable, and include a time frame for accomplishment.

organization breakdown structure (OBS) A structure used to assign responsibility for work packages.

organizational culture A system of shared norms, beliefs, values, and assumptions held by an organization's members.

organizational currencies A set of currencies used as a medium of exchange within organizations to influence behavior.

organizational politics Actions by individuals or groups of individuals to acquire, develop, and use power and other resources to obtain preferred outcomes when there is uncertainty or disagreement over choices.

outsourcing Contracting for the use of external sources (skills) to assist in implementing a project.

overhead costs Typically organization costs that are not directly linked to a specific project. These costs cover general expenses such as upper management, legal, market promotion, and accounting. Overhead costs are usually charged per unit of time or as a percent of labor or material costs.

P

parallel activity One or more activities that can be carried on concurrently or simultaneously.

partnering See project partnering.

partnering charter A formal document that states common goals as well as cooperative procedures used to achieved these goals which is signed by all parties working on a project.

path A sequence of connected activities.

payback method The time it takes to pay back the project investment (investment/net annual savings). The method does not consider the time value of money or the life of the investment.

performance review In general, all review methods of individual performance center on the technical and social skills brought to the project and team. These reviews stress personal improvement and are frequently used for salary and promotion decisions.

phase estimating This estimating method begins with a macro estimate for the project and then refines estimates for phases of the project as it is implemented.

phase project delivery   Delivering useful parts of a project in phases instead of when the project is entirely completed.

plan of record   The current official plan for the project in terms of scope, budget, and schedule.

plan value (PV)   The planned time-phased baseline of the value of the work scheduled. Previously this was called budgeted cost of work scheduled (BCWS).

precedence diagram method   A method used to construct a project network that uses nodes (e.g., a rectangle) to represent activities and connecting arrows to indicate dependencies.

principle of negotiation   A process of negotiation that aims to achieve win/win results.

priority system   The process used to select projects. The system uses selected criteria for evaluating and selecting projects that are strongly linked to higher-level strategies and objectives.

priority team   The group (sometimes the project office) responsible for selecting, overseeing, and updating project priority selection criteria.

proactive   Working within your sphere of influence to accomplish something.

process breakdown structure (PBS)   A phase-oriented grouping of project activities that defines the total scope of the project. Each descending level represents an increasingly detailed description of project work.

project   A complex, nonroutine, one-time effort to create a product or service limited by time, budget, and specifications.

project audit report   A report that includes classification of the project, analysis of information gathered, recommendations, lessons learned, and an appendix of backup information.

project cost–duration graph   A graph that plots project cost against time; it includes direct, indirect, and total cost for a project over a relevant range of time.

project interfaces   The intersections between a project and other groups of people both within and outside the organization.

project kickoff meeting   Typically the first meeting of the project team.

project life cycle   The stages found in all projects—definition, planning, execution, and delivery.

project management   The application of knowledge, skills, tools, and techniques to project activities to meet the project requirements.

project management office (PMO)   A centralized unit within an organization or department that oversees and improves the management of projects.

project manager   The individual responsible for managing a project.

project partnering   A nonbinding method of transforming contractual relationships into a cohesive, cooperative project team with a single set of goals and established procedures for resolving disputes in a timely manner.

project portfolio   Group of projects that have been selected for implementation balanced by project type, risk, and ranking by selected criteria.

project screening matrix   A matrix used to assess and compare the relative value of projects being considered for implementation.

project sponsor   Typically a high-ranking manager who champions and supports a project.

project vision   An image of what the project will accomplish.

projectitis   A social phenomenon in which project members exhibit inappropriately intense loyalty to the project.

projectized organization   An organizational structure in which core work is accomplished by project teams.

positive synergy   A characteristic of high-performance teams in which group performance is greater than the sum of individual contributions.

R

ratio (parametric) methods   Uses the ratio of past actual costs for similar work to estimate the cost for a potential project. This macro method of forecasting cost does not provide a sound basis for project cost control since it does not recognize differences among projects.

resource   Any person, groups, skill, equipment or material used to accomplish a task, work package, or activity.

resource-constrained project   A project that assumes resources are limited (fixed) and therefore time is variable.

responsibility matrix   A matrix whose intersection point shows the relationship between an activity (work package) and the person/group responsible for its completion.

risk   The chance that an undesirable project event will occur and the consequences of all its possible outcomes.

risk profile   A list of questions that addresses traditional areas of uncertainty on a project.

risk severity matrix   A tool used to assess the impact of risks on a project.

S

"sacred cow"   A project that is a favorite of a powerful management figure who is usually the champion for the project.

scenario analysis   A process in which potential risk events are identified and analyzed.

schedule performance index (SPI)   The ratio of the work performed to work scheduled (BCWP/BCWS).

schedule variance (SV)   The difference between the planned dollar value of the work actually completed and the value of the work scheduled to be completed at a given point in time (SV = BCWP − BCWS). Schedule variance contains no critical path information.

scope creep   The tendency for the scope of a project to expand once it has started.

scope statement   A definition of the end result or mission of a project. Scope statements typically include project objectives, deliverables, milestones, specifications, and limits and exclusions.

sharing risk   Allocating proportions of risk to different parties.

slack   Time an activity can be delayed before it becomes critical.

social network building   The process of identifying and building cooperative relationships with key people.

sociotechnical perspective   A focus on the interaction between tools/methods and people.

splitting   A scheduling technique in which work is interrupted on one activity and the resource is assigned to another activity for a period of time, then reassigned to work on the original activity.

stakeholder   Individuals and organizations that are actively involved in the project, or whose interests may be positively or negatively affected as a result of project execution or completion. They may also exert influence over the project and its results.

strong matrix   A matrix structure in which the project manager has primary control over project activities and functional managers support project work.

systems thinking   A holistic approach to viewing problems that emphasizes understanding the interactions among different problem factors.

T

task   See activity.

team-building   A process designed to improve the performance of a team.

team evaluation   Evaluating the performance of the project team using a minimum core of conditions in place before the project began. Evaluation practices should emphasize the team as a whole, while minimizing individual performance.

time and cost databases   Collection of actual versus estimated times and costs of work packages over many projects that are used for estimating new project tasks and their expected possible error.

time-constrained project   A project that assumes time is fixed and, if resources are needed, they will be added.

time-phased budgets   Planned costs that are broken down by distinct time periods (e.g., $5,000 per week) for a work package, as opposed to a budget for a whole job/project (6 months for a total of $130,000). Time phasing allows better cost control by measuring the actual rate of expenditure versus the planned expenditure rate over small pieces of the project.

total slack   The amount of time an activity can be delayed and not affect the project duration (TS = LS − ES or LF − EF).

transferring risk   Shifting responsibility for a risk to another party.

360-degree feedback   A multirater appraisal system based on performance information that is gathered from multiple sources (superiors, peers, subordinates, customers).

V

variance at completion (VAC)   Indicates expected actual cost over- or underrun at completion (VAC = BAC − EAC).

virtual project team   Spatially separated project team whose members are unable to communicate face to face. Communication is usually by electronic means.

W

weak matrix   A matrix structure in which functional managers have primary control over project activities and the project manager coordinates project work.

work breakdown structure (WBS)   A hierarchical method that successively subdivides the work of the project into smaller detail.

AC	Actual cost of the work completed		**KISS**	Keep it simple, stupid
ACWP	Actual cost of work performed		**LF**	Late finish
AOA	Activity on arrow		**LS**	Late start
AON	Activity on node		**MBWA**	Management by wandering around
BAC	Budget at completion		**NIH**	Not invented here
BATNA	Best alternative to a negotiated agreement		**NPV**	Net present value
BCWP	Budgeted cost of work performed		**OBS**	Organization breakdown structure
BCWS	Budgeted cost of work scheduled		**PBS**	Process breakdown structure
C-C	Critical-chain approach to project planning and management		**PCI**	Percent complete index
CPI	Cost performance index		**PCIB**	Percent complete index—budget costs
CPM	Critical path method		**PCIC**	Percent complete index—actual costs
CV	Cost variance		**PDM**	Precedence diagram method
DUR	Duration		**PERT**	Project evaluation review technique
EAC	Estimate at completion (with revised cost estimates)		**PMO**	Project management office
EF	Early finish		**PV**	Planned value of work scheduled
EPM	Enterprise project management		**RM**	Responsibility matrix
ES	Early start		**SL**	Slack
ETC	Estimate to complete		**SPI**	Schedule performance index
EV	Earned value		**SV**	Schedule variance
FAC	Forecast at completion		**TCPI**	To complete cost performance index
FF	Free float		**UV**	Usage variance
IFB	Invitation to bid		**VAC**	Variance at completion
			WBS	Work breakdown structure

$$t_e = \frac{a + 4m + b}{6}$$

$$\sigma_{te} = \left(\frac{b - a}{6}\right)$$

$$PCIB = \frac{EV}{BAC}$$

$$CV = EV - AC$$

$$CPI = \frac{EV}{AC}$$

$$FAC = \frac{(BAC - EV)}{\left(\dfrac{EV}{AC}\right)} + AC$$

$$TCPI = \frac{(BAC - EV)}{(BAC - AC)}$$

$$\sigma_{TE} = \sqrt{\Sigma \sigma_{te}^{2}}$$

$$z = \frac{T_S - T_E}{\sqrt{\Sigma \sigma_{te}^{2}}}$$

$$PCIC = \frac{AC}{EAC}$$

$$SV = EV - PV$$

$$SPI = \frac{EV}{PV}$$

$$VAC_f = BAC - FAC$$

$$VAC_e = BAC - EAC$$

Index